Paul

Paul

Life, Setting, Work, Letters

Edited by
Oda Wischmeyer

Translated by Helen S. Heron
with revisions by Dieter T. Roth

t & t clark

Published by T&T Clark International
A Continuum imprint
The Tower Building   80 Maiden Lane
11 York Road   Suite 704
London   New York
SE1 7NX   NY 10038

www.continuumbooks.com

All rights reserved. No part of this publication may be reproduced or transmitted in any form or by any means, electronic or mechanical, including photocopying, recording or any information storage or retrieval system, without permission in writing from the publishers.

© Oda Wischmeyer, with contributors, 2012

Oda Wischmeyer and contributors have asserted their right under the Copyright, Designs and Patents Act, 1988, to be identified as the Author of this work.

British Library Cataloguing-in-Publication Data
A catalogue record for this book is available from the British Library.

ISBN: HB: 978-0-567-55991-3
      PB: 978-0-567-63091-9

Typeset by Fakenham Prepress Solutions, Fakenham, Norfolk NR21 8NN
Printed and bound in Great Britain

Contents

Foreword vii
Acknowledgements viii

Part I
Historical, Religious, Cultural Contexts and Conditions

1. Introduction to Part I 3
   Oda Wischmeyer
2. The Political Situation at the Time of Paul: The Roman Empire 5
   Andreas Mehl
3. Contemporary Religions and Philosophical Schools 23
   Bernhard Heininger
4. The Jewishness of Paul 57
   Jörg Frey
5. The Life of Paul 97
   Eva Ebel
6. Paul's Missionary Activity 111
   Eva Ebel
7. The Person of Paul 121
   Eve-Marie Becker

Part II
Letters. Theology

8. Introduction to Part II 135
   Oda Wischmeyer
9. 1 Thessalonians 139
   Eva Ebel
10. 1 Corinthians 149
    Oda Wischmeyer
11. 2 Corinthians 173
    Eve-Marie Becker

12. Galatians *Jörg Frey*	199
13. The Letter to the Philippians *Lukas Bormann*	223
14. The Letter to Philemon *Lukas Bormann*	237
15. The Letter to the Romans *Oda Wischmeyer*	245
16. Themes of Pauline Theology *Oda Wischmeyer*	277

Part III
Reception of Paul

17. Introduction to Part III *Oda Wischmeyer*	307
18. The Reception of Paul in the First Century. The Deutero- and Trito-Pauline Letters and the Image of Paul in Acts *Bernhard Heininger*	309
19. The Reception of Paul in the Second Century *Andreas Lindemann*	339
20. The Reception of Paul in the History of the Church *Wolfgang Wischmeyer*	355
Authors	367
Index of Persons	369
Index of Cities	371

Foreword

Paul comes to us as a person from the past. Biblical scholarship has always aimed at understanding Paul as a person of his time, living and working within the diverse and multiform political, religious and cultural world to which he belonged. Brought up as a Greek speaking Jew in Asia Minor, probably educated in Jerusalem, and achieving a leading position in the religious politics of the *Sanhedrin,* Paul spent the 'second half' of his life travelling around Syria, Asia Minor and Greece as an agent or *apostolos* of Jesus Christ. As a founder of Christ-confessing communities Paul is situated between first century Judaism and the young Christ-confessing movement that would later on come to be known as Christianity.

The authors of this textbook seek to present Paul of Tarsus, the first Christian apostle whom we can come to know through his own writings, based on the content of his epistles. We understand Paul's letters as the earliest and most important source for reconstructing his person, his work, his communities and his religious interpretation of the world, or, in other words: his theology. In our view, Paul is regarded as having laid the foundations of Christian communities especially in the Western part of the Roman Empire – in cities such as Corinth, Philippi and Thessalonica – and as having shaped the faith, the hope, the basic theology, and the ethics of these communities. At the same time, however, Paul remains one of the most influential Jews of his time, contributing to the first century's Judaism and on equal footing with Philo of Alexandria and with Josephus.

Our textbook is written from a German, ecumenical, theological perspective, mainly by New Testament scholars, but also by scholars of Classics and Church History. The book includes a careful consideration of Paul's Jewishness as his religious and cultural background and persisting identity. The authors are aware of Jewish interpretations of Paul that differ from the Christian perspective[1]. The contributions present not only major themes in current research on Paul, but also offer substantial original contributions to particular topics. At the same time the authors strive towards a critical reconstruction of Paul's person and work, and a proper appreciation of his letters as the first documents of 'the beginnings of Christianity'.

This textbook offers students three perspectives or approaches for studying Paul. The *first* contextualizes Paul's person and work within the political,

---

1. See D. R. Langton, The Apostle Paul in the Jewish Imagination. A Study in Modern Jewish-Christian Relations, Cambridge 2010.

cultural, and, in particular, the religious and philosophical world of the early Roman Principate. The *second* approach focuses on Paul's texts. The authors offer detailed analyses of Paul's letters, especially their historical context, structure, content, impact and audience. In the authors' view this approach is the most important because it enables students to work independently and responsibly with the texts. Reception history functions as the *third* approach, due to the fact that Paul's missionary work and his letters have shaped the beginnings and the history of Christianity in a significant way. We cannot understand Christian theology, Christian ethics, or Christian communities apart from the history of Paul's impact.

Acknowledgments

We are especially grateful for the opportunity to have our textbook translated into English and would like to express our appreciation to those who helped transform our German manuscript into an English textbook for students of Biblical and Religious studies. Helen Heron M.A., Erlangen, took up the challenging task of translating the whole volume with its different subjects, ranging from Roman history, philosophy and religion and ancient Judaism on the one hand and the history of interpretation on the other. This translation was made possible by the funding received from the University of Erlangen-Nürnberg. Dr. Dieter T. Roth, Postdoctoral Research Fellow at the University of Mainz, undertook the important work of revising the translation, particularly with a view towards the use of specialized terminology in the field of New Testament studies. Dominic Mattos, senior editor in Biblical studies with T&T Clark, accompanied the whole process of recasting the German textbook into a shape that meets the needs of English language teaching of Biblical studies not only with great patience, but also tremendous kindness, backing and support. Maximilian Meier, PhD student at the University of Erlangen-Nürnberg, Anna Turton, editorial assistant with T&T Clark, and Joanne Murphy, production manager with Continuum, assisted in the preparation of the manuscript for publication. Thanks to all of them.

Our hope is that this textbook may be a scholarly guide for engagement with Paul and with his letters, which are the very beginning of later Christianity.

Oda Wischmeyer, Erlangen, June 2011

Part I

Historical, Religious, Cultural Contexts and Conditions

Chapter 1

Introduction to Part I
Oda Wischmeyer

Paul is the first and only apostle of the emerging Christian communities who puts things in writing.[1] In this function as an apostle who writes he has influenced the whole of Christianity up to the present day, and this book is designed to show him in this perspective. In his letters we encounter Paul as preacher of the Gospel, church organizer and communicator – in his own words simply as 'Apostle of Jesus Christ' – and at the same time as a person who even in writing continues to articulate, develop and reflect himself.

The broad classifications used for the understanding and interpretation of Paul – Paul the apostle, Paul the missionary, Paul the creator of Christianity, Paul the inventor of high Christology, Paul the theologian, Paul the religious hero – are all aspects of the 'many-faceted interpretation of Paul' for which Udo Schnelle called.[2] We have here chosen a perspective on Paul, the only apostle in early Christianity who put things into writing, which embraces the aspects mentioned. At the same time it does justice to the fact that the way to Paul lies in his letters in which he presents himself and interprets himself as an apostle.[3]

Paul's letters are the main sources for the reconstruction of his life and his mission. But we also reconstruct his person, his life and his work from other sources.

The following secondary sources and early witnesses to his influence can be added to his own letters:

- The Acts of the Apostles
- The deutero- and trito-Pauline letters

---

1. O. Wischmeyer (2004), 'Paulus als Autor', in: *id. Von Ben Sira zu Paulus, Gesammelte Aufsätze zu Texten, Theologie und Hermeneutik des Frühjudentums und des Neuen Testaments* (WUNT 173), ed. E.-M. Becker, Tübingen, 289–307.
2. U. Schnelle (2003), *Paulus. Leben und Denken*, Berlin/New York, 24.
3. In contrast to Luke, who does not describe his hero Paul as an apostle in Acts. Cf. here J. Frey (2005), 'Paulus und die Apostel. Zur Entwicklung des paulinischen Apostelbegriffs und zum Verhältnis des Heidenapostels zu seinen "Kollegen"', in: E.-M. Becker and P. Pilhofer (eds), *Biographie und Persönlichkeit des Paulus* (WUNT 187), Tübingen, 192–227.

- Reports and representations from early Christian writings, beginning with I Clement and leading into the apocryphal acts of the apostles.

Acts connects Paul to the route of the Gospel through the *oikumene* and divides Paul's life into three great missionary journeys. The deutero- and trito-Paulines take up his theological and church-leading activities and use his authority for the ordering of their congregations. The 'acts' of the apostles describe him anew in the categories of their time as miracle-worker and saint.

This book deals with the aspects named within the framework of a historical representation which combines the reconstruction of Paul's life and work with the interpretation of his letters.

The historical enquiry is given the most extensive interpretation and does most justice to the universal significance of Paul's person and work and the history of his influence which has now lasted almost 2,000 years. It integrates the *theological* perspective with those of *religious history* and *psychology* – i.e. reconstructing his confessing, argumentative and paraenetic speech about God and the world (theology) and examining his primarily religiously defined person, beginning with the so-called 'Damascus Road' experience (religious history and psychology).

The first part of this volume places Paul's person and work in his own time, first in the world of the early Roman Empire, which formed his political and cultural environment (Chapters 2 and 3). Here we concentrate on the world of politics, religions and philosophical schools that Paul encountered in his missionary activity. Particular interest is paid to contemporary Judaism from which he came (Chapter 4). Against this background we develop the picture of Paul from the sources with particular consideration of his own missionary activity and journeys (Chapters 5 and 6) and his person (Chapter 7).

Chapter 2

The Political Situation at the Time of Paul: The Roman Empire
Andreas Mehl

This chapter is intended to describe the historical framework within which Paul carried out his work in the development of Christianity. This framework was the Roman Empire, not simply Rome. Hence the emphasis will lie on the former and not, as was the case in Roman historiography, on the latter. Further, the task amounts to describing the situation during a particular period, from Augustus to Nero (44/27 BCE–68/69 CE). Admittedly historians find it difficult to describe situations to the extent that their main 'business' does not deal with things that remain the same, the 'long duration' (*longue durée*) of the French Annals School, but describes, explains and substantiates events, changes in the sense of fluctuations and developments over a shorter or longer period, in the ideal case historical processes leading at least retrospectively to a recognizable goal.

1
Constancy or Development?

The subject to be considered here actually makes it impossible to describe a pure situation. That might seem surprising; in the view of both non-Christian and Christian antiquity, in the time of Augustus, and through him, the Roman Empire had received at least in its internal structure a new form or constitution it was destined to retain for centuries. The modern historian of antiquity is certainly quite prepared to accept the reality contained in this view, but will also point out that the very constitutional changes pushed through by Augustus involved a compromise between Republic à la Rome and Monarchy à la Hellenism which virtually demanded further changes in form. This could, at least for a time, lead to a back and forth, to a fluctuation between Republic and Monarchy. It could also be put this way: The usual talk of the Roman 'Empire', which on the ancient pattern of interpretation is mostly taken as starting with Augustus, claims to describe a state in which, despite the designation, much is not yet 'Empire'. If, following modern custom, one talks here of the 'Emperor', it must be pointed out that only the terms '*Princeps*' and 'Principate', the man himself or his position in the first rank, are correct. Since between the time of Augustus and that of Nero († 68 CE) this position was exposed to changes that finally led towards Monarchy, even if not expressly hereditary Monarchy, the other Roman decision-making and executive institutions, the Senate and the senatorial offices (magistracies), were inevitably also exposed to change, as was the subordinate administrative machinery: the former running counter to the position of the *Princeps*, the latter in the sense of its extension, indeed of initial emergence. In fact, the emergence and extension of a governmental administration were made possible and perhaps even necessary through the development of the Principate to a Monarchy.

From the time of Augustus' reign, specifically after the annexation of Egypt, the territorial extent of the Empire might suggest constancy. But this is not really the case. On the one hand, the popular, yet long recognized as inappropriate, talk of Augustus' switch of foreign policy from expansion to conservation is misleading. Between Augustus and Trajan's taking up of office in 98 CE there were certainly no more conquests and founding of Provinces on a large scale, but both still happened. On the other hand, the way the agents at the time understood the structure of the Roman Empire and the view of modern ancient historians differ in a characteristic way. In the report of his deeds (*Res Gestae*), Augustus did not in fact establish a clear boundary for the Empire. In particular, countries ruled by their own princes appear as subject to his decisions so far as he appoints rulers there or members of the ruling houses find themselves as his guests or – more accurately – as hostages. From this perspective, even the kingdom of the Parthians, the only evenly matched opponent of Rome in the longer term, was subject to the commanding authority, i.e. to the *Imperium* of Rome. The vagueness of the concept cast in the two words *Imperium Romanum*, which one may all too quickly be inclined to misunderstand as direct rule over a clearly defined territory, allows much to be considered as part of the Roman Empire which must, according to the modern definition of a state, have been a land of its own. This comes halfway towards the Roman claim to world domination, which precisely in the time of Augustus was officially and semi-officially proclaimed and formed an element of Augustus' own legitimation to rule. The Roman conception of 'Empire' also means that for a modern view the border between imperial territory and the outside world can often not be drawn as a simple line but stretches through areas of decreasing exercise of authority to merely occasional exertion of influence. Today one would only accept those so-called Roman client-states as parts of the Roman Empire whose client status belonged to an early stage of their relationship to Rome and was sooner or later superseded by their transformation into a Province. Here we have indeed mentioned a development which led to areas outside Italy and dependent on Rome being made into Provinces. Although in the period under consideration Rome had command over a large number of Provinces, there was no standardized provincial control and by no means were all government measures at that time oriented to such control.

2
The Empire from the City of Rome to the Provinces and Beyond

In the history of the world Rome probably represents a unique case of the emergence of a great power and world empire from a city. Parallel to the growth of Rome's power and territorial control people flocked from increasingly more parts of the known world into the city, and there they continued practising various religions and cults, some tolerated by the Roman authorities, some forbidden, but in every case kept under observation. Rome, however, never became the intellectual capital of the Roman Empire. Its manner of governing was absolutely typical of the city as the germ-cell of an Empire: The People, Senate and Consuls were responsible for the city of Rome and for everything else at the same time. The recognition that this was not practical led already in the time of the Republic to the seconding of individual magistrates to administer territories annexed and controlled outside of the Italian peninsula – Provinces in the particular territorial meaning of this Latin word. From the time of Augustus special permanent posts were created for the city of Rome. These were concerned with administration and technology, e.g. the supply of water and grain for the city. Meanwhile the responsibility for the welfare of the city population still lay not with a separate authority but with the *Princeps*, in whom the government of the whole Empire was concentrated. His particular responsibility for the city of Rome can be seen in the fact that he had foodstuffs and even money distributed at his own expense to Roman citizens living in the city, and even distributed them himself. Further, not only the magistrates but he himself financed and organized games for the Roman urban population in the Circus and Amphitheatre, and from Claudius onwards the widening of the harbours at Ostia and Portus on both sides of the Tiber estuary was driven forward by the emperor for the better provision of Rome.

Only early in the first century BCE, and also only after bloody confrontations with large portions of the population of the Italian peninsula, was a further legally defined plane introduced between the Provinces and the city of Rome: Italy in this sense, and then in the later first century a significantly enlarged Italy reaching to the Alps and to Istria, became an area of Roman citizenship. From this enlarged citizenship area came, for example, the Augustan poet Virgil and the equally Augustan historiographer Livy. Augustus divided this Greater Italy administratively into 11 regions. The 'naturalization' of Italy considerably increased the number of Roman citizens. This was advantageous for recruitment to the legions, in which only Roman citizens served. After the loss of many Roman senators, indeed the disappearance of whole families from the ruling class in the civil wars during the transition from the Republic to the Principate, Italy with the prosperous families in its cities also became indispensable for the supply of senators. Vespasian (from 69 CE) was the first Emperor to come from such a family, Italian but not from the city of Rome, moreover not related to Augustus. Economically Italy was indispensable for Rome as a supplier of wares that could not be imported from overseas, such as fruit or meat.

Even a cursory glance at a map shows that the Roman Empire is a Mediterranean construction. The Italian peninsula projects into the Mediterranean, and the city of Rome – as in Greece, e.g. Athens – is close to the sea. On the other hand – here unlike Athens – it is connected to the sea by a navigable river, the Tiber. If Republican Rome initially established its direct rule on islands, especially Sicily, Sardinia and Corsica, and thereby developed the system of Provinces, it soon spread into the countries that bordered on the Mediterranean: in the west, Spain and later the south of France; to the south, North Africa ('Africa', the area around the ruins of Carthage); east of this Cyrenaica, governed together with Crete across the sea; in the Aegean, Macedonia with Achaia (Greece); on the other side of the Aegean, under the name of 'Asia', the kingdom of Pergamum inherited by the Roman people; later also Bithynia and at a very late date in the Balkans, Illyria; and finally in the east, Cilicia along with the island of Cyprus, and Syria. This overall view reveals not only the extent of Rome's reach but also the gaps it left. In the time of the Republic the ring of the Mediterranean countries was in no way completely under the direct rule of Rome, and it was still not so under Augustus in spite of further expansion. In a war in which the last rivalry of the civil war period was fought out between two Roman politicians and rulers, Mark Anthony and Octavian (Augustus), the last of the once great Hellenistic Empires, the kingdom of the Ptolemies under its queen, Cleopatra VII – i.e. its central country Egypt – was won in 30 BCE. This, however, was not made into a Province of the Roman people but became the personal possession of the victor. Several decades later under Caligula and Claudius, new conditions were created at the two opposite ends of the Mediterranean. In the principality of North African Mauretania which was dependent upon Rome, Augustus had founded colonies. These colonies provided the basis for the conversion of the territory in 40 CE into a Province, which only two years later was divided. In 46 CE the client principality of Thrace was also made into a Province.

The Province of Syria extended along the eastern coast of the Mediterranean; on the other side it reached to the steppes and the desert. It was governed by an imperial governor (*legatus Augusti pro praetore*). Within the Syrian sphere there were, however, areas of differing status. In particular there existed in the last years of the Roman Republic and the first decades of Augustus' rule the kingdom of Herod I, 'the Great', with its heartland of Judaea, standing in succession to the Hasmonean Monarchy and dependent on Rome. After the death of Herod in 4 BCE the territories of his kingdom underwent a variegated fortune in that they were repeatedly shared out under his successors. Judaea, however, as part of the Province of Syria was governed by a *praefectus* of equestrian rank. This was also the post of Pontius Pilate. At a later date Judaea was the Province of a procurator. The share in the administration which was normally given to the provincials was not exercised in Judaea by a provincial council in which the cities or clans in the Province were represented, but by the Sanhedrin (from the Greek *Synhedrion*, 'assembly') under the chairmanship of the High Priest in Jerusalem. The cult of the Emperor, quite understandable in the east as succeeding the Hellenistic cult of the ruler, did not have to be observed by the Jews in general and thus not in Judaea either. Consequently the local priests and provincial chief priest responsible for the cult of the Emperor in other places were not to be found in Judaea. In view of this Roman restraint, Caligula's idea that he should be worshipped in the Temple in Jerusalem had to arouse indignation and unrest. In general governors with tact and sensitivity were needed, who would avoid breaking taboos, particularly in the exercise of their legal supervision of the Sanhedrin together with the High Priest. But not all prefects and procurators fulfilled this requirement, and this contributed substantially to the Jewish revolt in the years 66–70 CE. The fact that for the most part the procurators of Judaea did not live in Jerusalem but in the Hellenistic city of Caesarea by the sea founded by Herod certainly averted tensions. The Roman administration of Judaea was particularly difficult in that among the Jews, in a mixture of politics and religion, there seethed animosity on the one hand against the foreign rule and on the other among themselves. The trial of Jesus itself, even if one feels that it was very unjust, shows what was within the framework of the Roman administration of the Empire a normal and functioning co-operation between the priestly Jewish 'establishment' and Rome, represented by its governor.

Even before the Romans had made the area of the Mediterranean completely into Provinces, they reached beyond it into the interior of Asia Minor, east of the Adriatic, and in Gaul on the far side of *Gallia Transalpina*, which lay on the Mediterranean. Thereby they came into contact with new nations and powers. In eastern Asia Minor and beyond it, Armenia became the bone of contention between Romans and Parthians. Within the period under discussion here the feud came to a head in the time of Nero. When the Romans pushed forward into Illyricum and farther east into Moesia up to the Danube they came into conflict with the Dacians, which repeatedly led to violent wars. Finally, already in the time of Caesar the conquest of Gaul led to confrontation with the Germans, and then under Augustus to the beginning of Roman expansion on the right bank of the Rhine. One may even speak here of a Province of *Germania*. Several defeats, of which that of Varus in the 'Teutoburg Forest' in 9 CE was only one, albeit particularly bloody, as well as other battles involving heavy losses and great expense caused Tiberius to call off all further military action in the area to the right of the Rhine after the campaign of 16 CE. He recalled the commander there, his nephew and adopted son Germanicus, and settled for loose client relationships allowing the possibility of sporadic Roman intervention in the governing arrangements of the Germanic tribes. A somewhat distant result of Gaul's becoming a Province was the annexation of Britain, initiated at the beginning of the reign of Claudius. A further consequence of the acquisition of Gaul and of the Roman interest in Germania as well as the area around the Danube is at first surprising when one looks at a map: When they conquered Gaul the Romans marched around the Alps. These, then, were not Roman. Yet they ran from south to north between Italy and Germania, and from west to east between Gaul and Illyricum. Hence their direct incorporation in the Roman Empire was a must. Because of the numerous small regions of settlement in the high mountainous regions many military operations were necessary over several decades to subdue the peoples of the western and central Alps. Several more decades, however, were to pass before permanent Provinces were established here and in the northern foothills of the Alps. The Province of *Raetia (et Vindelicia)*, for example, was only established in the period between Tiberius and Claudius.

These decades were full of measures for the organization and reorganization of the Provinces – in far more cases than those just mentioned. There were various reasons for this. On the one hand, the new division of power in Rome involved a distribution of the Provinces, some to Augustus, and some to the

Senate. Augustus received the restive Provinces or those which were threatened from without, together with the military forces stationed in them, while the Senate was allotted the pacified Provinces (27 BCE). In the following period this principle led, according to how things developed, to changes in the assignment of Provinces. In the imperial Provinces – with the exception of Egypt – there was a division between those in which at least one legion was stationed and those where there were only auxiliary troops. The former were governed by a *legatus Augusti pro praetore*, the latter by a *procurator*. The *legatus* belonged to the ranks of the Senate, the *procurator* came from the equestrian class which from the time of Augustus was used and advanced to serve the Empire. Already in 22 BCE Augustus handed over responsibility for Cyprus to the Senate; thereafter the island like other senatorial Provinces was governed by a *proconsul*. Conversely the island of Corsica was separated administratively from Sardinia, at the latest after rebellions in 69 CE. Sardinia remained senatorial; Corsica became an imperial Province and was given a *procurator*. As we can see here, Provinces were also divided or amalgamated and reformed territorially. It is hardly surprising that the final form of a Province was not reached immediately after it was conquered and annexed or was about to be. Take the case of the situation on the Rhine, for example: Only after the period handled here did the military districts established there become the two Provinces of *Germania Superior* and *Germania Inferior*. The maintaining, perhaps even the support of a client kingdom, or on the contrary its conversion into a Province, could be evoked by political and above all strategic considerations. However, one ought not to underestimate the personal contacts of a client-prince with Rome and his standing with the Emperor and his circle. In this way Herod Julius Agrippa I, who had grown up in Rome, received from Caligula first one, then two parts (*Tertrarchies*) of the former kingdom of Herod I, and Claudius, whom he had helped in the turbulent circumstances of his succession to rule, gave him the Province of Judaea as well, so that the whole of Herod's old kingdom was in his hands. Agrippa's further ambitions were admittedly stopped by the governor of Syria, behind whom we must suspect the imperial government. Agrippa's early death (44 CE) was followed by the appropriation of his kingdom. Judaea became a procuratorial Province. In 50 CE Agrippa's son, Marcus Julius Agrippa II, who also grew up in Rome, received parts of the Herodian kingdom. Judaea was not one of them, but Agrippa II, like his father, had supervision of the Temple in Jerusalem and the right to appoint the High Priest.

The proconsuls, *legati Augusti pro praetore* and the procurators of Provinces were responsible for the general administration and supervision of the law, and they confirmed or quashed the death sentences pronounced by provincial institutions on free men who did not possess Roman citizenship. They were not, however, responsible for finance. Non-municipal taxes and customs duties were leased by the Roman state to private persons or groups amalgamated into companies (*publicani*) who gathered them on the spot on their own account, or were managed by special procurators for the imperial coffers (*fiscus Caesaris*) and collected by their helpers. Since the former was a very problematic procedure which, incidentally, brought those who exercised it into discredit among the population of the Province, the latter gradually became the norm. Tax and customs duty areas and as a result the official districts of the *procuratores fisci* were not for the most part coterminous with the districts of the governors, but generally larger. The Emperor as commander-in-chief had a share in the profits of war, particularly in the territory of the conquered opponent. Consequently in all the Provinces there were extensive imperial domains. In particular, Octavian (Augustus) took Egypt as his personal property and so it did not constitute a Province of the Roman people. Finally the concession for the mining of precious metals was transferred from the Roman citizenry to the Emperor as their highest representative. Because of all these possessions and their use, further procurators were active throughout the empire to oversee the Emperor's estates. Civilian settlements grew up before the gates of the forts where military posts were stationed for a longer period. These came under the jurisdiction of the camp commander. All this means that the inhabitants of a Province faced at least two if not more representatives of Rome and their staff.

Yet the Provinces were not only administered from above. Local and regional units within a Province were self-governing. For the Province as a whole, an assembly of representatives of the smaller units functioned as a provincial assembly. Certainly this received instructions and had to put into action what it was told, and it had constantly to prove its loyalty to the Emperor by means of his cult. On the other hand, it negotiated with the governor and regulated the interests of the Province in the area remaining under its jurisdiction. The composition of the provincial parliaments followed the principle of the Roman Republic, neither democratic nor egalitarian but oligarchic and plutocratic: Men from wealthy, respected families represented the local units. Judaea was an exception in that the function of the provincial parliament was performed by the priestly council in Jerusalem, the Sanhedrin mentioned above. Yet its members belonged to a rank which, apart from their priestly position, could be compared with the notables in another Province. The real basis of the Empire, according to the will of its ruler, was represented by its cities as self-governing associations. These released the government in Rome from having to administer local units through Roman officials. Some cities became particularly significant as official residences of the provincial governors. In a world which was very concerned with rank and honour, titles were important. Cities could be raised to the status of a 'Metropolis'.

Nevertheless, in the early years of the first century CE the west was still far from having such a network of cities as had been woven in many regions in the east, at the latest in the Hellenistic period. Where there were no cities – e.g. in Gaul – the Romans used existing tribal organizations or created something similar to set up a form of 'administrative districts' (*civitates*) with a central place as the equivalent of cities, or cities were founded. Caesar began with the latter in Gaul, and his successors there and the Emperors continued the practice. In this way there arose in about a hundred years cities such as – in the order of their establishment – *Colonia Iulia Equestris* (Nyon on Lake Geneva), *Lugdunum* (Lyons), *Augusta Rauracorum* (Augst by Basel), *Augusta Treverorum* (Trier) and *Colonia Claudia Ara Agrippinensis* (Cologne). On the one hand, entirely new cities could be founded; these were, if not only nominal, colonies of veterans in which provision for battle-scarred legionaries was combined with their potential for military employment even after their retirement. Because veterans of legions possessed Roman citizenship such a colony was a *colonia civium Romanorum*, an outpost of Rome in a foreign place. On the other hand, an existing settlement of indigenous people or with a mixed population (*oppidum*) could be raised to the rank of a city according to Roman law (*municipium*). The latter measure tended towards the gradual Romanization, or rather the self-Romanization of the respective city population. The countryside, looked at in contrast to the city, belonged territorially and administratively to a city, a *civitas*, an imperial estate (*saltus*), or in the east also to a temple. The peasants who lived and worked there – if they were not slaves – could accordingly be citizens of the relevant city or its residents, tenants (*coloni*) or servants of the temple. The size and quality of a farm varied considerably in the Empire. In many places Roman senators in particular had wide estates, *latifundia*. North Africa, for example, was known for this.

There was a cultural gradient within the Roman Empire and cultural differences: between east and west, between border areas and the regions on the Mediterranean, between neighbouring Provinces, on a small scale between city and country, and even within a city where there was a mixed population such as in Rome, Alexandria at the mouth of the Nile or Antioch on the Orontes. Rome did not attempt to abolish all these differences; it even accepted them legally. But it had an interest that alongside their own culture as many people as possible also practised Roman behaviours and came to know and internalize certain Roman values, above all such as were provided by Roman legal conceptions and standards. A vehicle for this was the award of Roman citizenship (*civitas Romana*). During the civil wars this was frequently granted by Roman officials to award the ranks of their own supporters. Probably because of this, Augustus exercised restraint here. Claudius, however, regarded the spreading of citizenship as a cornerstone of the Roman Empire and acted accordingly. Wealthy families from the leading ranks of the *municipia* rose over a period of several generations to Roman citizenship and beyond this to the imperial elite of knights and senators. In this way Claudius' maxim proved to be true. Another way to receiving Roman citizenship was long and arduous: service in the auxiliary units of the Roman army and in the navy. Admittedly the number of Roman citizens in the Empire initially remained small, and among the freemen there remained for a long time the legal distinction between Roman citizens (*cives Romani*) and non-citizens (*peregrini*).

Certainly the question arises about social mobility apart from the acquisition of citizenship. One could – e.g. in Cyprus in the early days of the Empire – belong to a local, provincial elite without being a Roman citizen. One may imagine in general that in the east, where a city culture was widespread long before and apart from the Romans, urban society was far less oriented on Rome than in the cities of the west, which had only arisen or become cities through Rome. It was also possible to rise from the state of slavery. This can be explained among other things by the fact that, alongside background, property played a decisive part. A freedman and to a limited extent even a slave could acquire property, and not a few from this class of traders were successful in business and were able not only to buy their freedom but to amass affluence. The 'millionaire' Trimalchio in the 'Satyricon' written by Petronius during the reign of Nero was not freely invented but satirical exaggeration of this authentic type. It is also certain, however, that the great mass of slaves in the period under discussion here remained in bondage. Alongside social mobility was geographical mobility which was in part causally connected to it. Because of their occupation soldiers were probably the most mobile, admittedly not voluntarily, and with them also any relatives who accompanied them. The further expansion of the Empire and the reorganizations of the Provinces that were driven ahead in the early years of the Empire led to transfers of troops. We can not only read of these, along with their consequences for other people, on the votive inscriptions and epitaphs of Roman soldiers and veterans, but can also relate to them. Those too, who travelled by land or sea, with vehicles, on horses and mules, in litters or on foot were locally mobile. Journeys could be made not only to a shrine, but also to baths or spas. According to ancient guidebooks, journeys were undertaken for historical or artistic interest or non-intellectual pleasure. Geographical mobility, above all, led in many places to the mixing of people with various backgrounds and to cults leaving their region of origin and being followed in many places in the Roman Empire. Eastern cults spread in the west in a conspicuously one-sided movement. Such developments, however, must still have been insignificant in extent in the early Empire outside the city of Rome. Here, however, everyone and everything came together, so that Rome, so to speak, embodied the sum of the Provinces ethnically and religiously. Here a cult could attract attention by its collective public appearance. The Jewish community in Rome came into the sights of the imperial government when during the reign of Claudius internal Jewish conflicts were waged so violently that they or their consequences became publicly visible. Trade was also characterized by mobility: Bulk goods were admittedly clearly limited in how widely they could be traded without some politically motivated intervention; other wares, however, do not seem to have been impeded in their distribution even by the excise barriers between the customs areas of the Empire.

On the opportunities for people from the Provinces in the Roman Empire, we must not forget that they were subject to their Roman conquerors, and owed them life and limb. For this they had to pay tributes (*tributum*). These tributes – such as corn from North Africa and Egypt – were of benefit to Rome and the Romans, the army and officials but also, through propagandist redistribution by the Emperor, helped needy Provinces and cities, for example after natural disasters. On the whole of course, a man from the Provinces knew that he existed with his labour not only for himself but for Rome and the Empire and was reckoned with by Rome for this purpose. Collections of taxes, but also the rule of Rome in itself, could lead to discontent and rebellion. Here we may mention revolts in North Africa and Gaul in the time of Tiberius. The resistance movement initiated and led by the Cheruscan Arminius was seen by the Romans simply as a rebellion, but in the eyes of Arminius and his comrades-in-arms it was a legitimate fight for freedom; nonetheless, both of these views presuppose a control already exerted by the Romans. While there could be revolts against Roman control itself, an exercise of this control against Rome's wishes, its misuse by individuals or small groups, could also cause unrest and rebellion. Finally, ethnic or ideological groups living in close proximity could come into such conflict with each other that peace and order were affected. Such incidents occurred frequently with well-documented crises in the time of Caligula and Claudius between Greeks and Jews in Alexandria at the mouth of the Nile. In the Jewish rebellion from 66 CE several of the factors mentioned here combined. The imperial peace (*pax Augusta, pax Romana*), so impressively praised by the poet Virgil and used as a formula of imperial self-portrayal, was certainly an ideal, but not unmixed reality. For this one can partly hold the Roman control, in part the respective rebels, responsible.

Unrest and rebellion in the border areas always had an aspect that pointed beyond the borders. Admittedly, as already mentioned, the concept of 'border' is problematic when applied to Rome, particularly in the time of Augustus and his immediate successors. It is not compatible with the Roman and particularly the Augustan claim to a 'boundless Empire' (*imperium sine fine*). As long as Rome did not expressly or actually abstain totally from expansion, there might be borders of the areas that were in fact under control, particularly those occupied and secured by the legions, but the existence of client-states on the periphery blurred the illusion of a clearly defined boundary. Settlements, trading and military outposts in areas that were not yet Provinces were another factor. Finally, in regions where, as in North Africa or Syria, steppe merged into desert, these did not offer straightforward lines for borders, which were arbitrarily drawn. And if 'border' is a vague expression, there was an external world upon which Rome had only very limited control or indeed none at all: above all the islands beyond the English Channel or, after the beginning of the annexation of Britain, unconquered territory there such as Scotland and Ireland and the whole of the farther island world to the north up to *ultima Thule*; then free Germania, which for the Romans grew within a few decades from a seemingly small and controllable area to an uncontrollable wilderness of immeasurable extent; and in the east a large area which was the only extra-Roman territory known by the name of a single power, the kingdom of the Parthians. This last was also the one enemy evenly matched with the Romans. Although in the report of his actions Augustus gave the impression that because of his right of disposal over members of its royal house he had the kingdom of the Parthians – and even beyond them the Indians – under his control, all his successors in the period under discussion and after it had to deal with this kingdom and its rulers, and that by no means always on the offensive. Troubled border-areas already mentioned were Armenia and Syria. The last named region could be threatened in various ways: South of the sharp bend in the Euphrates near the town of Zeugma the distance from the clearly drawn border with the kingdom of the Parthians to the Mediterranean in the Bay of Issos was only about 150 kilometres. Between Syria and Mesopotamia there were ethnic transitions, and the nomads of the Syrian desert could opt for either side. Finally there were Jews not only in Judaea and throughout the Roman Empire but also in significant numbers in Babylonia, which belonged to the kingdom of the Parthians, and in the Hellenistic city of Seleucia on the Tigris and thereby in the immediate vicinity of the Parthian capital, Ctesiphon. Borders of the Roman Empire could be felt painfully by Rome and its rulers. Those who experienced this first were of course the inhabitants of a border Province attacked from without. The ponderous Roman military machine was certainly effective in retaliation, but not capable of immediate defence on or even beyond the border and so offered them only delayed protection.

3
The Government in Rome: Emperor, Senate and 'Ministries'

From Augustus on, *one* man held the reins in Rome and the Empire. He no longer held this position for one year only but permanently and, since abdication was not provided for, until he died. A person became *Princeps* – the contemporary designation for this man – through the meshing of certain conditions. These are the consequence of the fact that the main protagonists in the civil wars had lamed, even destroyed the Republic, but among the senators and citizens so much of a republican mentality still survived that the (undisguised) establishment of a Monarchy did not appear opportune. Corresponding to this ambiguous situation the conditions differed to a very high degree, and were in fact conflicting. Nowhere was it laid down that one had to be a member of a particular family to become *Princeps*, yet in fact this was the case: Augustus' successors belonged to his own Julio-Claudian family; that is, to one of its two branches going back partly to Augustus himself, partly to his wife and later widow, Livia. This was so strongly felt to be a requirement that Galba, the first Emperor to follow the last of the Julio-Claudian dynasty, Nero, is said to have called the Romans the 'inheritance of a family' or that somewhat later the historiographer Tacitus could express it so. Yet each new *Princeps* from the Julio-Claudian dynasty did not inherit his position and there was certainly no established line of succession to the Principate. But the successor did inherit one thing from his predecessors, whether related naturally or through adoption: his fortune, at least in large part. As victor in the civil wars Augustus became the richest man in Rome, and Rome's further annexations increased his possessions even more. Consequently his successors too were the richest men in Rome, and they further extended the imperial fortune, also by the confiscation of the property of leading men who were sentenced to death – justly or unjustly – for political offences. Long before Augustus, in the Roman Republic and particularly in the period of its destruction, the politicians in Rome, especially members of the Senate, had used their wealth for their own political advancement in competition with others. But now *one* man with unrivalled riches, in an unrivalled position, intervened with the aid of his wealth wherever it seemed to him useful and opportune; where convention, e.g. the addiction of the population of the city of Rome to games of various kinds, let this seem advisable; and finally where material help was associated with one of the functions devolved to him, such as the care of the poorer section of the citizenry (*cura plebis*). This all means that people other than the *Princeps*, particularly people outside his family, could on the one hand only sporadically keep pace with him in material generosity, and on the other did not dare to compete with him in such generosity.

A decisive step towards becoming *Princeps* was the initial appointment by the Senate, i.e. the vesting with rights and responsibilities such as had been transferred in particular to Augustus, and immediately also acclamation by the unit of the army stationed by the *Princeps*, the Praetorian Guard. Whichever of the two acted first determined the new *Princeps* or, from a military point of view, the new *Imperator*. The Senate embodied – from the standpoint of antiquity – the aristocratic element in the Roman Republic which up to the time of the civil wars safeguarded and upheld the leadership of Rome but had preserved only remnants into the Principate, much though senators might mourn for the Senate's lost controlling power. The Praetorian Guard, as Roman citizens under arms, could count as representatives of the Roman citizenry, but was regarded by the Senate as part of the armed forces which had appropriated power over *political* decisions. For the cluster of competences in Republican offices which made up the position of Augustus (and his successors) could only be granted by the Senate – with the consent of the citizenry – if one was somehow to remain within the constitutional tradition of the Republic, which did not elevate him *de jure* above the holders of the Republican offices still continuing to exist. In a broader sense there also belonged here the title of High Priest of the state-cult of Rome (*pontifex maximus*) which included the supervision of all the cults followed in Rome, and so also the actions of the Christians who were becoming established in the capital.

In 27 CE and again in later years the Senate transferred official powers and honours to Augustus. His first successor, Tiberius, likewise received his authority from the Senate – Tiberius himself insisted on this – in a very slow-moving process. However, the initiative for the appointment of the new *Princeps* soon shifted from the Senate to the armed forces. After the murder of Caligula, in a turbulent situation of civil war in which the re-introduction of the consular constitution without a *Princeps* was at least being discussed, Claudius was hailed as the new Emperor, initially by individual soldiers and then, after the populace assembled at many points in Rome had demanded *one* man at the head of the state and called Claudius' name, by the Praetorian Guard as a whole in their camp. For this Claudius rewarded them with money. Proclamation by the Praetorian Guard and payment by the one named as Emperor now became the custom. The murder of Claudius, commissioned by his wife Agrippina to bring her son Nero to power, was so managed that the announcement of Claudius' death and the proclamation of Nero as the new Emperor by the Praetorian Guard occurred simultaneously. The latter was again associated with a payment of money. Yet even after the initiative had passed to the soldiers, the authority of the new Emperor – after his proclamation by the army – was confirmed by a resolution of the Senate. In keeping with the Roman conception of law this followed as far as possible the precedents of the resolutions of the Senate for earlier Emperors.

The determination of the new Emperor was further complicated by the fact that not only the respective *Princeps*, first of all Augustus, took measures – and had them agreed to by the Senate – which built up a family member as successor before all eyes, but even women of the Julio-Claudian dynasty did or attempted this. Augustus' wife, Livia, is said to have been the first of them. Finally particular circumstances were involved in the transfer of the position of *Princeps* from one to another. These arose from the fact that the *Princeps* kept his position until he died, which meant that it was only available after his death. If one was dissatisfied with the current *Princeps*, as for example with Caligula, or wanted to replace him with another, an opening for a successor could only be brought about if someone killed the reigning *Princeps* or he killed himself. The first occurred in the brief period under discussion here two or possibly three times (37 CE Tiberius by Caligula [?]; 41 CE Caligula as the result of a conspiracy; 54 CE Claudius by his wife, Agrippina) and the second once (68 CE Nero, after the Praetorian Guard defected and the Senate declared him an enemy of the state). Seen in this way the Principate proved to be anything but a stable institution because the conditions under which it was awarded did not guarantee continuity. Nevertheless with each new Emperor it became increasingly established in the Roman state, and the attempt to do without it after the murder of Caligula remained merely an interlude.

The *Princeps* was the centre of all political and administrative decisions. He ruled together with the Senate, as well as with his small circle of advisers (*consilium principis*), which by no means consisted only of senators, and soon also with his cabinet. The Emperor had the Senate approve many matters by addressing them himself or through a representative. Here lay the seed by which the Senate declined to a mere committee of endorsement. Attempts by the Emperors Tiberius and Claudius to prevent this were condemned to failure. Only the Emperor, not the Senate, had the information necessary to prepare and decide upon political concerns of the Empire. Only the Emperor, not the Senate with its periodically summoned sessions, was the permanently active and accessible organ of government. The Emperor had the most positions to allocate, even to senators; consequently he received acquiescence. Tiberius was deeply affected by such behaviour; he could only have changed it by relinquishing his position and in so doing burying the institution of the 'Principate'. Specifically during his reign senators destroyed one another by denunciation. A favourite means for this was the charge of offending against the imperial majesty (*crimen laesae maiestatis*). Yet it was above all the extension of imperial rule that pushed the Senate, which from its Republican history had no real executive power, further and further aside in political events. This might have suggested the abolishing of the Senate; but at no point was this even considered. The *Princeps* needed the Senate as a political stage and the individual members of the Senate as officials for the administration of the Empire. The individual senators did not do badly under the *Princeps* if they received from him honourable and lucrative administrative posts and possibly their sons too entered into a career under and through the Emperor. Such a career culminated as before in the Consulate. This was admittedly now only an honour without any political or military decision-making powers; it was, however, followed by a prominent administrative position in Rome (e.g. the supervision of the water supply) or a governorship of an important Province, possibly several such positions in succession.

The lack of a governing executive in Rome was one of the structural defects of the Roman Republic as soon as it had developed into an Empire with outlying possessions – colonies in the modern sense. The decisive achievement for the Empire in the early period of the Caesars was the construction of institutions of government and administration that were destined to be extended and completed in the further course of the Roman Empire. For this, on the one hand, new institutions were set up alongside the still extant old ones and soon surpassed them in the extent of their responsibilities; thus, in financial administration the newly created *fiscus Caesaris* overtook the traditional *aerarium Saturni* of the Senate. Imperial money – with the Emperor or a close member of the imperial family on at least one side of the coins – came more and more into circulation and soon became the coinage as such. On the other hand, completely new institutions were created. In the measures taken for this there was a mixture of administrative and social factors of change: if the powerful in the declining Republic had established their personal administrative offices to which they appointed people they trusted irrespective of their status in the society of Republican Rome, this procedure took on an official character from the time of Augustus. Augustus appointed not senators but men from the second rank which in the Republic was not defined particularly in terms of political activity, namely that of the knights, to several positions culminating in the governorship of Egypt and in the command of the Praetorian Guard. He even raised this formerly diffuse group of Roman citizens into a rank of its own (*ordo equester*). Differently than in the case of the senators with the Senate, there was no group representation behind these men; they faced the Emperor as individuals and were consequently easier to employ. It is not surprising that all the Emperors after Augustus used knights extensively. The elevation to the rank of senator was naturally a reward for which a knight strove – and for the Emperor it was a means for the desired gradual social and mental reshaping of the Senate.

Admittedly not only the senators but also the knights were exposed to competition from the lower ranks. Many former slaves (*liberti*) were appointed to the emerging imperial offices which together made up the imperial cabinet. They came to these positions through the personal trust they had acquired by services in the closest proximity to the current Emperor. Without any support in society they were so dependent on their Emperor that at a change in the Principate they were in danger of losing their position or being called to account for something or other with possibly fatal results. The imperial freedmen were in no way restricted to inferior posts. When 'ministries' were formed under Claudius, freedmen rose to be heads of these and thereby became 'ministers'. Such were the one responsible for the *fiscus Caesaris* – *a rationibus*, the one dealing with submissions from the population – *a libellis*, and the one who oversaw the correspondence of the government with all the Roman officials throughout the Empire, particularly with the governors – *ab epistulis*. The last-mentioned function was soon divided between two 'ministers', those of *ab epistulis Latinis* and of *ab epistulis Graecis*. These responsibilities, strange-sounding compared with government cabinets today, are an indication of peculiarities in the Roman Empire and its government and administration: The eastern part of the Empire, which at least under the early Emperors was clearly more heavily populated, was represented in Rome by the office for correspondence in Greek. Rome recognized Greek alongside Latin as a second official language. In so far as the Empire was governed and administered by the offices for petitions and correspondence, it was not ruled through individual departments responsible for specific areas but according to reports or submissions received. The Emperor reacted with written answers to the actual cases, but the Roman understanding of law with its development of the general from the specific and individual gave these answers a general significance and in this way imperial decisions in individual cases were simultaneously general rules, i.e. laws.

Governing with the aid of petitions from the people needs its own explanation. As we can read in petitions to Ptolemaic kings that survive on papyrus, it stands in line with Hellenistic and so eastern tradition that one can go directly to the king if he is present and plead before him. When addressed as 'benefactor' or perhaps even as 'saviour', the king must react. The impossibility of meeting the king in person every time he was needed led to the written composition and submission of petitions by the supplicants through their local administrative offices. These passed the files upwards and they came back to them after they were processed, in the kingdom of the Ptolemies as a royal decision, in Rome as an imperial decision. In this way the process of petitioning was bureaucratized; under the Roman Emperor it led to the setting-up of a 'ministry' of its own. The work of the *a libellis* could lead to decisions in which the Emperor displayed the qualities of a ruler in the Hellenistic tradition. At the same time it was still possible in the Roman Empire to express petitions by word of mouth. Admittedly it was not individual inhabitants of the Empire but communities such as cities or tribes who could, with the consent of their governor, send embassies to Rome to present their common request there. Here the Senate provided a stage for the Emperor's reaction to demonstrate imperial benevolence, and so events of this kind were conducted and concluded, not without elements of show, in co-operation between the imperial government and the Senate in sessions of the latter – even if the decision had already been made in the circle of imperial advisers or the cabinet. A further possibility of applying to the Emperor existed only for the citizens of Rome: The right to confirm or repeal verdicts of death delivered by a court had been transferred from the Roman citizenry to the Emperor. As a Roman citizen condemned to death one could appeal to the Emperor. According the Acts of the Apostles Paul did this. Some researchers admittedly doubt the historicity of his rights as a Roman citizen and in consequence also of his appeal.

The institutionalization of the imperial government and administration with an advisory committee and cabinet may raise the question of what the first Emperors contributed to the running of the Roman state. Augustus' will and commitment to rule cannot be doubted. When Tiberius became Emperor at an advanced age he had exceptionally great experience; he did, however, spend many years of his reign outside Rome, during which he neither could nor would conduct day-to-day political and administrative business. One may question whether Caligula's mad doings were intended to provoke; but he certainly cannot be described as a reliable helmsman of the Roman Empire. Ancient historiography and biography have denigrated Claudius as an idiot dependent on women and freedmen, but there are statements by Claudius himself that show him to have been a ruler aware of his responsibility who reflected intelligently on problems. On his assumption of office Nero was young and not experienced in ruling in spite of all earlier introductions to publicly effective appearances before the Senate. He needed the guidance of competent men, but rid himself of them, partly even by their murder (especially Seneca). For the rest he occupied himself intensively in a style scandalous for a Roman senator with literature and music and pursued insanely ambitious building plans in Rome. These plans apparently even led him to have the city set on fire in an attempt to realize them (64 CE). From the answers given to the question posed above there results an astonishing conclusion: The state and its administration did not collapse because of Tiberius' absence, nor under the incompetence and idiosyncrasies of further Emperors. The imperial government with its 'ministries' and the functionaries at their individual posts in Rome and in the Empire must somehow have been very quickly welded together into an administrative machine which ran by itself, even under a 'bad' Emperor. And yet there was an Emperor, and the people were convinced that they needed him. For the east, accustomed to Monarchy in its Hellenistic form, he was something natural, not only as a human ruler but also as a god, and this became manifest already under Augustus in the provincial and municipal Cult of the Emperor.

Table 2.1
Roman Emperors from Augustus to Nero:
(for further data cf. Dietmar Kienast (1996), *Römische Kaisertabelle. Grundzüge einer römischen Kaiserchronologie*, Darmstadt²)

Augustus (*63 BCE)	Entry into politics 44 BCE; Consul for the first time 43 BCE; *Princeps* 27 BCE–14 CE
Tiberius (*42 BCE)	Co-regent with Augustus 4 CE: *Princeps* 14–37 CE
Caligula (*12 CE)	37–41 CE
Claudius (*10 BCE)	41–54 CE
Nero (*37 CE)	54–68 CE

References

Works of classical authors
Augustus (1979), *Res gestae divi Augusti: The achievements of the divine Augustus*. With an introduction and commentary by P. A. Brunt and J. M. Moore. Latin–English, Oxford: Oxford University Press.
Cassius Dio (Lucius Claudius Cassius Dio Cocceianus) (1914–27), *Dio's Roman History*. With an English translation by E. Cary, in nine volumes, London/Cambridge, MA: W Heinemann/Harvard University Press.
Flavius Josephus (Iosephus Flavius) (1926–65), *Josephus*. With an English translation by

H. St J. Thackeray, R. Marcus and L. H. Feldman, in nine volumes (I The Life. Against Apion, II–III The Jewish War, III–IX Jewish Antiquities), London/Cambridge, MA: W Heinemann/Harvard University Press.

Suetonius (Gaius Suetonius Tranquillus) (1992), *Suetonius*. With an English translation by J. C. Rolfe, in two volumes, Latin–English, Loeb classical library, Cambridge Mass.

Tacitus (Publius Cornelius Tacitus) (1925–37), *Tacitus*. The histories: with an English translation by Clifford F. Moore; the annals: with an English translation by John Jackson, in five volumes, Latin–English, Loeb classical library, Cambridge MA: Harvard University Press.

Collections of sources, especially documents

V. Ehrenberg and A. H. M. Jones (1955), Documents illustrating the reigns of Augustus and Tiberius, Oxford: Clarendon Press.

B. Levick (1985), *The Government of the Roman Empire. A Sourcebook*, London: Croom Helm.

E. Mary Smallwood (1967), Documents illustrating the principates of Gaius, Claudius and Nero, Cambridge: Cambridge University Press.

Literature

A. K. Bowman, E. Champlin and A. Lintott (1996), *The Augustan Empire, 43 B.C.–A.D. 69* (The Cambridge Ancient History, Second Edition, Volume X), Cambridge: Cambridge University Press.

D. Braund (1988), *The Administration of the Roman Empire (241 BC–AD 193)*, Exeter: University of Exeter.

J. Carcopino (1978), *Daily Life in Ancient Rome: The people and their city at the height of the empire*, edited by H. T. Rowell. Harmondsworth: Penguin.

M. D. H. Clark (2010), *Augustus, First Roman Emperor: Power, propaganda and the politics of survival*, Exeter.

R. Étienne (1994), *Pompeii: The day a city died*, translated by R. Daniel, London.

P. Garnsey and R. Saller (2001), *The Roman Empire: Economy, society and culture*, 5th edn, London.

A. W. Lintott (1993), *Imperium Romanum: Politics and administration*, London: Routledge

R. Mellor (2006), *Augustus and the Creation of the Roman Empire: A brief history with documents*, Boston: Bedford/St Martins.

F. Millar (2002), *Rome, the Greek World and the East, Vol. 1. The Roman Republic and the Augustean Revolution*, edited by H. M. Cotton and G. M. Rogers, Chapel Hill and London.

D. S. Potter (2007), *A Companion to the Roman Empire* (Blackwell Companions to the Ancient World), Malden, MA: Blackwell.

M. Rostovtzeff (1979), *The Social and Economic History of the Roman Empire*, 2nd edn, repr. Oxford: Clarendon Press.

Chapter 3

Contemporary Religions and Philosophical Schools
Bernhard Heininger

Paul was, and remained as long as he lived, a Jew. But he acted as an apostle to the Gentiles, i.e. the non-Jews. And the basis of his mission to the Gentiles was the abstention from 'converting' the Gentiles to ioudaismos: Hence he dealt with Gentiles who from a Jewish point of view simply remained Gentiles. This is what makes the question of the appearance of the 'paganism' Paul had to deal with so important since he began 'to bring about the obedience of faith among all the gentiles' (Rom. 1.5) and 'to proclaim God's Son among the gentiles' (Gal. 1.16).

'Even though there may be so-called gods in heaven or on earth – as in fact there are many gods and many lords – yet for us there is one God, the Father, from whom are all things and for whom we exist, and one Lord, Jesus Christ, through whom are all things and through whom we exist' (1 Cor. 8.5f.). This sentence, which comes in the context of the debate on food sacrificed to idols, reveals in rare clarity that Paul's mission and the development of his churches by no means took place in a vacuum and that the 'pagans' were anything but irreligious. The cities of Asia Minor and those in Greece in which Paul worked as a missionary and founded churches are – if we follow his biographer, Luke – full of altars and temples (cf. Acts 17.16) and sacrifices, and frequently conflicts arose from the contact with pagan religions. Yet what Paul and Barnabas experienced in Lystra because of a miracle of healing appears rather as comical (cf. Acts 14.8–18): They are taken for gods in human form, more precisely for Zeus (Barnabas) and Hermes (Paul); the people want to sacrifice to them, which the two can only prevent with difficulty. Then in Philippi it is really dangerous: According to Acts 16.16–24 the clash with a woman 'who had a spirit of divination' – i.e. who belonged to the ancient mantic group – results in Paul's imprisonment. And in Ephesus the silversmiths see their trade with the reproductions they have made of the temple of Artemis gravely endangered if Paul should be successful with his new teaching (Acts 19.23–40).[1]

This being said, we have only touched on some of the points that should interest us in what follows. In addition we shall look at the Mystery Cults, which are regularly mentioned as significant relative groups in the matters of Baptism or Eucharist; the worship of the emperor in its various forms, the philosophy of

---

1. On this cf. O. Wischmeyer (2004), 'Gottesglaube, Religionen und Monotheismus in der Apostelgeschichte', in *id., Von Ben Sira zu Paulus. Gesammelte Aufsätze zu Texten, Theologie und Hermeneutik des Frühjudentums und des Neuen Testaments* (WUNT 173), Tübingen, 329–51.

that period in the Empire with its diverse currents and finally Gnosis – which, towards the end of the first century or the beginning of the second century, became a problem (not only) for the Pauline churches and may have left its traces above all in the Pastoral Epistles (cf. 1 Tim. 6.20) – will also be topics. But we begin with the everyday religious life encountered by Paul everywhere on his missionary journeys to the Gentiles through the ancient world. By and large Paul's mission takes place in the eastern part of the Imperium Romanum. There the Greek religion of the Hellenistic epoch is dominant. In the towns the Roman state religion joins the others.[2] The larger cities have their special cults. Everywhere older, regional gods are worshipped alongside the Greek deities – often with Greek names and in syncretistic shape. The Jewish communities form their own institutional companies in the towns; their religion is understood as foreign and peculiar but is tolerated (*religio licita*).

1
Public Worship

Deities, Temples and Altars
In contrast to Paul, who knows several heavens (cf. 2 Cor. 12.2–4) but only one God (monotheism), pagan thought as a rule knows only one heaven but this is inhabited by many deities (polytheism). These deities, differing from humanity through their boundless knowledge, their superior power and finally through their immortality, are extremely specialized: Apollo, for example, who together with Athena had the largest number of principal shrines in the Greek cities, is the god of the seers and the 'owner' of the Delphic oracle, his sister Artemis the goddess of the hunt, Demeter the goddess of the grain, Dionysus the god of wine, etc. Yet the number of known deities who enjoy general worship remains easily comprehensible; already in antiquity they were combined into lists of 12, among which the list of the *Twelve Olympian Gods* is the best known (see Table 3.1). This list, however, is by no means canonical and is often altered: for example, Hestia and Hades are often numbered among the Twelve instead of Ares and Dionysus.[3]

Alongside the deities the Greeks also know other kinds of mysterious divine powers which intervene in human affairs either in a charitable or in a detrimental way: the *demons*. These represent a kind of intermediate being between humankind and gods. This is true also to a certain extent of the *heroes*, whose cultic significance is admittedly much greater than that of the demons (who in fact hardly appear in the cult). A hero is a dead man known by name who at one time did service for the community (frequently the founder of the Polis) and whose life and glorious death belong to a time past (e.g. Theseus). The rituals and feasts held in their honour are in no way inferior to the religious performances brought to the gods, and in many cases one expects from the heroes the same

2. J. Rüpke (2001), *Die Religion der Römer. Eine Einführung*, Munich.
3. Cf. L. Bruit Zaidman and P. Schmitt Pantel, *Religion*, 179–214.

as one also expects from the gods: They give oracles, heal, protect and punish. Often they have at their disposal their own cult-personnel, flourishing shrines and naturally their own mythology.

The gods and goddesses are worshipped in temples, which admittedly do not have a uniform shape. If one takes as a model the temple of Artemis at Ephesus mentioned above, one of the Seven Wonders of the World which, according to the travelling writer Pausanias, 'surpasses everything which men have built'[4] with its immense size, but of which no stone remains in place and which we can only reconstruct on the basis of ancient sources,[5] then we get the following picture: In the middle of a long rectangle up to which steps lead, there is a closed room (*cella*) which receives its light from an opening in the roof or through the high door which faces east. On the end wall of the *cella* stands the statue of the deity – in this case, Artemis – to whom the temple is dedicated. Further items of furniture are a table for the food of the god in the temple (*theoxenie*), a small incense altar and devotional gifts. This temple interior is intended as a residence for the deity which is represented by her religious effigy[6] and which further statues of divinities could join as devotional gifts; it is not, however, an assembly room for believers but is accessible only for the priests. Further rooms are possible behind the *cella*, (e.g. for priestly equipment or the temple treasure) and the whole is surrounded by one or more rows of columns.

Table 3.1
The Olympian Gods with their Greek and Roman Names

1. Zeus (Jupiter)	The father of the gods and humans
2. Hera (Juno)	His wife
3. Poseidon (Neptun)	Brother of Zeus and lord of the seas
4. Athena (Minerva)	Patron goddess of Athens, according to legend springing from the head of Zeus, an armed virgin and warrior but also a caring helper for women
5. Apollon (Apollo)	Son of Zeus, among other things at home in Delphi as the god of the oracle, usually depicted as a vigorous youth
6. Artemis (Diana)	His twin sister, ruler of the animal world and goddess of the hunt
7. Aphrodite (Venus)	The goddess of love
8. Hermes (Mercurius)	The messenger of the gods, patron of merchants and thieves; he also guides the souls of the dead to the underworld (*Mercury*)
9. Hephaistos (Vulcanus)	The smith, a god of fire and handwork (*Vulcan*)
10. Ares (Mars)	The grim god of war
11. Demeter (Ceres)	The goddess of the grain – already somewhat removed from the others because she is seldom mentioned in Homer but extremely important for the Mystery Cults
12. Dionysus (Bacchus)	The god of wine (*Dionysus*)

4. Pausanias, Descriptio Graecae, 4, 31, 8.
5. Cf. K. Brodersen (1996), *Die sieben Weltwunder. Legendäre Kunst- und Bauwerke der Antike* (BsR 2029), Munich, 70–7.
6. The effigy of Artemis of Ephesus is famous because of its many 'breasts'; presumably it was originally a matter of bull's testicles, a fetish intended specially to symbolize fertility.

Sacrifice

The actual religious life, however, took place in the open. Here stood the sacrificial altar upon which burned the sacrificial flame and upon which the gods' portion was burned in sacrifice. The favoured manner of communicating with the deity in antiquity is by sacrifice – or, put in another way: sacrifices in antiquity are a social and religious reality of prime importance; they accompany a person practically wherever he goes. The sacrifices are mainly animals (usually sheep and goats; the planned sacrifice of several bulls of which we read in Acts 14.13 belongs to the larger sacrifices); but there are also many sacrificial gifts of honey, oil, wine, bread, cakes, pastries or the first-fruits.[7] Drink offerings (libations) in particular belong to the earliest elements of Greek religion; one differentiates between spondai and choai. While the *spondē* was made principally as being well pleasing to the gods or to give protection from plagues or had a place in the context of symposia or before journeys, the choai were employed particularly in connection with cleansings and in the cult of the dead. In somewhat simplified terms one can say that the spondē was poured from a pitcher and some wine for the Olympian deities on the altar (alternatively also on the ground), and what remained was drunk, while in the choē a vessel for the chthonian deities and the dead was emptied out completely on the ground.

Which animals were appropriate for a sacrifice depended upon the occasion and the deity to be worshipped. The majority of the gods received cattle, sheep and goats. Demeter on the other hand traditionally was given pigs and piglets, Ares dogs, Aphrodite birds and Priapus,[8] for example, fish. The quality of the animal was crucial: it must be perfect and should not be coerced but should walk willingly when led in procession to the sacrificial altar. At the head of the procession was a girl, on her head a basket in which, hidden under barley and ribbons, was the sacrificial knife. Male adolescents led the animal to be sacrificed and a flautist gave the procession its rhythm. At the sacrificial altar all participants in the ceremony washed their hands in water. The priest recited the customary prayers and sprinkled water on the head of the sacrificial animal causing it to dip its head; this nodding was understood as consent to the following immolation. Then barley – the Romans also used salted whole corn (the so-called *mola salsa*) – was scattered into the fire on the altar together with some hair from the forehead of the sacrificial animal cut off earlier by the priest (pre-sacrifice) and thereby marked the beginning of the actual immolation. One of the participants stunned larger animals with a powerful blow of the sacrificial axe or hammer, the participants lifted the animal with its head turned upwards and the priest or another cult-functionary cut its throat with the sacrificial knife accompanied by the shrill ololygē cry of the women.[9] Smaller sacrificial animals

---

7. Our chief sources apart from literary texts (as e.g. Homer Il I, 458–68; Od 3, 445–63; 14, 413–38) and depictions on vases and dedicatory reliefs are also the analyses of the remains of ancient sacrifices, cf. J. Boessnec and J. Schäfer (1983), *Tierknochenfunde aus Didyma*, AuA 29, 611–51; (1986) AuA 32, 251–301.
8. Fertility god in Asia Minor.
9. Cf. Aeschylus, Sept 269: LSAM 12.26 (2nd century BCE: Pergamum).

were left to bleed to death on the altar and the blood of larger animals was collected in a bowl (sphageion) and then sprinkled on the altar.

Finally the sacrificial animal was cut into pieces and divided by the *mageiros* (slaughterer/cook); the thigh-bones were taken out and, covered with fat, were burned on the altar (the god's portion), assistants of the priest threaded the entrails (splanchna) onto skewers and distributed these among those making the sacrifice. Thereafter the remainder of the meat was divided into equal parts; one part remained reserved for the gods and the other pieces were distributed according to weight. Before they were eaten they were cooked in large pots and on occasion served in the temple's own restaurant as in the Asclepieion in Corinth;[10] in other cases the ritual permitted these pieces to be taken away and eaten outside the sacrificial place or sold in the meat market. The verse 1 Cor. 10.25 ('Eat whatever is sold in the meat market without raising any question on the ground of conscience') clearly presupposes such a practice.

Religious Associations
Many associations, which determine the social and religious reality after the collapse of the Polis or its organizing social structures, develop around such sacrificial acts and the common feasts that take place at their close. The ancient Greek term for the members of an association, orgeōnes, captures this connection well: It describes the 'sacrificial comrades' who come together in order to celebrate a sacrificial meal.[11] Such sacrificial meals take place at regularly recurring intervals, yearly for the feast of the deity for whom one had named oneself – well-known names of associations are for example the 'Dionysiastes' after the Greek god of wine, Dionysus, or the 'Serapiastes' after the Egyptian god Serapis – or for the celebration of the endowment of the cult, monthly or more frequently. It is obvious that the early Christian congregations who likewise met for a common meal could easily be mistaken by an outside observer for such a cult association, although in their own self-understanding they were more like an assembly of the free citizens of a Polis, the ekklēsia and named themselves as such, while this self-description of Greek associations hardly appears in the ancient sources. Looked at pragmatically, the Christian congregations, from an external perspective, differed from the Greek and Roman cult associations in so far as one was called to the common table a little more often (weekly for the celebration of the Eucharist).

As the statutes of associations, which have come down to us in inscriptions, show, these clubs were well organized or had clear structures, whereby in the majority of cases the offices tried to copy public life. At the top of the association

10. Cf. 1 Cor. 8.10; on this topic with the corresponding archaeological details cf. J. Fotopoulos (2003), *Food Offered to Idols in Roman Corinth. A Socio-Rhetorical Reconsideration of 1 Corinthians 8, 1–11* (WUNT II/151) Tübingen.

11. Other common terms for associations are thiasos, the festive association which organizes sacrifices, processions and other celebrations in honour of a deity, or eranos, the 'dining club' (in fact the meal with friends, each of whom contributes something). In Egypt the preferred term for an association is synodos; Philo uses it among other terms for the gatherings of the Therapeutae (Vit Cont 40). The Latin term for the association is *collegium*.

was a chairman who was elected either for a limited period or for life (prostatēs), also known as hiereus in religious groups. He was responsible for the running of the cult, the general meetings and the festive meals and for carrying out the decisions of the association. He had several different additional officials. According to the constitution of the Athenian Iobacchoi, a club of worshippers of Dionysus, these are the deputy priest (anthiereus), the Archibacchos, who assisted at the sacrifice or could represent the priest, the treasurer – obligatory for every association – and perhaps a leader of the dance; in addition there are personnel to ensure order.[12] There is also evidence that the clubs had scribes (grammateus/*scriba*). In addition, the Athenian inscription of the Iobacchoi records most precise rules for the procedure leading to membership and also knows a code of behaviour for assemblies; a constitution of a group which stems from Egypt and is dated towards the end of the Ptolemaic period even explicitly forbids the formation of factions (schismata), a phenomenon we know all too well from Corinth (cf. 1 Cor. 11.18).[13]

Many of the ancient associations known to us owe their existence to the endowment of a rich patron or patroness (*patronus/patrona*; the Greek counterparts are prostatēs or prostatis) who frequently put at their disposal not only the place for gatherings and cult place but also a piece of land for the burial of members who had died. Connected to this there was also as a rule the endowment of a founding capital from the interest of which the festive meals were financed and gifts of money could be distributed (cf. the founder's inscription reproduced here). This frequently entitled them to the honourable name of *pater* or *mater collegii* – 'father' or 'mother of the association'. It is quite natural within this family metaphor that the members of such a club should be called brother, adelphos, or sister, adelphē (so far as women were admitted). Again the comparison with the early Christian churches is perfectly obvious, particularly when one of them apparently records Phoebe, the diakonos and prostatis of the congregation at Cenchreae (cf. Rom 16.1f!), as a patroness among its numbers.[14]

The constitution of an association. The statute of the Society of Aesculapius and Hygeia:

Salvia Marcellina, the daughter of Caius, in memory of Fl. Apollonius, a procurator of

---

12. SIG³ 1109. An in-depth discussion of the constitution in G. Scheuermann (1996), *Gemeinde im Umbruch. Eine sozialgeschichtliche Studie zum Matthäusevangelium* (FzB 77), Würzburg, 17–20, 29–43. The inscription is dated towards the end of the 60s of the second century CE. The text can also be found in T. Schmeller (1995), *Hierarchie and Egalität. Eine sozialgeschichtliche Untersuchung paulinischer Gemeinden und griechisch-römischer Vereine* (SBS 162), Stuttgart, 110–15.On the details of the Iobacchoi cf. E. Ebel, *Attraktivität*, 76–150. further cf. M. Oehler (2005), 'Antikes Vereinswesen', in K. Scherberich (ed.), *Neues Testament und Antike Kultur II: Familie, Gesellschaft, Wirtschaft*, Neukirchen-Vluyn, 79–86.

13. PLondon 2710 = SGUÄ 7835.

14. The facts are admittedly not undisputed; in this regard I concur with the view of H.-J.Klauck (2003), 'Junia Theodora und die Gemeinde von Korinth', in *id.*, *Religion und Gesellschaft im frühen Christentum. Neutestamentliche Studien* (WUNT 152), Tübingen, 232–47 (245f.).

Augustus, who was the director of the state collection of paintings, and of his assistant Capito, a freedman of Augustus, her very best and good-hearted husband, donated to the Society of Aesculapius and Hygeia a small house with an extension, a marble statue of Aesculapius and a covered terrace so that the members of the society named could dine there. ... Likewise the same Marcellina donated the society 50,000 sesterces for 60 people on condition that no more than the number named would be admitted and that the places of dead members should be sold and free people admitted, or, if a member wished to bequeath his place to his son he should pay the half of the funeral money into the society's coffers; furthermore, they may not re-allocate the said money for other purposes, but with the interest from this sum they should celebrate at this place on the days mentioned below; if they have bought presents for 60 people from the (interest) income of this sum by common consent ..., then they should distribute gifts on the 19th September, the propitious birthday of our Augustus Antoninus Pius, the father of the fatherland: ... to C. Ofilius Hermes, the permanent Quinquennal, or to whomsoever may hold the position then, 3 denarii, to Aelius Zeno, the father of the society 3 denarii, to Salvia Marcellina, the mother of the society 3 denarii, to the non-contributory members 2 denarii each, to the curators 2 denarii each, and to the people 1 denarius each.

Likewise it was decided that on the 4th November, the birthday of the society, they should distribute the following sum from the income mentioned above at the statue of Mars (or: temple of Mars) to those assembled in the house of our society: to the Quinquennal 6 denarii, the father of the society 6 denarii, the non-contributory members each 4 denarii, the curators each 4 denarii, bread for 3 (asses); to the Quinquennal 4 and a half litres of wine, the father of the society 4 and a half litres, the non-contributory members each 3 litres, the curators each 3 litres, and to the people one and a half litres each.[15]

2
The Mystery Cults

The Concept
Among the religious groups the mystery cults represent a special genre for the understanding of early Christianity. The name 'mysteries' (from the Greek mystēria) describes a type of ritual celebration whose core – in the original sense of the word – remains 'secret'. They take place in hidden places, frequently at night. This kind of cult existed in addition to the official religion from the seventh century BCE to the fourth century CE, until Christianity, in the meantime having risen to be the state religion, brought about their end. Alongside the Eleusinian Mysteries, the ancient Mystery cult 'par excellence' that was tied to Eleusis, the Mysteries of Dionysus, Attis, Isis and Mithras were not tied to a particular locality and enjoyed a wide dissemination.

Because entry into the Mysteries was not open to all but was reserved for a special group of initiates, *initiation* represents a constitutive feature of this cult. Consequently *Walter Burkert* characterizes the Mystery Cults as 'rituals of

---
15. ILS II/2, 7213 (153 CE): text according to Schmeller, *Hierarchie* (n.12) 106–9; Quotation 106f.

initiation; this means that admission depends upon a personal ceremony which each individual has to undergo'.[16] Yet the initiation into the Mysteries was based on the free decision of the individual who expected to gain from this a kind of personal insurance against torments, particularly the fear of illness and death. How such an initiation took place can be shown paradigmatically from the example of the Eleusinian Mysteries. Eleusis was not simply the model for the other Mysteries; it is also the cult about which the ancient sources give the most detailed account.

The Mysteries of Eleusis
Characteristic of the Eleusinian initiation rites are the three steps of *Myesis* ('initiation'), *Telete* ('perfection') and *Epopteia* ('vision'). Two relief-friezes from the Imperial period – the so-called Lovatelli Urn and the Sarcophagus of Torre Nova[17] – give us information about the course of the first stage, i.e. the Myesis, which can be taken as the actual act of initiation. They show the one to be initiated – after the sacrifice of a piglet and a ritual purification – on a stool covered with a sheepskin, his head concealed under a cloth. A priestess holds a sheaf of corn over him (Lovatelli Urn) or brings a burning torch or torches near to his hand. Both signify the cleansing of the one to be initiated by air and fire and simultaneously refer to the legend of the foundation of the Eleusinian Mysteries – the abduction of Persephone, the daughter of Demeter, by the ruler of the underworld, Hades – which is recorded in the Homeric Demeter Hymn. As Demeter, searching for her abducted daughter enters the house of King Keleos,

> '(she) did not want to sit in the gleaming easy-chair, she waited in silence,
> lowered her eyes, until finally Jambe, the excellent experienced one
> pushed a sturdy chair over to her and covered it with a fleece
> which shone as if made of silver. She sat down on this,
> held her headscarf before her eyes with her hands and sat on the seat,
> full of distress for a long time and uttered no sound.'[18]

This means, however, that while the one being initiated reproduced the sacred tradition in the ritual he simultaneously gained a share in the destiny of the goddess and had the hope that his own fate may have a similar happy ending as is granted in the myth of the goddess.

Correspondences between myth and rite can also be found in the central Eleusinian festival in the month of Boedromion (September/October), the

---

16. W. Burkert, *Mysterienkulte*, 15; in a similar manner D. Zeller (1994), 'Article: Mysterien/ Mysterienreligionen', *TRE* 23, 504–26, here 504: The mysteries are illuminated from the rituals of initiation and reveal the structure of a *rite de passage*.
17. There is a fine depiction of the Lovatelli Urn in Burkert, *Mysterien*, illustrations 2–4; the Sarcophagus of Torre Nova can be seen inter alia in J.Leipoldt and W. Grundmann (⁶1987), *Umwelt des Urchristentums, Vol. 3: Bilder zum neutestamentlichen Zeitalter*, Berlin, illustration 34; there also (illustration 32) is the reproduction of a marble relief from Naples which to a large extent corresponds to the depiction on the sarcophagus.
18. Hom. Hymn, Dem 192–8.

so-called 'Great Mysteries'.[19] The ceremonial procession from Athens to Eleusis, covering a distance of 20 kilometres, could already be understood as a ritual repetition of Demeter's search for her daughter.[20] Associations with the myth can also be seen in the fasting and drinking of the Kykeon[21] mentioned in the Eleusinian Synthema: 'She (i.e. the goddess) greeted no-one either in word or gesture; without laughing, without eating, without drinking' until finally she is persuaded by Jambe and drinks the mixed drink 'because of the sacred custom' (Hom. Hym., Dem 199f., 211). In addition, the performance of the cultic drama (the abduction of Persephone) by the cult personnel at Eleusis is also to be taken into consideration.

Those being initiated experienced the high point of the festival in the *Telesterion*, a large covered assembly hall which provided space for about 3,000 people and which housed in its interior (not quite in the centre) a small chapel, the *anaktoron* (meaning roughly 'the house of the ruler'). According to a tradition recorded by Hippolytus the *anaktoron* opened at a fixed time, flames blazed upwards[22] and in their light the hierophant revealed a sacred object, while proclaiming in a loud voice the secret of the Mystery: 'The lady, Brimo has borne a holy boy Brimos, i.e. the strong one has borne the strong one.'[23] By 'the lady, Brimo' is meant either Demeter or Persephone, 'the holy boy Brimos' either Pluto, the personification of wealth, or the initiate, who becomes the child of the deity. The central object that was shown – if we continue to follow Hippolytus – is a cut ear of corn. Alternatively, the 'sacred object' could also be venerable statues of deities which would symbolize the epiphany of Demeter or the ascent of the Kore ('maiden'), as Persephone was often named, from the underworld. *Marion Giebel* suggests that the presenting of the corn (and also the objects in the 'chest' to which the Eleusinian synthema alludes, *v. supra*) and the epiphany of the Kore (however realized) should be separated from one another. She allocates the first to the *telete*, the latter to the *epopteia*.[24] This proposal makes sense without any

---

19. In contrast to the 'Lesser Mysteries' of Agrai, which were celebrated in the spring and during which the initiation took place in the first stage of consecration (Myesis). Scholia Aristophanes, Plutarch 848 Turchi, considers the Lesser Mysteries as 'a pre-purification (prokatharsis) and pre-sanctification (proagneusis) of the Great Mysteries'.

20. Cf. Lactantius, Inst Epit 18: 'Proserpina is sought in the night with lighted torches; when she is found the whole celebration comes to an end with rejoicing and waving of torches'; further evidence in W. E. Berner, *Initiationsriten*, 20.

21. Handed down by Clement of Alexandria, Protr 21,2: 'I fasted, I drank the mixed drink (Kykeon), I took from the chest, I "pottered about" and laid it then in the basket and from the basket into the chest again.' Such code- and passwords, which retrospectively capture a part of what takes place in the Mysteries can be found in all the Mystery Cults; they served the mystics as a kind of membership card, either for admission to the next stage of consecration or in everyday life.

22. Confirmed by Plutarch, Prof Virt 11 (Mor 81E): 'who reaches the interior and sees the great light, as e.g. when the Anaktoron opens ...'

23. Hippolytus, Refut V 8,39f.

24. M. Giebel, *Geheimnis*, 44–6. the classification suggested by Zeller, 'Article: Mysterien' (n.16), 505f., also remains possible. He suggests that the Telete belongs in the radius of the Synthema, while the display of the corn lies in the field of the Epoptie.

problem since, on the evidence of the ancient sources, the space of at least a year must lie between *telete* and *epopteia*. How the organization of this was then coped with, we do not know: All *mystai* had access to the *telesterion*. Perhaps the participants in the *telete* were sent out before the acts assigned to the *epopteia*, or their heads were covered.

Further Mystery Cults
For the other ancient mystery cults mentioned at the beginning of this section very similar observations can be made, which naturally has to do with the fact that the Eleusinian Mysteries, as the oldest cult which had existed for centuries, were a factor in giving them their form. Therefore before the actual initiation there are almost always preparatory rites as in Eleusis. These often include the instruction of those to be initiated, fasting (with sexual abstinence) and a purificatory bath. Naturally there were also details specific to the cult.

Already in antiquity the *galloi*, priests of the cult of Attis and Cybele, were infamous. They took the fundamental myth of their cult literally, danced in ecstasy to shrill music at orgiastic feasts and castrated themselves at the high point of their ecstasy.[25] The ritual marriage between the deity and the initiate possibly stands at the centre of the initiation into the Mysteries.[26] The Mithras Mysteries, interpreted variously in early research as a serious competitor to Christianity, have as their characteristic feature seven stages of initiation which represent the ascent of the soul through the different heavenly spheres: *corax* (raven), *nymphius* ('masculine bride'), *miles* (soldier), *leo* (lion), *perses* (Persian), *heliodromus* ('sun-runner') and *pater* (father). The cult, almost without exception restricted to men, was particularly popular among soldiers and traders (the large number of Mithraea – i.e. cultic grottoes – along the Roman borders allows us to make this assumption); in Rome and Ostia (18 Mithraea were found here) the number of Mithraea may have gone into the hundreds. Here we always have an elongated room, shut off from daylight, with a corridor in the middle and half-high, slightly inclined stone benches on both sides designed for 40–50, at the most 100 participants. On the end wall is the cult symbol (Mithras, sinking the dagger into the bull's side; from the bull's tail spring out ears of corn) and a small, low altar.

We are relatively well informed about the initiation into the Mysteries of the goddess Isis, who originally stemmed from Egypt but already in the first century CE had grown into the universal deity of the Mediterranean. Our information – presumably interspersed with autobiographical details – comes from the report

25. The myth is recorded in Ovid, Fasti 223–44; Catullus, Carmina 63, 1–26; 91–3: In revenge (because he was unfaithful to her) Cybele, a mother-goddess in Asia Minor, drove her young lover, Attis, into madness, with the result that he castrated himself and died as a result. At the request of Cybele, who afterwards repented of her atrocious deed, Zeus left Attis's corpse undecayed. His hair grows and the little finger moves. Attis thus became a 'living corpse'.

26. Cf. Clement of Alexandria, Propr 15,3: 'I ate from the tympanon, I drank from the cymbal, I carried the kernos around; I entered the inner room.' The Greek term rendered 'inner room' is pastos, which can also be translated as 'bridal chamber'.

of Apuleius (*c*.125–180 CE) in the 11th book of his *Metamorphoses*.[27] After the usual preparatory rites (with instruction on the old Egyptian script, purificatory bath and ten-day fast with renunciation of meat and wine) there finally comes the rite of initiation, which the hero of the story, Lucius, describes as follows:

> 'I approached the border zone of death, climbed over Proserpina's threshold and came back through all levels; around midnight I saw the sun shimmering in a white light, walked face to face with the gods of the dead and the gods of heaven and worshipped them in close proximity' (Apuleius, Met XI 23,7).

We may be allowed to interpret this as follows: The *mystai* join in a journey to Hades, a journey right to the entrance to the underworld, where Proserpina (Persephone) dwells. Thereby they symbolically die and achieve new life. The journey 'through the elements' (fire, water, air and earth, possibly also the ether) should perhaps indicate that the one to be initiated comes into contact with the constituents of the universe and now understands what holds the world together.[28] This interpretation is supported by archaeology in so far as the temples of Isis had underground rooms, corridors and crypts (proven for the Isaeum in Pompeii) on the walls of which are scenes from the underworld and the myth in which the killing and the continuing life of the husband of Isis, Osiris, is the central point in the underworld.[29]

Let us turn at the end of our overview of the ancient mystery cults to the Dionysus Mysteries, which are almost as old as those of Eleusis, but since they were not bound to a particular place were consequently already widespread at an early date.[30] In Rome they were at times forbidden because of the *Bacchanalian scandal* (186 BCE); the restrictions imposed because of this were, however, relaxed under Caesar and led to a multitude of Mystery groups in which the upper classes in particular adopted the cult. An inscription from Torre Nova (*c*.150 CE) lists more than 500 members of such an association; they are composed of a senator's family, his slaves and clients and are recorded according to their rank and position within the cult. The High Priestess is the lady of the house, Agrippinilla.[31] Further evidence is perhaps given by the so-called mystery villas, the best-known example being the Villa Item in Pompeii.

---

27. On this in detail, J. Gwyn Griffiths (1975), *Apuleius of Madauros: The Isis Book* (Metamorphoses, Book XI) (EPRO 39), Leiden.

28. Looking at Col and the adoration of the elements represented there by 'philosophy' one could also consider whether the initiation into the Isis Mysteries does not intend to lead to dealing with the elements without fear.

29. The myth is recorded in its essential outlines in Plutarch, Is et Os 12 – 19; cf. on this J. Gwyn Griffiths (1970), Plutarch's De Iside et Osiride, Cardiff.

30. The existence of the Dionysus Mysteries can be established with certainty in the fifth century BCE since Euripides, in his tragedy *The Bacchae*, first performed in 405 BCE, alludes to the Mysteries of Dionysus; but they are probably even older. The cult experienced particular support in Egypt where the Ptolomaeans desired from time to time to make the Dionysus Cult the state cult and tried to force the Jews to take part in the Mysteries. (Cf. 3 Macc. 2.27–30.)

31. The text is in L. Moretti, *Inscriptiones Graecae Urbis Romae* I (= IGUR I), N. 160.

Initiation into the mysteries took place at night, preferably in a cave or grotto in the open; before this took place, those to be initiated were instructed and fasted for ten days with sexual abstinence. To what extent the *Omophagia* (eating of raw meat) recorded in Euripides was still practised during the Empire is beyond our knowledge. According to Euripides' 'Bacchae' Dionysus himself practised *Sparagmos* (the tearing to shreds of living animals with one's bare hands or with the aid of various instruments) and *Omophagia* and his followers copied him.[32] From this we can infer a ritual in which the god's worshippers dismember a sacrificial animal and eat raw mouthfuls of it.[33] According to Clement of Alexandria they do this 'as a sign of the tearing-apart which Dionysus suffered at the hands of the Maenads' (Protr. 119,1) – i.e. in the eating of raw meat one is united with the divinity whose vitality one attempts in this way to make one's own. After the initiation, festivals by night take place at periodic intervals with elements such as dressing up, performance of parts of the myth, processions with dancing and music, drinking of wine and festive meals.

If we can assign to the mysteries of Dionysus the little gold Orphic-Bacchic plaques from the fifth/fourth centuries BCE – probably 'passports for the dead' to guide the Bacchantes on the way through the hereafter – then already at an early date particular hopes for the hereafter were bound up with the Dionysus Mysteries.[34] Plutarch confirms this during the time of the Empire: In his consolatory letter to his wife on the death of their daughter he refers to the initiation of both into the mysteries of Dionysus.[35] Clearly one expected a continuation of the celebration of the mysteries in the hereafter.

Mystery Cults and Pauline Churches
In view particularly of the Mysteries of Dionysus – the deity is in the wine; in the consumption of raw meat the initiates consume the deity – one can understand why the history-of-religions school derived the early Christian sacraments (baptism and Eucharist) from the Mystery Cults and explained the death and resurrection of Jesus against the background of the dying and revival of the deities of the mysteries.[36] But this kind of one-sided derivation does not do justice either to the religio-historical findings (the 'continuing to live' of Attis or Osiris

---

32. Euripides, Bacchantes 135–40, 735–47.
33. This conclusion can be drawn from a fragment of Euripides' drama, 'The Cretans' (frag. 472, 9–15 Nauck) although various cults may have run together here: 'I lead a holy life since I became an initiate of Zeus of Mount Ida and shepherd of Zagreus (= Dionysus) who revels by night. I performed the feast of raw meat (ōmophagous). I waved the torch of the Great Mother in the mountains. Having become holy I now call myself a Bacchant.'
34. Cf. C. Riedweg (1998), 'Initiation – Tod – Unterwelt. Beobachtungen zur Kommunikationssituation und narrativen Technik der orphisch-bakchischen Goldblättchen', in F. Graf (ed.), *Ansichten griechischen Rituale*, FS W.Burkert, Berlin, 359–98.
35. Plutarch, Consolatio ad uxorem 10 (Mor 611D).
36. Rudolf Bultmann, in his *Theologie des Neuen Testaments*, first published in 1953 and reprinted many times, still explained the sacraments totally from the Mystery cults. English translation: (2007), *Theology of the New Testament* (trans. K. Grobel), 2 vols, Waco: Baylor.

is different from the raising of Jesus from the dead) or to the textual findings. But on the other hand it is equally unreasonable to try to deny any influence of the mystery religions, particularly in the area of the Pauline churches.[37] The fact that the Corinthians understood the Lord's Supper in the sense of a mystery feast – the eating and drinking of the Eucharistic gifts of bread and wine create *communio* with Christ, understood as a cult hero like a deity of the *mysteries* – and that Paul corrected such an understanding ecclesiologically is, in my opinion, still the best explanation of 1 Cor. 10.16f. or the whole section on the Eucharist (1 Cor. 11.17–34). The situation appears similar in Rom. 6.3f., where Paul counters an understanding of baptism which again, in the manner of the mystery cults, connects it with participation in the fate of the deity, i.e. here in fact to the death *and* resurrection of Jesus (cf. on the other hand Col. 2.12f!). While Paul can assent wholeheartedly to the thought that in baptism the old man dies with the death of Christ, he puts limits on any present eschatology derived from the baptismal affirmation.[38] For him the imperative arises from the indicative.

3
Divination, Miracle, Magic

The Nature of the Oracle
Mystery religions, to quote Walter Burkert once again, were a 'personal option' from which one expected (certainly not only) a better life in the hereafter. Until then, however, there was usually time, and everyday life with its banal and less banal problems always had to be experienced and overcome anew. Here the ancient oracles came into play by offering help (in deciding) in almost every vicissitude in life. Oracles are prophecies that were given in particular places according to an established ritual and at established times when the deity was thought to be present; at the same time the term 'oracle' denotes the place where the prophecies are made. Altogether more than 60 locations, of varying degrees of significance, where oracles were delivered can be proved to have existed in the Greek world. The most famous oracle was without doubt that of Delphi in Greece, but the oracle of Ammon in the Oasis of Siva in Libya (which was visited by Alexander the Great among others) or the oracle of Apollo at Didyma near Miletus with its colossal temple were also known and famous far beyond their national boundaries.

The reasons for visiting an oracle were commensurately manifold: Frequently it was a matter of great political importance as in the time of the Persian Wars (490–479 BCE), just when the Delphic oracle was at the height of its fame, but far more often it was whether one should start out on a journey, whether

---

37. Zeller, however, does so in the article, 'Mysterien' (n.16) 522: 'In the area of the New Testament hardly any borrowing from the Mystery Cults can be demonstrated.'
38. Cf. against this a fragment of text in Firmicus Maternus, De errore profanorum 22.1, which is brought into connection with the mysteries of Osiris and is frequently quoted for Rom. 6.3f.: 'Be comforted, ye Mystes that the god is saved; for he will save you from troubles.'

one should buy a field, whether one should marry, etc.[39] The questioning of an oracle suggests itself particularly when misfortune and illness afflict the family. So a woman named Nikokratia asks the oracle of Zeus at Dodona in the north of Greece 'to which of the gods she should sacrifice more favourably and with better chances in order to be freed from her illness'.[40] A further example: The perhaps best-known hypochondriac of the second century CE, the Sophist and orator *Aelius Aristides* (117–180 CE), mentions in his *Hieroi Logoi*, the 'holy reports', a questioning of the oracle of Apollo in Claros on the Aegean coast when his sufferings once again became worse. From the prophet of the Clarian Apollo he receives in the 'holy night' – this stands verbatim in the text – the reply:

'We shall make you healthy and well for the honour of the fame of Asclepius of the noble city of Telephos, not far from the river Kaikos.'[41]

This is already a very complex answer, and here one could puzzle over the way and manner of the reception of the oracle and the metrical formulation of the words of the oracle in the same way as in the case of the Delphic Pythia, whose oracular speeches have been the subject of learned and less learned discussions since antiquity. Was the Pythia, the medium between the god of the Delphic oracle, Apollo, and the people, in a kind of trance when she delivered the oracle? Already in antiquity it was suspected that she chewed laurel and that this had a toxic effect, but neither leaf nor fruit of the laurel causes this. Plutarch, who was a priest at the shrine of Delphi, mentions a crevice in the interior of the temple over which the Pythia set herself. From this crevice emerged vapours and put the Pythia into a trance; but this, too, is refuted by archaeological and geological examinations. The crevice mentioned by Plutarch never existed. Consequently there is no basis for understanding the Pythia as a seer in a state of ecstasy. In general if we look at the ancient sources we see that as a rule one fell back on very simple and barely mysterious forms of proclaiming the oracle. Frequently, as

---

39. Cf. the selection and the supplementary list of questions of this kind put to the oracle in M. Totti (1985), *Ausgewählte Texte der Isis- und Sarapisreligion* (SubEpi 12), Hildesheim, 130–9; for the oracle at Dodona in Epirus the wide range of questions is demonstrated in several thousand examples of as yet unpublished lead tablets found there (cf. J. Rickenbach (1999), 'Dodona – eine der ältesten Orakelstätten der Antike', in A. Langer and A. Lutz [eds], *Orakel. Der Blick in die Zukunft* [Exhibition catalogue of the Rietberg Museum], Zürich, 44–9).

40. Preserved on a lead tablet from Dodona (fourth/third century BCE); text and translation as Nr. 126 in G. Pfohl (²1980), *Griechische Inschriften als Zeugnisse des privaten und öffentlichen Lebens*, Greek/German (TuscBü), Munich, 141f.

41. Aelius Aristides, Hieroi Logoi III 12; the translation follows H. O. Schröder (1986), *Publius Aelius Aristides: Heilige Berichte, Einleitung, deutsche Übersetzung und Kommentar* (Wiss. Kommentare zu griech. und lat. Schriftstellern), Heidelberg. On the procedure of the giving of the oracle both Tacitus, Ann II 54 and Jamblichus, Myst III 11 give a corresponding report: The priest of the oracle (prophētēs) descends into a cave, drinks from the water of a secret spring and gives aphorisms in reply to the questions which those who are seeking the oracle simply form into thoughts but must not voice. According to Jamblichus the event only took place on fixed dates.

for example at the oracle of Apollo at Corope, the question put to the oracle was in the form of a 'yes/no' question scratched onto a lead or wax tablet – should I or should I not? – and a decision was drawn by lot.

An oracle from Phratrai in the north of the Peloponnese related by Pausanias is really curious.[42] In the middle of the marketplace stood the marble statue of a bearded Hermes, in front of it a marble altar with bronze lamps. A person who wished to consult the god came in the evening, lit incense on the altar, filled the lamps with oil and lit them, laid a local coin on the altar to the right of the image and whispered in the ear of the god what he wished to ask. Then he left the marketplace, holding his ears. When he was outside the marketplace he took his hands from his ears, and whichever voice he heard first was taken for the oracle. Such random techniques offer little room for modern speculation. Even if one were sceptical about a direct intervention on the part of the gods or a fateful power, such practices were clearly comprehensible and provided help in making a decision in situations that could not be fully dealt with in a rational way.

Miraculous Healings
The Asclepian Shrines
Related to the oracles or a special type of them are the shrines of Asclepius. Asclepius, a son of the god Apollo and a human mother Koronis, a king's daughter,[43] is in the Greek pantheon responsible for healing. The places of his cult and healing were spread over the whole Roman Empire – among others was an Asclepion in Corinth;[44] their number was in the hundreds. In Epidaurus, the centre of the cult of Asclepius, mainly eye complaints, even blindness, and symptoms of paralysis were healed; from Kos, which was very closely connected with the medical school of the Asclepiads there, we know of a vegetable recipe against poisonous animals (Pliny, *Natural History* 20.264). As for Pergamum – a branch of Epidaurus, the heyday of which is dated in the second century CE when 'the whole of Asia' streamed there (Philostratos, *Life of Apollonius* 4.45) – Aelius Aristides in his 'Holy Reports' testifies to the treatment of indigestion, among other things. Here too, however, we find curious requests: one person asks that his hair may grow, another that he may be rid of lice and a third that headaches that have set in because of worry about winning in a forthcoming competition may be healed!

The character of these health resorts,[45] which were at the same time places of religious worship, can best be reconstructed by a (fictitious) tour. The shrine of Asclepius at Pergamum on the Aegean coast of modern Turkey can serve as an example. One reaches it, coming from the town, by the Holy Way and enters through a gateway into the actual temple area which is surrounded by columned halls. To the right is the library, to the left a circular temple dedicated

---

42. Pausanias VII 22.
43. Pindar, Pythian Odes 3.55–58; Plato, Republic 408 b–c.
44. Cf. Fotopoulos, *Food* (n.10).
45. Cf. on these K.Brodersen (ed.) (1999), *Antike Stätten am Mittelmeer* (Metzler Lexikon), Darmstadt, 305–8.

to Zeus Asclepius Soter, a kind of universal deity. There is also an older temple of Asclepius in the western area of the shrine. Further, there are various fountains and bathing places for cleansings and treatment as well as a theatre with room for around 3,500 visitors.

Typical characteristics of every shrine of Asclepius are, however, the incubation buildings, in Pergamum established opposite the older temple of Asclepius. These were bedrooms to which the patients went every evening led by the priest. They hoped for a vision during the night in which the god would either give instructions for a treatment which promised success or, even better, would accomplish a cure directly in the dream. Examples of these have been found on inscribed tablets from Epidaurus (end of the fourth century BCE). They contain around 70 reports of healings, of which some are presented here in more detail as illustrations and with the New Testament in mind:

> Hermodikos of Lampsakos, paralyzed in body. Asclepius healed him as he slept in the healing-room, and ordered him, when he went out, to bring a stone, the largest which he could carry, into the shrine. He then brought the one which now lies before the shrine.
>
> Alketas of Halieis. He was blind and had a vision. It seemed to him as if the god came to him and opened his eyes with his fingers. Then he saw the trees in the sanctuary for the first time. When it was daylight he came out, cured.
>
> A man from Argos, epileptic. This man, sleeping in the sanctuary, had a vision. He dreamt that the god stepped in front of him and pressed his ring on his mouth, nostrils and ears. And he became healthy.[46]

It is hardly possible to state precisely how these cures came about in the end. In principle with regard to the 'miraculous tales' from Epidaurus we must also reckon with exaggerations on the part of the priesthood, who later, for propaganda purposes, had the letters of thanks originally written on wood by the individual believers transferred onto stone. Yet cures accomplished in Epidaurus and other shrines of Asclepius remain a fact that cannot be denied. To explain them one suspects suggestion or autosuggestion where psychogenic causes of the illness exist and also the removal of psychological blockades. We also cannot rule out further manipulations on the patients during their sleep.

'Divine Humans'[47]

The temple medicine, at least in its origin, restricted the healing presence of the god to particular times and places. The 'divine humans', a kind of ancient

---

46. Quoted in R. Herzog (1931), 'Die Wunderheilungen von Epidauros. Ein Beitrag zur Geschichte der Medizin und der Religion' (*Philologus*. Supplement 12,3), Leipzig, Nrs. 15, 18, 62.

47. The term 'divine human' has come under increasing criticism in religious-historical terminology (cf. D. du Toit [1997], *Theios Anthropos. Zur Verwendung von 'Theios Anthropos' und sinnverwandten Ausdrücken in der Literatur der Kaiserzeit* [WUNT II/91], Tübingen): I use it here simply to characterize a particular type of miracle-worker.

Contemporary Religions and Philosophical Schools 39

shaman, were different. The decisive characteristic of these healers was their independence. Yet the origin of their therapies from folk-medicine connects them to the Asclepius shrines, although with the shamans the magical components come more to the fore. Empedocles, a legendary representative of this group from the fifth century BCE, is consequently traditionally considered not simply as a doctor but also as a soothsayer and 'sorcerer' who appears with claims to be divine:

> 'I travel around as an immortal god, no longer mortal ... Some ask me for prophecies, others ask for information in illnesses of every kind to hear a healing word.'[48]

Like Jesus later (cf. Mk 4.35–41!), Empedocles was also said to possess the ability to control the powers of nature; he is even said to have wakened the dead. So Heracleides Ponticos (fourth century BCE) reports in his work 'On the apparently dead or on illnesses' on the resuscitation by Empedocles of a woman who appeared no longer to have a pulse or to be breathing, who only differed from a dead person by the remnant of body heat, and who had been declared dead by the physicians.[49]

For our purposes Apollonius of Tyana is more important. Like Paul he lived in the first century CE. His biography, admittedly written only at the beginning of the third century CE by Philostratos, praises him as a man skilled in philosophy, astronomy, magic, prophecy and medicine. A series of 'miracles' are ascribed to Apollonius: He cures a dropsical patient by dietetic measures[50] or a manic youth through massive threats to the evil spirit of the illness.[51] And like Empedocles, Jesus or Paul according to Acts, Apollonius, too, raised the dead; admittedly the revival of a young woman from Rome, whose funeral procession Apollonius met by chance, is more like the raising of the young man from Nain in Lk. 7.11–17 than Acts 20.7–12:

> 'Lay the bier down, he said, I shall dry the tears which you are shedding for the girl ... But he simply touched her, spoke something mysterious and in this way wakened the girl from supposed death. The child spoke aloud and was taken back into her father's house ... When the girl's relatives presented Apollonius with 150,000 denarii he said that he gave them to the girl as a dowry' (Vit Ap 4, 45).

Finally, Apollonius also performed miracles of rescue: He protected Ephesus from the plague and several towns on the Hellespont from earthquakes (*Vit Ap* 4.10,41; 8.7,9).

---

48. Diogenes Laertius, Vit Phil 8,62.
49. Heracleides Ponticos, frg. 76–89; the fragments are printed in F. Wehrli (1969), *Die Schule des Aristoteles.Text und Kommentar, Heft VII: Herakleides Pontikos*, Basel/Stuttgart, 27–32.
50. Philostratos, Vit Ap 1,9; cf Lk 14. 1–6!
51. Philostratos, Vit Ap 4.20.

Magic

Apollonius' working of miracles was not always received positively in antiquity. How could we otherwise explain that his biographer, Philostratos, writing at the beginning of the third century CE, sees himself compelled to stand up for Apollonius against the charge of practising magic?[52] In this case the Hippocratic scientific medicine was responsible for the accusation of using magic. At a very early date they pushed the healer who cured by using ritual into the zone of magic, since he, as in the case of epilepsy, declared the illness to be caused by a demon (as possession) and trusted in prayer and incantation as forms of therapy. If one takes up this perspective one must also call Paul (and in any case Jesus) a magician, since in Acts 16.16–19 he drives a demon out of the fortune-telling slave at Philippi. And in fact Paul was also accused of being a magician, but only later, namely in the apocryphal Acts of Paul and Thecla, and for another reason; he brings women into his power through magic so that they no longer find pleasure in marriage.[53] Here we find mention of a form of ancient magic, the love spell, which in the vast majority of cases was practised by men in relation to women and with which it was a matter of making the 'object of desire' submissive. Other areas where damaging magic is used are court cases, contests or commercial transactions – i.e. always situations that develop in confrontation and whose outcome is uncertain.

So one attempts, for example, to impede the opponent in a court case by loss of speech and paralysis or wishes one's competitor at the race track a limping horse or a broken wheel, etc. As the magic papyri,[54] tablets with curses, cameos and figurines that have come down to us in great number verify, one called especially on the traditional gods of the underworld but also on Egyptian deities and those of Asia Minor (often also on Jao = Yahweh or Christ) and above all on demons. If this gives the impression that ancient magic was nothing more than a part of popular religiosity, the existence of books of magic (Acts 19.9!) shows otherwise, that magic was a professional field of study handed down in books with its own terminology. In the Graeco-Roman area specialists had this literature at their disposal, handed it down further and put their knowledge at the disposal of clients – certainly also for commercial purposes.

---

52. Cf. Philostratos, Vit Ap 1.2: 'Some even consider him a sorcerer (magon) because he kept company with the Babylonian magicians, the Indian Brahmans and the Egyptian Gymnosophists, and slander him with their completely false conception that he was knowledgeable in the violent arts.' Cf. also Dio Cassius 77.18,4 where Apollonius is accused of being goēs kai magos akribēs.

53. ActaTh 20; Acta Pl 7: 'He is a sorcerer (magos), away with him!' On this subject, also on the comparison with Apollonius, cf. here B. Heininger, *Im Dunstkreis der Magie: Paulus als Wundertäter nach der Apostelgeschichte*, in E.-M.Becker and P. Pilhofer (2005), *Biographie und Personlichkeit des Paulus* (WUNT 187) Tübingen, 271–91.

54. The classic collection is K. Preisendanz and A.Henrichs (eds) (1973/74), *Papyri Graecae Magicae – die griechischen Zauberpapyri* (SWC), Vol. 1–2, Stuttgart, reprinted 2001.

4
The Worship of the Emperor

History and Dissemination

We return once more to 1 Cor. 8.5f. The Pauline expression about the many so-called gods 'in heaven or *on earth*' can be interpreted as meaning that there are 'gods' not only in heaven but also on earth. This could be aimed at the cult of the ruler and emperor – i.e. at the custom of which we have evidence dating from the fourth century BCE of worshipping outstanding political leaders such as victorious commanders 'as gods'. At the time of the New Testament it is the Roman emperors who were given the same honour as the Olympian gods, particularly in the eastern part of the Empire: altars and temples were set up for them, priests engaged, sacrifices brought and festivals celebrated in their honour and in their name. In fact the idolizing of rulers within their lifetime was alien to Roman sensitivity (in contrast to Egypt, where the Pharaoh had always been worshipped as a son of god and the Ptolemies carried on this tradition willingly), but at the latest under Caesar the boundaries became blurred: an inscription from Ephesus celebrates him as 'the god appearing visibly (theon epiphanēn) descended from Ares and Aphrodite and general saviour (sōtēra) of human life';[55] in Rome after his victories over Pompey in North Africa and Spain he was given honours 'which went beyond the human measure' as his biographer, Suetonius, notes critically.[56] In the Quirinius Temple a statue of Caesar was to be erected with the inscription 'to the unconquered god';[57] at the games in the Circus Caesar's idol should be carried among those of the other gods. In addition, the Senate voted – still within his lifetime – that 'he should receive a god's cushion and statue, a house with a temple-pediment and its own priest',[58] which, however, was never carried out because of his murder.

His adopted son and successor, Octavian, who soon after his death had him raised by decree of the Senate to the status of a state god and thereafter could call himself *divi filius*, 'son of a deified one' (in Greek huios tou theou!) later as Caesar Augustus permitted similar honours for himself, admittedly not in Rome but in the east of the Empire – i.e. at the same time as Paul was at the height of his missionary activity.

Already in 29 BCE Augustus allowed the town of Pergamum to erect a temple for the *Dea Roma* (the personification of the Roman state) and himself; in Ephesus, where in the same year he had authorized the building of a temple for the *Dea Roma* and the *Divus Julius*, two further temples were erected for him: one in the temple area of Artemis (cf. Acts 19.23–40!) and another in a central position in the town. In Miletus there is also alongside a temple of Augustus an *Ara Augusti* in the centre of the court of the Bouleuterion; the temple in the

---

55. SIG³ 760 (48 BCE). Even more succinctly a contemporary inscription from Demetrias in Thessaly: 'Gaius Julius Caesar Emperor, God' (SEG XIV 474).
56. Suetonius, Divus Julius 76.
57. Dio Cassius 43,45,3.
58. Cicero, Phil. 2,110.

centre of Eresos on Lesbos is built 'for Augustus God Caesar'. But above all there is a series of inscriptions in Asia Minor which praise Augustus in the highest tones and refer to him as 'the Zeus of our ancestral religion and saviour of the whole human race' or, because the beginning of the year was to be transferred to his birthday (23 September), speak of the 'birthday of the god' (in the so-called Calendar Edict of Priene).[59]

Augustus' successor Tiberius (14–37 CE) then attended to the posthumous deification of his predecessor in Rome in that he introduced a rite, the so-called *consecratio*, which from that time on was granted to all the emperors so long as they did not fall prey to the *damnatio memoriae* (as e.g. Caligula or Nero): By the cremation of the corpse on the Campus Martius an eagle was released into the air and a witness swore that he had seen Augustus, as Proculus had once seen Romulus, rising up to heaven.[60] Tiberius ensured the spread and implementation of the cult of Augustus; for himself temples with priesthoods and cult can be proved in at least 11 towns in Asia Minor (e.g. in Smyrna). According to an honorific inscription from Myra he was considered by the inhabitants as a 'sublime god, son of sublime gods, lord of heaven and earth, benefactor and saviour of the whole world'.[61]

Both emperors in whose reign Paul's worldwide mission to the Gentiles substantially took place, Claudius (41–54 CE) and Nero (54–68 CE) were markedly restrained with regard to emperor-worship (this holds true at least for the young Nero). After the excesses of Caligula (37–41 CE), who soon after he succeeded to the rule behaved in the manner of a Hellenistic god-emperor, allowed himself to be addressed inter alia as 'Jupiter of Latium' and had his own temple built with priests and sacrifices,[62] clearly restraint was again called for. At any rate Claudius on several occasions rejected temples and priests for himself, although naturally he also, like Nero who followed him on the throne, was already addressed as 'god' during his lifetime.[63] Perhaps the restraint of these two rulers explains why Paul – compared to the later New Testament writings such as the book of Revelation[64] – clearly did not yet

59. OGIS 2,458 = I Priene 105.
60. Dio Cassius 56,42,3; 46,2: 'And the flames consumed it (i.e. the wood), but an eagle which was released flew up from it as if it carried the soul of Augustus heavenwards ... For her part she (i.e. Livia) donated a million sesterces to a certain Numericus Atticus, a Senator and one-time Praetor, who stated under oath that he had seen Augustus, as it is told of Proculus and Romulus, ascending into heaven.'
61. IGRR (= Inscriptiones Graecae ad res Romanas pertinentes) III 721.
62. Cf. Suetonius, Gaius Caligula 22,2–3: Recently, however, great doubt has been cast on Suetonius' depiction in A. Winterling (²2003), *Caligula. Eine Biographie*, Munich, 139–52. He writes in conclusion: 'Caligula was far from considering himself as a god or introducing an official emperor-cult in Rome. Rather he used occasional productions of his divinity to demonstrate in its absurdity the apprehensive yet hypocritical obsequiousness of the senatorial society to the Emperor in public – in front of a public of simple folk from the people which could not stifle its laughter over the people of high rank.'
63. Cf. PLond 1912; Scribonius Largus, Praef 60 for Claudius.
64. Relevant: H.-J. Klauck (1992), *Das Sendschreiben nach Pergamon und der Kaiserkult in der Johannesoffenbarung*, Bib. 73, 153–82.

have any problems with the cult of the emperor. A text such as Rom. 13.1–7, which calls for loyalty to the governing authorities, would otherwise hardly be possible!

Forms of Worship
On the other hand the worship of the emperor is for Paul and his missionary preaching a social reality (1 Cor. 8.5: 'so-called gods'!) of which he was aware wherever he went. In this connection Simon Price has spoken of how the public sphere was imprinted with the cult of the emperor: temples, altars and statues of the emperor were mainly in the centre of the town or, like the Temple of Trajan on the acropolis of Pergamum, situated in a prominent place so that one could not ignore them even if one tried. A town like Ephesus, for example, already had more than four temples for Emperors in the second century CE, a monumental altar for Antonine and various archways dedicated to the emperors ('The Arch of Hadrian'); four gymnasia were occupied in one way or another with the cult of the emperor. There were also, as in every town, a large number of statues of the emperor, which were situated in public buildings such as the library, the theatre or the town meeting place or simply lined the streets. And where there was no temple erected to the emperor, he was integrated into the traditional cults. In the shrine of Asclepius at Pergamum, for example, there was a niche in which a statue of the Emperor Hadrian was set up with the inscription 'the god Hadrian'. Another practice which today we might possibly describe as 'temple-sharing' was (normally) to place the image of the traditional god in the *cella* of the temple and a (smaller) statue of the emperor in a less important place. In an extreme case, the temple was divided: one half remained reserved for the traditional deity, and the other half belonged thenceforth to the emperor/his statue.

In saying this we have mentioned an important catchword: the central factor most closely connected to the cult of the emperor is the emperor's image (cf. Rev. 13.14f!) usually in the form of a statue. Sacrifices and festivals took place before the image; the portrait was garlanded and carried in processions.[65] Even in the 'sacrificial test' which Pliny the Younger had carried out to convict the Christians who had been denounced to him, the image of the emperor played a central part. Only those passed the test who

> 'following my (i.e. Pliny's) example called upon the gods and offered incense and wine to your image which I caused to be brought here together with the images of the gods, and they had also cursed Christ.' (Pliny, Ep X 96, 5)

For the implementation of the sacrifice as for the organization of the ritual in general priests were needed to supervise the correct course of the rites. In the provinces these were drawn from high-ranking local families for whom the office of priest in the cult of the emperor offered the possibility of distinguishing

---

65. Even in Palestine there were statues of the emperor, as e.g. in the harbour town of Caesarea Maritima extended by Herod; he also founded a temple for the emperor furnished with statues of Augustus and the Dea Roma (Jos Bell 1,414).

themselves and raising their own public prestige. Conversely, this bound these wealthy provincials even more closely to the imperial family and the idea of the Empire. To be High Priest in the cult of the emperor was a desirable goal. Apuleius of Madaura, for example, who has already been mentioned in several places, a highly educated man with a wealth of literary publications ranging from a treatise on the genius of Socrates to picaresque novels,[66] was *sacerdos provinciae*, i.e. High Priest of the cult of the emperor in his home town in North Africa in the second century CE. The office of High Priest was also open to women; the earliest inscription we have attesting this comes from Magnesia in Asia Minor and dates from between 40 and 59 CE – i.e. precisely in the main period of Paul's activity:

> The council [and the people honour] / Juliane, daughter of [Eus]tra[tos, of the son of Pha] / nostratos, the wife [of Al] / kiphronos, who was for A[sia Highprie] / st, who [became] the High Priestess / of Asia as first of the [women] ...[67]

The inscription not only confirms the admittance of a woman to the highest offices in the cult but also gives evidence of an amassing of offices, which was common for important families.

Religion frequently wins its attraction in that it offers something for the eyes and ears and not least for the stomach. In this respect the cult of the emperor is no exception. The main festival which takes place yearly on the emperor's birthday – alternatively the anniversary of his accession to the throne or the date of the foundation of the cult of the emperor in that particular town are also possible dates – perfectly meets such needs with sacrifices, processions and public feasts along with athletic and musical competitions. Tertullian's sarcastic account of such an imperial festival makes it impressively clear that such 'national holidays' were not dissimilar to today's public festivals, above all when they have a religious varnish:

> 'The Christians are considered to be enemies of the state because they do not give the Emperors any senseless, mendacious and presumptuous tributes, because as followers of the true religion they celebrate the Emperor's festivals in their hearts rather than in boisterousness. In truth it is a great honour to carry incense burners and padded chairs out into the streets, to hold feasts in the alleyways, to transform the whole town into a hot-food stall, to make the filth in the streets smell of wine, to run around in great numbers, playing practical jokes in brazenness and disgraceful obscenity ... Why do we not decorate our doorposts on the joyful days with laurel-wreaths and dull the daylight with torches? It is considered respectable when required by a public festival to give one's house the finery of a newly-opened brothel.' (Tertullian, *Apologeticum* 35)

---

66. Everything significant on the life and work of Apuleius can be found in J. Hammerstaedt et al. (2002), *Apuleius, De Magia/Über die Magie* (SAPERE 5), Darmstadt, 9–22.

67. I Magnesia 158: can be read in O. Kern (1900), *Die Inschriften von Magnesia am Maeander*, Berlin.

If the emperor was due to visit (for which we only have evidence with regard to Asia Minor from the second century CE) for his *adventus* / his parousia, the citizens decorated the town and a procession led by the town dignitaries went to meet him and lead him ceremonially into the town. The participants in the procession carried olive and palm branches, torches and incense.

Pauline and Deutero-Pauline Reception
The relevance of the cult of the emperor for the Corpus Paulinum certainly does not lie in the fact that particular Christological concepts – Jesus as 'son of God' or as sōtēr[68] – or ecclesiological ideas such as the church as a body with Christ as her head (Col. 1.18) might or even should be derived from the cult of the emperor, but far more in its significance as a foil for the reception of the Pauline and post-Pauline preaching. When for example Paul speaks in 1 Thess. 4.15–17 of the parousia tou theou in which the risen kyrios descends from heaven and the living along with the dead in Christ will be transported to meet him, the Thessalonians addressed certainly may have thought of the imperial *adventus* described above – particularly as the hero of their cult also bears the title kyrios which is quite usual in the cult of the emperor (naturally not only there)![69] There might be a similar reaction to 2 Tim. 1.10, where there is talk of the epiphaneia tou sōtēros hēmōn Christou Iēsou, the appearance of our Saviour Christ Jesus. Associations with the cult of the emperor appear almost inevitable for an inhabitant of the Roman Empire.

And sometimes it is worth looking very carefully. When Paul in 1 Cor. 11.20 describes the festive meal of the Corinthians as kyriakon deipnon, as a 'Lord's supper', the Corinthians may well have thought of associations with the emperor (worship). The rare adjective kyriakos, which in the New Testament only appears again in Rev. 1.10 ('the Lord's day') means literally 'that which belongs to the Lord', but in secular Greek it is used almost only in the sense of 'that which belongs to the emperor'.[70] This in turn does not inevitably mean that Paul borrowed the expression from the cult of the emperor – an old thesis proposed by Deissmann – but it is also not impossible.

5
Paul and the Philosophy of the Imperial Age

If the cult of the emperor represents a foil for the reception of particular Christological concepts, ecclesiological models and eschatological 'tentative attempts', this is true not only but above all in the area of ethics for philosophy, particularly in the imperial period. Here, too, we must reckon that Paul or his

---

68. Cf. 2 Tim. 1.10; Tit. 1.4; 2.13; 3.6.
69. For Nero cf. SIG³ 814.31: 'The Lord (kyrios) of the whole cosmos, Nero'; more generally Epictetes, Diss IV 1.12: 'the Lord of all, the Emperor (ho pantōn kyrios Kaisar)'.
70. Evidence in C, Spicq (1994), *Theological Lexicon of the New Testament II*, Peabody, 336–8.

disciples borrow from it, as conveyed through the filter of Hellenistic Judaism. But independently of the question whether Paul took over a thought from contemporary philosophy or not, the fact must be borne in mind that in his letters he frequently touches on themes that were the subject of detailed discussions, even whole diatribes ('treatises') by his contemporary philosophers.

An example is the Corinthian slogan about marriage quoted by Paul: 'It is well for a man not to touch a woman' (1 Cor. 7.1) and the answer to this that the apostle formulated (1 Cor. 7.2–5) leads right into the middle of Graeco-Roman discussions of marriage which – depending on the line of the particular philosophical school – receives very different answers. While e.g. the Cynics, according to Epictetus (Diss III 22.67–82) praise the unmarried state as the ideal, Musonius, a Roman Stoic who lived in the first century CE, recommends marriage for the purpose of 'companionship of life and the procreation of children'; this demands, as Musonius goes on to say, 'that they live together and generate children together and that neither has anything alone, not even his body' (Muson. XIIIa), a conception which comes fairly close to the Pauline argumentation in 1 Cor. 7.4. Plutarch, a Middle Platonist who likewise can be dated to the first and beginning of the second century CE, to name yet a third line, had even written a whole tract on questions relating to marriage, the so-called *Praecepta Coniugalia* ('Advice on Marriage').

That is why it is fitting that Paul's first biographer, Luke, has the Apostle to the Nations engage in conversation during his tour of Athens with representatives of the two leading philosophical schools of his time – the Epicureans and the Stoics (Acts 17.18) – and has him quoting a Stoic theologoumenon in his following speech on the Areopagus (Acts 17.22–31). For this reason our main interest in what follows is concerned with these two philosophical schools.

Epicurus and his School
Doctrine
How does a person find his 'life worth living', his eudaimonia? Epicurus, born on Samos 342/1 BCE and since 307/6 resident in Athens where he bought a house with a garden (kēpos) would no doubt answer: In that he tries to overcome his fears, always strives for pleasure – for pleasure (hēdonē) is the 'beginning and goal of the blissful life' (Men 128) – and wherever possible avoids pain. Already in antiquity this earned Epicurus the reproach that he was speaking out in favour of base Hedonism, a reproach which Epicurus undermined in the *Letter to Menoikeus* in which he advertised his doctrine as a way of leading a good life:

> If we say that pleasure is the goal, we do not mean the pleasures of the unrestrained and those which consist in consumption such as some people who do not know and admit this or interpret it maliciously but: to experience neither physical pain nor mental shock. For it is not drinking-sessions and a succession of processions and also not the enjoyment of boys and women, of fish and all the other things which a lavish table offers which generate the life of pleasure, but a sober intellect which works out the reasons for every choice and avoidance and drives away mere conjectures from which the most frequent shock encroaches upon the soul. (Men 131f.)

The explanation of nature,[71] theoretical cognitive reflections and basic ethical principles help the mind to shut out disquieting factors in that they show the unknown to be comprehensible, the unattainable to be irrelevant and the inevitable to be acceptable.[72] That we must die is a fact; but we can overcome the fear of death if, with Epicurus, we keep in mind that death 'is nothing which concerns us' (Men 124). For 'When "we" are, death is not there; when death is there, "we" are not. It therefore is of concern neither to the living nor to the dead since it is not there for the first and the latter are no longer there for it' (Men 125). It is similar with regard to fear of the gods/their punishments; the gods too, in the system of Epicurus, are something that does not really concern us. Certainly there are gods, but they live as blissful beings removed from time in intermediate worlds and do not care about human beings. Prayers and sacrifices do not reach them, although the Epicureans recommended participation in worship, but this should presumably serve to keep before one's eyes the objective of the blissful life that the gods personify. 'Thus the exercise of religions is given a function in terms of psychological health, perhaps even of social health too.'[73] In any case one can no longer threaten with such gods and sow the seeds of fear in a person. This means that where religion oppresses people Epicurus gives an indisputable contribution towards the necessary criticism of religion.

The Epicurean School
Epicurus gathered around himself from the beginning a circle of disciples, among them women and slaves who knew they were committed to the ideal of mutual friendship and joint search. *Askesis* and *Therapeia* – i.e. the practice of the way of life justified by philosophy and the assisting spiritual guidance (through individual conversations with accountability and intensive counselling) – characterize the common life and determine the particular attraction of the Epicurean school. At first there were branches in the Greek islands and in Asia Minor; with these Epicurus remained in contact through letters and occasional visits (Paul!). Otherwise – and this is in complete contrast to Paul – he led a secluded, quiet life which took to heart the principle he represented of lathe biōsas, 'live in seclusion' (frg. 551 Usener)[74] and avoided any wider political activity.

After his death Epicurus was given almost divine honours in his school. His birthday was celebrated as a commemoration day, and on the 20th of every month Epicurus decreed a festive gathering 'in memory of myself and

---

71. Epicurus' principal work was entitled 'On Nature' (Peri physeōs) and contained 37 books altogether; numerous fragments are preserved.

72. Cf. Kyriai Doxai ('Main Teachings') 12: 'It is not possible to cast off the fear of the most crucial legality if one has not understood the legality of the universe but suspects something on the basis of myths. Hence it is impossible to achieve unimpaired feelings of pleasure without natural science.'

73. H.-J. Klauck, *Context*, 393.

74. In an early writing Plutarch took a polemical look at this Epicurean precept for life, cf. Plutarch, Ist 'Lebe im Verborgenen' eine gute Lebensregel? With an introduction and interpreting essays by U. Berner, R. Feldmeier, B. Heininger and R. Hirsch-Luipold (2001), (SAPERE 1) Darmstadt.

Metrodoros' (cf. 1 Cor. 11.24f!).[75] The image of Epicurus, which combines in itself features of the father, the philosopher, the cult hero and the saviour – yes, even of God – was frequently reproduced and was intended to awaken in outsiders the desire to know more about this man. This was clearly successful time after time in the following centuries, for the school of Epicurus continued to exist until the middle of the first century CE.[76] Already in the first century BCE Epicureanism came to Rome in the figure of Philodemus of Gadara (c.110–40 BCE) who opened a new school at Herculaneum.

However, the philosophy of Epicurus was really made popular in Rome by Lucretius who described Epicurean physics in his didactic writing, *De rerum natura*. In Lucretius this is connected more strongly than in Epicurus with a sharp criticism of all traditional religion. This progressive attitude found many echoes in the Roman society of the Late Republic: Epicurean positions repeatedly appear in the writings of Cicero, poets such as Horace and Virgil develop sympathies for the teaching of Epicurus and even in the work of Seneca, who from his overall profile is certainly to be described as a Stoic, there are clear borrowings from Epicureism. At the time of the Augustan reformation with its revival of traditional values and cults Epicureism lost some of its significance; yet it remained present, particularly in the upper strata of society, and time and again won over influential circles. An example is Plotina, the wife of the Emperor Trajan.

The Stoa
History and Major Representatives
The predominant philosophy of the early imperial period was the *Stoa*. It owes its name to the stoa poikilē in Athens, the 'many-coloured hall' decorated with frescoes in which the founder of the philosophical line, Zeno of Kition, taught from *c*.300 BCE. His division of the Stoic system into three parts – into logic, physics and ethics – still existed in the imperial period, even if the outstanding representatives of Stoic philosophy at that time, Seneca (*c*.0–65 CE), who was active in the imperial court as tutor of Nero and from time to time also running government business, and the former slave Epictetus (*c*.50–120 CE), who after his expulsion from Rome taught in Nicopolis on the west coast of Greece, were in fact purely moral philosophers.

Together Seneca and Epictetus, with the – admittedly later – philosopher-ruler Marcus Aurelius usually dominate the perception of the Stoa in the imperial period because they left an extensive body of writings. But they are, as it were, only the tip of a 'Stoic iceberg'. To the Stoics writing in Greek during the Augustan period belong such well-known people as the historical philosopher Areius Didymus, the geographer Strabo or, possibly less well known, the grammarian Heraclitus, to whom we owe a still-preserved allegorizing reinterpretation of the Homeric tales of the gods. Cornutus drew up a summary of the Stoic theology drawn from interpretation of myths; the lectures of the Roman

---
75. Diogenes Laertius, Vit Phil 10,18.
76. In 51 CE a certain Patronus was the leader of the school; but towards the end of the 50s BCE the 'garden' was on the verge of ruin (Cicero, Fam 13,1,3; Att 5,11,6).

knight Musonius (25/30–100 CE) – unfortunately preserved only in fragments – come strikingly close to Paul.[77] Likewise only preserved in fragments is the 'Stoic Ethics' of Hierocles of Alexandria, written in the second century CE.[78] For Latin scholars alongside Seneca we should refer particularly to Manilius with his Stoic Astrology and to Persius.

The Telos-Formula and the Concept of Freedom
Like Epicureanism, Stoicism too was concerned with eudaimonia, the successful life in the face of a world that had become increasingly more complex. No matter how confusing this might be, the proverbial Stoic composure – in this connection the Stoics speak of the 'imperturbability of the soul' – can be achieved if one simply heeds the Stoic telos-formula: homologoumenōs (tē physei) zēn, 'live in harmony (with nature)'! There is no hidden ecological programme concealed behind this; it is simply the challenge to mankind to follow the divine Logos – i.e. the Stoic world principle. As logos spermatikos, which can also be envisaged as *Pneuma*, as a kind of delicate substance like fire, it penetrates everything that exists. It is detectable in the form of the (caring) divine providence (*providentia*) and fate (*fatum*) to which the wise Stoic should confidently devote himself and allow himself to be led – even when fate has its proverbial strokes in store and even if it means death. For the Stoics the world is a great stage upon which each must play his allotted part to the best of his ability.[79] Only in this way does the wise man win his identity and freedom. If, however, he resists the Logos he is in the grip of the emotions – among which, alongside desires and lust, the Stoics count fear and mourning – and then he is not free and does not achieve his destiny. The description of a dog tethered to a wagon attributed to Zeno and Chrysippus describes the Stoic conception of humankind aptly: either he runs willingly alongside or he is dragged along, but the wagon/its driver determines the direction![80] Or to quote Seneca: 'The fates lead the willing, the unwilling they pull along' (*Ep Mor* 107.11).

That such a drastic picture inevitably raises questions about the Stoic understanding of freedom is obvious. Does the talk of the wise Stoic, who not only bears the blows of fate laid upon him by providence 'a-pathetically' – i.e. dispassionately (without pain, anger or mourning) – but accepts them thankfully and so should win his identity (because he is living in harmony with the Logos and therefore in the end with himself) and freedom – does this not border on

---

77. R. Laurenti (1989) gives detailed information on the life and work of Musonius: 'Musonio, maestro di Epitetto', in ANRW II/36.3, 2105–46.

78. Cf. H. von Arnim (1906), *Hierokles. Ethische Elementarlehre* (Papyrus 9780) along with the ethical excerpts preserved in Stobaeus (Berliner Klassikertexte 4), Berlin.

79. Epictetus, Ench 17: 'Consider this: You have a role in a play, whose character is determined by the author, a short one when he wishes it short, a long one when he wishes it long. If he wants you to play a beggar, play this role sensitively; the same is true for a cripple, a ruler or an ordinary person. Your task is simply to play the part assigned to you well; it is up to another to choose it.' The parable of the journey (Ench 7) also argues in this sense; cf. for this and the whole topic H.-J. Klauck (1989), 'Dankbar leben, dankbar sterben. Eucharistein bei Epiktet', in *id., Gemeinde, Amt Sakrament. Neutestamentliche Perspektiven*, Würzburg, 373–90.

80. Handed down by Hippolytus, Ref Omn Haer I 21 (= SVF 2, 975).

cynicism? Such a perspective is perhaps too modern and fails to recognize the efforts of Stoicism to salvage personal freedom in a contemporary situation where the citizen of the Polis is to a large degree robbed of possibilities for political action. Hence for the Stoics, freedom is above all a 'mental problem' in so far as we must learn to differentiate what is within our power (ta eph hēmin) and what is not in our power (ta ouk eph hēmin). What is not in our power are all 'external factors': spouse, children, siblings, friends, landholding, clothing, house, our body. All of these, according to Epictetus in his great Diatribe on Freedom (*Diss* IV 1, 62–75), can be taken from us and frequently far sooner than we would like.[81] In fact all that we have in our hands is actually only our bearing and inner attitude to things – i.e. how we evaluate them and what status we grant them. Whether I am poor or rich, whether I am a slave or a free man in itself means nothing for my eudaimonia according to the Stoic conviction; it is the *attitude to things* (i.e. whether I fix my pleasure on the existence of my property or on my own worth) which is the decisive factor. Freedom is consequently transposed completely into the heart.

Suicide and Eschatology
It also belongs to Stoic freedom to put an end to one's own life if the situation makes it necessary. Other than Paul, who in Phil. 1.21–24 considers 'dying as gain' and expresses the wish 'to depart and be with Christ' but would never lay a hand upon himself, Seneca and Epictetus clearly contemplate the possibility of suicide:

> Wherever you look, there is the end of your unhappiness. Do you see that steeply falling place? From there one steps down into freedom ... Am I showing you solutions which are far too arduous and demand great courage and strength? You ask, what is the way to freedom? Every vein in your body![82]

Although Seneca had often thought of suicide in his younger years and ended his life at Nero's demand, neither he nor Epictetus speak of a longing for death from a vague weariness of life. The criterion for suicide is always logical (corresponding to the Logos), i.e. one must register strong signals of fate (a fatal illness, unbearable treatment by doctors, robbery and piracy, tyranny with torture and execution) which can be understood as nothing other than a request to end one's life. One's first duty is always to stand fast at the place where one is posted.

This attitude is all the more astonishing since Stoicism, completely contrary to the Platonic teaching on the immortality of the soul and also in contrast to the Judeo-Christian hope of resurrection, did not expect that the soul would live on after death. Certainly Seneca is not so radical on this point as is Epictetus, for whom soul and body dissolve into the elements after death (they become again a component of the primary material from which the world is made) while

---

81. A detailed discussion of the Epictetan Diatribe on Freedom can be found in S. Vollenweider (1989), *Freiheit als neue Schöpfung. Eine Untersuchung zur Eleutheria bei Paulus und in seiner Umwelt* (FRLANT 147), Göttingen, 23–104.
82. Seneca, De ira III 15,4; cf. also Epictetus, Diss I 24,20.

Seneca can imagine that the soul may exist for a limited period after death. But for him, too, this continued existence comes to an end at the next *Ekpyrosis*, i.e. the periodically recurring cosmic incineration in which the world is destroyed in a tremendous conflagration in order to be created anew thereafter.

6
Gnosis

Gnosis in the New Testament?

It is justified to ask to what extent the treatment of Gnosis has a place in a book on Paul. The outline of Gnostic doctrinal systems only become visible in the middle of the second century CE; the heyday of what we now subsume under Gnosis, however, comes much later, namely in the third/fourth century and reached its climax (and its end) in Manichaeism. On the other hand the term gnōsis appears frequently in First Corinthians[83] and the old thesis of a 'Gnosis in Corinth'[84] still occasionally finds supporters among modern interpreters. But neither the insistence upon gnōsis in the debate on food sacrificed to idols (cf. 1 Cor. 8.1–3,7,10f.) nor the deep respect shown in Corinth for spiritual-intellectual charismata such as gnōsis (cf. 1 Cor. 1.5; 12.8; 13.2; 14.6) nor the denial of the Resurrection (cf. 1 Cor. 15) should 'be expanded in the sense of a Gnostic gnōsis in a speculative mythological fashion'.[85]

Matters appear somewhat differently in the area of influence of the deutero- and trito-Paulines. At the end of the letter to Timothy the author asks 'Timothy' particularly to 'avoid the profane chatter and contradictions of what is falsely called knowledge (tēs pseudōnymou gnōseōs); by professing it some have missed the mark as regards the faith' (1 Tim. 6.20f.). Here the term gnōsis already stands for a clearly defined doctrine, the contours of which can be determined in rough outline (even if through the author's spectacles)[86] from further examples from the pastoral epistles: A strongly Jewish, perhaps even a Jewish-Christian, element is unmistakeable (Tit. 1.10) with a fateful interest in 'Jewish myths' and genealogies (Tit. 1.14; 1 Tim. 1.3f.); further, the adversaries are characterized by a strict ascetic trait. They forbid marriage and demand abstinence from foods (1

---

83. Ten instances in 1 Cor. alone; in the undisputed Pauline epistles there are three further examples in Rom., six in 2 Cor. and one in Phil. The statistics for the verb ginōskein reveal a less distinctive picture, but here, too, the Corinthian correspondence musters the largest number: Rom.: nine; 1 Cor.: 16; 2 Cor.: eight; Gal.: four; Phil.: five.

84. W. Schmithals (³1969), *Die Gnosis in Korinth. Eine Untersuchung zu den Korintherbriefen* (FRLANT 66), Göttingen; also *id*. (1984), *Neues Testament und Gnosis* (EdF 208), Darmstadt.

85. Cf. W. Schrage (1995), *Der erste Brief an die Korinther*, Vol 2: 1 Kor 6,12–11,16 (EKK 7/2), Zürich etc., 227.

86. Cf. J. Roloff (1988), *Der erste Brief an Timotheus* (EKK 15), Zürich etc., 228–39 (digression on the adversaries) according to whom the description of the adversaries in the Pastorals 'can be read almost as a case study of how the emergence of the Gnostic trend within the Gentile Christian congregations in the 1st century came about' *ibid*., 236.

Tim. 4.3). This all culminates, so to speak, in a present eschatology 'by claiming that the resurrection has already taken place' (2 Tim. 2.18).

If in what follows we attempt to shed a little light upon and supplement these sparse statements using not only Gnostic texts such as the writings from Nag Hammadi,[87] but also the writings of the Church Fathers and apocryphal 'Acts' of the apostles. In so doing, we must always bear in mind that in this particular case we are attempting to explain older texts using more recent ones – i.e. using a hermeneutical method which qua se is not legitimate or is at least dubious. This is precisely the difficulty in any New Testament consideration of Gnosis and the reason why the determination of the origin of Gnosis has not yet been satisfactorily resolved.

Outline of the System

The Greek word gnōsis means 'knowledge, awareness' and in Gnosis it has the same connotation. One could describe the Gnostics as a kind of ancient society of knowledge and information who, in contrast to us today, did not gather information indiscriminately or accumulate knowledge but purposefully sought answers to basic human questions. Clement of Alexandria, in his *Excerpta ex Theodoto*, a collection of Gnostic quotations and texts written around 200 CE, recorded seven such fundamental questions:

> Who were we? What have we become? Where were we? Where have we been cast? Whither are we rushing? From what have we been freed? What is birth, what is rebirth? (*Excerpta ex Theodoto* 78, 2)

The Gnostic Myth

The Gnostic myth[88] gives the following – very rough – answer to these: The world and humankind came into being as the result of a mistake or a programmatic error; *qua se* both were not planned in the Gnostic programme which, like a kind of endless loop, brings forth constantly new emanations ('outflows') of

---

87. Nag Hammadi is the name of a small town in the upper reaches of the Nile between Siut and Luxor. In 1945/46, 13 codices were found there with writings in Coptic and for the most part Gnostic content, inter alia the Gospel of Thomas and a previously unknown 'Acts' of the Apostles which bore the title 'The Deeds of Peter and the Twelve Apostles'. Altogether there are 52 individual works on around 1,200 pages. A complete German translation is now available: H.-M. Schenke, H.-G. Bethge and U. U. Kaiser (eds) (2001/2003), Nag Hammadi Deutsch, Bd 1 : NHC I,1 – V,1; Bd. 2 NHC V,2 – XII,1, BG 1 und 4. Eingeleitet und übersetzt von Mitgliedern des Berliner Arbeitskreises für Koptisch-Gnostische Studien (GCS NF 8.12 = Koptisch-gnostische Schriften 2/3), Berlin. Cf. J. M. Robinson (ed.), ([4]1996), The Nag Hammadi Library in English, Leiden/New York/Köln: Brill.

88. In fact there is no such thing as *the* Gnostic myth but rather a number of Gnostic myths. This is because Gnosis does not represent a uniform organization but falls apart into various 'schools' or, better, systems. The reports of the Church Fathers on the diverse Gnostic schools (cf. e.g. Irenaeus, *Adv Haer* I 25,1 – 31,2) must, however, be read with a healthy dose of historical scepticism. In my view at least the differentiation into Valentinian (after the Roman theologian, Valentinus) and Sethian (after the redeemer-figure, Seth) Gnosis makes sense. This allows various writings to be grouped.

the Divine. In Gnostic literature these emanations are called Aeons, and one of these Aeons, the heavenly Sophia (clearly, the personified Old Testament Wisdom is in the background) is in the end responsible for the whole disaster. Without the consent of the 'Spirit' – here a cipher for the highest god who as such can only be described in the negative ('un-limited', 'im-penetrable', 'im-mense', 'in-visible', 'un-utterable', etc.) – and also without the consent of her other half, her masculine–feminine spirit, allows a thought to emerge and become manifest, i.e. there occurs a kind of materialization of the spirit which, however – similar to a mutation in genetic reduplication – goes wrong:

> Her thought could not be inactive and her work emerged, imperfect and ugly because she had made it without her other half ... She pushed it away from her, away from that place so that none of the Immortals saw it, because she had given birth to it in ignorance. She bound it with a cloud of light and placed a throne in the middle of the cloud..., and she called it Jaldabaoth. (AJ BG 8502/2 37, 12 – 38, 14)[89]

The Jaldabaoth, as it were the Gnostic variant of the Old Testament Creator God and the Platonic Demiurge, immediately sets about to create a world opposite to the heavenly world, admittedly with active assistance from the highest god. Because Sophia's mistake must be made good, the highest god allows his reflection to appear 'in the form of a man in the water' – presumably the thought here is of the components of water in the lowest heaven (clouds) – which made a powerful impression upon Jaldabaoth and the seven Archons he had created and inspired them to create humankind:

> They saw in the water the appearance of the likeness and said to one another: Let us make a man like the picture and appearance of god. (AJ BG 8502/2 48,8–14; cf. Gen. 1.26!)

The result is a being consisting of a soul, but one which is not yet capable of life; only by a trick was Jaldabaoth brought to breathe 'something of the spirit which is in him' into it, which he then does: 'And so he blew into the body some of his spirit – that is the strength from the mother – and the body moved in that hour' (AJ BG 8502/2 51,16–52,1). The echoes of Gen. 2.7 are unmistakable, and yet there is a significant difference from the second biblical account of the Creation; as yet the Gnostic Adam is a being of soul and spirit who, because of

---

89. Here and in what follows I orient myself on the variant of the Gnostic myth as it is related in the *Apocryphon of John* (= AJ), one of the writings which can be assigned to Sethian Gnosis, which is handed down in four manuscripts. Three were found in Nag Hammadi, another was known earlier from a Coptic papyrus in Berlin (BG 8502/2). The manuscripts available witness to a longer (NHC II/1; IV/1) and a shorter (NHC III/1; BG 8502/2) version which for their part represent a translation of a Greek original. AJ belongs to the oldest original Coptic texts and might be dated to around 150 CE, perhaps even a little earlier. The translation and numbering offered in the English translation are based on the Berlin papyrus according to the edition of W. Till and H.-M. Schenke (1972), *Die gnostischen Schriften des Koptischen Papyrus Berolinensis. Herausgegeben, übersetzt und bearbeitet* (TU 60), Berlin.

the divine spark within him, is actually superior to his Creator.[90] Jaldabaoth and his Archons, in the meantime jealous of their creation, transplant the Adam of soul and spirit to 'the realms at the ground of all material' and give him a second, material body:

> They made once more a further shape, this time from earth, water, fire and wind (pneuma), that is, from matter, darkness, desire and the opposing spirit (pneuma). This is the fetter, this the grave of the bodily shape, made out of matter, which is cast upon man. (AJ BG 8502/2 55,3–13)

Soteriology: Liberation through Knowledge
What must have already become clear[91] from the expositions of the myth is that only the spirit of man, his transcendental core or – in mythical terms – his divine spark of light is capable of being redeemed while the material body and, in complete contrast to the Platonic tradition, even the soul as seat of the desires and passions remain behind when the spirit rises after death. In order for this to happen at all man needs knowledge, more precisely self-knowledge, of which, however, he is in himself incapable. Here Gnosis clearly moves away from the Socratic-Platonic philosophy. Man's entanglement in passions and desires, his inability to get out of the 'daily grind' and the constant danger of being drawn into the tumult of the world, are a hindrance to self-knowledge from the beginning. For this disastrous situation Gnosis invokes a series of images: The picture of the prison from which the person cannot free himself, the example of inebriation and, very prominent, the image of sleep from which the person must be awakened by a call – i.e. an external impulse, a 'revelation' which comes from beyond the cosmos. This call is uttered by the Revealer or Saviour figure which can be either an historical (Simon Magus) or a mythical character. Abstract forms such as Sophia or the Protenoia ('first idea') can also fulfil this function. Where Gnosis is infused with Christian elements (the heavenly) Christ naturally functions as a Redeemer-figure. This can happen in such a way that Christ is equated with one of the highest emanations of God, e.g. the 'Son of the First Father' who then descends to earth from the heavenly heights. The so-called 'Naasene Psalm' preserved in Hippolytus gives a good insight into such ideas:

> Then Jesus spoke: 'Look, Father, at this being pursued by evils who is wandering around on earth, far from your breath. It is trying to escape from the bitter chaos and does not know how it might prevail.
>
> For its sake, send me, Father! I shall descend, holding the seal, I shall stride through all the Aeons, I shall uncover all secrets ... and I shall reveal the secrets of the Holy Way which I have named Knowledge (gnōsis).'[92]

90. 'And the man glowed because of the shadow of the light which was in him and his mind rose above that of the one who had created him' (AJ BG 8502/2 54,5–8).
91. If one questions the myth it gives a further comprehensible reason why the soul lacks the ability to be freed: The soul – or, better, the individual parts of the soul – stem from the seven Archons, Cf. BG 8502/2 49,2 – 50,4!
92. Hippolytus, *Ref* V 10.2.

The knowledge made possible in this way, i.e. with the help of an external call, permits the Gnostic to find himself but is naturally not yet to be equated with the return to the heavenly realm of light. This occurs only at the moment of death through the ascent of the spirit already mentioned, which, however, is not without danger. The spirit which leaves the body behind on earth must pass through several heavens (and in each heaven leaves a part of itself behind until at the end only the pure, divine spirit remains); the demons, Archons and not least Jaldabaoth attempt to block the soul's way. The 'post-mortem' journey to heaven succeeds only by using particular aids such as incantations, magical signs, amulets or passwords which must be shown or recited in passing from one heaven to the next. The end of the world is then reached when all Gnostics have achieved knowledge – which means when all the spiritual particles have returned to the heavenly realm of light. What is left of the world then falls to pieces and vanishes, a process which is on occasion described after the pattern of the Stoic doctrine of Ekpyrosis.[93]

Question of Origin
If we again recall the original Gnostic texts – which are still hard to comprehend even after a second or third reading – a system becomes apparent which envisages a distant god (negative theology); introduces a host of further divine figures among which is also a creator god (Jaldabaoth) who is sometimes described as ignorant, sometimes as evil; subscribes to a fundamentally negative view of the world and matter; and portrays the disastrous situation of humanity or a particular class of humanity as a mythical drama from which, admittedly, liberation is possible. The magic word for this is gnōsis, 'knowledge' which, however, can only be achieved through an other-worldly redeemer-figure ('call') and which shows the Gnostic the way back to the heights.[94]

When and where did this system originate? The massive recourse to Old Testament traditions, particularly the story of Creation, the prominent role of Wisdom and also the marked correspondence with the pessimistic, dualistic view of the world found in Jewish Apocalypticism – there is no salvation in the world as we know it – point to a Jewish milieu or to one strongly influenced by Judaism. The proximity to the thought of the Jewish philosopher Philo of Alexandria also supports this interpretation: like Gnosis he uses Plato as a source of ideas and as a hermeneutical lens when dealing with Biblical texts. And finally, the findings in the Pastoral epistles also confirm this suggestion: The false doctrine they call 'Gnosis' clearly has a Jewish colouring (see above). A chronological ordering of Gnosis *before* Christianity cannot be substantiated by these arguments, nor even the simultaneous emergence of Christianity and Gnosis. The decisive obstacle to an early dating lies in the fact that we have no extant texts which are clearly of Gnostic provenance from the first century CE or even earlier; those which we know stem at the earliest from the middle of the second century CE. It is due to

---

93. Irenaeus, *Adv Haer* I 7,1.
94. Cf. C. Markschies (2000), Art. Gnosis/Gnostizismus. II. Christentum, RGG[4] 3, 1045–53.

this circumstance that the 'ecclesial-historical solution' going back to Adolf von Harnack is again becoming more popular. This understands Gnosis as an 'acute Hellenization' of the Christian faith in the 'laboratory' of the Christian theology of the first centuries (Markschies).

References

For abbreviations of ancient literature, authors and works, inscriptions and papyri cf. *The Oxford Classical Dictionary* (1996³), Oxford/New York: Oxford University Press. Brill's New Pauly. Encyclopaedia of the Ancient World, Leiden: Brill.

Public Worship (and General Literature)
W. Burkert (1985), *Greek Religion*, Cambridge, MA: Harvard University Press.
H.-J. Klauck (2000), *The Religious Context of Early Christianity. A Guide to Graeco-Roman Religions* (Studies in the New Testament and Its World), Edinburgh: T&T Clark.

Mystery Cults
W. Burkurt (1987), *Ancient Mystery Cults*, Cambridge, MA: Harvard University Press.
J. Godwin (1989), *Mystery Religions in the Ancient World*, London: HarperCollins.
M. W. Meyer (1987), *The Ancient Mysteries: A Sourcebook. Sacred Texts of the Mystery Religions of the Ancient Mediterranean World*, San Francisco: Harper & Row, pb. edition 1999.

Divination, Miracle, Magic
F. Graf (1996), *Gottesnähe und Schadenzauber. Die Magie in der griechisch-römischen Antike*, Munich: Beck.
F. Graf and S. Iles Johnston (1999), 'Art. Magie, Magier', *DNP* 7, 662–72.
H. W. Parke (1967), *Greek Oracles* (Classical History and Literature), London: Hutchinson.

The Worship of the Emperor
S. R. F. Price (1980), 'Between Man and God: Sacrifice in the Roman Imperial Cult', *JRS* 70, 28–43.
Ders. (1984, 1987), *Rituals and Power. The Roman Imperial Cult in Asia Minor*, Cambridge.

Paul and the Philosophy Prevalent in the Roman Empire
T. Engberg-Pedersen (2000), *Paul and the Stoics*, Louisville: Westminster John Knox Press.
M. Erler (1994), 'Epikur. Die epikureische Schule. Lukrez', in H. Flashar (Hg.), *Die hellenistische Philosophie. Erster Halbband* (Die Philosophie der Antike 4/1), Basel: Schwabe, 29–490.
M. Forschner (²1995), *Die stoische Ethik. Über den Zusammenhang von Natur-, Sprach- und Moralphilosophie im altstoischen System*, Darmstadt: Wissenschaftliche Buchgesellschaft.
A. A. Long and D. N. Sedley (2000), *Die hellenistischen Philosophen. Texte und Kommentare*, Stuttgart: Metzler, 29–522.
P. Steinmetz (1994), 'Die Stoa', in H. Flashar (Hg.), *Die hellenistische Philosophie. Zweiter Halbband* (Die Philosophie der Antike 4/2), Basel: Schwabe, 491–716.

Gnosis
K. L. King (2003), *What is Gnosticism?* Cambridge, MA: Harvard University Press.
C. Markschies (2001), *Die Gnosis* (BsR 2173), Munich: Beck.
Ders. (2000), *Art. Gnosis/Gnostizismus. II. Christentum*, RGG⁴ 3, 1045–53.
K. Rudolph (³1990), *Die Gnosis. Wesen und Geschichte einer spätantiken Religion* (UTB 1577), Göttingen: Vandenhoeck & Ruprecht.

Chapter 4

THE JEWISHNESS OF PAUL
Jörg Frey

As long as he lived Paul was a *Jew*, even as an apostle of Christ. There is nothing to support the assumption that he at any time called into question his affiliation, justified by birth, to God's chosen people 'Israel' (Rom. 11.1), to the 'Jews' (Gal. 2.15: Ioudaioi) and the relationship to his 'brothers' and 'kindred' (Rom. 9.3). Even if others doubted his loyalty to the Torah (cf. Rom. 3.31; Acts 21.21,28) he never saw himself as breaking the Law or as 'apostate'.

The common picture, inspired by the Lukan report of the turning point in Paul's life (Acts 9), of *the 'conversion' of the Jew Saul into the Christian Paul* is consequently *factually incorrect*. It contradicts not only Paul's own statements about himself but also Luke's picture of Paul (Acts 26.6ff.). The Judaism of Saul/Paul is therefore anything but a 'dark past'[1] which his 'enlightened' Christian self-understanding could leave behind. If Paul's Jewishness basically determines the shape of his education, if the Torah – practised from his early youth – determined his way of life *before* the turning point, then his existence as a Jew is the basis to which the apostle's thinking remains related. Consequently 'knowledge of Saul the *Jew* is a precondition of understanding Paul the *Christian*'[2] and his theology.

This being so, there arises a series of complex questions:

- How can we determine the *Jewish identity of the 'pre-Christian' Paul* (within the currents of contemporary Judaism)? Which concerns and themes shaped him?
- How can we determine his position within contemporary Judaism?
- How can we understand in this framework his statements on circumcision and the Law, on the fate of Israel and – central to his thinking – his Christology?

---

1. Thus J. Becker (1993), *Paul: Apostle to the Gentiles* Louisville: Westminster (trans. O. C. Dean; 1) 33. G. Strecker (2000), *Theology of the New Testament* (trans. E. Boring; New York: de Gruyter), 21 even infers from Gal. 1.13–24 and Phil. 3.3–11 that Paul's 'self-understanding included a fundamental break with Judaism'. Paul's pattern of contrast in some of his texts has led scholars to fatal misjudgements and implicitly fostered tendencies of a Christian anti-Judaism.

2. M. Hengel and R. Deines, *The Pre-Christian Paul*, xiii. – On the name 'Paul' see Chapter 5 on Paul's life by E. Ebel in this volume.

1
Paul's Jewishness according to his Own Testimony and the Acts of the Apostles

The basis of our knowledge of how Paul understood himself are the texts in which he speaks about his own Jewishness (particularly Gal. 1.13f.; Phil. 3.5f.; 2 Cor. 11.22f.; Rom. 11.1; further Gal. 2.15; Rom. 9.1–5) together with the Lukan statements (Acts 22.3; 23.6; 26.4f.) which must be critically included in a comprehensive historical appreciation.[3]

The Evidence about his Background
Let us begin with the longest text, the beginning of the speech for the defence which *Luke* in Acts 22.3 puts into the mouth of the apostle when he was arrested in Jerusalem, and which Paul is said to have given in Aramaic (tē Hebraidi dialektō).

> 'I am a Jew, born in Tarsus in Cilicia, but brought up in this city at the feet of Gamaliel, educated strictly (akribeia) according to our ancestral law, being zealous (zēlotēs) for God, just as all of you are today.'

In Acts 23.6 the Lukan Paul, in the scene before the Jewish Sanhedrin, states more precisely:

> 'I am a Pharisee, a son of Pharisees. I am on trial concerning the hope of the resurrection of the dead.'

In his last speech for the defence in Acts 26.4f. Luke has Paul say in addition:

> 'All the Jews know my way of life from my youth, a life spent from the beginning among my own people and in Jerusalem ... I have belonged to the strictest party (hairesis) of our religion and lived as a Pharisee.'

These texts provide a series of references to Paul's religious background which are confirmed by his own testimony (see 1.2): Paul appears as a *Jew*, more precisely as a member of the party of the *Pharisees*, whose observance of the

---

3. On the question of method: Since the time of the 'Tübingen School' in the nineteenth century (Ferdinand C. Baur) and its 'tendency criticism', it has been controversial how the Lukan statements are to be evaluated historically alongside the authentic Pauline texts. Following Baur numerous interpreters (e.g. from the Bultmann School) consider only Paul's own texts to be real sources while Acts is considered as a kind of 'secondary literature'. Yet even if the 'tendency' of the Lukan picture of Paul cannot be denied, Paul's letters (e.g. his autobiographical description in Gal. 1–2) are also by no means 'unbiased'. There is no 'pure' source. Hence the only thing we can do in a historical reconstruction is to include *all* possible sources (including Acts!) *critically*, i.e. taking into consideration their historical locus, their literary form and their intent. Where Paul and Luke differ, generally Paul deserves priority, but not everything which is not verifiable from the Pauline epistles can be considered as Lukan fiction.

Torah was considered to be *particularly strict*, and as a *zealot* for the fathers' statutes. According to the Lukan understanding Paul as a devout Jew is closely connected with the Holy City. He is accused there 'because he is still a Pharisee and orthodox Jew'.[4] Consequently the accusation of the zealous people of Jerusalem that he is a law-breaker and demagogue (Acts 21.27f; 24.5f.) is unsubstantiated as Luke sees it.

Luke alone provides further details: Only from him do we learn that Paul comes from Tarsus in Cilicia (Acts 9.11; 21.39; 22.3; cf. 9.30; 11.25). Paul himself only once mentions his long period of activity in the double province of Syria-Cilicia (Gal. 1.21) without naming Tarsus. He writes nothing about his birth and upbringing there. Only Luke mentions the Jewish name Saul, the old king's name of the tribe of Benjamin (Acts 9.4,11,17; 22.7,13; 26.12), while Paul himself always uses the name (possibly the *cognomen*) Paulos. It is also only from Acts that we learn of his *study* of the Torah *in Jerusalem* and his education to be a Pharisaic scribe in the house Rabbi Gamaliel I, the leading Pharisaic teacher of his time (cf. Acts 5.34). Yet we must not assess every detail unconfirmed by Paul's own words in his preserved letters as Lukan invention. Paul had little reason to mention these facts in his own writings. Implicitly, however, all three are supported by his own testimony.[5]

More difficult to evaluate is the claim of the Lukan Paul that he grew up in Jerusalem 'from my youth' so that 'all the Jews' know his way of life (Acts 26.4)[6] while Paul himself emphasizes in Gal. 1.22f. that he was personally unknown to the Jewish Christian congregations in Judaea. Consequently it is controversial when Paul was in Jerusalem and where he acquired his characteristic Jewish (and Greek) education: in Tarsus or in Jerusalem. While some interpreters follow Acts 22.3 and 26.4 and locate Paul in Jerusalem from his childhood,[7] others, referring to Gal. 1.22f., deny that he ever sojourned in Jerusalem before the turning point

---

4. Thus J. Jervell (1998), *Die Apostelgeschichte* (KEK 3; Göttingen: Vandenhoeck & Ruprecht), 591.

5. Paul's origin in Tarsus is hardly ever criticized as fictional, even by radical critics of the Lukan work, probably because it fits well into the overall image of the apostle to the Gentiles. In contrast with this, the information about Paul's sojourn in Jerusalem and the Pharisaic studies of the Law under Gamaliel were often rejected. The reason behind this is methodologically that the mention of Tarsus runs counter to Luke's tendency of 'judaizing' Paul's image while the reference to Gamaliel is in keeping with it. The different exegetical treatment of the two pieces of information also points to a long-standing exegetical tendency to see Paul in sharper contrast to contemporary Judaism than he actually was, a tendency which we can interpret as a subtle form of Christian anti-Judaism.

6. This is certainly a rhetorical exaggeration; cf. C. K. Barrett (1998), *A Critical and Exegetical Commentary on the Acts of the Apostles*, vol. II (ICC; Edinburgh: T&T Clark), 1151.

7. W. C. van Unnik (1973), 'Tarsus or Jerusalem', in van Unnik, *Sparsa Collecta*, vol. I (NovTSup 29; Leiden: Brill), 259–320 suspects that Paul's parents returned to Jerusalem with the child Paul; cf. also Haacker, 'Paul's Life', 21; Jervell, *Apostelgeschichte*, 542 (n.4). According to a tradition attested to by Jerome (*Vir. ill.* 5 [PL 23,646]; *Comm. Phlm.* 23 [PL 26,633f.]) Paul was even a Palestinian, born in Gischala in Galilee.

in his life.[8] Yet in Gal. 1 the question is simply whether the Jewish congregations knew Paul as a preacher or authorized his Gospel. In contrast Paul observes that they were only aware of the rumour about the conversion of the persecutor. Gal. 1.23 rather suggests that Paul had acted as a persecutor specifically in Judaea.[9]

The close connection to *Jerusalem*, which Paul rather minimizes in Gal. 1 in the interest of maintaining his independence of the apostles and the community there, is documented in the collection for 'the poor among the saints' in the Jerusalem church (Rom. 15.26), and the journey there, undertaken despite danger (Rom. 15.25), bear witness to his lasting ties to the Holy City. Moreover, Jerusalem plays a far greater role in his letters than Damascus or Antioch, not to mention Tarsus,[10] as can be seen in Rom. 15.19b where Paul describes his mission geographically as a circular movement 'from Jerusalem and as far around as Illyricum'. This confirms that Paul knew Jerusalem and had spent some time there for the study of the Law. Studying to become a Pharisaic scribe could scarcely have taken place anywhere other than in Jerusalem.[11]

It is not clear when Paul came to Jerusalem and whether his basic Jewish education took place there or in Tarsus. Although there were also possibilities for a Greek education in Jerusalem,[12] his good command of the language and his sovereign dealing with the Greek Bible support the view that he grew up in the Diaspora. He would then have come to Jerusalem as an adolescent to complete his education. At a later date a sister lived there (Acts 23.16ff.).

The Religious Dimension of his Background

How far are these details supported by Paul's own testimony? We do not possess any writings from the pre-Christian stage of his life, and the apostle mentions his earlier life only rarely and then in sharp contrast with his life as an apostle. This pattern of contrast is caused in Gal. 1.13f. and Phil. 3.3ff. by concrete conflicts. Consequently it is advisable to ascertain Paul's self-understanding from passages that are less antithetically phrased. For example, in the so-called 'Fool's Speech' Paul formulates what for him is basically a foolish 'contest' with other Jewish Christian missionaries (2 Cor. 11.22):

---

8. The argument originates in the article by W. Heitmüller (1912), 'Zum Problem Paulus und Jesus', ZNW 13: 320–37 and was adopted by Bultmann and his school. Cf. e.g. E. Haenchen (1977), *Die Apostelgeschichte* (15th ed.; KEK 3; Göttingen: Vandenhoeck & Ruprecht), 59–60 and also Strecker, *Theology* (n.1), 23–4. The view is also adopted in E. P. Sanders, *Paul*, 14–15.

9. Participation in the persecution of the Jerusalem 'Hellenists' (Acts 8.1) is more likely than a pursuit of persecution in Damascus or Tarsus; cf. Hengel and Deines, *The Pre-Christian Paul*, 167–76.

10. Cf. Hengel and Deines. *The Pre-Christian Paul*, 24–5.

11. Cf. here Hengel and Deines, *The Pre-Christian Paul*, 24–5. On the problem of 'Diaspora Pharisaism' see 2.2.4.

12. Cf. in detail M. Hengel and C. Markschies (1989), *The Hellenization of Judaea in the First Century after Christ* (trans. J. Bowden; London: SCM Press), 19–29; M. Hengel (1999), 'Jerusalem als jüdische und hellenistische Stadt', in Hengel, *Judaica, Hellenistica et Christiana. Kleine Schriften*, vol. II (WUNT 109; Tübingen: Mohr Siebeck), 115–56 (140ff.).

'Are they Israelites? So am I. Are they descendants of Abraham? So am I.'

Even more clearly – and in a completely unpolemical fashion – the apostle mentions his affiliation to Israel in Rom. 9–11 in connection with the statements on Israel's continuing election:

'... Has God rejected his people? By no means! I myself am an Israelite, a descendant of Abraham; a member of the tribe of Benjamin ...' (Rom. 11.1)

In this adoption of the idea of the 'remnant' (Rom. 11.2ff.; cf. 1 Kgs 19.18), the election of some of Israel (of whom Paul himself is an example), guarantees the continuing election of *the whole of Israel*.[13] Here Paul confesses positively without qualification that he is an *Israelite, a descendant of Abraham* and – what Luke ignores – from the old royal tribe of *Benjamin*.[14] In a similarly positive way he speaks in Rom. 9.3–5 of the 'Israelites' as his 'brothers',[15] his 'kindred according to the flesh' to whom according to biblical tradition there belonged a number of salvific possessions: the recognition as children of God (cf. Exod. 4.22; Hos. 11.1; Isa. 43.6 and frequently), the manifestation of his glory (cf. Exod. 14.4; 15.7; 16.7,10; 24.16; 40.34f. and frequently), the establishment of the covenant, the gift of the Law, the worship of the Temple (understood here positively as a *gift*), the promises and – emphasized – the Patriarchs (cf. Rom. 4; 9.6–13) and the bodily descent of the Messiah (cf. Rom. 1.3; also Lk. 2.29–32; Jn 4.22). These goods belong to the whole of Israel, and according to Rom. 11.29, permanently and irrevocably. Even in the face of the current resistance to salvation on the part of the majority of Israelites, for Paul this is not called into question. Consequently even as a Christian and apostle to the Gentiles he remains irrevocably attached to the whole of Israel in suffering (Rom. 9.2), intercession (Rom. 10.1), exemplary existence in faith (Rom. 11.1) and eschatological hope (Rom. 11.25–32).[16]

Within the framework of this understanding which he retained as long as he was active we can read the other statements about Israel and his earlier life in Ioudaismos in which the conflict with Jewish Christian opponents led him to brusque pejorative assertions: In Phil. 3.3–6 for example (similarly to 2 Cor. 11.22), while praising the advantages 'in the flesh' – i.e. with regard to descent

---

13. Cf. K. Haacker (2003), *The Theology of Paul's Letter to the Romans* (Cambridge: CUP), 77–96, also Haacker (1999), *Der Brief des Paulus an die Römer* (ThHK 6; Leipzig: Evangelische Verlagsanstalt), 220: 'Here it is taken for granted that faith in Jesus ... causes no break in a person's Jewish identity and does not alter the affiliation to the people of God.'

14. In connection with this the 'Benjaminite' name Saul points to a Jewish family proud of its pedigree and traditions.

15. Here the metaphorical use of family relations is used not in an inner-Christian but inner-Israelite sense. The kata sarka is a closer definition of syngeneis, not related in a qualifying manner to adelphoi.

16. Cf. Hengel and Deines, *Pre-Christian Paul*, 25–34; and more extensively Niebuhr, *Heidenapostel*.

and lifestyle – he agrees with this but then emphasizes the radical *revaluation* of these values which he has experienced in his own life:

> 'If anyone else has reason to be confident in the flesh, I have more: circumcised on the eighth day, a member of the people of Israel, of the tribe of Benjamin, a Hebrew born of Hebrews; as to the law, a Pharisee; as to zeal, a persecutor of the church, as to righteousness under the Law, blameless.'

In addition to the aspects already mentioned Paul presents himself as *a Hebrew born of Hebrews* – i.e. he is neither a proselyte nor a 'normal' Diaspora Jew but a scion of a Palestinian family which kept a firm hold of the traditions of their native country even in the Diaspora. This includes the knowledge and use of the Hebrew/Aramaic language and is combined in Paul with the approval of the Pharisaic interpretation and observance of the Law and his 'zeal' for the Torah and against its opponents.

In a similar confrontation Paul, in the 'autobiographical' section in Gal. 1.13f., recounts the 'pre-history' of the change in his life:

> 'You have heard, no doubt, of my earlier life in Judaism (en tō Ioudaismō). I was violently persecuting the church of God and was trying to destroy it. I advanced in Judaism beyond many among my people of the same age, for I was far more zealous for the traditions of my ancestors.'

Here, too, the exemplary Jewish identity nurtured in his youth, his zeal for the Torah is mentioned – admittedly focused on its effectiveness in the battle against the 'church of God', the followers of Jesus. The term Ioudaismos[17] here does not mean 'Judaism' (as in contrast to Christianity) but the vigorous defence of the Torah, the Temple and the religious traditions which arose against 'Hellenism' and had been fostered since the time of the Maccabaean Wars. The former activity as persecutor appears as part of an 'inner-Jewish confrontation about the question of the validity of the Torah'.[18] When Paul speaks of his 'earlier' way of life in this forceful action for the Jewish tradition and lifestyle, this does not mean that he has meantime given up or renounced his 'Judaism' – i.e. his affiliation to the people of God and the faith of the patriarchs – but rather that his 'zeal' – now regarded as false – has been turned into the opposite direction by God's intervention and through the revelation of Christ. Hence even in view of Gal. 1.13f. and Phil. 3.7f. we cannot say that Paul knew that he felt fundamentally separated from Judaism.[19] Rom. 9.3ff. and 11.1 clearly contradict this idea.

---

17. The term is not contrasted with Christanismos before Ignatius (*Magn.* 10,3; *Phld.* 6,1).
18. This is correctly stressed by Niebuhr, *Heidenapostel*, 24.
19. Contrary to Strecker, *Theology* (n.1), 21.

2
Paul's Position within the Framework of Contemporary Judaism

The Jewish Diaspora[20]
The fact that Paul came from Diaspora Judaism should not be interpreted as an indication of a 'non-Jewish' character as has often been done in the History of Religions School (with reference to his home town, Tarsus)[21] and also by some Jewish interpreters.[22] This would only be possible if the picture of a Jewish 'orthodoxy' were to apply in contrast to the 'assimilation Judaism' of the Diaspora. The relationships, however, are more complex.

On the one hand, the *influence of Hellenism on Palestinian Judaism* was fairly strong from the time of Alexander the Great[23] and the encounter with this cultural power (including the struggle with its supporters among the Jewish population and aristocracy) shaped the situation in Jewish Palestine so strongly, at the latest from the time of the Maccabean crisis, that the influence was even effective within the circles who decided to resist the Hellenistic culture (such as the Qumran community). On the other hand the self-assured Judaism in the

---

20. Literature on Diaspora Judaism: E. Schürer (1986), *The History of the Jewish People in the Age of Jesus Christ*, vol. III/1 (rev. and ed. by G. Vermes, F. Millar and M. Goodman; Edinburgh: T&T Clark), 1–176; J. M. G. Barclay (1996), *The Jews in the Mediterranean Diaspora* (Edinburgh: T&T Clark); E. S. Gruen (2002), *Diaspora: Jews amidst Greeks and Romans* (Cambridge: Harvard University Press); on *Asia Minor* see Schürer, *History*, 17–36; P. R. Trebilco (1991), *Jewish Communities in Asia Minor* (SNTSMS 69; Cambridge: CUP); Barclay, *Jews*, 259–81. On the (mostly later) epigraphical evidence see the compendium by W. Ameling (ed.) (2004), *Inscriptiones Judaicae Orientis*, vol. II: *Kleinasien* (TSAJ 99; Tübingen: Mohr Siebeck).

21. The argument was first introduced by H. Böhlig (1913), *Die Geisteskultur von Tarsus im augustinischen Zeitalter mit Berücksightigung der paulinischen Schriften* (FRLANT 19; Göttingen: Vandenhoeck & Ruprecht), who thought that Paul had 'remarkably misjudged or at least very one-sidedly judged Judaism as it was represented by the Rabbis' (164), and wanted to explain Pauline theology from the Hellenistic syncretism of the town of Tarsus.

22. H.-J. Schoeps (1961), *Paul: The Theology of the Apostle in the Light of Jewish Religious History* (German original 1959; trans. H. Knight; London: Lutterworth) saw Paul as an 'assimilation Jew of the Hellenistic Diaspora', who was 'far removed from the patriarchal ideas of faith', and, as a consequence, gave a 'distorted picture of the Jewish law' (see p. 213ff. in English edition). Even more negatively, H. Maccoby (1986), *The Mythmaker: Paul and the Invention of Christianity* (New York: Harper & Row), describes Paul as a Gentile convert who introduced concepts of Hellenistic religion and thus 'created' Christianity. Maccoby, however, accepts the polemical information from late Jewish Christian fragments, but dismisses the data given in Luke. Notably, recent Jewish interpreters of Paul draw a much more positive picture of Paul's Judaism, cf. e.g. Segal, *Paul the Convert*, or Boyarin, *Radical Jew*. See the survey by S. Meissner (1996), *Die Heimholung des Ketzers. Studien zur jüdischen Auseinandersetzung mit Paulus* (WUNT II/87; Tübingen: Mohr Siebeck).

23. This influence stretches from the language and culture that found their way in through the adoption of Greek forms of commerce and administration such as the Ptolemaic system of leasing the gathering of taxes up to architecture in the Hasmonean or Herodian period. See fundamentally M. Hengel (1974), *Judaism and Hellenism: Studies in Their Encounter in Palestine in the Early Hellenistic Period* (trans. J. Bowden; 2 vols; London: SCM); Hengel and Markschies, *Hellenization* (n.12); Hengel, 'Jerusalem' (n.12).

Diaspora largely resisted assimilation to the pagan world and developed *forms of an independent Jewish identity distinct from its surroundings*.

Numerically the Jewish Diaspora was larger than the Jewish population of Palestine. For this reason we cannot consider Palestinian Judaism alone as the 'real' Judaism.[24] *Geographically* the Diaspora extended from Mesopotamia to Italy and Rome with main centres in Syria, Egypt and the Cyrenaica as well as in Asia Minor. The origins in Mesopotamia and Egypt reach back to the time of the Exile.[25]

The *Diaspora in Asia Minor* from which Paul came and which probably also existed already prior to the Hellenistic Age[26] had grown significantly under the Seleucids.[27] So in the Roman period there was already an old, self-assured Jewish community in almost all the towns in the province of Asia and the regions on the south coast of Asia Minor, including Tarsus in Cilicia where Paul grew up.[28] Jews lived in the towns as a rule as an independent ethnic group (ethnos, politeuma)[29] with their own laws[30] and sometimes they also had municipal civil rights.[31] The Jews enjoyed tolerance for the most part under the Ptolemies and Seleucids.[32] After the Romans took over power their privileges were repeatedly confirmed by the Senate or the emperor as we can see from a series of edicts proclaimed

---

24. Cf. Barclay, *Jews* (n.20), 4 n.1: 'probably several million by the first century CE.' Philo, *Flacc.* 41 – admittedly not very reliable – speaks of a million Jews in Egypt; cf. also the numbers in Jos. *Bell.* II, 561 and VII, 368. M. Avi-Yonah (1976), *The Jews of Palestine* (Oxford: Blackwell) estimates for the period after 135 the number to be *c*.1.3 million Jews. Admittedly even rough numbers are difficult to confirm.

25. Possibly we should speak here of a 'Judaean' Diaspora. We should think here not only of the Diaspora in Mesopotamia which goes back to the deportations but also particularly of the Jewish military colony on the Nile island of *Elephantine* in Upper Egypt where in the fifth century BCE there existed for a time a *Jahu*-Temple with connections to Samaria and Jerusalem; see J. Frey (1999), 'Temple and Rival Temple: The Cases of Elephantine, Garizim, and Leontopolis', in *Gemeinde ohne Tempel – Community Without Temple* (ed. B. Ego, A. Lange and P. Pilhofer; WUNT 118, Tübingen: Mohr Siebeck), 171–203.

26. Aristotle is reported to have met in Asia Minor in the mid-fourth century BCE a highly educated 'Greek' Jew according to Clearchus in Jos. *C. Ap.* I, 176–82.

27. Antiochus the Great is said to have settled 2,000 Jewish families from the east in Phrygia and Lydia (Jos. *Ant.* XII, 147–53); others followed as traders, manual workers, slaves or freedmen.

28. On the community in Tarsus see Hengel and Schwemer, *Paul*, 158–61. On the Jews in Cilicia cf. Philo, *Leg.* 281; Acts 6.9.

29. Other terms we encounter are oi Ioudaioi, katoikia, laos, synodos and later synagōgē (see Schürer, *History* III/1 [n.20], 87–91; and more recently C. Claussen (2002), *Versammlung, Gemeinde, Synagoge: Das hellenistisch-jüdische Umfeld der frühchristlichen Gemeinden* [SUNT 27; Göttingen: Vandenhoeck & Ruprecht], 146–50).

30. According to Jos. *Bell.* 110 (cf. *Ant.* XII, 119–24; *C. Ap.* II, 39) in Antioch the laws of the Antiochene Jews were written on bronze tablets.

31. According to Jos. *Ant.* XII, 119 Seleucus I Nicator (until 280 BCE) conferred civil rights on the Jews in the towns he founded in Asia Minor and Syria. Whether this is historically correct is, however, questionable.

32. To this extent the attempted suppression of the Jewish religion by Antiochus IV is an exception.

by the Senate or emperor cited by Josephus.[33] The following *privileges* for the Diaspora are mentioned:

Table 4.1

General	*Life according to the 'Law of their Fathers'* and Jewish customs
Religious	The observance of religious traditions and of the Sabbath, and the right of assembly
Legal	internal *self-administration* their own internal *jurisdiction* (court of arbitration, synagogue punishment)
Financial	the right to build religious and secular *buildings* the raising of taxes and the transfer of 'sacred monies' (*Temple tax*) to Jerusalem
Military	freedom from Roman *military service* (which brought them into contact with idols and military standards)

An exemption from *emperor-worship* often mentioned in the secondary literature cannot be found among these edicts because in the early years of the Empire Rome imposed no obligation to worship the emperor (hence no 'exemption' was needed). Generally abstinence from the worship of the emperor was included in the tolerance of Jewish customs. Jews could always say that the daily sacrifice and prayers in the Temple were carried out *pro salute Caesaris*.[34]

The repeated confirmation of these privileges by Rome admittedly shows that the status of the Jewish community in the towns was by no means assured but was questioned again and again. Their non-participation in elements of public and social life together with the transfer of money to Jerusalem could stir up mistrust and resentment as is shown by the pogroms in Alexandria in 38 CE described by Philo.[35]

The Jewish community in the Diaspora was primarily defined by 'ethnic' *affiliation*, yet non-Jews could also decide to live according to Jewish customs (Jos. *C. Ap.* II, 210) and join the community in varying degrees. They did not always decide to undergo a formal conversion[36] through which, as 'proselytes',

---

33. The texts are given with a commentary in M. Pucci Ben Zeev (1998), *Jewish Rights in the Roman World* (TSAJ 74; Tübingen: Mohr Siebeck); see in particular the compilation in 374–7.

34. Jos. *C. Ap.* II, 77f.; Philo, *Leg.* 356 and *passim*. Other groups in Greece and Egypt also sacrificed 'for' the emperor (cf. evidence in Pucci Ben Zeev, *Jewish Rights* [n.33], 475f.; on the problem of a Jewish 'privilege' in this regard, ibid., 471–81). The conflicts under Caligula (cf. Philo, *Leg.* 132–54, 353–7), however, reveal that there could be no definite legal certainty on this point.

35. Philo, *Flacc.* On this see Barclay, *Jews* (n.20), 40ff. On ancient anti-Judaism see P. Schäfer (1997), *Judaeophobia: Attitudes Toward the Jews in the Ancient World* (Cambridge: Harvard University Press); cf. the sources in M. Stern (ed.) (1974–1984), *Greek and Latin Authors on Jews and Judaism*, vol. I–III (Jerusalem: The Israel Academy of Sciences and Humanities).

36. A 'prime example' is the conversion of the royal house of Adiabene, cf. Jos. *Ant.* XX, 17–96. For males the conversion was connected to circumcision. There was no corresponding ceremonial act for females – what was decisive was that they followed Jewish customs; see D. R. Schwartz (2007), 'Doing like the Jews and Becoming a Jew: Josephus on Gentile Women', in

they became full members of the Jewish community. But the faith in the One God and the adoption of the central ethical requirements could also be accomplished without this formal act (with its social consequences caused by the Jewish purity and dietary laws) so that a larger number of people remained linked to the synagogue as 'God-fearers' (theosebeis, sebomenoi ton theon), i.e. as 'sympathizers', guests and not least as benefactors of the synagogue without taking upon themselves the personal, social and political restrictions connected to circumcision.[37] These circles were later one of the most important groups to be addressed by the early Christian (and also the Pauline) mission.

On the other side the communities of the Diaspora by no means displayed a total assimilation to their surroundings but rather a clear *delimitation* in that their laws relating to food and purity restricted to a very large degree mealtime fellowship (and consequently many other social connections) with non-Jews, and as a rule mixed marriages were not accepted or marriage into the community generally could only take place on condition of conversion to Judaism.[38]

The *organization* of the communities could vary, from a loose connection of individuals to well-organized congregations with organized functionaries (archēsynagōgos, presbyteros, archōn),[39] their own buildings, archives, courts and burial places and 'official' relationships to the respective Polis. Meeting places were frequently private houses; larger communities had their own 'prayer houses' (proseuchē, synagōgē).[40] For the most part there also existed a social and economic network that was necessary for life in the Diaspora because of the dietary and purity laws (e.g. for the provision of oil, meat and other foodstuffs). The institution of the Synagogue with regular prayers and the study of the Scriptures made a distinctive impression on the identity of the Diaspora communities. Independently of the worship in the Jerusalem Temple, *spoken services* without sacrifice were developed, with readings and interpretation of Scripture, prayers and Psalms,[41] the weekly *celebration of the Sabbath* and

---

Jewish Identity in the Greco-Roman World (ed. J. Frey, D. R. Schwartz and S. Gripentrog; AJEC 71; Leiden: Brill), 93–110. Evidence for the so-called 'proselyte baptism' exists only from the time after 70 CE. Its origin was probably the ceremonial immersion required for the necessary thanksgiving sacrifice in the Temple which then became a ritual in itself.

37. Cf. on the 'God-fearers' F. Siegert (1983), 'Gottesfürchtige und Sympathisanten', *JSJ* 4: 109–64; J. Reynolds and R. Tannenbaum (1987), *Jews and God-fearers at Aphrodisias* (Cambridge: Cambridge Philological Society); Hengel and Schwemer, *Paul*, 60–71; Donaldson, *Judaism*, 469–82.

38. Cf. Barclay, *Jews* (n.20), 410–12. Jos. *Ant.* XX, 139, 145f. shows that circumcision was required before marriage into the Herodian clan.

39. See C. Claussen (2003), 'Meeting, Community, Synagogue', in *The Ancient Synagogue: From its Origins until 200 C.E.* (ed. B. Olsson and M. Zetterholm; ConBNT 39; Stockholm: Almquist & Wiksell), 144–67 (159–61); more extensively Claussen, *Versammlung* (n.29), 256–93.

40. On the origin of the synagogue in the Egyptian Diaspora in the third century cf. M. Hengel, 'Proseuche und Synagoge', in Hengel, *Judaica* (n.12), 171–95; Claussen, *Versammlung* (n.29), 151–65; on the terms see also Claussen, 'Meeting, Community, Synagogue', 150–2.

41. This spoken service was a novelty in ancient religion; cf. Hengel, 'Proseuche', and

the celebration of other religious feasts, which had great social significance.[42] The raising of the Temple tax of a half-shekel (cf. Exod. 30.11–16)[43] and the transfer of this money and other gifts to the Jerusalem shrine – often connected to pilgrimages to the holy feasts in Jerusalem (cf. Acts 2.5–11) – shows the great significance the connection to the 'mother-country' had even for the Jews in the Diaspora.[44] The *religious character* of Diaspora Judaism was determined by the Scriptures (primarily the Mosaic *'Law'*) which was read in the Greek version, the *Septuagint* (LXX). For this translation, Diaspora Jews claimed the same authority and quality of revelation as for the Hebrew text, not simply a derivative authority.[45] At home and in the Sabbath meetings the *'Law'* was studied, and Moses was the central authority and figure of identification. This raised the Jewish faith and its ethics in age and worth above the philosophical traditions of the Greeks. In broad unanimity Diaspora Judaism rejected the pictorial polytheistic cults. The separation from pagan banquets based on the laws of purity and diet, the practice of circumcision of all newborn male children (and with it the symbolically marked limitation of sexual relationships) and the keeping of the Sabbath were effective *signs of Jewish identity* in the Diaspora. For Paul the significance of this *Diaspora-Jewish identity* can scarcely be overestimated. He uses the Greek language of his day, the Koine, syntactically correctly and without conspicuous translations of Semitisms, sometimes even with creative poetic power (e.g. in 1 Cor. 13). His epistles certainly do not follow any school-rhetoric but yet communicate in a rhetorically skilful manner, sometimes in the style of argumentation of the *diatribe* (cf. Rom. 1.18 – 2.11; 2.17–24; 7.1–5 and often) as probably also used in synagogue sermons.[46] Paul cites the *Scriptures* in Greek according to the LXX or according to different textual forms in a sovereign combination of passages and adaptation of the wording, so that we may assume in the background not only his own verbal activity as a teacher but also a familiarity established in his early youth.[47] Alongside these he uses quite naturally

further in J. C. Salzmann (1994), *Lehren und Ermahnen* (WUNT II/59; Tübingen: Mohr Siebeck), 450–9.

42. On Philo see J. Leonhardt (2001), *Jewish Worship in Philo* (TSAJ 84; Tübingen: Mohr Siebeck).

43. On the significance of this tax cf. Barclay, *Jews* (n.20), 417f. and Philo, *Spec.* I, 77–8. The transformation of the Temple tax into the *fiscus Iudaicus*, a penalty tax which had to be paid to the temple of Jupiter Capitolinus in Rome after 71 CE, eventually made it necessary that all Jews, men, women and children, were publicly identified as such by 'status lists' – which made the Jews even more aware of their special position in Roman society. Cf. M. Heemstra (2010), *The* fiscus Judaicus *and the Parting of the Ways* (WUNT II/277; Tübingen: Mohr Siebeck).

44. Barclay, *Jews* (n.20), 418f.

45. Cf. *Let. Aris.* 310f and especially Philo, *Mos.* II, 33–4. On the Septuagint see M. Hengel (2002), *The Septuagint as Christian Scripture: Its Prehistory and the Problem of Its Canon* (Grand Rapids: Baker Academic); N. Fernández Marcos (2000), *The Septuagint in Context* (Leiden: Brill).

46. For examples of synagogual sermons see F. Siegert (1992), *Drei hellenistisch-jüdische Predigten*, vol. II (WUNT 61; Tübingen: Mohr Siebeck).

47. For quotations from Isaiah, Job and 1 Kings we may assume the use of a revised

metaphors and imagery from the Hellenistic world, e.g. the Greek metaphor of the 'inner nature' (2 Cor. 4.16; Rom. 7.22) or the image of the competition in a gymnasium (1 Cor. 9.24–27). The continued use of motifs from Hellenistic-Jewish preaching can be seen in passages such as 1 Thess. 1.9 (the turning from idols to the true God) or also 1 Cor. 8.4–6 (which is actually a variation of the *Shema Jisrael*).[48] Only as a *Diaspora* Jew was Paul later in a position to exercise his effectiveness as apostle to the Gentiles – an effectiveness transcending borders and cultures.

The Jewish Religious Parties in Palestine and Pharisaism

In his own self-witness and in Acts Paul is presented as a *Pharisee* (Phil. 3.5: kata nomon Pharisaios, cf. Acts 23.6). The education under Rabbi Gamaliel I, the leading Pharisaic teacher of his time, referred to in Acts 22.3, mentions the link even more precisely. But how is Pharisaism characterized? And how can the classification as a Pharisee be combined with Paul's identity as a Diaspora Jew?

The Jewish Religious Parties according to Josephus

Our information about the religious currents in Palestine around the latest years BCE and the earliest years CE comes above all from Flavius Josephus. In his *Antiquities of the Jews* (*Ant.*) and his *History of the Jewish War* (*Bell.*) he speaks of three 'religious parties' (haireseis)[49] which, comparable to the Greek schools of philosophy, stand alongside one another in Judaism: *Pharisees, Sadducees* and *Essenes*.[50] As a further group he names the so-called 'fourth philosophy', the *Zealots*, who decisively determined the development up until the Jewish War. According to Josephus they concurred with the Pharisees in all essential points apart from their relentless struggle for (political) freedom.[51] In the light of the catastrophe, Josephus, himself a onetime guerrilla who then deserted to the Romans, distanced himself from the Zealots, while he portrays the Essenes as an ideal community of philosophers and the Pharisees as a politically active party. Pharisees, Sadducees and Essenes are described in Greek terms and charac-

---

version more in accordance with the Hebrew text, cf. Hengel and Deines, *The Pre-Christian Paul*, 25 and 60.

48. On this, cf. E. Waaler (2008), *The* Shema *and the First Commandment in First Corinthians* (WUNT II/253; Tübingen: Mohr Siebeck).

49. The term here should not be translated as 'sect' in the sense of 'marginal' groups in contrast with a kind of mainstream religion. All three movements were probably quite influential.

50. These remarks are schematic, but are not therefore historically useless. Cf. alongside the particularly problematic autobiographical report in Josephus, *Vita* 10f, the 'Three Schools Report' in *Bell.* II, 119–66; *Ant.* XIII, 171–3, 288, 298; XVIII, 11–22. In *Bell.* II, 119–61 the Essenes are treated in a particularly extensive way – doubtless because of his processing of the sources. On the question of sources cf. R. Bergmeier (1993), *Die Essener-Berichte des Flavius Josephus* (Kampen: Kok Pharos); on the three groups cf. also G. Stemberger (1995), *Jewish Contemporaries of Jesus: Pharisees, Sadducees, Essenes* (Minneapolis: Fortress).

51. Jos. *Ant.* XVIII, 23. On this group see the foundational study by M. Hengel (1989), *The Zealots: Investigations into the Jewish Freedom Movement in the period from Herod I until 70 A.D.* (trans. D. Smith; Edinburgh: T&T Clark).

terized according to their position on fate and their belief in the immortality of the soul.[52]

Table 4.2

	Pharisees	Sadducees	Essenes
Fate/freedom of will (heimarmenē)	Fate and personal action	No fate only personal action	Everything happens according to fate and divine determining[53]
Immortality of the soul (What is meant here are the concepts in Palestinian Judaism of the Resurrection of the dead and the Judgement.)	Immortality of the soul, reward	No immortality No reward	Immortality of the soul
parelleled with	Stoics	Epicureans	Pythagoreans

Was there a 'Common Judaism'?
In view of the discrepancies not only between the Judaism of Palestine and that of the Diaspora but also within Palestinian Judaism it is questionable whether and to what extent we can or cannot speak of a unity of 'the' Judaism (or of a more or less 'mainstream' Judaism shared by all). While E. P. Sanders put forward the view that a 'common Judaism' characterized by Covenant and Torah could form this unity,[54] J. Neusner and others talk of 'Judaisms' in the plural.[55]

---

52. In the Greek terms we see a reflection of what Palestinian Judaism called the 'resurrection of the dead' (cf. Dan 12.2 and its tradition history). Whether and to what extent the Qumran community taught the resurrection of the dead is uncertain. Arguments for such a belief could be the frequency of the book of Daniel and related texts (admittedly not authored by the community) in the Qumran library (see esp. 4Q521 2 ii 12; and the Pseudo-Ezechiel text 4Q 385 2 8f.) and also their mode of burial. This is strongly advocated by E. Puech (1993), *La croyance des Esséniens en la vie future: immortalité, résurrection, vie éternelle?* (2 vols.; EBib 21/22; Paris: Editions Gabalda; more cautious is J. J. Collins (1997), *Apocalypticism in the Dead Sea Scrolls* (London: Routledge), 111–28; see also G. W. E. Nickelsburg, 'Resurrection', in *Encyclopedia of the Dead Sea Scrolls* 2:764–7 and most recently A. Hogeterp (2009), *Expectations of the End: A Comparative Study of Eschatological, Apocalyptic and Messianic ideas in the Dead Sea Scrolls* (STDJ 83; Leiden and Boston: Brill), 247–93.
53. Here we can see reflected in the Greek terms the belief in predestination held by the Qumran community (and expressed programmatically in the Treatise on the Two Spirits 1QS III 13 – IV 26).
54. Sanders, *Paul and Palestinian Judaism*; Sanders (1992), *Judaism, Practice and Belief 63 BCE – 66 CE* (London: SCM); see also the critical review in Hengel and Deines (2001), 'E. P. Sanders' "Common Judaism"'; and the anthology *Justification and Variegated Nomism*, vol. I: *The Complexities of Second Temple Judaism* (ed. D. A. Carson, P. T. O'Brien and M. Seifrid; WUNT II/140; Tübingen: Mohr Siebeck).
55. J. Neusner (1990), 'From Judaism to Judaisms. My Approach to the History of Judaism', in Neusner, *Ancient Judaism, Debates and Disputes* (Atlanta: Scholars), 181–221.

In actual fact the *plurality*, indeed the *divergence* within the Judaism of antiquity cannot be marginalized. It affects not only the relationship between Palestine and the Diaspora but also Palestinian Judaism before 70 CE.

- At the latest from the time of the Maccabean Wars there exists the problem of the 'apostates' among their own people who collaborated with the oppressors and played a part in creating the people's religious affliction.[56] To combat this there arose, following the example of Phinehas (Num. 25), the 'zeal' of Mattathias and his sons, the Maccabeans (1 Macc. 2.24ff.). Their example of zeal for the Law and Sanctuary remained vivid and influenced the movement of the Zealots[57] and perhaps even the 'zeal' (zēloun) of Paul the persecutor.[58]
- Pharisees and Sadducees (aristocracy) did deadly battle with one another in the time of the Hasmoneans. Their participation in the 'Sanhedrin' (under the leadership of the Sadducees) cannot conceal the wide distance between them: the Sadducees rejected the prophets and the writings which the Pharisees read, and they denounced the Messianic hope, belief in the resurrection and a final judgement and much more.
- The members of the Qumran community ('Essenes'), who by no means lived only near the Dead Sea, considered the Temple to be polluted and the priesthood there as illegitimate and refused to participate in the sacrificial cult. They saw God's 'Covenant' as fulfilled only in their community; other Israelites were not considered as belonging to this 'Covenant' and were ritually cursed in regular covenant rites (1 QS II, 1–18). At least here the divergent interpretations of the Torah and the radicalized (purity) Halakha split apart the entities 'Israel' and 'Covenant'.

To be sure common Jewish beliefs in contrast to the pagan world cannot be denied: monotheism and the (variously interpreted) Torah can serve as fundamental features in this perspective.[59] But there can be no talk of any coherent unity or of a 'common Judaism' focused on the Temple and Torah in view of Qumran or the rivalry between the Pharisees and Sadducees.

Pharisaism and its Significance

What was the character and significance of Pharisaism before the destruction

---

56. On this see Hengel, *Judaism and Hellenism* (n.23) who takes up Elias Bikerman's view that the religious persecution under Antiochus IV arose not only from the politics of that pagan ruler but also because of the agitation of the Hellenistic reformers in Jerusalem (who were Jews).

57. Hengel, *Zealots* (n.51), 149ff.

58. Cf. Hengel, *Zealots* (n.51), 177; on Paul see M. R. Fairchild (1999), 'Paul's pre-Christian Zealot Associations: A Re-Examination of Gal 1.14 and Acts 22.3', *NTS* 45: 514–32; T. Seland (2002), 'Saul of Tarsus and Early Zelotism: Reading Gal. 1.13–14 in Light of Philo's Writings', *Bib* 83: 449–71.

59. To justify his proposal Sanders must marginalize both the Essenes and the Pharisees as phenomena of peripheral importance; cf. the criticism by Hengel and Deines, 'E. P. Sanders' "Common Judaism"'.

of the Temple in 70 CE? After all, Josephus says that the Pharisees had a great influence on the people (*Ant.* XVIII, 15). Both in Josephus (44 times) and in the New Testament (99 times) the Pharisees are the religious party who are most often mentioned. The state of research is controversial:[60]

- *Earlier Jewish and Christian research* assumed a *'normative Judaism' of (Pharisaic) Rabbinic character* before the year 70. This can no longer be maintained today since this picture is based on an uncritical use of the rabbinic texts which were only edited long after 70 – i.e. the partial projection into the past period before the destruction of the Temple of conditions existing later. In Palestine before 70 there was *no normative Judaism* but, as the Qumran discoveries in particular have shown, there was a plurality of positions which spread far beyond the three 'schools' of Josephus.
- Within the frame of his thesis of a 'Common Judaism' characterized by Temple and Torah, E. P. Sanders wants to estimate *the influence of the Pharisees as being very modest*, so that in the end the Temple priesthood appears as the leading group within Judaism before 70. This position partly resulted through the lack of reliable primary Pharisaic sources and consequently met with some acceptance. Josephus' clear remark about the influence of the Pharisees on the people (*Ant.* XVIII. 15) and the frequency with which they are mentioned not only in the New Testament but also in Josephus stand in the way of this interpretation.
- *Jacob Neusner* discerned a position between these 'extremes' which he wanted to depict as a development of Pharisaism from a primarily political 'party' to a movement which was characteristically religious after 70 (*'from politics to piety'*).[61]
- Yet we can detect religious concerns in the reports on the early years of the Pharisees (Jos. *Ant.* XIII, 289, 297), and conversely we encounter them in political contexts in the Herodian period, so that the development is questionable. A retreat to 'mere' piety cannot be confirmed.

Fundamental *sources* for our knowledge of Pharisaism before 70 are some remarks in the works of Josephus.[62] These can be supplemented by comments from the literature of Qumran and the New Testament, whereby in both cases we

---

60. Literature on Pharisaism: R. Deines, 'Pharisees', *The Eerdmans Dictionary of Early Judaism* 1061-3; Deines, 'The Pharisees between "Judaisms" and "Common Judaism"', in *Justification* (n.54), 443–504; on the historical analysis of the traditions, J. Neusner (1971), *The Rabbinic Traditions about the Pharisees before 70* (3 vols; Leiden: Brill), and the criticism by P. Schäfer (1991), 'Der vorrabbinische Pharisäismus', in *Paulus und das antike Judentum* (ed. M. Hengel and U. Heckel; WUNT 58; Tübingen: Mohr Siebeck), 125–72 (126–32).

61. J. Neusner (1979), *From Politics to Piety. The Emergence of Pharisaic Judaism* (2nd ed.; New York: Ktav).

62. Whether Josephus himself was really a Pharisee as he claims in *Vita* 10–12 is questionable. Nevertheless he is a contemporary eyewitness. To be sure specific biases in his depiction of Pharisees must be taken into consideration, moreover the statements in *Bell.* and *Ant.* are not uniform: in *Bell.* Josephus is more strongly apologetic than in the later *Ant.* Cf. S.

must reckon with polemic distortions,[63] from rabbinic literature – the historical evaluation of which is questionable[64] – and from archaeological data.[65] The psalms of Solomon and the Aramaic 'Scroll of Fasting' (*Megillat Ta'anit*) are frequently attributed to Pharisaism. Other texts such as e.g. 4 Ezra show certain similarities with Pharisaic concepts, but can scarcely derive from these circles.

The *name* Pharisaioi (Hebrew perushim, Aramaic perishayya, from the Hebrew prsh 'separate', 'discriminate', 'specify'), was possibly used initially by others to describe 'those who are separated', i.e. who differ from the main body of the people not following that kind of observance, or 'those who specify', i.e. precisely interpret the law, e.g. between pure and impure.[66] Their *history* can be clarified only in part. Presumably they stem from the offshoots of the Hasidic piety movement (1 Macc. 2.42; 7.12; 2 Macc. 14.6). Josephus mentions them as a distinctive group for the first time under the Hasmonean Jonathan (*Ant.* XIII, 171ff.), i.e. in the middle of the second century BCE. In the time of John Hyrcanus (135–104 BCE) they are mentioned in a 'school anecdote' which tells of the break with the Hasmoneans as a political party (*Ant.* XIII, 288–98).[67]

Mason (1991), *Flavius Josephus on the Pharisees* (Leiden: Brill); Schäfer, 'Pharisäismus' (n. 60). The most important texts are discussed in Stemberger, *Contemporaries* (n.50).

63. In the Qumran texts the Pharisees are perhaps referred to under the polemical pseudonym of 'those who seek smooth things' (CD I, 18f; 1 QHᵃ X, 35 [= II, 32 Sukenik] and frequently in Nahum-Pesher 4QpNah = 4Q169) as representatives of a (from an Essene point of view) too lax attitude to the question of purity, a practice of the Torah too strongly interested in practicability and in conformity with the political and cultic conditions. On this see A. I. Baumgarten, 'Seekers After Smooth Things', *Encyclopedia of the Dead Sea Scrolls* 2:857–9; Baumgarten, 'Pharisees', *ibid.*, 2:657–63. In the Gospels they are increasingly depicted as the opponents of Jesus, most clearly in Matthew (cf. Mt. 23.13 and more frequently). The stereotype 'Woe to you, scribes and Pharisees, hypocrites! ...' indicates intensified confrontations of the early Christians with this current (before and after 70) and at the same time their significance as representatives of substantial Jewish positions in this epoch.

64. It is questionable which traditions from the earlier period can really be related to the Pharisees, for the name perushim is seldom applied by the Rabbis – and then rather negatively. They speak rather of the 'wise men' (hakhamim). This demonstrates the extent of the transformation between the 'pre-rabbinic' Pharisaism and the later rabbinic elite.

65. R. Deines (1993), *Jüdische Steingefässe und pharisäische Frömmigkeit* (WUNT II/53; Tübingen: Mohr Siebeck), concludes from the archaeological finds of stone jars (cf. Jn 2.6) in Judaea and Galilee that Pharisaic piety was quite widespread. According to the Pharisaic halakha, stone jars, unlike clay jars and vessels, did not become impure (and useless) through contact with anything impure. Thus the use of the (more expensive) stone jars can show that this kind of Pharisaic interpretation was followed.

66. Cf. E. Schürer (1979), *The History of the Jewish People in the Age of Jesus Christ*, vol. III/2 (rev. and ed. by G. Vermes, F. Millar and M. Goodman; Edinburgh: T&T Clark), 396f.; Deines, 'Pharisees' (n.60), 1061. The expression 'we have separated ourselves (parashnu) from the mass of the people' is encountered in parallel form in the early 'Essene' halakhic text 4QMMT C 7, where the rigid position of this community compared with the addressee (possibly the High Priest then in office) is expounded.

67. The conflict probably arose when Hyrcanus attempted to institutionalize permanently the merging of the office of High Priest with the political-military leadership. The opposition to this clearly had religious grounds. A similar situation somewhat earlier probably led to the separation of the 'Essenes': the usurpation of the office of High Priest by Jonathan in 152 BCE.

Here their interest in the religious life of the people can be discerned when it is reported that they handed down to the people unwritten, oral legal regulations based on the traditions of the fathers (XIII, 297) which were rejected by the Sadducees. In spite of the clash with the Hasmoneans (in the civil war under Alexander Jannaeus) they came to terms with the political conditions whenever possible, and under Salome Alexandra they came to have political influence, at least for a certain time. Possibly in 6 CE a radical theocratic branch split off and developed to a group of its own later named 'Zealots' (XVIII, 3ff.). In the New Testament period the Pharisees were a minority in the '*Synhedrion*', alongside the Sadducees (cf. Acts 23.6–9; also Acts 5.38; Jn 7.50). *Structurally* the Pharisaic movement was more a loose community without definite rules of admission etc. within which, however, there were also closer groupings. Their importance is not to be measured simply by the number of their members but by the influence which this 'elite' had on the people. As Josephus remarks (*Ant.* XVIII, 15.17) this was because their 'closeness to the people' was greater than that of the aristocratic circle of the Sadducees and of the Essenes who required strict purity and dissociation from outsiders. In contrast to these one can perhaps not describe Pharisaism before 70 CE as a 'people's movement' but yet as an influential *religious revival movement* oriented towards the people and interested in the sanctification of daily life in Land of Israel.[68] Later Pharisaism merged into the rabbinic reconstitution of Palestinian Judaism.

Table 4.3

Characteristics of Pharisaic Teaching and Practice[69]		
'oral Torah'	In addition to the written Torah legal regulations were handed down to the people from the 'traditions of the elders' *Contrast to the Sadducees*	Jos. *Ant.* XIII, 296f.,408; v. basically *m. Avot* I, 1 cf. Mk 7.3,5,8f.,13
	Flexibility in the interpretation of the Law (attention to practicability for the people) *Contrast to the Sadducees/Essenes*	polemically in Qumran: 'those who seek smooth things ...' CD I, 18f.; 1 QH II,15,32; 4,7–10; 4QpNah
	Leniency in administration of Justice (i.e. no rigour, rather practicability)	Jos. *Ant.* XIII, 294 (cf. Acts 5.38f.)

---

68. Hengel and Deines, *The Pre-Christian Paul*, 30 speak of a 'Palestinian lay holiness movement'.
69. Cf. Deines, 'Pharisees' (n.60), 1062f. who lists the predominant themes of Pharisaic interest: purity, tithing, fasting, Sabbath observance, proper religious behaviour in public, and teaching others.

	Characteristics of Pharisaic Teaching and Practice	
'Canon'	Alongside the Pentateuch they *recognized the prophets and other writings* (they counted as part of the 'oral Torah' and consequently share in the Mosaic authority)	Jos. *Ant.* XIII, 297f.
Eschatology	Belief in a resurrection of the dead and an eschatological Judgement (These topoi are not to be found in the Pentateuch) *Difference to the Sadducees*	Jos. *Bell.* II, 163; *Ant.* XVIII, 14 *m. Sanhedrin* X, 1 (cf. Dan. 12.2f.; *Pss. sol.* 3.11f.); Mk 12.18f.; Acts 23.6,6; 26.5
	Belief in angels	Acts 23.8 (cf. Daniel)
	Messianic expectation (but no uniform conceptualization)	Jos. *Ant.* XVII, 43–5; *Pss. sol.* 17–18
Fate and Freedom	Belief in fate *and* freedom to do what is good/ethical responsibility – i.e. rejection of a total Determinism *Middle position between the Sadducees and Essenes*	Jos. *Bell.* II, 162f.; *Ant.* XIII, 171; cf. *Pss. sol.* 9.3–5; *m. Avot* III, 15 cf. also Phil. 2.12f.
	Practice of Striving for righteousness, God's Piety pleasing and piety (not exclusively Pharisaic ideals)	Jos. *Ant.* XIII, 289–91; XIV, 176; *Bell.* II, 163 cf. Mt. 5.20; Lk. 16.15.
Observance of the Torah	Meticulousness (akribeia) in its interpretation, particularly in relation to the purity-halakha, the contribution of the tithe (for foodstuffs) and the Sabbath	Jos. *Bell.* I, 110; II, 162; *Ant.* XVII, 41; *Vita* 191, 198; cf. Phil. 3.5; Acts 22.3; 26.5; on the tithe, Mt. 23.23; on purity Mk 7.1ff.
	Practice of fasting and praying	The Scroll of Fasts (Megillat Taanit) *Pss. sol.* 3.7f.; cf. Lk. 18.12.
Purity-Halakha	Extension of the priestly rules of purity to the daily life of the whole of Israel	*m. Kelim* I, 6–9 etc.
Relation to the Eretz Israel	With the aim of the priestly purity of Israel the connection with the Eretz Israel was obvious since only there could this cleanness be lived[70]	*m. Sotah* IX, 15 etc.

70. Thus Hengel and Deines, *The Pre-Christian Paul*, 31–4; cf. G. Stemberger (1990), 'Die Bedeutung des "Landes Israel" in der rabbinischen Tradition', in Stemberger, *Studien zum rabbinischen Judentum* (SBAB 10; Stuttgart: Katholisches Bibelwerk), 321–56 (324ff.).

Characteristics of Pharisaic Teaching and Practice		
Study of the Torah	Interests in the instruction of the people; fostering of witness to the Writings and the Law; encouragement of the study of the Torah	*m. Avot* I, 1,4,6,12f.,16; II, 4ff. cf. Gal. 1.13; Phil. 4.6.

On the Problem of 'Diaspora Pharisaism'
The interest of the Pharisees in the holiness of *Eretz Israel* casts doubts on the term 'Diaspora Pharisaism' which is sometimes used in research. This term is occasionally introduced by scholars who consider Paul as an 'assimilation Jew' or hold the note about his study in Jerusalem to be a Lukan fiction[71] so that they have to explain how Paul can call himself a Pharisee if he had no close relations with the land of Israel. In fact, however, there is *neither a certain proof of Pharisees resident in the Diaspora nor even 'for the existence of Pharisaic schools outwith Palestine' before 70* CE.[72]

The frequently cited references to journeys of scribes in the Diaspora (e.g. Mt. 23.15) rather show that those scribes did not permanently reside outside of the land of Israel, and the Pharisees who fled the land before Alexander Jannaeus (Jos. *Bell*. I, 98) returned as soon as possible to their motherland because in foreign parts there was always the threat of ritual impurity. Houses of teaching outside Palestine first arose as a result of the catastrophes of 70 CE and 132–135 CE. For the earlier period it is significant that King Izates of Adiabene, who converted to the Jewish faith, sent five of his sons to Jerusalem so that they might be educated in Hebrew and in the Torah (Jos. *Ant*. XX, 71). This confirms the situation we assume for Paul. He could only receive an education as a Pharisaic scribe in the mother country.

3
Paul's Jewish Background and his Confrontation with the Distinctive Marks of Jewish Identity

As a Pharisee Paul did *not stand on the edge of the Judaism* of his time, but was in a movement which sought to encourage Jewish life and Jewish identity and thereby to correspond to the divine election. Paul's Jewish identity and his Pharisaic background left lasting traces in the work and theology of the apostle.

For a Pharisee the study of the 'Law' and the endeavour to see it put into practice (Phil. 3.5) was a crucial concern. Hence it is understandable that he reflected more profoundly on the problems of *law and justice* than all other

---
71. Cf. also K. Berger (1988), 'Jesus als Pharisäer und frühe Christen als Pharisäer', *NovT* 30: 231–62 (254–61). Without rejecting the sojourn in Jerusalem also Schnelle, *Apostle Paul*, 64–9. But see the criticism in Hengel and Deines, *The Pre-Christian Paul*, 29–34.
72. Hengel and Deines, *The Pre-Christian Paul*, 33–4.

early Christian authors. This reflection did not arise only in the conflicts of his later years but must have *determined his thinking and working since his calling or since his early experiences of mission*, even if written documents of his view can only be ascertained later.

To Paul's Pharisaic inheritance there also belonged the specific form of belief in the *resurrection of the dead*. This apocalyptic hope was popularized in Palestine by the Maccabean crisis (Dan. 12.2f.; 2 Macc. 7) and the pharisaic movement, while in the Diaspora cosmic expectations rather receded over against an individual belief in the afterlife.[73] The formulaic speech of the 'God, who gives life to the dead' (Rom. 4.17) is reminiscent of the second of the 18 Benedictions of the *Shmoneh Esreh* (which belonged to the daily prayers in the synagogue) and the confession of God 'who raised Jesus ... from the dead' (Rom. 4.24; 8.11) puts this in concrete terms with regard to Jesus.

If Paul understands the Resurrection of Christ as the beginning of the general resurrection (1 Cor. 15.20) this presumes the apocalyptic collective understanding. Against the denial of the resurrection (1 Cor. 15.12) which is only comprehensible from particular forms of the Greek mindset, Paul tries to explain the totally different kind of *corporality* of the resurrection life (1 Cor. 15.35–49). A separation of soul and body or of the spiritual and material parts of humans would have been hardly thinkable for him.[74] This also speaks for the fact that he could understand the Resurrection of the 'buried' Jesus (cf. the formulation in 1 Cor. 15.3) in no other way than bodily.

The *integral anthropology* recognizable here, according to which a person not only *has* a body but *is* a body,[75] as he or she *is* also soul, heart or mind, is due not only to a general biblical but to a concrete Palestinian-Jewish inheritance.

Traces of the apostle's Jewish identity can be seen in many other aspects of his *piety, strategy of mission, argumentation and theology*. These can be mentioned here only very eclectically and in outline:

- His *self-understanding as apostle to the Gentiles* and the *Jewish division of the world into Jews and Gentiles* or *Jews and Greeks* and then the practice of preaching 'to the Jews first and then to the Greeks' (Rom. 1.16);

---

73. 2 Macc. forms an exception. Mention of the resurrection is avoided in 4 Macc., and it fades likewise in Sap, in Philo and in JosAs. Cf. G. W. E. Nickelsburg (2006), *Resurrection, Immortality and Eternal Life in Intertestamental Judaism and Early Christianity* (expanded ed.; Cambridge: Harvard University Press); on Paul see M. Hengel (2001), 'Das Begräbnis Jesu bei Paulus und die leibliche Auferstehung aus dem Grabe', in *Auferstehung – Resurrection* (ed. F. Avemarie and H. Lichtenberger; WUNT 135; Tübingen: Mohr Siebeck), 119–83 (esp. 150–72).

74. Cf. Hengel, 'Das Begräbnis Jesu bei Paulus' (n.73), 149.

75. Cf. basically R. Bultmann (2007), *Theology of the New Testament* (trans. K. Grobel; 2 vols; Waco: Baylor), 1.190–227; on the anthropological concepts in the Old Testament, H. W. Wolff (1974), *Anthropology of the Old Testament* (London: SCM); on Paul see U. Schnelle, *Apostle Paul*, 494ff.

- *the fundamental reference to Israel's Bible* for the contents of the Gospel of Christ and especially for the fact that this Gospel is also for the Gentiles (Rom. 15.14–21 and often);
- the description of his call *following the call of the prophets* (Gal. 1.15f.) and his self-understanding as the *eschatological bringer of joy* (Isa. 52.7) who proclaims the promised universal salvation among the peoples;
- the *takeover of forms and terms of Jewish religious propaganda* for the mission to the Gentiles (renunciation of idols, return to the living God; cf. 1 Thess. 1.9f.) and the brusque *negative valuation of the pagan cults*;
- the reception of *eschatological-geographic conceptions* according to which Zion is not only the starting point of the message of salvation (Rom. 15.19) but also the eschatological destination (Rom. 11.26f.) and which are based on the (Palestinian) early Jewish reception of the Table of Nations (Gen. 10);[76]
- the taking up of the *practice of writing advisory letters to congregations*[77] (among others) attested to in contemporary Judaism as well as individual components of the epistolary formulae, particularly the 'oriental' prescript and the salutation with the phrase charis kai eirēnē inspired by the Jewish peace greeting (cf. 2 Bar. 78.2);
- the reception of manifold *requirements and methods of Jewish biblical exegesis at that time* (Qal Wa-homer in Rom 5.9f. and elsewhere; Gezerah shavah in Rom. 4.1–12 and elsewhere, Midrash-exegesis in Gal. 3.6–14 and Rom. 4; typology in 1 Cor. 10.1–13; allegory in Gal. 4.21–31);
- the independent *reception of manifold apocalyptic traditions and modes of thought* (Parousia; the Day of the Lord; two aeons; relation of the kingdom of Christ and the Kingdom of God in 1 Cor. 15.23–28; resurrection and judgement; new creation) as well as an understanding of time which expected the Parousia in the present lifetime (1 Thess. 4.17; 1 Cor. 15.52f.);
- the *taking up of Palestinian Jewish discourses* which can be recognized in significant *linguistic parallels from the library of Qumran* (e.g. on the 'righteousness of God' in 1QS X, 25; XI, 12; 1QM IV, 6; on erga nomou in 4QMMT C 27, on the connection of 'flesh' and sin in 1QS XI, 9–14, the Hodayot and Palestinian Wisdom Literature[78]).

Paul's Jewish identity can be observed in the specific way in which he discusses the most distinctive markers of Jewish identity, circumcision and the Torah.[79] Even in his 'criticism of the Torah' he does not reach for

---

76. On this cf. J. M. Scott, *Paul and the Nations*, 136ff.
77. 2 Macc. 1.1–9; 2 Macc. 1.10–21.18 etc.
78. On this J. Frey (2002), 'Flesh and Spirit in the Palestinian Jewish Sapiential Tradition and in the Qumran Texts: An Inquiry into the Background of Pauline Usage', in *The Wisdom Texts from Qumran and the Development of Sapiential Thought. Studies in Wisdom at Qumran and Its Relationship to Sapiential Thought in the Ancient Near East, the Hebrew Bible, Ancient Judaism and the New Testament* (ed. C. Hempel, A. Lange and H. Lichtenberger; BETL 159; Leuven: Peeters), 367–404.
79. Further features of Jewish identity were the Sabbath and (in the Diaspora) the Temple tax.

'pagan' or progressive arguments but applies motifs from the internal Jewish discussion about the Torah to the situation of the Christian communities and the questions that have arisen there.

Circumcision

Circumcision[80] was, from the time of the Exile, and reinforced after the crisis under Antiochus IV Epiphanes, the physical, enduring sign for men of their Jewish identity. Greeks and Romans considered it to be a stigma. Hence in the Roman Empire it came to be 'the exclusive *nota Iudaica*'[81] which was not dispensed with even in the Diaspora.[82] Male converts became Jews through this act and with it proselytes simultaneously agreed to take over the *complete* Torah, while uncircumcised 'god-fearers' had to observe it only partially (avoidance of idolatry, ethical behaviour) as far as possible but were not obliged to observe the social limitations (table-fellowship, business and marital relationships).

If the early Christian preaching, on reaching people born as Gentiles, occasionally refrained from circumcising them[83] (cf. Acts 10.1–11.18) and only later practised a more well-considered *circumcision-free mission to the Gentiles*, this offered a great *potential for conflict*. This practice conferred great success on the Christian mission and gave rise to the (understandable) envy of the local synagogues; it also offered explosive potential for the community of circumcised and uncircumcised followers of Jesus in so far as the circumcised considered themselves still bound to the purity and food laws of the Torah while the uncircumcised did not comply or only partially complied with the requirements laid down there. In particular the early Christian community in Jerusalem came under enormous pressures of loyalty through contacts with the uncircumcised, which were heightened even further by the strained political situation in Judaea before 70 CE.

The agitation of the 'judaizing' opponents to the practice represented by the community of Antioch and carried further by Paul (Acts 15.1,5; Gal. 2.3; 5.2,11f.; 6.12–15) was directed towards the adoption of circumcision because it would also carry an obligation to follow the other Torah laws. In Gal. Paul

---

80. See N. E. Livesey (2010), *Circumcision as a Malleable Symbol* (WUNT II/295; Tübingen: Mohr Siebeck); and in more detail A. Blaschke (1998), *Beschneidung* (TANZ 28; Tübingen/Basel: Francke); there on Paul: 361–425.

81. Blaschke, *Beschneidung* (n.80), 360.

82. Philo also insists on its implementation among the Jews (*Migr.* 89–94) and proselytes (*QE* 2.2). Negligence of circumcision occurs only in the time of the Maccabees and then by radical allegorists in Alexandria, against whom Philo argues in *Migr.* 89–94 (Blaschke, *Beschneidung* [n.80], 210–14). On circumcision in Philo, see also Livesey, *Circumcision* (n.80), 41–76.

83. Presumably the practice arose relatively early; one could consider believing Gentiles as god-fearers. The practice had to be reflected upon more seriously, however, at the latest when the number of the Gentile Christians grew. Cf. F. W. Horn (1996), 'Der Verzicht auf die Beschneidung im frühen Christentum', *NTS* 42: 479–505.

counters this agitation consistently with an argumentation on the significance and function of the Law.

It is to be assumed that Paul, who considered himself a Jew (Gal. 2.15), was circumcised according to tradition (Phil. 3.5) and accepted the practice of circumcision among the Jews (Acts 16.3),[84] and likewise accepted the preaching of Christ's message to the Jews (Gal. 2.7) in a form in which the practice of circumcision and observance of the Torah were retained.

In terms of the history of salvation Paul acknowledges that for Jews circumcision is a sign of God's care (Rom. 3.2; 9.4f.). The historical *prae*, however, is no soteriological *plus*: In relation to salvation (or judgement) circumcision is only of use when one follows the Torah (Rom. 2.25) which is the only criterion of the assessment at the Last Judgement.[85] But in view of the actual sinfulness of all circumcision is of *no* help (Rom. 3.9ff.). It is not a quasi-sacramental sign of participation in salvation, nor a basis of any 'certainty' of election, nor any ground for 'boasting' (Rom. 2.17). It has *no soteriological value in itself* but is decisively *relativized*.[86]

Because of God's new creation in Christ, being circumcised or uncircumcised is no longer soteriologically relevant (Gal. 5.6; 6.15). A change in the 'status' given by circumcision or reconstruction of the foreskin ('epispasmos') after becoming a Christian is superfluous (1 Cor. 7.17–19). A subsequent circumcision would also be a denial of the sufficiency of faith or of Christ's work of salvation (Gal. 5.2) which would result in the loss of salvation (Gal. 5.4).

Consequently Paul counters those who call for a supplementary circumcision of Gentile Christians with *sarcastic polemic*: He describes them as 'dogs', 'workers of evil' and 'mutilators of the flesh' (katatomē); they would do better to let themselves be 'mutilated' (i.e. castrated) (Gal. 5.12).[87]

Paul cites his own example *autobiographically* to show the soteriological worthlessness of circumcision (Phil. 3.4ff.). On the other hand he claims a state of being circumcised *in the figurative sense* for *Jewish and Gentile Christians* (Rom. 2.28-30; Phil. 3.3). This is:

- not *outwardly visible* (en tō phanerō) but *inwardly* (en tō kryptō);
- not *in the flesh* (en sarki), but a circumcision *of the heart* (peritomē kardias);
- not *in the letter* (en grammati), but *in the spirit* (en pneumati);
- not for the *praise of men*, but *(for the praise) of God*.

---

84. On the historicity of Timothy's circumcision see Blaschke, *Beschneidung* (n.80), 460–3. The act corresponds to 1 Cor. 9.20, 'to the Jews I became as a Jew'. The rumour that Paul advised Jewish Christians against circumcising their children (Acts 21.21; cf. Barn 9.4) is historically improbable.

85. Vice versa the uncircumcised who fulfils the Law will become (figuratively) circumcised (Rom. 2.26f.).

86. In the understanding of the sinfulness of all (Rom. 2.3) the soteriological use of circumcision is in reality *negated* (see Blaschke, *Beschneidung* [n.80], 414).

87. This polemical tone is missing in Rom. because apparently no one in Rome demanded the circumcision of Gentile Christians.

This talk of the *circumcision of the heart* (Rom. 2.29) goes back to numerous biblical and early Jewish parallels.[88] It defines afresh who is *truly* 'a Jew' (Rom. 2.28) or 'Israel of God' (Gal. 6.16). The external circumcision contributes nothing beyond this.

The soteriological worthlessness of circumcision is also substantiated by the biblical *example of Abraham* (Rom. 4). His circumcision (Gen. 17) follows only after the promise of righteousness for the faithful (Gen. 15.6). It is a retrospective 'seal of faith' (Rom. 4.11) which is granted to *the uncircumcised*. In this way Scripture finally confirms justification *without works* (here: circumcision).

This *relativization of the fundamental Jewish identity marker of circumcision*, admittedly offensive for contemporary Jews, ensues argumentatively *in the framework of Jewish questioning and traditions*:

- In agreement with the Judaism of his day,[89] Paul takes for granted *the close connection of Torah and circumcision*: Circumcision is not simply a 'supplement' but commits Jews and proselytes on principle to obey the *whole* Torah (Gal. 5.3).[90]
- An element of the Jewish argumentation is also the halakhic *distinction between Jews and Gentiles*: The Law is not the same for all; only Jews (and proselytes) are obliged to follow the Torah. The uncircumcised are not. In Gal. 5.11 Paul takes this distinction for granted.[91]
- The question of the Gentile (Christian) participation in salvation implicitly *raises discussions which Diaspora Judaism, too, had to solve*. Here too the question arose as to how Gentiles could belong to God's people. For Paul the 'god-fearers model' of a 'second-class membership' is inacceptable; Gentile Christians (like the proselytes in the synagogue) should rather have an *unrestricted* participation in the congregation. But if this should not be possible *without* circumcision and obligation to obey the Torah, then there exists a *new definition of the 'requirements for admission'*.[92] Paul justifies this *soteriologically* (the vicarious and salvific death of Jesus), *pneumatologically* (the manifestation of the Spirit to the uncircumcised) and *exegetically* (the promise came before the Law; believers are children of Abraham).[93]

The Law and the Question about the Basis of Paul's Criticism of the Law

Central questions about the understanding of the Torah are bound up with the

88. Cf. Ezek. 44.7,9; Jer. 9.24f.: further Philo, *QE* 2.2; *QG* 3.46 and other passages.
89. Cf. Jos. *Ant.* XIII, 257f., 318f.; XX, 139.
90. This was doubtless what the 'Judaistic' agitators had in mind when they wanted to make Gentile Christian converts into proselytes and bind them to the Torah by circumcision to solve the problem of 'mixed' congregations (Acts 15.5). In Gal., Paul makes his readers forcefully aware of the consequences of such a step.
91. Cf. Tomson, *Paul and the Jewish Law*, 261.
92. Cf. T. L. Donaldson (1997), *Paul and the Gentiles* (Minneapolis: Fortress), 215–48.
93. Cf. Blaschke, *Beschneidung* (n.80), 395.

problem of circumcision: the Torah (Thorah = instruction), in Greek usually nomos (law),[94] was of central significance for all Jewish groups (not only for the Pharisees). This was intensified in Palestine from the time of the Maccabean crisis, but 'Moses' was the authority in the Diaspora too. To this extent the Torah constituted Jewish identity, although its interpretation and practice (and therewith the 'proper' interpretation of Jewish life) were fiercely disputed among individual groups (see 2 b) 2). Its mediation to the people through promulgation and teaching and its defence against its opponents were central concerns of the Pharisees, concerns which the 'pre-Christian' Paul also advocated.[95] But also with the question as to *how* the Torah was to be properly interpreted, with the struggle for its understanding and status in the face of the Christ-event, Paul *moves within the framework of the Jewish discussions of his time*.[96]

1   Some aspects of the contemporary Jewish understanding of the Torah must be emphasized:[97]
   • For contemporary Jewish, particularly Pharisaic thinking, the Torah is naturally *from God*. It is the proclamation of his holy will and at the same time *his gift to Israel* through which this people is honoured *above all nations*. It witnesses to God's electing love to Israel.
   • The Torah revealed on Sinai is simultaneously identical with *pre-existent Wisdom*, the *world-order* created by God before the Creation of the world, the pre-existent 'construction plan' of the Creation.[98] Because of its pre-existence the Patriarchs could already follow the commandments of the Moses-Torah,[99] and God's first words to humanity (Gen. 2.15–17) were identified with the Torah.[100]

---

94. The literature on the Torah in Second Temple Judaism is immense: Cf. Schürer, *History* (n.66), 464ff.; E. P. Sanders (1990), *Jewish Law from Jesus to the Mishnah* (London: SCM); Sanders, *Judaism* (n.54); F. Avemarie (1996), *Tora und Leben: Untersuchungen zur Heilsbedeutung der Tora in der frühen rabbinischen Literatur* (TSAJ 55; Tübingen: Mohr Siebeck); particularly with regard to Paul see H. Lichtenberger (1996), 'Das Tora-Verständnis im Judentum zur Zeit des Paulus', in *Paul and the Mosaic Law* (ed. J. D. G. Dunn; WUNT 89; Tübingen: Mohr Siebeck), 7–24.
95. Consequently Paul belonged to the most influential group in the (Palestinian) Judaism of his time (cf. Deines, 'Pharisees' [n.60], 503f.). For this reason the assumption that he grossly misunderstood Judaism is a groundless misrepresentation. Paul must have remembered his own earlier practices.
96. The Jewish historian of religion, A. F. Segal rightly emphasizes this in 'Paul's Jewish Presuppositions', 161.
97. In this I follow P. Stuhlmacher, *Biblische Theologie des Neuen Testaments*, vol. 1: *Grundlegung: Von Jesus zu Paulus*, 257–61.
98. On the 'ontology of the law' cf. Hengel, *Judaism and Hellenism* (n.23), 292ff.; on the pre-existence of the Torah G. Schimanowski (1985), *Weisheit und Messias* (WUNT II/17; Tübingen: Mohr Siebeck), 69ff., 216ff.
99. Cf. Sir. 44, 19–21; *Jub.* 6.11–14; 21.1–25; 2 Bar. 57.2.
100. Cf. the Targumim (*Neofiti I* and *Yerušalmi I*) on Genesis 2.15; also Jos. *Ant.* I, 41–7; Philo, *Leg.* I, 90ff.; 4 Ezra 3.7; 7.11 et al. On the commandment to Adam in Paradise see

- The Torah was *given* to Israel *with a positive purpose, for life*. It should preserve and regulate the life of Israel before God.[101]
- The Torah is the *yardstick of the Last Judgement* for Israel and the nations.[102] Obedience to it is relevant to judgement. To this extent the Torah will also exist to the end of the world. Conversely in early Judaism righteousness remains always related to the Torah.
- The Torah with its individual commandments is regarded in principle as *practicable and accomplishable*.[103] In spite of human frailty and sin (for which 'repentance' and a rite of atonement are provided) Judaism (except for the Essenes) is convinced that each person can choose what is good and keep the commandments.

2 Paul at many points refers to this understanding of the Torah and assumes it for himself or his interlocutor[104] – admittedly there ensue significant modifications:
- For Paul, too, the Torah is the revealed will of God (Rom. 2.17f.), God's Word (cf. Rom. 3.2) and his gift (Rom. 9.4) which honours Israel before all nations. It is '*holy ... just and good*' (Rom. 7.12). Paul can even call it – in an unparalleled expression[105] – 'spiritual' (pneumatikos) (Rom. 7.14).
- Paul, too, can connect the Torah with the world order which found its expression in the Creation (Rom. 1.20) and in the conscience of the Gentiles (Rom. 2.14f.); he also knows and uses the tradition that Adam encountered the Torah Law in Paradise (Rom. 7.7–11).
- For Paul, too, the Torah is the yardstick of the Last Judgement (Rom. 2.6ff., 12f.); Gal. 5.19–23). The question of its correct interpretation and fulfilment appears for him on the *forensic* and *apocalyptic* horizon.[106]
- Paul, too, takes for granted the opinion that the Torah was given for life (Rom. 7.10). But in view of the Christ-event he cannot adopt that statement in its entirety. There is another obstacle to its positive intention – which he does not dispute: *In reality the Law has brought death* (Rom. 7.10). *There is no Law that could be effective for life* (Gal. 3.21). In this respect the Law is '*incapable*' (Rom. 8.2f.).
- Before his conversion Paul had also taken for granted that the Law could be

---

in detail H. Lichtenberger (2004), *Das Ich Adams und das Ich der Menschheit* (WUNT 64; Tübingen: Mohr Siebeck), 203–41.

101. Sir. 17.11 calls it nomos zōēs, *Pss. Sol.* 14.2 speaks of the Law 'which God has commanded us to live by'; cf also *2 Bar.* 38.2.

102. Cf. 4 Ezra 7.37, 70–73; *2 Bar.* 48.27, 38–40, 46f. According to 4QMMT C 31, these works of the Torah 'will be counted as righteousness'.

103. Cf. Sir. 15.15; *Pss. Sol.* 9. 4–7; 4 Ezra 8.56–61; *m. Avot* III, 15. Cf. also Paul's pre-Christian vision of himself in Phil. 3.6f. and Rom. 2.17–20. The apostle, however, thinks differently; see Rom. 7.15ff.

104. See Stuhlmacher, *Biblische Theologie* (n.97), 257–61.

105. Thus Lichtenberger, *Das Ich Adams* (n.100), 139–42.

106. Stuhlmacher, *Biblische Theologie* (n.97), 262f. rightly emphasizes this.

carried out in full. But in view of his knowledge of Christ such advantages are worthless (Phil. 3.7ff.). What is more: In reality *no one truly fulfils the Law*; everyone – Jews like Gentiles – is a sinner (Rom. 3.9ff.,23) and even the desire to do good leads to the opposite under the power of sin (Rom. 7.14ff.).

With this 'pessimistic' anthropology Paul differs from the majority of contemporary Jewish positions. Admittedly this does not mean that this position is 'un-Jewish': some statements from Qumran[107] come very close to Paul in the knowledge of humankind's fundamental sinfulness. They stand there alongside the profession of divine grace, which would be granted to the prayer inter alia in the proper understanding of the Torah. Here we can see in detail analogies and significant differences to Paul.

The Pauline statement can only be understood against his *Pharisaic background*.[108] To this is added the fundamental fact of the *experience of his conversion* and with this his new-won insight in the encounter with Christ.[109] Certainly some questions (such as the circumcision of Gentile converts) only arise in the course of his mission, and conflicts (the 'Apostolic Council', the 'Incident at Antioch', the crisis in Galatia) caused Paul to intensify individual arguments, but we can assume that the converted Pharisee, who very quickly began to work as an independent preacher of the message of salvation, *already at an early date after Damascus* critically reflected on his view of the relationship of the Torah to Christ and therewith the scope of the Torah. A historical interpretation and one which is objectively appropriate must take into account the *relationship* of the statements *to their situation and* see the *fundamental nature* of the reflection against the background of Paul's experience of Christ.

3 Admittedly there are some insoluble *tensions in the Pauline statements about the Law*:[110]
  - *Origin*: Naturally Paul assumes that the *Torah* comes *from God* (Rom. 7.22; 8.7). Yet in Gal. 3.19f. he says that the order was given *by angels through a mediator* (Moses). This statement also takes up Jewish traditions (Deut. 33.2 LXX; *Jub.* 1.27–9; Philo, *Somn.* I, 140–4; cf. Acts 7.53) which admittedly are not meant derogatively.

---

107. 1 QS XI, 9f.; 1 QM IV, 4; XII, 12; 1 QH^a V, 30f. (= XIII, 13f. in the old enumeration); cf. J. Frey, 'Flesh and Spirit' (n.78); cf. already J. Becker (1964), *Das Heil Gottes* (SUNT 3; Göttingen: Vandenhoeck & Ruprecht), 111f., 248.

108. In Gal. 1.14 Paul explicitly names the 'traditions of the Fathers', i.e. the oral tradition of interpretation which likewise was part of the Torah according to the Pharisaic and later rabbinic understanding.

109. Cf. M. Hengel (2004), 'The Stance of the Apostle Paul toward the Law in the Unknown Years between Damascus and Antioch', in *Justification and Variegated Nomism*, vol. II: *The Paradoxes of Paul* (ed. D. A. Carson, P. T. O'Brien and M. Seifrid; WUNT II/181; Tübingen: Mohr Siebeck), 75–103.

110. These tensions were particularly stressed by H. Räisänen (1997), *Paul and the Law* (WUNT 29; Tübingen: Mohr Siebeck).

- *Function*: In Rom. 7.10 Paul stresses that the Law 'was given for life' to mankind. In Gal 3.19 he emphasizes on the contrary that the Law was added (to the Promise) *'because of transgressions'*, for recognition (Rom. 3.20), even for 'increase' of sin (Rom. 5.20; cf. 1 Cor. 15.56). Here he speaks of a negative effect, in Gal. 3.19 even of a negative intention of the Law.
- *Area of validity*: Paul fundamentally distinguishes between Jews 'under the Law' and Gentiles who are 'not under the Law' (Rom. 2.12ff.; 9.20f.): to this extent the Law is an advantage for Israel (Rom. 2.14,18; 9.4). On the other hand he reckons that Gentiles, too, may fulfil the Law and that at the last Judgement all – Jews and Gentiles – will be judged according to the yardstick of the Law (1 Cor. 7.19; cf. Rom. 2.6–10).[111]
- *Period of validity*: On several occasions Paul underlines the temporal limitations of the Law: It was only added 430 years after the Promise (Gal. 3.17) and according to Gal. 3.25 its 'preserving' function ends with the coming of faith. Gal. 4.5 speaks of the redemption of those under the Law (cf. Rom. 7.1–6; 8.1), those who are ruled by the Spirit are 'not under the Law' (Gal. 5.18) and Rom. 10.4 probably means: 'Christ is the *end* of the Law' (not its goal). On the other hand Paul explicitly denies that he desires to abolish the Law (Rom. 3.31). At least it remains valid for him – as for Jewish conviction – as the yardstick in the Last Judgement.
- *How it can be fulfilled*: The statements about the universality of sin (Rom. 1.18–3.20) and Rom. 7 do not claim that it cannot be fulfilled but say that it is not fulfilled in reality. On the other hand Rom. 2.14f. reckons with a (partial or only hypothetical) fulfilment by Gentiles. Individual texts, however, say that those who believe in Christ now fulfil the legal demands of the Torah in a new manner in the Spirit (Gal. 5.14ff.; Rom. 8.4; 13.8–10).
- *Quality*: The statements that are extremely critical of the Torah (particularly in Gal.), which connect the Law with bondage, formulate its purpose with regard to (increase of) sin or count it as one of the 'world elements' (Gal. 4.3), are contrary to the unparalleled climactic statement that the Law is not only 'holy ... just and good' (Rom. 7.12) but even 'spiritual' (Rom. 7.14).

Neither the assumption that the Pauline statements are constantly incoherent[112] nor the solution of the tensions in a conjectural material 'development' from Gal. to Rom.[113] provides a satisfactory solution here. Even the reference to the

---

111. The question as to how far the Law is in force for the Gentiles or whether Gentiles can count as righteous according to the Law is also raised in Judaism. Gentiles will also become righteous through the Torah but have to observe only a few commandments: cf. Segal, 'Paul's Jewish Presuppositions', 166.

112. Thus Räisänen, *Paul* (n.110); against this, however, cf. the fundamental criticism in T. E. van Spanje (1999), *Inconsistency in Paul* (WUNT II/110; Tübingen: Mohr Siebeck).

113. Cf. H. Hübner (1986), *Law in Paul's Thought* (2nd ed.; Edinburgh: T&T Clark). Certainly the polemical accent is stronger in Gal., but the statements in Rom. are no less critical

rhetorical intention of individual statements can only smooth out some of the tensions (e.g. in relation to Gal. 3.15–20).[114]

4 The key question is, *to what extent is the Torah still valid in view of the Christ-event*, or how can we determine its place in relation to the crucified and risen Christ?
On the basis of his calling, Paul had to recognize that the circle of those whom God considers 'righteous' has been defined anew by God's eschatological dealings in Christ: Circumcision and observance of the Law can no longer be the criterion. He himself, the converted persecutor, was called by Christ past the Torah, i.e. 'without the Law'. This has consequences:

- Admittedly there is no *abrogatio legis* in the sense that the Torah might no longer serve as an orientation and only the commandment of love is in force (Rom. 13.10).[115] Paul never intended to abolish the Torah. This would be a Marcionite tendency, 'more Pauline than Paul'. Against this idea Paul states that the Law will be carried out as before (Rom. 2.13) and is valid as a yardstick in the Last Judgement.
- The opposite view (which arose above all in the field of Christian-Jewish dialogue) that Paul carries on the Jewish understanding of the Torah with scarcely a break – i.e. that the Law is established through faith (cf. Rom. 3.31) – seems even less appropriate, if Paul's strongly critical statements on the Torah are considered.
- It is interesting that Paul makes no differentiation within the Torah, e.g. between the cultic or ethical Torah or between commandments which are to be followed literally and those which are to be understood allegorically. In the end he considers the Torah as a unity.

The soteriological and anthropological aspects of the Pauline perception of the Law can no longer be presented in this connection. Looking at the concrete practice of his mission, the substantial observation is that Paul clearly *accepted observance of the Torah by Jewish Christians without a second thought* (even if in his own missionary practice according to 1 Cor. 9.21 he can leave it out of consideration as far as he himself is concerned); his opposition only arises where the Jewish Christian observance wants to limit the complete right of inclusion of Gentile Christians within the congregation.

Just as Paul in Gal. (and in the 'Incident at Antioch' in Gal. 2.11ff.) defends the full right of Gentile Christians to share in the community (even without fulfilling the legal 'minimal demands') he also defends vice versa in Rom. 14f. the

---

of the Torah than those in Gal. On other theses on development (which for the most part proceed from a late dating of Gal.) cf. the contribution on Gal. in this volume (Chapter 8).

114. On the rhetorical explanation for some of the tensions see L. Thurén (2000), *Derhetorizing Paul* (WUNT 124; Tübingen: Mohr Siebeck), 80–4 and *passim*; see also van Spanje, *Inconsistency* (n.112), 251f.

115. On this thesis, which was particularly prominent in Protestant research, e.g. the Bultmann school, cf. the discussion in F. Hahn (2005), *Theologie des Neuen Testaments*, vol. 1: *Die Vielfalt des Neuen Testaments* (2nd ed.; Tübingen: Mohr Siebeck), 233f.

right of Christians of Jewish origin to retain as Christians their traditional Jewish lifestyle through abstaining from meat and keeping the Sabbath. Paul argues in this way in the interest of the love and unity of the congregation, although he himself has come to be convinced that to the pure all food is pure and all days are alike.

Consequently for Paul *Israel's specific signs of identity have lost their soteriological and their ecclesiological* (in a mixed congregation divisive) *significance*. From a Jewish point of view this means admittedly a fundamental qualification of elements which appear impossible to relinquish for the vast majority of his Jewish contemporaries. With this position the apostle could appear to both Jews and Christians as apostate. Although he regarded himself as a 'Hebrew of the Hebrews' and although he himself fought tirelessly for the unity of Jewish and Gentile Christians, perhaps he made the greatest contribution to the fact that the ways between the increasingly Gentile Christian church and Judaism ultimately separated.[116]

4
On the So-called 'New Perspective on Paul'[117]

During the past 30 years, the debate on Law and Justification in Paul has moved in a direction that has been called (for the first time by J. D. G. Dunn[118]) the 'New Perspective on Paul'. Especially exegetes in British and North-American scholarship[119] have followed this 'new' way of looking at matters, hailed by many as 'revolutionary' and as a 'change of paradigm' (with brusque polemics against the 'old', especially the German and Lutheran interpretation), with the result that there now exists a many-voiced choir of 'new' and even 'newer'[120] perspectives which are in essence only in agreement in their rejection of the 'old' view. In continental European and especially German-speaking scholarship with its strong bond to the Reformation tradition, the reception was rather hesitant and critical,[121] which was also due to the one-sidedness of some advocates of the

---

116. W. D. Davies, 'Paul: From the Jewish Point of View', 730; cf. J. M. G. Barclay (1995), 'Paul among Diaspora Jews: Anomaly or Apostate?' *JSNT* 60: 89–120.

117. Cf. the balanced discussion in Westerholm, *Perspectives*; Westerholm, 'The "New Perspective" at Twenty-Five', in *Justification* (n.54), 1–38; Yinger, *New Perspective*. On the increasing discussion in continental Europe see M. Bachmann (ed.) (2005), *Lutherische und neue Paulusperspektive* (WUNT 182; Tübingen: Mohr Siebeck).

118. J. D. G. Dunn (1983), 'The New Perspective on Paul', *BJRL* 65: 95–122; now in Dunn, *The New Perspective on Paul*, 89–110.

119. Cf. the list in Westerholm, 'New Perspective at Twenty-Five' (n.117).

120. Cf. A. J. M. Wedderburn (2005), 'Eine neuere Paulusperspektive?' in *Biographie und Persönlichkeit des Paulus* (ed. E.-M. Becker and P. Pilhofer; WUNT 187; Tübingen: Mohr Siebeck), 46–64, who discusses the works of, e.g., John Gager, Lloyd Gaston and Stanley Stowers.

121. See e.g. H. Hübner (1985), 'Was heißt bei Paulus Werke des Gesetzes?' in *Glaube und Eschatologie*. Festschrift W. G. Kümmel (ed. E. Grässer and O. Merk; Tübingen: Mohr Siebeck), 121–33; E. Lohse (1997), 'Theologie der Rechtfertigung im kritischen Disput – zu einigen

The Jewishness of Paul

new views and the somewhat superficial interpretations presented there. In the meantime a critical debate has also developed in the Anglo-Saxon world that led to a more differentiated discussion and more balanced evaluations,[122] and the valuable insights as well as the problematic one-sidedness of the so-called 'New Perspective' are now being discussed with greater frankness.

1. As the negative foil (which is not always fairly described, nor even properly understood) there serves the classical picture of the *'Lutheran Paul'*[123] considered to be minted by *Augustine* and *Luther* (or also Calvin and – important for the English-speaking world – John Wesley) and represented in the twentieth century especially by the interpretation of *Bultmann*. This line (which is in fact an oversimplification) is generally said to be characterized by a *negative image of Judaism* as a religion of Law and Works[124] and a *negative anthropology* according to which humankind is totally unable to hold its own before God through works. Consequently salvation comes through grace alone, i.e. through faith in Christ without works. As the pivotal interest in this line of interpretation the *question about individual salvation* is identified. Since in Lutheran theology the *Doctrine of Justification* counts as *articulus stantis et cadentis ecclesiae* (the article with which the church stands and falls), *Paul* became the main doctrinal authority for this central concern.[125] This implies, admittedly, the danger of a reading of Paul which is overloaded dogmatically and which projects the questions of later generations anachronistically upon the apostle.

   In his Lutheran and especially *existential* interpretation of Paul, Rudolf Bultmann begins *anthropologically* with the concepts that describe the human condition 'prior to the revelation of faith'[126] (body, soul, spirit, heart, flesh, sin, death, Law) in order then to display the existence 'under faith' under the concepts of 'righteousness', 'grace', 'faith' and 'freedom'. Here faith is understood as a change in the understanding of existence, from an understanding that is assured by the self and is consequently unsuccessful to a new under-

---

neueren Perspektiven in der Interpretation der Theologie des Apostels Paulus', *GGA* 249: 67–81; see also Hengel and Deines, 'E.P. Sanders' "Common Judaism"'; and P. Stuhlmacher (2001), *Paul's Doctrine of Justification. A Challenge to the New Perspective*. With an essay by Donald Hagner (Downer's Grove: IVP).

122. See especially the discussion in Westerholm, *Perspectives* (n.117); further, in particular S. J. Gathercole (2002), *Where is Boasting? Early Jewish Soteriology and Paul's Response in Romans 1–5* (Grand Rapids: Eerdmans); the criticism of the 'New Perspective' (particularly from conservative exegetes) was collected in the two volumes *Justification and Variegated Nomism* (n.54 and 109).

123. Cf. Westerholm, *Perspectives* (n.117), 3–97, especially the summary 88–97.

124. This description goes back to F. Weber (1880), *System der altsynagogalen palästinischen Theologie* (Leipzig: Dörffling & Franke) and was handed down by scholars such as Wilhelm Bousset, Emil Schürer and Paul Billerbeck to Bultmann and later theologians.

125. On the comparison Luther – Paul cf. V. Stolle (2002), *Luther und Paulus. Die exegetischen und hermeneutischen Grundlagen der Lutherischen Rechtfertigungslehre im Paulinismus Luthers* (ABG 10; Leipzig: Evangelische Verlagsanstalt).

126. Bultmann, *Theology* (n.75), 1.190.

standing which is bestowed and for which the person is indebted to God or Christ. It should be noted, however, that the appropriateness of Bultmann's anthropological understanding of Paul was energetically contested by other Lutheran exegetes (e.g. his former student Ernst Käsemann). The problem is that *the particular types of Judaism as they existed in Paul's time are now generalized*: 'Judaism' becomes the cipher for the human inclination (possible in any religion) to secure one's own existence by one's own activity ('works'). Consequently it becomes the prototype of a religion of the natural person and as such it serves as a dark foil against which Paul's message (in Bultmann's interpretation) can be described. Although Bultmann's interpretation adopted some important aspects of the reformers' views, especially in the view of justification, it is nevertheless a reduction, with its focus on anthropology rather than Christology, and also with its existentialist terminology and the rejection of any salvation-historical perspective.

2 The 'criticism' of the scholars who developed the 'New Perspective' focuses on various points, above all on the *individualist view of salvation* and on the *depiction of Judaism* which – already in Luther – was heavily overlaid by the controversies of the sixteenth century.

- *Krister Stendahl*: The first step in the criticism of the 'Lutheran' Paul was made in an essay by the later Lutheran bishop of Stockholm, Krister Stendahl.[127] He pointed out that in Paul 'Justification' should not be restricted to the question of the individual acquisition of salvation ('How do I obtain a merciful God?'). Unlike the young Luther the 'pre-Christian' Paul was not tormented by pangs of conscience. Paul had a 'robust' conscience and regarded himself as irreproachable in his actions for the Torah and Jewish tradition. Misinterpretations arose through the introduction of the 'Western' tradition of 'examining the conscience' coined by Augustine. According to Stendahl the Pauline understanding of justification and law arose from issues of his missionary work. What place have the Gentiles in God's plan for salvation in view of the Christ-event? Thus, the Pauline teaching on justification is not the basis of Paul's theology but was only developed in view of practical issues of his mission.

- *Ed P. Sanders*: The influential work by Sanders, *Paul and Palestinian Judaism*,[128] is often regarded as the 'watershed' between the 'old' and the 'new' perspectives. In this work, Sanders attacked in an effective polemics *the negative image of Judaism as a religion of 'righteousness through works'* as he found it in the earlier, particularly German, research. When comparing Paul and contemporary Judaism, Sanders adopted the method of a relatively abstract comparison of the respective structure of the religious system of Judaism and of Paul: The structure is made up only

---

127. K. Stendahl (1963), 'The Apostle Paul and the Introspective Conscience of the West', *HTR* 56: 199–215; also in Stendahl (1977), *Jews and Gentiles and Other Essays* (London: SCM), 78–96.

128. Sanders, *Paul and Palestinian Judaism*; Sanders (1983), *Paul, the Law and the Jewish People* (London: SCM); Sanders, *Paul*.

by two fundamental elements: '*getting in*' and '*staying in*', i.e. how does a person get into the state of 'salvation' (or 'covenant') and how does he or she manage to stay within that state?

On the basis of an examination of texts from *c*.200 BCE to 200 CE Sanders claimed that *Judaism* commonly had a basic structure which was largely valid for all relevant Jewish groups (therefore: 'Common Judaism'). This structure is described as 'Covenantal Nomism': here entry is based on *election* or the 'covenant' (and consequently on God's mercy) and to remain therein demands observance of the Torah. What is decisive, however, is that election comes before the Torah. Not the action but the *election is constitutive for salvation*. Sanders, therefore, rejects the view that the law was ever a 'way of salvation'. Thus Judaism in antiquity between Ben Sira and the Mishna appears as a 'religion of mercy'. This 'new' portrayal of (Palestinian) Judaism was adopted with much approval in scholarship because it offered a possibility to discontinue traditional anti-Jewish clichés.

According to Sanders the view represented by Paul is in structural analogy with Jewish Covenantal Nomism: *Entry into Salvation comes through grace, while Judgement is enacted according to works*, hence works are not necessary for the attainment of salvation but only to 'remain therein'. Having determined both 'systems' in a general analogy, Sanders can define afresh the issue between Paul and his fellow Jews: what Paul criticizes in Judaism is not a 'righteousness through works' (which did not exist). 'This is what Paul finds wrong in Judaism: it is not Christianity.'[129] With Christ in mind the Law had to become problematic for Paul. Hence he came 'from solution to plight', not vice versa. And so, because of his conviction that salvation is only possible through faith in Christ, Paul challenges the power to save of Israel's Election, Covenant and Law. What separates him from Judaism is basically his *christocentric Soteriology*. Sanders characterizes this as *participatory Soteriology*. Its central idea is not juridical justification but the *life in Christ*, participation.

- *James D. G. Dunn*, who originally introduced the *term* 'New Perspective on Paul',[130] takes up Sanders' understanding of Jewish covenantal nomism but states Paul's position more precisely: In sociological terms, he understands the Law, and particularly the aspects of circumcision, purity and dietary laws and the Sabbath not only as *identity markers* but also as *boundary markers*, i.e. as regulations pertaining to an ethical and social delimitation. They serve to uphold Israel's special position among the nations. Hence the term 'works of the Law' (Gal. 2.16 etc.) is primarily interpreted as denoting the laws that provide the delimitation of Jews from non-Jews, particularly the rules for purity and food. If this is correct, Paul criticizes the Jewish position not

---

129. Sanders, *Paul and Palestinian Judaism*, 552.
130. Dunn, 'New Perspective' (n.118); cf. his retrospective: Dunn, 'The New Perspective on Paul; Whence, What and Whither?' in Dunn, *New Perspective* (n.118), 1–80, and the collected essays there; also Dunn, *Theology*.

for the attempt to achieve 'righteousness through works' but because of the striving for ethnic-social separation. The problem is not the 'self-righteous' referral to 'works' but the glory of Israel's Election in separation from the nations. Hence what is important for Paul is the universality of the message of salvation, the surmounting of ethnic barriers, namely the question of how the Gentiles may belong to the People of God without having to become Jews.

- *Francis B. Watson*: An even more sociologically oriented version of the 'New Perspective' has been developed by Francis B. Watson.[131] Even more than Dunn he points out that Paul has been read too often and too strongly in the interest of systematic theology and Christian doctrine, with the effect that the concrete social reality behind his epistles was not seen sufficiently. According to Watson's reconstruction, Paul started his mission among the Gentiles after the mission among the Jews had failed. To prevent another failure, Paul then reduced the requirements for Gentile converts. Gal. and Rom. are composed to defend the practice of life and mission within those Gentile Christian communities. In this view, the term 'works of the law' points to the Jewish lifestyle in general, not to particular 'boundary markers'. Paul ultimately aims at separating his Gentile Christian communities from Judaism, not at an integration of Jewish and Gentile Christians. Theologically this view leads to a reassessment of ethics: If the contrast of 'faith' and 'works' is primarily related to the contrast of Gentiles and Jews, there is no further reason to deny the soteriological relevance of works within Christian life.[132]

There is no need to describe the vast variety of other views and scholarly aspects developed within the framework of the so-called 'New Perspective' or deliberately going beyond that framework.[133]

3 The many-voiced *criticism of the 'New Perspective'* can be summarized in a number of points:
   - *'Common Judaism'* (see 2 b) 2): even though criticism of the 'old' distorted picture of Judaism is justified and necessary, Sanders' argument is based on a partly one-sided selection of sources and polemical rhetoric.[134] Methodologically, the abstract focus on very simple fundamental struc-

---

131. F. B. Watson (1986), *Paul, Judaism and the Gentiles: A Sociological Approach* (SNTSMS 56; Cambridge: CUP); see now the revised and expanded new edition: Watson (2007), *Paul, Judaism and the Gentiles: Beyond the New Perspective* (Grand Rapids: Eerdmans).

132. Watson, *Paul* (rev. ed.; n.131), 353f.

133. This concerns on the one hand developments and modifications of the 'New Perspective' as represented for instance by N. T. Wright and D. A. Campbell (cf. Wright [1997], *What Saint Paul Really Said* [Grand Rapids: Eerdmans]; Wright [2005], *Paul: Fresh Perspectives* [London: SPCK]; Campbell [2009], *The Deliverance of God: An Apocalyptic Rereading of Justification in Paul* [Grand Rapids: Eerdmans]) and on the other hand more radical approaches like those of John Gager, Lloyd Gaston and Stanley Stowers (as referred to by Wedderburn, 'Eine neuere Paulusperspektive?').

134. Hengel and Deines refer to this in 'E.P. Sanders' "Common Judaism"', 477–9.

tures leads to a levelling of specific differences, to a putative Common Judaism behind the texts which no longer concurs with the historical reality.[135] Later investigations show that the Judaism of that period was more varied and less schematic in its classification of the Torah and salvation than Sanders admits.[136]

- *'Covenantal Nomism' and the question of a 'soteriological' significance of the fulfilment of the Torah*: It is completely incontestable according to early Jewish texts that judgement takes place according to works. From numerous texts it emerges that the 'soteriological' significance of the Torah and its fulfilment were more highly evaluated.[137] It is of secondary importance that matters of the fulfilment of the Torah were not a question of 'getting in' but of 'staying in', when they are finally relevant for the decision in the Last Judgement. The Jewish texts cannot so easily be brought into one line as Sanders wishes to do, and the question of salvation frequently remains connected to human activity. *Friedrich Avemarie* formulates concisely for the early Rabbinic texts: 'The principle of retaliation remains unbroken: Nowhere is it in doubt that fulfilling the Law will be rewarded and infringement will be punished' – even if it is again and again said 'that better obedience is not motivated by reward but happens for the sake of God or the Law itself'.[138]

- *'Works of the Law' as simply 'boundary markers'?* Dunn's limitation of the expression *'works of the Law'* to the concrete 'boundary markers' such as circumcision and the regulations regarding food (i.e. those directions in the Torah which led to the distinguishing of the Jewish and Gentile Christians) found many critics. This might historically fit to the context of Gal. 2.16f. but at least Rom. 3.20 demands a more fundamental reflection. This can also be discerned in Gal. 2.21. In the meantime Dunn has modified his view; the expression can describe *all* the works demanded by the Law, although some certainly become a 'test case' to a special degree.[139] See below on the semantics of erga nomou.

- *The object of boasting.* Simon Gathercole in particular, disagreeing with his teacher, Dunn, emphasizes that the 'boasting' which Paul condemns as being 'excluded' cannot be viewed as limited to the 'national' aspect

---

135. Thus the methodological critique in H.-M. Rieger (1996), 'Eine Religion der Gnade. Zur "Bundesnominismus"-Theorie von E. P. Sanders', in *Bund und Tora* (ed. F. Avemarie and H. Lichtenberger; WUNT 92; Tübingen: Mohr Siebeck), 129–61 (140–6).

136. Cf. in detail *Justification and Variegated Nomism* (n.54).

137. Cf. on this Gathercole, *Where is boasting* (n.122), 37–169; on the Tannaitic texts Avemarie, *Tora und Leben* (n.94), 38–44, 291–4, 582f.; P. S. Alexander, 'Torah and Salvation in Tannaitic Literature' in *Justification and Variegated Nomism* (n.54), 261–301.

138. Avemarie, *Tora und Leben* (n.94), 578. Cf. also Avemarie (1999), 'Erwählung und Vergeltung: Zur optionalen Struktur rabbinischer Soteriologie', NTS 45: 108–26.

139. Dunn, 'The New Perspective: Whence, What and Whither?' (n.130), 1–88 (25f.). According to P. Stuhlmacher, '"Christus Jesus ist hier, der gestorben ist, ja vielmehr der auch auferweckt ist, der zur Rechten Gottes ist und uns vertritt"' in *Auferstehung* (n.73), 351–61 (357–8) it is a matter of 'legal rules' in Gal. 2.16 and Rom. 3.20.

of Israel's Election but also includes the active obedience associated with that Election.[140] In view of the widespread expectation of the Judgement 'according to works' (which Paul shared) such a confidence in Israel's Election *and* obedience is by no means unfounded. This means that the question of individual salvation, central for the 'Lutheran' interpretation of Paul, is somewhat rehabilitated: Paul is also concerned about each person's standing before God – not simply about the inclusion of the Gentiles in the People of God.[141]

- *The eschatological dimension*: Many exegetes are of the opinion that the focus of the 'New Perspective' on sociological categories (identity, dissociation, restriction, etc.) has reduced the awareness of the fact that Paul (with his contemporaries) was convinced that the struggles were about matters that were relevant eschatologically. In Paul's view, each person faces Judgement in which – according to Jewish tradition – works are decisive, and in this viewpoint the forensic terminology (righteousness/justification) has its place.[142] This is based on pre-Pauline traditions (Rom. 4.25; 8.34) and points back to biblical models (cf., e.g., Isa. 53).[143]
- *Differences in anthropology*: *Timo Laato* locates a considerable difference between Paul and contemporary Judaism in *anthropology*.[144] The 'New Perspective' takes too little account of the question of the human capability to do good: While for the most part Judaism (exception: Essenes/Qumran) takes for granted that man is free to choose the good and withstand the 'evil inclination', for Paul the Adamic person finds himself in the situation where he does not do the good which he desires to do. If anthropological premises of the 'religious systems' differ, the result is differences in their Soteriology as well. While 'cooperation' is included in Jewish thinking, this is excluded for Paul in view of faith.

4 A central point in the discussion is the syntagma 'works of the Law' (erga nomou Gal. 2.16; 3.2,5,10; Rom. 3.20,28; Phil. 3.9):
- *Bultmann* related the term to *human endeavour*, 'to man's effort to achieve his salvation by keeping the Law'.[145] Even the striving to fulfil the Torah is accordingly unsuccessful and sinful. This cannot be Paul's position. Today almost all exegetes dissociate themselves from this.
- *Dunn* interprets the syntagma used in Gal. 2.16 as denoting concrete 'boundary markers' such as circumcision and the dietary laws – i.e. those instructions in the Torah which separate Jews from Gentiles and which

---

140. Gathercole, *Where is Boasting?* (n.122), 194. Cf. also S. Grindheim (2005), *The Crux of Election: Paul's Critique of the Jewish Confidence in the Election of Israel* (WUNT II/202; Tübingen: Mohr Siebeck) (see the summary 198–200).

141. Cf. also Westerholm, *Perspectives* (n.117), 440–5.

142. Cf. Stuhlmacher, 'Christus Jesus' (n.139), 353f.; cf. also Wright, *What Saint Paul Really Said* (n.133), 17f.

143. Stuhlmacher, 'Christus Jesus' (n.139), 355f.

144. T. Laato, *Paul and Judaism*.

145. Bultmann, *Theology* (n.75), 1.264.

led e.g. in the 'Incident at Antioch' or also in Galatia to the separation of Jewish and Gentile Christians.
- *Michael Bachmann* endeavoured in several attempts[146] to prove semantically that erga nomou describes exclusively *halakhoth*, concrete *rules* in the Torah but *under no circumstances human actions*. Paul, however, presupposes that rules are laid down for action – i.e. to be carried out.[147]
- *Friedrich Avemarie* and *A. Andrew Das*[148] understand the expression in the sense of *deeds* corresponding to the Law.
- *Klaus Haacker*[149] finally desires to apply the expression specifically to *ritual actions* conforming to the Law – distinguished from ethical 'good works'.

A special part in the critical analysis is played by the parallels in Qumran in the early Essene halakhic letter 4 QMMT C 27–31, in which the speaker – sometimes suspected to be the 'Teacher of Righteousness' – conveys to the opposite side, perhaps the High Priest, some very specific halakhoth which give the reason for the separation of his own faction:

> We have (indeed) sent you some of the precepts of the Torah according to our decision, for your welfare and the welfare of your people. For we have seen (that) you have wisdom and knowledge of the Torah. Consider all these things and ask Him that He strengthen your will and remove from you the plans of evil and the device of Belial, so that you may rejoice at the end of time, finding that some of our practices are correct. And this will be counted as a virtuous deed of yours, since you will be doing what is righteous and good in His eyes, for your own welfare and for the welfare of Israel.[150]

This single exact parallel to the construction for which we have no other evidence in Greek shows that Paul terminologically refers to a Palestinian-Jewish halakhic discussion. We can see this from the following:

- The context in 4QMMT is *halakhic*: It deals with individual requirements which are of a ritual character here. It is, however, questionable whether the ritual context must delimit the expression to cultic (as opposed to ethical) aspects.
- It deals with *particular requirements* which are at the root of the separation of two groups, i.e. with (here inner-Jewish) 'boundary markers'. According to Dunn a similar situation can be suspected in Gal. 2.16.

---

146. M. Bachmann (2008), *Anti-Judaism in Galatians?: Exegetical Studies on a Polemical Letter and on Paul's Theology* (trans. R. Brawley; Grand Rapids: Eerdmans); Bachmann, 'Keil oder Mikroskop? Zur jüngeren Diskussion um den Ausdruck "Werke des Gesetzes"' in *Lutherische und neue Paulusperspektive* (n.117), 69–134.

147. Bachmann, 'Keil oder Mikroskop?' (n.117), 73.

148. F. Avemarie (2001), 'Die Werke des Gesetzes im Spiegel des Jakobusbriefs: A Very Old Perspective on Paul', *ZTK* 98: 282–309; A. A. Das, *Paul and the Jews*, 40–2.

149. Haacker, *Brief* (n.13), 83f.

150. E. Qimron and J. Strugnell (1994), *Qumran Cave 4. V: Miqṣat Ma'aśe ha-Torah* (DJD 10; Oxford: Clarendon), 62–3.

- The construction as such can best be translated as *'precepts'* – but a pronounced dissociation from 'deeds' seems inappropriate since it is clear that these regulations are *laid down to be followed*: The 'works' are done by the one group; they should be done by the other.
- The corresponding action, the *fulfilling* of these regulations (but not simply of these but of 'what is upright and good in his eyes') should in the end 'be *reckoned for righteousness*' by God.

In summarizing we can say that regulations and obedience to them cannot be separated. The corresponding action will be reckoned for righteousness. Hence even in Paul's soteriological principle, 'no human being will be justified by the works of the Law' (Gal. 2.16; Rom. 3.20), action conforming to the Law is in view. This simply cannot be limited to some distinguishing regulations but affects life under Torah as *a whole*.

Credit is without doubt owed to the 'New Perspective' in that it has effectively challenged the transmitted caricature of Judaism as a religion of 'righteousness through works' and has brought the uncritical discussion of the 'Law as Way of Salvation' lastingly into question. In contrast with the reception history of Paul's theology we can see from Jewish sources that for contemporary Jews the Torah meant joy, not a burden, vocation, not slavery. On the basis of the latest research it should be unequivocally impossible to describe the Judaism of the time of Jesus as a 'religion of total self-redemption'[151] and to accuse it of 'righteousness through works' and ritualism. Such verdicts are neo-protestant rather than Lutheran and contradict the Jewish self-perception. It is also a gain that the danger of bringing later questions into the interpretation of Paul is now perceived more acutely. Before generalizing Paul's statements into timeless teaching, the historical location and rhetorical context of the texts must first be considered seriously. The sociological categories, as Dunn, too, acknowledges, must not step into the place of theological reflection. The theologian Paul cannot be reduced to intentions that are simply drawn from practical aspects of mission or focused on the 'politics' of the church.[152] He developed his theology against the background of his biography and knowledge of Christ, and his views on the human nature and also on human sinfulness are deeper than the representatives of the 'New Perspective' wished to admit. Further discussion should not omit the 'theological' issues in favour of merely sociological terms but take both dimensions seriously, as in Paul's thought theology, biography and mission come together: his Jewish education, his experience of Christ, and the further reflection of this experience and the later developments and conflicts in his missionary work.

---

151. Thus still P. Billerbeck (1928), *Kommentar zum Neuen Testament aus Talmud und Midrasch*, vol. IV/1 (Munich: Beck), 6.
152. Cf. Lohse, 'Theologie der Rechtfertigung' (n.121), 76.

Bibliography

D. Boyarin (1994), *A Radical Jew: Paul and the Politics of Identity*, Berkeley: UCP.
A. A. Das (2003), *Paul and the Jews*, Peabody: Hendrickson.
W. D. Davies (1999), 'Paul: From the Jewish Point of View', in W. Horbury, W. D. Davies and J. Sturdy (eds) *The Cambridge History of Judaism*, vol. III: *The Early Roman Period*, Cambridge: CUP, 678–730.
T. L. Donaldson (2007), *Judaism and the Gentiles: Jewish Patterns of Universalism (to 135 CE)*, Waco: Baylor.
J. D. G. Dunn (1998), *The Theology of Paul the Apostle*, Grand Rapids: Eerdmans.
—(2005), *The New Perspective on Paul*, Wissenschaftliche Untersuchungen zum Neuen Testament 185, Tübingen: Mohr Siebeck.
J. Frey (2007), 'Paul's Jewish Identity', in J. Frey, D. R. Schwartz and S. Gripentrog (eds), *Jewish Identity in the Greco-Roman World*, Ancient Judaism and Early Christianity 71, Leiden: Brill, 285–321.
K. Haacker (2003), 'Paul's Life and Work', in J. D. G. Dunn (ed.), *The Cambridge Companion to St. Paul*, Cambridge: CUP, 19–33.
M. Hengel and R. Deines (1995), 'E. P. Sanders' "Common Judaism", Jesus, and the Pharisees', *Journal of Theological Studies* 46: 1–70.
—(1991), *The Pre-Christian Paul*, London: SCM.
M. Hengel and A. M. Schwemer (1997), *Paul Between Damascus and Antioch: The Unknown Years* trans. J. Bowden, London: SCM.
T. Laato (1995), *Paul and Judaism: An Anthropological Approach*. South Florida Studies in the History of Judaism 115, Atlanta: Scholars.
K.-W. Niebuhr (1992), *Heidenapostel aus Israel. Die jüdische Identität des Paulus nach ihrer Darstellung in seinen Briefen*. Wissenschaftliche Untersuchungen zum Neuen Testament 62, Tübingen: Mohr Siebeck.
R. Riesner (1997), *Paul's Early Period: Chronology, Mission Strategy, Theology*, trans. D. W. Stott, Grand Rapids: Eerdmans.
E. P. Sanders (1977), *Paul and Palestinian Judaism: A Comparison of Patterns of Religion*, London: SCM.
—(1991), *Paul*, Oxford: OUP.
U. Schnelle (2005), *Apostle Paul: His Life and Theology*, trans. M. E. Boring, Grand Rapids: Baker.
J. Scott (1995), *Paul and the Nations: The Old Testament and Jewish Background of Paul's Mission to the Nations with Special Reference to the Destination of Galatians*. Wissenschaftliche Untersuchungen zum Neuen Testament 84, Tübingen: Mohr Siebeck.
A. F. Segal, (1988), *Paul the Convert: The Apostolate and Apostasy of Saul the Pharisee*, New Haven: YUP.
—(2003) 'Paul's Jewish Presuppositions', in J. D. G. Dunn (ed.), *The Cambridge Companion to St. Paul*, Cambridge: CUP, 159–77.
P. J. Tomson (1990), *Paul and the Jewish Law: Halakha in the Letters of the Apostle to the Gentiles*. Compendia rerum iudaicarum ad Novum Testamentum 3/1, Assen: van Gorcum.
S. Westerholm (2004), *Perspectives Old and New on Paul: The 'Lutheran' Paul and His Critics*, Grand Rapids: Eerdmans.
K. Yinger (2011), *The New Perspective on Paul: An Introduction*, Eugene: Cascade Books.

Chapter 5

THE LIFE OF PAUL
Eva Ebel

For information on the life of Paul there are two sources available: the seven letters acknowledged as truly Pauline (Rom., 1 Cor., 2 Cor., Gal., Phil., 1 Thess., Phlm.) which give his own self-witness; and the Acts of the Apostles by Luke as the witness of a stranger. Luke probably did not know Paul personally and only wrote his work several decades after Paul's death. Consequently what is said in the epistles has priority in time and content, although these, too, are not a neutral representation of Paul's life and work and are not intended to be complete. Paul only gives biographical details when he wishes to use these for his argumentation, and shades them accordingly. Paul's statements about his own person are very sketchy, and that is why the Lucan details are indispensable for a biography of Paul. Further, Acts alone makes it possible to fix the chronology of the Apostle's life. In his work Luke makes use of numerous local traditions – admittedly after selecting and editing them to suit his purpose. This means that Acts must be examined critically against the background of the primary sources.

1
Chronology

Neither the date of Paul's birth nor that of his death is recorded in the writings of the New Testament; none of his letters is dated. Hence to achieve the complete chronology of his life one must bring into play references to such people and events as can be dated with the help of non-biblical sources.

1 Here the starting point is the so-called *Gallio Inscription*. Lucius Iunius Gallio Annaeanus appears in Acts 18.12 as proconsul of Achaia (anthypatos tēs Achaias). Achaia was a senatorial province, i.e. in the normal case the Senate annually chose a new governor who presumably took up office on 1 July.[1] The period of office of Gallio, the elder brother of the philosopher, Seneca, can be determined with relative certainty from an inscription – unfortunately only

---

1. According to Cassius Dio 57,14,5 Tiberius decreed this. He reports that Claudius specified that the governor depart from Rome, initially at the beginning of April (60,11,6), then in the middle of April (60,17,3).

preserved in fragments – found at Delphi:[2] It presumably lasted from the early summer of 51 till the early summer of 52.

The letter of the Emperor Claudius which is documented in the inscription is about a matter relating to the town of Delphi and is addressed to the town either during the proconsulate of Gallio or that of his successor in office. The document is dated on the 26th acclamation of Claudius as *imperator* and – though this is uncertain from the text – on the 12th conferment on him of tribunal authority. The *tribunicia potestas* was conferred upon a new emperor immediately upon his assumption of office; its number is therefore identical with the current year of office. Claudius' 12th year of office began on 25 January 52 and ended on 24 January 53. Since the 27th acclamation as *imperator* took place before 1 August 52, the letter must have been drawn up earlier, i.e. in the summer of 52. The date of writing therefore must have been somewhere between 25 January and the early summer of 52. Because of the length of the procedure of appointment treated in the letter it is more likely that Gallio's period of office as proconsul did not commence in the early summer of 52 but lasted from the early summer of 51 until the early summer of 52, and that Claudius' rescript was only drawn up after Gallio's retirement from office.[3]

According to Acts 18.11 Paul spends a total of 18 months in Corinth during his first visit. If he was living there during Gallio's period of office as proconsul, his sojourn there lasted at the earliest from the autumn of 49 until the summer of 51 and at the latest from the spring of 52 until the winter of 53/54. This period can be further narrowed down by two observations: The Lucan narrative gives the impression first that the Jews had speculated on the inexperience of the newly arrived governor, and second that Paul did not remain much longer in the city after these events (cf. Acts 18.18: eti prosmeinas hēmeras hikanas). Hence the incident probably took place in the first phase of Gallio's governorship and towards the end of Paul's first visit to Corinth which consequently is to be dated in the summer of the year 51.

---

2. The definitive edition of the so-called Gallio Inscription was made by A. Plassart (1970), 'Lettre de l'empereur Claude au gouverneur d'Achaïe (en 52)', in *Les inscriptions du temple du IVe siècle* (Fouilles de Delphes III/4), Paris: École française d'Athenes, 26–32 (Nr. 286). H. Conzelmann (1987), *Acts of the Apostles* (Hermeneia), Philadelphia, 152f. provides an English translation. Basic are the observations of A. Deissmann (1957), *Paul: A Study in Social and Religious History*, New York, 261–86 with photographs of the fragments as frontispiece of the book. Among recent works on Pauline chronology one should look at R. Jewett (1979), *A Chronology of Paul's Life*, Philadelphia, 38–40; G. Lüdemann (1984), *Paul, Apostle to the Gentiles. Studies in Chronology*, London, 163f. (for a detailed analysis of Lüdemann's argumentation cf. D. Slingerland, Acts 18:1–17 and Luedemann's 'Pauline Chronology', *JBL* 109 [1990], 686–90; J. Murphy-O'Connor (1993), 'Paul and Gallio', *JBL* 112: 315–17; R. Riesner, *Paul's Early Period*, 202–11; H. Omerzu, *Prozeß*, 247–52.

3. A period of office which lasted more than a year is possible, but in the case of Gallio is most unlikely since, according to a note written by his brother Seneca, he fell ill with fever in Achaia (Epistulae 104,6). We can more readily conjecture that Gallio left Achaia prematurely, as e.g. Riesner, *Early Period*, 207 supposes.

2 This is confirmed by a further detail about Paul's stay in Corinth which can be read in Acts 18.2: While there Paul meets Aquila and Priscilla who 'recently' (prosphatōs) have come from Italy since, because of an edict issued by Claudius (dia to diatetachenai) all Jews have had to leave Rome.[4]

The earliest literary reference after Acts for an expulsion of Jews from Rome under the Emperor Claudius is to be found only in the second century in Suetonius: *Iudaeos impulsore Chresto assidue tumulantis Roma expulit* (Claudius 25,4).[5] In the fifth century Orosius first quotes the passage from Suetonius – though in the *interpretatio Christiana* with the form *Christo* – and then dates it 'in the ninth year' of Claudius, i.e. the time between 25 January 49 and 24 January 50 (Historia adversum paganos 7,6,15).

The so-called Claudius Edict is dated by most commentators to the year 49 CE on the basis of the evidence in Suetonius and Orosius.[6] We can then suppose that the married couple, Aquila and Priscilla, arrived in Corinth either in that same year or at the beginning of the following. Paul arrived in the city 'not long afterwards', most probably then in 50 CE and remained there for 18 months until the late summer of 51 CE.

3 Quintus Sergius Paul(l)us was proconsul of Cyprus from 46 to 48 CE.[7] In Acts 13.7 Luke has Paul preach successfully before the governor, hence his time in Cyprus must have fallen within this period.

4 The change of office from Felix to Festus (Acts 24.27) is the basis for dating the events that Luke relates in the final quarter of his Acts of the Apostles and

---

4. On the manifold problems of the so-called Claudius Edict, cf. Riesner, *Early Period*, 157–201; H. Botermann (1996), *Das Judenedikt des Kaisers Claudius. Römischer Staat und Christiani im 1. Jahrhundert* (Hermes.E 71), Stuttgart, and D. Alvarez Cineira, *Religionspolitik*, 194–216.

5. This can be translated either as causal, 'He expelled the Jews from Rome because, driven by Chrestus, they constantly created unrest' or with a limiting relative clause, 'He expelled the Jews from Rome who, driven by Chrestus, constantly created unrest.' *Chrestus* is in all probability a mistake in spelling or hearing for *Christus* and is meant to refer to Jesus Christ. One must bear in mind that 'Chrestus' was a common name for a slave in Rome, though we have no evidence of a Jew who bore this name; cf. here in detail Botermann, *Judenedikt* (n.4), 87–95 and Alvarez Cineira, *Religionspolitik*, 201–6.

6. A different, earlier dating is based on Cassius Dio who records (60,6,6) that the Jews in Rome were prohibited from assembling, presumably in the first year of Claudius' reign, i.e. 41 CE. It is extremely questionable whether the 'expulsion' (Acts and Suetonius) and the 'prohibition of assembly' (Cassius Dio) are identical. Lüdemann, *Paul* (n.2), 164–71, however, considers this to be the date of Paul's first sojourn in Corinth which must be distinguished from a second stay during Gallio's period of office.

7. Cf. H. Halfmann (1982), 'Die Senatoren aus den kleinasiatischen Provinzen', in *Atti del Colloquio Internationale AIEGL su Epigrafia e Ordine Senatorio* (EOS) 2, Rome, 101f.; D. A. Campbell (2005), 'Possible inscriptional attestation to Sergius Paul(l)us (Acts 13:6–12) and the implications for Pauline chronology', *JThS* 56, 1–29. Campbell, however, puts (guardedly) Sergius Paul(l)us' stay during or before 37 CE. On the question of historicity see below, p. 101f. with n.11.

which lead Paul as a prisoner from Jerusalem by way of Caesarea to Rome. The sources give no definite information about the actual date, but much speaks for the year 59 CE.[8]

Around the comparatively certain date of Paul's first stay in Corinth and the change in governors, the relative details in the letters and Acts can be so arranged as to produce the course of Paul's life represented on p. 108.[9]

2
Paul's Background and his Social and Legal Status

Just as the information in the Pauline epistles and Acts is so detailed on Paul's activity first as persecutor of the Christian congregations and then as Christian missionary, so the details about his background are fragmentary: Neither the year of his birth nor his social and legal status nor the educational level and profession of the apostle are certain. The assessment of the last stage of Paul's life in which, according to Luke, he reached Rome from Jerusalem via Caesarea Maritima as a prisoner, is extremely complicated (Acts 21–28).

The *year of Paul's birth* cannot be deduced from his letters, and Luke also is silent on this point. The statement in Phlm. 9 that he is now an elderly man (presbytēs) does not allow any precise calculations.[10]

Paul gives no concrete information about his *family*, not even the names of his parents or possible siblings can be ascertained from his letters.[11] If the Lucan mention of a nephew in Acts 23.16 has a historical basis, then Paul had at least one sister who lived in Jerusalem. He himself according to his own words is unmarried (1 Cor. 7.1, 8; 9.5).

Likewise Paul gives us no information as to his *birthplace*, unlike Acts. The

---

8. On this problem cf. Schürer (1973), *The History of the Jewish People in the Age of Jesus Christ (175 BC–AD 135).* A New English Version revised and edited by G. Vermes and F. Millar, Vol. I, Edinburgh, 465–8; Jewett, *Chronology* (n.2), 40–4 and Omerzu, *Prozeß*, 405f. Lüdemann, *Paul* (n.2), 192f., n.104, pleads for an earlier dating in the year 54 CE, however, cf. 32 n.6.

9. Here we offer a kind of consense model. It is not possible within the framework of this book to discuss the multitude of versions put forward. Selected aspects are treated in Chapter 6 in this volume, on Paul's missionary journeys.

10. According to Philo, De opificio mundi 3, the term presbytēs, 'old man', was used from the 49th year. If we follow the dating of the epistle to Philemon by L. Bormann in this volume (cf. Chapter 9), Paul would then have been born a few years after the birth of Christ.

11. The name Paulos is a Latin *cognomen* and *praenomen*, here Graecized. Two further bearers of this name in the Palestine of the first century are known (T. Ilan [2002], *Lexicon of Jewish names in late Antiquity I. Palestine 330 BCE – 200 CE* [TSAJ 91], Tübingen, 336). These are names of Herodians. Paul therefore had a Hellenistic second name which was most likely assumed because it sounded similar to Sa'ul. Further in: R. Bauckham, 'Paul and Other Jews with Latin Names in the New Testament', in A. Christophersen (2002), *Paul, Luke and the Graeco-Roman World. Essays in Honour of Alexander J. M. Wedderburn* (JSNT.S 217), Sheffield, 202–20.

town of Tarsus in Cilicia is twice named there as Paul's home town (Acts 21.39; 22.3; cf. 9.11), whereby in the first mention he is explicitly described as a 'citizen' (politēs) of the town. For a faithful Jew it is not possible for religious reasons to accept all the prerogatives connected with the civil rights of a Greek city, since public events (theatre, festivals, competitions, etc.) just like political offices always have a religious component. Consequently the Jewish residents of a town have no civil rights in the full sense.[12] We must therefore reject as extremely unlikely the idea that Paul had unlimited *civil rights in Tarsus*.[13] If one does not wish to suspect a Lucan construction here, we might consider an alternative interpretation, that politēs is used in an inexact sense simply as a designation of origin.[14] Nothing speaks against the historicity of this Cilician city being the apostle's home town.[15] We can interpret the apostle's repeated sojourns in Cilicia as an indication of a close connection to Tarsus.[16]

Decisive for the evaluation of Paul's social background and legal situation is the question whether he possesses the *civil rights of a Roman* or not. He himself says nothing on this subject, which is not surprising because it was not relevant to the correspondence between the apostle and his churches.[17] Only Luke calls Paul a *civis Romanus* (Acts 16.37f.; 22.25–29; 23.27). To corroborate the plausibility of this statement or to question it a large number of statements from the Pauline letters and Acts – or the lack of particular statements – are enlisted as evidence.[18] The aim here is either to find a clear reference for or against Roman citizenship or at least the proof of an affiliation to a higher or lower social class. The juristic questions particularly linked to the process cannot be answered with complete certainty, since Roman law in the first century CE is changing radically

---

12. Noethlichs, *Jude Paulus*, 64–7; this is why, with regard to Paul's civil rights in Tarsus, he speaks of 'the semblance of a problem' (67).

13. H. W. Tajra, *Trial*, 78–80 and Omerzu, *Prozeß*, 34–6 reject the idea; Hengel, *Pre-Christian Paul*, 4–6 is positive but restrained.

14. This corresponds to a large extent to the use of politēs in the LXX, in the New Testament and in Josephus. Cf. Hengel, *Pre-Christian Paul*, 6; Omerzu, *Prozeß*, 35f.

15. Jerome hands down the so-called Gischala Tradition, according to which Paul was not born in Tarsus but only came there in his youth: Paul's parents emigrated (*commigrare*; De viris illustribus 5,1) to Tarsus after Jewish Gischala was taken by the Romans or were carried off there (*transferri*: Commentarius in epistulam ad Philemonem). It is scarcely possible to connect this account with verifiable wartime events around the time of Paul's birth; cf. on this Haacker, *Werdegang*, 828–30; Omerzu, *Prozeß*, 37–9; Noethlichs, *Jude Paulus*, 56 with n.8.

16. Paul himself comments on this in Gal. 1.21; Luke in Acts 9.30; 11.25; 15.41.

17. Haacker, *Werdegang*, 843 sees in the second person plural teleite in Rom. 13.6a perhaps 'a – discreet – allusion' by the apostle to the *civitas Romana*, since Paul as a Roman citizen is not obliged to pay *tributum* (phoros) whereas his addressees, who thereby are to be seen as non-citizens, are.

18. The articles on Paul's rights as a Roman citizen and the individual questions connected with this are innumerable: As examples of the most recent I mention Hengel, *Pre-Christian Paul*, 6–15 (affirming); Stegemann, *Apostel*, 200–29 (rejecting); Haacker, *Werdegang*, 831–47 (affirming); Omerzu, *Prozeß*, 17–52 (affirming); Schnelle, *Apostle Paul*, 60–61 (affirming). On the relevance of the arguments for one versed in the history of antiquity cf. Noethlichs, *Jude Paulus*, 67–84 (rejecting).

because of the transition from Republic to Principate and there are very few sources.[19]

The following aspects are directly connected with the rights and duties of a *civis Romanus* and are consequently of prime importance for the assessment of the question of Paul's rights as a Roman citizen:

- The *name*: A Roman citizen is recognizable by his tripartite name, consisting of *praenomen, nomen gentile* and *cognomen*. At no place is Paul called by a triple name. *Pro*: This lack can be put down to the style of Paul's correspondence and that of the author of Acts, Luke.[20] *Contra*: Paul did not have a tripartite name and consequently no rights as a Roman citizen.
- The *ill-treatment* at the hands of the Jewish and Roman authorities: Paul himself reports that he underwent five times the synagogal punishment in the form of 39 lashes and was beaten with rods three times (2 Cor. 11.24f.). The latter must relate to the action of the Roman authorities. Luke bears witness to this in Acts 16.22. *Pro*: With regard to the synagogal measures, this was a question of an internal Jewish conflict; to appeal to his status as a Roman citizen at this point would have been a provocation. The flagellations by Roman officials are illegal infringements which were not an isolated case in the Roman Empire. It is difficult to prove one's Roman citizenship – a relevant document can easily be lost, particularly when one is travelling. Paul sees himself as participating in the suffering of Jesus (Gal. 6.17) and consequently accepts these pains. *Contra*: The flagellation of a Roman citizen is prohibited by law. It is difficult to imagine that one and the same person should be the victim three times of such an official irregularity.
- The *course of the trial*: Luke certainly attributes Roman citizenship to Paul but he does not connect a legal step within the process directly to this status. If the outward course as Luke reports it is historical we must clarify whether Roman citizenship is the necessary requirement for this or not. *Pro*: An appeal to the emperor is the privilege of Roman citizens exclusively. *Contra*: The particularly explosive nature of the case is sufficient reason for handing Paul over to Rome.
- The compatibility of strict *Judaism* and the rights of a Roman citizen: Jews are freed from certain obligations that are incumbent upon Roman citizens

---

19. On the questions about the *provocatio* and *appellatio* in the first century CE cf. Omerzu, *Prozeß*, 53–109; Noethlichs, *Jude Paulus*, 70–3. Basic for historical research is the article by T. Mommsen (1901), 'Die Rechtsverhältnisse des Apostels Paulus', ZNW 2, 81–96. A new approach on the legal questions was first offered by J. Bleicken (1962), *Senatsgericht und Kaisergericht. Eine Studie zur Entwicklung des Prozessrechtes im frühen Prinzipat* (AAWG.Ph III 53), Göttingen.

20. D. B. Saddington (2000), 'The sorts of names used by auxiliaries in the early principate', in G. Alföldy, B. Dobson and W. Eck (eds), *Kaiser, Heer und Gesellschaft in der Römischen Kaiserzeit* (Heidelberger Althistorische Beiträge und Epigraphische Studien 31), Stuttgart, 163–78 points to the fact that not only Paul but also Josephus, whose Roman citizenship is undisputed, never introduced himself with the *tria nomina* (166). This means the *tria nomina* argument cannot be brought into play against Paul's Roman citizenship.

(the worship of the emperor, military service). *Pro*: These concessions to the Jewish religion make it possible, even for a strict Pharisee, to hold Roman citizenship. *Contra*: In spite of this alleviation for Jews it is not possible for a Pharisee to reconcile the dictates of his faith with the demands on a Roman citizen.

Less significant on the other hand are the following points which are brought up from time to time:

- The *knowledge of Latin*: A Roman citizen should have the mastery of Latin. It is doubtful whether Paul has mastery of more than certain fragments of Latin which he inevitably picked up on his journeys. *Pro*: In the east of the Imperium Romanum Greek is the normal language even in official matters. *Contra*: Precisely under Claudius sanctions were imposed upon those ignorant of Latin.
- The choice of the *routes of his journeys*: Paul travels by preference on Roman roads and chooses as places for his missionary activities Roman colonies such as the Pisidian Antioch, Philippi and Corinth. *Pro*: Paul as a Roman citizen knows his way particularly well in towns with a Roman character. *Contra*: Paul chooses these ways because they make for fast progress and these destinations because they can be most easily reached using the existing infrastructure.

In addition the following points are offered to fit Paul into a particular social class:

- His *occupation*: According to Acts 18.3 Paul is a skēnopoios.[21] It is not clear when Paul learned this trade – before his calling or during his activity as a missionary. *Pro*: skēnopoios describes a manufacturer of fine leather products who had access to high social ranks. Paul's working at a trade corresponds to the principles of his theological education. *Contra*: Here it means an ordinary tentmaker who belongs to the lower class of society. Proofs for such combination of training as a scribe and as a craftsman only occur at a later date.
- His *education*: In his letters Paul quotes the LXX. According to Acts 22.3 he was educated in Jerusalem at the feet of Rabbi Gamaliel. *Pro*: Paul's use of the Scriptures lets us conclude that he had a good education and therewith an elevated social position. For a Diaspora Jew the possibility of an education in Jerusalem demanded a considerable financial investment.

According to Acts 22.28 Paul has had Roman citizenship from the time he was born – i.e. his father was already a Roman citizen. The *civitas Romana* can be attained by birth and adoption as well as through being set free (*manumissio*) from captivity or slavery, or awarded at the end of one's military service (*missio*

---

21. For Paul's tentmaking cf. R. F. Hock (2007), *The Social Context of Paul's Ministry. Tentmaking and Apostleship*, Minneapolis.

honesta). From the time of Claudius trade in Roman citizenship steadily increased (cf. Acts 22.28). If the Lucan account is to be taken as historical, freeing from captivity is most usually considered as the most likely way for Paul's father to have attained Roman citizenship.[22]

If one looks at the discussion as a whole there is no conclusive argument that Paul was a Roman citizen. On the contrary, within the conception of Luke's two-part work and particularly in Acts it appears quite possible that Luke attributes the *civitas Romana* to Paul in order to bring him on stage as a prime example of the compatibility of Christianity and Roman citizenship. Although he often came into serious conflict with the Roman authorities as e.g. in Philippi and met not only positive state administrators like Gallio but also negatively characterized officials such as Felix, the apostle held to the Roman judicial system and insisted on a trial before the emperor (Acts 25.9–12; cf. 25.20f., 25, 32). Therewith Acts receives an apologetic character: Christians should be able to live in the Imperium Romanum without being repressed by the state because they in particular, like the apostle Paul, prove to be exemplary citizens.[23]

3
Paul the Jew, Pharisee and Persecutor of Christians

According to his own account Paul belonged to the People of Israel, more precisely to the tribe of Benjamin (Phil. 3.5; Rom. 11.1). As a strict Pharisee and zealot for the Law (Gal. 1.14; Phil. 3.5f.; cf. Acts 22.3; 23.6) he persecuted the new, developing Christian churches – here Paul's own statements and Acts concur. There are, however, differences as to where these persecutions took place.

When Paul looks back at his actions against the Christians he does not name a place (Gal. 1.13, 23; Phil. 3.6; 1 Cor. 15.9). He uses in a stereotyped fashion the verb diōkein, 'pursue', which is intensified in Gal. 1.13, 23 by the addition of porthein, 'destroy', and as object he names the ekklēsia (tou theou), the 'church (of God)'.

Luke reports that as a young man (neanias) Paul was present in Jerusalem when Stephen was stoned (Acts 7.58) and that he 'approved' (syneudokein) of this killing (Acts 8.1; cf. 22.20). In the period following Paul appears as a zealous persecutor: He goes from house to house and commits men and women from the Jerusalem church to prison; this action is described as an attempt to 'destroy' (lymainesthai in the imperfect *de conatu*) (Acts 8.3f.; cf. 9.1; 22.4, 19; 26.10).

---

22. Hengel, *Pre-Christian Paul*, 14f. with reference to the Gischala Tradition, which gives evidence that already in the Early Church this was assumed, as also Riesner, *Early Period*, 152f. It cannot, however, then be explained how Paul could have already been born as a Roman citizen if he was only carried off with his parents as a child (*adulescentulus*) according to Jerome in his commentary on Philemon.

23. It is often emphasized that from the Roman point of view no crime worthy of punishment can be proved against Paul; cf. in the framework of his trial Acts 23.29; 25.25; 26.31 and already earlier at Acts 18.14–17.

Luke's endeavour to portray the later Christian missionary as an extremely resolute and cruel persecutor of the first Christians is unmistakable.

This localization to Jerusalem is surprising if we look at Gal. 1.22: There Paul writes that before the council of the apostles he was unknown by sight to the churches of Judaea (agnooumenos tō prosōpō). If Paul was in fact a leading figure in the persecution of the Jerusalem church he should have been a person who was known, even notorious, in Judaea.[24]

In view of this finding the Lucan presentation with its characteristic concentration upon Jerusalem must be put in doubt: it is much more likely that Paul's anti-Christian activities are to be located in Damascus.[25] Acts 9.2 speaks of an authorization from the Sanhedrin for Paul to move against Christians in Damascus. Even if according to Luke this was prevented by Paul's conversion, this note still refers to a persecuting activity of Paul in that city. Above all Paul himself implies this in Gal. 1.17: After his conversion he went to Arabia and then *returned* to Damascus (palin hypestrepsa).

4
Paul the Christian: His Calling

Paul's Damascus experience is proverbial. However, what precisely do the biblical sources let us know about the event?

Paul certainly reports several times on his calling (1 Cor. 9.1; 15.8; Gal. 1.12–16), but only reveals in doing so that it involved an appearance of Christ, and dispenses with details of time and place. His concern is exclusively argumentative; it lies in proving his independence from human, particularly Jerusalem authorities (cf. Gal. 1.16b–17a), but not in a most impressive possible description for its own sake. Paul connects the experience of this manifestation directly with his commission to Christ to the Gentiles (Gal. 1.16).

By contrast Luke's threefold report on this turning point in Paul's life is extremely detailed (Acts 9.3–19; 22.6–21; 26.12–18). The events are first of all included in the third person in the narrative of Acts; the repetitions are to be found as reports in the first person in Paul's speeches before the people in the Jerusalem Temple and before the Roman Procurator Festus, King Agrippa and his sister Berenice. All three versions place the event on the road to Damascus and name a shining light. They unanimously report the question by a heavenly voice, 'Saul, Saul,[26] why do you persecute me?', the counter-question, 'Who

---

24. Hengel, *Pre-Christian Paul*, 77 seeks to defuse this argument by interpreting the persecution in terms of internal controversies within the Greek-speaking synagogues in Jerusalem: 'The earliest Christian "Hebrews" in Jerusalem, not to mention those in Jewish Palestine, remained relatively unaffected by these "internal" controversies within the Greek-speaking synagogues of Jerusalem.' Cf. also M. Hengel and A. M. Schwemer, *Paul*, 35–8.

25. Thus too among others J. Becker, *Paulus*, 63; Schnelle, *Apostle Paul*, 84–85; however Hengel, *Pre-Christian Paul*, 72–9, holds fast to the historicity of the Lucan presentation.

26. Luke uses the form Saoul exclusively in the scenes of his calling (Acts 9.4; 22.7; 26.14), otherwise the Greek form Saoulos (Acts 7.8; 8.1, 3; 9.1, 8, 11, 22, 24; 11.25, 30;

are you, Lord?' and the reply of the heavenly voice, 'I am Jesus whom you are persecuting.' According to Acts 9.7 his companions see nothing, but hear the voice; according to Acts 22.9 and 26.14 they see the light, but hear nothing.

The setting of the events by Paul and Luke is characteristic: What matters for the apostle, as 1 Cor. 15.3–11 proves, is the appearance of the Son of God to him in the succession of the Easter appearances before the apostles. Luke by contrast sees a clear caesura between the appearances of the risen Christ before the Ascension and the appearance to Paul. Significantly, he also reports Paul's subsequent baptism (Acts 9.18; cf. 22.16), whereas Paul himself makes no mention of a possible baptism.

5
Paul's End

The final quarter of the Acts of the Apostles is devoted to Paul's arrest in Jerusalem, his imprisonment there and in Caesarea Maritima, his trial before the Roman procurators Felix and Festus and his transfer to Rome. The story ends with Paul's unhindered preaching in Rome (Acts 28.31: meta pasēs parrēsias akōlytōs) which according to Luke lasted two years. It fits with Luke's apologetic goal to pass in silence over Paul's death, which is assumed in the farewell speech in Miletus (Acts 20.25, 38).

The next records of the further fate of the apostle are to be found in the first letter of Clement, a writing of the Roman congregation to the church in Corinth which is counted among the Apostolic Fathers. In 1 Clem 5.5–7 we read:

> Because of jealousy and strife Paul demonstrated the crown of patience: Seven times in chains, exiled, stoned, ambassador in East as in West, he received noble fame for his faith. He taught the whole world righteousness, and he came to the limit of the West and gave testimony before the leaders; so is he departed from the world and came to the holy place – the greatest model of patience.

The precise circumstances of his death are not to be gleaned from these lines, but the preceding and following statements make martyrdom likely.[27] Whether or not one takes the Lucan account of the trial as historical or rather visualizes

---

12.25; 13.1, 2, 7, 9). The last of these says: 'Saul, who is also (called) Paul' (Saulos de, ho kai Paulos); in the continuation only the form Paulos is used. The call is thus by no means a case of a proverbial change 'from Saul to Paul'. On the name 'Paul' see above n.11.

27. In the introduction to the remarks on Peter and Paul we read: 'Because of jealousy and envy the greatest and most righteous pillars were persecuted and struggled unto death' (1 Clem. 5.2). Further examples relating to the two outstanding figures are introduced with the following sentence: 'These men whose walk was pleasing to God were accompanied by a great host of the elect, who endured many pains and tortures by reason of jealousy and became an excellent example among us' (1 Clem. 6.1). On this passage in the text cf. H. Löhr (2001), 'Zur Paulus-Notiz in 1 Clem. 5.5–7', in F. W. Horn (ed.), *Das Ende des Paulus. Historische, theologische und literaturgeschichtliche Aspekte* (BZNW 106), Berlin/New York, 197–213.

Paul's handing over as being for political reasons which do not presuppose his Roman citizenship,[28] Rome is unanimously seen as the final station on his way, particularly as there is no alternative tradition. Whether his death represents a juridical act in the framework of his trial[29] or belongs in the context of measures against the Christians cannot be definitively answered. This holds in particular for any possible connection with the moves against the Christians under Nero in the year 64 CE after the burning of Rome (cf. Tacitus, *Annales* 15.44.2–5; Suetonius, *Nero* 16,2; 38,1–3), for the first letter of Clement at any rate does not suggest anything of the kind.[30]

References

Monographs

D. Alvarez Cineira (1999), *Die Religionspolitik des Kaisers Claudius und die paulinische Mission* (HBS 19), Freiburg: Herder.

J. Becker (1989), *Paulus. Der Apostel der Völker* (UTB 2014), Tübingen: J. C. B. Mohr.

M. Hengel and A. M. Schwemer (1997), *Paul Between Damascus and Antioch. The Unknown Years*, Louisville, KY: Westminster John Knox Press.

R. F. Hock (2007), *The Social Context of Paul's Ministry. Tentmaking and Apostleship*, Minneapolis, MN: Fortress Press.

J. Murphy-O'Connor (2004), *Paul: His Story*, Oxford: Oxford University Press.

H. Omerzu (2002), *Der Prozeß des Paulus. Eine exegetische und rechtshistorische Untersuchung der Apostelgeschichte* (BZNW 115), Berlin/New York: De Gruyter.

R. Riesner (1998), *Paul's Early Period: Chronology, Mission Strategy, Theology*, Grand Rapids, MI: Eerdmans.

U. Schnelle (2005), *Apostle Paul: His Life and Theology*, Grand Rapids, MI: Baker Academic.

H. W. Tajra (1989), *The Trial of St. Paul. A Juridical Exegesis of the Second Half of the Acts of the Apostles* (WUNT 2/35), Tübingen: J. C. B. Mohr.

Essays and Encyclopedia Articles

K. Haacker (1995), 'Zum Werdegang des Apostels Paulus: Biographische Daten und ihre theologische Relevanz', *ANRW* II 26.2, 815–938.1924–1933.

M. Hengel (1991), *The Pre-Christian Paul*. In collaboration with Roland Deines, London: SCM Press; Philadelphia: Trinity Press International.

F. W. Horn (ed.) (2001), *Das Ende des Paulus. Historische, theologische und literaturgeschichtliche Aspekte* (BZNW 106), Berlin/New York: De Gruyter.

K. L. Noethlichs (2000), 'Der Jude Paulus – ein Tarser und ein Römer?' in R. von Haehling (ed.), *Rom und das himmlische Jerusalem. Die frühen Christen zwischen Anpassung und Ablehnung*, Darmstadt: Wissenschaftliche Buchgesellschaft, 53–84.

W. Stegemann (1987), 'War der Apostel Paulus ein römischer Bürger?' *ZNW* 78, 200–29.

---

28. Thus for example Stegemann, *Apostel*, 212f.; Noethlichs, *Jude Paulus*, 79.
29. Omerzu, *Prozeß*, 508.
30. Becker, *Paulus*, 506 argues for Paul's death before the events of 64 CE; Schnelle, *Apostle Paul*, 386 suspects that his death occurred 'in the setting of a persecution of Christians between 62–64 CE in the time of Nero'.

Table 5.1

	Rome		Paul		Palestine
30–14 BCE	*Emperor Augustus* (cf. Lk. 2.1)		Birth	37–34 BCE	Herod the Great (cf. Mt. 2.1; Lk. 1.5)
14–37 CE	*Emperor Tiberius* (cf. Lk. 3.1)		Education	30	Death of Jesus
		32	Persecution of Christians Call (Gal. 1.15f.; 1 Cor. 15.8) Arabia and Damascus (Gal. 1.17)		
		35	Jerusalem (Gal. 1.18: three years later; 15 days)		
37–41	*Emperor Gaius = Caligula*		Syria and Cilicia (Gal. 1.21)		
41–54	*Emperor Claudius* (cf. Acts 11.28)		Antioch (Acts 11.26: one year) *1st missionary journey:*	44	Death of Agrippa I (Acts 12.20–23)
46–48	Quintus Sergius Paul[l]us Proconsul	44–47	Cyprus and Asia Minor (Acts 13f.) Antioch (Acts 14.28: not a brief time) Apostles' Council in Jerusalem (Gal. 2.1: 14 years later; Acts 15.4–29) Antioch (Gal. 2.11; Acts 15.30–35)		
		48			
49	Claudius' Edict (Acts 18.12)	49/50	*2nd missionary journey:* Syria, Cilicia (Acts 15.40) Asia Minor, Macedonia and Achaia (Acts 16f.)	50	Agrippa II becomes king of Chalcis (cf. Acts 25.13 – 26.32)
51/52	Gallio Proconsul of Achaia (Acts 18.12)	50–52	Corinth (Acts 18.11: 18 months) *3rd missionary journey:*	52–59	Felix Procurator of Judaea, Idumaea and Samaria (cf. Acts 23.26)
		52–54/55	Ephesus (Acts 19.10: two years; 20.31: three years)		

54–68	*Emperor Nero*		Macedonia and Achaia (Acts 20.3: three months)	59	Change of governor from Felix to Porcius Festus (Acts 24.27)
			Asia Minor (Acts 20)		
		57	Caesarea (Acts 21.10: several days)		
		57–59	Jerusalem (Acts 21.15 – 23.30)		
		59–60	Caesarea (Acts 24.27: two years)		
		60–?	Transfer to Rome (Acts 27)		
			Rome (Acts 28.30: two years)		

Chapter 6

Paul's Missionary Activity
Eva Ebel

The success and geographically wide extension of Paul's missionary activity are based not least on the apostle's untiring journeys which took him by land and sea through the eastern Mediterranean. The outward circumstances of these journeys, the routes we can recognize and the companions on his travels will be discussed in this chapter.

1
Travel in the Early Empire

In order to found new churches and to visit them again the apostle journeys by land and by sea around the eastern Mediterranean. If he himself is unable to visit a church his fellow workers and church members act as messengers and set out on behalf of the apostle or their own community to deliver letters, questions, instructions and money since the Roman post carried only government letters.[1] Indispensible for communication are also people who are constantly travelling on business journeys and in the course of these take care of the exchange of news between the individual congregations.[2]

They all profit from the fact that the military and economic needs of the Imperium Romanum demand the extension of the existing roads to a dense network upon which one can travel by foot, on a mount or in a carriage.[3] On these roads a traveller can presumably cover on average 20 to 30 kilometres per day, but might be delayed or completely prevented from journeying further by snow in the mountains and rivers overflowing their banks.[4] It appears that

---

1. 1 Thess. 3.1f., 6: Timothy hastens from Athens to Thessalonica and meets Paul again in Corinth. Phil. 2.25; 4.18: Epaphroditus is responsible for the exchange of news and financial support between Paul and the church at Philippi.
2. As an example of these we have 'Chloe's people' in 1 Cor. 1.11.
3. For an introduction to the topic 'Travel in the Roman Empire' cf. L. Casson, *Travel*, 115–329.
4. On the record of achievements which are registered in ancient literature on the one hand and the average speed of travel of ancient travellers on the other, cf. R. Riesner, *Early Period*, 307–17.

Paul always travelled by foot when he was on land,[5] for the use of a mount or a carriage is attested neither by his own letters nor by the Acts of the Apostles.

Shipping in the Mediterranean is suspended during the winter months (cf. Vegetius, *De re militari* 4,39: *maria clauduntur*),[6] but it is also not without danger during the rest of the year. It is difficult to foresee the time necessary for a voyage because of the changeable weather situation.[7]

But it is not only weather conditions which represent a danger to the life of travellers by land and by sea, as Paul himself relates in a list of adverse circumstances (2 Cor. 11.25–27):

> '... three times I was shipwrecked (nauagein); for a night and a day I was adrift at sea; on frequent journeys on foot (hodoiporiai) I was in danger from rivers, danger from bandits (lēstai) ..., danger in the city, danger in the wilderness, danger at sea ..., in toil and hardship, through many a sleepless night, hungry and thirsty, often without food, cold and naked ...'[8]

The possessions they have with them – but also the travellers themselves – are booty much sought after by bands of robbers and pirates whom even the Roman troops can scarcely control.

2
Paul's Journeys

If one asks for the exact routes of Paul's journeys, it is not possible to harmonize what the apostle writes in his letters and the journeys Luke describes in Acts, the so-called 'missionary journeys'. When comparing these two sources one finds not only contradictions which cannot be co-ordinated but also details that are given exclusively in Paul's epistles or in Acts and which therefore must be critically interpreted.

While Paul, for example, in his own description emphasizes that after his conversion he did not go to Jerusalem but into Arabia and to Damascus and only visited Jerusalem three years later (Gal. 2.17f.), Paul's way according to Luke led a few days after his conversion and flight from Damascus to Jerusalem,

---

5. Together with the passage cited in the following, 1 Cor. 11.26, we point to Acts 20.13: Paul prefers to go by foot (pezeuein) rather than aboard ship.
6. The wintering (paracheimazein) of ships in a suitable harbour is mentioned in Acts 27.12 and 28.11.
7. Riesner, *Early Period*, 312–17, gives a list of journey times under optimal circumstances for selected routes as witnessed in ancient sources and looks more closely, with Paul in mind, at the relevant stretches from Troas to Neapolis (Acts 16.11 and 20.6), from Greece to Palestine (Acts 20 and 21) and from Corinth to Rome (information on the circumstances in Rome, the transport of the letter to the Romans).
8. For the dangers of Paul's travels cf. R. Schellenberg (2011), '"Danger in the Wilderness, Danger at Sea": Paul and Perils of Travel', in P. A. Harland (ed.), *Travel and Religion in Antiquity* (Studies in Christianity and Judaism 21), Waterloo, 141–61.

where he was brought by Barnabas to the disciples (Acts 9.26f.). The intentions of the authors could not be more different. Whereas Paul wishes to show his independence from Jerusalem and the church there, Luke, also with Paul in mind, wants to depict Jerusalem and the circle of 12 as the starting point and guarantee of the Christian message. In doubtful cases Paul's own witness should be given priority, yet this example coming already from the early stage of the Christian Paul shows that even the biographical sections of his letters do not give an objective picture of his life but are marked by the purpose of his statement on the particular occasion.

When considering the historicity of Acts it would seem to be advisable to examine the separate sections individually and not to enhance or devalue the whole document with one sweeping statement. At many places we can discern traditions that are of great historical value which Luke has collected and edited for his work. The names of places and the description of the routes of Paul's journeys are far more extensive in Acts than the details about these in the Pauline letters. This is particularly true for Acts 16.12–17, in which the place names are listed as in an itinerary for travellers – which gave rise to the so-called 'Itinerary Hypothesis' to explain the 'we'-sections in Acts.[9]

Where the historical content may be challenged are deviations in Acts from the Pauline epistles which establish a connection of the apostle with Jerusalem. Alongside the example already mentioned in Acts 9.26f. there is also Paul's visit to Jerusalem which Luke reports in passing in Acts 18.22 with the aid of confusing details of a journey: Although the real destination of Paul's sea voyage begun in Ephesus is, according to Acts 18.18, Syria, the apostle arrives at Caesarea Maritima, i.e. in Palestine. After that Paul by no means sets off northwards but 'goes up (to Jerusalem) and greets the church' (anabas kai aspasamenos tēn ekklēsian) before he goes down to Antioch on the Orontes. Luke does not give a closer definition of 'the church', but 'to go up' is the *terminus technicus* for going to Jerusalem; hence at this point Luke perhaps integrates into his account a short visit to Jerusalem.[10]

On the other hand it is characteristic of Luke to incorporate in his account in particular Paul's contact with important personalities or with those whose attitude to the new Christian teaching was positive. Evidence of this endeavour can be seen e.g. in Acts 13.4–12, in the report of the sojourn of the missionaries, Paul and Barnabas, on Cyprus and the conversion of the Roman governor, Sergius Paullus: the apostle's own letters give no evidence of this.[11]

9. On the Itinerary Hypothesis cf. J. Wehnert (1999), *Die Wir-Passagen der Apostelgeschichte* (GTA 40), Göttingen; D.-A. Koch (1999), 'Kollektenbericht, "Wir"-Bericht und Itinerar. Neue Überlegungen zu einem alten Problem', NTS 45, 367–90; U. Schnelle (1998), *The History and Theology of the New Testament Writings*, London, 266–70.

10. We must differentiate between the interpretations of the 'going up' as a visit by Paul to Jerusalem instead of a simple ascent from a harbour to the town to which it belongs on the one hand and on the other the historical probability ascribed to a visit to Jerusalem. E. Haenchen (1977), *Die Apostelgeschichte* (KEK 3), Göttingen, 525f., however, votes against the historicity of a visit to Jerusalem at this particular time.

11. According to G. Lüdemann (1989), *Early Christianity according to the Traditions in*

Disregarding these reservations, the following routes of Paul's three so-called missionary journeys can be derived from the statements in Acts:

- Paul makes the *first* missionary journey (Acts 13.1 – 14.28) as companion of Barnabas; initially (to Acts 13.13) John Mark is also with them. The way leads from Antioch on the Orontes (13.1–3) and its harbour Seleucia (13.4) first by ship to Cyprus (13.4–12) with the towns of Salamis (13.5) and Paphos (13.6–12). After landing in Pamphylia the missionaries travel via the stages Perga (13.13f.), Pisidian Antioch (13.14–50), Iconium (13.51 – 14.6), Lystra (14.6–20) and Derbe (14.6f.). From there they return via Lystra, Iconium and Pisidian Antioch (14.21–24), Perga and Attalia (14.25), where Paul and Barnabas again board ship for Antioch on the Orontes (14.26–28).
- The *second* missionary journey (Acts 15.36 – 18.22), on which Paul is accompanied by Silas and later (from 16.3) also by Timothy, again begins from Antioch on the Orontes (Acts 15.36–40). The missionaries journey through Syria and Cilicia (15.41) to Derbe and Lystra (16.1–3), and then, after detours through the countryside of Phrygia, Galatia (16.6) and Mysia (16.7f.) reach Alexandria Troas (16.8–11). Then they travel by sea past Samothrace (16.11) to Neapolis (16.11) and from there on the Via Egnatia to Philippi (16.12–40), via Amphipolis and Apollonia (17.1) to Thessalonica (17.1–9), Beroea (17.10–13), Athens (17.15–34) and Corinth (18.1–18). From its harbour, Cenchreae (18.18), they travel further by ship to Ephesus (18.19–21) and Caesarea Maritima (18.22), although the actual goal was Syria (18.18). Afterwards the apostle goes, initially on foot, to Jerusalem (18.22) and finally returns to his point of departure, Antioch on the Orontes (18.22).
- On the *third* missionary journey (Acts 18.23 – 19.40), which cannot be clearly demarcated, Paul journeys from Antioch on the Orontes (18.23) to Galatia and Phrygia (18.23) and then on to Ephesus (19.1–40) where he spends two years (19.10), which can be seen as the end of the third journey.[12]

Alternatively the following road to Jerusalem can also be added.[13] From Ephesus Paul turns again towards Macedonia (Acts 20.1f.) and Greece (20.2f.), makes his way back through Macedonia (20.3), in particular Philippi (20.6), and then travels by ship to Alexandria Troas (20.6–12). Overland the apostle goes to Assos (20.13f.) and then travels further, again by ship, to Mitylene (20.14), past Chios, touches at Samos (20.15) and comes to Miletus (20.15–38). Stations on the following sea journey are the islands of Cos and Rhodes and the town of

Acts. A Commentary, London, 152–8, Paul's mission to Cyprus is a Lucan construct that has been created on the basis of Barnabas' Cypriot origins (Acts 4.36), his mission on Cyprus with Mark and his co-operation with Paul.

12. This is how e.g. G. Schille (1989), *Die Apostelgeschichte des Lukas* (ThHK 5), Berlin, 372 subdivides Paul's activity. Schnelle, *History* (n.8), 260 makes a break already before Demetrius' rebellion and entitles Acts 19.21 – 21.17 'Paul on the way to Jerusalem (and Rome)'.

13. Thus e.g. W. Marxsen (1978[4]), *Einleitung in das Neue Testament. Eine Einführung in ihre Probleme*, Gütersloh, 168.

Patara (21.1) before Paul lands in Tyre (21.3–6). The route then leads by way of Ptolemais (21.7) and Caesarea Maritima (21.8–14) to his destination, Jerusalem (21.17).

The following table is a synopsis of Paul's missionary journeys according to Acts. In the representation of the routes the names of towns are in *italics* and the most important towns are in **bold type**.

Table 6.1

	1st Journey (Acts 13.1 – 14.28)	2nd Journey (Acts 15.36 – 18.22)	3rd Journey (Acts 18.23 – 19.40)
Companion(s)	Barnabas (John Mark)	Silas Timothy	
Starting point	*Antioch/Orontes*	*Antioch/Orontes*	*Antioch/Orontes*
Route	Cyprus *Salamis* *Paphos* Pamphilia *Perge* *Antioch* (Pisidia) *Iconium* *Lystra* *Derbe* *Lystra* *Iconium* *Antioch* (Pisidia) *Perge* *Attalia* *Antioch/Orontes*	Syria Cilicia *Derbe* and *Lystra* Phrygia Galatia Mysia *Alexandria Troas* *Samothrace* *Neapolis* **Philippi** *Amphipolis* *Apollonia* **Thessalonica** *Beroea* *Athens* **Corinth**/*Cenchraea* *Ephesus* *Caesarea Maritima* *Jerusalem* *Antioch/Orontes*	Galatia Phrygia *Ephesus*

These so-called missionary journeys cover the period of time in which Paul writes the letters handed down in the New Testament or the period of his life to which he looks back in his letters (particularly in Gal. 1f.); hence here it is possible to make a critical comparison of the two sources. It is a different matter when we look at Paul's 'journey' as a Roman prisoner from Jerusalem to Caesarea Maritima (Acts 23.25–35) and thence to Rome (Acts 27f.). Acts is the only source for this phase of Paul's life, the juridical course of the trial and the details of the sea voyage. The autobiographical report ends – if one understands the letter to the Romans as the last of Paul's extant epistles – with the comment that the apostle intends to journey to Spain via Rome after he has handed over the money collected for Jerusalem (Rom. 15.23f., 28).

According to Luke the course of Paul's transferral to Rome appears as follows: From Caesarea Maritima (Acts 27.1) the journey goes by way of Sidon (27.3) along past Cyprus (27.4), along the coast of Cilicia and Pamphylia (27.5) to Myra in Lycia (27.6). There the group changes to a ship coming from Alexandria and heading for Italy (27.6). This part of the journey proves difficult until they reach Cnidus (27.7). Then they sail south along the coast of Crete until they come to 'Fair Havens' (kaloi limenes) near the city of Lasaea, where they anchor but do not spend the winter (27.8–13). On the next stage of the journey to suitable winter quarters the south wind changes (27.13) and with a strong north-easterly (27.14) they pass the island of Cauda (27.16). The ship drifts for 14 days in the Adriatic until it lands at Malta[14] (27.27 – 28.11). After three months the group boards a ship from Alexandria which has wintered off the coast of Malta (28.11). After a stop in Syracuse (28.12) the route goes along the Italian coast via Rhegium and Puteoli (28.13f.). The journey on land finally leads by way of the Appian Forum and Three Taverns (28.15) to Rome (28.16).

If one doubts the historical content of the Lucan report about Paul's arrest, imprisonment and transportation to Rome not simply in details but as a whole, when we look at the extra-biblical evidence for the apostle's death in the capital (especially in 1 Clem. 5,5–7[15]) there arises the question of how else Paul could have reached Rome. There are no other reports of his journey there.

3
Paul's Travelling Companions and Colleagues

At no point during his missionary activity does Paul journey alone. Without the co-operation and aid of other men and women his endeavours would not have had such a lasting success, and contact with the congregations could not have been maintained. Around 50 people who are mentioned by name in the Pauline letters or Acts are clearly described as Paul's fellow-workers (synergoi) or can be classified as such.[16]

Paul begins his missionary activity at the behest of the church in Antioch on the Orontes. In Acts 13.1 Barnabas, Simeon who was called Niger, Lucius of Cyrene and Manaean, who had been brought up with Herod Antipas, are named together with Paul as prophets and teachers (prophētai kai didaskaloi) of the church. The church sends Barnabas and Paul together on the first missionary journey described above and to the assembly of the apostles in Jerusalem,

---

14. H. Warnecke (1987), *Die tatsächliche Romfahrt des Paulus* (SBS 127), Stuttgart, interprets the Greek name of the island Melitē as meaning not Malta but the western Greek island of Cephallenia, more precisely as the Phoenician settlement of Melitē on the peninsula of Argostolis. For criticism of this cf. J. Wehnert (1990), 'Gestrandet. Zu einer neuen These über den Schiffbruch des Apostels Paulus auf dem Weg nach Rom' (Apg 27–28), *ZThK* 87, 67–99.

15. Here cf. Chapter 5, 'The Life of Paul' in this volume.

16. W.-H. Ollrog, *Paulus*, 1 with n.2 and n.3. On the description as synergos cf. Ollrog, *Paulus*, 63–72.

whereby Barnabas[17] is initially the leader as we can deduce from the fact that he is named before Paul in Acts 11.30; 12.25 and 13.1, 2, 7. Both share the principle that they should not be provided for by the congregations but should earn their own living (1 Cor. 9.6). The system of teamwork obviously proves successful, for even after he parts company with Barnabas (Acts 15.36–39; cf. Gal. 2.13) Paul continues in this way. He immediately makes Silas/Silvanus[18] his companion (Acts 15.40) and later in Derbe wins Timothy[19] as well (Acts 16.1–3).

These two men constitute the closest circle of the apostle's co-workers after he detached himself from the church at Antioch, and also appear as co-authors of the epistles to the churches in whose foundation they were energetically involved: Both are named in the prescript of 1 Thess., Timothy alone as co-sender of 2 Cor., Phil. and Phlm.[20] How invaluable they were for the Pauline mission and how deeply the apostle trusted them can be seen for example in Paul's recommendation of Timothy to the Christians at Philippi (Phil. 2.20–22):

> 'I have no one like him who is so completely one soul (isopsychos) with me, who will be genuinely concerned for your welfare. All of them are seeking their own interests, not those of Jesus Christ. But Timothy's worth you know, how like a son with a father he has served with me in the work of the gospel.'

This characterization shows clearly why Timothy more than anyone else is suited to take action in the spirit of Paul and also to settle tricky situations in the churches by himself as Paul's representative (Corinth: 1 Cor. 4.17; 16.10f.; Thessalonica: 1 Thess. 3.2f.; Philippi: Phil. 2.20–22).

Among Paul's more independently active fellow-workers the married couple, Aquila and Prisca/Priscilla,[21] have a prominent place; although mentioned only a few times in the New Testament documents they allow us insights into the spectrum of the missionary work. They are a missionary couple, i.e. they reflect a model of missionary life which Paul declines for himself but which he concedes to Peter and the other apostles (1 Cor. 9.5). It is conspicuous that, with one exception (1 Cor. 16.19), Prisca is always mentioned before her husband and thereby is presumably emphasized as the driving force. The example of Prisca makes it clear that women play a major part in spreading the gospel, founding

---

17. On Barnabas cf. Ollrog, *Paulus*, 14–17; M. Öhler (2003), *Barnabas, die historische Person und ihre Rezeption in der Apostelgeschichte* (WUNT 156), Tübingen; B. Kollmann (2004), *Joseph Barnabas: His Life and Legacy*, Collegeville.

18. On the forms of the name Silas (in Acts) and Silvanus (in Paul's letters) cf. n.6 in Chapter 9 on 1 Thess. in this volume. On Silvanus cf. Ollrog, *Paulus*, 17–20.

19. On Timothy cf. Ollrog, *Paulus*, 20–3.

20. Alongside Timothy and Silvanus only Sosthenes appears as a co-sender of a Pauline letter. The mention of him in 1 Cor., however, according to Ollrog, *Paulus*, 22 n.77, is not 'conditioned by his function' but is 'conditioned by the situation' since Sosthenes, as a member of the Corinthian church, stands emphatically behind Paul's words.

21. In his letters Paul uses the form Priska (Rom. 16.3; 1 Cor. 16.19) while in Acts the diminutive form Priskilla appears (Acts 18.2, 18, 26). On Prisca and Aquila cf. Ollrog, *Paulus*, 24–7.

Christian churches and, not least, in supporting Paul.²² This couple stays for longer periods in one place in order to build up a house-church there: After they have to leave Rome they settle first in Corinth (Acts 18.3) and then move to Ephesus (1 Cor. 16.19).²³ Meanwhile they earn their living, like Paul, as 'tentmakers' (Acts 18.3: skēnopoios).

Table 6.2

Names	Biblical references
Barnabas	Acts 11.30; 12.25; 13.1, 2, 7; 15.36–39 1 Cor. 9.6
Silas (Silvanus)	Acts 15.40 1 Thess. 1.1
Timothy	Acts 16.1–3 1 Thess. 1.1; 3.2f. 1 Cor. 4.14; 16.10f. 2 Cor. 1.1 Phil. 1.1; 2.19–22 Phlm. 1
Prisca and Aquila	Acts 18.2, 18, 26 1 Cor. 16.19 Rom. 16.3
Phoebe	Rom. 16.1f.
Junia(s)	Rom. 16.7

4
Paul's Achievements through his Journeys

The number of miles Paul covered in the service of preaching the gospel is beyond measure; the dangers and deprivations he endured in the process can hardly be counted. Along with Paul's theological achievement the logistic and physical strains which, despite illness (Gal. 4.13f.; 2 Cor. 12.7), he undertakes for his missionary work deserve the highest respect. Together with the dangers of travelling as such, personal characteristics make the life of the itinerant

---

22. In a similar way as Paul praises Prisca along with her husband Aquila for their commitment to him personally (Rom. 16.3–5), he also stresses that the deaconess, Phoebe (hē diakonos), stood by him (Rom 16.1f.).

23. Depending upon whether one takes Rom. 16 as the end of the letter addressed to Rome or considers it as an addition or an appendix to a copy sent to Ephesus, Rom. 16.3–5 is either proof that the couple returned to Rome some years later and founded a church there, or a renewed confirmation of their house-church in Ephesus. Cf. here Chapter 14 on Romans by O. Wischmeyer in this volume.

missionary more difficult: the apostle finances his livelihood, as he constantly emphasizes, from what he earns by the work of his own hands (1 Thess. 2.9; cf. 1 Cor. 4.12):

> 'You remember our labour (kopos) and toil (mochthos), brothers: We worked (ergazesthai) night and day, so that we might not burden any of you while we proclaimed to you the Gospel of God.'

Financial dependence upon his churches would have called into question Paul's apostolic freedom and authority and pulled him into proximity with other itinerant preachers of his time who pursued economic interests and used dishonest methods (1 Thess. 2.1–12; 1 Cor. 9.3–18). The only exception is the church at Philippi, whose material gifts Paul accepts willingly (2 Cor. 11.7–9; Phil. 4.10, 15f.). As well as independence this way of life as a travelling missionary offers a further advantage: Because of his skilled trade the apostle can make contacts when he arrives as a newcomer in a town and in this way find a first target group for his preaching (Acts 18.2f.).

In his missionary endeavours Paul orients himself on the extent and travelling routes of the Imperium Romanum: As to the first, it is his wish to found churches in central places – and these are often the capitals of the particular Roman province such as Thessalonica (cf. 1 Thess.; Acts 16) and Corinth (cf. 1 Cor.; Acts 18). After this has taken place he travels on and leaves the further development of the church and the foundation of other churches in the surrounding area to local Christians or other missionaries (1 Cor. 3.6). On the other side, the routes and consequently the choice of places for his proclamation are determined by the system of Roman roads – thus Philippi, Thessalonica and Beroea (Acts 16f.) all lie on the Via Egnatia.

On his travels in the eastern part of the Roman Empire, even if he increasingly visits towns with a Roman character such as Antioch *ad Pisidiam* and Philippi,[24] Paul can communicate everywhere with the aid of the Greek language and in many places meet Jewish people or sympathizers with Judaism who are familiar with a monotheistic religion and have an open attitude to the Christian ideas which go back to Judaism. Yet after concluding his mission in the eastern part of the Roman empire (Rom. 15.19, 23) Paul's vision goes via the capital, Rome (Rom. 15.23) to Spain on the western edge of the Imperium Romanum and likewise of the then known world (Rom. 15.24, 28) The plans directed towards Spain demand a modification of the apostle's missionary concept: There it would neither have been possible for Paul to preach his message in Greek, nor could synagogues have been the starting point of his missionary endeavours.[25] As this

---

24. For a comparison of these two *coloniae* and Paul's possible preparation for Rome and Spain cf. P. Pilhofer (2002), 'Antiochien und Philippi. Zwei römische Kolonien auf dem Weg des Paulus nach Spanien', in *id.*, *Die frühen Christen und ihre Welt, Greifswalder Aufsätze 1996–2001* (WUNT 145), Tübingen, 154–65.

25. Cf. here *A. Reichert*, Der Römerbrief als Gratwanderung. Eine Untersuchung zur Abfassungsproblematik (FRLANT 194), Göttingen 2001, 83–91.

makes very clear, it is not a continuing progress on tested routes but the universal proclamation which is the idea behind Paul's strategy of mission.

References

L. Casson (1994), *Travel in the Ancient World*, London/Baltimore: Johns Hopkins University Press.
A. v. Harnack (1904), *The Mission and Expansion of Christianity in the First Three Centuries*, London: Williams & Norgate; New York: G. P. Putnam.
W.-H. Ollrog (1979), *Paulus und seine Mitarbeiter: Untersuchungen zu Theorie und Praxis der paulinischen Mission* (WMANT 50), Neukirchen-Vluyn: Neukirchener Verlag.
R. Riesner (1998), *Paul's Early Period: Chronology, Mission Strategy, Theology*, Grand Rapids, MI: Eerdmans.
E. P. Sanders (1991), *Paul*, Oxford/New York: Oxford University Press.

Chapter 7

THE PERSON OF PAUL
Eve-Marie Becker

The questions concerning the person of Paul are fundamental ones which are, however, rarely handled in current Pauline research.[1] They have their place between the reconstruction of Pauline *biography* and ancient research on *character*.

A 'biography' establishes the details of the life and deeds of a person. Ancient 'character' research works in the sense of finding an anthropological typologization. A representation of the *'person'*, however, tries on the one hand to describe intrinsic features – i.e. permanent characteristic features – of an individual historical figure, and on the other hand to work out the interactions between the one-off biographical incidents and the permanent characteristics of the historical figure.

Adolf Deissmann, for example, attempts the like when in his book on Paul (1911) he dedicates a whole chapter to Paul the 'human' and in it laments the comparatively scant interest shown by nineteenth-century research in Paul the human, i.e. the person of Paul.[2] In this description of Paul, borne as it is by Deissmann's social emotiveness, essential aspects of his historical influence already shine through. Deissmann sees Paul as a 'personality' who is important and whose influence is lasting in the history of religion and culture. In so doing he is moving in the history of research within the context of the school of the

---

1. But cf. most recently the contributions in E.-M. Becker and P. Pilhofer, *Biographie*. B. J. Malina and J. H. Neyrey, *Portraits* should be understood as a contribution to research on the social and cultural history of persons. E.-M. Becker (forthcoming), 'Art. Person des Paulus', in F. W. Horn (ed.) *Paulus Handbuch,* Tübingen. Cf. recently. V. H. T. Nguyen (2008), 'Paul and his contemporaries as social critics of the Roman stress on persona. A study of 2 Corinthians, Epictetus, and Valerius MaximusAuthor(s)', *Tyndale Bulletin* 59, 157–60.

2. A. Deissmann (1911), *Paulus. Eine kultur- und religionsgeschichtliche Skizze*, Tübingen, esp. 35–8. In the search for 'the contours of this human' Deissmann comes to the following description: 'An ancient Anatolian Paul, a *homo novus*, who grows out of the mass of many little people and, ignored by all the men of letters in his pagan environment, is destined to become a leading personality in the history of the world, a *homo religiosus*, at one and the same time a model of mysticism and the most sober practician, a prophet and brooder who, crucified in Christ in this world, is immortal as a citizen and wayfarer of the world, and as a world philosopher has an influence up to the present day...', V. Cf. also the fundamentally similar observations in W. Wrede (1904/ ²1907), *Paulus*, Halle, 'Preface', in which Wrede makes it clear that he is concerned inter alia to depict Paul's 'personality'.

History of Religion.³ In the meantime, however, a terminological distinction must be made between the description of Paul as a 'personality' – which implies an appreciation and assessment in the history of civilization – and the description of him as a 'person'.⁴

1
Paul as a Person: his Physical Appearance

The question about Paul as a person begins with speculations about his outward appearance, since we possess neither contemporary depictions nor descriptions – for either theological or cultural reasons.⁵ Hence we know nothing about his appearance. The *Acta Pauli* dating from the end of the second century CE provide for the first time a literary description of the Pauline appearance which became famous in the ages following:

> And a man named Onesiphorus, who had heard that Paul was coming to Iconium, went to meet Paul with his children, Simmias and Zeno, and his wife, Lektra, to offer him hospitality. Titus had told him what Paul looked like, because he had not seen him before in the flesh, only in the spirit. And he went to the royal road which leads to Lystra, took up position there to wait for him and looked at everyone who passed to see whether they fitted Titus' description. But he saw Paul coming: A man short in build with a bald head and bowed legs, with a noble bearing, his eyebrows meeting and a small nose which protruded a little, full of kindness; for one moment he seemed like a man, the next he had the face of an angel. (*Acta Pl* 3,2–3)⁶

The various 'Acts' of the Apostles serve particularly to entertain their Christian readers and consequently reflect what were the interests of the Christian readership of their time. Clearly Paul's appearance was a fundamental part of this interest at the end of the second century.

Iconography mediates a lively impression of which 'pictures' of Paul have

---

3. On this cf. O. Merk, 'Die Persönlichkeit des Paulus in der Religionsgeschichtlichen Schule', in Becker and Pilhofer, *Biographie*, 29–45.
4. Cf. here W. Sparn, 'Einführung in die Thematik "Biographie und Persönlichkeit des Paulus"', in Becker and Pilhofer, *Biographie*, 9–28.
5. Deissmann, *Paulus* (n.2), 39 surmises theological-eschatological reasons for this lack of information: 'Who should have thought in his day to record his features for posterity when the face of the Master himself had not even once been perpetuated? ... the whole mood of the early Christian era was far too dominated by the new Age to come than that one could think of the interest of future earthly generations in the outward appearance of the Saviour and his apostles.' On the emergence of Christian portraiture in general cf. H. P. L'Orange (1982 [Oslo edn 1947]), *Apotheosis in Ancient Portraiture*, New Rochelle (New York); E. Dinkler (1938), *Die ersten Petrusdarstellungen. Ein archäologischer Beitrag zur Geschichte des Petrusprimats*, Marburg.
6. From the German translation by W. Schneemelcher (1997), 'Paulusakten', in *id.* (ed.), *Neutestamentliche Apokryphen II, Apostolisches, Apokalypsen und Verwandtes*, Tübingen,⁶ 193–241, here 216.

The Person of Paul

impressed and shaped art. Paul's features are already distinct around 400 CE, which is in fact probably connected to the picture in the 'Acts':

> While the old and early representations portray Paul as short, with a bald head and long beard, very prominent forehead and a Roman nose, representations of the modern era show a tall man giving the impression of great physical strength ... This picture of Paul then has a head, the form of which is not unlike that of Christ, with parted or curled hair, a longer beard in two strands and more aged features ... The longer beard which comes to a point is derived from the beard of the philosophers.[7]

There is also an analogy in the literary reception of Paul to the iconographic element last mentioned: Paul's pseudo-epigraphical correspondence with the Stoic philosopher, Seneca, which perhaps dates from the fourth century CE, is intended to give prominence to the philosophical erudition and significance of the apostle to the Gentiles.[8] Hence we cannot grasp the historical person of Paul from iconography but solely from literary sources. Here the collected writings in the New Testament which have a direct connection to Paul (authentic Pauline epistles) or are brought into such (Acts; the Deutero- and Trito-Paulines) turn out to be the most important sources.

2
Paul as a Person: his Characteristics

The Acts of the Apostles bring Paul narratively before our eyes. Paul himself is present in his letters, in his argumentation, admonition and also in his statements about himself. How can he be understood and defined as a *person*, i.e. in his essential personal features?

Philosophical Anthropology[9] names particular human characteristics which constitute a human being. This involves the distinction between the person and the external world and a (somehow constituted) awareness of this differentiation. Thus the person is constituted over against other people and the world. Fundamental categories in which personality can be understood are: 'consciousness', 'the ability to suffer/illness', 'the adoption of perspectives', 'memory' and 'freedom of will'/responsibility and self-awareness. In other

---

7. M. Lechner (1976), 'Article: *Paulus*', LCI 8, 128–47, 131.
8. Cf. recently: A. Fürst (2006), *Der apokryphe Briefwechsel zwischen Seneca und Paulus. Zusammen mit dem Brief des Mordecai an Alexander und dem Brief des Annaeus Seneca über Hochmut und Götterbilder, eingeleitet, übersetzt und mit interpretierenden Essays versehen von A. Fürst et al.* (SAPERE XI), Tübingen. Paul's relationship with the philosophical tradition has been investigated in terms of rhetoric or philosophical teaching: Cf. on this e.g. H. D. Betz (1972), *Der Apostel Paulus und die sokratische Tradition. Eine exegetische Untersuchung zu seiner 'Apologie' 2. Korinther 10–13* (BHTh 45), Tübingen; T. Engberg-Pedersen (2010), *Cosmology and Self in the Apostle Paul. The Material Spirit*, Oxford.
9. Here cf. H.-P. Schütt (2003), 'Article: Person II Philosophisch-anthropologisch', RGG [4]6, 1121–3; G. Figal (2002), 'Article: Mensch III. Philosophisch', RGG 5, 1054–7.

words: A 'person' is capable of reflecting his/her strengths and potential as well as his/her weaknesses and constraints.

Some examples of these constituents of 'personality' can be given from his letters.

- *Consciousness*: Paul busies himself as a letter-writer, i.e. he acts with consciousness and intention. He allows addressees to participate in the process of his cognition (cf. e.g. the use of gignōskein in 1 Cor. 13.12; 2 Cor. 2.9; 5.16) and reflects specifically on this (2 Cor. 1.12–14).
- *Ability to suffer/illness*: In Gal. and 2 Cor. Paul singles out his illness as a central theme: In Gal. 6.17 he calls them the 'marks of Jesus' (stigmata tou Iēsou), in 2 Cor. 12 as 'a thorn ... in the flesh' (skolops tē sarki, v. 7) as a messenger of Satan who beats him with fists. Paul admits his suffering and ability to suffer. He also refers to this, e.g. in the so-called 'Peristasis catalogues' (see below). What is more, he thematizes the illness of his fellow-workers (Phil 2.25ff.). Besides, Paul uses various somatic expressions for either self-description (1 Cor. 15.8: ēktroma) or communicating his emotional state in his correspondence ('tears' e.g. in 2 Cor. 2.4).
- *The adoption of perspectives*: Frequently in his letters Paul actively adopts the perspectives of his communities (e.g. 1 Cor. 7.1; 15.12ff.; 2 Cor. 7.5ff.) and thereby sometimes of several churches at the same time (e.g. 2 Cor. 9.2). He also reflects, more or less critically, the ministry of competing missionaries (Phil. 1.15–18; 2 Cor. 10–13).
- *Memory*: When Paul reports, for example, on his missionary journeys (2 Cor. 1.8ff.) or reminds his readers of his earlier activity in the congregation (1 Cor. 2.1ff.) he is showing 'memory' and makes the collective recollection an integral part of the story of the foundation and leading of the church. In Gal. 1 and 2 he looks back to his calling and the events which followed it. In 1 Thess. 1.9f. he recalls his missionary activities in Macedonia and thus establishes a kind of a 'communicative memory'.[10]
- *Freedom of will/responsibility*: Paul stresses that he is humanly independent (e.g. 1 Cor. 9.1,19). This is also true in principle for his addressees (1 Cor. 7.37). This freedom, however, is relationally anchored: it is at one and the same time a freedom *from something* and a freedom *for something*. Paul puts the 'freedom from' in relation to the Law (Rom. 6.7: apo tēs hamartias; 7.6: apo tou nomou). The 'freedom for' is put in relation to the various aspects of Christian existence, particularly to Christ himself (1 Cor. 7.22; 9.1). The 'freedom for' manifests itself above all in Paul's existence as an apostle (1 Cor. 9.1) as responsibility to someone (Christ) and for something (e.g. building up the churches).
- *Awareness of the self*: In the argumentation in his letters Paul manifests a pronounced awareness of himself. This is particularly clear in the frequent use of the first person singular and especially of the personal pronoun egō

---

10. Concerning this expression cf. J. Assmann (2000), *Religion und kulturelles Gedächtnis. Zehn Studien*. Munich, 12.

– above all in 1 Cor. 7; 2 Cor. 11f.; Rom. 7.[11] Accordingly Paul introduces the presumably oldest, extremely sharp letter of the Corinthian correspondence – 2 Cor. 10–13 – emphatically with autos de egō Paulos parakalō hymas (2 Cor. 10.1). The very language expresses the *personally* responsible defence of Paul before the Corinthian congregation.

Alongside Paul's awareness of himself and his personal responsibility for proclaiming the gospel and guiding the churches we also find the phenomenon of the restriction of his self-identity (see also 1 Cor. 15.8). In Gal. 2.20 Paul almost annuls his self-identity in favour of Christ: '… it is no longer I who live, but it is Christ who lives in me'. This is preceded in v. 19 with the insight: 'For through the Law I died to the Law, so that I might live to God. I have been crucified with Christ'. Hence the existence in the form of Christ for which Paul strives virtually demands the disintegration of the personal identity determined by the 'flesh' (sarx): 'For I know that nothing good dwells within me, that is, in my flesh' (Rom. 7.18) – Paul describes the pre-Christian 'self' as 'fleshly', i.e. as a 'self' determined by sin (to kakon, Rom. 7.21).

3
Paul as Author and Autobiographic Writer: the Person on Himself

We encounter Paul as the writer of a total of seven preserved letters. Thereby Paul is the earliest Christian author in a literary sense. The literary character of the Pauline epistles can be seen inter alia in their autobiographical content:[12] Paul makes statements in various ways about his career (Gal. 1.10ff.; Phil. 3.5ff.), his religious experiences such as e.g. his experience with ecstasy (2 Cor. 12), his experience of suffering in the so-called 'Peristasis catalogues' (e.g. 1 Cor. 4.10–13; 2 Cor. 4.7–10; 11.23–25), his life as an apostle (1 Cor. 9) or his experience with the Corinthian church and the Corinthian correspondence in general (2 Cor. 2 and 7).

Autobiographical writing does not simply have a literary aspect but is closely connected to the development of the 'personality'; for autobiographical writing presupposes and at the same time leads to individualization, i.e. the experience of one's own individuality. The *Confessions* of Augustine have become a classic example of this: A person who experiences himself as an individual forms himself autobiographically and simultaneously emerges through his autobiographical writing as an individual person.[13] Individualization and autobiography are mutually dependent and constitute substantial elements of the 'person'. With

---

11. The personal pronoun egō occurs twice in 1 Thess., 20 times in Rom., 32 times in 1 Cor., 19 times in 2 Cor., ten times in Gal., six times in Phil. and four times in Phlm.
12. On this cf. various contributions in Becker and Pilhofer, *Biographie*.
13. D. Mendels (2004), *Memory in Jewish, Pagan and Christian Societies of the Graeco-Roman World* (Library of Second Temple Studies 45), London/New York, xi, speaks here of an 'individual memory'.

this first of all a *general anthropological* aspect of autobiographical writings is named which in the meantime is also reflected on by *narrative theory*: In this way we can discover an identity of the great 'author', 'narrator' and 'person' in autobiographical or autodiegetic texts.[14]

A *historical* or *literature-historical* aspect can be added: in that the person Paul experiences and forms himself in writing as an individual, he reveals himself in a special way in his context as a person in antiquity. For autobiographical writing – with a few exceptions (such as Caesar, Augustus, Nicolas of Damascus, Flavius Josephus and later Augustine) – is generally not widespread in the ancient world.[15] This is particularly true of Jewish authors.

4
Paul as Apostle: the Person of Paul and Other People

Paul's apostolicity is the decisive intrinsic feature of the Pauline personality. The term apostolos (e.g. Rom. 1.1; 1 Cor. 1.1 etc.) for Paul himself can hardly be considered as a title but should be understood as a 'description of his profession'. It goes along with a vocation, must prove its worth compared with fellow apostles or hostile/false apostles and stands in the service of building up the communities and guiding them.

Paul and Christ

Paul's apostolicity goes back to a calling (e.g. klētos: Rom. 1.1; 1 Cor. 1.1; aphōrismenos: Rom. 1.1; cf. Gal. 1.15) or a divine revelation (apokalypsis) of the Son of God, Jesus Christ (Gal. 1.12,15; cf. 2 Cor. 1.1) *ad personam*. From that time on Paul considers himself directly dependent on Jesus Christ – the term 'apostle' is more precisely qualified by a *genitivus qualitatis* (Iēsou Christou) (1 Cor. 1.1; 2 Cor. 1.1). This 'professional qualification' which distinguishes Paul from other, competing or even hostile, apostles is linked to Paul's whole person and existence; thus Paul describes himself as virtually 'a slave of Jesus Christ' (doulos, Rom. 1.1; Phil. 1.1). This subordination to Christ, however, at the same time becomes for Paul a co-ordination with Christ: Paul considers the sufferings connected with his apostolate (e.g. 2 Cor. 4.7ff.) *and* his own illness (Gal. 6.17) as an analogy to the suffering and resurrection of Jesus Christ.

Hence with regard to the person of Jesus Christ Paul sees himself in an extremely close relationship. On the one hand he lives in dependence on Christ, in bondage, lowliness and with many kinds of suffering (e.g. Gal. 2.19; 2 Cor. 1.5), on the other hand as one of the Chosen, in boundless freedom and personal proximity to Christ (2 Cor. 5.20; 11.10; Gal. 2.4).[16]

14. Cf. G. Genette (1992), *Fiktion und Diktion*, Munich, esp. 80–3 with reference to P. Lejeune (1980), *Le Pacte autobiographique*, Paris.
15. Cf. K. Jansen-Winkeln, H. Görgemanns and W. Berschin (1997), 'Article: Autobiographie', *DNP* 2, 348–53.
16. The psychological tension under which Paul stands is examined closely in M.

Paul and the Apostles

Paul's apostleship certainly goes back to a vocation *ad personam* (cf. also 1 Cor. 15.8f.), but from the very beginning it is not a unique or unrivalled appointment: The risen Christ was seen by the other 'apostles' *before* Paul (1 Cor. 15.7); and Paul's missionary work in Corinth initially took place in a clash with the activity of other apostles (e.g. Apollos, 1 Cor. 1.12ff.) and later in serious conflict with opposed or competing missionaries whom Paul takes pains to expose as 'super-apostles' (2 Cor. 11.5; 12.11) or even as 'false apostles' (pseudapostoloi 2 Cor. 11.13), who 'disguise' themselves as apostles of Christ (2 Cor. 11.13).

In the struggles with the opposed apostles in Corinth Paul argues uniquely with his whole 'person': He refers to his suffering and ability to suffer (2 Cor. 11.23ff.), to an intimate prayer-dialogue with Christ (2 Cor. 12.8f.) and to the apostolic 'signs' he performed in Corinth (2 Cor. 12.12). He makes his own personal 'weakness' (astheneia), sharply criticized by the Corinthians (2 Cor. 10.10), the basis and characteristic feature of his apostolate (e.g. 2 Cor. 11.30): for only in personal weakness can the 'power of Christ' (dynamis tou Christou, e.g. 2 Cor. 12.9) be visible in the apostolic existence.

Paul and the Churches

Paul's apostolic existence moves in the tension between 'I' and 'we'. Paul is called as an individual and bears personal responsibility for the development and guidance of his churches (e.g. 2 Cor. 10–13; Phil. 1.12ff.) Hence Paul considers himself as a 'spiritual father' and 'guardian' (paidagōgos) of the Corinthian community (1 Cor. 4.15) and addresses the congregation as 'beloved children' (1 Cor. 4.4; 2 Cor. 6.13). But Paul does not desire to be 'lord' over the faith of the Corinthians but their 'helper' (synergos, 2 Cor. 1.24). At the same time Paul also calls individuals among his fellow-workers his 'sons' (e.g. Timothy, 1 Cor. 4.17; Onesimus, Phlm. 10). The fact that in his letters Paul frequently also uses the first person plural shows on the one hand that he includes his closest colleagues directly in his thoughts and actions (e.g. 2 Cor. 1.1; 1.8ff.; 6.1ff.; Phil. 1.1). On the other hand, in using 'we' Paul again is expressing his direct unity with his addressees (e.g. 2 Cor. 1.3ff.; Rom. 6.1ff.).

Over and above this, 'I' and 'we' can also be understood as referring to Christ-believing people in general (e.g. Rom. 7.7ff.). The transitions between a specific and a general use of the personal pronouns in the Pauline epistles are fluid. This shows clearly that the Pauline apostolate stands not only in the tension between individual experience or personal responsibility and supra-individual community but also in the tension between actual experience and a general Christ-believing interpretation and management of life.

Göttel-Leypold and J. H. Demling, 'Die Persönlichkeitsstruktur des Paulus nach seinen Selbstzeugnissen', in Becker and Pilhofer, *Biographie*, 125–48.

5
Paul as a Jew and as an Apostle of Jesus Christ: the 'Break' in his Person

We know Paul the apostle of Jesus Christ. At the same time Paul reports on several occasions on his origins in Judaism. Paul belongs by birth to the minority of the ethnos tōn Ioudaiōn within the frame of the *Imperium Romanum*, more precisely to Diaspora Judaism.[17]

Paul comes from Pharisaic Judaism (Phil. 3.5; Acts 22.3) and later describes himself as an assiduous 'persecutor' and 'destroyer' of the ekklēsia tou theou (Gal. 1.13,23; Phil. 3.6; cf. also Acts 22.4ff.). In this respect Luke tells of Paul's 'approval' of the death of the earliest Christ-confessing martyr, Stephen (Acts 8.1).

Through his calling Paul becomes a follower and later leading personality of a new Jewish hairesis: the small group of the Christianoi, as Luke names them (Acts 11.26 and 28.22). Thereby he is a member of a new religious group which is still diffuse. He devotes himself entirely to its service and plays a decisive role in its dissemination. He finds himself additionally – while still belonging ethnically to the Jewish minority – in the marginal status of a member of the Christ-believing communities, endangered on account of Jews as well as the Roman authorities.

Paul's person continuously stands in the tension between 'Judaism' and 'Christ-believing communities'. Paul's commission (Gal. 1.15), described by Luke as a 'conversion' (cf. Acts 9; 22; 26), leads to a 'break' in the Pauline biography.[18] From a Jewish point of view Paul the apostle of Jesus Christ is a Jew who has broken away, a so-called renegade. This naturally brings him disapproval and in some circumstances hatred on the part of the Jews and in the end leads to his arrest in Jerusalem according to Luke (Acts 21.27ff.). From the Gentile point of view he initially represents something like a schismatic Jew. His religious affiliation is unclear and forces him to make this constantly clear and to articulate it in language and argument.

Paul himself interprets this biographical break with aphorizō, as 'a setting apart' (Rom. 1.1; Gal. 1.15) and transfers it back to his prenatal state (ek koilias mētros mou, Gal. 1.15; cf. 1 Cor. 15.8). In modern terms, he suffered a 'break' in his personality through modifying his religion. His own perception, however, is rather that of a rebirth or even a prenatal predestination even if in Phil. 3.7f. and in Gal. 1.13f. he can express the revelation of Jesus Christ in the language of

---

17. Cf. here Chapter 4 by J. Frey in this volume.
18. On the matter of this biographical break we can establish an interesting parallel development – in the context of ancient Judaism – in the early Jewish historiographer, Flavius Josephus: Josephus' departure from Palestine and his turning to the imperial dynasty of the Flavians can be connected with the fact that Josephus is the author of the only ancient Jewish autobiography (*Vita*). Consequently 'broken biography' and autobiographical writing with the aim of *apologia* are clearly to be found in close connection in Josephus – in Paul, too, there are signs of these. Here, there arises in a special way the interplay between inflection and reflection. Apart from ancient Judaism this connection of biographical 'break' and autobiographical writing is particularly clear in Augustine's *Confessiones*. On this cf. Augustinus (1990), *Confessiones*, ed. L. Verheijen (CCSL 27), Turnholt, esp. conf. 8.8ff.

brusque discontinuity. In this way Paul, commissioned to be an apostle, does not call into question his Jewish background and affiliation to Judaism even when he sees himself – in contrast to Peter – as called to preach the gospel among the 'uncircumcised' (Gal. 2.7–10).

Paul calls himself: 'a Hebrew, Israelite, descendant of Abraham' (2 Cor. 11.22; cf. also Rom. 4.1), 'circumcised on the eighth day, a member of the people of Israel, of the tribe of Benjamin, a Hebrew born of Hebrews' (Phil. 3.5) or a 'brother of the Israelites according to the flesh' (Rom. 9.3f.). Here circumcision proves to be constitutive for Paul. It is a permanent physical sign and at the same time a central theme, particularly in Rom. and Gal. (cf. Rom. 2–4; Gal. 2.5). Yet while Paul knows that 'according to the flesh' he belongs permanently to the people of Israel (Phil. 3.3f.) and is able to say: 'We are Jews by birth (physei) and not Gentile sinners' (Gal. 2.15), he defines Christian existence as a 'spiritual' circumcision, namely as a service of God and glory of Jesus Christ (Phil. 3.3ff.). Consequently for Paul's way of thinking circumcision remains on the one hand an essential distinguishing feature between Jewish Christ-believers and Gentile Christ-believers, and the 'Gentiles' are described in an abbreviation as 'uncircumcised' and the Jews as 'circumcised' (Gal. 2.7: akrobystia – peritomē). On the other hand Paul demonstrates the dubious theological nature of the relevance of the differentiation between 'circumcised' and 'uncircumcised': '... if those who are uncircumcised keep the requirements of the Law, will not their uncircumcision be regarded as circumcision?' (Rom. 2.26). This is why Paul's conception is that 'a person is a Jew who is one inwardly, and real circumcision is a matter of the heart – it is spiritual and not literal' (peritomē kardias en pneumati ou grammati, Rom. 2.29).

Thus Paul moves existentially and personally between Judaism and his earlier and later Jewish-Christians on the one side and Gentile Christians on the other *and* at the same time theologically moves beyond these definitions when he formulates a theological differentiation between affiliation to Judaism and belief in Jesus Christ (Rom 9–11). In Rom 7.7-25 Paul pushes this differentiation so far that in the end he formulates a foundational text of Christian anthropology beyond the alternatives of 'Jew – non-Jew'.

6
Paul and his Body: Recognizing and Transcending Limitations of the Person I

Paul's manner of thinking frequently deals theoretically *and* metaphorically with concepts from the area of 'body' and 'bodiliness (sarx, sōma).[19] Paul is aware of and names the limits of his own personal physicality and that of humanity as a whole and frees it from such limits by defining it anew in the light of Christ.

Paul sees his own physical being restricted by his *illness* (particularly: 2 Cor. 12.1–10) and the *sufferings* experienced which he mentions in the 'circumstances'

---

19. Cf. here the already classic approach to the representation of Paul in R. Bultmann, *Theologie*; Id. *Theology*, particularly §17ff.

(2 Cor. 11.23ff.). He interprets this experience of physical suffering and weakness in a threefold way: *First*, in a pragmatic way, he purposefully takes pride in his weakness (astheneia, 2 Cor. 11.30) and validates this interpretation by referring to Christ (2 Cor. 12.9f.). But he uncompromisingly dismisses the criticism raised in Corinth against his weak bodily presence (2 Cor. 10.10) by referring to his authority as an apostle (2 Cor. 10.11). *Second*, Paul considers his own personal experiences of suffering to be an analogy of Christ and consequently understands them as a part of the life of one who would emulate Christ (2 Cor. 1.5f.). *Third*, Paul surely starts from his own personal experiences of suffering when he ponders on the limitations of all physical existence – the creation (Rom. 8.18ff.) and human existence as a whole (2 Cor. 5.1ff.).

Paul considers his disappointing personal – i.e. physical – presence in Corinth as a precondition of his *letter-writing* (2 Cor. 10.1; 13.10), when he contrasts bodily absence with the proximity of letters which he calls a presence in the spirit (1 Cor. 5.3: egō ... apōn tō sōmati parion de tō pneumati). That is why, particularly in 2 Cor., Paul tells the Corinthians of his emotional state, i.e. he lets them participate in his physical existence through a letter: He writes 'with many tears' (2 Cor. 2.4) and shows the Corinthians his 'heart' which is 'wide open' (2 Cor. 6.11).

Finally, Paul makes physicality a *theological theme* when he connects the terminology of 'body' with his biography (1 Cor. 15.8), as well as with soteriology and ethics, and transfers it to ecclesiology (1 Cor. 12). For pre-Christian and Christian existence it is a fact that a life according to the flesh (kata sarka) brings death, is alienation from God and runs counter to a life kata pneuma (Rom. 8.1ff.). In fact the sending of the Son of God condemned the sins of the 'flesh' and made possible a life in the spirit of Christ. Thus mortal bodies will also be given life through the spirit of the One 'who raised Christ from the dead' (Rom. 8.11). Yet even for an existence as a Christ-believing person there remains the danger of falling victim to the 'desires' and 'works' of the flesh (Gal. 5.13ff.). Consequently recognizing the limitations of human bodiliness and transcending those limitations are a central theme in Pauline *soteriology and ethics*.

In 1 Cor. 12.12ff. Paul transfers the imagery of physicality to *ecclesiology*: He describes the church as sōma Christou. This metaphor has a twofold function: At one and the same time Paul makes Christ 'incarnate' present in the ekklēsia and combines the individual members of the church to a 'somatic' unity. Thus it is clear that the various gifts of grace (charismata) given to the individual members of the church must be led back collectively to the grace of Christ (Rom. 12.6: echontes de charismata kata tēn charin ...).

7
Paul and the Eschaton: Recognizing and Transcending Limitations of the Person II

The anticipation of the eschaton had aspects for Paul which were both supra-individual and individual or personal. A 'development' in Paul's thought can be observed in respect of his eschatological ideas.

First, with regard to supra-individual aspects: In 1 Thess. 4.13ff. Paul expresses the expectation of an imminent parousia of the Lord which will occur within his lifetime and that of his addressees and which will take place through being 'caught up' (harpazō, 1 Thess. 4.17). The resurrection of the dead and those who are still alive being 'caught up' points to the permanent community with the Kyrios. In 1 Cor. 15.51ff. Paul speaks of a 'transformation' (allassō, 1 Cor. 15.51) of human existence which is not brought into direct connection with the parousia. Here it is more a matter of the vanquishing of death, for the 'mortal' will put on 'immortality' (1 Cor. 15.54ff.).

In Phil. the imprisoned Paul (Phil. 1.7,13f.) admittedly also formulates individual eschatological expectations (Phil. 3.11) that transcend ties to somatic as well as geographical conditions (Phil. 3.20f.). But above all Paul expresses his own personal longing for death: The yearning to die arises because he desires to be with Christ (Phil. 1.21ff.). Perhaps the delay in the coming of the parousia is here connected with his individual wish to die. At the same time Paul shifts from supra-individual eschatological ideas to the expectation of transcending his individual personal limitations.

In particular, Paul describes experiences of limitation and transcendence of his personhood under four aspects:

1 *Illness and suffering* lead to the questioning of the person and personal strength. Paul understands the word of the Lord which he received: 'My grace is sufficient for you, for power is made perfect in weakness' (2 Cor. 12.9) as a fundamental interpretation and confirmation of his own personal existence.

2 Paul sees Christian existence in a permanent *tension between life and death*. This tension, i.e. what is in principle the restriction of Christian existence, is connected with a person's mortality and serves the revelation of Jesus Christ: 'For while we live, we are always being given up to death for Jesus' sake, so that the life of Jesus may be made visible in our mortal flesh' (2 Cor. 4.11). But Paul can also reverse this fundamental insight into the relationship of mortality and revelation: it is a characteristic of those who serve God, 'as dying ... (to be) alive' (2 Cor. 6.9). To be dead to sin, the 'wages' of which are death (Rom. 6.23), means to be 'alive to God in Christ Jesus' (Rom. 6.11).

3 The conformity of Pauline existence to the model of Christ leads to a dissolution of the personal structure determined by the flesh. Paul expresses this emphatically in the formula: '*Christ ... in me*' (en emoi Christos, Gal. 2.20).

4 In 1 Cor. 13 Paul makes *eschatological statements* concerning experiencing and transcending limitations of the person. At first glance these statements are admittedly of a general anthropological kind, but behind them we can also detect biographical experiences and expectations. The eschatological statements (1 Cor. 13.8ff.) lead into reflections on the 'now and not yet' of the person and his/her cognitive capacity: 'Now I know only in part; then I will know fully, even as I have been fully known' (1 Cor. 13.12). Thus for Paul understanding in general (2 Cor. 1.13) as well as the final knowledge of the person remains an eschatological property.

References

E.-M. Becker and P. Pilhofer (Hg.) (2005/2009), *Biographie und Persönlichkeit des Paulus* (WUNT 187), Tübingen: Mohr Siebeck.

R. Bultmann (1984), *Theologie des Neuen Testaments* (UTB 630), Tübingen: J. C. B. Mohr.[9]

—(2007), *Theology of the New Testament*. With a New Introduction by R. Morgan. 2 vols. Translated by K. Grobel, Waco, TX: Baylor University Press.

B. J. Malina and J. H. Neyrey (1996), *Portraits of Paul: An Archaeology of Ancient Personality*, Louisville, KY: Westminster John Knox Press.

Part II

Letters. Theology

Chapter 8

INTRODUCTION TO PART II
Oda Wischmeyer

From around 50 CE Paul communicated with the Christian churches by means of letters. These letters, which he wrote to the churches he had founded in Thessalonica, Corinth, Philippi and Galatia as well as to the Christians in Rome whom he did not know personally, represent the beginning of Christian literature and theology.

Paul himself initially strove to communicate by letter with his churches in the period of time until the Second Coming of the Lord Jesus Christ or in the time remaining until his own premature death in the service of proclamation. Consequently his letters are personal writings related to the prevailing situation and to his addressees – as it were literature to be used and applied, but yet always written under an apostolic signature, i.e. in the authority of the Apostle of Jesus Christ, as Paul understood himself. This gives his epistles an official tone even when he writes in such a personal way as in 2 Corinthians.

This is particularly clear in the letter to Philemon, in which Paul requests the Christian house-owner and slave-holder to take back his runaway slave, Onesimus, without punishing him. In spite of the personal reason Paul begins the short letter in a very official way:

> Paul, a prisoner of Jesus Christ, and Timothy, our brother, to Philemon our dear friend and co-worker, to Apphia our sister, to Archippus our fellow-soldier, and to the church in your house: Grace to you and peace from God our Father and the Lord Jesus Christ!

This official tone is present to a far greater extent in his longer epistles, especially in Romans. Paul definitely conceived these epistles as open letters to the Christian assembly (ekklēsia) at the time in the provincial capital or the capital of the Empire. The letters were intended to be passed on to the churches in the vicinity. They were read aloud, discussed, understood, misunderstood, not understood, suspected or opposed. 2 Cor. 10.10 affords us an insight into the reactions to the letters:

> For they say, his letters are weighty and strong, but his bodily presence is weak and his speech contemptible.

At all events his letters gave cause for questions and further expositions in following letters and consequently served to construct a theology. The so-called

Corinthian Correspondence is evidence of this process. 2 Peter represents a final echo of the complex history of inner-New Testament understanding of the Pauline epistles. In 2 Pet. 3.15f. we read:

> ... regard the patience of our Lord as salvation. So our beloved brother Paul wrote to you according to the wisdom given him, speaking of this as he does in all his letters. There are some things in them hard to understand (dysnoēta), which the ignorant and unstable twist ...

In recent years research on letters has very successfully and precisely located the Pauline epistles in the early Jewish, Greco-Roman and early Christian epistolary culture, literature and theory of the early Empire.[1] When Paul uses a shorter or more extensive letter as a means of written communication,[2] he is acting like a literary figure or philosopher, possibly even as a diplomat, politician or religious leader.[3] At the same time he writes in a way which is popular, understandable, communicative and encouraging. Each of his extant letters is different and original, adapted to the communicative situation. With the letter Paul is using a multiform literary medium which allows him every freedom and at the same time secures the maximum effect on his addressees.[4] His epistles were successful and became formative for the style and theology of the second and third generation of Christian missionaries, church-leaders and teachers. They were preserved and collected. The first collections of Pauline letters formed the core of the later canon.[5]

The Pauline letters are literary bearers of information, communication, argumentation and instruction.

Information – e.g. on the common collection for Jerusalem – gives the young churches a feeling of reciprocal knowledge and communal spirit. *Communication* replaces and bridges the absence of the apostle and deepens the relationship between the apostle and the churches. *Argumentation* acquaints the churches with the fundamental principles and consequences of the apostolic preaching and should protect them from what Paul understands as the false preaching of

---

1. H.-J. Klauck (2006) *Ancient Letter Writing and the New Testament: A Guide to Context and Exegesis*. With the collaboration of Daniel W. Bailey, Waco, TX.: Baylor University Press.
2. E.-M. Becker (2004), *Letter Hermeneutics in 2 Corinthians. Studies in Literarkritik and Communication Theory* (JSNT. Suppl. Series 279). T&T Clark: London/New York.
3. Cf. the letters which Paul carries with him on behalf of the Sanhedrin (Acts 9.2). Cf. also the Bar Kochba correspondence and the so-called Diaspora letters, cf. I. Taatz (1991), *Frühjüdische Briefe* (NTOA 16), Freiburg/Göttingen.
4. O. Wischmeyer (2004), 'Paulus als Autor', in: *id., Von Ben Sira zu Paulus. Gesammelte Aufsätze zu Texten, Theologie und Hermeneutik des Frühjudentums und des Neuen Testaments* (WUNT 173), Tübingen, 289–307.
5. H. v. Lips (2004), *Der neutestamentliche Kanon. Seine Bedeutung und Geschichte*, Zurich.

opposed missionaries. Research on rhetoric in the past generation has brought new, deeper insights into the public, argumentative and communicative structure and into the textual pragmatics of the letters.[6] Finally, *instruction* is effective for the lives of young Christians in a confused religious and social world in which Paul gives the churches paraenetic advice for the Christian life within and outside of the church.

The argumentative passages in the Pauline letters open up theological themes, concepts and strategies of argumentation; the paraenetic passages open themes and areas of Christian ethics. In this way Paul laid a foundation for Christian theology and ethics.

Part II of this book is structured correspondingly. First the letters are described in what was probably their original order (Chapters 9–15). Chapter 16 gives an introduction to the theological and ethical themes of the letters.

---

6. Cf. on research into rhetoric the literature on the contributions to Rom. (Chapter 15) and 2 Cor. (Chapter 11) in this volume.

Chapter 9

1 Thessalonians
Eva Ebel

Table 9.1

Sender	Paul (1.1) Co-senders: Silvanus, Timothy (1.1)
Addressees	Church at Thessalonica: the majority Gentile-Christians
Situation of origin	Beginning of Paul's missionary work in Corinth
Occasion	Questions about the Parousia in Thessalonica
Place of writing	Corinth (*not named explicitly*)
Date	50 CE
Opposition	----------
Themes	Foundation of the church, Parousia, necessity of working

Broad structure	Opening of the letter 1.1 Prescript
	                                       1.2–10 Proemium as thanksgiving
	Body of the letter 2.1 – 3.13 1st Main Part: Thanks
	                                      4.1 – 5.24 2nd Main Part: Paraenesis
	Close of the letter 5.25–28 Postscript

1
Approaching the Text

The Content and Transmission of the Text

In the Nestle text the first letter to the Thessalonians contains 1,472 words, which in the latest edition of Nestle-Aland fill approximately eight printed sides.[1] Certain sections of the letter have come down to us in the papyri P[46] (*c*.200), P[30] (third century), P[65] (third century) and P[61] (*c*.700). The significant majuscules Sinaiticus (ℵ 01, fourth century), Alexandrinus (A 02, fifth century), Vaticanus (B 03, fourth

---

1.   Cf. R. Morgenthaler (1958), *Statistik des neutestamentlichen Wortschatzes*, Zürich/Frankfurt, 168.

century) and D 06 (sixth century) offer the complete text. There are gaps in C 04 (fifth century) and I 016 (fifth century).

Analysis of the Text

The prescript of 1 Thessalonians is shorter than all the other Pauline epistolary openings. The statement about the sender (*superscriptio*) is particularly unpretentious: Paul ascribes neither to himself nor to his two co-senders, Timothy and Silvanus, a title such as 'Apostle'; all three stand side by side without distinction.

The eucharistoumen which opens the proemium in 1.2 is characteristic of the further contents of the epistle. In this letter the writer's gratitude to his addressees can be found not only at the beginning – as a transition, so to speak, to the actual body of the letter – but in 2.13 there is a second eucharistoumen and in 3.9 it is again mentioned with eucharistia and thereby becomes an actual theme of the letter. Consequently it is difficult to separate the proemium and the body of the letter. It seems reasonable to see a clear break in 2.1 since here the Christians in Thessalonica are addressed directly and a reflection on Paul's preaching begins which is more fundamental.

The central themes of the letter are already mentioned in the proemium, which consequently contains 1.2–10: First, there is a thankful recollection of Paul's activity in Thessalonica (1.2–5) and the reaction of the Thessalonians (1.6). Then the present function of their church as a shining example in Macedonia and Achaia and 'in every place' is stressed (1.7f.). Finally, after a renewed recollection of the 'coming' (eisodos) of the Christian missionaries into Thessalonica (1.9) which is cleverly introduced rhetorically by a *praeteritio* (1.8c), an allusion is made to the coming Judgement (1.10).

In 2.1 Paul again takes up the key-word eisodos but turns away from the situation in Thessalonica in that he first goes into details about his negative experiences in Philippi which preceded the founding of the church there and then goes far afield in a general *apologia* for his work as a preacher (2.1–12). In support of his own self-representation in which, with the aid of antitheses, he dissociates himself sharply from dishonest itinerant preachers,[2] Paul on the one hand refers repeatedly to the Thessalonian Christians' knowledge (2.1f., 5, 9–11) and on the other he names God as witness (2.5, 10). After renewed thanks for the acceptance of God's word (2.13), the sufferings of the Christians in Thessalonica are thematized as a perceptible consequence of this (2.14–16).

From Paul's close relationship with this church and the knowledge of their suffering there then follows the apostle's strong desire to visit them again, but he is twice prevented from so doing by 'Satan' (2.17–20). In his need Paul grasps two alternative means of communication: first, to find out finally the state of the Thessalonians' faith he sends Timothy there (3.1–6). His report is a reason for rejoicing, but to remedy the still existing 'lack in faith' (ta hysterēmata tēs pisteōs) Paul then writes the letter before us to the church (3.7–10).

---

2. On the dissociation from Cynic itinerant preachers portrayed in exemplary fashion in the writings of Dio Chrysostom, cf. A. J. Malherbe (1970), '"Gentle as a Nurse". The Cynic background to 1 Thess ii', *NT* 12, 203–17.

The first main section of the epistle devoted to thanks concludes with a wishful prayer in 3.11–13, which on the one hand is again related to Paul's wish to visit them, but on the other hand links into the following second main section with the key-words 'holiness' (hagiōsynē) and 'strengthen your hearts' (stērizai hymōn tas kardias).

The first sentence of the second part points very clearly to its contents with the predicates erōtōmen and parakaloumen: it is a pleading exhortation to the Christians in Thessalonica. The central concept of the section 4.1–8, which is focused on the avoidance of fornication (porneia) and greed, is 'holiness' (4.3, 4, 7; hagiasmos). By means of the second *praeteritio* of the letter Paul then turns to 'brotherly love' (philadelphia), which the Thessalonians make effective in the whole of Macedonia, far beyond the circle of their community. In the same way as in the two following sections the apostle begins his remarks with peri, so that the impression arises that he is working through a list of topics that have been given to him or that he himself has selected.

The indubitably most famous section of 1 Thessalonians is devoted to the fate of the deceased Christians (4.13–18) at the Parousia of the Lord (4.15: parousia tou kyriou). Appended to this are thoughts on the 'times and seasons' of the 'day of the Lord' (5.1–11). Both sections are closed with an exhortation to mutual encouragement and admonition (4.18; 5.11).

After these very special expositions, the consequence of which should be a life in vigilance and sobriety, Paul gives some general instructions for the life of individual Christians and that of the congregation (5.12–22) before he also concludes the second main part of 1 Thessalonians with a wishful prayer (5.23f.).

Conspicuous in the postscript to this letter (5.25–28) is the request for prayer for Paul and his fellow workers and the lack of greetings from other Christians.

In spite of the fact that the contents of this letter clearly fall into two parts, there are also elements that overlap. Dominant throughout the epistle is the eschatological perspective: Already in the first main section Paul alludes to the Parousia of Christ (1.10; 2.19; 3.13) which is treated in detail in the second major part (4.3–18; 5.1–11).[3] Further, all the instructions for the life of the members of the church are given in expectation of the imminent arrival of the Lord, so that especially the call to be 'blameless' (amemptōs) is twice linked directly to the Parousia (3.13; 5.23).

In this letter we find many examples of metaphors relating to family: The salutation 'brother' (adelphos) is not used so often in any other epistle.[4]

---

3. The term parousia in relation to Jesus Christ is found in the *corpus Paulinum* as well as in 1 Thess. 2.19; 3.13; 4.15; 5.23 only in 1 Cor. 15.23 – i.e. in his later letters Paul abstains almost completely from using the word which in secular Greek is used to describe both the epiphany of a god and the visit of a worldly ruler (cf. A. Oepke [1959], 'Article parousia, *ThWNT* 5, 856–69; W. Radl [²1992], 'Article parousia', *EWNT* 3, 102–5). T. Holtz, 1 Thess., 120, brings into play Paul's increasing knowledge of the Greek world: 'It would appear that Paul gained knowledge particularly in the field of apocalyptic ideas and terminology which caused him to employ a more restrained way of expressing himself in his later letters.'

4. Adelphos appears in 1.4; 2.1, 9, 14, 17; 3.2, 7; 4.1, 6, 10, 13; 5.1, 4, 12, 14, 25, 26, 27; in 4.9 we also have philadelphia.

Moreover, Paul describes his relationship to the church as that of a father to his children, who comforts and admonishes them (2.11f.): Consequently he is 'orphaned' (2.17: orphanos) by the separation from the congregation.[5]

Structure

From these observations on the text we have the following structure of the first letter to the Thessalonians:

Table 9.2

Beginning	1.1	Prescript
of the letter	1.2–10	Proemium as thanksgiving
Body of the letter	2.1–3.13	1st main part: Thanks
	2.1–12	Apologia for Paul's preaching
	2.13–16	The acceptance of the word of God and its consequences
	2.17–20	Paul's prevented visit
	3.1–6	The sending of Timothy
	3.7–10	Timothy's report
	3.11–13	Prayerful wish
	4.1–5.24	2nd main part: Paraenesis
	4.1–8	Avoidance of fornication and greed
	4.9–12	Brotherly love
	4.13–18	The fate of the deceased at the Parousia
	5.1–11	The time of the Parousia
	5.12–22	Life in the congregation
	5.23f.	Prayerful wish
Ending of the letter	5.25–28	Postscript

2
The Genesis of the Text

In the prescript Silvanus and Timothy appear along with Paul as co-senders. Paul emerges as a single person on three occasions (2.18; 3.5; 5.27), otherwise the third person Plural is maintained – but in 3.1, for example, only Paul can be meant by the 'we'. Hence Silvanus and Timothy are responsible for the form and contents of the letter to a limited extent.

Both, however, do not appear without reason as co-senders of the epistle, for they, too, have a special connection to the church in Thessalonica: Their participation in the mission in Macedonia can be deduced not only from 1 Thessalonians but also from 2 Cor. 1.19. There is, admittedly, some uncertainty about the precise role Timothy played because of the report on the second missionary journey in Acts: While Silas/Silvanus[6] appears repeatedly as

---

5. For family metaphors in 1 Thess. cf. C. Gerber (2005), *Paulus und seine Kinder* (BZNW 136), Berlin/New York, 270–343.

6. Silouanos = Silvanus is the Latinized form of the Aramaic name *Siloni*, the Greek

Paul's companion, Timothy[7] is not mentioned by name either in the section on Philippi (Acts 16.11–40) or in that on Thessalonica (Acts 17.1–9), and in the section on Beroea (Acts 17.10–15) he is only mentioned when, together with Silas, he remains behind there while Paul sets out for Athens (Acts 17.14). Does Luke tacitly assume that Timothy was a co-founder of this church along with Paul and Silvanus, or was Timothy active in other places independently of the two missionaries? Paul praises Timothy's reliability and congeniality of spirit (isopsychos) in the highest tones, hence there was no one more suitable than Timothy to visit churches on Paul's behalf and to take action there as Paul would have wished, but yet autonomously (1 Thess. 3.1–6; Phil. 2.19–23; 1 Cor. 4.17).

Paul describes the foundation of the church in the Macedonian port of Thessalonica – which reveals a wide spectrum of pagan cults[8] – as a renunciation of 'idols' (eidōla) and a turning to the true and living God (1.9). Since he was born a Jew he could never have accused Jewish Christians of being guilty earlier of 'idolatry', therefore with this summary reference he reveals that very many members of the church in Thessalonica are Gentile Christians. The lack of any direct quotations from the Old Testament in the whole of 1 Thessalonians also points to this. In Acts, on the other hand, we are told that Paul preached in the Synagogue[9] (Acts 17.2f.) and was particularly successful among the Greek god-fearers (Acts 17.4), while the leader of the synagogue, Jason, gave him shelter (Acts 17.7). Taking both reports together gives the picture of a church composed mainly of Gentiles of whom no small part had sympathized with Judaism before their conversion to Christianity.

As far as the duration of the sojourn of Paul and his fellow workers in the town is concerned, the accounts in 1 Thessalonians and Acts cannot automatically be brought into accord. According to Luke, Paul's activity in Thessalonica is limited to a few weeks since he preaches in the synagogue on three Sabbaths (Acts 17.2) and then must leave the town precipitately for Beroea after the Jews have instigated a revolt of the mob (Acts 17.5, 10). Paul's own self-witness on the other hand speaks of a longer stay: The apostle stresses that he works for his living (2.1–12) and in another place reports that he twice received financial support from Philippi during this period (Phil. 4.16).

Already at the time of its foundation the church is exposed to persecution

---

form of which is Silas. Hence in all probability the Silas of Acts and the Silvanus of the Pauline epistles are identical. On this fellow worker of Paul cf. W.-H. Ollrog (1979), *Paulus und seine Mitarbeiter. Untersuchungen zur Theorie und Praxis der paulinischen Mission* (WMANT 50), Neukirchen-Vluyn, 17–20.

7. On this co-worker of Paul cf. Ollrog, *Paulus* (n.6), 20–3.
8. On Thessalonica cf. C. vom Brocke, *Thessaloniki*; K. P. Donfried, *Cults*, and *id*., *Paul*, 21–48.
9. The earliest evidence for a synagogue in Thessalonica is an inscription on a sarcophagus from the beginning of the third century BCE in which even synagogai in the plural are mentioned; cf. here P. M. Nigdelis (1994), 'Synagoge(n) und Gemeinde der Juden in Thessaloniki: Fragen aufgrund einer neuen jüdischen Grabinschrift der Kaiserzeit', *ZPE* 102, 297–306. On the Jews in Thessalonica cf. vom Brocke, *Thessaloniki*, 217–33.

(thlipsis, 1.6). This experience continued after the departure of their founder (2.14f.) and demanded the apostle's pastoral encouragement. But two attempts to visit his congregation failed not long (pros kairon hōras) after he had left Thessalonica (2.17f.), so that Paul sends his fellow worker, Timothy, from Athens to strengthen the Christians in Thessalonica and attain certain knowledge of their faith (3.1–5). Paul expresses his praise and thanksgiving for the positive report which Timothy can give on his return (3.6) in the letter we have to hand. What is more, he tells of prevailing uncertainties and exhorts the church in view of the unchanged, difficult relationship with their pagan environment to live a righteous life in unity among themselves which appears trustworthy to those who do not belong to the church (4.10–12).

The location where the three senders met again – and consequently the place where 1 Thessalonians was written – is not named explicitly. According to 1 Cor. 1.19, Paul, Silvanus and Timothy are working together in Corinth, hence this town is taken as the place where 1 Thessalonians was written. Since there is no greeting from members of the Corinthian church in the postscript – i.e. no intensive communication structures have developed as yet – it was probably written towards the beginning of Paul's activity in Corinth in the year 50 CE.

3
Exegesis of the Text

The section 2.14–16 embodies a problematical passage within 1 Thessalonians. At the beginning the suffering of the Thessalonians which their symphyletai, their compatriots in Phyle,[10] have caused them is equated (2.14) with that which the churches in Judaea endured at the hands of 'the Jews' (hoi Ioudaioi). Then follow five accusations against these people: They killed Jesus and the prophets, persecuted 'us' – i.e. Paul and his fellow workers – displeased God and were hostile to everyone (2.15); they filled up the measure of their sins by hindering the proclamation of the gospel to the gentiles (2.16a, b). Consequently God's wrath (orgē) has at last (eis telos) overtaken them (2.16). These statements in 1 Thessalonians are difficult to reconcile with the position of Paul as seen in the letter to the Romans, for there the possibility of salvation for Israel continues to exist (Rom. 11.25–32).

Various solutions are suggested for the dilemma that results from this difference. Ferdinand Christian Baur, for various reasons, particularly on the basis of these verses, declares the whole of 1 Thessalonians as 'not Pauline'.[11] Birger A. Pearson,[12] among others, dismisses this thesis and considers instead an interpolation. In the argumentation for this the following reasons are brought

---

10. vom Brocke, *Thessaloniki*, 152–66.
11. F. C. Baur (1867), *Paulus. Der Apostel Jesu Christi. Sein Leben und Wirken, seine Briefe und seine Lehre*, Vol. 1, Leipzig, 96f.
12. B. A. Pearson (1971), '1 Thessalonians 2:13–16: A Deutero-Pauline Interpolation', *HThR* 64, 79–94.

into play: the Aorist ephthasen describes something that happened in the past; the only meaningful grounds for wrath would be the destruction of Jerusalem in 70 CE and 2.16c is consequently secondary for chronological reasons. If one does not wish to restrict the interpolation to 2.16c it becomes particularly difficult to determine its extent: 2.15 and 2.16 are closely connected and therefore can scarcely be separated; the parallelization of suffering in 2.14 seems somewhat laboured and cannot be explained as an obvious later continuation; 2.14 appears necessary to explain the effectiveness of the Thessalonians' faith mentioned in 2.13; if one extracts 2.13–16 from the text there is no definite train of thought connecting 2.12 to 2.17. Literary-critical considerations therefore can in no way corroborate the thesis of an interpolation;[13] rather they suggest that 2.14–16 are part of the original letter and consequently must be ascribed to Paul.

Hence exegesis stands before the task of explaining the anti-Jewish passage at the historical level. It appears that Paul makes the Jews living in Thessalonica responsible for the troubles afflicting the church there which is very dear to him. This interpretation of the church's situation and his own negative experiences in the past – which he also lets drop here (2.15) – and possibly currently relevant at the time the letter was written could be suspected as background for such a violent attack on 'the Jews'. As zealously (zēlos) as Paul once adhered to the Jewish Law and persecuted the Christian churches (Phil. 3.6), so now he reacts violently when he sees the proclamation of the gospel to the gentiles endangered by the Jews (2.16b). The accusations raised here in 2.14–16 depend on the one hand on widespread anti-Jewish polemics expressed both by the Jews themselves (the killing of the prophets) and also by non-Jews (*odium humani generis*[14]); on the other hand Paul adds personal details (persecution of his own person, not pleasing to the sight of God, prevention of proclamation to the Gentiles). If one does not allow the apostle to speak in the prophetic Aorist,[15] an interpretation of the orgē in terms of a historical event as relating to the destruction of Jerusalem is ruled out; that he was thinking of a concrete historical event at all is scarcely probable.[16] On the contrary Paul's personal

---

13. For criticism of the hypothesis of an interpolation cf. I. Broer (1983), '"Antisemitismus" und Judenpolemik im Neuen Testament. Ein Beitrag zum besseren Verständnis von 1 Thess. 2, 14–16', in B. G. Gemper (ed.), *Religion und Verantwortung als Elemente gesellschaftlicher Ordnung. Für Karl Klein zum 70. Geburtstag* (Beiheft zu den Siegener Studien), Siegen, 734–72; here 741–6, and *id*. (1990), '"Der ganze Zorn ist schon über sie gekommen": Bemerkungen zur Interpolationshypothese und zur Interpretation von 1 Thess 2,14–16', in R. F. Chandler (ed.), *The Thessalonian Correspondence* (BEThL 87), Leuven, 137–59; here 137–48 and Holtz, *1 Thess.*, 27, 96f.

14. Cf. on this at a later date Tacitus, *Annales* 15,44,4: here the accusation used against the Christians. A collection of relevant texts about Jews in M. Stern (ed.), *Greek and Latin Authors on Jews and Judaism*, 3 vols, Jerusalem 1974–1984.

15. E. von Dobschütz (1909), *Die Thessalonicher-Briefe* (KEK 10) Göttingen, 116.

16. E. Bammel (1955), 'Judenverfolgung und Naherwartung. Zur Eschatologie des Ersten Thessalonicherbriefs', *ZThK* 56, 294–315 (reprinted in *id*. [1997], *Judaica und Paulina. Kleine Schriften II*, [Mit einem Nachwort von] P. Pilhofer [WUNT 91], Tübingen, 237–58); here 295–301, thinks of the expulsion of the Jews from Rome under the Emperor Claudius (cf. Acts 18.2).

consternation and the intervention on the part of the Jews which he interpreted as endangering his lifework lend plausibility to the suspicion that the Aorist ephthasen is intended to express, in prophetic terms, the certainty of the eschatological judgement on the Jews.[17]

The real reason for the first epistle to the Thessalonians is the problem that Paul describes in 4.13–18 and concerns those 'who have fallen asleep' (4.13: peri tōn koimōmenōn).[18] On the visit when he founded the church Paul proclaimed the imminent Parousia of the Lord without considering the fact that members of the congregation could die before the Parousia. Now, however, at least one death has occurred and the church is worried about the fate of those who have died before the Parousia.

As answer to this situation Paul first refers to their common belief in the death and resurrection of Jesus which makes it impossible that God should forget those who have passed away (4.14). Then, as confirmation, he quotes a 'word of the Lord' (logos kyriou) that there will be no 'precedence' given to the living over the dead at the Parousia (4.15). The formulation 'we who are alive, those who are left' which Paul chooses in 4.15 and again in 4.17 reveals his strong imminent expectation in this phase of his activity. Paul had inserted at least the second classification 'those who are alive' in contrast to the dead into a tradition which presumably does not go back to a saying of Jesus but is a post-Easter creation. The apostle describes the dawning of the Parousia in apocalyptic motifs before he – almost casually – mentions the resurrection of the dead (4.16) as prerequisite for the common rapture of all (4.17). For Paul as a one-time Pharisee this is obvious – but this is in no way comprehensible for the Gentile Christian members of the Thessalonian church. Paul can solve the problem that has arisen in Thessalonica by remembering his own Jewish roots, but his one-time Gentile readers needed more extensive explanations.[19] But for Paul himself this is not the main concern: he is concerned with an undifferentiating rapture of the living Christians and those who have already died (hoi nekroi en Christō) who must be raised from the dead for this purpose. The connection of the resurrection and the Parousia serves to refute ideas that the dead will be disadvantaged because the Parousia could pass them by: everyone, dead or alive, will be together with the Lord forever (4.17: syn kyriō esometha).

Paul's remarks are by no means a complete representation of the events at the Parousia or even of the resurrection. Many questions remain open: How will the resurrection take place? What does 'together with the Lord' imply? What will happen to non-Christians? The apostle goes into questions connected to the Parousia and resurrection only to the extent to which they are important for the actual problem in Thessalonica. He breaks off as soon as he has achieved the

---

17. Broer, *Antisemitismus* (n.13), 763–6; *id.*, Zorn (n.13), 158; Holtz, *1 Thess.*, 108f.; U. Schnelle, *Apostle Paul*, 179f.
18. For this passage cf. D. Luckensmeyer, *Eschatology*.
19. W. Marxsen, *1 Thess.*, 63–8.

goal of his argumentation: nothing could be farther from his mind than giving a dogmatic foundation of this theme.

In the following section (5.1–11) Paul deals additionally with only one aspect – the 'times and seasons' (peri de tōn chronōn kai kairōn): the 'day of the Lord' (hēmera kyriou) will come unpredictably like a thief in the night (5.2, 4), so that there is a need for constant vigilance and sobriety (5.6). But in this connection also the apostle returns to the central idea of the previous section (5.9f.): The Christians are destined for salvation since Jesus Christ died for them so that, awake or asleep (eite grēgorōmen eite katheudōmen) – i.e. alive or dead – they will live with him (syn autō zēsōmen).

Two perspectives characterize the first letter to the Thessalonians: the look back to the activity of Paul and his fellow workers when founding the church there and the look forward to the imminent Parousia.

The apostle emphasizes his commitment to preaching and his honesty (1.5; 2.1–12) which can be seen not least in his working for his livelihood (2.9). The enthusiastic acceptance of the gospel by the Thessalonians is in keeping with this engagement (1.9; 2.1, 13). The close relationship between the church and its founders which results from this, which can be seen in exemplary fashion in the metaphor of the father (2.11f.), endures even after they have parted. The Christians in Thessalonica are especially 'imitators' (mimētai) in suffering of Paul who, for his part, follows the example of Christ (1.6; cf. 1 Cor. 4.16). The church is currently, as Paul predicted (3.4), marked by 'troubles' (2.14; 3.3f.) and oriented on the future. In view of the imminent arrival of the Lord who will save the faithful (1.10) it is necessary that they live a life pleasing to God (4.1), blameless (3.13; 5.23: amemptōs) and in holiness (4.3, 4, 7: hagiasmos).

4
Evaluation

The first letter to the Thessalonians is the oldest extant Pauline epistle. Both in form and content it displays some differences from the apostle's later letters.

The prescript of this letter is simpler than any other: Neither the senders nor the recipients are given a title or any other closer definition. In particular it is not necessary for Paul to prove his apostleship. Certainly he is aware that there are competing itinerant preachers (2.1–12), but these do not call into question his rank as apostle and consequently his authority with respect to the church. As the use of apostolos in 1 Thess. 2.7 verifies, Paul is aware of his special position and also knows how to include it in his argumentation.

It is conspicuous that some theological concepts which to a large extent characterize Paul's later writings such as Law (nomos) and sin (hamartia), cross/ crucify (root staur-) and righteousness/make righteous (root dik-) are missing in this letter.[20] In spite of this terminological lack the themes of judgement and justification are constantly present in the first letter to the Thessalonians: Paul

---

20. Cf. on this deficiency and its significance U. Schnelle, *Der erste Thessalonicherbrief*.

writes about the coming wrath (orgē) of God (1.9; 5.9; cf. 2.16); in contrast to this stands salvation (sōtēria) through Jesus Christ who died for us (hyper hēmōn, 5.9). In this letter, however, Paul expresses himself in such a way on the theme of judgement that we cannot say that here we have simply a preliminary stage of the understanding of justification developed in Galatians and Romans: Here we can recognize a comprehensive, independent outline in which the Law is not mentioned.

References

Commentaries

F. F. Bruce (1982), *1 and 2 Thessalonians* (WBC 45), Waco, TX: Word Books.

T. Holtz (³1998), *Der erste Brief an die Thessalonicher* (EKK 13), Zürich: Benziger.

A. Malherbe (2000), *The Letters to the Thessalonians* (AncB), New York: Doubleday.

W. Marxsen (1979), *Der erste Brief an die Thessalonicher* (ZBK.NT 11.1), Zürich: Theologischer Verlag.

Monographs

C. vom Brocke (2001), *Thessaloniki – Stadt des Kassander und Gemeinde des Paulus. Eine frühe christliche Gemeinde in ihrer heidnischen Umwelt* (WUNT II/125), Tübingen: Mohr Siebeck.

K. P. Donfried (2002), *Paul, Thessalonica, and Early Christianity*, Grand Rapids, MI: Eerdmans.

H.-J. Klauck (2006), *Ancient Letter Writing and the New Testament: A Guide to Context and Exegesis*. With the collaboration of Daniel W. Bailey, Waco, TX: Baylor University Press.

D. Luckensmeyer (2009), *The Eschatology of First Thessalonians* (NTOA 71), Göttingen.

U. Schnelle (2005), *Apostle Paul: His Life and Theology*, Grand Rapids, MI: Baker Academic, 171–191.

Essays and Encyclopedia Articles

K. P. Donfried (1985), 'The Cults of Thessalonica and the Thessalonian Correspondence', *NTS* 31, 336–56.

U. Schnelle (1986), 'Der erste Thessalonicherbrief und die Entstehung der paulinischen Anthropologie', *NTS* 32, 207–24.

Review of Research

S. Schreiber (2007), 'Früher Paulus mit Spätfolgen. Eine Bilanz zur neuesten Thessalonicher-Forschung', *ThRev* 103, 267–84.

Chapter 10

1 CORINTHIANS
Oda Wischmeyer

Table 10.1

Sender	Paul (1.1; 16.21) Co-sender: Sosthenes (1.1)
Addressees	The church in Corinth, Christians in Corinth (1.2)
Situation of origin	A longer sojourn in Ephesus by Paul during the third missionary journey and a planned journey to Macedonia
Occasion	Questions posed by the Corinthian community
Place of writing	Ephesus (16.8)
Date	Spring of 55 CE
Opposition	No outside opponents, tendencies within the community towards schism
Themes	Main theme: Unity of the congregation, the congregation as a Christian community (see the broad outline for more detail)

Broad outline	Opening of the letter	1.1–3 1.4–9	*Epistolary prescript* *Epistolary proemium*
Body of the letter 1.10 – 16.12		I: 1.10 – 4.21	Exhortation for unity in the congregation
		II: 5–6	Prohibition of sexual immorality in the church
		III: 7	Instruction on gender questions in the church
		IV: 8–11	Instruction on the eating of meat sacrificed to idols
		V: 12–14	Instruction on the spiritual gifts in the church
		VI: 15	Treatise on the resurrection of the dead
		VII: 16.1–12	Questions about the collection

Conclusion	16.13–24	16.13–18	Concluding *paraenesis*
		16.19–20	Greetings
		16.21–24	*Epistolary ending*

1
Approaching the Text

The Content and Transmission of the Text

In the Nestle text the first letter to the Corinthians contains 6,807 words[1] on approximately 30 printed pages. Consequently it is the second longest Pauline epistle and only a little shorter than the letter to the Romans. The following important Early Church majuscules hand down the text: ℵ 01 (fourth century), A 02 (fifth century), B 03 (fourth century), C 04 (fifth century, with gaps), D 06 (sixth century, one small gap). Parts of 1 Corinthians can be found in the following papyri: Þ11 (seventh century), 14 (fifth century), 15 (third/fourth century), 34 (seventh century), 46 (the oldest witness, *c*.200, Dublin, Chester Beatty Library II; Ann Arbor, University of Michigan, Inv. 6238, text almost complete), 61 (*c*.700), 68 (?seventh century), 123 (fourth century, P.Oxy. 4844).[2] 1 Corinthians can be found in the early canonical lists and has been commented on since the time of Origen.

Analysis of the Text

The letter begins with the author giving his own name and that of the co-sender, Sosthenes (1.1) and concludes with a greeting originally written in his own hand (16.21–24).

The text of the letter displays structural features which clearly have precedence:

Table 10.2

1.4	eucharistō	There follows the topical *thanksgiving* for the community.
1.10	parakalō	The letter from 1.10 – 14.40 stands under this key word of admonition/exhortation.
15.1	gnōrizō	*The topic of resurrection* in ch. 15 comes under this catchword.

Therefore in keeping with Paul's self-understanding the epistle contains

---

1. According to E. Morgenthaler (1958), *Statistik des neutestamentlichen Wortschatzes*, Zürich/Frankfurt am Main, 164 §3.
2. According to B. and K. Aland, J. Karavidopoulos, C.M. Martini, B.M. Metzger (eds) (2001), *Nestle-Aland, Novum Testamentum Graece post Eberhard et Erwin Nestle editione vicesima septima revisa communiter*, 27th, rev. edn, Stuttgart, and Institut für Neutestamentliche Textforschung an der Universität Münster: Continuation of the Manuscript List.

exhortations at the beginning[3] and towards the end detailed 'information'[4] or report on the resurrection of the dead.

Particularly important for the divisions in the text is the phrase peri de ('concerning'):

Table 10.3

7.1	peri de ōn egrapsate	Theme: male and female[5]
7.25	peri de tōn parthenōn	Theme: young unmarried women
8.1	peri de tōn eidōlothytōn	Theme: meat from pagan sacrifices
8.4	peri tēs brōseōs tōn eidōlothytōn	Theme: eating of sacrificial meat
12.1	peri de tōn pneumatikōn	Theme: spiritual gifts and the service of God
16.1	peri de tēs logeias	Theme: the collection
16.12	peri de Apollō tou adelphou	Theme: Apollos' journey to Corinth

The phrase peri de is encountered from chapter 7 on. This makes a clear division in the letter as a whole. The phrases mark the themes on which the Corinthians require instruction – either in their own view or in that of Paul.[6] Hence the epistle has broad didactic sections in addition to its paraenetic character.[7]

Further signs of partition of the text are the references to conditions in the church of which Paul has 'heard' (1.11; 5.1; 11.18 taking up 1.11). Here he refers thematically to factions (chapters 1–4), sexual immorality (5.1ff.) and Eucharistic traditions (11.17ff.).[8] In 5.9,11 Paul mentions a letter which he has previously written to their church.

Structure

The letter is arranged according to the normal pattern of the Pauline epistles (*epistolary construction*):

---

3. Cf. also the reversion to parakalō in 16.15: Here Paul confirms indirectly that he has written a paraenetic letter.
4. Gnōrizō can be translated as 'proclaim publicly, announce'.
5. Here Paul refers to a letter which the Corinthians have written to him.
6. But observe the earlier uses of ouk oidate inter alia in 3.16; 5.6; 6.2,3,9,15,19. The paraenesis in 1 – 6 already had strong noetic-didactic features.
7. Cf. the noetic verbs eidenai (8.1,4; 11.3; 12.2), ouk agnoein (12.1) and gnōrizein (12.3; cf. 15.1).
8. Cf. also 15.12: Paul has heard that some members are saying: 'There is no resurrection of the dead'.

Table 10.4

1.1–3	*Epistolary prescript*	Introduction to the letter
1.4–9	*Epistolary proemium* shaped as thanksgiving	

1.10 – 15.58		Body of the letter

16.1–18	Concluding *paraenesis*	
16.19–20	Greetings	Conclusion of the letter
16.21–24	Epistolary *eschatocoll* (*subscriptio*)[9]	

The internal arrangement of chapters 1–15 has already been described.

Themes

It is difficult to name a continuous topic or even *one* particular theme as the most important theme of the epistle because of its markedly close connection to the church and the situation there as well as the variety of topics mentioned. Moreover, *one* uniform theme presumes the literary unity of the text before us or at least makes this unity probable. The question of the unity of the letter, however, can only be clarified later. At this point I only ask about the theme or topic of the letter *as it exists*. Naturally exegetes come to diverse conclusions:[10]

Table 10.5

Conzelmann	'The "Last Things" are the theme of the letter which holds all the other topics together'.[11]
Schrage	'A proper Theology of the Cross and Eschatology', 'theology ... oriented towards practice', 'Agape'.[12]
Lindemann	'A single theme ... the ekklēsia itself and therein oikodomē'.[13]
Schnelle	'The unity of the church grounded in Jesus Christ in the face of their actual disunity'.[14]

9. With U. Schnelle (^{5}2005), *Einleitung in das Neue Testament*, Göttingen The History and Theology of the New Testament, 61. Cf. *ibid.*, 61–73 on the form of the ancient letter in general and in Paul's usage.

10. Cf. further R. A. Horsley (1998), *1 Corinthians*, (ANTC 7), Nashville, 22: 'Paul wrote his letter to address the problem of divisions that had arisen within the recently founded Corinthian assembly'. Similarly B. Witherington (1995), *Conflict and community in Corinth. A social-rhetorical commentary on 1 and 2 Corinthians*, Grand Rapids, 73: 'Paul is in the midst of trying to create community and dissipate conflict in the Corinthian community'; and 75: 'In order to overcome these sources of discord Paul gives in his letter a lengthy discourse on concord or reconciliation using deliberative rhetoric.'

11. H. Conzelmann (^{2}1981), *Der erste Brief an die Korinther* (KEK 5), Göttingen, 27.

12. W. Schrage, *Der erste Brief an die Korinther* (EKK 7/1–4), Neukirchen-Vluyn 1991–2001, vol. 1, p. v.

13. A. Lindemann (2001), *Der Erste Korintherbrief* (HNT 9), Tübingen, 15.

14. U. Schnelle (^{5}2005), *Einleitung in das Neue Testament*, Göttingen, 70.

Betz/Mitchell	'Verse 1:10 is the prothesis or thesis statement of the argument of the entire letter, which calls on the Corinthians to end their factions and be reconciled with one another'.[15]
Thiselton	The 'unifying issue in 1 Corinthians was that of an overrealized eschatology'. In addition Thiselton stresses the sociological and cultural aspects: 'I now perceive how this theological misperception combined with the seductive infiltration into the Christian church of cultural attitudes derived from secular or non-Christian Corinth as a city'.[16]
Fitzmyer	The message of the cross 'puts Christ himself at the center of soteriology, God's new mode of salvation, and all else in Pauline teaching has to be understood in relation to it. That is why the sketch of Pauline teaching in this letter also has to take as its starting point that message of the cross, "we proclaim Christ crucified"'.[17]

The table shows clearly that the commentators perceive the text in different ways. Conzelmann, Schrage and Fitzmyer look for the basic theological theme which controls all Paul's individual themes and argumentation and determine the content. This is also true of Lindemann, whose suggestion for a solution, however, is more concrete and less theological: the church and her increase are the subject of the letter. Schnelle, Betz and Mitchell, and Thiselton put the situation and the self-understanding of the Corinthian church in the central position and, in varying degrees, come to the same conclusion: the theme lies as it were on the surface of the text. It relates to the actual situation of the church which is characterized by strife, tendencies to secede and members' overestimation of their own spiritual capacities. Against this Paul urges them to unity and reconciliation as Christian ways of behaviour.

These different positions provide us with an important insight into the themes of 1 Corinthians. The letter has a central topical theme: the unity of the congregation (Schnelle et al.) and – more forcefully – the congregation as a Christian community (Lindemann). But at the same time a fundamental theological conviction lies behind the various paraenetic peri de-sections and the thematic main section of the letter which can be defined with Conzelmann as eschatological – in a narrow sense – or with Schrage and Fitzmyer – even more narrowly – as a theology of the cross and eschatology.

The reference to the 'coming revelation of our Lord, Jesus Christ' in the *proemium* makes it clear that Paul understands his presence and his own activity,

---

15. H. D. Betz and M. M. Mitchell, *Art. Corinthians, First Epistle to the*, ABD I (1992), 1139–48, 1143.

16. A. C. Thiselton (2000), *The First Epistle to the Corinthians. A Commentary on the Greek Text*. The New International Greek New Testament Commentary. Eerdmans: Grand Rapids, Mich./Cambridge, UK, 40.

17. J. A. Fitzmyer (2008), *First Corinthians. The Anchor Yale Bible 32*, Yale University Press: New Haven and London, 70.

154 Paul

just as the fate of the church, in relation to the resurrected, ruling and returning Lord Jesus Christ. The theology of the cross in chapters 1 and 2 is a more specific but also thematically dominant theologumenon connected to the commensurate explanation of the essence of the proclamation of Christ (1.17ff.).

Semantic Fields

In accordance with its clear thematic structure (peri de) the epistle uses very differentiated semantic fields which sometimes take over from one another, sometimes are entwined and again and again refer to one another. These semantic fields open up the individual themes of the letter and how these are connected and consequently deserve particular attention. Here I present only the most important semantic fields.[18]

Chapters 1–4 are dominated by two extensive semantic fields which stand antithetically to one another:

Table 10.6

Gifts of the Corinthians		God's way of acting and communicating
logos	↔	logos tou staurou
gnōsis		
sophia/sophos/sophia kosmou	↔	sophia tou theou = mōria tou kērygmatos/ to mōron tou theou
dynamis	↔	dynamis theou = to asthenes tou theou
pneuma tou kosmou	↔	pneuma tou theou
Behaviour of the Corinthians	↔	*Behaviour of the Apostle*
kauchēsis		
zēlos/eris		
physioun		
Replete/rich/clever/to be esteemed	↔	mōroi dia Christou
basileuein	↔	condemned to death
ta onta	↔	ta mē onta
anthrōpos sarkinos	↔	anthrōpos pneumatikos
↓		↓
Factions within the church		Paul and other Apostles

Chapters 5 and 6 arrange the following words thematically: sexual immorality etc. (porneia) – flesh (sarx) – vices (5.10f. and 6.9f.) as well as food – nourishment (brōma) – stomach (koilia) – eating – common meals (synesthiein). Paul gives this group of words a disparaging to clearly negative evaluation, condemning them. This group is contrasted with the body (sōma), which is associated with concepts and metaphors that have a very positive sense: the saints (6.1f.) – eschatological judges (6.3) – the Kingdom of God (6.9f.) – sanctified – washed clean – justified (6.11) – resurrection (6.14) – their bodies as members of the body of Christ (ta sōmata hymōn melē Christou 6.15) and temple of the Holy Spirit (6.19).

---

18. I cannot go into the numerous metaphors here.

1 Corinthians

The theme porneia occurs once more in chapter 7. There gender themes are central. The group of words relating to gender includes: man (anēr, anthrōpos) – woman – virgin – to marry – to be unmarried.

Chapters 8–10 continue 5–6 and 7. Once again the subject is nourishment (brōsis), now about meals with meat sacrificed to idols: eidōlothyton. In this connection Paul discusses in detail the limits of gnōsis as knowledge of God, the exousia and the eleutheria of Christians. Limits to this freedom are again porneia, eidōlolatria and other vices (cf. chapters 5 and 6) as well as the demons and foreign gods (8.1–6) who also belong in this negative, dangerous area. 8.1b points back to chapter 1 and forward to chapter 13.

Chapter 11 once again addresses meals, this time the Lord's Supper. Again their being the sōma Christou and the Judgement are brought in to clarify the topic.

Finally, Chapter 15 contains the vocabulary of resurrection or raising from the dead in connection with the antithetically constructed cosmological-eschatological semantic field which is related to the fate of the body (sōma):

Table 10.7

earthly	heavenly
mortal	immortal
perishable	imperishable
first man	second man
Adam	Christ (already also in vv. 20–28)

There also appear apocalyptic concepts in connection with the resurrection of the dead in the Last Days: Death – end – might – rule – force – kingdom – enemy – destroy – subordinate (vv. 20–28; cf. 50–55 – last trumpet – the dead).

Heterogeneous as the individual themes may appear, particular basic ideas or themes which can be seen in the vocabulary run through the *whole letter*: Unity (koinōnia, no schismata), church (ekklēsia), brother (adelphos), apostle (apostolos), strong/weak (dynamis/astheneia), body (sōma/sōma Christou – melē), events of the Last Days (Resurrection of Jesus Christ, the raising of the dead, the Day of the Lord, the Last Judgement), Spirit/gifts of the Spirit/spiritual (pneuma/ pneumatika – charismata/ pneumatikos).

Communication and Rhetoric
Communication
The first epistle to the Corinthians is a letter which is to a great extent communicative: it contains several *levels of communication*. The four levels can be graphically represented in the following way:

Table 10.8

Level 1	Communicative level (central level)
Level 2	Level reinforcing the communication ↓ ↓ Metaphors etc. lists etc. autobiographical details tradition
Level 3	Meta-communicative level
Level 4	Trans-communicative level

1. The central level is that of the *direct paraenetic-didactic communication* with the Corinthian church or individual factions within the congregation. The addressees – 'the church of God in Corinth' (*v. infra*) – are spoken to and admonished or instructed on this level (e.g. 1.10; 5.1; 7.1; 8.1; 10.1; 10.14; 11.1–3; 12.1; 14.1; 15.1). Paul refers to news from the church, letters between himself and the church, addresses current incidents within the congregation, quotes things which have been said in the church (*v. supra*) and admonishes and teaches the congregation persistently on the relevant current controversial topics.
2. In addition to this the reader observes a second level: The *level of the short passages which are also communicative*, and serve to provide a better understanding of or to illustrate individual arguments or admonitions. The following passages bear this meta-argumentative and likewise meta-paraenetic character:

Table 10.9

3.10.15	Detailed *metaphor* from the field of house-construction, located apocalyptically
5.6.8	*Metaphor* from the area of the Passover Feast
7.17.23	*Thematic digression* evoked by the cue 'calling'
9.7f.	*Rhetorical question* in connection with the theme 'proceeds of work'; from the areas of warfare – wine-growing – livestock ownership
9.9ff.	*Interpretation of the Torah* in the area of 'proceeds of work'
9.24–27	*Metaphor* from the sphere of running
10.1–10	*Midrash-like* reversion to the Torah: Episodes from the Exodus
12.14–26	*Fable*[19] related to the human body
14.7f.	*Metaphor* from the field of music
14.10f.	*Metaphor* from the area of speech

19. The term 'fable' describes an 'independent, short, epic-didactic form of fiction, mainly about animals ... which as an exemplary tale illustrates a truth well known in general ... by using an example in a figurative depiction and, particularly through anthropomorphic transposition of human characteristics ... achieves ethically didactic effects'. G. von Wilpert ([8]2001),

1 Corinthians

In this field there also belong the lists of vices, peristases, virtues and charismata:

Table 10.10

1.26.29	Antithetical list: strong – weak etc.
5.10.11	List of vices in nominal form
6.9f.	"
10.7–10	List of vices in verbal form within the frame of the Midrash on Exodus (*v. supra*)
12.8–10	List of charismata
12.28f.	"
12.29f.	" in verbal form in rhetorical questions
13.1–3	List of charismata
13.4–7	List of virtues in verbal form
[14.1–33	Numerous mentions of the various charismata]

These passages readily make use of definite literary figures of speech: metaphor, rhetorical question, biblical exegesis, fable, lists from various themes and tradition.

A further group of texts has a place here: the likewise *communicative autobiographical* passages. Again and again Paul writes brief or longer (ch. 9) autobiographical sections to make his *paraeneses*, teaching and commands more vigorous by connecting them with his own person or exemplifying them in his own life.[20] These sections can be found in: 1.14–17; 2.1–5: 3.1–4; 4.1–4; [4.9–13 *v. supra* – list of peristases]; 4.14–16; 7.7; 9.1–27; 11.1; 15.8f.; 15.30ff.

Finally, Paul frequently in his communication makes use of *tradition*[21] (paradosis) or makes reference to a word of the Lord to make his exhortations or teaching clearer or more binding. Here the following passages are affected:

Sachwörterbuch der Literatur, Stuttgart, 254. Paul chooses the human body rather than the animal kingdom as a demonstration, cf. Livy II 32, 9–12 (more detail in Lindemann, *Der Erste Korintherbrief*, 275–7).

20. Cf. especially 4.16 and 11.1: mimētai mou ginesthe. He sees himself as an example of a Christian existence – not merely in the moral sense but in his whole way of living.

21. Cf. also the references to the tradition concerning baptism 1.30; 6.11; 12.13 (cf. Schnelle, *Einleitung*, 66f.).

Table 10.11

7.10f.	Prohibition of divorce/word of the Lord
9.14	Maintenance of the apostle
11.2	General reminder of the tradition which Paul has handed down to the church
11.23b–25	Paradosis of the Lord's Supper
15.3b–5	Paradosis of the Resurrection

3. The fact that there are frequent meta-communicative passages in which Paul explains his *paraeneses* and teaching corresponds to Paul's great need to communicate in this letter. This *third level of metacommunication* can be found in the following texts:

Table 10.12

2.6.9	Introductory remark on the understanding of the expression sophia theou
3.1f.	Reference to the earlier communication with the Corinthians
4.6	Instruction for the proper understanding of 3.5 – 4.5
4.14	Instruction for the proper understanding of 4.7–13
5.9–13	Instruction for the proper understanding of his earlier letter to the Corinthians
7.6,10,12, 17b, 25f., 35,40b	Precise allusions to the authorization of his orders and advice on each occasion
10.19	Instruction for the proper understanding of 10.14–18
12.31b	Instruction for the proper reading of ch. 13
14.20	Comment on understanding or insight
15.51	Comment on understanding the following passage

4. Finally, a *fourth level* is not directly connected to communication but formulates a *meta-communicative surplus*[22] of Paul's theology. I call this the *trans-communicative level* because here Paul is no longer concerned with communication but attempts to represent his theological thematic *beyond* communication. There are four such passages:

---

22. On the term 'meta-communicative surplus' cf. E.-M. Becker (2004), *Letter Hermeneutics in 2 Corinthians. Studies in* Literarkritik *and Communication Theory*. Journal for the Study of New Testament Supplement Series 279. London/New York: T&T Clark International, 89 and 111.

Table 10.13

1.18–25	Theological description of the apostolic preaching as that of the logos tou staurou
2.6–16	Theological description of sophia
13	Theological-ethical description of agapē as the greatest charisma
15.35–49	Theological description of the resurrection body

In these texts we encounter the real 'theological' statements in 1 Corinthians.

Rhetoric

Rhetoric is a central component of Greco-Roman culture.[23] As the 'art of persuasion, as totality of rules and regulations through the application of which the public is convinced' rhetoric was the basis of every ancient address. Originally applied in the fields of politics and law, 'rhetoric developed in the Hellenistic period and in Rome into an *ars dicendi* ("the art of speaking") which in its focussing on every kind of linguistic expression represents no less than an extensive theory and practice of human communication'.[24] Rhetorical elements and strategies made their way into literature. Hans Dieter Betz has discovered rhetorical elements and strategies in the Pauline letters and thereby made clear the proximity of the Pauline epistles to Hellenistic-Roman literature. Betz and Margaret M. Mitchell represent the rhetorical composition of the letter as follows:[25]

Table 10.14

[1.1–3	The beginning of the epistle, *v. supra*]
1.4–9	*Exordium*, the introduction (ends thematically with a call to koinōnia/ sense of community)
1.10.17	*Narratio*, the argument or formulation of the contents (v. 10 is the prothesis, the thesis: 'all of you be in agreement')
1.18.15.57	*Argumentatio* or *probatio*, the evidentiary implementation
15.58	*Peroratio*, the effective conclusion
[16.1–24	Closing of the letter, *v. supra*]

Ancient rhetorical theory works with three *genera dicendi* which are affiliated with the main public institutions, occasions and situations: the *genus iudicale*, the speech in court, the *genus deliberativum*, the counselling speech, and the *genus demonstrativum*, the speech for a special celebration. According to Betz and Mitchell the rhetorical character of the letter is deliberative: 'a deliberative

---

23. C. Walde and M. Weissenberger (2001), 'Article "Rhetorik"', *DNP* 10, 958–87; short introduction in H.-J. Klauck, *Ancient Letter Writing*.
24. Walde and Weissenberger, *Rhetorik* (n. 23) 959f.
25. H. D. Betz and M. M. Mitchell, *Corinthians*, 1145.

letter convincing the Corinthians to be reconciled and end their factionalism'.[26] The *genus deliberativum*, the symbouleutic (advisory) speech 'has its seat in the council meeting. It advises in the matter of taking a decision'[27]. Paul consequently in his letter addresses the ekklēsia in Corinth in the tone of a council meeting and appeals to their sense and faculty of judgement. This gives his epistle both an official and rational character extending far beyond the tone of a letter of friendship.

2
The Genesis of the Text

Author, Addressees and Historical Situation
The *author* of the letter before us is Paul (1.1 and 16.21). In the original epistle Paul wrote 16.21 in his own hand; for the rest, he dictated the letter. The authenticity of the letter is determined less by the address and greeting than by the numerous autobiographical passages (*v. supra*) which make the epistle one of the most important sources for the life of Paul and the story of his mission.

The *addressees* according to 1.1 are in the first place the ekklēsia of God in Corinth[28] and then all other 'saints', i.e. Christians.[29] This surprisingly wide circle of addressees makes it clear that 1 Corinthians should not only be understood in relation to the situation and actual addressees but claims general significance. The problems of the Corinthians are not simply 'personal' problems *of one community* which therefore are subject to Paul's pastoral discretion, but concern all Christians and ought also be made known to all Christians. Hence Paul was not thinking only of single communities and their problems but also of a 'Christian public'.

After the successful foundation of the ekklēsia in Corinth Paul continued his mission in Asia Minor (Acts 18.18ff., 19). In Ephesus he constantly exchanged news with Corinth, so that he was able to gain a nuanced picture of the *situation in the church*. How far this picture reproduces the reality we do not know. Paul assumes that the congregation at Corinth has developed very soon after his departure to a self-assured community rich in spirit (1.4–7 assessed positively, 4.6–10 negatively). In Ephesus he hears varying reports. 'Chloe's people' visit him and inform him of factions among the congregation gathering around particular persons, which he perceives as 'schisms' or factions (1.10; cf. 11.18 – apparently particularly clear at the celebration of the Lord's Supper). He has heard of a particular case of 'sexual immorality' which he does not tolerate

26. Ibid., 1143.
27. H.-J. Klauck, *Ancient Letter Writing*.
28. On Corinth cf. D.-A. Koch (2005), 'Korinth', in K. Erlemann et al. (eds), *Neues Testament und Antike Kultur II: Familie, Gesellschaft, Wirtschaft*, Neukirchen-Vluyn, 159–62 (lit.); in this volume cf. Chapter 11 by E.-M. Becker on 2 Corinthians.
29. On the 'somewhat overloaded *adscriptio*' [sc. address] cf. Lindemann, *Korintherbrief*, 26f.

(5.1ff.) and of liberties which the women in the assembly of the congregation have the nerve to take (11.1–16: praying with head unveiled, 14.33b–35; speaking in the assembly)[30] which he also forbids, and further, of disagreement, formation of groups and social inconsiderateness at the Lord's Supper (11.18ff.). 'Some' say that there is no resurrection of the dead (15.12). The group around the rich and influential Stephanas, the first convert in Corinth (1.16) visits him in Ephesus (16.15–18), and he desires to strengthen their authority (16.16). What is more, members of the congregation have turned to him in letters with questions because there is some uncertainty on questions of marriage (7.1).

Paul attempts to understand these somewhat heterogeneous items of news as an expression of *one actual situation* in Corinth: *disunity*. Consequently the letter can be understood with Margaret M. Mitchell as 'deliberative argument for concord' (1.10).[31]

Date and Place of Writing

According to 16.8 Paul dictates the letter in Ephesus. In 15.32 he refers to a deadly danger in which he found himself in Ephesus.

In the account in Acts Paul stayed for a longer period in Ephesus during his third missionary journey, so that Ephesus became a centre of his activity. In chapter 16 he mentions his projected further journey to Macedonia to receive the collection for Jerusalem. Within the framework of the Pauline chronology is seems reasonable to suppose that Paul made one sojourn in Ephesus *'from the summer of 52 until the spring of 55'*.[32] Since he talks of journeying further, it is more likely to assume the date of writing in the spring of 55 CE.[33]

Unity and Process of Editing

The first letter to the Corinthians is a part of the so-called Corinthian Correspondence – i.e. of the exchange of letters between Paul and the church in Corinth.[34] The first letter of Paul to Corinth which no longer exists is assumed by various exegetes to form a part of 1 Corinthians as we have it.[35] But analysis of the semantic and conceptual fields as well as the levels of communication

30. If this text is not a gloss (*v. infra*).
31. M. M. Mitchell (2001), 'Article: Corinthians', *RPP* 3, (Clu–Deu) 489–491, here 490.
32. With U. Schnelle, *Paulus*, 54. Cf. there for the grounds for this supposition.
33. The reference to Pentecost (Jewish Feast of Weeks, 50 days after Passover) allows us to think of the spring. According to 5.7f. it is possible that it was written before the Feast of the Passover.
34. Cf. the mention of a letter *before* 1 Corinthians (in 1 Cor. 5.9) and a letter from the church to Paul (in 1 Cor. 7.1).
35. Cf. the hypotheses for division in Schnelle, *History*, 62f. On the grounds for dividing the letter cf. Mitchell, *Korintherbriefe* (n.26), 1690: (1) 'detected breaks', e.g. in the plans for journeying, (2) duplications, e.g. chs 8 and 10, (3) 'formal grounds particularly in relation to the expression peri de [*v. supra*] ..., which according to some experts delimits an "answering letter"'. Schnelle, *History*, 63–66 names the following arguments: (1) The difference between 1.11 and 16.15–18, (2)1.1 – 4.21 can represent one writing coherent within itself, (3) theological tensions in 5.11. Mitchell and Schnelle plausibly dismiss the arguments.

and rhetoric makes it highly likely that the letter was produced as a unity, while the extremely heterogeneous hypotheses for division are not illuminating either materially or in terms of the technical history of the emergence of the letter.[36]

The question of glosses in 1 Corinthians is more difficult. If we assume glosses[37] we also presuppose one who makes glosses (an editor) and must name him. The question is important for how we judge 14.33b–36. Verses 34 and 35 offer problems for textual criticism,[38] but in particular their content cannot be connected to 11.2–16, where the woman naturally speaks when she prays or utters prophetically. On the other hand, 14.34f. forbids women to speak prophetically in the church assembly. 14.34 can be explained as a gloss, but this judgement naturally remains hypothetical. The one who made the glosses might be sought in the vicinity of the first letter to Timothy (cf. 1 Tim. 2.10–13).[39]

3
Exegesis of the Text[40]

Overview of the Text

In the prescript Paul introduces himself expressly as an apostle and writes together with Sosthenes[41] to the local church in Corinth.[42]

The *proemium* is formed as a thanksgiving. Paul gives thanks for the wealth of spiritual gifts among the Corinthians (charisma, gift of grace) and refers to 'the end' – i.e. the eschatological return of Jesus Christ their Lord.

In a first part of the letter Paul exhorts the Corinthian congregation to *unity* and the avoidance of divisions (1.10). He contends vehemently against the building of factions in Corinth around individual apostles including himself.[43]

He makes clear various facts about his own person. First, he has from Christ (1.1) the precise, restricted task of preaching the gospel (euangelizesthai 1.17); second, he founded the church (3.5ff.; 4.15ff.) and together with the other

---

36. This holds true for the hypotheses for dividing 1 Cor. since J. Weiss (1977), *Der Erste Korintherbrief* (KEK 5), Göttingen [1910], XL–XLIII. Weiss rightly emphasizes that we do not have the originals but only 'examples of an ecclesiastical collection'. But how could a complicated construction such as he and others suggest have come into existence? Hypotheses of division must unconditionally offer plausible suggestions for how the final form came into being.

37. Schnelle, *History*, 64 considers 6.14 to be an interpolation. Lindemann, *Korintherbrief*, 147, rejects this on good grounds.

38. The witness of the so-called 'Western' text (D, F, G) bring both these verses only after v. 40.

39. Cf. the detailed representation in Lindemann, *Korintherbrief*, 317–21.

40. For exegetical details cf. the commentaries. I shall refer in particular to the commentary of Lindemann in order to acquaint students with an Anglo-Saxon exegetical education with the German exegetical discussion on 1 Corinthians.

41. Sosthenes appears nowhere else in the epistles. Perhaps he is identical with the Sosthenes in Acts 18.17 (cf. Lindemann, *Korintherbrief*, 26).

42. On the extension of the circle of addressees cf. Lindemann, *Korintherbrief*, 26f.

43. See here 3.2.

apostles is a 'servant of Christ' and 'steward of God's mysteries' (4.1ff.). This is the extent of the basic instruction.[44]

Paul *reinforces* several points: first of all the *nature of his preaching of the gospel* (1.18–25[45]), the form of the church (1.26ff.; 3.1ff.; 3.16ff.; 4.6ff.) and his own existence as an apostle of Christ (2.1ff.; 4.6ff. list sufferings endured in the apostolic life). Both the preaching and the form of the church as well as his own life and that of his fellow apostles are placed by Paul under a theological criterion: The cross of Christ, i.e. the fact that Jesus was executed on the cross. He makes this scandalous (1.23) juridical fact of the greatest significance for Christian theology and for Christian existence. For Christian theology, wisdom (sophia), the instrument given at the creation for knowledge of God, is re-evaluated and counted as foolishness (1.18ff.). At the same time, the enhancement of the preaching about Jesus Christ – which Paul deliberately, in an abbreviated, trenchant way, names the logos tou staurou (1.18) – is deemed the true wisdom, namely the wisdom of God. He also alludes to the social form of the church – many simple members – and to his own missionary activity in Corinth – simple preaching about the crucified Christ:[46] God's wisdom of the cross answers the weakness of the Christians. The reversal of the wisdom given to mankind at the creation into folly, however, does not mean that God is not wise and that he does not act wisely. Paul emphasizes the continuity of the wisdom of God (2.6ff.) but brings out once again its special close connection with the death of Jesus (2.6–9).

The doctrine of the first part of the epistle is clear: it closes with a summarizing admonition (nouthetō[n] 4.14) to take to heart the injunctions of this part of the letter (4.14–21).[47]

Chapters 5 and 6 represent a *second thematic constellation* and relate further to negative reports about the congregation.

First, in Paul's opinion a member of the church has contravened every (!) form of marriage legislation[48] without this troubling the congregation. Paul demands that he should be excluded from the church. This takes place in a 'sacred, spiritual legal act';[49] it is not simply a matter of expulsion from the church but it is a 'dynamistic ceremony'[50] in which the sacredness of the ekklēsia is understood as virtually physical: The holy church must be protected from desecration by

---

44. This corresponds in essence to the first central level of communication (*v. supra* 1.6).

45. This corresponds basically to the trans-communicative level. 1.18–25 is a brief, theologically didactic text on the proper understanding of the preaching in Christ.

46. In 2.2 we again have the deliberate abbreviation of the preaching of Christ to the crucifixion. The complete old tradition can be read in 15.3–5, there *without* reference to the manner of death.

47. Here the extended metaphor of the teacher is dominant: Paul, not the apostle but the paidagōgos, even more: the father (v. 14), Timothy his 'son', the Corinthians the children and pupils (v. 21).

48. On legal questions *v. infra*.

49. H. Conzelmann, *Brief*, 124.

50. *Ibid.*, 125.

sin.[51] At the same time Paul makes it clear that the righteousness i.e. the cleanliness from heinous sins (vv. 10,11 list of vices) or the detachment from such sins only applies within the church. Hence he is not demanding a flight from reality but, with reference to the Last Judgement (v. 13), gives the example of a polarity of spheres; the Christians 'inside' (positive), the non-Christians 'outside' (negative vv. 12f.).

Second, the members of the congregation are taking legal action before the local judges,[52] perhaps to the best of their knowledge and belief. Paul forbids this practice almost furiously when he once again conjures up the Last Judgement (v. 3) and the holiness of the church (v. 11), but virtually leaves open to the Corinthians the choice between a renunciation of legal action and their own courts of arbitration. The conclusion of the second part is made up of an extended general reflection on the sanctity of the body (sōma) and a differentiation between two – superficially comparable – physical phenomena: eating and so-called immorality (6.12–20). Paul assesses eating as an outward phenomenon,[53] that has no significance for the Christian treatment of the body, but on the basis of Gen. 2.24 he considers immorality as an inward phenomenon (v. 18)[54] that destroys the spiritual righteousness of the Christian (v. 19). The common maxim 'All things are lawful for me, but not all things are helpful' (v. 12) and the brief reference to the problem of food anticipates the questions treated in the fourth part.

The doctrine in the text here presents a clear and sharp demand to refrain from all types of extramarital sexual love since for Paul they come under the verdict of immorality (v. 18: pheugete tēn porneian).

With chapter 7 there begin Paul's peri de-instructions. This chapter embodies in itself a *third* part: an *instruction on* – as we put it today – *questions of 'gender'*. Verses 1–7 deal with sexuality within Christian marriage. Paul permits sexuality but would prefer that Christian couples lived without sexual relations. He advises the unmarried not to marry but permits marriage (8,9). For those who are married he gives instruction from the Lord: there should be no divorce and no remarriage for those who are already divorced (10,11)! Paul himself gives moderate rules for marriages between Christians and non-Christians (12–16).[55] Verses 17–24 are a digression in that they are not concerned with the theme of gender but take up the motif 'remain as it is' (vv. 12ff. with regard to marriage) to require that the religious and social status quo is maintained.[56] Verses 25–38 treat the marriage of 'virgins'. Clearly this is a matter 'of a particular type of

---

51. The metaphor of sour dough is ethically transformed in this connection (v. 8) but is initially laid out in a material sense (v. 6).

52. Here it is perhaps a question of trials which were conducted and decided by private judges, i.e. Romans or Greeks resident in Corinth (cf. J. Bleicken (⁴1995), *Verfassungs- und Sozialgeschichte des römischen Kaiserreiches 1* (UTB 838), Paderborn, 186ff.

53. Cf. the Jesus tradition in Mk 7.14–23.

54. Cf. the Jesus tradition in Mk 7.20–23.

55. Strangely the prohibition of divorce does not apply in 'mixed marriages'. Cf. in detail Lindemann, *Korintherbrief*, 166f.

56. The argumentation is initially ethical (v. 19) but then christological (v. 22).

betrothal'.⁵⁷ Once again Paul employs the status quo argument: Marriage vows should be kept. But his doctrine consists of several layers. In his opinion (v. 25) renunciation of marriage is even better (v. 38) than the status quo. The explanation for this advice is eschatological (vv. 29–35).⁵⁸ Verses 39 and 40 apply the same graded system of values to widows. The instruction closes with a clear bias towards the unmarried state.⁵⁹

Chapters 8–11 make up the fourth part of the epistolary expositions. The peri de at the beginning names eidōlothyton as the theme of this section. Paul attempts to tackle the problem of to what extent the gnōsis of the Christians who eat meat offered to idols in the knowledge 'that an idol has no real existence' i.e. 'that there are no heathen gods' (8.4)⁶⁰ can run free. Those previously heathen who have become Christians appear to be eating meat offered to idols *'now'* because they wish to demonstrate their liberty (v. 9) and their knowledge (v. 10). Initially (8.1–6) Paul formulates the basic theological knowledge (oidamen) on this theme. The content of this basic knowledge is (1) the gnōsis: ouden eidolon en kosmō kai oudeis theos ei mē eis (v. 4); (2) the awareness of the subordination of this gnōsis to the agapē for fellow Christians (vv. 1–3). Paul's very differentiated argumentation in what follows moves between gnōsis and agapē. At the same time he already touches upon the theme of chapters 12–14. In chapter 8 Paul compares the Christians' gnōsis with their *conscience* (syneidēsis). Not all the Christian Gentiles are so certain that there are no eidōla in the world and suffer from a wounded conscience because they still lack the true freedom from idolatry/worship of strange gods – i.e. they are afraid when they eat, and eat contrary to their conscience. In such a difficult case Paul again gives the same advice as in chapter 7: namely, to remain by the status quo, this time in refraining from eating meat offered to idols. For: 'Food will not commend us to God' (8.8).⁶¹

Chapter 9 is an autobiographical *exemplum*.⁶² In its third section (vv. 23–33) chapter 10 returns to the peri de-theme of eating meat offered to idols. The doctrine is clear: Paul differentiates between simply buying at the market (v. 25) and eating when invited by 'unbelievers' (v. 27) on the one hand and renunciation of eating sacrificial meat when a fellow Christian expresses explicit misgivings (v. 28) on the other. This differentiated instruction is not based on the material

---

57. Lindemann, *Korintherbrief*, 176.
58. The style is apocalyptic: 'The Kairos is short' and 'the form of this world is passing away'.
59. Verse 40 for widows, cf. vv. 27 and 38 for men/youths v. 34 for the betrothed virgin and the unmarried woman. In 7.1,7 Paul gives precedence – also with reference to his own personal way of life – to celibacy, but does not impose it.
60. 8.1–6 is a clash of the monotheistic Paul with Greco-Roman polytheism from a Jewish perspective (8.6b christological).
61. Observe once more the eschatological expression.
62. Important autobiographical details: v. 5 (in contrast to the apostles, the brothers of Jesus and Peter, Paul is unmarried); vv. 12–18 (Paul did not allow himself to be supported financially in Corinth, the reason: v. 17); vv. 19–23 (Paul's differing ways of living a religious life demanded by his missionary activity).

question of whether a Christian may or may not eat 'meat sacrificed to idols'[63] but on the conscience of the fellow Christian. Here Paul is *in principle* arguing theologically but *in fact* pastorally.

Earlier in 10.1–13 and 14–22 Paul gives precedence to two theological considerations associated with the question of sacrificial meat. In verses 1–13 he warns of the dangers of idolatry, immorality, temptation and 'grumbling' against God in pointing to Israel's fate while wandering through the desert.[64] In verses 14–22 he brings the Lord's Supper directly into play. The doctrine reads: Christians who participate in the Lord's Supper cannot take part in temple feasts which are clearly dedicated to a religious purpose, and certainly not because the gods worshipped there 'are something' (v. 19) but because with such meals the common relationship of Christians, understood physically, with the Lord Jesus Christ is destroyed.[65]

With 11.1 the theme of eidōlothyton is essentially concluded. In 10.32 – 11.1a Paul, taking up 9.21–23, refers again to his way of life – 'all things to all men' (9.22) – which he presents to the church as exemplary.

In 11.2–34, in a thematic supplement to the question of meat offered to idols, he adds an exhortation on the proper way to eat the kyriakon deipnon (v. 20). Earlier he settles – so to speak in passing, introduced by a catchword (mimētai mou 11.1a and panta mou memnēsthe 11.2) – in a short passage (11.1b–16) a particular aspect of congregational practice (synētheia 11.16): A woman should not pray or make prophetic speeches without 'authority on her head'.[66] In unveiled praying of the women in the Corinthian congregation Paul sees a violation of 'church practice' (v. 16). Then he diagnoses grave violations in the celebration of the Lord's Supper. In this connection he goes back even farther: namely to the theme of divisions (11.18f.) which he has treated in detail in the first part of his epistle. Verse 23 gives a precise guideline: the members of the church should *wait* for one another and then eat the kyriakon deipnon *together*. This is the doctrinal point of chapter 11. Paul sets the basis for the order in vv. 23b–25(26) in the recording of the Last Supper which he himself received[67] and handed on to the Corinthians.[68] The Lord's Supper demands a worthy (v. 27)

---

63. For Paul this question is clarified theologically: One may eat *any* meat since there are no 'idols'/gods: 8.1–6.

64. A midrash on the passages in Exodus (cf. Nestle-Aland). The point is: the people of Israel already had baptism (v. 2) and the Lord's Supper (v. 4) in a spiritual form, and yet despite this God allowed them to perish (v. 5). Paul uses the story in Exodus explicitly typologically: tauta de typoi hēmōn engenēthēsan (v. 6) i.e. Christians, too, are not immune to deterioration because of baptism and the Lord's Supper and should not deal too carelessly with the question of eidōlothyton. In v. 11 he again also refers to the Last Days.

65. The idea of participation, koinōnia, v. 20. Paul uses the same idea in 11.17–34 in another expression.

66. The text remains unclear. Some scholars argue that it is not so much a matter of a veil but rather of *long* hair and in certain circumstances of a particularly conservative hairstyle. On the details of the line of reasoning cf. Lindemann, *Korintherbrief* 237–47 (Lit.).

67. Not from Jesus himself but from the church's tradition which goes back to Jesus (Lindemann, *Korintherbrief*, 253).

68. On the wording and history of the tradition of the Lord's Supper in Paul cf.

and appropriate (v. 29) manner which does justice to the body and blood of the Lord (v. 27), i.e. his sacrificial death for the community. The habitual practice in Corinth – that each member of the congregation partakes of his idion deipnon within the celebration of the Lord's Supper instead of the members waiting for one another[69] – contravenes the intention and purpose of Jesus' sacrifice.[70]

Now Paul comes to a fifth part: peri de tōn pneumatikōn (concerning spiritual gifts) to which are devoted chapters 12–14. Here, after chapters 7 and 8–11, Paul writes a third thematic instruction (ou thelō hymas agnoein) which is carefully constructed and carried through. As in chapter 8, he begins with a fundamental orientation on the Spirit of God (8.1–3) and a theological discourse on the variety of gifts and the unity of the Spirit who produces these gifts (8.4–11). Paul clarifies this proportional relationship in vv. 12–26 with the allegory of the body and the members which he promptly relates persuasively to the congregation. In vv. 27–31 he applies the argumentation pragmatically to the situation of the church in Corinth by emphasizing the variation and function of the offices and spiritual gifts – both treated together in vv. 28ff.

In chapter 13 he refers in a manner critical of charismata to *love* as the greatest of the spiritual gifts (cf. 8.1). In that he also interprets the virtue of love like hope and faith as a charisma he opens up the possibility of treating the spiritual phenomena *ethically*. Chapter 14 relates this 'ethical turn' in the spiritual gifts above all to the most important ways of speaking in the communal worship. The Corinthians favour the direct *glossolalia* effected by the Spirit.[71] Paul points them to *prophecy* as a 'theologically authoritative form of speech with convincing content',[72] which in contrast to glossolalia is communicative, i.e. understandable and edifying for the congregation (14.4). For Paul glossolalia suffers in that it lacks the ability to communicate and because it is related only to the person speaking.

Part 6 contains chapter 15 and can be understood as a thematically strongly unified treatise on the resurrection of the dead. The cause of this is that 'some' Corinthians are saying: anastasis nekrōn ouk estin (v. 12). In 15.1–11 Paul prefaces this statement of the situation with a fundamental argumentation as in chapters 8 and 12.[73] Here it is a matter of a tradition in the church as in 11.23ff., this time about the wording of the euangelion-paradosis (15.3–5).[74] From the tradition about Christ, i.e. from the death of Jesus and his resurrection – which is disputed in Corinth – Paul concludes in 15.12–19 the universal raising from the dead. He understands Christ's resurrection not as the unique fate of a cult-hero, Christ, who will allow his followers to participate in some way in his risen life,

---

Lindemann, *Korintherbrief*, 256ff.

69. Here see the clear remarks in Lindemann, *Korintherbrief*, 252f. – Cf. *supra* on 10.14ff. (koinōnia tou sōmatos tou Christou).

70. Observe also the eschatological argument in vv. 29–32.

71. Cf. on this Lindemann, *Korintherbrief*, 297ff.

72. Lindemann, *Korintherbrief*, 299.

73. V. *supra* on the relevant chapters.

74. On the original form of the confession, which is probably contained in vv. 3b–5a, cf. Lindemann, *Korintherbrief*, 328–30.

but as the universal event which – analogous to the creation of Adam – initiates the Last Days for mankind: vv. 20–28. The *first* argumentative stress clearly lies on the 'all' in 15.22.[75] In Paul's view Christ is not a hero of a group but an apocalyptic ruler of the world who brings the whole of creation back to life (5.26 the destruction of death) before he gives his rule back to God. Here Paul combines the apocalyptic ideas of a ruler at the end of time and the general resurrection of the dead in the Last Days.

In 15.29–34 he adds personal arguments: the baptism on behalf of the dead in Corinth and his own constant danger of death only make sense if the dead are raised.

If verses 1–34 were concerned with the *fact* of the resurrection, verses 35–49 ask about the '*how*': 'Is a bodily resurrection conceivable or believable?'[76] The *second* accent in the argument is on the resurrection of the body. Paul argues along the lines of an analogy with the Creation (vv. 36–41) on the resurrection of the dead (vv. 42–49) whereby, in spite of the continuity in principle between Creation and New Creation – which guarantees the identity of the sōmata – he establishes a discontinuity between the creaturely, corporeal-physical-earthly body and the spiritual-heavenly body as also applies for Jesus Christ.

Paul closes the treatise with an apocalyptic revelation passage (vv. 50–55) which once again concentrates his argument, gives it full authority and directs it to the circle of addressees ('we'): pantes de allagēsometha. For Paul and the church it holds good that before or after their physical death they 'will be changed' into imperishability and immortality.[77]

A short seventh part deals with the topic of the collection (logeia) with which Paul has been concerned since the council of Jerusalem (Acts 15; Gal. 2.10) and his plans for journeys connected with this.

The theme of the collection is once again opened with peri de (16.1). Paul appeals for individual savings and intends to have the total amount on his next visit either sent to the Christian community in Jerusalem or to accompany it himself[78] – which is what actually happened. A final peri de applies to Apollos (v. 12) upon whose visit in Corinth Paul has no influence. Verses 13–18 contain topical and current exhortations. Verses 19 and 20 contain greetings from the Christians in the province of 'Asia', 21 Paul's personally written greeting, 22 a topical curse, 23, in antithesis to this, a blessing, and in 24 Paul closes the epistle 'with a reference to his agapē for the addressees for which there is no parallel in the entire Corpus Paulinum'.[79]

---

75. In contrast to this, Lindemann, *Korintherbrief*, 339 assumes the accent upon the dead.

76. To what extent Paul is here opposing different ideas in the Corinthian group cannot be inferred from the text since Paul does not return to the opinion of the tines. Whether Lindemann (*Korintherbrief*, 372f.) gives an accurate description of the Corinthian group when he calls them 'spiritual enthusiasts' (373) can remain open.

77. Lindemann, *Korintherbrief*, 363, rightly points out that here Paul (speaks) 'with emphasis of himself and the addressees, without any reference (positive or negative) to other people'.

78. On the historical details cf. Lindemann, *Korintherbrief*, 374ff.

79. Lindemann, *Korintherbrief*, 389.

1 Corinthians

Exegetical Problems
The first letter to the Corinthians contains numerous exegetical problems, which have led to various attempts at solution. I specify some prominent examples in what follows.[80]

I begin with two general problems.

1. *The literary unity* has been challenged since J. Weiss. The foundations for this are the variety of topics and new beginnings together with the reference to an earlier letter. G. Sellin submitted a hypothesis of division which has attracted much attention. He reconstructs three letters: A, the earlier letter; B, the answering letter; and C, a further letter.[81] Currently Schnelle, Lindemann, Schrage, Mitchell, Thiselton, Fitzmyer et al. opt for the unity of the epistle based on observations of method, content and rhetoric. The model of differentiated levels of communication submitted above[82] supports this thesis of unity.

2. The *religious profile of the Corinthian church* is composed of varying and in part contradictory aspects:[83] spiritual enthusiasm, sexual asceticism, gnōsis, ecstatic glossolalia, casual behaviour of women in the service of worship. Alongside these there are aspects of sexual carefreeness (ch. 5) and a careless, provocative contact with meals of sacrificial meat and also with the Lord's Supper. In addition there is the rejection of the resurrection of the dead by 'some'. From this some exegetes develop a religio-historical profile. Schmithals speaks of Christian Gnostics,[84] Sellin of Alexandrian Jewish Wisdom Theology.[85] Schnelle pleads for an 'endogenous development in Corinth', the basis of which is 'a way of thinking oriented on the sacraments [baptism and the Lord's Supper]'[86] which is close to that of the Mystery religions.

There follow selected individual problems:

3. the *factions* in Corinth (1.12)[87]
4. the religio-historical location of sophia in 1.18 – 2.16 and 3.18ff.[88]

---

80. Most of the problems have already been mentioned in the course of this account. Here I arrange them once more schematically and refer to further literature.
81. 'Earlier letter' A: 11.2–34; 5.1–8; 6.12–20; 9.24 – 10.22; 6.1–11; 'Answering letter' B: 5.9–13; 7.1 – 9.23; 10.23 – 11.1; chs 12–16 without 14.33b–36; C: chapters 1–4; Cf. G. Sellin (1987), 'Hauptprobleme des Ersten Korintherbriefes', *ANRW II* 25.4, 2940–3044: 2996–3023. As introduction to the hypotheses of division, Lindemann, *Korintherbrief*, 3–6.
82. Cf. above 1.6.1 Communication.
83. Cf. Sellin, *Hauptprobleme*, 3016ff.
84. W. Schmithals (1971), *Gnosticism in Corinth*, Abington Press: Nashville, Ten. Cf. in general Schnelle, *Einleitung*, 66–70.
85. G. Sellin (1986), *Der Streit um die Auferstehung der Toten* (FRLANT 138), Göttingen.
86. Schnelle, *Einleitung*, 67–68 with n. 204.
87. Cf. Lindemann, *Korintherbrief*, 39–41.
88. Ibid. 92f.

5. the case of an extraordinary *sexual transgression* in 5.1–5[89]
6. the position of *slaves* in a socio-historical respect[90]
7. the *Lord's Supper* among the Corinthians and from Paul's perspective[91]
8. the significance of Paul's instructions for the manner of praying of the women in 11.1–16[92] (veil or particular *hairstyle*)
9. the authenticity of the *command for silence* given to the women in 14.34f.[93]
10. the *tradition of the* euangelion (problems of the reconstruction) in 15.2b–5.[94]

The problems of the chapter on resurrection have already been discussed in the exegetical analysis.

4
Problems of Interpretation

The Pauline letters are not theological compendia which are only *then* sufficiently interpreted when one has described their construction, thematic and statements. They are – and here there is agreement – writings that are related to the situation and to the addressees. This is particularly true of the first letter to the Corinthians, the content of which is consistently determined by the situation of the church in Corinth. This relation to the situation is the key to the interpretation of the document but at the same time it also represents the main problem for an appropriate interpretation. For the situation in Corinth can only be reconstructed – if at all – from the letter that should then explain it!

The following models of interpretation[95] attempt in varying ways to handle this hermeneutically circular problem:

1. the *literary-critical* interpretation, which resolves the uncertainties in the reconstruction of what took place between the apostle and congregation by reconstructing different letters
2. the *religio-historical* interpretation, which wants to explain the religious ideas of the Corinthian community and its groups (schismata) from the world of Hellenistic Roman religion and the blending of this with Paul's missionary preaching
3. the *socio-historical* interpretation, which derives the different viewpoints of the Corinthians and Paul from their social environment,[96] their sociological structures (religious associations), and the common cultural values and

---

89. Ibid. 123f.
90. Ibid. 174f.
91. Ibid. 252f. and 256–8.
92. Ibid. 238–47 (detailed exegetical analysis).
93. Ibid. 319–21 (question of a gloss).
94. Ibid. 328–30.
95. In the commentaries several models are brought into play simultaneously. Here I give a simplified representation of ideal types.
96. See W. A. Meeks (1983), *The Social World of the Apostle Paul*. New Haven: Yale University Press.

concepts that they share with their pagan environment, especially concerning the concept of body and of honour and shame[97]
4. the *scientific-communicative* interpretation, which understands Paul's epistle as an expression of the specific situation of the apostle's communication with the church he founded
5. the *rhetorical* interpretation, which reads the letter as a literary instrument by means of which Paul advises the Corinthian ekklēsia.[98]

This contribution takes account particularly of the communicative and rhetorical elements in the letter,[99] and in its analysis comes in addition to the evaluation of the theological statements[100] and the differentiated pragmatics of the text. Such a *diversified method of interpretation* does most justice to the requirements of this great letter to an Early Christian community.

5
Evaluation

The first letter to the Corinthians shows Paul's communicative, rhetorical, argumentative, community-guiding, paraenetic and educational as well as specifically theological abilities in its co-operation and relation to a group of addressees who are extremely close to him. The letter is evidence of the combination of a treatment of questions – related to the situation but also containing a personal emotional element – which have arisen in the everyday life of the Corinthian missionary church with basic theological considerations which Paul first expresses conceptually and in literary form and into the evolution of which the letter provides an insight. Paul admonishes and instructs the church in Corinth on the basis of what the community has heard about the death and resurrection of Jesus and about the Lord's Supper, the tradition that he himself received and passed on to the church in Corinth. He interprets baptism and develops his ethical reflections on the basis of words of the Lord, general customs in the communities, his own experience, insight and lifestyle. He corrects convictions, behaviour and customs of the Corinthians, sometimes brusquely, apodictically and in a restrictive way, sometimes in a subtly differentiated manner and relatively liberally.

To Paul the church appears as a strong, growing community, which, however, tends to form groups. Its richness of spiritual gifts characterizes and distinguishes but also endangers it.

As he tackles particular defects (chs 1–6) and questions posed by the

---

97. See D. B. Martin (1995), *The Corinthian Body*. New Haven: Yale University Press. The commentary of A. C. Thiselton stresses these concepts and makes them the basis of his interpretation (40–1).

98. M. M. Mitchell (1992), *Paul and the Rhetoric of Reconcialiation: An Exegetical Investigation of the Language and Composition of 1 Corinthians*. Tübingen: Mohr, and Louisville: Westminster/Knox.

99. See the commentary of A. C. Thiselton (41–52).

100. See the commentary of J. A. Fitzmyer (69–92).

congregation (7–14) as well as the idiosyncratic opinion of one group on the resurrection (15), Paul develops certain theological insights: the significance of the *body of Christ and their own body* for the present and future of Christians, the necessity of a *Christian ethos*, which facilitates questions of gender, social co-existence in the church, the form of common worship and discriminating dealings with the – numerically overwhelming – non-Christians without damaging their own Christian identity. He describes the Christian ethos in connection with the spiritual gifts as agapē. Agapē forms the *one* pole of Christian existence, the *other* Paul sees in the eschatological detachment from the world which corresponds to the world's *situation in the Last Days* which he describes in chapter 7: ho kairos synestalmenos estin (7.29: the appointed time has drawn closer) and paragei gar to schēma tou kosmou toutou (7.31: for the form of this world is passing away). Consequently the Christians' *faith* and *hope* are directed not to this life but to the future life in the form of immortality (15.35–49).

References

Commentaries

H. Conzelmann (²1981), *Der erste Brief an die Korinther. Kritisch-Exegetischer Kommentar zum Neuen Testament 5*. Göttingen: Vandenhoek & Ruprecht.

J. A. Fitzmyer (2008), *First Corinthians. The Anchor Yale Bible 32*. New Haven, CT and London: Yale University Press.

R. A. Horsley (1998), *1 Corinthians. Abingdon New Testament Commentary 7*, Nashville, TN: Abingdon Press.

A. Lindemann (2001), *Der Erste Korintherbrief. Handbuch zum Neuen Testament 9*. Tübingen: Mohr.

W. Schrage (1991.1995.1999.2001), *Der erste Brief an die Korinther. Evangelisch Katholischer Kommentar zum Neuen Testament 7/1-4*. Neukirchen-Vluyn: Neukirchener Verlag.

A. C. Thiselton (2000), *The First Epistle to the Corinthians. A Commentary on the Greek Text. The New International Greek New Testament Commentary*. Grand Rapids, MI/Cambridge: Eerdmans.

J. Weiß ([1910] 1977), *Der Erste Korintherbrief. Kritisch-Exegetischer Kommentar zum Neuen Testament 5*. Göttingen: Vandenhoek & Ruprecht.

B. Witherington III (1995), *Conflict and community in Corinth. A social-rhetorical commentary on 1 and 2 Corinthians*. Grand Rapids, MI: Eerdmans.

Monographs

H.-J. Klauck (2006), *Ancient Letter Writing and the New Testament: A Guide to Context and Exegesis*, with the collaboration of Daniel W. Bailey, Waco, TX: Baylor: University Press.

D. B. Martin (1995), *The Corinthian Body*. New Haven, CT: Yale University Press.

W. Schmithals (1971), *Gnosticism in Corinth*. Nashville, TN: Abingdon Press.

U. Schnelle (2005), *Apostle Paul. His Life and Theology*. Grand Rapids, MI: Baker Academic.

Essays and Encyclopedia Articles

H. D. Betz and M. M. Mitchell (1992), 'Article: Corinthians, First Epistle to the', *ABD I*, 1139–48.

M. M. Mitchell (2001), 'Article: Corinthians', *RPP* 3, (Clu–Deu), 489–494.

Chapter 11

2 Corinthians

Eve-Marie Becker

Table 11.1

Sender	Paul (1.1; 13.10) Co-sender: Timothy (1.1)			
Addressees	Church in Corinth Christians in Achaia			
Situation of origin	Continuation of Paul's written communication with the church in Corinth during his absence			
Occasion of writing	A disruption of Paul's relationship to the Corinthian congregation			
Place of writing	Macedonia (*not named explicitly*)			
Date	Terminus post quem: 55 CE (1 Corinthians) Terminus ante quem: 56/57 CE (Paul's third visit to Corinth)			
Opposition	*Presumably*: itinerant Christian preachers of Jewish-Hellenistic origin			
Themes	Prehistory, apostolicity, relationship of Paul to the Corinthian church, eschatology, the collection, Paul's life as an apostle			
Broad division	Opening of the letter	1.1, 2		*Epistolary prescript*
			1.3–11	Eulogy and opening
	Body of the letter	1.12 – 13.10	1.12–7.4	*Apologia* and *narratio*
			7.5–16	Explanation of the defence
			8.1–24	'Collection letter' (1)
			9.1–15	'Collection letter' (2)
			10–13.10	*Apologia* for Paul's ministry and person
Conclusion of the letter	13.11	Concluding *parenesis*		
	13.12	Greetings		
	13.13	*Epistolary eschatocol*		

1
Approaching the Text

The Content and Transmission of the Text

The 'canonical' 2 Corinthians in the Nestle text contains approximately 4,448 words[1] and takes up *c*.20 pages. Consequently it represents the third longest of Paul's epistles. In spite of insignificant variations in the *superscriptiones* (1 Cor. 1.1: Paul and Sosthenes; 2 Cor. 1.1: Paul and Timothy) and in the *adscriptiones* (1 Cor. 1.2: 'the church of God at Corinth'; 2 Cor. 1.1: 'the church of God at Corinth, with all the saints in the whole of Achaia'), 1 and 2 Corinthians are addressed to circles of addressees which are to a large extent identical and represent the oldest and most extensive of the extant early Christian correspondence with churches.

2 Corinthians is first handed down with only minor omissions in ⲣ46 (*c*.200 CE).[2] ⲣ46 is of considerable importance for the earliest evidence *and* transmission of the text of 2 Corinthians, for alongside ⲣ46 Marcion or Tertullian and possibly the canon Muratori represent the earliest *witnesses* for the comprehensive rendition of the canonical 2 Corinthians. Apart from ⲣ46 there are no references to 2 Corinthians in the papyri[3] which date from before the important early church majuscules. What is transmitted in the majuscules up to around the fifth century is the text of 2 Corinthians contained in Sinaiticus (א 01 fourth century), in Vaticanus (B 03, fourth century), in D 06 (sixth century), in Alexandrinus (A 02, fifth century with one large omission), in C 04 (fifth century with various omissions), in I 016 (fifth century; some verses) and in 048 (fifth century in parts: 2 Cor. 4.7–6.8; 8.9–18; 8.21–10.6).

Analysis of the Text

2 Corinthians begins with Paul's naming of himself as author of the letter and of Timothy as co-sender (2 Cor. 1.1). The letter ends with a trinitarian/triadic blessing which is by no means typical of the Pauline epistles (2 Cor. 13.14).[4]

In the text of the letter there are higher-level structural elements. In contrast to the structural elements in 1 Corinthians, they provide, however, formal i.e. epistolary rather than contextual structures.

---

1. Cf. R. Morgenthaler (1958), *Statistik des neutestamentlichen Wortschatzes*. Zürich/Frankfurt, 164.

2. Cf. on the rendition in ⲣ46: K. Junack et al. (eds) (1989), *Das Neue Testament auf Papyrus II. Die paulinischen Briefe Teil 1: Röm., 1 Kor., 2 Kor.* (ANTF 12), Berlin/New York.

3. The only other papyri known to us until now, which hand down parts of 2 Cor., are: ⲣ34 (2 Cor. 5.18ff.; 10.13f.; 11.2ff.*), dated only in the seventh century; ⲣ99 (2 Cor. 1.3–6; 1.6–17; 1.20–24; 2.1–9; 2.9–5.13; 5.13–6.3; 6.3–8.13; 8.14–22; 9.2–11.8; 11.9–23; 11.26–13.11), dated around 400 CE; ⲣ117 (2 Cor. 7.6–8; 7.9–11), dated in the fourth/fifth century; ⲣ124 (2 Cor. 11.1–4; 11.6–9), dated in the sixth century. Cf. Institut für Neutestamentliche Textforschung an der Universität Münster: Continuation of the Manuscript List.

4. For a similar motif cf. at best e.g. Phil. 2.1 (koinōnia pneumatos).

2 Corinthians

Table 11.2

1.3	eulogētos	Eulogy in the opening of the letter
1.8	ou gar thelomen hymas agnoein	'Disclosure' formula
8.1	gnōrizomen de hymin	Opening of the first 'collection letter'
9.1	peri men gar tēs diakonias	Opening of the second 'collection letter'
10.1	autos de egō Paulos parakalō	Opening of the *apologia*

2 Corinthians 8, 9 and 10ff. can be set apart from their immediate contexts by these introductory expressions and possibly understood as independent epistolary unities. 2 Corinthians 1–7 on the other hand can, if we look at their form, represent *at first glance* a textual unity, i.e. one which at least as far as a letter is concerned cannot be further subdivided. In contrast to 1 Corinthians this textual unity is not structured by various formally characteristic thematic prefaces (e.g. peri-phrases) but is formed throughout as an argument of Paul with the Corinthian church and as a reflection of his communicative relationship with the Corinthians. This confrontation, however, is interrupted first on the grammatical-syntactic level of the text:

Table 11.3

2.13	...exēlthon eis Makedonian
2.14	tō de theō charis ...
6.13	...platynthēte kai hymeis
6.14	mē ginesthe heterozygountes apistois ...
7.1	...epitelountes hagiōsynēn en phobō theou
7.2	chōrēsate hēmas ...
7.4	...tē chara epi pasa tē thlipsei hēmōn
7.5	kai gar elthontōn hēmōn eis Makedonian

Secondly, we can suspect different communication situations within 2 Cor. 1–7, as e.g.

| 2.1ff. | ekrina....kai egrapsa touto auto... ek gar pollēs thlipseōs kai synochēs kardias egrapsa |
| 7.9,13 | nyn chairō ... dia touto parakeklēmetha |

The observation of incohesions in form and in language and syntax within the letter as a whole – 2 Cor. 1–13 – and within chapters 1–7 raise doubts about the original unity of the canonical 2 Corinthians and lead to the conjecture that it is a compilation of what were originally several separate epistles.

Structure

The structure of the canonical 2 Corinthians as a complete letter can best be undertaken according to the customary *epistolographic scheme* employed for the subdivision of the Pauline epistles:

Table 11.4

Epistolographic division into three parts		Subdivision Schnelle[5]
Opening of the letter	1.1–11	1.1 – 2.17
Prescript (superscriptio, adscriptio, charis-formula)	1.1,2	1.1,2
Eulogy	1.3–7	1.3–7 *Proemium*
'Disclosure' formula	1.8–11	1.8–2.17 *Epistolary self-testimonial*
Body of the letter	1.12–13.10	3.1–12.13
Close of the letter	13.11–13	12.14–13.13
Closing words	13.11,12	12.14–13.10 *Apostolic parousia* 13.11 *Closing parenesis* 13.12 *Greetings*
Tripartite blessing	13.13	13.13 *Eschatocol*

The attempt to make an *accurate subdivision* of the letter *with regard to its subject matter* mirrors how the whole letter is marked by the reflection of Paul's relationship to the Corinthian church and – apart from the topic of the collection (chs 8 and 9) – how it contains hardly any independent themes or argumentation.

In comparison with other suggestions for subdivision (M. E. Thrall, F. J. Matera), the following *similarities* are broadly apparent: The epistolographic forms of *beginning and closing of the letter* are delimited in like manner. Chapters 8 and 9 are taken as independent sections in the letter. 2 Cor. 10.1ff. marks a new unit of subdivision. 2 Cor. 7.5–16 is assessed as an independent section in the context of the body of the letter which begins in 1.12ff.

Differences arise particularly in the *internal subdivision of 1.12–7.4*: The majority of interpreters (as also Thrall, Matera) separate 2 Cor. 2.13 and 2.14 and consequently make 2.14 begin an independent section of the epistle. My suggestions for subdivision on the other hand take 2 Cor. 1.12–7.4 as a cohesive section of the letter. These suggestions for division – as will be seen later – are closely connected with *Literarkritik*.

Themes

Particularly in comparison with 1 Corinthians the character and theme of 2 Corinthians is clear: 1 Cor. does *not* reveal *one* leading topic but shows '[a]

---

5. U. Schnelle, *History*,[5] 78, combines the delimitation by the formal epistolographic elements with a subdivision of the letter according to its contents.

markedly close connection to the church and the situation there as well as [a] variety of topics mentioned'.[6] 1 Cor. is an expression of Paul's lively discussion of the theological and ethical questions relating to facts and behaviour that have arisen in the Corinthian church.

In 2 Corinthians the *pertinence to the congregation* is intensified particularly by forms of address (e.g. 6.11;[7] 7.2) and in the direct relationship to the apostle Paul himself (e.g. 1.12ff.; 2.1ff. 7.4ff.), i.e. on the one hand to the *person of Paul* (10.10f.; 12.1ff.) and on the other to his *service as apostle* (e.g. 3.1ff.; 4.1ff.; 5.1ff.; 6.1ff.). 2 Corinthians' *relation to the situation* can be seen in the variety of situations of conflict and communication. Instead of a multitude of theological and ethical topics as in 1 Cor., in 2 Cor. we encounter *numerous diverse 'approaches'* to Paul's apologetic self-defence and to the reflection of his relationship to the Corinthian church. The (apostolic-) theological (e.g. 4.1ff.), Christological (e.g. 5.20f.), anthropological (e.g. 4.7ff.) or eschatological (e.g. 5.1–10) statements arise essentially from the meta-communicative coherence of the argumentation.

Since 2 Cor., or the individual letters contained in 2 Cor., tend to be dated later than 1 Cor., the difference in themes between the two letters provides information on the *history and development of the Corinthian correspondence* and Paul's relationship to the Corinthian community. While 1 Cor. is characterized by theological and ethical questions and arguments related to actual situations (e.g. legal issues: 1 Cor. 6; meat sacrificed to idols: 1 Cor. 8; resurrection: 1 Cor. 15), it is Paul's communication with the Corinthians itself – which has been disrupted and endangered on the one hand by a distressing visit to Corinth (2 Cor. 2) and on the other hand by the intrusion and activity of hostile missionaries and so called 'super-(lative) apostles' (2 Cor. 11) – that becomes the central theme of 2 Cor.: 'The letter we call 2 Corinthians abounds with fascinating insights into the activity and mind of the Apostle Paul'.[8]

The topic common to 1 and 2 Corinthians is made up of two aspects: (1) The discussion of the function of the apostleship and the lifestyle of the apostle (1 Cor. 9; e.g. 2 Cor. 11.5ff.); (2) the advance notice of the collection for the early Christian community in Jerusalem (1 Cor. 16.1ff.) which is again taken up by the administrative writing(s) on the request for and implementation of the collection in 2 Cor. 8 and 9.

Semantic Fields

The semantic fields or the semantic inventory of the text of 2 Corinthians stem predominantly from the area of 'boasting', 'glorifying' and 'commending'. Moreover they are connected to *emotional* attitudes, *experiences of mission and journeying*, the definition of the apostolic and in particular of the Pauline *self-understanding* as well as the reflection of verbal and written *communication*.

---

6. Described in this way by O. Wischmeyer in Chapter 10 in this volume.
7. The form of address Korinthioi in 2 Cor. 6.11 is the only such emphatic vocative in the authentic Pauline letters apart from the invective ō anoētai Galatai (Gal. 3.1).
8. H. D. Betz, 'Article: Corinthians', 1148.

Moreover in chapters 8 and 9 we find a *special vocabulary* (cf. also 1 Cor. 16.1ff.; Rom. 15.25ff.) connected to the request for contributions to the collection.

Table 11.5

Semantic fields	Lexemes	Examples
Boasting/glorifying/ commending etc.	kauch-	1.12–14; 5.12; 10.8ff.; 11.10ff.; 12.1ff.
	synistēmi	3.1; 4.2; 6.4; 7.11; 10.12ff.
Emotional attitudes/ experiences negative	lyp-, thlipsis, dakryon metamelomai	2.1ff.; 6.11ff.; 7.2ff.
positive	chairō, chara, agapē parakalō	1.3ff.; 7.7ff.; 13.9ff.
Experiences of mission and journeying Journeys and activity	erchomai, Asia, Makedonia, Ioudaia Trōas	1.8f.; 1.15ff.; 2.12f. 7.5ff.
Peristases	en plēgais, en phylakais	6.4ff.; 11.23ff.
Plans for journeys and visits		12.14ff.
Apostolic ministry	synerg-, diak-, kēryg- presbeuomen (pseud)apostol-	1.19,24; 3.3ff.; 4.1ff.; 5.11ff.; 6.1ff.; 10.12ff.; 11.4ff.
The Pauline self- understanding	asthen-, sperma Abraam apokal-, skolops	10.10f.; 11.22; 12.1ff.
Reflection on verbal and written communication	laleō, graphō, ana/ epiginōskō apōn, parōn	1.12–14; 2.3ff.; 3.1–3; 6.11ff.; 7.8ff.; 10.9–11; 13.10
Donation for the collection	ptōcheia, ploutos, periss-, diakonia, eulogia dotēs, leitourgia.	Chs 8–9.

The question as to whether the frequency of the lexemes belonging to these semantic fields, their semantics and function remain constant or change in the different sections of the letter is related to the question of the original unity of 2 Cor. since it must be examined whether the usage of the vocabulary allows us to conclude that different contexts exist for the various sections. Hence the analysis of the semantic fields proves to be a considerable *factor in arguments for the cohesion or lack of cohesion when assessing the literary unity of the canonical 2 Cor.*

From the reflection on the communicative relationship with the Corinthian community, significant theological statements arise – described below as 'meta-communicative surplus' – e.g. on the apostolic ministry. Thereby they develop their own particular theological dynamics which they base on striking semantic antitheses. An example of this is 2 Cor. 3.4–18:

Table 11.6
Connection to the theme of recommendation (2.14ff.; 3.1ff.) and the thesis:
The hikanotēs of the apostle comes from God

diakonoi kainēs diathēkēs	↔	'old covenant'
↓		↓
pneuma	↔	gramma
↓		↓
zōopoiei	↔	apoktennei
↓		↓
diakonia tou pneumatos	↔	diakonia tou thanatou
↓		↓
diakonia tēs dikaiosynēs	↔	diakonia tēs katakriseōs
↓		↓
to menon en doxē	↔	to katargoumenon dia doxēs
↓		↓
anakekalymmenō prosōpō	↔	kalymma epi tēn kardian

Closing reason:
ho de kyrios to pneuma estin ou de pneuma kyriou, eleutheria

Communication and Rhetoric
Communication

2 Corinthians is to a far greater extent than 1 Corinthians a communicative writing. As has already been emphasized on several occasions Paul is at pains to determine his relationship as an apostle *and* as a person to the Christian congregation in view of the distressing incidents in Corinth (ch. 2) and the confrontation with hostile apostles (ch. 11). This determination of relationship falls into the area of *meta-communication*. Thus we can differentiate three substantial levels of communication in 2 Cor.: (1) the level of written communication which takes the place of a personal visit; (2) the level of meta-communication where Paul explicitly reflects upon the relationship with the church at Corinth; (3) the level of meta-communicative surplus on which Paul implements and interprets the meta-communication with theological content.

1. The level of *written communication* is extremely limited in 2 Corinthians: Paul simply reports on the experiences in his missionary activity and informs the Corinthians of his frustrated or future plans for travelling.

Table 11.7

1.8ff.; 2.12ff.; 7.5ff.	Experiences from his missionary/church-guiding activity
1.15ff.	Frustrated/altered plans for a journey
12.14; 13.1ff.	Plans for future journeys

2. The level of *meta-communication* makes up the most extensive textual level in 2 Corinthians. It has at least three central aspects: It contains reflections on the 'level of relationship' between Paul and the Corinthians, observations on the 'apostolic ministry and on the person of Paul himself' and 'epistolary-hermeneutically relevant statements' on the function of letter-writing.

Table 11.8

	Level of relationship: Paul – the Corinthian community:
2.1ff.	Recognition of Paul's love for the Corinthians
6.11ff.; 7.2ff.	Emotional appeal to the congregation at Corinth
8.8	Paul gives no epitagē
	Apostolic ministry:
2.14ff.	eilikrineia of the service of an apostle
4.1ff.	Function of the office of apostle
6.1ff.	Servant of God
	Person of Paul:
10.9ff.	Paul assesses letters and personal activity as of equal importance
11.7f.	Paul acted in Corinth without receiving any financial support
11.5ff.	Paul stands in conflict with so-called 'super-apostles'
11.22	Paul as an Israelite and descendant of Abraham
12.1ff.	Paul's experience of revelation.
	Epistolary-hermeneutic reflections:
1.12–14	The interdependence of writing and understanding
2.1ff.; 9f.	Writing to avoid a distressing visit and to discover if they have been reliable
3.1ff.	The function of letters of commendation
7.8f.	Letter-writing leads to regret
10.9ff.	The letters are put on the same level as the apostolic activity

3. Out of the meta-communication there emerges a *meta-communicative surplus* on a third textual level.[9] In the course of meta-communicative reflections Paul formulates theological components which on the one hand serve to support the argument of the meta-communicative statements and on the other lead to the formulation of independent theological statements. The

---

9. On the concept cf. E.-M. Becker, *Letter Hermeneutics*, e.g. 84–6. In this book I have offered a more comprehensive analysis of 2 Cor. where questions of *Literarkritik* and the reconstruction of the letter's prehistory are interconnected with the analysis of communication and Paul's epistolary hermeneutics.

following representation of the theological aspects of meta-communicative surplus (marked in italics) takes up the three aspects of meta-communication mentioned above:

Table 11.9

	Level of relationship: Paul – the Corinthian congregation
6.11ff.; 6.14ff.; 7.1ff.	Emotional appeal to the Corinthian congregation [*with reference to a double comparison of righteousness and iniquity*]
8.8ff.	Paul does not give orders; *it is a matter of recognizing the mercy of Christ*
	Apostolic office:
4.1–6; 4.7ff.; 5.1ff.	the function of the apostolic office *with reference to the context of the proclamation, the pressure of Christian existence and its eschatological perspective*
	Paul's person:
11.5ff., 12ff.	Paul stands in conflict with so-called 'super-apostles', *who are described as servants of Satan*
12.1–10	Paul's experience of revelation *leads into a saying of the Lord*
	Epistolary-hermeneutic considerations:
1.12–14	he interdependence of writing and understanding *with an eschatological outlook*
2.5–11	Writing to avoid a distressing visit and to know that they have proved themselves *with a look at the forgiveness of Christ and the work of Satan*
3.1ff.; 4ff.	The function of letters of recommendation *looking at the difference between 'stony' and 'fleshly' and the 'new covenant' of the Spirit*
7.8ff.	Letter-writing leads to regret *and to a sadness according to the will of God*
10.9ff.; 12ff.	The letters are put on the same level as the apostolic work, *the commendation comes from the* kyrios

In 1 Corinthians the level that deals with theological and ethical questions is dominant in the communication with the Corinthians: a large part of the theological and ethical doctrinal statements and admonitions take place on the level of direct communication in the letter.[10] At the same time, in 1 Corinthians there are also aspects of meta-communication and meta-communicative surplus which arise from or enter into meta-communicative connections (cf. 1 Cor. 8.1–6). 2 Corinthians on the other hand is dominated by the meta-communicative character of Paul's argument with the Corinthian community and the hostile missionaries and apostles active there.

Hence the history of Paul's communication with the Corinthian community in the two letters to the Corinthians reveals a development from a confrontation which was predominantly pertinent (theological and ethical instruction and

---

10. Wischmeyer, Chapter 10, this volume speaks here of a level of communication and of trans-communication/theology.

admonition) in 1 Cor. to a defence of Paul as an apostle and as a person and to an increasing determination of his relationship to the church at Corinth.

Rhetoric

In recent years, exegetes have analysed 2 Corinthians more intensively from the aspect of rhetoric. Rhetorical analyses of the text investigate rhetorical strategies.[11] Rhetorical analysis has either suggested a rhetorical pattern for the letter as a whole and stressed the unity of 2 Cor.,[12] or it has been implemented to support the perception of 2 Cor. as a collection of what were originally separate letters: then individual rhetorical analyses are advocated, particularly for 2 Cor. 8 and 9, the two writings about the collection that can be classified among Paul's 'administrative correspondence' (H. D. Betz; cf. similarly M. E. Thrall):[13]

Table 11.10

2 Cor. 8	Betz	Thrall
8.1–5	*Exordium*/Introduction	*Exordium*
8.6	*Narratio*/Statement of facts	*Narratio*
8.7,8	*Propositio*/Proposition	*Propositio*
8.9–15	*Probatio*/Proofs	*Probatio*
8.16–23	Legal section; Commendation and authorization of the envoys	
8.16–22	The commendations	Commendation of the envoys
8.23	The authorizations	Their authorization
8.24	*Peroratio*	*Peroratio*
2 Cor. 9	Betz	Thrall
9.1,2	*Exordium*/Introduction	*Exordium*
9.3–5a	*Narratio*/Statement of facts	*Narratio*
9.5bc	*Propositio*/Proposition	*Propositio*
9.6–14	*Probatio*/Proofs	*Probatio*
	Peroratio/Peroration	*Peroratio*

11. Cf. e.g. L. L. Welborn (2001), 'Paul's appeal to the emotions in 2 Corinthians 1.1–2.13; 7.5–16', *JSNT* 82, 31–60.

12. Thus e.g. B. Witherington (1995), *Conflict & Community in Corinth. A Socio-Rhetorical Commentary on 1 and 2 Corinthians*, Grand Rapids (Mi), particularly 333; J. D. H. Amador (2000), 'Revisiting 2 Corinthians. Rhetoric and the Case for Unity', *NTS* 46, 92–111; F. M. Young and D. F. Ford (1987), *Meaning and Truth in 2 Corinthians*, Grand Rapids, esp. 44. In regard to more general questions: I. H. Jones (2008), 'Rhetorical Criticism and the Unity of 2 Corinthians. One "Epilogue" or More?', *NTS* 54, 496–524.

13. Cf. H. D. Betz, *2 Corinthians 8 and 9*, e.g. 139; M. E. Thrall, *Second Epistle*, 37 and 40.

2
The Genesis of the Text

Prehistory

The possibly complicated (history of the) genesis of 2 Corinthians raises in a special way the question of the prehistory of the letter. In this connection the chronology of the Pauline communication with the church at Corinth must be presented, at least in the period of time from the writing of 1 Cor. to the genesis of 2 Cor. In doing this we must take into consideration the hypotheses for the reconstruction of the Corinthian correspondence discussed below which already have implications for the structuring of the canonical 2 Cor.

First I take up two prominent suggestions discussed in research (M. E. Thrall; G. Bornkamm) and follow them with a reconstruction of my own:

Reconstruction of the chronology of the events after the writing of 1 Cor. (according to M. E. Thrall):[14]

Table 11.11

Year/Date	Events	Letters
April 55	1 Cor. sent	1 Cor.
June 55	*Interim visit*: Paul returns to Ephesus	
July/August 55	Drafting of the tearful letter, Paul goes to Macedonia	not preserved
Aug./Sept. 55	Titus returns with good news and meets Paul	
March 56	*Letter* and sending of Titus	2 Cor. 1–8
June/July 56	'Collection letter'	2 Cor. 9
July/August 56	News reaches Paul in	Macedonia
Aug./Sept. 56	*Letter*	2 Cor. 10–13
Sept./Oct. 56	Paul travels to Corinth and spends the winter 56/57 there.	

---

14. Cf. here Thrall, *Second Epistle*, 77.

Reconstruction of the chronology of 2 Cor. (according to G. Bornkamm):[15]

Table 11.12

Events	Letters/Parts of letters
Apologia Drawn up in Ephesus before the *interim visit* and incident in Corinth	2 Cor. 2.14–6.13; 7.2–4
Excerpts from the *tearful letter* in Ephesus Return of Titus from Corinth with fresh news	2 Cor. 10–13
Placatory letter in Macedonia	2 Cor. 1.1–2.13; 7.5–8.24
'Collection letter' to the churches in Achaia	2 Cor. 9

Reconstruction of the chronology of the events between 1 and 2 Cor. (according to E.-M. Becker):[16]

Table 11.13

Year/Date	Events	Letters/Verification
54/55	Writing of 1 Cor. from Ephesus	**1 Cor.**; 1 Cor. 16.8
	Interim visit to Corinth and distress 'Tearful letter'	2 Cor. 2.1ff. **2 Cor. 1.1–7.4**; 2 Cor. 2.3f.; 8f.
	Fresh news brought by Titus	2 Cor. 7.6f.
	A letter by Paul	**2 Cor. 7.5–16**; 2 Cor. 7.8f.; 12f.
	'Collection letters'	**2 Cor. 8–9**
	Verbal attacks on Paul in Corinth	2 Cor. 10.10; 11.16
	Paul's final letter	**2 Cor. 10–13**
At the latest winter 56/57	Planning and execution of the third visit	2 Cor. 12.14; 13.1

The suggestions reveal that the reconstruction of the chronology of the events between the writing of 1 and 2 Corinthians is closely connected to *Literarkritik*. In particular the following evaluations have a decisive effect upon the reconstruction of the chronology *and* on the written correspondence:

- The approximate dating of the *interim visit* with the incident in Corinth: Does this interim visit take place before the writing of the parts of the letter

---

15. Cf. here G. Bornkamm, *Vorgeschichte*, 162ff.
16. Cf. here Becker, *Letter Hermeneutics*, 66.

of 2 Cor. (Thrall; E.-M. Becker), or have parts of 2 Cor. already been written before Paul's *interim visit* in Corinth (Bornkamm)?
- The identification of the situation behind *2 Cor. 1–7*: Do chapters 1–7 reflect a largely homogeneous situation of writing (Thrall) or can the changes of mood be traced back to situations of its composition that were inevitably different (Bornkamm; E.-M. Becker) and, if so, where can these changes be established in the text of the letter (between 2.13 and 2.14, 7.4 and 7.5: Bornkamm; only between 7.4 and 7.5: E.-M. Becker)?
- The identification and reconstruction of the so-called *tearful letter* (2 Cor. 2.3f.): Has the tearful letter been lost (Thrall) or is it a part of the canonical 2 Cor. (chs 10–13: Bornkamm; 2 Cor. 1.1–7.4: E.-M. Becker)?
- The classification of *chs 8–9*: Are the 'collection letters' independent components of the Corinthian correspondence (E.-M. Becker; in part, Thrall; as a whole, Betz)[17] or were they written and sent together with a complete letter or with partial letters (Bornkamm; in part, Thrall)?
- The diverse suggestions are in agreement that the *third visit to Corinth* which Paul announced in 2 Cor. 12.14ff. and 13.1ff. is not documented in the Corinthian correspondence itself (cf. however Rom. 15.26ff. as a reference to the receipt of the collection from Macedonia and Achaia).

Author, Addressees and Historical Situation
The *Pauline authorship* of the canonical 2 Cor. (cf. 1.1; 13.10) as a whole is currently not disputed. As co-sender Paul names Timothy (1.1). To this extent we may suspect *co-authorship* in the drafting of the letter or at least of individual parts of the letter. *2 Cor 6.14–7.1* is considered by some researchers as a post-Pauline interpolation, i.e. as an editorial insertion (e.g. H.-J. Klauck; U. Schnelle).[18]

The presupposed target group named in the *adscriptio* in 2 Cor. 1.1 is largely identical with that presupposed in 1 Cor. 1.2. The differences in the details of the two *adscriptiones*:

---

17. Cf. here Betz, 'Article: Corinthians', 1150; *id.*, '2 Corinthians 8 and 9'. Similar to this: E. Gräßer (2002), *Der zweite Brief an die Korinther. Kapitel 1,1–7,16* (ÖTK 8/1), Gütersloh, 34f.
18. Cf. H.-J.Klauck (³1994), *2 Korintherbrief* (NEB 8), Würzburg, 8; Schnelle, *Einleitung*,⁵ 101f. Cf. also: S. J. Hultgren (2003), '2 Cor. 6.14–7.1 and Rev. 21.3–8. Evidence for the Ephesian redaction of 2 Corinthians', *NTS* 49, 39–56. Differently: M. D. Goulder (1994), '2 Cor. 6:14–7:1 as an Integral Part of 2 Corinthians', *NT* 36, 47–57.

Table 11.14

1 Cor. 1.2	2 Cor. 1.1
...tē ekklēsia tou theou tē ousē en Korinthō hēgiasmenois en Christō Iēsou, klētois hagiois, syn pasin tois epikaloumenois to onoma tou kyriou hēmōn Iēsou Christou en panti topō autōn kai hēmōn	... tē ekklēsia tou theou tē ousē en Korinthō
	syn tois hagiois pasin tois ousin en holē tē Achaia

are, however, interpreted and evaluated differently:

- H.-J. Klauck explains the abbreviated address to the Corinthian church in 2 Cor. 1.1 in comparison with 1 Cor. 1.2 as due to the less ecclesiologically oriented nature of 2 Cor. as a whole.[19]
- H. Windisch understands the *extension of the target group* in 2 Cor. 1 beyond Corinth to Achaia as evidence that 2 Corinthians – in like manner to Galatians – was conceived as a circular letter.[20] M. E. Thrall on the other hand thinks that the extension of the adscription in 2 Cor. 1 points to a larger audience of Christians in the vicinity of Corinth who are in contact with the Corinthian community.[21] H. D. Betz sees in the double naming of addressees in 2 Cor. 1.1 an indication that 2 Cor. 9 represents a separate 'collection letter' directed especially to Achaia.[22]

On the *structure and significance of the Corinthian church*: Paul himself founded the church at Corinth (Acts 18.1ff.) around 50 CE[23] on his second missionary journey (Acts 15ff.) which took him to Europe (Acts 16.9) – first to Macedonia (Philippi, Thessalonica) then by way of Athens (Acts 17.15ff.) to the Peloponnese. The stay in Corinth during which the founding took place lasted around a year and a half.

Corinth[24] – founded anew in 44 BCE by Caesar as a civilian Roman colony (*Colonia Laus Iulia Corinthus*) and settled with freedmen and veterans, after 27 BCE capital of the province of Achaia and seat of a proconsul – advanced in

19. Cf. H.-J.Klauck, *Korintherbrief* (n.18), 17.
20. Cf. H. Windisch, *Korintherbrief*, 35.
21. Cf. Thrall, *Second Epistle*, 88.
22. Cf. Betz, *2 Corinthians 8 and 9*.
23. The dating of this stay in Corinth can be made relatively precisely from the so-called Gallio Inscription found at Delphi – in Acts 18.12 reference is made to Gallio's proconsulship in Achaia. Cf. as a whole the contribution on the life of Paul in Chapter 5 of this volume by E. Ebel.
24. On Corinth cf. D.-A. Koch (2005), 'Korinth', in *Neues Testament und Antike Kultur II: Familie, Gesellschaft, Wirtschaft*, Neukirchen-Vluyn, 159–62 (Lit.).

the time of the Empire to be the largest and richest town in Hellas. Two factors in particular – as well as its favourable geographical and geopolitical situation – allowed Corinth to become an important, prosperous town: the erection of monumental buildings in the time of Augustus (31 BCE–14 CE) and Tiberius (14 – 37 CE) and the organization of the Isthmian Games.[25]

Philo (Legatio ad Gaium, 281) reports on a large, lively Jewish community in Corinth in the first century CE. Through the activity of competing judaizing missionaries (2 Cor. 11.22) who had settled in Corinth (2 Cor. 11.20) and whom Paul calls 'super-apostles' (2 Cor. 11.5) the Christian community in Corinth, which is actually more Gentile-Christian (cf. esp. 1 Cor. 8) apparently falls into the area of conflict of the Jewish-Christian congregations (cf. also Acts 20.3).

In contrast to these missionaries Paul refuses economic support from the Corinthian community (cf. also Acts 18.2f.) in order on the one hand to be independent and on the other to make clear that, from the inescapability of his calling, he is an apostle of Jesus Christ. And so he works for his living, preaches without remuneration and is merely supported by gifts from the community in Philippi (cf. Phil. 4.10ff.; 2 Cor. 11.7ff.). This causes displeasure since the Corinthians consider their bounden duty to provide (for him) as violated.[26] During his absence in person Paul communicates with the Corinthians by means of letters written in Greek which, although Latin has been the official language in the province since 44 BCE, remains the language of trade and social life. 1 and 2 Corinthians document the history and development of an early Christian Pauline church in the first half of the 50s in the European part of Paul's missionary area.

Date and Place of Writing

In contrast to 1 Corinthians (cf. 16.8: en Ephesō heōs tēs pentēkostēs) in 2 Cor. there are no direct references to the time and place of its writing. The dating of 2 Cor. or the individual letters contained in 2 Cor. can consequently only be done by implication, i.e. on the basis of a linking of *absolute* (cf. the Gallio Inscription and Acts 18) with the *relative Pauline chronology*, including the *reconstruction of the chronology of the Corinthian correspondence* and the statements about *plans for journeys and places of sojourn* which can be ascertained in particular from 2 Cor. As *terminus post quem* for the formation of the parts of letters in 2 Cor. is the writing of 1 Cor. (*c*.55 CE), *terminus ad quem* is Paul's third and final visit to Corinth (at the latest 56/57 CE).

In 1 Cor. 16.5 Paul announces a visit to Corinth after his journey through Macedonia. On the basis of the mention of Macedonia in 2 Cor. 2.13; 7.5 and

---

25. On the significance of Corinth during the Imperial period: 'The temples of the ancient city remained intact; they were, however, enriched in the Roman period by public buildings, new temples and other shrines. The agora was fashioned on the model of a Roman forum and thereby received a monumental appearance while the city as a whole expanded to a great extent', D. I. Pallas, 'Article: Korinth', 746.

26. Cf. on this matter as a whole G. Theissen (1975), 'Legitimation und Lebensunterhalt. Ein Beitrag zur Soziologie urchristlicher Missionare', *NTS* 21, 192–221.

the references to Macedonia in 2 Cor. 8.1; 9.2, the drafting of substantial parts of letters can be presumed to have taken place in *Macedonia*.[27]

Unity and Processes of Editing
The literary unity of 2 Cor. has been controversial for 200 years[28] and has given rise to a multitude of different hypotheses for division up to present-day research. The following observations speak *against* the assertion of the *unity of the letter*[29] and *for* the question of the history of the development of a possible collection of letters:

1. We have positive evidence of the canonical 2 Cor. in a connected form only from towards the end of the second century. Consequently around 150 years of the history of the text and its transmission lie in darkness. Source criticism and the redaction history of the letter might contribute to throwing light on this period.
2. Numerous literary and *situational indications* point to the segmentation of 2 Cor. and lead us to suspect that in 2 Cor. we have a collection of what were originally several separate letters:

- We observe linguistic, semantic and thematic incohesions in chapters 1–7 and 10–13.
- We need to ask: Are 2 Cor. 8 and 9 a duplication or were they originally separate letters about the collection?
- There are various references to several letters to the Corinthians (e.g. 1 Cor. 5.9; 2 Cor. 10.10) so that the existing canonical letters (1 and 2 Cor.) by no means represent the whole correspondence.
- We need to value 2 Cor. 2 and 7 carefully: Do 2 Cor. 2.3ff. and 7.8ff. refer to the same situation of writing, or do they deal with different situations which are possibly related to the so-called 'tearful letter'?
- Literary breaks are assumed between 2 Cor. 2.13 and 2.14 and between 2 Cor. 7.4 and 7.5 which occasionally lead to 7.5 being understood as following after 2.13 (R. Bultmann).
- Does 2 Cor. 6.14–7.1 belong to the original Pauline document, or is it a post-Pauline interpolation?
- These observations lead to 2 Cor. being understood as a compilation of letters and to a search for the *reconstruction of the original form of the text* of the letters contained in 2 Cor.

---

27. So e.g. Thrall, *Second Epistle*, 74f.; F. J. Matera, *II Corinthians*, 20.
28. For a survey of the research cf. R. Bieringer (1994), 'Teilungshypothesen zum 2 Korintherbrief. Ein Forschungsüberblick', in *id.*, with J. Lambrecht (eds), *Studies on 2 Corinthians* (BEThL 62), Leuven, 67–105. To the literary-critical complications in 2 Cor. in general: J. Dunn (1998), *The Pauline Letters: The Cambridge Companion to Biblical Interpretation*, ed. J. Barton, Cambridge (repr. 1999), 276–89, 282.
29. The unity of the letter is accepted by e.g. J. Lambrecht, *Second Corinthians*, 9.

The following models of *Literarkritik* division are the subject of discussion at present:[30]

Table 11.15
Division of the letter into two: e.g. H.-J. Klauck (NEB)[31]

10–13 (tearful letter)	1–9 (conciliatory letter)

In a similar manner (setting apart chs 8–9) but *reversing the classification*: H. Windisch (KEK), M. E. Thrall (ICC)[32]

1–9 [or 1–8] [9]	10–13

More complex composite models: e.g. R. Bultmann (KEK special volume)[33]

2.14–7.4 (without 6.14–7.1); 9; 10–13 (tearful letter)	1.1–2.13; 7.5–16; 8 (conciliatory letter)

G. Bornkamm (similar hypotheses: D. Georgi; M. M. Mitchell, RGG 4th edition) makes his reconstruction – as seen above – expressly from a reconstruction of the *chronology of the events* and arrives at the following division of the letter:[34]

2.14–6.13; 7.2–4 Apologia	10–13 Excerpts from the tearful letter	1.1–2.13; 7.5–8.24 Conciliatory letter	ch. 9

Concatenation of the individual letters while they were being copied: E.-M. Becker:

1.1–7.4 (without 6.14–7.1) tearful letter	7.5–16 letter because of fresh news	8–9 letters about the collection	10–13 final letter

Result and Perspectives of the Historical Reconstruction
The historical reconstruction of the Corinthian correspondence occurs because of the perception of situative and literary incohesions in the text of the letter and aims to throw light on the history of the text of 2 Corinthians, comprehensible at the earliest at the end of the second century, from the time of the drafting of the partial letters. Hence the historical reconstruction has two essential (historical and *literarhistorische*) aspects which I name in conclusion:

1) Pauline chronology and the chronology of the events in Corinth
The historical reconstruction of the Corinthian correspondence and the events at the time is of considerable importance for the chronology of Paul's activity in the first half of the 50s. The model for division that I have proposed leads in the end, combined with the *dates of the Pauline chronology* and the *plans for journeys* contained in 1 and 2 Cor., to the following chronology of the events:[35]

---

30. In what follows hypotheses from the more/most recent literature are cited.
31. Cf. Klauck, *Korintherbrief* (n.18), 9.
32. Cf. Windisch, *Korintherbrief*, 11–21; Thrall, *Second Epistle*, 74ff.
33. Cf. R. Bultmann, *Brief*, 23.
34. Cf. Bornkamm, *Vorgeschichte*, 162ff.
35. The following table is an extension of the model in: Becker, *Letter Hermeneutics*, 65f.

Table 11.16

Year (c.)	Events	Evidence in the text
50	Paul's mission in Corinth and the founding of the church	1 Cor. 2.1; Acts 18.1ff.
	Stay in Corinth for *c*.1½ years	Acts 18.11
52–55	Earlier **letter** by Paul (not preserved)	1 Cor. 5.9
	Paul in Ephesus; during this period three kinds of reports from Corinth	1 Cor. 16.8; cf. Acts 18.19ff.
	> letter from the Corinthians	> 1 Cor. 7.1
	> Chloe's people	> 1 Cor. 1.11
	> Corinthian delegation	> 1 Cor. 16.17
55	**Letter** from Paul to the Corinthians from Ephesus = **1 Cor.**	1 Cor. 16.8
	containing plans for journeys: Macedonia – Corinth – escort from Corinth (to Judaea?)	1 Cor. 16.5ff.; cf. Acts 19.21
	Later planned journeys: Corinth – Macedonia – Corinth – escort to Judaea	2 Cor. 1.15f.
	Actual journeys:	(Acts 20.1ff.)
	> Difficulties in the province of Asia	> 2 Cor. 1.8
	> preaching in Troas	> 2 Cor. 2.12
	> from Troas to Macedonia	> 2 Cor. 2.13
	> only a short visit to Corinth (= Interim visit = 2nd visit?)	> 2 Cor. 1.15; 2.1ff.
	>> then: affront and departure to Macedonia (?)	>> 2 Cor. 2.5ff.; 1.16
	>> initially no further visit to Corinth planned	>> 2 Cor. 2.1ff.
	Letter by Paul from Macedonia = **Tearful letter: 2 Cor. 1.1–7.4** (= **2 Cor. A**)	2 Cor. 2.3f
	Fresh reports by Titus in Macedonia on the effect of the tearful letter: consequently: **letter** from Paul = **2 Cor. 7.5–16** (= **2 Cor. B**)	2 Cor. 7.5ff.
	'**Collection letters**' from Macedonia = **2 Cor. 8, 9** (= **2 Cor. C and D**)	2 Cor. 8.1; 9.2
	New attacks on Paul in Corinth and the influence of hostile missionaries	2 Cor. 10.10; 11.5ff., 16
	Letter by Paul from Macedonia = Apologia: **2 Cor. 10–13** (= **2 Cor. E**)	2 Cor. 10.11; 13.10
	containing: announcement of the third visit to Corinth, which is still to come	2 Cor. 12.14ff.; 13.1
55/56 or 56/57	3rd and final visit and sojourn by Paul *in Corinth*	Rom. (15.26ff.); 16.1, 22f.

2) Pauline correspondence with Corinthians and its transmission and collection

The assumption that the canonical 2 Cor. represents a compilation of what were originally four or five separate letters throws light on the one hand upon the character of the Corinthian correspondence and on the other on the transmission and collection of the Pauline letters in Corinth.

Clearly Paul conducts a lively epistolary correspondence which consists of several (2 Cor. 10.9f) – in part no longer preserved (1 Cor. 5.9) – letters from Ephesus and Macedonia together with answering letters from the Corinthian congregation (1 Cor. 7.1). 1 and 2 Cor. document a considerable component of this *extensive and lively correspondence* with the Corinthian community. The compilation of the letters could possibly have taken place in the course of the copying of the individual letters which were possibly written on wax-tablets, with the aim of *conserving, transmitting and collecting* them in Corinth up until about 70 CE.[36] Here an interlinking copy with the omission of prescripts and epistolary conclusions appears more plausible than complex 'interlocking models' which presume a conceptual editorial processing of the letters.[37]

3
Exegesis of the Text

Overview of the Text
The following depiction attempts to give an account of the contents and structure of the letter to a large extent independently of *Literarkritik* and historical suggestions for reconstruction.

In contrast to the reference to his being called to the ministry of apostle in 1 Cor. 1.1 (klētos apostolos) in 2 Cor. 1.1 Paul uses the term 'apostle' without any comparable defining participial or adjectival modifier. The further use of the apostolos-term in 2 Cor. (e.g. 8.23; 11.5; 12.11) however shows that, at the time when 2 Cor. was written, apostolos was understood and used, certainly as a 'description of a profession' but not as a rigidly defined form of address. Paul's commission and authorization emerge from the closer attributive definition of the term 'apostle' in the *superscriptio*, not from a putative 'title of apostle'. What

---

36. Later processes of copying – presumably up to the end of the first century – served rather to produce transcongregational 'proto-corpora' from the congregational 'small corpora' of Pauline letters in which compilations of letters had possibly already been made; on this cf. K. Aland's observations (1979): 'Die Entstehung des Corpus Paulinum', in *id.*, *Neutestamentliche Entwürfe* (TB 63), Munich, 302–50. In general to the issue of compilation: H.-J. Klauck (2003), 'Compilation of Letters in Cicero's Correspondence', in J. T. Fitzgerald et al. (eds), *Early Christianity and Classical Culture. Comparative Studies in Honor of A. J. Malherbe* (NTS 110), Leiden/Boston, 131–55, and finally on the discussion also: T. Schmeller (2004), *Die Cicerobriefe und die Frage nach der Einheitlichkeit des 2 Korintherbriefs*, ZNW 95, 181–208.

37. So, e.g. Bornkamm's idea, *Vorgeschichte*, 186.

'apostle' means in term of authority is rather more still under dispute.[38] There is therefore just as little ground for attributing an 'official character' to 2 Cor. on the basis of the prescript.

The proemium (2 Cor. 1.3–7) is formed as a eulogy (eulogētos) and anticipates a central lexeme of the emotional mood of 2 Cor. 1–7 (e.g. thlipsis, parakalein). The so-called '*disclosure*'-formula[39] (2 Cor. 1.8: ou gar thelomen hymas agnoein…) which follows it gives indications of the author's intention and leads into the body of the letter: Paul reports on the torments he suffered in the province of Asia and asks the Corinthians to pray for him (deēsis, 1.11)

2 Cor. 1.12–14 opens the body of the letter or initially functions as an introduction to the first individual letter.[40] On the basis of its fundamentally epistolary-hermeneutic function 1.12ff. can, however, also be taken as a 'general theme' of the epistle as a whole or even as a 'thesis' of the letter.[41]

In 2 Cor. 1.15ff. Paul reports on his changed plans for a journey, originally in part compatible with 1 Cor. 16.5ff., and justifies the changes with the avoidance of a further visit (2 Cor. 2.1ff.) in view of the grief and affront he experienced during a visit to Corinth (2 Cor. 2.5ff.).

The apostolic self-defence that begins in 2 Cor. 2.14ff. leads to significant theological statements: on the reflection about the office of apostle within the 'new covenant' (3.4ff.). Further: on the definition of the office of apostle in relation to the gospel (4.1ff.), to Christ (4.7ff.; 5.11ff.), in view of the Eschaton (5.1ff.) and with regard to the apostolic existence (6.1ff.).

In 2 Cor. 7.5ff. there is a recognizable 'change of mood' which goes back to the effect in Corinth of the tearful letter.

In 2 Cor. 8–9 Paul requests that the Corinthian church/the churches in Achaia (2 Cor. 9.2) implement the collection for the original church in Jerusalem (1 Cor. 16.2ff.; Rom. 15.26) to which he has committed himself at the meeting of the apostles (Gal. 2.10)[42] and which is described as a 'service for the saints' (2 Cor. 9.1: diakonia eis tous hagious). Paul tries to attract the donation of the Corinthians by referring to the eagerness of the Macedonian churches (2 Cor. 8.1; Rom. 15.26) just as he emphasizes the willingness of the churches in Achaia when he is canvassing for donations in Macedonia (2 Cor. 9.2: prothymia). Thus Paul whets the zēlos (2 Cor. 9.2) of the churches in Achaia and Macedonia.

---

38. On this cf. already O. Roller (1933), *Das Formular der paulinischen Briefe. Ein Beitrag zur Lehre vom antiken Briefe*, Stuttgart, 99f.; W. G. Doty (1973), *Letters in Primitive Christianity*, Philadelphia, 30.

39. Cf. on this concept H.-J. Klauck (1998), *Die antike Briefliteratur und das Neue Testament* (UTB 2022), Paderborn etc., 154. *Cf.* id. (2006), *Ancient letters and the New Testament: a guide to context and exegesis*, Waco.

40. Cf. Thrall, *Second Epistle*, 128ff.

41. Thus C. Wolff (1989), *Der zweite Brief des Paulus an die Korinther* (ThHK 7), Berlin, 29.

42. On the history, function and significance of the collection cf. D. Georgi (1965), *Die Geschichte der Kollekte des Paulus für Jerusalem* (ThF 38), Hamburg; S. Joubert (2000), *Paul as Benefactor. Reciprocity, Strategy and Theological Reflection in Paul's Collection* (WUNT 2.124), Tübingen.

Simultaneously he gives donations to the collection a *theological interpretation*:[43] the donation will be understood as charis (2 Cor. 8.1–7) and is voluntary (2 Cor. 8.8–12). It makes community a reality (2 Cor. 8.13–15) and is a 'proof of love' (2 Cor. 8.24: endeixis tēs agapēs). It presupposes trust in God (2 Cor. 9.6–10) and works toward the praise of God (2 Cor. 9.11–15). The *official character* of the writings about the collection which H. D. Betz stresses[44] can be seen particularly in the references to the formal correctness in the implementation of the collection (2 Cor. 8.16ff.).

2 Cor. 10–13 can be described as a Pauline apologia: Paul is at pains to establish the legitimacy of his apostolic office[45] *and* to defend his own person. The so-called 'Four Chapter Letter' has been described as 'the sharpest which Paul ever wrote'.[46] While Paul in defining his apostolic office within 2 Cor. 1–7 frequently writes in the first person plural (cf 2 Cor. 3.1ff.; 3.4ff.; 4.1ff.; 4.7ff.; 5.1ff. etc.), 2 Cor. 10–13 are characterized by a defence in which he takes personal responsibility and which is structured in the first person singular. This is introduced already in 10.1 with programmatic clarity: autos de egō Paulos parakalō hymas. Lexemes from the root asthen- predominate in the Four Chapter Letter (altogether 14 instances) but are lacking in the earlier parts of the epistle (2 Cor. 1–9). On the other hand the leading lexeme in chapters 1–7, paraklēsis (nine times in all, twice in ch. 8) does not occur in 2 Cor. 10–13. These examples of semantic and linguistic differences particularly between 2 Cor. 1–7 and 10–13 point to a changed situation of writing and an increase in conflicts between Paul and the Corinthians.

In 2 Cor. 10.1–11 Paul threatens with his apostolic authority (10.8 exousia) which he proposes to use when present in Corinth. It serves inter alia to punish disobedience (10.6: ekdikēsai pasan parakoēn). This threat is directed against the current opinion in Corinth that only Paul's letters, not his personal presence (10.9f.) are weighty and strong (10.11).

In 2 Cor. 10.12ff. Paul begins by comparing his apostolate with that of his opponents and establishes that his apostolic kauchēsis and commendation (synhist-) are founded on God/the kyrios (10.13,18).

2 Cor. 11.1–12.10 or to 12.13 are termed a so-called '*Fool's Discourse*':[47] This speech is characterized by lexemes from the root aphr-, and at its end Paul describes himself as a 'fool' (12.11: gegona aphrōn). The Fool's Discourse is defined by four important themes which are significant for the social and religious history of the Corinthian congregation, in particular, however, for Paul's biography:

---

43. Cf. here the subdivision of 2 Cor. 8–9 in Bultmann, *Brief*, 255ff.
44. Cf. Betz, *2 Corinthians 8 and 9*.
45. On this cf. the still stimulating essay by E. Käsemann: *Legitimität*.
46. Thus H.-M. Schenke and K. M. Fischer (1978), *Einleitung in die Schriften des Neuen Testaments I: Die Schriften des Paulus und die Schriften des Paulinismus*, Gütersloh, 109.
47. Cf. for a detailed stylistic and argumentative analysis of the Fool's Discourse: J. Zmijewski, *Stil*.

- Paul tackles the problem of the *hostile missionaries* who are active in Corinth and comments on their religious profile. He polemicizes against his opponents in designating them as 'super(lative) apostles' (e.g. 11.5: hyperlian apostoloi; 11.13: pseudapostoloi), namely as false and cunning workers who disguise themselves as apostles of Christ but are in reality servants of Satan (11.15). *Ex negativo*, i.e. from the perspective of the Pauline invective, we may suspect: his opponents commend themselves (so already in 10.12), they preach another Jesus and another gospel (11.4) and allow themselves to be maintained by the Corinthian community (vv. 11.7ff.). They are Hebrews and call themselves children of Abraham (11.22) and boast about their own merits (vv. 11.30). Scholars come to various conclusions about their precise identity. They are taken to be Gnostics (W. Schmithals), Spiritualists (J. L. Sumney), delegates of the Jerusalem church (E. Käsemann) or Jewish-Christian missionaries (D. Georgi).[48] The opponents can be described in their general tendency as competing Christian 'itinerant missionaries with a Jewish-Hellenistic background'.[49]
- Presumably Paul justifies his *lifestyle* in a programmatic differentiation from that of his opponents, i.e. particularly in his abstention from receiving financial support from the Corinthian congregation (11.7ff.; thus already in 1 Cor. 9; cf. also Phil. 4.11ff.; Acts 18.2f.). Paul understands the *peristases* he has experienced as part of the life of an apostle (11.23ff.) and interprets them for the Corinthians as a legitimation of his apostolicity in the sense of the 'theology of weakness' (11.30).
- In connection with the kauchēsis 'imposed' upon him by the Corinthians (12.1,11) Paul reports in the form of an autobiographical *narratio* (O.Wischmeyer) on the revelations he has experienced and his *apostolic commission* (12.1–10).[50] This *narratio* differs from the brief form of legitimization of his apostolicity normally employed by Paul as witness to the resurrection (1 Cor. 15.8ff.; Rom. 1.4f.) or as called by Christ (Gal. 1.12).
- Within the context of this autobiographical *narratio* Paul mentions and interprets his *'illness'* (elsewhere: Gal. 4.13f.: 6.17; possibly 2 Cor. 10.10) which

---

48. Cf. for a brief survey: Thrall, *Second Epistle*, 671ff. Cf. W. Schmithals (^{3}1969), *Die Gnosis in Korinth. Eine Untersuchung zu den Korintherbriefen*, Göttingen, 277ff.; J. L. Sumney (1990), *Identifying Paul's Opponents. The Question of Method in 2 Corinthians* (JSNT.S 40), Sheffield, 183; Käsemann, *Legitimität*, 34ff.; D. Georgi (1964), *Die Gegner des Paulus im 2 Korintherbrief. Studien zu der religiösen Propaganda in der Spätantike* (WMANT 11), Neukirchen-Vluyn, 301. To more recent identifications of Paul's opponents cf.: L. L. Welborn (2009), 'Paul's Caricature of his Chief Rival as a Pompous Parasite in 2 Corinthians 11.20', *JSNT* 32, 39–56; T. R. Blanton (2010), 'Spirit and Covenant Renewal. A Theologoumenon of Paul's Opponents', *JBL* 129, 129–51 identifies Paul's opponents as advocators for a 'covenant renewal theologoumenon', 147f.

49. Thus G. Strecker, 'Die Legitimität des paulinischen Apostolates nach 2 Korinther 10–13', *NTS* 38 (1992), 566–86, 572.

50. Cf. O. Wischmeyer (2004), '2 Korinther 12.1–10. Ein autobiographisch-theologischer Text des Paulus', in *Ead., Von Ben Sira zu Paulus. Gesammelte Aufsätze zu Texten, Theologie und Hermeneutik des Frühjudentums und des Neuen Testaments*, ed. E.-M. Becker (WUNT 173), Tübingen, 277–88.

in 2 Cor. 12 he describes as a 'thorn in the flesh' (12.7: skolops tē sarki), as a 'messenger of Satan' which pricks him so that he cannot become too arrogant (hyperairomai). In a prayer addressed to God Paul receives the reply that in future the grace of Christ should be sufficient for him (12.9). Thus Paul understands his personal weakness (astheneia) and the *peristases* he endures (12.10) as a locus for the perfecting of the charis and the dynamis of Christ (12.9: teleitai).

In 2 Cor. 12.14–13.10 Paul deals mainly with the announcement of his third visit to Corinth and explains the reasons for and aim of his *apologia* (12.19: oikodomē) as well as the function of the written defence (13.10).

Considering the apologetic sharpness of chapters 10.1–13.10, the ending of the epistle in 2 Cor. 13.11–13 (greetings and wishes) appears to be extremely brief and contains only in the triadic charis-formula (13.13) an unusual formal-epistolographic and theological feature.

Exegetical Problems
I have already named at the appropriate places the exegetical problems connected to the division, reconstruction and interpretation of 2 Corinthians. Here I give a brief résumé:

- In spite of programmatic attempts to postulate the *literary unity* of 2 Cor., I view the question of the original form of 2 Cor. and the genesis of a compilation of letters is unavoidable on source-critical, *literarhistorische*, redaction-, and text-historical grounds.
- The acceptance of the idea of a *compilation of letters* is connected with the reconstruction of the original sequence of the letters and the questions of the reasons for, the function of, and the technical production of the Corinthian collection of letters.
- The assumption of individual letters being compiled is also connected to the reconstruction of varying situations when they were written and *a chronology of the events relating to Corinth*.
- The originality of 2 Cor 6.14–7.1 remains controversial for *Literarkritik* and redaction criticism.
- The *determination of* Paul's *opponents*, particularly in 2 Cor. 10–13 on the one hand gives information on the historical social and religious structure of the Corinthian community, and on the other must be dealt with within the framework of the so-called research on invective.[51]
- The obligation to give *donations to the collection* for the early church in Jerusalem which Paul formulates in the majority of his epistles – to which Acts makes *no* reference – is thematized in most detail in 2 Cor. (chapters 8–9). The interpretation of 2 Cor. is consequently engaged with the question of the function, significance and result of the collection of the donations.

---

51. On this in general cf. W.-L. Liebermann (1998), 'Article: Invektive', *DNP* 5, 1049–51.

2 Cor. contains the most extensive number of *Paul's statements about himself*, on his self-understanding as apostle and as person, as e.g. also on his illness. The 'theology of weakness' deduced from this with regard to his apostleship (2 Cor. 11.30; 12.9) corresponds to the 'theology of the Cross' formulated in 1 Cor. 1.18ff. Hence Paul puts his own apostolic self-understanding in an explicit relationship to his Christology (cf. 2 Cor. 4.7ff.). Biography and theology/autobiography and apostolic self-understanding on the one hand and Christology on the other build a contingent prospect of interpretation.[52]

4
Problems of Interpretation

The interpretation of 2 Cor. in many cases is confined in its extremes to an evaluation of the theological statements *or* to the perception of the collection of letters as a 'quarry' for the historical reconstruction of the Corinthian correspondence.[53] Every interpretation of a text is, to be sure, determined by hermeneutical assumptions and methodical (pre-) decisions. Yet the interpretation and exegesis of 2 Cor. should be made in the awareness and consideration of the variety of heuristic questions and methodical approaches to the text produced by research on Paul. As such should be mentioned:

1. *Literarkritik* and the *literarhistorische* interpretation which aims to reconstruct the epistolary correspondence and the genesis of the collection of letters (in the context of a Pauline 'school')
2. the *historically* oriented interpretation which attempts to reconstruct the chronology of the events in Corinth
3. the *socio-* and *religio-historical* interpretation which tries to ascertain the religious profile of the Corinthian community in the area of conflict of Pauline character and the influence of hostile missionaries
4. the *autobiographical* interpretation which scrutinizes Paul's statements about himself in 2 Cor. in respect of their literary form, their biographical value or their apostolic-theological content
5. the *rhetorical* interpretation which understands Paul as a letter-writer who structures his letters to push through his apostolic authority e.g. against his opponents (2 Cor. 10–13) or in the matter of the collection (2 Cor. 8–9)
6. the interpretation *based on the science of communication and letter hermeneutics* which, on the basis of the Corinthian Correspondence, sketches the early Christian development of the gospel preached verbally to theological epistolary literature which makes ethical demands on the congregation[54]

---

52. Here cf. also Chapter 7 by E.-M. Becker on the 'Person of Paul' in this volume. Cf. also various essays in E.-M. Becker and P. Pilhofer (eds), *Biographie und Persönlichkeit*.

53. The tendency can be discerned in Bornkamm; it is pronounced in W. Schmithals (1984), *Die Briefe des Paulus in ihrer ursprünglichen Form*, Zürich.

54. Cf. once again Becker, *Letter Hermeneutics*. Cf. also recently: M. M. Mitchell (2003),

7. the *theological* interpretation which, to a large extent leaving out of account the contextuality of the letter/the individual letters, aims to interpret theological, Christological or similar statements in 2 Cor.

The contribution before you takes into consideration the communicative and letter-hermeneutic elements in particular and attempts to combine *Literarkritik, literarhistorische* and hermeneutical questions: It aims at exposing first how Pauline theology arises in the frame of meta-communication, and secondly to reconstruct and explain the historical and source history of the collection of letters contained in 2 Cor.

5
Evaluation

2 Cor. – in spite of the complexity of the specialized questions thrown up by Pauline exegesis – can scarcely be overrated in relation to its *significance for the theology of the New Testament*.[55] This significance can be seen in two aspects which I formulate from a historical perspective:

- The canonical 2 Cor. provides the most extensive insight into the historical and theological *history* of early Christian communities and the emergence of early Christian literature and theology on the basis of epistolary correspondence.
- 2 Cor. gives the deepest insight into Paul's *biography*, his literary i.e. also autobiographical self-understanding, his linking of theology of the apostolate and Christology, and reflects in the history of the transmission of the text in the *Corpus Paulinum* the trans-congregational impact and authority of the apostle beyond the 50s of the first century.

References

Commentaries
H. D. Betz (1985), *2 Corinthians 8 and 9. A Commentary on Two Administrative Letters of the Apostle Paul* (Hermeneia), Philadelphia: Fortress Press.
R. Bultmann[2] (1987), *Der zweite Brief an die Korinther*, hg. v. E. Dinkler (KEK Sonderbd.), Göttingen: Vandenhoeck & Ruprecht.
J. Lambrecht (1999), *Second Corinthians* (Sacra Pagina 8), Collegeville, MN: Liturgical Press.
F. J. Matera (2003), *II Corinthians. A Commentary* (The New Testament Library), Louisville/London: Westminster John Knox.

'The Corinthian Correspondence and the Birth of Pauline Hermeneutics', in T. J. Burke and J. K. Elliot (eds), *Paul and the Corinthians. Essays in Honour of M. Thrall*, Leiden/Boston, 17–53; Ead. (2010), *Paul, the Corinthians, and the Birth of Christian Hermeneutics*, Cambridge.

55. On this cf. the considerations of the significance of 2 Cor. for the theology of R. Bultmann by E. Dinkler, in Bultmann, *Brief*, 11. For a comprehensive bibliography on the studies in 2 Cor. cf.: R. Bieringer et al., *2 Corinthians*.

M. E. Thrall (1994/2000), *The Second Epistle to the Corinthians* Vol. 1/Vol. 2 (ICC), Edinburgh: T&T Clark.

H. Windisch (1970), *Der zweite Korintherbrief. Neudruck der 9. Aufl. 1924*, hg. v. G. Strecker (KEK 9), Göttingen: Vandenhoeck & Ruprecht.

Monographs and Anthologies

E.-M. Becker (2004), *Letter Hermeneutics in Second Corinthians. Studies in Literarkritik and communication theory* (JSNT.S 279), London/New York.

E.-M. Becker and P. Pilhofer (eds) (2005/2009), *Biographie und Persönlichkeit des Paulus* (WUNT 187), Tübingen: Mohr Siebeck.

R. Bieringer et al. (2008), *2 Corinthians. A Bibliography* (Biblical Tools and Studies 5), Leuven: Peeters.

U. Schnelle[5] (2005), *Einleitung in das Neue Testament* (UTB 1830), Göttingen: Vandenhoeck & Ruprecht.

J. Zmijewski (1978), *Der Stil der paulinischen ‚Narrenrede'. Analyse der Sprachgestaltung in 2 Kor 11,1–12,10 als Beitrag zur Methodik von Stiluntersuchungen neutestamentlicher Texte* (BBB 52), Cologne/Bonn: Hanstein.

Essays and Encyclopedia Articles

H. D. Betz (1992), 'Art. Corinthians, Second Epistle to the', *ABD* 1, 1148–54.

G. Bornkamm (1971), 'Die Vorgeschichte des sogenannten Zweiten Korintherbriefes', in *Geschichte und Glaube. Zweiter Teil. Ges. Aufsätze Bd. IV* (BEvTh 53), Munich, 162–94.

E. Käsemann (1942), 'Die Legitimität des Apostels. Eine Untersuchung zu II Korinther 10–13', *ZNW* 41, 33–71.

D. I. Pallas (1990), 'Art. Korinth', *RBK* 4, 746–811.

Chapter 12

GALATIANS
Jörg Frey

Table 12.1

Sender	Paul (1.1)		
Addressees	Probably the churches founded by Paul on the south coast of Asia Minor		
Situation when written	*No explicit reference in the letter*		
Occasion	A judaizing counter-mission in the Galatian churches, demand by the opponents for circumcision		
Place of writing	Ephesus or Macedonia/Achaia (*no explicit reference in the letter*)		
Date	50–55/56 CE (*no explicit reference in the letter*)		
Opponents	Hellenistic Jewish-*Christians* (or circumcised Gentile Christians) who think *circumcision and the Law* indispensable for faith in Jesus and consequently challenge Paul's '*apostolic authority*'		
Themes	The independence and divine authorization of Paul's Gospel Justification by faith Life in freedom from the Law and in the Spirit		
Broad division	Beginning of the letter	1.1–5 1.6–10	*Epistolary prescript* *Epistolary proemium*: no thanksgiving, but rebuke
	Body of the letter	1.11 – 2.21	*Autobiographical section*: The independence and divine of the Pauline Gospel
		3.1 – 5.12	*Theological-argumentative section*: Justification by faith (or: Why the Galatians should not yield to the demand for circumcision)
		5.13 – 6.10	*Paraenetic section*: Life in the Spirit and in freedom from the Law

Closing of the letter	6.11	Note that the postscript is written in Paul's own handwriting
	6.12–15	Repetition of his own position
	6.16f.	Closing *paraenesis*
	6.18	Concluding blessing

1
Approaching the Text

The Content and Transmission of the Text

With 2,220 words and *c.*10 pages in Nestle the letter to the Galatians is barely a third of the length of the letter to the Romans. Like Romans it is attested to in the major majuscules ℵ 01, A 02, B 03, C 04 (incomplete), D 06 and with gaps in the papyri Þ 46 (*c.*200) and Þ 51. Even earlier the text can be found in Marcion (*c.*140) from whose dogmatically 'purified' edition of Paul's letters ('*apostolos*') there are quotations from 1.1 – 6.17 in Tertullian (*Adversus Marcionem*).[1] In Marcion's edition and probably also in its source Gal. was the first of the Pauline epistles (followed by 1 and 2 Cor. and Rom.).[2] In the list of the Canon Muratori (*c.*200) it is inserted after 1 and 2 Cor., Eph., Phil. and Col.; in Þ 46 after Rom., Heb., 1 and 2 Cor., Eph. The usual sequence today, which is roughly oriented on the length of the letters, only develops later. Gal. offers no particular problems for textual criticism.

Analysis and Structure

- The text is encompassed in an *epistolary* frame which gives it the obvious form of a letter. Within Gal. itself there are also references to the epistolary situation – the spatial separation of the author from the addressees (e.g. the 'wish to come to them' in 4.20). In the *prescript* the expansion of the *superscriptio* to emphasize *Paul's authority* and his mission (1.1) is remarkable as well as the weighty soteriological expansion of the *salutation* along with a unique modification in the *proemium*, namely the insertion of a sharp rebuke where normally the thanksgiving for the church is formulated (1.6). In the *ending of the letter* should be observed *the autographic subscript* (6.11) (in the original recognizable from the chirography).
- The *body of the letter* begins with an *autobiographical section* (1.11 – 2.21) which can, however, be precisely related to the aim of the argumentation of the letter. Here it serves to *prove the independence and divine authority* of the gospel preached by Paul. Paul reports on his 'pre-Christian' years as

---

1. U. Schmid (1995), *Marcion und sein Apostolos* (ANTF 25; Berlin/New York: de Gruyter), 1/315–19.
2. Ibid., 294–6.

persecutor of the church (1.13f.), his 'calling' (1.15f.) and – gathered together but in chronological order[3] – on phases of his activity in the following years, including the meeting of the apostles in Jerusalem (Gal. 2. 1–10) (the so-called 'Jerusalem Conference' or 'Apostolic Council') and a confrontation with Peter in Antioch (the so-called 'Incident at Antioch': Gal. 2.11–14). The last report merges into a fundamental exposition of the theme of justification by faith (2.15–21).

- Following the formulation of the theme in 2.15–21 there is a theological-argumentative section which then merges into an ethical-paraenetic section. In both, the subject is *'Justification by Faith'* and its practical consequences for living. Several times Paul gives theological reasons why the Galatians should not bow to the demand for circumcision. Here the delimitation of the various arguments is not always clear.[4] Here, 'dogmatics' and 'ethics' cannot be clearly separated. The section which discusses the questions of circumcision and the Law ends with the appeal to resist the demand for circumcision (Gal. 5.1f.) and a sharp, ironic attack on the teachers of false doctrine (5.12: 'they should mutilate [= castrate] themselves').

- The *Paraenesis* in which the *life in freedom from the Law and in the Spirit* is described in more detail begins in 5.13f. This section also is related to the situation to the extent that Paul does not tackle concrete ethical failings (as in 1 Cor. etc.) but counters the implicit accusation that freedom from the Law serves only the sarx, i.e. human self-indulgence, and thereby is a pretext for sin.

Table 12.2

1.1–10	Beginning of the letter	
1.1–5	*Prescript*	stresses the *divine authority of Paul's apostolic office* (1. 1) extended by a confessional 'formula of self-sacrifice' (1.4)
1.6–10	*Proemium*	immediately refers to the actual critical situation: no thanksgiving, but rebuke (1.6: 'I am astonished') Theme: *'another Gospel'* – a curse ('anathema') on possible preachers of such
1.11 – 2.21	Autobiographical section: The independence and divine authority of the Pauline Gospel	
1.11,12	'Subject': the *divine origin* of the Gospel which Paul preaches	

---

3. Cf. the temporal adverbs (epeita 1.18,21; 2.1), details of time (1.18; 2.1) and the extension in 2.11.

4. It is debated, e.g. whether 3.19–25 is 'only' a digression or is more closely connected to 3.26 – 4.7 (R. N. Longenecker) and whether the paraenesis begins already in 5.1 (H. D. Betz) or whether 5.1–12 does not in fact contain the concluding demand to draw the consequences from the argumentation, i.e. not to follow the demand for circumcision (cf. 6.12–15).

1.13–24	On the life of the apostle before and after his vocation (vv. 13f.: the 'pre-Christian' Paul; vv. 15f.: call; v. 17: in Arabia; vv. 18f.: first visit to Jerusalem; v. 21: in Syria and Cilicia) → Aim: Proof of the *independence* from humans of the Pauline Gospel
2.1–10	On the meeting of the apostles in Jerusalem ('Apostolic Council'): → Aim: Proof of the *recognition* by the Jerusalem 'pillars' of Paul's apostolate and his (Law-free) Gospel for the Gentiles
2.11–21	On the 'Incident at Antioch': → Aim: The defence of the *normative validity* of the (v. 14: for the Gentiles 'Law-free') Gospel even over against Peter From 14b: (fictitious) speech of Paul to Peter (v. 15): *Justification by faith*, not through the Law/'works'
3.1 – 5.12	**Theological-argumentative section: Justification by faith (or: Why the Galatians should not yield to the demand for circumcision)**
3.1–5	*Argument from experience*: The Spirit was given to the Galatians because of the preaching of faith, not because they did 'works of the Law'
3.6–14	*Proof from Scripture*: Faith was reckoned to *Abraham* as righteousness. The promise of blessing given to him is granted in Christ to believers
3.15–18	*Analogy* from secular legal practice (*argumentum ad hominem*; cf. v. 15): The Law later added (through Moses) does not rescind the legally valid promise given earlier (to Abraham)
3.19–25	*Excursus*: The (temporally limited) function of the Law: it is a 'disciplinarian' (paidagōgos) for Christ until the 'coming' of faith (i.e. of Christ)
3.26–29	*Argument from experience*: The *baptism* they have experienced points to the reality of their status as children of God and to the surmounting of ethnic and social barriers (3.28: no longer Jew/Greek, slave/free, male/female; cf. 5.6)
4.1–7	*Consequence*: the children of God are also heirs of the promise, of the Spirit (4.6: 'Abba'), they are no (longer) slaves but free. Key statement: 4.4: The sending of the Son as 'turning-point of the ages'
4.8–20	*Warning against relapse* and solicitation of the 'friendship' of the Galatians
4.21–31	*Proof from Scripture: the Allegory of Hagar and Sara*: The believers are children of the free woman
5.1–12	*Appeal* to refrain from circumcision (Alternatives: Freedom/slavery)
5.13 – 6.10	**Paraenetic section: Life in the Spirit and in freedom from the Law**
5.13f.	Exhortation to love as a way of fulfilling the Law in freedom
5.15–24	The ethical alternatives: 'works of the flesh'/'fruit of the Spirit'

5.25 – 6.10	Various exhortations for life 'in the Spirit'	
6.11–18	Closing of the letter (autographic subscript)	with a 'reference to his own handwriting' (6.11); repetition of his own position (6.12–15); exhortation (6.16f.) and concluding blessing (6.18)

Semantic Fields, Themes and Central Contrasts

- euangelion: Central concepts in Gal. 1–2 are euangelion (seven times) / euangelizesthai (six times in Gal. 1–2). Euangelion (Gospel) describes the saving message of God's justifying activity in the Cross and Resurrection of Christ which was revealed and authorized by God, preached by Paul and accepted by the Galatians. For Paul the 'truth' which cannot be denied lies herein: that it is unconditional and consequently 'free of the Law' (for Gentiles). In the situation of confrontation with the demand for circumcision of the Gentiles and therewith their obligation to the Jewish Law, Paul phrases in brusque antitheses:[5]

Table 12.3

1.7	'Gospel of Christ'	1.6	an 'other gospel' which would be no gospel at all
1.11	the Gospel preached by me (cf. 2.2: 'the Gospel which I preach among the Gentiles')	1.8,9	we/an angel/anyone preached differently to what we preached/ contrary to that which you received
1.11f. cf. 1.1	not from/through men but through Jesus Christ/ God or through 'revelation'		human/seeking human favour (cf. 1.10, there probably as a reproach made by Paul's opponents)
2.7,14	the truth of the Gospel		[untruth]

- A second central concept in Gal. is made up of the words relating to 'justice'/'Justification': dikaios, dikaiosyne and in particular the verb dikaioun/ dikaiousthai (eight times, concentrated in 2.16f.). Here, too, sharp alternatives are expressed:

---

5. The distinction in 2.7 (perhaps adopted from earlier usage) 'Gospel to the uncircumcised' (= Gentiles) / 'Gospel to the circumcised' (= Jews) does not describe a difference in the content of the gospel. It simply distinguishes between different addressees, Jews and Gentiles, whereas the gospel itself is fundamentally the same.

Table 12.4

2.16	through faith in Christ (ek/dia pisteōs Christou)	2.16	by works of the Law
2.17	en Christō	3.11	en nomō (cf. 5.4: severed from Christ)
3.8,11,21	ek pisteōs (cf. 3.6: like Abraham because of his faith)	3.21	ek nomou (cf. 2.21: dia nomou)

- The antithesis 'works (of the Law)' – 'faith (in Christ)' (2.16) is continued:

Table 12.5

2.16	be just(ified)	'by works of the Law'	'through faith in Christ'
3.2,5	receiving of the Spirit/powerful effects	'by works of the Law'	'by hearing with faith'
3.10	Life (existence)	'by works of the Law' (= life under the curse)	[3.14: ransomed from the curse by Christ]

- The central term in Gal. is nomos (32 times). It occurs particularly in Gal. 2.16–21 and 3–4. Here we encounter combinations such as 'by works of the Law' (2.16 [three times]; 3.2,5,10), but also analogous to this in 3.11; 5.4 'by the Law' (en nomō) or 'under the Law' (4.21; 5.18 – there in contrast to life 'through the Spirit'). Central antitheses are formulated in the words about the Law. They all aim to refute the thesis that the law still remains in force after the coming of Christ.

Table 12.6

3.17f.	chronological sequence	Law (430 years later)	Promise (given earlier, consequently remains valid)
3.21f.	difference in function	Law consigns all things under sin	Promise is given to those who believe in Christ
3.23	the order of salvation history	Law guarded us until faith/Christ came	Faith came, was revealed with the coming of Christ

A central soteriological statement is formulated in 4.4: Christ was 'set under the Law' in order to redeem those who were [living] 'under the Law'. In an exemplary 'I' statement in 2.19 Paul says: 'I through the Law died *to the Law*, that I might live to God.'

The talk of the 'law of Christ' in Gal. 6.2 is a conspicuous phrase – and one that is important for Pauline ethics. It makes clear that for Paul nomos does not have only negative connotations. But we can scarcely obtain a systematic definition of the relationship between 'law' and 'paraenesis' from the polemical argument in Gal.

- A further antithesis, which characterizes Gal. 4.21–31 and 5.1–12, is the juxtaposition of freedom and slavery. This is first introduced in the allegory of Hagar/Sara.

Table 12.7

4.22	two sons of Abraham	[Ishmael] from the slave (Hagar)	[Isaac] from the free woman (Sara)
4.23	begotten in different ways	'according to the flesh' (= by human will)	'through promise' (= by the will of God)
4.24–26	allegorical interpretation	[Hagar]: Mt Sinai: the present Jerusalem slavery	[Sara]: (Zion) our mother the heavenly Jerusalem the free

The point of the description is that those who believe are children of the promise, i.e. they are children of the free woman (4.31) therefore are free (from the Law). In view of the opponents' demands 5.1f. expresses the consequence, with the antithesis 'set free for freedom' – 'again under the yoke of slavery'. The adoption of circumcision would bring with it again the obligation to the Law (in total) and therewith the return to bondage.

- In the paraenetical section Paul forms a further antithesis between 'Spirit' and 'flesh' which is basic for his anthropology. Here 'flesh' does not mean, as in the Old Testament, the creaturely frailness of humanity, and also not the physical or even sexual dimension, but mankind's striving – even in its most spiritual impulses – contrary to the will of God (and thereby as sinful).

Table 12.8

'Basic situation'	5.17 Flesh and Spirit are opposed to one another (so that a person is not his own master)	
ethical alternatives	5.22f. Fruit of the Spirit (Catalogue of virtues)	5.9–21 Works of the flesh (Catalogue of vices)
eschatological consequence	6.8 sow to the Spirit → reap eternal life	6.8 sow to the flesh → reap corruption
paraenetic aim	5.13f. Love (= fulfilment of the Law; fruit of the Spirit 5.16 'live in the Spirit' 5.18 'be moved by the Spirit' 5.25 'walk by the Spirit'	5.13 freedom not as an opportunity (aphormē) for the flesh 5.16–24: not gratifying the desires of the flesh; having crucified the flesh with its desires.

Communication, Genre and Rhetoric

Rhetoric and Epistolography: Many formulations in Gal. suggest a speech (1.9; 3.15; 4.1 etc.). Yet Gal. is a letter and not simply a 'speech in an envelope'.[6] It is admittedly the one among the Pauline epistles in which the fruitfulness of the categories of classical rhetoric can be most clearly seen. In his pioneering commentary *Hans Dieter Betz* classified Gal. as an *apologetic* epistle in the rhetorical *genus iudiciale* (dikanikon), i.e. the 'courtroom speech' which demands a verdict. According to this concept the letter takes the place of the speech for the defence by the absent apostle:

Table 12.9

1.1–5		epistolary prescript
1.6–11	*exordium*	introduction (to the speech)
1.12 – 2.14	*narratio*	statement of facts (here: explanation of the 'prehistory' of the conflict)
2.15–21	*propositio*	proposition (= theme, with points of agreement and disagreement)
3.1 – 4.31	*probatio*	proofs (in 6 steps of argumentation)
5.1 – 6.10	*exhortatio*	exhortation (strictly speaking not a part of the courtroom speech)
6.11–18		epistolary postscript (in the function of a *conclusio*)

The scholarly discussion of this approach has demonstrated the limits of rhetorical analysis of the New Testament letters. Only the autobiographical section is 'apologetic',[7] therefore other authors classify the letter not as a courtroom speech but as an 'advisory' speech belonging to the *genus deliberativum* (symbouleutikon).[8] The paraenesis, however, belongs more to the field of Moral Philosophy than to Rhetoric, and in 4.12–20 we encounter *topoi* of the ancient friendship letter. A schematic application of the categories of ancient rhetoric will consequently hardly do justice to Gal., particularly since ancient rhetoric also distinguishes between letters and speeches. We only have knowledge, however, of 'rules' formulated for epistolography in later antiquity. Thus the categories of ancient rhetoric can help to explain the function of individual sections of a letter but do not offer a master-key to the Pauline epistles.[9]

6. Thus the thesis proposed by V. Jegher-Bucher (1991), *Der Galaterbrief auf dem Hintergrund antiker Epistolographie und Rhetorik* (ATANT 78; Zurich: TVZ), 204.
7. H.-J. Klauck (2006), *Ancient Letters and the New Testament* (Waco: Baylor), 315.
8. G. A. Kennedy (1984), *New Testament Interpretation through Rhetorical Criticism* (SR; Chapel Hill: University of North Carolina Press), 145–7; F. Vouga (1988), 'Zur rhetorischen Gattung des Galaterbriefes', *ZNW* 79: 291–2.
9. Cf. further R. D. Anderson (1999), *Ancient Rhetorical Theory and Paul* (CBET 18; Leuven); J. S. Vos (2002), *Die Kunst der Argumentation bei Paulus* (WUNT 149; Tübingen:

2
The Genesis of the Text

Author, Addressees and Historical Situation
Author and Authenticity
The *authenticity* of Gal. is not disputed today. Its *literary integrity* is also almost unanimously accepted. Only a few[10] consider the possibility of interpolations or that Gal. is a compilation of various pieces. The note about Paul's own handwriting in Gal. 6.11 may suggest that a 'secretary' (possibly as 'co-sender'; cf. 1.2) played a part. It remains unclear what effect such a 'scribe' had on the form (cf. Rom. 16.22). The fact that even the sarcastic attack in 5.12 was not moderated allows us to assume that virtually no reworking took place. The apostle himself is fully responsible for the form and content of the letter.

The Question of the Addressees: The Region or the (Southern Part of the) Province of 'Galatia'?
The determination and location of the *addressees* is highly controversial: differently than the rest of the genuine Pauline epistles, Gal. is not directed to an individual church but to several congregations in Galatia (1.2; cf. 1 Cor. 16.1) which Paul knows and founded (1.8; 4.13f.,19). The addressees are addressed as 'Galatians' (Galatai: 3.1), but it is controversial which *addressees* in which *region* are meant.[11]

- According to the *North Galatian* Hypothesis (*Region Hypothesis*) Galatians is addressed to the inhabitants of the *'Region' Galatia in central Anatolia* around the towns Ancyra (today's Ankara), Pessinus and Tavium, who got their names from the Celtic tribes who penetrated this area in the third century BCE.[12] The people of that area were slightly Hellenized, though in the few towns the population probably was mixed. In the first century there is no proof of a Jewish Diaspora worth mentioning in that region.[13] According to Acts 16.6; 18.23 Paul travelled through 'the region of Galatia', which could

---

Mohr Siebeck); D. F. Tolmie (2004), *Persuading the Galatians. A Text-Centred Rhetorical Analysis of a Pauline Letter* (WUNT II/190; Tübingen; Mohr Siebeck).

10. Most recently T. Witulski, *Adressaten*, who in Gal. 4.8–20 sees an interpolation, the purpose of which was to turn the Gentile Christians (in south Galatia!) from a relapse into paganism, in this case the newly introduced cult of the emperor.

11. For this, cf. the commentaries and introductions, and in more detail C. Breytenbach, *Paulus*; J. M. Scott, *Paul*.

12. 'Galatai is a variant form for Keltoi and denotes Gaels', Breytenbach, *Paulus*, 149.

13. The earliest datable Jewish gravestones in Galatia stem from the fifth/sixth centuries CE (see W. Ameling [ed.] [2004], *Inscriptiones Judaicae Orientis*, vol. II: *Kleinasien* [TSAJ 99; Tübingen: Mohr Siebeck], 335–41), an inscription, which is perhaps Jewish, stems from the third century CE (Breytenbach, *Paulus*, 145). At the time when the Jewish Diaspora in Asia Minor began (third century BCE) the area lay outside the Seleucid Empire as an un-Hellenized region controlled by Celtic tribes (Breytenbach, *Paulus*, 146).

apply to this area, on his second and third so-called missionary journeys. On the other hand Luke makes no mention of Paul *founding* churches there.
- According to the *South Galatian Hypothesis (Province Hypothesis)* Galatians is addressed to the inhabitants of the Roman *Provincia Galatiae* which, along with the region of Galatia (the seat of the governor was Ancyra), *also* included the area right up to the south coast of Asia Minor, i.e. *parts of Pamphylia, Pisidia, Isauria and Lycaonia*. Here there was an old Jewish Diaspora of considerable strength.[14] Towns in this area (Antioch in Pisidia, Iconium, Lystra, Derbe and Perge) are mentioned in Acts 13f. as stations of the First Missionary Journey of Paul and Barnabas. Accordingly both founded churches there and visited them again on their return journey.

The present state of scholarship is convoluted and the alternatives are difficult to clarify from the sources (Gal. and Acts). The decision also depends upon the historical assessment of Acts. The question of the addressees is important for the dating of Gal., for identifying the opposing preachers and the situation in the church. While Anglo-Saxon research has favoured the south Galatian hypothesis for a long time,[15] German research to a large extent followed the north Galatian,[16] but in recent years the number of supporters for the Provincial Hypothesis is increasing.[17] Behind the option for the 'Region' often lay scepticism about the historical value of Acts, while representatives of the 'province' hypothesis on the other hand were 'suspected' of trying to 'harmonize' Paul uncritically with Acts. In the end both hypotheses have to use details from Acts. If, however, scholars take the first missionary journey in Acts 13–14 for a Lucan invention (inter alia because Paul does not mention it in Gal. 1.21), the churches on the south coast of Asia Minor are ruled out. But since on the other hand Gal. 1 is primarily interested in the relationship to Jerusalem and one cannot expect a complete enumeration in this 'autobiographical' report, this result[18] 'is not enough to rule

---

14. Cf. Acts 13.14 and 14.1 (Synagogues in Antioch in Pisidia and Iconium); 16.1,3; further 1 Macc. 15.23; Philo, *Legatio ad Gaium* 281 and the list in Acts 2.10 as well as some inscriptions that are difficult to date; cf. E. Schürer (1986), *The History of the Jewish People in the Age of Jesus Christ*, vol. III/1 (rev. and ed. by G. Vermes, F. Millar and M. Goodman; Edinburgh: T&T Clark), 30–4; P. R. Trebilco (1991), *Jewish Communities in Asia Minor* (SNTSMS 69; Cambridge: CUP); Ameling, *Inscriptiones* (n.13), 449–69.

15. Basic: W. Ramsay (1899), *A Historical Commentary on St. Paul's Epistle to the Galatians* (London: Hodder and Stoughton). Cf. the detailed argumentation in R. N. Longenecker, *Galatians*, lxi–lxxii.

16. So the introductions by Kümmel (n.21), Vielhauer (n.37) and Schnelle (n.36) and the commentaries by H. Schlier, *Brief*; H. D. Betz, *Galatians*; F. Mussner, *Galaterbrief*; and F. Vouga, *Galater*; also the monograph by U. Borse, *Standort*.

17. See the more recent monographs by Breytenbach, *Paulus*; Scott, *Paul*; Witulski, *Adressaten*; and Schäfer, *Paulus*; also C. Hemer (1989), *The Book of Acts in the Setting of Hellenistic History* (WUNT 49; Tübingen: Mohr Siebeck), 277–307; R. Riesner (1998), *Paul's Early Period* (trans. D. W. Stott; Grand Rapids: Eerdmans), 280–91.

18. J. Jervell (1998), *Die Apostelgeschichte* (KEK 3; Göttingen: Vandenhoeck & Ruprecht), 343.

out the historicity of that missionary activity'.[19] Hence a decision in favour of the 'Region' and against the 'Province' (or its southern parts) cannot be reached through criticism of Acts.

Reasons for the *Region Hypothesis* (a) are given – which are in part also reversible:

Table 12.10

+ From the time of the Church Fathers (Ambrosiaster, fourth century), Gal. is connected with the *region* of Galatia (or with the churches mentioned in Acts 16.6 and 18.23).	– But these remarks take for granted later reorganizations of the Roman Province[20] and are of little proof for the time of Paul.
+ In his autobiographical report in 1.21 Paul does not say that he visited the addressees at the time in question. If the towns in southern Galatia were meant, Paul could have said: 'then I went into Syria, Cilicia *and to you*'.[21]	– But did he *have to* formulate it thus? The argument takes too little account of the specific interests of Gal. 1.
+ On several occasions Paul stresses that *he* founded the churches, even that he 'gave birth' to them (4.19). Should he not have also mentioned Barnabas if he is addressing the churches named in Acts 13f.?	– All the same, Barnabas is mentioned three times in Gal. 2 (vv. 1,9,13) which suggests that the churches addressed have a relationship to Barnabas (in accordance with Acts 13f.).
+ In Luke the southern regions of the Province of Galatia are called Pisidia and Lycaonia (Acts 13.14; 14.6,11,24), while Luke names the more northern area the 'Galatian region'.[22]	– But does this apply for Paul, too, who usually uses the names of the Provinces?

---

19. G. Lüdemann (1989), *Early Christianity according to the Traditions of Acts* (trans. J. Bowden; Minneapolis: Fortress, 157); cf. Jervell, *Apostelgeschichte* (n.18), 342f.; M. Hengel and A. M. Schwemer (1997), *Paul Between Damascus and Antioch* (trans. J. Bowden; London: SCM), 260–1; cf. in detail Breytenbach, *Paulus*, 5–93; Riesner, *Paul's Early Period* (n.17), 280–94.

20. Already in 74 CE Pisidia was separated from Galatia; in 297 CE a new province of Pisidia was created with the capital Antioch: This province included the whole southern Galatian area, so that the province of Galatia was in fact restricted to the region in central Anatolia. Cf. Longenecker, *Galatians*, lxiii; Breytenbach, *Paulus*, 99.

21. Thus W. G. Kümmel (1975), Introduction to the New Testament: Quelle & Meyer, 295.

22. Cf. Acts 16.6; 18.23. It remains unclear to what the term applies in 1 Pet. 1.1 or 2 Tim. 4.10 (cf. Schlier, *Brief*, 16).

+ For a long time it was maintained that the use of Galatia to denote the southern area was 'not usual' at that period.	– Yet evidence of the literary and official use of Galatia for the whole province and its inhabitants at the time of Paul definitely exists.[23] The linguistic usage is no longer a conclusive argument that the inhabitants of the province who belonged to different ethnic groups could not be addressed together as Galatai.[24]
+ As the strongest argument it is cited that it would be 'unthinkable ... that Paul in 3.1 would have addressed e.g. Pisidians or Lycaonians as "foolish Galatians"'.[25]	– Yet the greatest acrimony lies in the adjective anoētos. For the rest, we can hardly expect that in such a polemical letter Paul would have paid any attention to 'political correctness'. Consequently the argument is weak.

Consequently several arguments for the *Province Hypothesis* (b) deserve renewed consideration:

+ Paul normally uses the names of Roman provinces; he only uses names of regions for areas in the east such as Arabia and Judaea (Gal. 1.17,22; 1 Thess. 2.14)[26] and 'Spania' in the west (Rom. 15.24). All other names are related to administrative units.

+ Paul talks of the 'churches of Galatia' in 1 Cor. 16.1 also (in a context in which he normally uses only the names of provinces) in relation to the order for a collection for Jerusalem. According to Acts 20.4 there was among the bearers of the collection a representative of the churches in southern Galatia, namely Gaius from Derbe. This, too, speaks for the southern region.

+ In Acts there is no clear reference to any missionary activity by Paul in the Galatian region. The formulations in Acts 16.6–8 and 18.23 might also not mean exactly the same area but may presuppose varying routes. Only in Acts 16.6 is it taken for granted that Paul passed through the northern area. Acts 18.23 might also relate to the southern regions.[27]

+ A Pauline missionary activity in the region of Galatia would be inconsistent with the missionary strategy according to which Paul normally worked in larger towns and used these as a 'base'.[28]

+ If the addressees were not only Gentile Christians but – as Gal. 3.27f. appears to assume – a 'mixed' congregation of Jewish and Gentile Christians with a majority of

23. Hemer, *Book* (n.17), 290–307; Scott, *Paul*, 192–3; Breytenbach, *Paulus*, 149–52; Witulski, *Adressaten*, 17–23; Schäfer, *Paulus* 312–13.
24. Breytenbach, *Paulus*, 152–5 wants to see in the Galatai inhabitants in southern Galatia who are of Celtic origin.
25. H. Hübner, 'Galaterbrief', TRE 12:5–14 (6); in a similar manner Kümmel, *Introduction* (n.21), 298.
26. 'Arabia' is used for the region of the Nabataeans outside of the Roman Empire; Judaea was a part of the Province of Syria.
27. Schäfer, *Paulus*, 302–3.
28. Riesner, *Paul's Early Period* (n.17), 283–4.

Gentile Christians, this is more likely in the towns on the coast than in the north where there were hardly any Jewish communities. Likewise the activity of Jewish-Christian missionaries trying to influence the Pauline churches to their way of thinking is more plausible there where there were synagogues and the contacts to the mother country (Jerusalem) were relatively close.

+ The frequent mentions of Barnabas in Gal. 2 (vv. 1,9,13) can be explained if the addressees knew him as a missionary. – Certainly Paul does not name him as co-founder of the church but this can be explained from the situation of the letter in which Paul is fighting for 'his' gospel. Besides, the parting from Barnabas lies quite some time in the past.

+ If Paul's geographical agenda (Rom. 15.19) is determined by early Jewish tradition (the Table of the Nations), it is interesting that Josephus (*Ant.* I, 123–6) relates Gomer, the son of Japheth, to the 'nation' of the Galatians, and the southern parts of the Province (Paphlagonia) with the sons of Gomer.[29] This shows how, from a Jewish perspective, the ethnic groups in the province could be 'genealogically' integrated. This makes the argument untenable that Galatai could mean only the Celtic inhabitants of the region.[30]

On the whole it appears that there is a growing tendency in scholarship in favour of locating the addressees in the missionary areas on the south coast of Asia Minor.[31] They are rather to be looked for in the areas around Antioch in Pisidia, Iconium etc. where there existed churches where the majority were Gentile Christians with a certain Jewish Christian element alongside a self-assured Jewish Diaspora. Their establishment dates back to the mission organized from Antioch by Barnabas and Paul before the 'Apostolic Council'.

Date and Place of Writing

Gal. does not contain any explicit references to the *date* and *place of writing*. The calculation depends rather on three factors: a) the decision on the *question of the addressees*,[32] b) the *synchronization with Acts*, above all in respect of Paul's journeys to Jerusalem, and c) *evidence of the relative sequence* of the Pauline letters. In research almost all variants are represented from an extremely early date before the 'Apostolic Council' (before 48/49 CE) to a late date after the letter to the Romans (57 CE). The most probable solutions could be calculations which place Gal. *before* 1 Cor., *between* 1 Cor. and 2 Cor. or – the most favoured dating in current German research – *after* 2 Cor. but *before* Rom.
- Textual evidence: Gal. 1.6 and 4.13 offer no useful indications. The fact that the Galatians
- turn away from the Pauline Gospel 'so quickly' (1.6) cannot be cited as proof

---

29. Scott, *Paul*, 214–15.
30. Riesner, *Paul's Early Period* (n.17), 283. Cf. also Schäfer, *Paulus*, 314–15.
31. With the examinations by Hemer, *Book* (n.17); Riesner, *Paul's Early Period* (n.17); Scott, *Paul* and Breytenbach, *Paulus*, according to Hengel and Schwemer, *Paul* (n.19), 475 n.1359, it even appears that 'the old disputed questions should really finally have been settled'.
32. A date *before* the Second Missionary Journey (Acts 16.6) is only possible on the basis of the Province Hypothesis; conversely this can be combined with a later date for the writing of Gal.

of an early dating, and to proteron (4.13) can mean 'first' or 'for the first time' so that we cannot clarify whether Paul visited the churches only once or indeed twice.

- *The synchronization with Acts*: If the incident mentioned in Gal. 2.1–10 is identical with that related in Acts 15 – which the fundamental similarities still support – then Gal. was written after this incident, i.e. after 48 CE. Only if the journey described in Gal. 2.1–10 was identified with the journey to Jerusalem by Paul and Barnabas mentioned in Acts 11.27–30[33] would an earlier calculation be conceivable. If the 'Incident at Antioch' (Gal. 2.11f.) took place very soon after the 'Apostolic Council', Gal. could have been written before 1 Thess. and consequently be the oldest Pauline epistle.[34] Yet much can be said for positioning this event later, i.e. after the Second Missionary Journey.[35] As the period of time for the writing of Gal. would then come into question *the Third Missionary Journey, i.e. (at the earliest) the sojourn in Ephesus (from 52 CE) or the time in Macedonia and Achaia (55/56 CE)*.

Still to be explained the relationship to 1 and 2 Cor. and Rom. The *remarks about the collection* for Jerusalem and the *thematic proximity (and difference) to Rom.* might serve as arguments.

- The *remarks about the collection*: The collection is mentioned in 1 Cor. 16.1ff. 2 Cor. 8–9 urges it on and Rom. 15.25–27 reports its completion in Macedonia and Achaia. According to 1 Cor. 16.1 Paul has also ordered the collection in Galatia. The question then is, what does Gal. 2.10 mean ('the very thing I was eager to do') within this framework? If one understands the remark in the sense that the collection in Galatia was already concluded when Gal. was written, this leads to a date after 2 Cor.[36] If it is merely about the readiness he declared at that time to carry out the collection, then Gal. might have been written before 1 Cor.[37] The question is difficult to answer since it remains uncertain whether the Galatians participated in the collection. They

---

33. This was eagerly represented by conservative researchers such as T. Zahn from Erlangen but by no means only by such. Cf. I. H. Marshall (1980), *The Acts of the Apostles* (TNTC; Grand Rapids: Eerdmans), 242–7; Bruce, *Galatians*, 19–32; see also C. K. Barrett (1994), *A Critical and Exegetical Commentary on the Acts of the Apostles*, vol. I (ICC; Edinburgh: T&T Clark), 560–6. Schäfer, *Paulus*, desires to see in Gal. 2.1–10 a first 'Apostolic Council' *before* the later Council described in Acts 15 but still assigns a late date to Gal.

34. Thus (presupposing the Province Hypothesis) the conjecture in Bruce, *Galatians*, 22; Howard, *Crisis*, ix; Breytenbach, *Paulus*, 172.

35. Hengel and Schwemer, *Paul* (n.19), 242; A. J. M. Wedderburn (2003), *A History of the First Christians* (Edinburgh: T&T Clark), 98–9.

36. J. B. Lightfoot (1890), *Saint Paul's Epistle to the Galatians* (10th ed.; London: Macmillan), 55; U. Schnelle (2005), *Apostle Paul. His Life and Theology* (trans. and rev. by M. E. Boring; Grand Rapids: Baker Academic), 270–1; T. Söding (1997), 'Zur Chronologie der paulinischen Briefe', in Söding, *Das Wort vom Kreuz* (WUNT 93; Tübingen: Mohr Siebeck), 3–30 (29); Schäfer, *Paulus*, 25–6.

37. Thus J. L. Martyn, *Galatians*, 222–8; D. Georgi (1992), *Remembering the Poor: The History of Paul's Collection for Jerusalem* (Nashville: Abingdon).

are not mentioned in Rom. 15.25–27.[38] Whether the conflict had curbed their willingness or whether the collection was already finished at that point in time remains unclear. Yet 1 Cor. 16.1 appears to be undisturbed by the conflicts thematized in Gal. But this, too, does not speak for a later dating of Gal.: Paul might simply not have seen any reason for thematizing the Galatian conflicts in a letter to the Corinthians. Hence the references to the collection do not provide a solid basis for the dating of Galatians.

- The *thematic-theological argument* is brought into play more often: There are close analogies between Gal. and Rom. in the themes of the doctrine of the Law and Justification as well as in individual ideas and motifs.[39] The explanation in Rom. appears less agitated and is thematically extended. From this we deduce that Gal. was written before Rom.[40] The question remains whether one can consequently conclude a close temporal proximity to Rom., i.e. a formulation after 1 and 2 Cor.[41] Then Galatians would have been written around 55/56 CE in Macedonia or Corinth.

There are, however, *considerable uncertainties*: The factual differences between Gal. and Rom. cannot be underestimated, so that a temporal proximity does not necessarily follow from closeness in theme. If a theological 'development' of Paul is deduced from the late formation of Gal., the argument usually becomes circular. The decisive question is whether Paul first developed and phrased his view of Justification at that time and because of the Galatian crisis. The reasons for thinking that it was already at least conceived during his earlier activity and could have been reflected upon theologically are, however, important,[42] and in 1 and 2 Cor., too, in spite of quite different problems in the church, there are the beginnings of theological reflection on Justification.[43] The argument from the history of theology cannot support the burden of explaining a late composition

---

38. Nevertheless a representative of a community in (south) Galatia is mentioned as accompanying Paul in Acts 20.4.

39. Cf. Schnelle, *Apostle Paul*, 277–95 (n.36); *Borse*, Standort.

40. Differently Vouga, *Galater*, 3–5.11, who sees in Gal. the combination of the thoughts in 1 and 2 Cor. and Rom., see F. Vouga (1996), 'Der Galaterbrief: kein Brief an die Galater', in *Schrift und Tradition*. Festschrift J. Ernst (ed. K. Backhaus; Paderborn: Schöningh), 243–58.

41. If one assumes that 2 Cor. and Phil. are made up of parts of letters, some segments of both letters could have been written at a time close to Gal. (following U. Borse, F. Mussner [*Galaterbrief*, 10–11] places Gal. after 2 Cor. 1–9 and before 2 Cor. 10–13); yet the assumption of division on such thematic grounds is circular and consequently problematic.

42. Cf., critically against such a late dating S. Kim (1981), *The Origin of Paul's Gospel* (WUNT II/4; Tübingen: Mohr Siebeck); Hengel and Schwemer, *Paul*, 11–15; C. Dietzfelbinger (1985), *Die Berufung des Paulus* (WMANT 58; Neukirchen-Vluyn: Neukirchener), 115–16; F. Hahn (2006), 'Gibt es eine Entwicklung in den Aussagen über die Rechtfertigung bei Paulus?' in *Studien zum Neuen Testament* vol. II (ed. J. Frey and J. Schlegel; WUNT 192; Tübingen: Mohr Siebeck), 271–98.

43. Cf. e.g. 1 Cor. 4.1–5; 9.20–23 and the remark in 1 Cor. 15.56 – which is readily excluded as a gloss by representatives of the development theory.

of Gal. It is, in fact, impossible to substantiate a precise dating of Gal. within the period of 50–55/6 CE and in relation to 1 and 2 Cor. and Rom.[44]

The Situation of the Churches Addressed

The *situation of the communication* can be ascertained only from the letter itself. Its reconstruction takes for granted that Paul had accurate information about the situation and assumes that his polemical argumentation reproduces a virtually undistorted picture of the position of his opponents. There exists an 'eternal triangle': Paul is writing to churches influenced by other missionaries and who have given ear to their message (1.6–9; 4.9,17,21; 5.4; 6.12f.). With such people Paul argues only indirectly. He has nothing in common with them: More precisely, the 'anathema', the eschatological curse in 1.9 is aimed at them.

The opponents are demanding the *circumcision* of the Gentiles who have come to faith in Christ (6.12f.; cf. 5.1–12 and frequently) with which is connected – at least to a certain extent[45] – the *observance* of the Torah (4.21) which comprises the keeping of the *rules relating to food and purity* (2.11–16; cf. Acts 15.20,9) a *calendar of cultic festivals* ('Calendar piety': 4.10) in addition to further *ethical demands*. Behind this lies a theology which sees an affiliation to the People of the Covenant and participation in the divine promises made possible *exclusively* through circumcision (i.e. to be Jewish or become a proselyte). One who is circumcised like Abraham will be a 'son of Abraham'. The Torah is the God-given way of life for Israel: To comply with it is the expression and necessary implication of affiliation to this Covenant. In this way Gentile Christians are co-opted by circumcision in the manner of Jewish proselytes into the People of God. According to a widespread Jewish standpoint (cf. also Acts 15.1f.) the opening for non-Jews could only be put into practice under this condition. From this point of view, however, the *legitimacy of Paul's circumcision-free mission to the Gentiles is fundamentally challenged* – which for Paul is contrary to the consultations with the Jerusalem 'pillars'.

The opponents were certainly Hellenistic (i.e. Greek-speaking) Jewish *Christians* (or circumcised, i.e. one-time Gentile Christians who have become proselytes), not simply Jews,[46] else they could hardly have impressed the churches. They saw no tension but rather a necessary connection between faith in Jesus and the obligation for circumcision and the Law (cf. a similar position in Mt. 5.17ff.). Presumably they referred to the authority of the mother-church in Jerusalem, from whose position Paul had, as they saw it, distanced himself. Consequently they contested Paul's full 'apostolic' status and thus undermined his authority. That their preaching and theology is an 'other gospel' (and that means *no* gospel) is a Pauline perception. The missionaries no doubt saw themselves as mediators of all the implications of the gospel of Christ for the Gentile peoples. They could

---

44. So also Betz, *Galatians*, 12.
45. That the addressees would be obliged to obey the *whole* of the Law (5.3) is a Pauline interpretation. It is unlikely that the opponents set such an uncompromising demand. Gal. 6.13 speaks against this.
46. So, however, now Nanos, *Irony*, 281–3.

accuse Paul of not introducing the churches he founded completely into the covenant of salvation and the obligations this brought (i.e. of withholding from them the 'total salvation' of the Covenant) to make grace 'cheap'.[47] Here we have a *fundamental criticism of the Pauline gospel* and a *final questioning of his earlier and further-planned mission*. The unprecedented polemic of the argumentation in Gal. corresponds to such a challenge.

The opponents certainly placed themselves in a relationship to the mother-church in Jerusalem,[48] which, due to the rapid mission to the Gentiles, faced increasing political pressure in Judaea for a certain expression of loyalty and thus pursued a 'revival of Jewish self-understanding' that consequently had to be impressed upon the Gentile Christian churches[49] – possibly also in modification of their attitude concerning the decisions of the 'Apostolic Council'.[50] Consequently Paul sees himself in a position where the agreements made with the other apostles are called into question by his opponents (and the people behind them) – and under the circumstances of their position the universal mission which he conducted would be impossible, the fruits of his activity would be destroyed. But it is not a matter of Paul's person or even his 'glory' but of a decisive theological question, 'the appropriate understanding of, and response to, God's saving act in Christ'.[51] The conflict should therefore be thought through *theologically*.

3
Exegesis of the Text

Overview of the Text (Lines of Argumentation)
Nowhere else does Paul underline so emphatically the authority of his *office as apostle* as at the beginning of Gal. His office is not of human origin or assigned by human mediation but was given directly by Christ and God (1.1). 'His' gospel, too, (as he preached it, as the Galatians have accepted it and as it is revealed in what follows)[52] is based on divine revelation (1.11f.) so that even heavenly powers do not have the authority to alter it (1.8). Elsewhere, too, Paul claims that the gospel he has preached is the yardstick for all further proclamation (cf. 1 Cor. 3.10). Opinions are divided about this claim. Here the question is whether

---

47. The success of the early Christian mission, particularly among the 'God-fearers' who hitherto had shied away from the final step of conversion to Judaism, circumcision, can make such ideas comprehensible.
48. There is, however, no recognizable specific connection to James or even to Peter.
49. Thus Schnelle, *Apostle Paul* (n.36), 273–6.
50. The Apostles' Decree handed down by Luke (Acts 15.29) also appears to originate from such attempts at modification. On this cf. J. Wehnert (1997), *Die Reinheit des 'christlichen Gottesvolkes' aus Juden und Heiden* (FRLANT 173; Göttingen: Vandenhoeck & Ruprecht).
51. Schnelle, *Apostle Paul* (n.36), 276.
52. The continuity stressed in 1.8f. makes the assumption appear problematical that in Gal. Paul is taking a new position with regard to the Law, developed because of the Galatian crisis.

deliverance (1.4) or 'Justification' (2.16) comes through Christ *alone* or whether other elements ('circumcision', 'fulfilment of the Law', proving oneself ethically) must be added (for the reason that otherwise salvation would be incomplete or even ineffective). If one believes this, God's saving act in Christ is not understood in its real depth. The interpretation of Paul by the Reformers (Luther, Calvin) is right in drawing this theological consequence, even if it must be corrected in some aspects (as e.g. in their view of Judaism).[53]

The 'autobiographical' section 1.11 – 12.21 serves to *prove the divine authority and normative validity* of the Pauline proclamation of the gospel (free of circumcision and the Law for Gentiles) and its independence of all human authority. The section is consequently everything other than a historical report 'free of bias'.[54] It is rather so that all the elements are related to the theme and situation of the letter and embedded in the argumentation.

For the *independence* of the Pauline gospel, which was not 'taken over' or 'learned' from tradition but was 'revealed' by God (1.12,16) the following grounds are offered:

Paul's change of life from being a zealot for the "traditions of my ancestors" (Torah) and from persecutor to preacher is a work of God, not humanly produced[55]. It is a matter of a call which is based wholly on the will of God (1.15 analogous to the prophets: Jer. 1.5; Isa. 49.1). Paul is called (by God) to be an Apostle (Rom. 1.1).

After his calling he did not 'immediately' follow human counsel (1.16), he did not get in touch with the 'apostles before him' (v. 17) but began an independent proclamation, first in 'Arabia' (the realm of the Nabataeans), then in 'Syria and Cilicia' (the regions around Tarsus and Antioch).[56]

His first visit to Jerusalem[57] took place only three years later, was brief and merely led to his making the acquaintance of Peter and James. The churches in Judaea did not know him and had only heard of his change of life (1.22f.). Hence Paul is independent of the apostles and the mother-church in Jerusalem. This

---

53. On the discussion of the so-called 'New Perspective' of Paul v. the article on 'The Jewishness of Paul' see Chapter 4 in this volume.

54. This is significant when we consider the differences from the report in Acts (e.g. in the number of Paul's journeys to Jerusalem and in the report of the meeting of the apostles in Acts 15). It would scarcely be proper to give priority in principle in the matter of historicity to Gal. 1–2 before Acts. Both witnesses should be interpreted critically within their respective contexts.

55. The pre-Christian Paul was not oppressed under the 'burden' of the Law, entertained no doubt about the necessity of following it precisely and no knowledge that it could not be fulfilled. He certainly does not 'despair' of the Law (cf. Phil. 3.4–6), and his change of lifestyle is not a human 'decision'. All such categories are uncalled for here.

56. Paul was an *independent* missionary before he entered the service of the Antioch church (Acts 13.2).

57. Paul of course means: after his call. One should not, on the basis of this remark, challenge the fact that Paul had already been in Jerusalem studying the Torah in the Pharisaic school (Acts 22.3).

also means that his gospel cannot be 'corrected' or 'supplemented' by standards taken from there.

For the rest Paul knows that he is at one with the other apostles in his proclamation (1 Cor. 15.11). The report on the meeting of the apostles in Jerusalem (the relation of which to Acts 15 is *historically* complex) is an attempt to substantiate this even in the controversial question of the demand for circumcision:

- 'Those who count' in the Jerusalem church have endorsed Paul's apostolate and his mission to the Gentiles as brought about by God (2.7–9).
- Even the uncircumcised Gentile Christian, Titus, whom Paul took with him as a 'demonstration', was not urged to be circumcised by the people in Jerusalem. In this, too, Paul perceives his practice of a circumcision-free mission to be accepted.
- The only condition which Paul accepts is the request to look after the poor (i.e. the impoverished mother-church) – which he then set about doing energetically in his efforts for the collection.

It does not appear that the practical problems of the community made up of Jewish and Gentile Christians were solved by the meeting of the apostles. They only become apparent later in the question of how to deal with the laws relating to food and purity to which the Jewish Christians still felt themselves tied. The practice of the church in Antioch in which the majority of members was Gentile Christian appears initially to have been a 'liberal' implementation, i.e. a lowering of the barriers in favour of the communal meal for all (without laying any special requirements on the Gentiles).[58] The relinquishing of table-fellowship by Peter and other Jewish Christians caused by fear of the visitors from Jerusalem must have caused their previous practice to appear illegitimate (2.18). This would not merely snub the Gentile Christians but would in the end question their participation in Salvation. Consequently for Paul the 'truth of the gospel' is at stake. Thus the incident serves as an example with which Paul at the same time thematizes the problem that, with the circumcision demanded by the 'Judaists' the Galatians would likewise go back under the Law and thereby renounce the freedom they have previously enjoyed as false. Therefore both in the 'Incident at Antioch' and at this point in time in Galatia it is fundamentally a matter of 'Justification by faith', not by 'works of the Law'.

Starting out from the biblical precept that 'no person is just' in God's eyes (Ps. 142.2b LXX) Paul states clearly that this is (also) true regarding the fulfilment of the rules of the Law ('by works of the Law', 2.16). With this in sight – which according to Paul is also necessary for Jewish Christians (such as himself and Peter) – the soteriological quality of the Mosaic Law or the soteriological value of fulfilling its regulations is fundamentally challenged. In the exemplary 'I'-form

---

58. Such consideration for the Jewish-Christians was then demanded in Acts 15.20,29 (cf. 21.25) in the context of the 'Jerusalem Conference' in the 'Apostolic Decree' which probably stemmed from Jerusalem tradition, the *Halakot* for Gentiles (or according to Lev. 17f. for the 'strangers' living in Israel) formulated following the commandment given to Noah (Gen. 9.4).

Paul maps out a double guideline of the new life in Christ (2.19) with reference to Christ's self-offering in his cross (2.20) and the soteriological words about dying with him:

- I through the Law died to the Law – crucified with Christ.
- I live to God; by faith in the Son of God; Christ lives in me.

The complex theological argumentation related to his own experience from 3.1 has the aim of convincing the Galatians *not to yield to the demand for circumcision*.

Table 12.11

Paul recalls his own experience ...	... that the Galatians have received the Spirit and experienced its effects (3.2,5), were assured of their being children of God through baptism (3.27) and know in Christ of the overcoming of old religious and social barriers (3.28).
Paul uses scripture to argue ...	... that the promise given to Abraham promises blessing for the Gentiles (3.8; cf. Gen. 12.3) and that it does not bind to the Law but to faith (3.6; cf. Gen. 15,6; see also Rom. 4.3). A second argument – albeit a somewhat daring allegory from Scripture (4.21–31) – wishes to make clear that, according to the story of Abraham's wives/sons, those who believe can count as children of Abraham and consequently are not slaves but free.
Paul argues in legal terms but at the same time in terms of the history of salvation ...	... that the Mosaic Law was imposed only 430 years after the promise was given to Abraham and consequently cannot dissolve or put under an additional condition at a later date the legally valid legacy which is to be received in faith (3.17f.).
In a multitude of ways Paul underlines *inferiority* and *insufficiency* of the Mosaic Law compared to the Promise given in Christ:	In respect of its *mediation*: it was given by the (many) angels,[59] whereas the promise to Abraham was given by the One God himself (3.19f.). In respect of its *power*: It cannot make alive (3.21; cf. Rom. 8.3). In respect of its *function*: It was not meant to bring 'justice' and life in a positive but in a negative sense, namely 'consign all things to sin' (3.22), i.e. reveal sin.

---

59. The gift of the Law through angels can also be found in Jewish statements (*Jub.* 1.29; Jos. *Ant.* XV, 136; Rabbinic traditions; cf. Acts 7.53; Heb. 2.2) but there they are not valued pejoratively.

Galatians

> In respect of its *relation to faith*: Its task is to guard 'us' (i.e. Israel) as a 'custodian'[60] and watchman 'until Christ came' (3.23f.).
> In respect of its *temporal limitation*: its function has ended with the coming of faith (Christ). Believers are no longer under the 'custodian' (3.25). Hence the Law is not eternal and everlasting[61] but is limited temporally.

Paul can count the Law as belonging to the powers which order the world, the *'elemental spirits'* (4.3 stoicheia tou kosmou) and make it parallel in a certain way to the pagan gods once worshipped by the Galatians (4.8f.).

Paul emphasizes in a radical way the Law's *obligatory character*. Anyone who does not observe it is under the curse (Gal. 3.10; cf. Deut. 27.26). Consequently all who live by 'works of the Law' are under the curse. Paul the Christian believes that there can be no perfect fulfilling of the Law which did not bring this curse upon itself. All are sinners (cf. Rom. 3.10ff.,23).

Paul uses *soteriological* arguments with the *motif of representation*: As the Crucified One Christ took the curse upon himself, became the accursed, to redeem 'us' from the curse of the Law (3.13). Thereby believers are 'redeemed from the curse of the Law, even from the Law itself (4.5), with Christ they have 'died' to the Law (2.19).

This means: A return under the Law would mean a return to slavery (5.1) and to the obligation to obey the *whole* Law (5.3). It would mean a *nullification of grace* (2.21); *the loss of the salvation brought about in Christ* (5.4). It would all have been 'in vain' (2.21; 3.4; 4.11). Consequently the demand for circumcision is diametrically opposed to the 'truth of the gospel'.

In the paraenetic section 5.13 – 6.10 Paul wants to counter the obvious accusation that freedom from the Law means freedom for the human 'desires'[62] conflicting with God. Fulfilment of the *whole* Law is given rather in the commandment of love (Lev. 19.18) and love is at the same time the first and decisive 'fruit of the spirit'. The individual paraeneses (6.1–10: helpful rebuke, bearing one another's burdens, humility, doing good) consequently put this command of love in concrete terms.

The ending in Paul's own handwriting (6.11–18) in addition to a renewed attack on his opponents (6.12f.) summarizes once again the more important points in the letter: In Christ the boundary-line between circumcision and uncircumcision (i.e. Jews and Gentiles) has been soteriologically surmounted; a *new creation* is established (6.15.; cf. 2 Cor. 5.17).

---

60. The word paidagōgos here means the slave who guarded young boys and if need be punished them but did not teach them.
61. This was the widespread view in contemporary Judaism.
62. 'Desire' is at the same time a key concept in the Ten Commandments.

Exegetical Problems
Individual exegetical problems which cannot be discussed here in detail are:

1. The interpretation of the use of erga nomou and the Pauline statement that 'no flesh' (i.e. no one) can be justified ex ergōn nomou.[63]
2. The debate on the translation and interpretation of the genitive pistis Christou, which centres on the question whether the phrase refers to 'faith in Christ' (objective genitive) or to 'the faithfulness of Christ' (subjective genitive). While the traditional view underlines the incompatibility of 'works of the Law' and 'faith' with respect to salvation (cf. Gal. 2.16), the subjective understanding emphasizes within the framework of a 'representative Christology' that 'Jesus Christ, like Abraham, is justified ek pisteos and that we, as a consequence, are justified *in* him ..., as a result of his faithfulness.'[64] Although the subjective understanding has numerous supporters, especially in the English-speaking world, philological and theological reasons strongly support the view that the term primarily points to the believers' faithful relationship with Christ as the only mode in which, according to Paul's theology, salvation is received.
3. The relationship of the teaching on the Law in Gal. and that set out in Rom. which is no less fundamental but in individual elements has a much more positive, less polemical, view of the Law. Here the question arises whether Paul misunderstood the Judaism of his day, whether he has given up his Jewish identity or whether – in spite of all polemic – he is still moving within the bounds of the internal Jewish discussion.
4. In Gal. 5.1ff. but also in 5.13 *freedom* is introduced as a fundamental concept of life in Christ. From the alternatives Law/freedom in the perspective of Pauline ethics, the task arises of giving an appropriate place to the *Indicative* of the promise of salvation and the *Imperative* of the paraeneses (cf. 5.13: love as fulfilment of the Law). This task is made more difficult by Paul's use in Gal. 6.2 of the phrase 'law of Christ'.

4
Evaluation

Gal. is often considered as the 'most Pauline' of Paul's epistles. It belongs with 1 and 2 Cor. and Rom. to the *'major letters'* and with 2 Cor. to the so-called *'combat letters'* in which Paul battles for the recognition of his apostolate

---

63. On this see Bachmann, *Anti-Judaism*, 19–84, as well as the contribution 'Paul and Judaism' in this volume, p. ???.

64. Hays, *The Faith of Jesus Christ*, 151; cf. recently D. Heliso (2007), *Pistis and the Righteous One* (WUNT II/235; Mohr Siebeck), 216–23. See for a critique and for further discussion K. F. Ulrichs (2007), *Christusglaube* (WUNT II/227; Tübingen: Mohr Siebeck); B. Schliesser (2007), *Abraham's Faith in Romans 4* (WUNT II/224; Tübingen: Mohr Siebeck), 257–80; M. Bird and P. Sprinkle (2010), *The Faith of Jesus Christ* (ed. M. Bird and P. Sprinkle; Peabody: Hendrickson).

and for 'his' gospel. This letter is central for the understanding of Paul's biography and for the interpretation of his theology. It has determined the perception of Paul and his impact in the history of theology. Antitheses such as 'gospel' and 'Law' (Marcion; Luther), 'Paulinism' and 'Judaism' (F. C. Baur) or even 'Christianity' and 'Judaism'[65] are often formulated with reference to Gal. The debate on the attitude to the Law of one who believes in Christ or even on the relationship between faith and ethics goes back in basic details to Gal. Consequently the exegesis of Galatians still has systematic theological implications.

References

Commentaries

H. D. Betz (1979), *Galatians*. Hermeneia. Philadelphia: Fortress Press.

F. F. Bruce (1982), *The Epistle to the Galatians*. New International Greek Testament Commentary. Grand Rapids, MI: Eerdmans.

J. D. G. Dunn (1993), *The Epistle to the Galatians*. Black's New Testament Commentary. London: A & C Black.

R. Y. K. Fung (1988), *The Epistle to the Galatians*. New International Commentary on the New Testament. Grand Rapids, MI: Eerdmans.

H. Lietzmann (1971), *An die Galater*. Handbuch zum Neuen Testament 10. 4th ed. Tübingen: Mohr Siebeck.

R. N. Longenecker (1990), *Galatians*. Word Biblical Commentary 41. Dallas: Word.

J. L. Martyn (1998), *Galatians*. Anchor Bible 33A. New York: Doubleday.

F. Matera (1992), *Galatians*. Sacra Pagina 9. Collegeville, MN: Liturgical Press.

F. Mussner (1981), *Der Galaterbrief*. Herders theologischer Kommentar zum Neuen Testament 9. 4th ed. Freiburg: Herder.

H. Schlier (1971) *Der Brief an die Galater*. Kritisch-exegetischer Kommentar über das Neue Testament 7. 5th ed. Göttingen: Vandenhoeck & Ruprecht.

F. Vouga (1998) *An die Galater*. Handbuch zum Neuen Testament 10. Tübingen: Mohr Siebeck.

B. Witherington (2004), *Grace in Galatia: A Commentary on Paul's Letter to the Galatians*. London: T&T Clark.

---

65. In Gal. the term Ioudaismos (1.13f.) can be found for a way of life oriented on the Torah, but not Christianismos. This juxtaposition occurs first at the beginning of the second century CE in Ignatius (*Magn.* 8,1; 10,1–3; *Phld.* 6,1) and even there does not signify two different religions. But one of the effects of Gal. is that it is frequently introduced to account for the break between 'Christianity' and 'Judaism'.

Monographs

M. Bachmann (2008), *Anti-Judaism in Galatians?: Exegetical Studies on a Polemical Letter and on Paul's Theology*. Translated by R. Brawley. Grand Rapids: Eerdmans.

—(1992), *Sünder oder Übertreter: Studien zur Argumentation in Gal 2,15ff*. Wissenschaftliche Untersuchungen zum Neuen Testament 59. Tübingen: Mohr Siebeck.

J. M. G. Barclay (1988), *Obeying the Truth: Paul's Ethics in Galatians*. Studies of the New Testament and Its World. Edinburgh: T&T Clark.

U. Borse (1972), *Der Standort des Galaterbriefes*. Bonner biblische Beiträge 41. Köln/Bonn: Hanstein.

C. Breytenbach (1996) *Paulus und Barnabas in der Provinz Galatien: Studien zu Apostelgeschichte 13f; 16,6; 18,23 und den Adressaten des Galaterbriefes*. Arbeiten zur Geschichte des antiken Judentums und des Urchristentums 38. Leiden: Brill.

H.-J. Eckstein (1996), *Verheißung und Gesetz: Eine exegetische Studie zu Gal 2,15–4,7*. Wissenschaftliche Untersuchungen zum Neuen Testament 86. Tübingen: Mohr Siebeck.

I. J. Elmer (2009), *Paul, Jerusalem and the Judaisers: The Galatian Crisis in Its Broadest Historical Context*. Wissenschaftliche Untersuchungen zum Neuen Testament II/258. Tübingen: Mohr Siebeck.

J. K. Hardin (2008), *Galatians and the Imperial Cult: A Critical Analysis of the First-Century Social Context of Paul's Letter*. Wissenschaftliche Untersuchungen zum Neuen Testament II/237. Tübingen: Mohr Siebeck.

R. B. Hays (2002), *The Faith of Jesus Christ: The Narrative Substructure of Galatians 3.1-4.11*. 2nd ed. The Biblical Resource Series. Grand Rapids: Eerdmans.

G. E. Howard (1990), *Paul: Crisis in Galatia. A Study in Early Christian Theology*. Society for New Testament Studies Monograph Series 35. 2nd ed. Cambridge: CUP.

D. Kremendahl (2000), *Die Botschaft der Form: Zum Verhältnis von antiker Epistolographie und Rhetorik im Galaterbrief*. Novum Testamentum et orbis antiquus 45. Göttingen: Vandenhoeck & Ruprecht.

M. D. Nanos (2002), *The Irony of Galatians: Paul's Letter in First-Century Context*. Minneapolis: Fortress.

R. Schäfer (2004), *Paulus bis zum Apostelkonzil: Ein Beitrag zur Einleitung in den Galaterbrief, zur Geschichte der Jesusbewegung und zur Pauluschronologie*. Wissenschaftliche Untersuchungen zum Neuen Testament II/179. Tübingen: Mohr Siebeck.

J. M. Scott (1995), *Paul and the Nations: The Old Testament and Jewish Background of Paul's Mission to the Nations with Special Reference to the Destination of Galatians*. Wissenschaftliche Untersuchungen zum Neuen Testament 84. Tübingen: Mohr Siebeck.

A. Wechsler (1991), *Geschichtsbild und Apostelstreit: Eine forschungsgeschichtliche und exegetische Studie über den antiochenischen Zwischenfall (Gal 2,11–14)*. Beihefte zur Zeitschrift für die neutestamentliche Wissenschaft 62. Berlin: de Gruyter.

Chapter 13

The Letter to the Philippians
Lukas Bormann

Table 13.1

Sender	Paul and Timothy (1.1)		
Addressees	Christians with their leaders and helpers in Philippi		
Situation of origin	Paul in prison		
Occasion	Thanks for help sent by the Philippians		
Place of origin	Ephesus, traditionally Rome (not explicitly named)		
Date	Spring 55 CE, traditionally 60 CE		
Opposition	3.2: 'dogs', 'evil-workers'; 3.18 'enemies of the cross of Christ'		
Themes	Participation in the eschatological event of the proclamation of the gospel		
Broad division the letter	Beginning of	1.1f. 1.3–11	*Epistolary prescript* *Epistolary proemium* as thanksgiving
	Body of the letter	1.12 – 4.20	Proclamation of the gospel, arrest, opponents and thanksgiving
	Ending of the letter	4.21–23	Final greetings

1
Approaching the Text

The Content and Transmission of the Text
Philippians contains approximately 1,624 words[1] and taking up around eight Nestle pages is one of the shorter Pauline letters. The oldest larger papyrus

---

1. R. Morgenthaler (1983), *Statistik des neutestamentlichen Wortschatzes*, Zürich, 164.

which has come down to us containing Pauline epistles, the Chester Beatty II (Þ46) contains virtually the whole of Philippians barring minor omissions (1.1,5–15,17–28; 1.30 – 2.12,14–27; 2.29 – 3.8,10–21; 4.2–12,14–23).[2] Further papyri (Þ16 and Þ61) attest a few additional verses to those preserved in Þ46. The manuscripts authoritative for the New Testament text in modern critical editions, the majuscule manuscripts Sinaiticus (א or 01) and Vaticanus (B or 03) contain the whole of the letter to the Philippians.[3]

The manuscripts raise no far-reaching text-critical problems.[4] The extension of the addressees in 1.1 to bishops and deacons is occasionally described as a post-Pauline gloss, without this assumption having backing from the manuscripts.[5]

Already in the letter of Polycarp (around 110 CE) there is mention of several letters which Paul wrote to the church at Philippi (Polyc 3.2: egrapsen epistolas). Recent studies have contended that the letter to the Philippians was used by Colossians.[6]

Analysis of the Text
The letter to the Philippians is not a literary epistle but a document which is part of an intensive, varied exchange relationship. It supports the lively communication between the church at Philippi and its founder, the apostle Paul. Personal information is communicated: Paul's arrest, Epaphroditus' state of health, the plans of Timothy, Epaphroditus and Paul; finally the references to Euodia, Syntyche, the nameless 'fellow workers' and Clement along with the greetings from a group of imperial slaves show the close integration of the letter in the current events concerning Paul, his environment and the Philippians. This lively communication, however, is now bound by Paul into a chronological structure not determined by these events but through the 'day of (Jesus) Christ' (1.6,10; 2.16). For the communication represented in Philippians the important fact is: 'The Lord is at hand!' (4.5). The church has been drawn into this temporal horizon from the moment of Paul's initial proclamation. She is a part of the eschatological event of Christ becoming reality which was initiated by God. Within the frame of this eschatologically interpreted present time a proclamation of the gospel takes place in which Paul and the church act together. The structuring of the relationship between the apostle and the church occurs after the pattern of the Christ-event. Phil. 2.6–11, certainly the most important individual passage in the letter to the Philippians, in this sense comprises the heart of the letter. The Christ-event is formulated poetically (the Song or Christ-hymn) and

---

2. K.Aland et al. (eds) ([27]1993), *Novum Testamentum Graece*, Stuttgart, 686; cf. K. Aland and B. Aland (1995), *The Text of the New Testament. An Introduction to the Critical Editions and to the Theory and Practice of Modern Textual Criticism*, Grand Rapids, 83–102.
3. Survey in J. Gnilka ([4]1987), *Der Philipperbrief, der Philemonbrief* (HThK X 3/4), Freiburg i.Br., 26f.
4. M. Bockmuehl, *Epistle*, 40f.; J. Reumann, *Philippians*, 7f.
5. Bockmuehl, *Epistle*, 53; Reumann, *Philippians*, 86.
6. O. Leppä (2003), *The making of Colossians* (SESJ 86), Göttingen, 209–17; 247–9.

demands an attitude among the recipients which goes beyond the exchange of information.

Structure

The structure of the epistle can be seen to a large extent independently of decisions about its controversial literary unity. The shifts in theme are clear. Those who hold to the unity of the letter ascribe these to a change in style or topic; those who hold to the hypothesis of a collection of fragments see here a change in the situation of the epistolary communication.

The prescript in Phil. 1.1f. and the closing greetings in 4.21–23 form the framework. In 4.4–7 and 4.8f. there are introductions to the ending of the letter which each close with a wish for peace (cf. 4.7 with 4.9).

Between the prescript (1.1f.) and the closing greetings (4.21–23) there are three arguments that are complete in themselves. In 1.3 – 2.30 Paul thematizes the *new situation of the proclamation of the gospel created by his arrest*. The proclamation of the gospel has, because of external circumstances, become a situation of probation and battle which brings serious problems for the apostle and his churches. The new beginning in 3.1 is either the close of this passage or should be understood as a transition to the second dominant theme in the letter: *The endangering of the gospel-compliant imitation of Christ*. In 3.2 – 4.1 the apostle tackles the problem of *false ways of interpreting the emulation of Christ*. The opposed position – which we cannot grasp with certainty – is usually connected with a Jewish-Christian mission that demanded circumcision and observance of the Law. The section 4.2–9, which in itself appears somewhat extraneous, is best understood as an introduction to the ending of the letter. 4.2f. gives a personal exhortation to unity (to auto phronein). 4.4–7 and 4.8f. initiate the close of the letter. 4.10–20 on the other hand forms an argument complete in itself which deals with the *support* Paul has received from the Philippians. At the centre stand his thanks. From this there emerges the following structure:

Table 13.2

1.1f.	Prescript
1.3–11	Proemium, thanksgiving
1.12 – 3.1	Proclamation of the gospel and arrest
3.2 – 4.1	Imitation of Christ
4.2f.	Exhortations to particular people
4.4–7	1st introduction to the close of a letter
4.8f.	2nd introduction to the close of a letter
4.10–20	Letter of thanksgiving
4.21–23	Closing greetings

Themes

The letter to the Philippians deals with the *situation of the proclamation of the gospel* as it is determined by the arrest of Paul, the helping and missionary activity of the Philippian church and finally by controversies over the form of the congregation's imitation of Christ. In this situation, discussion of the state of the proclamation of Christ is experiencing an intensification through the possible death of Paul, through the heightened situation of conflict with the governing authorities which the Philippians are causing through their loyalty to Paul and through opponents who are endangering the consistent imitation of Christ. In this situation the document serves the 'mutual ascertainment of the common participation in the Gospel'.[7]

Paul succeeds in taking up the conflicts of the situation in his theological argumentation, whereby they gain fundamental significance. In the effects the letter has had historically, the reflections on individual death (1.1–26), the so-called Christ-hymn (2.6–11) and the thoughts on righteousness through faith (3.7–11) are central. The Pauline argumentation is characterized by the intense eschatological expectation of the Day of Christ and the Parousia of Christ connected with it. The efforts for the proclamation of the gospel are put in this horizon, and its form should be oriented on the fate of Christ.

Semantic Fields

The letter to the Philippians belongs with 1 Thess. and Phlm. to the small group of Pauline epistles which do not contain any explicit quotations.[8] Nowhere in Philippians does Paul refer to Scripture (graphē) as such or to individual biblical books. Although quotations and references to Old Testament texts are missing there are numerous allusions to the Old Testament.[9] The allusions are defined by matching orders of up to five words (Phil. 1.19 and Job 13.16 LXX: touto moi apobēsetai eis sōtērian)[10] and by succinct syntactic constructions (Phil. 2.10f. and Isa. 45.23: pan gony kampsē ... kai pasa glōssa exhomologēsetai).[11] The linguistic connection to the Old Testament texts which in the end is minimal is now and again utilized to draw conclusions about the historical readers of the Letter to the Philippians: 'In Philippians there is little evidence that there was a significant Jewish presence within the Philippian Christian community; there are no clear allusions to the Hebrew scripture and the proper names in the letter are Greek and Latin (...).'[12]

The letter to the Philippians is characterized by an independent theological argumentation by Paul related to the situation which receives its linguistic succinctness from his interpretation of the Christ-event. The noun most often

---

7. H. Balz (1996), 'Art. Philipperbrief', *TRE* 26, 504–13, 509.
8. Bockmuehl, *Epistle*, 9.
9. J. Reumann, *Old Testament*, 189f.
10. R. B. Hays (1989), *Echoes of Scripture in the Letters of Paul*. New Haven/London, 21–4.
11. O. Hofius, *Christushymnus*, 70.
12. R. S. Ascough, *Associations*, 203.

used is 'Christos' (Christos 37; cf. Rom.: 65), the name 'Jesus' also occurs frequently (Iēsous 22; cf. Rom.: 37) and only then does the name of 'God' follow (theos 24; cf. Rom.: 153).[13] In the letter to the Romans the proportion of the occurrences of the names of God and Christ is somewhat reversed (Phil. 59:24; Rom. 102:153).[14] The statistical findings support the material observation that in the letter to the Romans Paul in the end orients his argumentation on ideas of God[15] while in the letter to the Philippians the Christ-event is central. Paul desires to express the dynamics of the eschatological horizon shown in the Christ-event in the life of the apostle and of the Christian community in order to drive forward the activity of the Philippian church in the proclamation of the gospel.

Here the linguistic field of 'rejoicing' plays a special part: chara (1.4,25; 2.2,29; 4.1); syncharein (1.18; 2.17,18,28; 3.1; 4.1,10). It is to be found exclusively outside the polemics in 3.2 – 4.1 and describes the manner of acting as a Christian in the proclamation of the gospel: collective rejoicing. The practice of solidarity in medial and material communication is expressed in the semantic field of koinōnia for 'joint partnership': koinōnia (1.5; 2.1; 3.10); synkoinōnos, synkoinōnein (1.7; 4.14); koinōnein (4.15). The shape of this partnership is described by the semantic field of 'form, model, being made like, imitate': morphē (2.6f.); symmorphizesthai (3.10); symmorphos (3.21); homoiōma (2.7); schēma (2.7); symmimētai (3.17); typos (3.17); metaschēmatizein (3.21). The social and political dimension of the community's life is underlined by the use of concepts that have a military or political ring: synathlein (1.27; 4.3); agōn (1.30); politeuesthe (1.27); politeuma (3.10). This entire practice of solidarity in imitation of the Christ-event is oriented on the Day of Christ: hēmera Christou (1.6,10; 2.16).

Communication and Rhetoric
Communication
The Philippian correspondence reflects the intensive mutual exchange of information between Paul and the Christian community at Philippi, in which spoken communication was only a part. Financial support, visits and the correspondence itself witness to varied means of direct communication. If one attempts to identify the communication mentioned in the letter to the Philippians one must bear in mind the following events: Paul's first visit accompanied by persecution and torture (1 Thess. 2.2; Acts 16.11–40); afterwards the Philippians on several occasions provided financial support for Paul's mission in Thessalonica (4.16); Epaphroditus, the envoy of the Christian community and bearer of a further gift (4.18), is with Paul when he is arrested (2.25); the Philippians know that Epaphroditus is ill and he for his part has heard how worried they are in Philippi about him (2.26); Paul wants to send Timothy (2.19) and Epaphroditus

---

13. Morgenthaler, *Statistik* (n.1), 105, 107, 156.
14. *Ibid.*, 164, 168.
15. Cf. 'Overview of the text' in Chapter 15 on the letter to the Romans by O. Wischmeyer, this volume.

to Philippi (2.28); finally, he announces that he himself intends to visit them (2.24).[16]

The communication by letter cannot be separated from these actual contacts which constantly determine the background for the interpretation of what is said in the letter. An interpretation of the letter oriented on the text in a narrower sense – whether based on epistolography, rhetoric or literary studies as is again and again attempted – tends to marginalize the comprehensible, factual and historical relationship of the chain of incidents.

The relationship which is stabilized and proved by the financial exchanges is accompanied by open-heartedness and rejoicing (2.18; 3.1; 4.4). The Christ-event makes possible a participatory sense of community which even now in its fulfilment imparts a share in the eschatological joy.

The close community relationship is controlled in a few places where Paul introduces admonishments or slight rebukes. In 4.2f. Euodia and Syntyche are admonished to co-operate, and a 'yokefellow' (syzygos), nameless but directly addressed in the second person, should again work together with the community of Paul's fellow workers without prejudice. In 4.10 there is a certain ironical hint of Paul's impatience that the Philippians' support has failed to appear for some time. Here he is making small corrections in the relationships between the people connected to the proclamation of the gospel. The sharp polemics into which Paul launches in Phil. 3.2–21 is clearly far different from this. Personal, defamatory insults (3.2) and polemical, dissociative rhetoric (3.18f.) predominate in this section. The play on words between katatomē (amputation or mutilation) and peritomē (circumcision) is intended to disparage his opponents personally but is not a devaluation of circumcision *qua se*, which Paul immediately claims for himself (3.2,5).

Rhetoric

The rhetorical analysis of the Pauline epistles which commenced in the promising interpretation of the letter to the Galatians was also applied on numerous occasions to the letter to the Philippians. Alexander sees the letter to the Philippians as a 'family letter' which 'could transform itself into a homily (ch. 3) and back again (ch. 4)'.[17] Brucker believes that Philippians is a 'rhetorically complete document of the advisory genre'. The abrupt change of style corresponds to ancient rhetorical theory and is intended to 'achieve a contrast'.[18]

---

16. Reumann, *Philippians*, 7.
17. L. Alexander, *Letter-Forms*, 245.
18. R. Brucker (1997), '"Christushymnen" oder "epideiktische Passagen"? Studien zum Stilwechsel im Neuen Testament und seiner Umwelt' (*FRLANT* 176), Göttingen, 326, 348–50.

2
The Genesis of the Text

Author, Addressees and Historical Situation

It has seldom been contested that Paul was the author. Nevertheless F. C. Baur did not number the letter to the Philippians among the genuine Pauline epistles, because its Christology were determined by the 'speculative ideas of Gnosis'.[19] Such criticism has not been raised in more recent times. Paul and Timothy are named as senders (1.1). Timothy's influence on the form of the text, however, must have been minimal; possibly when writing 1.14–17 and 2.19–30 Paul fell back on information from Timothy. Timothy was no doubt also intended to be the bearer of the letter. At any rate Paul sees himself as having cause to write a few words of recommendation (2.20–22). It seems reasonable to suppose that he intended shortly to start out for Philippi with Epaphroditus, the envoy of the Christian community there (2.28f.).

The details about the addressees are noticeably expanded. Paul is writing to 'the saints in Christ Jesus who are at Philippi with the overseers and deacons'.[20] This throws a first light on the conditions in the community. The episkopoi kai diakonoi appear to perform functions that arise from the particular structure of organization in the Philippian church. The fact that episkopos is missing in the other genuine Pauline epistles underlines the fact that here we are dealing with a function which developed in the church there. The description of a function as that of an episkopos was very common and most likely refers to financial tasks relating to administration and organization. The addressees face the apostle who founded their church as a Christian community which itself determines its own internal structures and actively develops them.

At this point the question constantly arises as to the Jewish or Gentile background of the community. As sensible as such a question is, it is nevertheless usually loaded by preconceptions about Judaism or paganism which are in themselves open to question. Acts 16.13 at any rate expressly reports on the linking of the Pauline mission with a Jewish-inspired place of prayer for women outside the town. At the same time Acts is also aware that the seller of purple goods from Thyatira named Lydia who had herself and her household baptized was a god-fearer and not a Jewess (Acts 16.14f.).[21] In addition, the prison guard converted by the apostles would probably have been a *servus publicus*, a slave owned by the authorities who had a Roman-Hellenistic background (Acts 16.32–34). In the letter to the Philippians itself we find exclusively names that belong to the Roman-Hellenistic world: Euodia, Syntyche, Clement and above all the heathen name Epaphroditus (derived from the name of the goddess Aphrodite). Even the slaves greeted in 4.22 or the freedmen from the Imperial House (*domus Augusti*) would have been very well acquainted with the religious-

---

19. F. C. Baur (1864), *Vorlesungen über neutestamentliche Theologie*, ed. F. F. Baur, Leipzig, 267.
20. On Philippi cf. Bockmuehl, *Epistle*, 2–10.
21. Bockmuehl, *Epistle*, 8–10.

political propaganda of the Julian-Claudian house. An all too narrow separation of the Jewish and Gentile ways of living in any case does not make sense outside of the Palestinian heartland of Judaism, Judaea and Galilee.[22] It is striking that in the letter to the Philippians Paul trusts in the ethical decisions of the community (2.15; 4.8). If one compares this with 1 Corinthians, one would have to say that the deficits of pagan ethics did not have to be corrected in Philippi. It is possible that the polemics in Phil. 3.2ff. speak for a Jewish background. Circumcision and the Law appear to be among the controversial issues here. This only makes sense against the background of a certain familiarity with Judaism. But circumcision and the Jewish Law belong on the other hand to the best-attested general knowledge of Judaism in pagan texts which have little other information on it. What is more, in Phil. 3.8–10 Paul abstains from separating himself from 'works of the Law' (cf. Phil. 3.9 with Gal. 2.16; Rom. 3.28).

In consequence one can say that there was sympathy in the community with the Jewish idea of God and with the Jewish lifestyle, but its cultural and political character was determined by the Roman-Hellenistic world.

Date and Place of Writing

The letter to the Philippians gives no explicit information on when and where it was written. It is also difficult to draw conclusions from remarks elsewhere, so that even the place of Philippians in the relative chronology of the Pauline epistles cannot be determined with certainty. The reading of the majority of texts in the Koine provides in the *subscriptio* the remark 'written from Rome' and thereby defines the traditional view of the letters written from prison – Eph., Phil., Col. and Phlm. (and also 2 Tim.) – which are said to have been written in Rome (Euseb. h.e. II 22). Critical research on this usually comes to other conclusions. The two genuinely Pauline epistles among the letters from prison, Philippians and Philemon, are located on the grounds of the situation of arrest described either in Rome (Bockmuehl, Schnelle), Caesarea (Lohmeyer) or in one of the imprisonments in Ephesus implied in 2 Cor. 1.8 or 1 Cor. 15.32 (Gnilka, Reumann, Walter). At the heart of the discussion lies the intense communication between the Christian community and the apostle, the naming of the location 'praetorium' (1.13) and the use of the term describing people as those of 'Caesar's household' (4.22). Paul's energetic travels do not speak conclusively against Rome, but 'praetorium' and 'Caesar's household' likewise do not speak conclusively for Rome.

Because of this open argument, internal developments in Paul's theological statements are from time to time used to date or to fit the letter into the relative chronology of the Pauline epistles, but here, too, there is nothing really decisive produced. The eschatological mood of Philippians is most clearly matched in the early 1 Thess. while the expectation of the death of the individual in Phil. 1.19–26 is in a certain way discordant with 1 Thess. 4.13–17 and 1 Cor. 15.50–54. But from this we cannot base a development or some sort of change in Paul's thinking which can then be chronologically evaluated, for what he said on each occasion

---

22. M. Goodman (ed.) (1998), *Jews in a Graeco-Roman World*, Oxford.

was determined by the situation. Incidentally, an examination of the older academic writings from Baur through Ewald, Lüttgert, Michaelis and Dibelius up to Lohmeyer warns against a dating based on the development of theological ideas. The topics judged to be conclusive here range from Gnostic speculation through a doctrine of perfection to the idea of martyrdom. It is rather the statements that relate to the factual, temporal context which should be decisive, and here the standpoints discussed hardly change. In the end the argument from the intense relationship of interchange between Paul and the Philippians should be decisive. The contacts mentioned consist of deliveries of financial aid, visits of envoys from the community who are informed about the situation and three journeys to Philippi which are proposed (of Timothy, Epaphroditus and Paul himself). If one also assumes that the letter to the Philippians probably represents a correspondence of three letters, there emerges an even more intensive network of communication. Those who consider here an imprisonment in Rome as probable tend to assume exceptionally high speeds of travelling rather than the average achievement repeated on several occasions.[23] Consequently priority should be given to the letter's having been written in Ephesus. Michaelis was the first to substantiate in detail the Ephesus thesis, which has been well received.[24]

Paul was in Ephesus around 52 and 55 (Acts 19.8–10). 1 Cor. assumes that the imprisonment had ended, but it was still written in Ephesus and names Pentecost as the date of departure (1 Cor. 16.8). Hence the correspondence with the Philippians must have been written earlier, so that one can date the Letter to the Philippians roughly at the same time as the letter to Philemon in the spring of 55 CE.

Unity and the Process of Editing

Various arguments against the unity of the letter to the Philippians have been asserted. Starting points are the abrupt change of style and situation occurring in 3.2, the completeness of 4.10–20 and the situational tensions it involves. The stylistic peculiarities are often explained laboriously by those who hold to the unity of the epistle. Even if one takes into account here the loose series of topics in ancient letters, the transitions from the invitation to rejoice in 3.1 to the wild insults in 3.2, and again from the sharp polemic in 3.18f. to the sensitive, personal *paraenesis* in 4.2f. and to the cry of joy in 4.4, are difficult to understand. Some commentators who maintain the literary unity admit here at least that there was an interruption in the writing or that new information turned up in order to explain the clear change in the situation.[25]

A similar argument arises with regard to 4.10–20. Why does Paul deal in so much detail with Epaphroditus in 2.25–30, praising his action in bringing a gift from the community at Philippi, yet only in 4.10–20 give thanks for the support of the Philippians which he brought (4.18)? Why does he say in a businesslike

---

23. U. Schnelle (2005), *Apostle Paul. His Life and Theology*, Grand Rapids, Mich., 369. Rome–Philippi: 14 days by ship or four weeks overland.
24. W. Michaelis (1935), *Der Brief des Paulus an die Philipper* (ThHK 11), Leipzig, 2–6.
25. Bockmuehl, *Epistle*, 25.

tone that he 'now', directly after receiving the gift, has enough (4.18) when, according to 2.25–30 there have been several communications between the place of his imprisonment and Philippi on the state of Epaphroditus' health, which would not only put several weeks between the receipt of the gift and the thanks for it but would also suppose several unused opportunities for giving thanks? These discrepancies are so grave that they form the basis for the important literary and historical thesis of the disunity of the letter to the Philippians.[26] One can reckon with three letter-parts: Letter A 4.10–23 (a letter of thanks); Letter B 1.1–3; 4.2–7 (a letter from prison); Letter C 3.2 – 4.1.8f. (against teachers of false doctrine). If one does not wish to follow this division, like Markus Bockmuehl and Udo Schnelle, the division of the contents which it expresses still remains important: Phil. 1 and 2 = a letter from prison; Phil. 3 = polemics against opponents; Phil. 4.10–20 = expression of thanks.

Table 13.3

	Letter A	Letter B	Letter C
Bormann's proposal, Similarly Bornkamm and Schmithals	4.10–23	1.2 – 3.1 4.2–7	3.2 – 4.1,8f.
Reumann's proposal	4.10–20	1.1 – 3.1 + parts of 4.1–9 + 4.21–23	3.2–21+ parts of 4.1–9
General proposal	1 + 2	3	4.10–20

3
Exegesis of the Text

Overview of the Text

By naming the apostle and Timothy on the one side and the saints, overseers and helpers of the Philippian church on the other, the prescript (1.1f.) emphasizes the variety of mutual relationships. The detailed proemium (1.3–11) strengthens this aspect with the thanks for the 'partnership in the gospel from the first day until now' (1.5). Paul emphasizes that this partnership remains secure despite his imprisonment and is part of the eschatological event initiated by God (1.7). After this programmatic introduction he turns to the consequences of his arrest for the proclamation of the gospel (1.12 – 3.1). According to 1.12–18 Paul's imprisonment is promoting the proclamation of the gospel 'throughout the whole *praetorium*' (1.13), but the conditions outside are not developing entirely as Paul would have liked. Here it does not appear to be a matter of fundamental controversies; if this were so Paul's mild criticism would be inexplicable. In 1.19–26 he reflects upon his own situation. He anticipates his death and weighs

26. Reumann, *Philippians*, 7–13.

up the meaning of life and death for the proclamation of the gospel. Both are valuable. Death brings one nearer to Christ; the life of the apostle will strengthen the Christian community and increase its eschatological glory.

In 1.27–30 he intensifies the attachment of the church to the gospel in a terminology which is sometimes aggressive: They can expect adversaries, conflict and suffering. In all this Paul stresses the unity of the church and the solidarity of its proclamation of the gospel with his apostolate. It is 'the same conflict' (1.30).

In 2.1–18 the unity of the church stands at the centre. It is connected to the past, to the Christ-event described in 2.6–11. The so-called 'Hymn' is certainly the most significant text in this document. Hofius divides it into two strophes (6–8 and 9–11) and sees it formed by the poetic means of the *parallelismus membrorum*.[27] In so doing he stresses the Old Testament-Jewish background of this figure of speech. Others see Graeco-Hellenistic models or totally deny any poetic formation.[28] At any rate it is certain that in vv. 6–8 a downward movement (abasement) through the assumption of human form unto death is described which is then followed by an upward movement (exaltation) which leads to universal veneration. The special quality of the composition makes one suspect that Paul did not pen this hymn himself but took it over. There are, however, no conclusive arguments for this.

Through the reference to the destiny of Christ and its future consummation in the universal *proskynesis*, the community is bound into this event. In order to illustrate the dimension of this Paul does not shrink in 2.12–19 from using astral mythology (2.15) or the terminology of sacrifice (2.17).

In 2.19–30 Timothy's plans for journeying and the condition of Epaphroditus who has been ill and has now recovered are described. The stereotyped formulation in 3.1 either closes this part or is intended to introduce the new section.

The section 3.2 – 4.1 is admittedly encased by 3.2 and 3.18f. with exceedingly sharp polemics (3.2 'dogs', 'evil-workers'; 3.18 'enemies of the Cross of Christ') but the central issue is the imitation of Christ which is in accordance with the gospel. The statements in 3.7–11 are significant theologically. The central concept of 'righteousness' describes the type of relationship to humanity desired by God. This relationship does not stem from the righteousness of the Law but from the righteousness of God which is imparted by the faithfulness of God in Christ or through faith in Christ. It leads to a consummation of the existence of the believer, in the forming of which Christ's fate is emulated. The believer is conformed to the death of Christ in order to enter God's movement of power which brings about resurrection.

Under this assumption Paul can then speak of whether there may already be people who are perfect (3.12–16). In this respect he sees himself quite confidently as an example and invites the Philippians to do as he does but under no circumstances to follow his opponents whom he now calls 'enemies of the Cross of Christ'. Apparently the opponents are avoiding a form of proclamation of

---

27. O. Hofius (1991), *Der Christushymnus Philipper 2,6–11. Untersuchungen zu Gestalt und Aussage eines urchristlichen Psalms* (WUNT 17), Tübingen 2. ed., 4–12.
28. Cf. Brucker, *Christushymnen*, 307–19 (a detailed discussion of the problem).

the gospel which could provoke persecution (3.17–19). Here Paul is uncompromising. The community's connection of loyalty refers to a heavenly citizenship and does not depend upon demands of political loyalty. Christ is the true centre of power (3.20f.).

4.1 leads up to passages that deal with relationships within the congregation. After an admonition to particular persons in 4.2f. there follow two others which are kept more general (4.4–7 and 4.8f.). The last two begin an ending to a letter, but instead in 4.10–20 there is a letter of thanks, which is complete in itself, in which Paul thanks the Philippians, in formulations that are sometimes ambivalent, for support brought by Epaphroditus.

The closing greetings in 4.21–23 are particularly significant. Here Paul puts emphasis on people from the *domus Caesaris* or *domus imperatoris* (hoi ek tēs Kaisaros oikias). The expression means the members of the imperial household and to this belong in the first place the slaves and freedmen of the Julian-Claudian dynasty. Here we are dealing with thousands who attend to the interests of the *domus imperatoris* throughout the Roman Empire. That such people greet the Philippians 'especially' underlines the fact that the Christian community at Philippi also made use of the social connections which were due to the social conditions in the Roman world in proclaiming the gospel.

Exegetical Problems

To the questions still open belong at least the literary unity of the letter and the place where it was written. This has been commented on in detail above.

Ancient models of social communication provide further aid in determining more closely the exchange with the Philippian church. A complete identification is ruled out from the start because of the intrinsic dynamics of the Christ-event. The ancient understanding of friendship is helpful[29] as is that of the benefactor,[30] the Roman grouping based on partnership (societas/koinōnia)[31] and the client-relationship.[32]

On the other hand the ancient kind of association which is often brought into play was as a rule restricted to very specific areas of life and does not come up to the intensity or commitment of the social relationships prevailing in the Pauline communities.[33]

The statements on the righteousness of God are of particular importance for explaining Paul's understanding of faith (3.7–11). The counter-positioning of righteousness through the Law as personal righteousness and righteousness through faith as God's righteousness seemingly supports a reforming interpretation of righteousness through faith, and lends it a certain emotiveness through

---

29. J. T. Fitzgerald (ed.) (1996), 'Friendship, flattery and frankness of speech' (*NTS* 82), Leiden etc., 83–160.
30. S. Joubert (2000), *Paul as Benefactor* (WUNT II/ 124), Tübingen.
31. J. P. Sampley (1980), *Pauline Partnership in Christ*, Philadelphia.
32. L. Bormann, *Philippi*, 161–224.
33. E. Ebel (2004), *Die Attraktivität früher christlicher Gemeinden* (WUNT II/ 178), Tübingen, 38–75, 217f.; T. Schmeller (1995), *Hierarchie und Egalität* (SBS 162), Stuttgart, 24–53, 94f.

Paul's sharp biographical rhetoric. But it also supports an interpretation of pistis as the faithfulness and loyalty of Christ.[34]

The section 2.6–11 raises special questions. Its linguistic form (genre, division into strophes), the historical tradition of its origin (Isa. 52f.; Wisdom) and its religio-historical classification are still much debated today as before.

The more recent discussion on the letter as a whole is characterized by the question of a political theology in the letter to the Philippians. There is much to be said for the view that the co-operative proclamation of the gospel by the apostle and the Philippian community was understood, at least by the people around them, as opposition to the religious-political propaganda of the Julian-Claudian dynasty.[35]

4
Evaluation

The letter to the Philippians achieves its own character through the close connection of Christology, apostolic existence and the life of the Christian community. The apostle is conformed to the Christ-event depicted in Phil. 2.6–11; in this and not through his own personality he becomes the example (topos) which looks for emulators (symmimētai) precisely in the execution of the practice of solidarity within the Christian community and in mission. The temporal horizon set by the Christ-event at the universal *proskynesis* (2.11) which will be accomplished on the Day of Christ gives the statements in the letter their special intensity. According to the letter to the Philippians Christian existence is the imitation of Christ, *imitatio Christi*. But because of the danger of a Christo-centric constriction which is raised in Philippians one must remember that the Christ-event itself can only be understood in the horizon of the total biblical account. Not least the reversion to Isa. 45.23 in Phil. 2.10f. makes this clear.

This emphasis in the letter to the Philippians is taken up in the letter to the Colossians and independently continued. Col., in its wake Eph., and independently of them 2 Tim., take up the situation of writing given in the letters to the Philippians and to Philemon, namely that Paul was in prison. The actual situation of imprisonment in Phil. and Phlm. becomes a literary encouragement to write further – now, however, fictional – letters from prison.

---

34. N. Walter (1998), 'Der Brief an die Philipper', in ders./E. Reinmuth and P. Lampe, *Die Briefe an die Philipper, Thessalonicher und an Philemon* (NTD 8/2), Göttingen, 5–101, 80.

35. M. Tellbe (2001), *Paul between Synagogue and State* (CB.NT 34), Stockholm, 210–78.

References

Commentaries

M. Bockmühl (2007), *Epistle to the Philippians*. Black's NT Commentary. London: Continuum.

G. D. Fee (1995), *Paul's Letter to the Philippians*. 3rd ed. New International Comm. on the NT, Grand Rapids, MI: Eerdmans.

R. Martin (2002), *The Epistle of Paul to the Philippians. An Introduction and Commentary*. 2nd ed. Tyndale Comentary Series. Grand Rapids, MI: Eerdmans.

P. T. O'Brien (1991), *The Epistle to the Philippians. A commentary on the Greek text* (NIGTC 11), Grand Rapids, MI: Eerdmans.

J. Reumann (2008), *Philippians. A new translation with introduction and commentary*, Anchor Bible 33B, New Haven, CT: Yale University Press.

Monographs

R. S. Ascough (2003), *Paul's Macedonian Associations. The Social Context of Philippians and 1 Thessalonians* (WUNT II/161), Tübingen: Mohr Siebeck.

L. Bormann (1995), *Philippi – Stadt und Christengemeinde zur Zeit des Paulus* (NT.S 78), Leiden: Brill.

R. P. Martin (2005), *Carmen Christi. Philippians ii. 5–11 in recent interpretation and in the setting of early Christian worship*, Cambridge/New York: Cambridge University Press.

P. Oakes (2001), *Philippians. From people to letter* (MSSNTS 110), Cambridge: Cambridge University Press.

D. Peterlin (1995), *Paul's letter to the Philippians in the Light of Disunity in the Church* (NT.S 79), Leiden: Brill.

L. Portefaix (1988), *Sisters rejoice. Paul's letter to the Philippians and Luke-Acts as seen by first-century women* (CB.NT 20), Stockholm: Almqvist & Wiksell.

Essays and Encyclopedia Articles

L. Alexander (2004), 'Hellenistic Letter-Forms and the Structure of Philippians', in Stanley E. Porter, Craig A. Evans (eds), *The Pauline Writings*. London: Continuum, 232–46.

D. E. Aune (2003), 'Art. Letter to the Philippians', in *The Westminster Dictionary of New Testament and Early Christian Literature*. Louisville, KY: Westminster John Knox, 356–9.

J. Reumann (2006), 'The (Greek) Old Testament in Philippians: 1:1–9 as Parade Example– Allusion, Echo, Proverb?' in S. Sang-won (Hg.), *History and Exegesis: New Testament essays in honor of Dr. E. Earle Ellis*, London: Continuum, 189–200.

Chapter 14

THE LETTER TO PHILEMON
Lukas Bormann

Table 14.1

Sender	Paul and Timothy (1.1)		
Addressees	Philemon, Apphia, Archippus and Philemon's house-church		
Situation of writing	Paul in prison		
Reason for writing	Return of Onesimus		
Place of writing	Ephesus, traditionally: Rome (*not explicitly named*)		
Date	Spring 55 CE, traditionally 60 CE		
Opponents	–		
Topics	Social status and social relationships within the Christian community		
Broad division	Beginning of the letter	1–3 4–7	*Epistolary prescript* *Epistolary proemium* as thanksgiving
	Body of the letter	8–20	The return of Onesimus
	Close of the letter	21–25 21f. 23–5	Closing exhortation Closing greetings

1
Approaching the Text

The Content and Transmission of the Text

The letter to Philemon contains approximately 328 words.[1] With less than two pages in Nestle-Aland it is the shortest of the extant Pauline epistles. The papyri

---

1. R. Morgenthaler (³1983), *Statistik des neutestamentlichen Wortschatzes*, Zürich, 164.

provide only an incomplete picture of the text (𝔓 61, 𝔓 87).² The more recent critical editions of the Greek New Testament base their reconstruction of the text of Philemon substantially on the majuscule manuscript Sinaiticus (ℵ or 01) but also consult Alexandrinus (A or 02) and the Codex Ephraemi rescriptus (C or 04). The letter to Philemon is missing in its entirety from Vaticanus (B or 03). The critical text of Philemon offers only a few variant readings. The quality of the text in the extant manuscripts is judged to be very good.³

The letter to Philemon was already accepted in the Corpus Paulinum.⁴ The names of the persons in the prescript and in the list of those to be greeted are taken up in Col. (4.7–17) and in 2 Tim. (4.10–21) and extended.⁵ Together with the letter to the Philippians Philemon is the real model for a series of fictitious letters from prison (Eph., Col., 2 Tim.).

Analysis of the Text

The text thematizes and defines relationships. Paul describes the relationship between the slave Onesimus, his owner Philemon and himself. The relationships are defined by mutual obligations and understood as a relationship of reciprocal exchange. The behaviour of Onesimus, who had run away from his master, has created a debt which was still owed. It is thanks to Paul that Philemon belongs to the eschatological community and in this sense he is indebted to Paul (19).

Onesimus should now return to Philemon and should be accepted again by him (17). This acceptance is impeded by a financial loss caused by the departure of Onesimus. Philemon should either release Onesimus from this debt of his own free will or he should demand payment of it from Paul. Here Paul is acting according to what he says in 1 Cor. 6.1–8. In everyday, worldly problems (biōtika) there are two possibilities: relinquishment of rights or a wise decision on the case. Paul offers to solve the financial legal conflict between Onesimus and Philemon by his own financial intervention but expects that Philemon will voluntarily relinquish his rights.

Structure

The structure given above is sufficient. It is only controversial with regard to the closing section. Paul closely combines his request to Philemon 'to do more' (21) with the announcement of his own arrival (22). Nevertheless some interpreters take 21 (Lampe; Wolter) or even 21f. (Hübner) as belonging to the body of the letter, others see already in 21 the beginning of the closing part of the epistle (Bruce, Dunn, Fitzmyer, Wengst, Wilson). Since the definite argumentation is

---

2. K. Aland (ed.) (²⁷1993), *Novum Testamentum Graece*, Stuttgart, 686–9; cf. K. Aland and B. Aland (1995), *The Text of the New Testament. An Introduction to the Critical Editions and to the Theory and Practice of Modern Textual Criticism*, Grand Rapids, 57, 83–102.

3. K. Aland (ed.) (1991), *Text und Textwert der griechischen Handschriften des Neuen Testaments* II/4, Berlin/New York, 374; J. A. Fitzmyer, *Letter*, 7.

4. P. Pokorný (1991), *Colossians. A Commentary*, Peabody.

5. A. Weiser (2003), *Der zweite Brief an Timotheus* (EKK 16/1), Neukirchen-Vluyn, 328–30.

really concluded in verse 20 one should then preferably consider verse 21 as part of the ending of the letter and avoid a ripping apart of verses 21 and 22.

Theme
The topic of the epistle can be outlined in a few words. Onesimus, Philemon's slave, is with Paul. Paul sends him back to Philemon with a letter in which he asks Philemon to take him back again. Paul is prepared to take over the financial debt incurred by the absence of Onesimus. He offers to take over the costs for Philemon, but reminds him that he, Philemon, is in (spiritual) debt to Paul. Paul leaves it up to Philemon to offset the financial debt with the spiritual or to call in the costs from Paul.

The restoration of the social relationship is a prerequisite for the integration of Onesimus in the Christian community. Paul thematizes the legal financial conflict between slave-owner and slave in the frame of the eschatological proclamation of the gospel.

Semantic Fields
Concepts from the language of commerce stand out: 'share/sharer in a partnership', koinōnia (6); koinōnos (17); debts (pros-)opheilein(18f.); put on account, ellogein (18); pay compensation, apotinein (18). They serve to bring the conversation round in a fair way to the legal financial problem and to relate it to the reality in Christ. It is a matter of the sharing in faith (6: hē koinōnia tēs pisteōs) which is also realized in social, legal and economic reciprocation.

Along with the terminology of friendship typical of the Pauline epistles the concept ta splanchna which occurs three times (7, 12, 20) in this short letter is particularly significant. In most commentaries it is translated as 'heart'. It designates literally the entrails and means the seat of the emotions which arise through social involvement (compassion, love). They are a part of a person's identity. It is the Ego in its self-awareness which is determined by social connections.

2
The Genesis of the Text

In Phlm. Paul mentions his imprisonment five times (1, 9, 10, 13, 23). This imprisonment is a consequence of his preaching the gospel (13). The situation is identical with that in Phil. (Phil. 1.17). The question of where it was written, however, must not necessarily be connected to the discussion on where Phil. was written. The plans for journeying in Phlm. 22 cannot easily be made to agree with what is written in Phil. 2.24. This divergence, however, can be sufficiently explained by a certain temporal interval. The factual conditions in Phlm. clearly indicate a certain proximity of the place of imprisonment to Philemon's place of residence. According to Col. 4.9,17 there are members of the church in Colossae named Onesimus and Archippus. Thus, much speaks for the traditional opinion that the letter was addressed to Colossae (*subscriptio*). Colossae lies about 170

240   Paul

kilometres from Ephesus. Consequently Phlm. like Phil. would have been written during the imprisonment at Ephesus.[6]

In its address the epistle is intended for Philemon, Apphia, Aristarchus and Philemon's house-church. Although Philemon is addressed throughout in the second person singular it appears that the letter was to be made public to a certain extent. As the time of writing, the end of the Ephesian imprisonment must be considered, that means the spring of 55 CE.

3
Exegesis of the Text

Overview of the Text
The greeting at the beginning provides full details of the senders and addressees. In each case the names are assigned titular-like descriptions: Paul is 'a prisoner for Christ Jesus', Timothy 'brother', Philemon 'fellow worker', Apphia 'sister' and Archippus 'fellow soldier'. Apphia and Archippus are members of Philemon's house-church. Here already the ambiguity of the letter is clear. The constellation of persons and their social relationships refer both to worldly connection (en sarki) and to connections within the Christian community (en kyriō) (16). Paul argues on both levels and brings them into relation to one another.

The thanksgiving puts Philemon in a good light: his acts of love (5, 7: agapē) and his faith (5f: pistis) promote good (6: to agathon) for the members of the Christian community so that it creates refreshment in all their feelings (7: ta splanchna). The heart of this action is the 'community based on partnership created by your faith' (6: hē koinōnia tēs pisteōs sou), i.e. the practice of solidarity.[7]

In 8–14 a first course of argumentation is carried out which combines the ideas prepared in 5–7 (the practice of solidarity) with the depiction of the situation in 1–3 (imprisonment) and relates to the case to be clarified. Paul styles himself as a helpless supplicant (8f.) whereby the real gravity of his request is rhetorically intensified. It is in Philemon's hands to influence Paul's feelings (ta splanchna) which are bound up with the well-being of Onesimus (12) by doing what is 'required' (8: to anēkon) and 'good' (14: to agathon). Paul asks from Philemon what is ethically imperative because of the change in Onesimus. Onesimus has become Paul's 'child' (10), has changed from being useless to being useful (11) and could be active in Philemon's place in the diakonia (preaching of the gospel

---

6.   Fitzmyer, *Letter*, 11; R. P. Martin, *Colossians*, 149; R. McL. Wilson, *Colossians*, 326; P. Lampe (1998), 'Der Brief an Philemon', in ders./N. Walter and E. Reinmuth, *Die Briefe an die Philipper, Thessalonicher und an Philemon* (NTD 8/2), Göttingen, 209–32, 205; E. Lohse ([14]1968), *Die Briefe an die Kolosser und an Philemon* (KEK 9,2), Göttingen, 264; M. Wolter (1993), *Der Brief an die Kolosser. Der Brief an Philemon* (ÖTK 12), Gütersloh, 238; differently J. D. Dunn, *Epistles*, 307f.; F. F. Bruce, *Epistles*, 196.

7.   K. Wengst (2005), *Der Brief an Philemon* (Theol. Komm. zum NT 16), Stuttgart, 55: 'selfless loyalty'; Wolter, *Brief*, 251: 'the community which has grown up through your sharing in the faith'.

or practical service?).[8] Paul expects Philemon to set Onesimus free and send him back. The linguistic form and manner of arguing in 8–14 raise the impression that here it is a matter of an everyday natural occurrence which Paul presents to Philemon courteously and respectfully.

The explosive force of the case of Onesimus only becomes clear in 15–20. Onesimus is doulos, a slave, and has run away from his master (15f.). Paul sends him back as a brother (16) and asks that Philemon receive him as a partner (17: koinōnos). The change in the status of Onesimus in the reality of Christ and in the social reality is described in the use of the terms 'brother' and 'partner'. Philemon must carry out in the social reality the implications of the integration of Onesimus in the freeing reality of Christ. If financial obstacles stand in the way of this step Paul is prepared to sweep them out of the way. In the language of commerce Paul commits himself to taking over the costs created by Onesimus (18f.). Through the clarification of the social and financial connections which still has to be confirmed by Philemon, that for which Philemon is known will be fulfilled for Paul (7): it will rejoice his whole heart (20). The social consequences of the reality in Christ are changes in status. Onesimus, from being a slave, will become a brother and partner. Philemon gives up his status as master.[9] The economic requirement is the undertaking to pay the financial costs connected with this. Paul asserts definitely that he will do so but would like to encourage Philemon to waive his claim. There is no mention of a criminal charge (the running away of a slave?) or a personal legal step (setting free). For the case at hand they have no significance.

In the ending of the letter Paul reopens the conflict that has already basically been settled by speaking of the 'more' that Philemon will do. There is some reason to believe that Paul does not mean this 'purely rhetorically'.[10] He has opened for Philemon a great deal of scope and expects that he will use it to do 'more' in the sharing of the reality in Christ. This could mean a greater financial engagement and the return of Onesimus.

In the closing greetings light is thrown upon Paul's situation. Epaphras is also a prisoner, and his fellow workers Mark, Aristarchus, Demas and Luke are with him.

Exegetical Problems

The letter contains problems of exegesis to the extent that the Pauline formulations do not permit us to see precisely which actual legal and economic conditions are in his mind. But Paul himself intended this openness. He does not wish to 'command' (8) but to invite Philemon's acting through love (5, 7, 9: agapē) so that he does 'more' (21) than is required (8: to anēkon). The candour is laid down in the writing. It gives Philemon space to decide for himself. The reader today, however, would like to know what Paul is aiming for. To make

---

8. Wolter, *Brief*, 266: proclamation of the gospel; Lampe, *Brief*, 218: as helper in a practical sense.
9. Lampe, *Brief*, 218–24.
10. Wolter, *Brief*, 279.

progress here numerous hypothetical possibilities have been considered. Some are laid out in the text: relinquishment of status, waiving legal claims and increased participation in the proclamation of the gospel.

4
Problems of Interpretation

The letter to Philemon is part of an extensive communication between Paul, Onesimus and the house-church around Philemon and Apphia. The matters treated in it relate to social, legal and economic conditions which are not easy to reconstruct. Paul has precise knowledge of these conditions; but he thematizes them consistently against the background of the message of the gospel. The blurring caused by this makes it more difficult to assess the concrete material consequences of the Pauline document. On the other hand the theological argumentation remains vague if one cannot see clearly the consequences it had for the social reality of the slave, Onesimus. One would like to know what the Pauline gospel says about the personal legal status of the slave Onesimus.

The assessment is additionally made more difficult by the fact that today exclusively negative connotations are connected to slavery. Personal, legal and economic freedom count today as a fundamental requirement for a humane structuring of life. The ancient texts are completely ambivalent in this respect. There are very few proofs of an express 'desire for freedom' among slaves.[11]

The ending of the status of slave in Greek law led to the legal, to a large extent unprotected, status of the 'resident alien', the metoikos (Athens).[12] According to Roman law, one freed by a Roman citizen acquired civil rights but at the same time the personal legal transition from *servus* to *libertus* did not put an end to the asymmetric relationship between master and slave. The freedman remained as before subordinate in certain personal rights to the one born free. In every case a relationship of loyalty was maintained from which rights and duties were derived as before.[13] Frequently the relationship of client remained the economic basis of the freedman. In both cases, in the Roman as in the Hellenistic practice, the social and economic situation before the freeing decided the worth and importance of the legal process. For the slave qualified in trade and industry or craft and possibly already prosperous, new perspectives are opened by his being freed; for the old, exhausted household slaves and those who are simple labourers being freed can lead to penury.

If one accepts these conditions it becomes clear that in the letter to Philemon it is not a question of the personal legal status of Onesimus but of the restoration of the social, economic and legal bases of his life. The integration into the community of Christ is in this case likewise the reintegration into Philemon's

---

11. I. Weiler (2003), *Die Beendigung des Sklavenstatus im Altertum. Ein Beitrag zur vergleichenden Sozialgeschichte* (Forschungen zur antiken Sklaverei 36), Stuttgart, 115–45.
12. Weiler, *Beendigung* (n. 11), 175–7.
13. Weiler, *Beendigung* (n. 11), 173–213; Wolter, *Brief*, 234.

household. But Paul expects more from Philemon here than the re-establishment of the status quo ante. This would then not relate – as is often assumed – to the freeing of Onesimus but to the granting of a social, legal and economic security which goes beyond the conditions through which Onesimus was forced to leave Philemon's household. The definition of koinōnia is central here. Paul desires the social equality of Philemon and Onesimus as participants in a community of partnership (koinōnia).[14]

5
Evaluation

The letter to Philemon affords insights into the consequences which the proclamation of the gospel has on the social reality. Social asymmetries do not remain untouched by the fellowship in Christ. The house-church (kat oikon ekklēsia) also changes the social relationships within the ancient household (oikos). For Paul the basis of his argumentation is now both the material-legal concept of the *societas*/koinōnia and the rule for dealing with material-legal conflicts (1 Cor. 6.1–8). Egalitarian structures of ancient social reality are taken up in the formation of the reality in Christ.

References

Commentaries
J. D. Dunn (1996), *The Epistles to the Colossians and to Philemon* (NIGTC), Grand Rapids, MI: Eerdmans.
J. A. Fitzmyer (2000), *The Letter to Philemon* (AB 34C), New York: Doubleday.
R. P. Martin (1974), *Colossians and Philemon* (NCB), London: Oliphants.
R. McL. Wilson (2005), *A Critical and Exegetical Commentary on Colossians and Philemon* (ICC), London: T&T Clark.
F. Segovia and R. S. Sugirtharajah (2007), *A postcolonial commentary on the New Testament writings*, London: T&T Clark.

Monographs
J. M. G. Barclay (1997), *Colossians and Philemon*, Sheffield: Sheffield Academic Press.
K. R. Bradley (1994), *Slavery and Society at Rome*, Cambridge: Cambridge University Press.
R. J. Cassidy (2001), *Paul in Chains. Roman Imprisonment and the Letters of St. Paul*, New York: Crossroad Publishing.

Essays and Encyclopedia Articles
D. E. Aune (2003), 'Art. Letter to the Philippians', in *The Westminster Dictionary of New Testament and Early Christian Literature*. Louisville, KY: Westminster John Knox, 354–6.
D. F. Tolmie (ed.) (2010), 'Philemon in perspective. Interpreting a Pauline letter' (*BZNW* 169), Berlin/New York: de Gruyter.

---

14. Wolter, *Brief*, 231–5; 272f.

Chapter 15

THE LETTER TO THE ROMANS
Oda Wischmeyer

Table 15.1

Sender	Paul (1.1) dictates the letter to Tertius (16.22)
Addressees	Christians in Rome (1.7): predominantly Gentile Christians
Situation of origin	The end of Paul's missionary activity in the east, a planned mission in Spain (15.14ff.)
Occasion	Preparation for the visit to Rome
Place of writing	Corinth (cf. 16.23 with 1 Cor. 1.16 and Acts 20.2f.: Gaius)
Date	56 CE
Opponents	–
Themes	Paul's apostolate, the gospel, faith, the righteousness of God, Jews and Greeks as participants in the righteousness of God, Israel, the relationship to the Imperium Romanum, strength and weakness, Paul's mission
Broad outline	Opening of the letter	1.1–7	*Epistolary prescript*
		1.8–12	*Epistolary proemium* as thanksgiving
		1.13–15	Epistolary self-recommendation
	Body of the letter	1.16 – 11.26	Theological themes
		12.1 – 15.13	General exhortations
	Letter ending/ Letter endings (?)	15.14–29	'Apostolic Parousia'[1]
		15.30–33a	First closing exhortation and wish for peace
		15.33b	First Amen
		16.1–16	First list of greetings
		16.17–20a	Second closing, exhortation, and eschatological peace perspective

1. U. Schnelle, *History*, 115.

16.20b	First wish for grace
16.21–23	Second list of greetings (greetings from co-workers)
[16.24	Second wish for grace and second Amen]
[16.25–27	Closing doxology and third Amen]

The section 15.30 – 16.27 is particularly finely structured:

Table 15.2

15.30–33a	15.33b	16.1–16	16.17–20a
1st closing exhortation and peace greeting	1st Amen	1st list of greetings	Closing exhortation and prospect of peace
16.20b	16.21–23	16.24	16.25–27
1st wish for grace	2nd list of greetings	2nd wish for grace and 2nd Amen	Closing doxology and 3rd Amen

1
Approaching the Text

The Content and Transmission of the Text
In the Nestle text the letter to the Romans contains 7,094 words and *c.*31 pages. It is the longest Pauline epistle with the largest vocabulary.[2] The following important early church majuscules transmit the text:[3] ℵ 01 (fourth century), A 02 (fifth century), B 03 (fourth century), C 04 (fifth century, incomplete), D 05 (sixth century, 1.1–6 missing). Parts of the letter to the Romans can be found in the following papyri: Ρ10 (fourth century), 27 (third century, Rom. 8 and 9, Cambridge, P.Oxy. 1355), 40 (third century, Rom. 1–4;6;9, Heidelberg P.Bad. 57 Inv. 45), 46 (the oldest witness, *c.*200, Dublin Chester Beatty Library, P. Chester Beatty II; Ann Arbor, University of Michigan, Inv. 6238), 94 (fifth/sixth centuries), 113 (Rom. 2, *c.*250, Oxford P.Oxy. 4497). The letter occurs in the early lists of the Canon and has been commented on since Origen.

The letter to the Romans presents some significant problems for textual criticism in chapters 14–16, which must be discussed at the outset. The major questions concern the original ending and the original place and textual relationship of 16.24 (the wish for grace 2), 16.25–27 (the doxology) and 16.20b (the wish for grace 1).[4] In the Nestle text the letter closes in several stages:

2. R. Morgenthaler (1958), *Statistik des neutestamentlichen Wortschatzes*, Zürich/Frankfurt, 164 § 3.
3. Nestle-Aland (2001), *Novum Testamentum Graece post Eberhard et Erwin Nestle editione vicesima septima revisa communiter*, ed. B. and K. Aland, J. Karavidopoulos, C. M. Martini and B. M. Metzger, 27th, rev. ed., Stuttgart. Cf. J. A. Fitzmyer, *Romans*, 44–7.
4. Standard: K. Aland (1979), 'Der Schluß und die ursprüngliche Gestalt des Römerbriefs',

Table 15.3

16.20a	16.20b	16.21–23	16.25–27
Eschatological prospect	wish for grace 1	list of greetings 2	doxology and Amen 3.

16.24 (wish for grace 2 and Amen 2) is not in the text in Nestle but in the apparatus.

The references set in italics are disputed either in respect to their originality or their original placement. The text-critical picture of these passages appears as follows:

Table 15.4

15.1 – 16.27	16.20b	16.24	16.25–27
	Wish for grace 1	wish for grace 2	doxology
Missing in Marcion (acc. to Origen)	missing in D*vid, F, G	missing in Þ46, Þ61, ℵ, A, B,C	missing in F, G
	comes after 16.20a in Þ46, ℵ, A, B, C, Ψ, minuscule 33, majority text	comes after 16.23 in Ψ, majority text, F, D, G	comes after 14.23 in Ψ, majority text
		comes after 16.27 in P and minuscule 33	comes after 15.33 in Þ46
			comes after 14.23 and 15.33 in 1506 (here 16.1–24 are missing)
			comes after 14.23 and 16.23 in A, P, minuscule 33
			comes after 16.23 in Þ61, ℵ, B, C, D

in *Neutestamentliche Entwürfe* (ThB 63), Munich, 284–301. In brief: Fitzmyer, *Romans*, 48ff.

From this we can deduce – in a simplified form – the following variants of the ending:

- Romans comes to an end in 14.23 (Marcion).
- The wish for grace 2 (16.24) is the end of Romans. The doxology is missing.
- The sequence of the text is: 1.1 – 14.23; 15.1 – 16.23; 16.24 (D 06 [source], F, G).
- The letter to the Romans closes with the wish for grace 2 (16.24). The doxology is placed earlier.
- The sequence of the text is: 1.1 – 14.23; doxology 16.25–27; 15.1 – 16.23,24 (majority text).
- The close of the letter to the Romans is the doxology. The wish for grace 2 is missing.
- The sequence of the text is: 1.1 – 14.23; 15.1 – 16.23; doxology 16.25–27 (א, B, C).
- The close of the letter to the Romans is the doxology, which also has a place earlier (double attestation). The wish for grace 2 is missing.
- The sequence of the text is 1.1 – 14.23; doxology 16.25–27; 15.1 – 16.23; doxology 16.25–27 (A, P, 33).
- The greeting in 16.23 is the ending of the letter to the Romans. The doxology comes earlier. The wish for grace 2 is missing.
- The sequence of the text is: 1.1 – 15.33; doxology 16.25–27; 16.1–23 (Ƿ46).
- The doxology concludes the letter to the Romans, preceded by the wish for grace 2.
- The sequence of the text is: 1.1 – 14.23; 15.1 – 16.23,24; doxology 25–27 (D 06).

It is clear that the doxology (16.25–27) and the wish for grace 2 (16.24) are frequently missing or can be positioned at different points and possibly were not part of the original ending of the letter. The wish for grace 1 (16.20b) on the other hand is missing only in the 'western' text.[5] The subscriptio pros Romaious is missing in Ƿ46. It is a later addition. The abridged version in Marcion appears to be of his own making.

Analysis of the Text
The letter begins with the author's naming of himself. He introduces himself in detail (1.1–7) and concludes in the Nestle text with a first wish for grace (16.20b), greetings (16.21–23) and – at least in a later form of the text – with a detailed doxology (16.25–27).[6]

The text of the letter clearly reveals higher level structural elements:

---

5. With Fitzmyer, *Romans*, 50: 'The best that one can say about the original form of Romans from a textcritical viewpoint is that it most likely contained 1:1–16:23'.
6. 15.33 already contains a wish for peace.

Table 15.5

Verses	Marks of textual division	Themes
1.8	prōton ... eucharistō	There follows the topical thanksgiving for the Christian community.
1.18	apokalyptetai orgē theou	There follows a bipartite explanation of the human condition: first, the current condition of humanity ('actual condition').
3.21	nyni de ...dikaiosynē theou pephanerōtai	Second, an analogous explanation of the new condition of a people, if they believe in Jesus Christ ('state of faith').
9.1ff.	alētheian legō en Christō ...hyper tōn adelphōn mou tōn syggenōn mou kata sarka, hoi tines eisin Israēlitai	After the hymn-like passage in 8.31–39 there follows a further explanation on the theme 'my brothers, my kinsmen by race' – the Israelites etc.
12.1	parakalō	Chs 12–15 stand under the key-word 'exhortation' (cf. a resumption in 15.30).
16.3	aspasasthe	Ch. 16 contains detailed lists of greetings.

The marks of division verify the division of the letter into two parts:

Table 15.6

	1.16 – 11.34	12.1 – 15.33	
1.1–15 Self-introduction	thematic expositions	exhortations	16 greetings

Structure

The letter is designed according to the usual form of the Pauline epistles (*v. supra*). Compared with the other Pauline letters the following is striking:

1 The beginning of the epistle is very clearly expanded by the self-introduction (1.1–7) and self-recommendation (1.13–15) of the apostle.
2 The two-level structure of theological account (1.16–1.36) and exhortation (12–15) – also known theologically as the 'Indicative-Imperative pattern'[7] – is found only in this letter.[8]
3 The epistolary ending appears confused and redundant.

---

7. Formulation following R. Bultmann, *Theology*, § 38. There, however, it is meant theologically and not with regard to division.
8. 1 Thess. 4.1ff.: paraenesis but no coherent theological explanation preceding it. Gal. 5.1ff.: paraenesis, but not marked as such. Gal. 1–4 is also not a coherent theological explanation.

The following representation shows the particularly clear suggestion for partition according to themes proposed by J. A. Fitzmyer:[9]

Table 15.7

1.1–15	Introduction
1.16 – 11.36	I Instructive part
12.1 – 15.13	II Admonishing part
15.14–33	III Planning
16.1–23	IV Conclusion
16.25–27	V Doxology

The suggestions for division made in the important commentaries of Käsemann, Fitzmyer, Wilckens, Lohse, Dunn,[10] and Jewett differ in particular on two questions:

First, it is controversial whether 1.16/18 – 15.13 consist of an instructing and an exhortatory part – in each case with subdivisions – or represent a loose succession of individual thematic sections within one general topic. Fitzmyer and Wilckens are of the first opinion while Lohse and Dunn choose the second alternative, as did Käsemann before them.

Secondly, the place of chapter 5 in particular is disputed. Does it belong to a first part (chs 1–5), the foundation of the gospel in the revelation of the righteousness of God – thus Wilckens and Dunn – or to a second part (chs 5–8), the development of righteousness through faith as a reality – so Käsemann and Lohse? If one follows the signs of textual division two things are obvious: First, the structure of the argumentation in chapters 1.18 – 8.39 is so dense that only verses 8.31–39 create a conclusion. Secondly, from the signs of division in the text a division of the structure seems most plausible, which takes 1.18 – 3.31 as a unified foundational explanation and interprets chapters 4–8 as a discussion of problems raised by the explanation in 1.13 – 3.21. This discussion takes up questions raised in 4.1 ('What shall we say about Abraham?'), 6.1 ('What shall we say then? Are we to continue in sin that grace may abound?'), 7.7 ('What then shall we say? That the law is sin?') and 8.31 ('What then shall we say to this [summarizing]?') and in each case answered in detail.

Consequently there is the suggestion of a slight caesura in 6.1, but on the other hand chapters 4–8 represent such a closely connected argumentation that only an analysis of the rhetoric and argument can give deeper insights into the construction of the text.[11]

Themes

The division of the epistle into two parts of theological account and paraenesis together with the tightly woven topic of chapters 1–8 create the framework for

---

9. I follow Fitzmyer, *Romans*, and make no suggestion of my own for partition.
10. For the commentaries see the references.
11. The proposal for structuring Romans by R. Jewett will be discussed below.

the question of the subject of the letter to the Romans. At the same time several factors must be taken into consideration: the letter to the Romans is the only Pauline epistle not addressed either to a church that he founded or to a person of his acquaintance, and accordingly does not predominantly pursue special concerns. Furthermore it is the longest letter and one which for long stretches is purely theological and argues without any explicit reference to the addressees. Finally, in the passages of the letter relating directly to the addressees, Paul states differing purposes of the correspondence: in 1.1–7 and 1.8–15 he is preparing for a visit to Rome with the intent of preaching the gospel to the Roman Gentile Christians (1.5f.,15) while in 15.22–29 he expresses the hope that he will receive support from the Christian community in Rome for his planned mission to Spain. A survey of important positions on the question of the theme of the letter to the Romans facilitates our approach to putting the question:

Table 15.8

Käsemann (1980[4])	The righteousness of God (p. v and vi)
Wilckens (1978–1982)	The 'Gospel' with its central content: the 'righteousness of God for each one who has faith' (p. 16)
Dunn (1988)	'It is … the tension between 'Jew first but also Greek' 1:16, which Paul experienced in his own person …, which also provides an integrating motif for the whole letter' (p. lxii); 'law is the chief secondary theme running through the whole letter' (*ibid.*)
Fitzmyer (1993)	The verses 1.16,17 'announce the major theme of the letter' (p. 253)
Lohse (2003)	'Account of the proof of the Gospel …, with which he looks back at his previous activity and explains what holds good for his further apostolic service' (p. 45); 'a summary of the Gospel' (*ibid.*)
Jewett (2007)	J. is primarily concerned with the purpose of the letter: The 'reflections about the practical exigencies of the Spanish mission are crucial for understanding the letter as a whole' (91). As to the leading theological theme he reads 1.16,17 as the '*Propositio*: the thesis about the gospel as the powerful embodiment of the righteousness of God' (136).

It is undisputed that the central theme of the letter is addressed in 1.16,17. *Eduard Lohse* uses the felicitous term '*propositio generalis*'.[12] The propositio relates three different elements to one another: the gospel, the righteousness of God and the participants in this, Jews and Greeks. Exegetes, however, evaluate these elements differently. It is striking that two supplemental aspects in the prescript, Paul's office as apostle[13] and faith – which also occur in the propositio – are given less attention. Furthermore, it should be noted that exegetes clearly express reservations about the question of a central topic. From what has been

---

12. E. Lohse, *Brief*, 76. Lohse takes up J.-N. Aletti (1991), *Comment Dieu est-il juste? Clefs pour interpréter l'épître aux Romains*, Paris, 36.

13. In 15.15f. Paul returns once again in a metacommunicative statement to his apostolate.

said it follows that any determination of the theme of the letter to the Romans must take into account the five features mentioned. It is important to see that the letter to the Romans is not devoted to one theme which can be explained but to a thesis – the *propositio generalis* in 1.16f. – which is implemented rigorously.

This impression is deepened if one also takes into account the debate on the purpose for which the letter was written.[14] This debate has been going on since the important article by *Ferdinand Christian Baur* (1792–1860),[15] 'Über Zweck und Veranlassung des Römerbriefs'.[16] Baur pointed out that it was 'not very likely that the Apostle wrote the Letter to the Romans without a particular external reason but simply with a general intention of giving a comprehensive, coherent representation of the truth of the Gospel'.[17] Consequently, since Baur the analysis of the situation of the Christian community and of Paul is considered to be a necessary prerequisite for interpreting the letter. Baur starts from the fact that all the Pauline epistles are related to the prevailing situation and assumes that this is also true for the letter to the Romans. In so doing he puts – unlike the Lutheran tradition of interpretation – chapters 9–11 at the centre of his reflections. He sees these chapters not as a clash with Judaism but with the Jewish Christians who have been shaken by Paul's successful mission to the Gentiles in Achaia and Asia Minor. 'The Apostle's letter sent to the Christian community in Rome is therefore devoted to this topic because it has its place there through the prejudice of the Jewish Christians in this community as in no other against the Apostle's effectiveness.'[18]

The discussion about the purpose for which the letter to the Romans was written has led since the time of F. C. Baur to very diverse proposals,[19] of which the most important are represented in tabular form:

Table 15.9

Baur	Confrontation with Jewish Christians in Rome who desire to exclude the Gentiles from the Law-free Gospel (Context: A disagreement between the Jewish Christians and Paul as the missionary who does not bind the Gentiles to the Law)
Bornkamm, Jervell, Wilckens	Jerusalem as the secret address of the letter to the Romans and (Context: anticipated confrontation of Paul with the Jewish Christians in Rome; the 'Testament of Paul'[20])

14. Lit.: Introductory, Schnelle, 12 cf. *History*.
15. Cf. U. Köpf (1998), 'Article: Baur, Ferdinand, Christian,' *RPP*1 647–49.
16. F. C. Baur (1963), 'Über Zweck und Veranlassung des Römerbriefs und die damit zusammenhängenden Verhältnisse der römischen Gemeinde', in *id.*, *Ausgewählte Werke in Einzelausgaben*, ed. by K. Scholder, Vol 1: Historisch-kritische Untersuchungen zum Neuen Testament mit einer Einführung von E. Käsemann, Stuttgart/Bad Cannstatt, 147–266.
17. *Ibid.*, 153.
18. *Ibid.*, 165.
19. Cf. the compilation by K. P. Donfried (ed.) (1977) *The Romans Debate*, Minneapolis; A. J. M. Wedderburn (1988), *The Reasons for Romans*, Edinburgh; A brief presentation in Schnelle, *Einleitung*, 133f. See also Jewett, *Romans*, 80–91.
20. G. Bornkamm (1971), *Der Römerbrief als Testament des Paulus. Geschichte und*

Stuhlmacher[21]	Apologia against Jewish Christian opponents who are already acting against Paul in Rome (Context: the continuing argument of Paul with Jewish Christian opponents who cast suspicion on him in Rome and hinder his missionary plans)
Jewett	'The letter seeks to elicit support for Paul's forthcoming mission to Spain' (p. 80).

The table shows clearly the extent to which, since F. C. Baur, reasons for the writing of the letter have been found in Paul's political, ecclesiastical and personal situation. Eduard Lohse by contrast took up the Reformation esteem for the doctrine of Justification contained in the letter to the Romans as *'caput et summa universae doctrinae Christianae,'* as Melanchthon formulated it,[22] and pointed to the theological significance of the letter, but at the same time emphasized in his commentary the situational features of the letter at the point of intersection between Paul's plans for journeys and missionary activities in Rome and Spain and his imminent journey to Jerusalem with the collection.[23]

Wedderburn, Fitzmyer, Schnelle and Dunn assume a number of reasons for writing. Dunn sees a missionary, an apologetic and a pastoral purpose;[24] Fitzmyer names six factors which caused the letter to be written.[25]

The positions described show clearly that, analogous to the five central thematic concerns, the question of the *one purpose* of the letter to the Romans must be replaced by the account of the *various factors* that led to the writing of the letter.

Semantic Fields
In the letter to the Romans certain theological terms occur frequently in a striking way:

Glaube II. Gesammelte Aufsätze IV (BEvTh), Munich, 120–39, here: 139.
21. P. Stuhlmacher (²1966), *Gerechtigkeit Gottes bei Paulus* (FRLANT 87), Göttingen.
22. Philipp Melanchthon (1848), 'Disputatio orationis in ep. ad Rom.', in C. G. Bretschneider (ed.), *Philippi Melanchthonis opera quae supersunt omnia*, Vol 15, Halle, 445. Cf. E. Lohse (1993), *Summa Evangelii – zu Veranlassung und Thematik des Römerbriefs* (NAWG.PH 1.3), Göttingen, 89–119. Melanchthon, however, is speaking of Justification, not of the letter to the Romans itself, as E. Lohse suggests.
23. Lohse, *Brief*, 42–5. (On p. 45 Lohse turns against the phrase 'Testament of Paul'.)
24. J. D. G. Dunn, *Romans*, liv–lviii.
25. Fitzmyer, *Romans*, 79; Schnelle, *Einleitung*, 132. Wedderburn, *Reasons* (n. 19), 142 speaks of a 'cluster of different interlocking factors: the presence of both Judaizing and Law-free Christians in the church there, ... the present situation of Paul, the visit to Jerusalem now being undertaken and the prospect of a future visit to Rome. All played their part in provoking Paul to write to the Roman Christians as he did.'

nomos, hamartia, pistis, dikaiosynē, ethnos, anthrōpos and sarx.[26] The two words theos and egō appear most often.[27]

Chapters 1.18 – 3.20 reveal a style that is strongly juridical: righteousness (dikaiosynē), court (krima), law (nomos), sin (hamartia) and condemnation build the framework which redefines the gospel in its revelation of the dikaiosynē theou (1.16f.).[28]

Communication, Genre and Rhetoric
Communication

Paul writes to 'all God's beloved in Rome, who are called to be saints'. At the start he describes them as 'brethren' (1.13), but in the following argumentation he seldom addresses the Christians in Rome as brothers.[29] The foundational chapters – 1.16 – 6.23 – function without any further personal address, though from 6.11 the apostle is in places involved in an argumentative dialogue with the addressees.[30]

Paul, however, establishes the real situation in the proemium (1.8–12 epistolary thanksgiving; 1.13–15 epistolary self-recommendation) and in the ending of the letter (15.14 with a salutation – 16.24 is probably secondary). In this respect 15.15 is the key statement in the letter: Paul is writing to Christians in Rome, whom he does not know personally and who were not evangelized by him, by virtue and on the basis of the grace given to him by God to be a leitourgos (an official or priest) of Christ Jesus among the brethren. Here we have a so-called meta-communicative/letter hermeneutic statement by Paul.[31] Hence he is writing officially as a representative of Jesus Christ, which the prescript,

---

26. Cf. Morgenthaler, *Statistik* (n. 2), 168: Frequency table in the Pauline epistles. Of *c.*7,100 words in Rom. we encounter: the one Jewish identity-marker nomos 72 times (16th place overall, after theos the most frequent noun!), hamartia 48 times, pistis 40 times, dikaiosynē 33 times, ethnos 29 times, sarx 26 times: nomos, pistis and sarx also occur more frequently than usual in Gal. The terms correlative to ethnos/ethnoi (cf. also Hellēn six times) are Ioudaios (11 times) and Israēl (11 times). The terms euangelion (nine times) and apostolos (three times, rather infrequent, cf. 1 Cor.: ten times) which we encounter in the prescript and in the *propositio* are not excessively frequent in the letter to the Romans. The same holds true of the further identity-marker peritomē (14 times in Rom., seven times in Gal., 35 times in all in the New Testament). The third Jewish identity-marker, the Sabbath, is not mentioned at all in Rom. (cf. however 15.5f.). The fourth, the laws relating to food, is treated thematically in chapter 14.

27. Theos 153 times, egō 90 times; theos is the most frequent name in Paul (548 times), egō and hēmeis, each occurring 397 times, lie in second place.

28. Further concepts are also met: adikia, anapologētos, alētheia, pseudos, hamartanein, krinein, ergon tou nomou, syneidēsis, apologeisthai, dikaios, proaitiasthai, hypodikos, katēgorein.

29. 7.1,4; 8.12; 10.1; 11.25; 12.1; 15.14,30; 16.17.

30. Up until then there is also no further implicit relation to the addressees. In 6.11 there is an explicit 'you' (hymeis, as also in 7.4; 8.9; 11.30; 16.17).

31. Cf. E.-M. Becker (2004), 'Letter Hermeneutics in 2 Corinthians. Studies in *Literarkritik* and Communication Theory', *Journal for the Study of the New Testament* Supplement Series 279. London/New York: T&T Clark International, 75: 'Epistolary hermeneutics arise as a meta-communicative explication of the aspect of relationship in a medially transmitted written communication'.

constructed around the concept of apostle, already shows clearly.[32] His theme is – in writing as well as verbally – the Gospel of Jesus Christ (1.15; 1.16ff.). The beginning of the letter-ending, the so-called apostolic parousia (15.14–29), also witnesses to this: here Paul explains to the Romans his plans for journeys in the service of proclaiming the gospel, in the course of which he desires to make their acquaintance personally. In so doing he gives precedence to personal before written communication. Hence the letter to the Romans, other than the Corinthian epistles, is not a part of a two-sided communication, an epistolary correspondence or an exchange of messengers and envoys, but it opens a communication – and that under the conditions determined by his preaching of the gospel to the Gentiles as an apostle of Jesus Christ.

Chapter 16[33] makes this clear in the conclusion. First Paul commends Phoebe, who perhaps is the bearer of the letter.[34] Then, in a list of greetings, he introduces various people or groups of people whom he knows in Rome. He mentions 24 Roman Christians by name.[35] This list of greetings – unusual for Paul – is due to the unusual communicative situation of the letter: 'Precisely *because* Romans 1–15 is singular, so also is Romans 16!' (P. Lampe).[36] In addition there are greetings from eight people who are mentioned by name – co-workers with Paul and important Christians from the church in Corinth (16.21–23).

These links to a personal communication however do not change the official character of the letter, which is once again given expression by 16.16: 'All the churches of Christ greet you'.

The Questions of Genre
The question of the literary genre of the letter to the Romans can only be discussed in connection with the following three factors: the general ancient conception of genre, epistolography and rhetoric.[37]

The classical Greek theory of genre[38] provides no possibility of assigning the letter to the Romans to one literary genre. It is the opposite way around: the letter to

32. Cf. also 1.11,13–15.
33. On the source-critical question see 2.3.
34. R. Jewett, *Romans*, 941–8, underlines Phoebe's status as diakonos and as 'Missionary Patroness' (941): 'The Roman recipients of the letter would understand her to be recommended as the patroness of the Spanish mission, which Paul had announced in the preceding chapter' (947).
35. Aristobulus (16.10) and Narcissus are not Christians (16.11) but house-managers who have in their household Christian slaves or freedmen known to Paul. Cf. P. Lampe, *From Paul to Valentinus*, 153–83. On the social status and leading role of Prisca and Aquila (Acts 18.2) cf. R. Jewett, *Romans*, 954–60. On Andronikos and Junia(s) cf. *ibid*. 961–4. Jewett affirms the textual variant Iounia (female) instead of Iounias (male) and emphasizes her apostolic rank: 'All we can say with certainty is that this couple had functioned as Christian apostles for more than two decades before Paul wrote this letter' (964).
36. *Ibid.*, 155.
37. See the essays in: K. P. Donfried (ed.) (1977) (²1991), *The Romans Debate*. Minneapolis: Augsburg.
38. Foremost: Aristotle, *Poetics*; cf. R. Hunter and P. R. Hardie (1999), 'Art. Lit. Gattung', *DNP* 7, 260–6.

the Romans itself built a model for a genre. The great post-Pauline Christian letters to churches from the Deutero-Paulines through the letter to the Hebrews up to the first letter of Clement follow its style. Attempts to classify the letter to the Romans as a philosophical exhortation (*logos protreptikos*)[39] or as a literary testament[40] have not been able to gain acceptance. On the contrary the letter to the Romans is predominantly understood from its epistolary structure and located in the ancient theory of letters. Here the various micro-genres are presented: the epistolary essay, the diplomatic document, the letter of self-testimonial, the friendly letter.[41] It is clear that in this assignment the genre 'letter' appears to be sub-divided according to differing purposes as was usual in ancient epistolary theory.[42] Letters which had a clearly-defined purpose – e.g. petitions, letters of condolence, threatening letters – were in practice rarely of such length as the letter to the Romans. Here diverse purposes and registers flow one into the other. Thus, according to the ancient terminology 1.18 – 3.20 is a typos katēgorikos, a letter of indictment; 3.21 – 8.29 would be a typos aitiologikos, a letter giving grounds for the indictment; 12.1 – 15.13 a typos symbouleutios or nouthetētikos, an admonitory or reprimanding letter, while in 15.14ff. – 16 motifs of friendship, recommendation and petition appear.[43] Robert Jewett argues for reading Romans as an ambassadorial letter.[44] His proposal fits with the terminology of the opening (1.1–7) and with Paul's self-interpretation as ambassador or agent of God (15.14–21).[45]

From what has been said it appears that on the one hand the letter to the Romans belongs to the genre of the ancient letter which from the Hellenistic period received attention as a literary letter because of its style, ethics and psychology,[46] but on the other it is the writing of a man who had read neither manuals on epistolography nor writers of Greek letters. If the letter to the Romans nevertheless may count as a literary text which is superior with regard to its content and language,[47] the reason for this lies in Paul's literary

---

39. D. E. Aune (1991), 'Romans as a Logos Protreptikos in the Context of Ancient Religions and Philosophical Propaganda', in M. Hengel and U. Heckel (eds), *Paulus und das antike Judentum* (WUNT 58), Tübingen: Mohr, 91–121.

40. Bornkamm, *Römerbrief* (n. 20), 120–39.

41. Cf. F. W. Horn (1995), 'Paulusforschung', in *id.* (ed.), *Bilanz und Perspektiven gegenwärtiger Auslegung des Neuen Testaments. Symposium zum 65. Geburtstag von Georg Strecker* (BZNW 75), Berlin/NewYork, 30–59, 35 n. 16. Further: H.-J. Klauck (2006), *Ancient Letter Writing and the New Testament: A Guide to Context and Exegesis*. With the collaboration of Daniel W. Bailey, Waco, Tx.: Baylor.

42. Klauck, *Ancient Letter Writing*.

43. On all motifs cf. Klauck, *Ancient Letter Writing*.

44. R. Jewett (1982), 'Romans as an Ambassadorial Letter', in Interpretation XXXVI, 5–20. See also R. Jewett, *Romans*, 42–6. Jewett interprets *apostolos* as expressing a particular 'diplomatic role' (45) and gathers from this term 'that the use of such rhetoric would be a natural expression of Paul's self-identity' (46).

45. R. Jewett, *Romans*, 906s, with reference to C. Spicq (1994), *Theological Lexicon of the New Testament 2*. Peabody Mass.: Hendrickson Publ., 382.

46. Klauck, *Ancient Letter Writing*.

47. O. Wischmeyer (2004), 'Paulus als Autor', in *id.*, *Von Ben Sira zu Paulus. Gesammelte Aufsätze zu Texten, Theologie und Hermeneutik des Frühjudentums und des Neuen Testaments*

and theological innovative productivity. With this writing he goes beyond the rest of his correspondence and places it in the type of the theological letter alongside the type of the philosophical-literary letter (Plato, Epicurus, Cicero, Seneca).

Rhetoric[48]

The letter to the Romans can be seen in long stretches as a well-ordered literary or epistolary speech on the righteousness of God in the light of the gospel (1.16f.). American exegetes in particular interpret the letter to the Romans as an argumentative speech or as argumentation. In 1997 Wilhelm Wuellner outlined 'Paul's Rhetoric of Argumentation'[49] in a contribution which received much attention. He put aside the question of the literary genre and emphasized instead the significance of the function of the rhetorical argumentation for the understanding of the letter: 'Not theories of literary forms, but theories of rhetorical argumentation, will offer us solutions to the problem of Romans'.[50]

His suggestion for division is:

Table 15.10

1.1–15	Exordium (Identical with the prescript)
1.16,17	Transitus
1.18 – 15.13	Confirmatio
15.14 – 16.23	Peroratio (Identical with the postscript)

Wuellner occupies himself particularly with the paraenetic section of the letter. He sees 12.1 – 15.13 as a practical obligation for the addressees: 'Argumentative thought (exordium and probatio in Rom. 1:1–15 and 1:16 – 11:36) relates argumentative appeal to commitment (paraenesis in Rom. 12:1 – 15:13)'.[51] In

---

(WUNT 173), ed. by E.-M. Becker, Tübingen: Mohr, 289–307, esp. 303: 'In the Letter to the Romans Paul is to a greater and more deliberate degree a literary author than in his other letters.'

48. Cf. on this p. XXX (on rhetoric in 1 Cor.).
49. W. Wuellner (1976), 'Paul's Rhetoric of Argumentation in Romans', *CBQ* 38, 330–51 = K.P. Donfried (ed.) (1977) (²1991), *The Romans Debate*, Minneapolis, 133–46 = Edinburgh, 128–46; S. E. Porter (1993), 'The Theoretical Justification for Application of Rhetorical Categories to Pauline Epistolary Literature', in *id.* and T. H. Olbright (eds), *Rhetoric and the New Testament. Essays from the 1992 Heidelberg Conference* (JSNT.S 90), Sheffield, 100–22; C. J. Classen, *St Paul's Epistles and Ancient Greek and Roman Rhetoric*, 265–91. Fundamental for Paul is: H. D. Betz (1986), 'The Problem of Rhetoric and Theology According to the Apostle Paul', in A. Vanhoye (ed.), *L'Apôtre Paul. Personalité, Style et Conception du Ministère* (BEThL 73), Leuven, 16–48.
50. Wuellner, *Rhetoric²* (n. 44), 132.
51. *Ibid.*, 143.

the rhetorical argumentation, according to Wuellner, we have an exemplum or paradigma.[52]

With a certain circumspection E. Lohse follows Wuellner and suggests as division:

Table 15.11

1.1–15	Exordium
1.16f.	Propositio (a section of general instruction, understood by Lohse in a somewhat restricted form as a thesis)
1.18 – 15.13	Argumentatio (section containing evidence)
15.14 – 16.23	Peroratio[53]

It is clear that this rhetorical analysis does not take us farther than the classical proposals for division according to themes. The question of the rhetorical genre of the epistle is also difficult. Of the three genera that Aristotle describes in his 'Rhetoric' (*genus iudicale*, the speech in court; *genus deliberativum*, the counselling speech; *genus demonstrativum*, the speech for a special celebration), none fit the letter to the Romans as a whole. Wuellner pleads for a *genus demonstrativum*, the speech for a special occasion (Greek epideiktikon): 'Romans is epideictic'.[54] He understands the speech in this case as the rhetorical effort to achieve an intensive approval of and allegiance to his propositio among his readers, as it were, the 'OK' of the listeners.[55] Lohse follows Wuellner – again cautiously.[56] Jewett pleads for a genus of 'Evangelical persuasion'.[57] James D. G. Dunn contradicts this classification which in fact remains very vague.[58] He points rather to the Pauline individuality of writing and arguing, which cannot be assigned to any rhetorical genre: 'the chief force of the letter lives in its distinctive Pauline art and content'.[59] According to Wuellner Paul wishes to refute objections to his understanding of the Law, i.e. he wants to reinforce his

---

52. *Ibid.*, 144.
53. Lohse, *Brief*, 96. Lohse uses the terminology more usual in German textbooks (cf. H. Lausberg ([10]1990), *Elemente der literarischen Rhetorik*, esp. 29). Cf. in general Lohse, *Brief*, 94–7 and lit. 94 n. 39; Horn, *Paulusforschung* (n. 38), there 34–40 on the rhetorical analysis of the letter to the Romans. Jewett, *Romans*, vii–ix, offers a similar, but more precise description of the structure. He divides the probatio (1.18 – 15.13) into four proofs (1.18 – 4.25; 5.1 – 8.39; 9.1 – 11.36; 12.1 – 15.13). The unit of 15.14 – 16.24 serves as peroratio.
54. Wuellner, *Rhetoric*[2] (n. 44), 135.
55. *Ibid.*, 139.
56. Lohse, *Brief*, 95.
57. Jewett, *Romans*, 23–46.
58. Dunn, *Romans 1–8*, lix.
59. *Ibid.* Further: J. D. G. Dunn, 'Paul's Epistle to the Romans: An Analysis of Structure and Argument', *ANRW* II 25.4, 2842–90.

argumentation. But more important is the observation that at least the text of 1.18 – 3.20 is a pure court speech – and that not a speech for the defence but a speech for the prosecution which leads into a verdict of universal guilt (address: 2.1,17; verdict of guilt: 3.19b). These facts show the weakness of the general proposal for interpretation made by Wuellner.[60]

In fact, the letter to the Romans can neither be meaningfully divided rhetorically nor can it be assigned as a whole to one rhetorical genre. But Wuellner's reference to the argumentative structure of the letter as a whole and to the skill of the individual arguments, which is best analysed in the commentaries, remains important. J. A. Fitzmyer rightly points to the fact that Paul dictated the letter and that 'Paul's style is more that of an orator than of a writer ... Romans was meant to be read aloud, more as a formal lecture than a literary essay-letter'.[61] This again points back to the structure of communication and the question of genre. Consequentially R. Jewett discusses 'the genre of Romans in relation to its epistolary type'.[62] He follows Wuellner's epideictic theory but refines it: 'Among the letters of Paul, Romans is a unique fusion of the "ambassadorial letter" with several of the other subtypes of the genre: the paraenetic letter, the hortatory letter, and the philosophical diatribe'.[63] Jewett however ignores the important parts of the *genus iudicale* in Romans.

2
The Genesis of the Text

Author, Addressees and Historical Situation
The author of the letter before us is Paul (1.1). Paul dictated the letter to Tertius who himself sends greetings to the Roman Christians in 16.22.

In the prescript (1.1–7), in the thanksgiving (1.8–15) and in the conclusion of the letter (15.14ff.) Paul presents himself clearly to his readers: his apostolate, his mission to the Gentiles, his earlier and current plans for journeys, mission and preaching. Important for his biography are particularly the statements in 15.17–32 about his previous personal portrayal of his mission, on the collection and his forthcoming journey to Jerusalem as well as the planned mission to Spain which Paul mentions exclusively in 15.24 and 28.

The addressees are 'all God's beloved in Rome, who are called to be saints' (1.7). Paul is not writing to one ekklēsia in Rome since there were already several house-churches in the capital as is shown by the list of greetings in chapter 16.[64] The story

---

60. Cf. the discussion in: Jewett, *Romans*, 42–6.
61. Fitzmyer, *Romans*, 92. Cf. Jewett, *Romans*, 22s. discusses the engagement of Tertius, the secretary, and Phoebe, Paul's patron in Corinth, in the whole process of writing, delivering and performing the letter.
62. Jewett, *Romans*, 42.
63. Jewett, *Romans*, 44.
64. Paul mentions the following important locations: the house-church (ekklēsia kat oikon autōn) of Aquila and Prisca in 16.5, the 'brethren' in vv. 14 and 15 'who belong to the family of Aristobolus' (v. 10) and those 'who belong to the family of Narcissus' (v. 11).

of the genesis of the Christian communities in Rome is shrouded in mystery. We know nothing about their founder or the date of their origin. It is, however, clear that these are connected with two factors: with the large Jewish congregation in Rome and with the trade in which individual Christians must have engaged in the capital from an early date. At any rate Paul finds several house-churches already there and assumes that he will find support in Rome for his mission to Spain.

We know four important dates for the history of Judaism in Rome[65] and for the early Christians in Rome:[66]

Table 15.12

19 CE	41 CE	49 CE	Oct 54 CE
Expulsion of the Jews under Tiberius	Prohibition of Jewish assemblies by Claudius	Edict of Claudius: expulsion of Jews	Death of Claudius; the repeal of the edict
Tacitus Annals II, 85; Suetonius, Vita Tiberii 36	Dio Cassius, Roman History LX 6,6	Suetonius, Vita Claudii 25.4 (Dating according to Orosius, Historia adv. Paganos VII 6,15)	Suetonius, Vita Neronis 33.1

The repeated restrictions upon Jewish assemblies or temporary expulsions of Jews from Rome give evidence of the numerical mass of Jews in Rome and how they were perceived by the Romans.

Were the majority of the Roman Christians at the time when Paul was writing his letter Jewish or Gentile Christians? The majority of researchers assume with Peter Lampe the following situation: 'After the separation from the synagogues, at the latest at the time of the writing of the letter to the Romans, Gentile Christians (in a large measure probably former *sebomenoi*) predominated. Several times Paul assumes that the urban Roman Christians, in general, come from paganism.[67] These univocal expressions must be given methodological

---

Lampe, *From Paul to Valentinus*, 359: 'Thus, in capital city of Rome, we count five different Christian islands. If we assume that the other fourteen people of Romans 16 do not belong to any of these five crystallization points and that they hardly could all have belonged to only one other additional circle, then this results in at least seven separate islands of Christianity. At least an eighth may be added to this when Paul sojourned in Rome and gathered Christians in his rented accommodation (see above, on Acts 28.30f). There is nowhere any indication of a central location for the different groups scattered over the city. Each circle of Christians may have conducted worship services by itself in a house or apartment, so that it can be referred to as a house community.'

65. On Rome cf. P. Lampe (2005), 'Rom – Hauptstadt und größte Metropole des römischen Reiches', in K. Erlemann et al. (eds), *Neues Testament und Antike Kultur II: Familie. Gesellschaft. Wirtschaft*, Neukirchen-Vluyn, 165–71 (lit.).

66. Cf. E. Schürer (1973–1987), *The History of the Jewish People in the Age of Jesus Christ (175 B.C. – A.D. 135)*. A New English Version revised and edited by G. Vermes and F. Millar, 3 vols, Edinburgh.

67. Reference to 1.5f., 13–15; 11.13, 17f., 24, 28, 30f., 15.15f., 18; cf. also 15.9ff.; 6.17–21 and 1.18ff, Further: Acts 28.23–31.

priority in the face of the impression elsewhere in the letter's contents of its being written primarily for a Jewish-Christian readership.'[68] As far as the social affiliation of the Roman Christians is concerned, we know of free business people (Aquila and Prisca) but predominantly of slaves or freedmen.[69] They came for the most part from the Greek-speaking east of the Roman Empire and were peregrini.

We know nothing about the size of the communities. However, they must have been large enough for Paul to hope for support from them and for the Roman authorities at the time of Nero to know the Christians as a distinctive religious organization.

Paul himself describes precisely in 15.14ff. the situation in which he wrote the letter: He is at the end of his mission in the eastern part of the Empire and now intends to carry out a mission in Spain. The Christians in Rome should 'send him' there (15.24), i.e. give him financial, linguistic and geographical support in Latin-speaking Spain. He is probably thinking of the connections the Roman Christians have in the western parts of the Empire. Before his journey to Rome he is planning a visit to Jerusalem 'to deliver the collection' to the community there (15.28). He states clearly that this journey will be dangerous because of the 'unbelievers' (15.31), i.e. the Jews.

Date and Place of Writing

The majority of researchers assume that Paul dictated the letter to his fellow Christian, Tertius, in the house of Gaius in Corinth in the spring of 56 CE (Acts 20.2f.; Rom. 16.1f.,23).

Unity and Process of Editing

Chapters 1–15 are considered as being a coherent text by the majority of exegetes. Chapter 16 on the other hand has for a long time repeatedly been considered as a problem for source criticism and is interpreted by various exegetes as a writing of Paul to Ephesus.[70] The following significant hypotheses are represented in this connection:

---

68. Lampe, *From Paul to Valentinus*, 70. R. Jewett, *Romans*, gives an updated outline of 'The History and Orientation of the Christian Communities in Rome' (59–74), in particular on the house tenement churches.

69. Ibid., 141–64.

70. Cf. W.-H. Ollrog (1980), 'Die Abfassungsverhältnisse von Röm 16', in D. Lührmann and G. Strecker (eds), *Kirche. Festschrift für Günther Bornkamm zum 75 Geburtstag*, Tübingen, 221–44, there n. 1: first in D. Schulz (1829), Rezensionen zu: *Eichhorn*, Einleitung in das Neue Testament, und *De Wette*, Lehrbuch der historisch-kritischen Einleitung in die kanonischen Bücher des Neuen Testaments, ThStKr 2, 563–636. In Ollrog all details and bibliographical references on the list. On Trobisch and Theißen cf. Theißen, *Das Neue Testament* (n. 37), 56: Theißen suspects that Paul sent the letter to the Romans to Rome as a journalistic testament and at the same time sent copies to Corinth and Ephesus. For the Christian community in Ephesus he added a chapter specifically for them – chapter 16. The basis of this hypothesis can be found in D. Trobisch (2001) *Paul's Letter Collection*, Quiet Waters Publications.

Table 15.13

Rom. 16	Independent writing to Ephesus, later appended to Romans	Deissmann/Schmithals/Marxsen/Käsemann/Vielhauer/Trobisch/Theissen
Rom. 1–15/ Rom. 16	General doctrinal writing to Rome which was sent to Ephesus along with Rom. 16	Manson
Rom. 16	Collection of various letter fragments	Feine-Behm/Michaelis

Against this the majority of exegetes support the unity of Rom. 1–16, particularly since there is no manuscript which ends with chapter 15 and because 'the joining together of two letters with completely different addresses (would be) ... completely unique in early Christian epistolary literature'.[71]

Here we can only mention[72] the question of possible glosses in the letter to the Romans (especially 16.17–20a and 7.25b). The assumption of a glossator remains historically problematical.

Traditions

In the letter to the Romans Paul frequently makes use of early Christian traditions in connection with his argumentation without, however, expressly indicating these as such as in 1 Cor. Linguistic arguments and arguments from historical motifs give every reason to evaluate at least the following texts as early Christian tradition: 1.3b,4a; 3.25,26a; 4.25; 6.3f.

3
Exegesis of the Text

Overview of the Text

Paul introduces himself in the prescript (1.1–7) in detail and as an apostle to the Gentiles – a theologically significant designation – to whom the Christians in Rome also belong. He writes the letter without any co-sender/co-author.

In the two-part proemium (1.8–15) Paul thanks God for the Christians in Rome, because their faith is known everywhere. Paul also informs them of his plans for visiting them and his self-understanding as a preacher of the gospel for Greeks and non-Greeks.

---

71. Ollrog, *Abfassungsverhältnisse* (n. 62), 234. – Yet Ollrog thinks that 16.17–20a (the polemic against false doctrine) and 16.25–27 (the final doxology) are later glosses from the time of the first letter of Clement (*c*.96 CE). Jewett, *Romans*, 941s., quotes Ollrog and argues: 'The inclusion of the transitional particle de ("now") relates these verses to the foregoing in a manner that precludes the possibility of the recommendation standing alone'.

72. On 16.17ff. v. n. 63. On 7.25b cf. H. Lichtenberger (1997), 'Der Beginn der Auslegungsgeschichte von Röm 7: Rom. 7.25b', ZNW 88, 284–95. In general: R. Bultmann (1967), *Glossen im Römerbrief, in: Exegetica. Aufsätze zur Erforschung des Neuen Testaments*, Tübingen, 278–84.

Part I: Rom. 1–11
The first part of the letter to the Romans is devoted throughout to a general, argumentative instruction. Salutations to the Roman audience are rare[73] and not crucial for the line of argument. The persons addressed in chapter 1 are generic: 'O man' (2.1; cf. 9.20), 'You Jew' (2.17), 'You' (11.17–24). The many questions that in places mount up (2.3; 3.1,9,27,29; 4.1; 6.1,15; 7.7,13,24; 8.31–35; 9.14,19,20,21,30,32; 10.14 – 15.19; 11.1,3,4,7,11) are a rhetorical stylistic device. They serve the argumentation, not the personal communication.

Paul's instructive document to Rome (1.16 – 11.35) builds a clearly argumentative unity: the *propositio generalis* in 1.16f. is developed in what follows in its significance for Gentiles and Jews (chs 1–3), defended by Scripture (ch. 4) and applied in detail to Christians (chs 5–8)[74] and Jews (chs 9–11). The unit of argumentation closes with the hymn in 11.33–35 and an 'Amen'. The very detailed structure of the argumentation in Part I cannot be gone over here but will now be represented merely in its basic points.

The starting-point is 1.16,17:

> Ou gar epaischynomai to euangelion, dynamis gar theou estin
> eis sōtērian panti tō pisteuonti, Ioudaiō te prōton kai Hellēni:
> dikaiosynē gar theou en autō apokalyptetai ek pisteōs eis pistin,
> kathōs gegraptai: ho de dikaios ek pisteōs zēsetai.

The sentences are initially the theological basis (gar v. 16) for Paul's personal announcement in his self-introduction, 'to preach the gospel to you also who are in Rome'. Consequently the sentences stand on the one hand in the biographical context. On the other hand they open (gar v. 18) the instructive discourse in chapters 1 to 11. The statements 1.16,17 formulate the basic theological conviction that the gospel unfolds its soteriological power for every person who believes: i.e. it is effective (in fact) first for Jews but then (in the same way) for non-Jews. The new generic term 'pisteuōn' – 'everyone who has faith' – consequently has priority over the classical religious dual pair of concepts in Judaism: 'Jews – non-Jews'.

This *propositio* must implicitly explain a point: The nature of human righteousness before God. The Jews were convinced that this resulted from fulfilling the Law and was valid for the Israelites whose forefather was Abraham. Paul by contrast makes it clear that the righteousness revealed in his proclamation of the gospel does not come from fulfilling the Law but simply from faith. In saying this, from a Jewish point of view he is fundamentally questioning the function and validity of the Law. This represents the uniform theological compass of chapters 1–11. 1.18 – 3.31 develop – as has been said already – this *propositio generalis* for Jews and non-Jews and for all humankind against the background of the divine avenging justice. In 3.28-31 Paul summarizes this argumentation again: Jews and non-Jews will be justified before God through faith.

---

73. *V. supra*, n. 29. Important is only 7.1. The Adelphoi-address comes in 7.1,4; 8.12,29; 9.3; 10.1; 11.25. Cf. by contrast the very frequent use of the Adelphoi-address in 1 Cor.!

74. Note the 'we' in 5.1 which has already been prepared for in ch. 4: 4.16; esp. 4.24.

Rom. 1–3

In chapters 1–3 Paul works in a bewildering way with different anthropological co-ordinate systems: on one occasion with the Jewish pair of terms 'Jews' and 'non-Jews' and the rhetorical address 'you … Jew' (2.14), at another time with the meta-concept 'humankind' and the rhetorical address 'O man' (2.1). He connects these two co-ordinate systems to one another – not in theory but in the rhetorical-argumentative execution – in order to include in the whole argument both the religious theme of 'Jews – non-Jews' and the anthropological theme of 'humankind' beyond this religious dualism. In the course of this the individual sections of argumentation each make their own points which cannot be systematized one with another. Nevertheless the individual texts in 1.18 – 3.20 build a rhetorical unity. Paul writes in the manner of the prosecuting speech in court and arrives at a general verdict of guilty before God for the whole kosmos (3.20) – against the background of the divine criminal court, whose standard of righteousness mankind cannot meet.

1.18–32 appears initially in the form of an apocalyptic court speech on God's righteousness as judgemental wrath upon those people who, although they know better, worship creatures instead of the Creator. As the Jews see this, these are the Gentiles even if Paul does not express this here. The exposition closes with the proclamation of the divine sentence of death on the Gentiles (v. 32).

In 2.1–10 there follows a direct indictment of all the people who judge others and themselves do the very thing for which they condemn others. For such people Paul swears that the Last Judgement will be one of punishment and wrath. There is certainly a place for deliverance in the concept of the Last Judgement (2.7,10), for in this part of the argumentation Paul is not interested in the general condemnation of the Gentiles but is thinking of those people who condemn others regardless of any ethical warrant.

In 2.11–16[75] Paul extends these partial perspectives to a general statement on anthropology and the ethics of behaviour that are derived from a new understanding of God: God no longer judges people according to their religion – i.e. whether they are Jews or Gentiles – but independently of this.[76] In this connection Paul develops a new as it were post-Jewish general human concept of the Law (v. 14) which is no longer related to the entirety of Israel's Torah but to the performance of what is ethically understood as good,[77] i.e. of the Moral Law. Correlate to this general moral law is the conscience of the individual, irrespective of his ethical religious affiliation to Jews or Gentiles. Hence though Paul does not say so here, the single person comes on the scene as a morally responsible individual (cf. ch. 7).

---

75. On this cf. O. Wischmeyer (2006), 'Römer 2.1–24 als Teil der Gerichtsrede des Paulus gegen die Menschheit', *NTS* 52.

76. Verse 11: God shows no prosopōlēmpsia in the sense of connecting his judgement to religious protestations but looks solely at people's conduct.

77. Paul does not put this into words, but from his argumentation it emerges that he is thinking of the 'Moral Law' which the Gentiles – who neither know the Torah nor can carry it out – also fulfil. Consequently Paul presumes a correspondence between the ethics of the Torah and the ethics of the Gentile rules for life.

In 2.17–24 Paul addresses reproachfully an ideal Jew, i.e. a Jewish teacher or Pharisee and unmasks him as a hypocrite in the sense of the general accusation in 2.1–10. In the subsequent text, 2.25–29 he makes it clear that, in the structure of Jewish Covenantal Nomism,[78] the *fulfilment* of the Law stands above the sign of the Covenant, circumcision, and consequently is of no advantage for the Jewish hypocrite. Paul detaches the concept of circumcision, analogous to the extension of the concept of the Law in 2.12–16, from the ritual Jewish connection and asserts the possibility of an 'internal' i.e. ethical circumcision for Gentiles whom, in so saying, he considers to be participants in God's Covenant which now no longer belongs primarily to the Jews. The train of thought in Rom. 2.12–16 and 2.25–29 represents a revolutionary transference of Covenantal Nomism to non-Jews. Paul claims that Gentiles, too, can keep the Law inwardly and be inwardly circumcised. This assertion is fundamental and must immediately provoke the objection: In the face of Paul's thesis does Jewish Covenantal Nomism still have any significance or soteriological value?

Paul answers this objection in 3.1–8. This is a first indication of the problem to come in chapters 9–11. The Jews' advantage lies in the entrustment (episteuthēsan) with the logia tou theou (v. 2).[79] In the passive form episteuthēsan Paul already indicates the soteriological turn in his argument which begins explicitly in 3.21ff. In 3.1–8 Paul does not judge the Jews by their fulfilment of the Law but rather from the faithfulness of God which he advances for Israel independently of their unfaithfulness. This argument of saving grace, however, is dangerous because it could contribute to the obstinacy of the Jews (vv. 5,8). Consequently Paul makes it clear: It is certainly true that the unfaithfulness of the Israelites does not revoke God's faithfulness to Israel, but on the other hand neither is Israel's unfaithfulness a part of the divine plan of salvation nor does God's judging wrath represent an injustice to Israel. Without a doubt his judging wrath is just.

In 3.9–20 Paul presents the conclusion of his indictment[80] and in verse 9 brings the verdict of guilty: 'Jews and Greeks[81] are all under the power of sin'. He cites a succession of quotations from Scripture based on Eccl. 7.20: ouk estin dikaios oude eis.[82] Paul stresses that these statements of condemnation were made by the Law itself so that 'the whole kosmos may be held accountable to God' (v. 19). Hereby the indictment which expounds the unrighteousness of all humankind in the face of God's Last Judgement comes to an end (1.18 – 3.20).[83]

With 3.21–26 Paul recognizes the fundamental change in the behaviour of God which he sees in the coming of Jesus Christ. He formulates this change in a very demanding, linguistically complex text which builds the positive core

78. Cf. on this Chapter 4 in this volume by J. Frey, 'The Jewishness of Paul'.
79. The list in 3.1 is not continued.
80. Verse 9 proaitiasthai = 'to accuse beforehand'.
81. Here Hellēnes instead of ethnoi (cf. likewise in 1.16; 2.9,10).
82. This is the most extensive series of quotations in Paul.
83. 3.20b anticipates the thoughts in chapter 7 on the real function of the Law: it cannot create righteousness for mankind since it itself has uttered the verdict on the unrighteousness of humanity, but it exposes sin as a manifestation of unrighteousness.

of chapters 1–4 and explicates the *propositio generalis* Christologically. God justifies those people who believe in Jesus Christ. Faith in Jesus Christ detaches righteousness from fulfilment of the Law, which is impossible. Paul describes the significance of Jesus Christ for this radically new definition of righteousness in the terminology of sacrifice as atonement (vv. 24,25). Faith is the possibility of salvation for all humanity (v. 22). Here Paul takes up again the universal perspective of 2.12–16; 2.25–29 and 3.9–18 – this time in a positive sense.

In 3.27–31 he discusses briefly a further Jewish objection (cf. 3.1ff.) 'What becomes of our boasting' (v. 27)? The important motif of boasting belongs for Paul to the fulfilling of the Law (4.2). Faith needs and engenders no boasting. In 3.28 Paul once again sums up in a positive way his thesis on the gospel (1.16f.). It provides righteousness for people regardless of their affiliation to the People of Israel. This righteousness before God is constituted through faith.[84] To sum up: in chapter 3 Paul substitutes the Jewish concept – as he himself interprets it – of God's covenant and human righteousness by the new concept of God's sacrifice in Jesus Christ on the one hand and faith on the other.

Rom. 4
In this chapter Paul defends the *propositio generalis* from Scripture with the example of the forefather of Israel: Abraham.

Paul argues in four sections: 4.1–8,9–12,13–17 and 18–25. With Gen. 15.6 he proves that Abraham achieved righteousness not through works but through his faith. At the same time he emphasizes that Abraham was considered as justified by faith before he was circumcised – because of his faith. In doing so Paul removes the two supports of Jewish Covenantal Nomism (as before in 2.12–16 and 2.25–29): the Law and circumcision. In a similar manner he connects the promise of inheritance ('inherit the kosmos' v. 13; cf. v. 17 following Gen. 17.5) to Abraham's righteousness through faith. By this interpretation Abraham, from being the forefather of Israel, becomes the 'father of many nations' (v. 18). Here, too, Paul unshackles a central Jewish perspective – the 'Patriarchs' and the 'Promise' (cf. 9.4 and 5) by placing Abraham in the history of 'humanity'. At the same time in so doing he draws the history of the human race into the patriarchal history of Israel. In the final section of the argument he elucidates the concept of faith contained in the *propositio generalis* using the exemplary faith of Abraham. Paul ends the proof from Scripture with a reference to the analogous faith of the Christians.

Rom. 5–8
In this section, which is closely worked out in detail, Paul's argument comes to the situation of the Christians ('we'), the fact of whose salvation (nyni de) he has already described in 3.21–26. 5.1 summarizes this new situation before God and then leads into the new theme: the life of the justified Christians in peace with God in the conditions of the old world. The chapters constitute an argumentative

---

84. In a closing remark Paul tackles a further objection and in anticipation makes it clear that the Law is not overthrown by faith (cf. ch. 2).

unit. On the one hand Paul sets out the 'peace with God' positively, but he must from time to time deal with the real and theoretical problems which stand in the way of the assertion that Christians live in peace with God. It is a question of the things which rule humanity as it is, stamped with the old Adam, which Paul concentrates in death, sin and the Law.[85] The discussion of this problem takes up the most space in the discussion. Paul argues meticulously in short blocks but does not lose sight of the aim of the argument. In principle the statements in 5.1 hold true for the status of the Christians:

Dikaiōthentes oun ek pisteōs eirēnēn echomen pros ton theon dia tou kyriou hēmōn Iēsou Christou and 8.1: ouden ara nyn katakrima tois en Christō Iēsou.

That is: the situation of judgement and eschatological condemnation, under which, according to chapter 3, all humans stand, is annulled for Christians and replaced by an eschatologically ordered peace with God.

In 5.2–5 Paul describes the Christian existence in this peace established by Christ, first in a programmatic way as life in hope (elpis 5.4f.) related to the earthly and to the eschatological existence. In 8.18–30 he takes this perspective up again in more detail. In this section Paul makes it very clear that the Christian existence is twofold: as earthly it is marked by 'hardship' and 'suffering' (thlipsis 5.3; pathēmata 8.18), as eschatological by 'glory' (doxa 8.18). Between 5.2–5 and 8.18–30 Paul tackles various questions that arise about the status of peace for Christians in the twofold structure between earthly and eschatological existence. The eschatologically ordained peace with God has been established by the death of Jesus Christ. Paul develops this basic fact in 5.6–11 in terms of the theology of sacrifice (v. 9). In 5.12–21 he considers the 'grace and gift' (v. 15: charis kai dōrea) that Christ has brought to humankind in the comparison with and in the relation to Adam, whom he interprets as an archetype or foreshadowing of Christ (typos tou mellontos, v. 14). In this section Paul combines diverse themes and reflections in a condensed form. Basically he assigns human history with regard to salvation collectively or in a participatory way[86] initially to the first human, Adam, and his destiny of death (many died through one man's trespass) then to the destiny of grace created by the righteousness (dikaiōsis v. 18) of Christ (through one man's death many will be saved[87]). Adam and Christ each behave reciprocally in the opposite way to the other. Moreover, Paul connects to

---

85. Observe particularly 5.17; 6.12; 7.24f. and 8.1f. on the things that rule the old world and the future components of freedom from death, sin and Law. Note also the future tense in 8.11: zōopoiēsei.

86. On the concept of participation cf. especially the standard work by E. P. Sanders (1977), *Paul and Palestinian Judaism. A Comparison of Pattern of Religion*, London: SCM.

87. Five parallel proofs Adam–Christ:
Two main clauses with opposed structure of exceeding:
v. 15 Through the one man ... – through the grace of the one man, Jesus Christ ...
v. 16 From the one man ... – the grace ...
Three analogous clauses bearing witness:
v. 17 because of one man's trespass ... – through the one man, Jesus Christ ...
v. 18 through the one man's trespass ... – through the one man, Jesus Christ ...
v. 19 through one man's disobedience ... – through one man's obedience ...

this panorama of salvation the theme of sin, death and the Law which dominates chapters 6 and 7. Sin and death are connected to Adam and are communicated from him to all people, even to those who lived before Moses who did not know the Law (5.12–14). The Law, which does not belong to this connection with Adam but was first given through Moses, then caused an increase in the sin (5.20,21) it was intended to prohibit.

In 6.1–14 Paul deals with the theme of Adam's sin and death, now in connection with the main theme of chapters 5–8: the earthly existence of Christians ('We', 6.1). He expresses one fact in various arguments: Christians have died to sin (v. 2). The arguments are of a participatory kind: the baptism into Christ's death (vv. 3f.), participation in his crucifixion (v. 6), dying with Christ (v. 8). Result: 'So you also must consider yourselves dead to sin and alive to God in Christ Jesus' (v. 11). After this description of their situation there follows a short paraenesis in 6.12–14, at the end of which the theme of the Law is taken up once again. The thesis is: 'You are not under law but under grace' (6.14).

6.15–23 states the consequences of this fact which is repeated in v. 15 in relation to continuing sin, here represented as a power in itself.[88] Paul stresses the possibility for Christians to live in righteousness (vv. 18,19) in spite of the authority of sin[89] which by its all-embracing quality extends to all 'Adamites', i.e. all humankind.

In chapter 7 Paul continues the topic 'You have died to sin' which reflects back to Adam in the following variation: 'You have died to the Law' (7.6). This means that Paul is now referring back to Moses without mentioning his name. 7.1–6 brings first an analogy from the law of inheritance, which clarifies the reality of the new legal circumstances that a death can create. Paul tackles the problem of the relationship of sin and Law in greater depth in 7.7–24. In 7.7–13 the Law is understood as that factor which first makes sin 'alive' (v. 9). Here Paul is writing an Adamic-Mosaic ideal autobiography in describing his fate at first generically as 'humankind' and then as 'Jew under the Law'. This 'I' dies the death of Adam and all the people after him since the 'I' broke the Commandment 'You shall not covet' (abbreviation for the Ten Commandments) and consequently has become a slave to death (cf. chapters 1–3). This is true for the time after Adam as for the time after Moses. In this section of the argument Paul makes a decisive differentiation: The Law and the Commandment are 'holy, just and good' (v. 12) as given by God.[90] Sin as it is revealed by the Commandment is on the other hand 'sinful beyond measure' – i.e. directed against God.

In 7.14–24 Paul adds an analogous train of thought for added protection of the Law. The Law is not only holy but is also 'spiritual' (v. 14) since it is

---

88. In v. 22 sin and God face one another as having equal rights (already in 6.10).
89. Metaphor of authority, e.g. 5.20f.; 6.6 and frequently (service to sin); metaphor of weapons, 6.12–14; metaphor of slaves, 6.15–22; metaphor of wages, 6.23.
90. Cf. here O. Wischmeyer (2005), 'Paulus als Ich-Erzähler. Ein Beitrag zu seiner Person, seiner Biographie und seiner Theologie', in E.-M. Becker and P. Pilhofer (eds), *Biographie und Persönlichkeit des Paulus* (WUNT 187), Tübingen, 88–105.

from God. For humanity – Mosaic humanity – this signifies a lapse into sin and death (v. 24). To illustrate this Paul writes 'a psychological, confessional ideal autobiography' in which he portrays himself as being a 'split person': 'Here Paul diagnoses himself autobiographically as a pious Jew with a split personality. The centre of his will has been destroyed, so that desire and action diverge'.[91] The reason for this cleft is the alienation of the ego which is 'understood as having been taken over by the power of sin'.[92] Consequently the 'spiritual' factor of the 'Law' given by God cannot produce good in the person because his will has been annulled by the 'fleshly' factor of 'sin' which works against God (vv. 19,20).[93] Here Paul is again thinking 'adamically' in the sense of the Fall of Man. Hence as a result there remains once again only the sentence of death in 1.32, which, however, has already been repealed in principle in 3.21–26 and in relation to existence in 5.1ff.: taleipōros egō anthrōpos: tis me rysetai ek tou sōmatos tou thanatou toutou? (v. 24). The answer comes in 7.25: 'Thanks be to God through Jesus Christ our Lord'. Salvation has come from outside: through Christ. Here it is clear: the Law is certainly spiritual but it cannot transmit participatory spirit and recreate people spiritually.

This lies in Christ alone and in his power to save. Herewith Paul has finally established the connection to 5.1–5 and can now in 8.1–17 depict the acquittal of Christians and the status of their life and peace (*v. supra* on 5.1). He defines freedom (from the rule of the Law, sin and death) as a manner of the eschatological existence of Christians and describes the Spirit as the characteristic factor of this existence. Hope corresponds to the Spirit. Hereby it is a fact: The statements in chapter 8 are only valid under the assumption that Christ is risen and functions as the 'new Adam'. If this is not so, chapter 8 would depict a fantasy. After a summarizing review of the theme of sin – Law – death (vv. 2 and 3a) and Christ's act of salvation (v. 3b) as well as of the antithesis of 'flesh' i.e. human or 'I'-existence and 'Spirit' i.e. participation in Christ (vv. 4–8 cf. 6.11ff., 16ff.) Paul addresses the Roman Christians ('You' in v. 9) about their 'spiritual life'. The participatory idea now becomes prominent. The 'spiritual life' has two aspects: a present and a future. Paul speaks to the Romans directly about their expectation of resurrection (v. 11) and about their earthly life as 'children of God' (vv. 14ff.) characterized by freedom but also by suffering (cf. 5.3).

8.18–30 sketches an eschatological picture of hope extended to the cosmos (*v. supra*). Now Paul understands the Christians initially as part of the Creation and

---

91. Cf. O. Wischmeyer (2003), 'Menschsein. Neues Testament', in *Id.* and C. Frevel, *Menschsein, Perspektiven des Alten und Neuen Testaments* (Die Neue Echter Bibel. Themen 11), Würzburg, 91f., quotation: p. 92. Cf. also R. v. Bendemann (2004), 'Die kritische Diastase von Wissen, Wollen und Handeln. Traditionsgeschichtliche Spurensuche eines hellenistischen Topos in Römer 7', ZNW 95, 35–63. Detailed standard work: H. Lichtenberger (2004), *Das Ich Adams und das Ich der Menschheit. Studien zum Menschenbild in Römer 7* (WUNT 164), Tübingen.

92. Wischmeyer, *Menschsein* (n. 82), 92.

93. With 7.5,18,25 the anthropological concept 'flesh' (sarx) comes into play. In Paul 'flesh' means 'the person, the human being' (2 Cor. 7.5), but often is denoted in a negative way.

points to the future destiny of freedom and glory for the whole of creation (v. 21f.), in which the Christians will be the beginning (v. 19). But more important for Paul than this eschatological perspective is, near the close of this section, once again the Christians' life in suffering and hope (vv. 23ff.) which is realized particularly in prayer (vv. 26ff.).

In 8.31–39 Paul concludes his remarks on the situation of the Christians. Once again he opens up the perspective of the Last Judgement in 1.18, and in 'a section which rings like a hymn'[94] closes his conviction of the salvation of the Christians which he has already formulated in 3.21–26; 5.1 and 8.1 with a fourfold series of tis-questions (8.31,33,34,35) and two peristases-like statements (v. 35 and vv. 38,39). No matter how far afield Paul goes, even to the cosmos in Rom. 8, at the end stands the formulation of his precise conviction: the Christians are righteous before God (8.33). This righteousness is described as a present existence in suffering (vv. 35f.) and a future existence in glory (v. 18).[95] This proves the *propositio generalis* for the Christians.

Rom. 9–11

These chapters now discuss, without a lengthy transition, the *propositio generalis* and its interpretation in 3.21ff. for the Jews. What does it mean for the Jews that 'the righteousness of God through faith in Jesus Christ (comes) for all who believe' (3.22)?

Paul considers this fundamental question in three lines of argument (chapters 9, 10 and 11) which he introduces in each case with a particular reference to his own person. The conclusion forms a hymn-like prayer (11.33f.).

Paul begins the new argument with a rhetorically emotional introduction in 9.1–5, a 'declaration like an oath',[96] a gesture of self-cursing and a list of the advantages remaining to Israel (vv. 4 and 5). This list provides the basis for the following remarks: Paul solemnly makes it clear that Israel is and remains the People of 'the Covenant and the Law' (v. 4). In relation to the preceding chapter 8 it is just as important that Paul also describes the Israelites as possessing 'sonship' and 'glory' (v. 4) – the same eschatological predicates of salvation that Paul has granted to the Christians in chapter 8. This detail shows even more clearly that in the following chapters Paul is wrestling with the basic problem of his Christian understanding of what is true: 'What place do the Jews have in this truth established by Christ?' (3.21–26).

In diverse question and answer passages that are highly rhetorically structured he comes to a clear conclusion in 11.26: kai houtōs pas Israēl sōthēsetai. The line of argument that leads to this conclusion is laid out as follows:

9.6–13: Paul attempts to distinguish between 'false' and 'true' Israelites and between Abraham's descendants and his real children. The motif of gracious

---

94. Lohse, *Brief*, 254.
95. 8.38 once again opens up the cosmic perspective, this time, however, more in the sense of the dangers to be overcome.
96. Lohse, *Brief*, 265.

election behind this differentiation is set out in 9.14–29. Sonship depends in the end solely upon God's mercy (v. 18). The metaphor of the potter underlines God's free choice in mercy (vv. 20ff. following Isa. 29.16 LXX). Here Paul portrays the history of salvation in such a way that God prepared 'vessels of mercy' for 'glory' from Jews and Gentiles (vv. 23f.) He supports these thoughts critical of Israel with various quotations from the prophets (vv. 25–29). In 9.30–33 he draws a first preliminary result which refers back to the *propositio generalis*: Israel has not attained righteousness because it understood righteousness as coming from works of the Law. By contrast the Gentiles who have faith in Christ have achieved righteousness because this comes from faith (cf. 1.16f. and 3.21ff.). This means: from the perspective of the dikaiosynē theou the Jews do not attain redemption.

In chapter 10 Paul reflects further on this point. 10.1–4 repeats in a personal reinforcement the verdict of chapter 9. 10.5–13 again consolidates this verdict in the contrast between righteousness from the law and righteousness through faith. This takes place in a mixture of scriptural quotations and their interpretation as relating to Christ and the proclamation of the gospel (Deut. 30.12,14 and Ps. 106.26 LXX). 10.9f. ties righteousness firmly and exclusively to the belief in Jesus and faith in his Resurrection. In 10.14–21 Paul expands the theme of the proclamation of the gospel and points to the fact that it is soteriologically necessary (cf. 1.15 and 1.16f. *propositio generalis*). At the same time he testifies that the gospel was also proclaimed to Israel. Paul explains the fact that the majority of the Jews did not accept the message of the gospel by referring to the prophetic theology of obstinacy (Deut. 32.21 LXX; Isa. 65.1 LXX; Isa. 65.2 LXX). So this line of argumentation also ends with the verdict that Israel is obstinate.

Nevertheless Paul adds a third and final line of argument which he again connects with his own person, this time referring to the fact that he himself is an Israelite, 11.1. The – in the train of argumentation very surprising – thesis, emphasized rhetorically by its form as a negated question, stands at the beginning in 11.2: 'God has not rejected his People'. In 11.3–24 Paul deals with the thesis that God has not rejected Israel. In the process several arguments follow one another: In 11.3–5 he attempts to argue on the basis of the Old Testament theology of Election and Remnant. This way, however, leads back again to the theory of Election and obstinacy in chapter 10 (11.6,7) which Paul again supports with several combinations of scriptural quotations (11.8–10).

Consequently in 11.11–16 he begins again by ascribing a salvific meaning to the 'fall' of Israel: Through their fall salvation (sōtēria) has come to the Gentiles (11.11); for it was only because the Jews did not achieve righteousness that the possibility arose for God to turn to the Gentiles. But Paul does not stop here. Instead, he looks ahead to the plērōma autōn (v. 12), i.e. to the time when all Israel will be saved. In this section he addresses the Gentile-Christians in Rome directly and explains to them his own position as a (Jewish) apostle to the Gentiles (v. 13). *He understands his mission to the*

272 Paul

Gentiles as an antecedent to the conversion of the Jews which he believes to be God's final intention.[97]

In 11.17–24, taking up the root–branches metaphor in v. 16, he inserts a speech in the form of a diatribe to a Gentile – who should be understood generically[98] – in which he makes clear from the metaphor of the wild and the grafted olive tree that the roots (i.e. figuratively Israel) always support the branches that are grafted on (i.e. figuratively the Gentile Christians). In so saying Paul demands respect for Israel and reverence for the 'loving kindness' and 'earnestness' of God (v. 22).

Paul formulates explicitly in 11.25–27 the perspective that the whole of Israel will be saved, which positively complements 11.1: When all the Gentiles are saved 'all Israel will also be saved' (v. 26). He emphasizes this statement of hope with Isa. 59.20 and Isa. 27.9. This section is initially formed as an apocalyptic mystērion (cf. 1 Cor. 15.5ff.) This means: Paul here formulates the eschatological fact 'pas Israēl sōthēsetai' against all appearances, against the world as it is, even against his own reason.[99]

In 11.28–34 Paul again addresses the Christians in Rome directly about their earlier paganism and clarifies their current complicated position with regard to the Jews who are in fact 'enemies' because they obstruct the gospel, but in the history of salvation are and remain 'beloved' of God. This is particularly significant, especially in Rome with its large Jewish population which itself is often the target of temporary expulsion by the Roman authorities.

In 11.32 Paul brings all of the expositions in chapters 1–11 to their goal: synekleisen gar ho theos tous pantas eis apeitheian, hina tous pantas eleēsē: 'For God has consigned all men to disobedience that he may have mercy upon all.' Here there exists a so-called inclusion. Paul is referring to 3.19: 'The whole kosmos is guilty before God'. To the guilt of the Jews and the Gentiles God answers with his mercy in Jesus Christ which first justifies the Gentiles who have faith in Christ and then will save all the Jews. It remains open whether Paul is in the end thinking of a so-called universal reconciliation, i.e. a deliverance of all the Gentiles. But his perspective – as frequently in the letter to the Romans – is universal: 11.15. Likewise it also remains open how exactly one must conceive the salvation of all the Jews – whether through faith in Jesus Christ or in an eschatological deliverance. Paul speaks here of the mystērion. This must all the more be respected when Paul himself closes with a short hymn in which he extols the incomprehensibility of God.

Part II: Rom. 12.1 – 15.13
After the teaching comes the admonition.[100] Paul begins directly with the mercy of

---

97. At this point he certainly has this in view.
98. Cf. the style of 2.1 and 2.17 as well as 9.20.
99. Cf. here 1 Cor. 2.6–16: here, too, Paul reveals a mystērion, namely the circumstance that the crucifixion of Jesus was the wisdom of God. This paradoxical secret is disclosed to the Christians and Paul only by the Spirit of God himself.
100. Parakalein = 'to admonish'.

God with which he concluded the doctrinal part in 11.32.[101] In chapters 12 and 13 he gives general and particular instructions for the Christian life. In chapter 14.1 – 15.13 he deals in more detail with the problem in the church of the so-called 'strong' and 'weak'.

In 12.1,2 Paul formulates a general basis of Christian ethics: righteousness (v. 1), distance from the 'world' (v. 2a) and fulfilment of God's will – i.e. doing what is good, acceptable and perfect (v. 2b). This means that he himself is aware of how things stand and he introduces the Roman Christians, too, to the fact that there is a Christian ethic which has the will of God as its guideline. It is not a purely spiritual ethic but is somatic. Distancing itself from the main currents of the world it resists them and is totally and fundamentally committed to what is good. Paul now sets out in individual paraenetic sections what this general 'good' can look like. The sequence is somewhat loose. Paul does not give a new law but gives pieces of advice which seem to him to be important. 13.1–7 and 14.1–23 could relate in detail to the situation in the Roman house-churches. On the whole the paraenesis has a more general character.

In 13.1–7 Paul gives general advice on the civil duties owed to the authorities. In Rome, where religious and philosophical groups from the east of the Imperium Romanum are always treated as a risk-factor, this topic is always particularly significant.[102] Paul writes from a Jewish perspective: Jews are good citizens; the same is true of the Christ-believing members of the Roman house-churches. In 13.8–10 Paul connects his ethics to the ethos of the Decalogue and in so doing with the theme of the Law in Part I of the epistle. He centres the Decalogue and all commandments on the commandment of love in Lev. 19.18. In this way he comes to a general Christian ethic of brotherly love (v. 8) on the basis of the love commandment. Paul thereby inaugurates a new understanding of the Law which now, within the framework of the Christian ethics in the commandment of brotherly love, definitely expresses the will of God (12.2) and can be fulfilled.[103] Paul closes the general part of the paraenesis with an eschatological exhortation in 13.11–14.

In Chapter 14 he deals with the problem of the co-existence of 'stronger' and 'weaker' in the church which we know from the first letter to the Corinthians. The co-existence of Jewish Christian or Jewish Christian influenced members of the community together with Gentile Christians would have caused similar

---

101. 11.32 eleein = 'to have mercy on'; 12.1 oiktirmos = 'mercy'.

102. The section is connected with the theme of good–evil. Christians should also always unwaveringly do 'what is good', e.g. as citizens or servants of the authorities. The state or the Roman officials were considered to be servants of God and thereby deprived of their autonomous power so that they could also not be demonized as e.g. in the Revelation of John. Cf. also O. Wischmeyer, 'Staat und Christen nach Römer 13.1–7. Ein neuer hermeneutischer Zugang', in *id.*, *Ben Sira*, 229–42.

103. Cf. Lohse, *Brief*, 360–2. But at the same time it is important that in the Pauline ethic the Jewish understanding of the Law is fundamentally changed. Paul certainly rehabilitates the Law (3.31) but by understanding the 'Law of God' (7.25) in the freedom of the Spirit ('Law of the Spirit' 8.2) as the commandment of love.

difficulties in Rome as in Corinth, Galatia and elsewhere.[104] Paul's warning not to judge one another is important here because he has already in 2.1ff. and 2.17ff. identified such behaviour by Gentiles and Jews as a mortal sin. In the 'Kingdom of God' it is not mutual judgement which prevails, but toleration, renunciation of pushing through one's own freedom, and peace and joy (v. 17).

In 15.1–6 and 7–13 Paul enhances Christologically this manner of behaving in the oikodomē (v. 2) which he considers of fundamental importance. In 7–13 he again takes up the theme of Jews–Gentiles which in the end is behind the clash between 'strong' and 'weak' by pointing to Christ who 'became a servant to the Jews' (v. 8) while the Gentiles should glorify God because of the mercy shown through him (v. 9). Paul closes the paraenesis with a prayerful wish.

Part III: Rom. 15.14–33
Paul now comes to the explicitly communicative part of the epistle and takes up the prescript: 15.14–21. He addresses the Christians in Rome very politely and makes his part clear just as politely in this letter: he simply 'reminds' the Roman Christians of a few things. Then he refers to his office as apostle to the Gentiles (vv. 17–21, cf. 1.5) and makes it clear that he can pride himself on an extremely successful mission to the Gentiles in the whole eastern part of the Imperium Romanum (v. 17).[105] In 15.22–33 he develops his plans for Spain, reports on the journey to Jerusalem with the collection and makes it clear that he is exposing himself to danger there.[106] He closes with a prayer for peace (v. 33).[107]

Exegetical Problems
The most important problems for exegesis concern neither the literary unity of the letter to the Romans[108] nor contemporary historical or biographical questions but basic questions of Pauline theology. In this connection I mention the following problems:

1 Paul's position with respect to the Law (also in relation to the letter to the Galatians) in Rom. 2–8 (particularly chapter 7) and 13.8 (for Christian ethics)[109]
2 the picture of atonement in 3.21–26
3 the proper interpretation and significance of the 'Doctrine of Justification' (Rom. 3.21f.) within the framework of Paul's entire theology[110]
4 the appropriate interpretation of the 'I' in Rom. 7 (a typical or personal 'I'? a non-Christian or Christian 'I'?)
5 the extent of pas Israēl and the modalities of its eschatological deliverance according to Rom. 11.26a (through faith in Jesus Christ or by a special way?)

104. The problem of sacrificial meat: 14.2f.; the problem of holy days: 14.5.
105. Cf. 1.16, the *propositio generalis*: 'I am not ashamed of the Gospel'.
106. Verse 31 reveals the 'practical' side of the Israel question for Paul himself.
107. Chapter 16 has already been discussed under textual criticism (1.1) and historical situation (2.1).
108. V. *supra*, p. XXX.
109. Cf. also Chapter 12 by J. Frey on the letter to the Galatians in this volume.
110. V. n. 101 and my contribution on Paul's theology, Chapter 16 in this volume.

6 the appropriate interpretation of Rom. 13.1–7 ('loyal to the state'? 'loyal to the authorities'? 'conformity ethics'? 'position in the context'?).

4
Problems of Interpretation

The problems and models of interpreting the letter to the Romans are connected to two facts that both arise from the specific character of the epistle. On the one hand the interpretation of the letter has always been determined to a particularly high degree by the prevailing theology of the exegetes or, vice versa, has decisively influenced their theology – as e.g. in the case of Luther. On the other hand the letter to the Romans is frequently understood less as a letter and more as a theological compendium and accordingly treated as a doctrinal document. The great debates on the understanding of the theological concepts – the 'righteousness of God', the Law, sin and Israel as well as the anthropology and its conceptuality – are to a large extent derived from the exegesis of the letter to the Romans. This is true from Origen[111] through numerous commentaries on the letter to the Romans by the Reformers[112] up to Karl Barth's *Commentary on Romans* (1922²) and the commentary of the Italian philosopher, Giorgio Agamben (2000).[113]

Alongside this runs a separate radical historical line of interpretation which was prominently initiated by Ferdinand Christian Baur. This is dedicated to the purpose and reason for the letter to the Romans and led into the widespread debate on 'the reason for Romans' which has been continued up to the latest commentary by Robert Jewett.

5
Evaluation

The letter to the Romans is the one of Paul's writings (and of the New Testament as a whole) which founded and inaugurated the theological thinking of Christianity. This thinking is concerned with the relationship between God and man, initially from the Israelite perspective of the history of salvation and then from a Christological perspective which is at the same time present and eschatological. Paul combines the two perspectives when he interprets the God of Israel, the God of the patriarchs, the covenant and the Law and the promise, as the Father of Jesus Christ. From this he draws far-reaching conclusions for the relationship of humanity to God. The 'righteousness' owed to God, which neither Jews nor Gentiles practise, is supplied vicariously by Jesus Christ. If they

---

111. Cf. Lohse, *Brief*, 13.
112. Cf. *ibid.*, 14.
113. G. Agamben (2000), *Il tempo che resta. Un commentato alla Lettera ai Romani*, Turin; (2006) *Die Zeit, die bleibt. Ein Kommentar zum Römerbrief*, Frankfurt.

have faith in him, Jews as well as Gentiles have entry into a new, eschatological life in righteousness before God. These facts Paul calls 'gospel'. They comprise the core of his proclamation. He sets out in revolutionary reflections the consequences of this Christological shift, anthropologically as they relate to humanity, to life, death and eschatological destiny, and in respect of the history of salvation as they affect Israel and the Law. These reflections have two vanishing points: (1) All people who become Christians – he names this attitude 'faith' – live in eschatological peace with God and in the state of righteousness. (2) The whole of Israel will also achieve this state. A universal anthropology and a universal soteriology correspond to one another. Both are connected to the universal grace and mercy of God, which Paul is convinced are finally revealed in Jesus Christ.

References

Commentaries
J. D. G. Dunn (1988), *Romans*, 2 Bde (WBC 38), Dallas, TX: Word Books.
J. A. Fitzmyer S.J. (1993), *Romans. A New Translation with Introduction and Commentary* (AncB 33), New York: Doubleday.
R. Jewett (2007), *Romans. A Commentary*. Hermeneia. Minneapolis, MN: Fortress Press.
E. Käsemann (1994), *Commentary of Romans*, Grand Rapids, MI: Eerdmans.
E. Lohse (2003), *Der Brief an die Römer* (KEK 4), Göttingen: Vandenhoeck & Ruprecht.
U. Wilckens (1978–1982), *Der Brief an die Römer*, 3 Bde (EKK 6), Zürich: Benziger.

Monographs and Anthologies
R. Bultmann (^{5}1984), *Theologie des Neuen Testaments* (UTB 630), Tübingen: Mohr, English translation (2007), *Theology of the New Testament* (trans. K. Grobel), 2 vols, Waco, TX: Baylor University Press.
K. P. Donfried (ed.) (1977), *The Romans Debate*, Minneapolis, MN: Augsburg.
J. D. G. Dunn (1998), *The Theology of Paul the Apostle*, Edinburgh: T&T Clark.
—(2005), *New Perspective on Paul. Collected Essays* (WUNT 185), Tübingen: Mohr Siebeck.
P. Lampe (^{2}2003), *From Paul to Valentinus*, London: Continuum.
U. Schnelle (^{5}1998), *The History and Theology of the New Testament Writings*, London: SCM.
P. Stuhlmacher (^{2}1996), *Gerechtigkeit Gottes bei Paulus* (FRLANT 87), Göttingen: Vandenhoeck & Ruprecht.
M. Theobald (2000), *Der Römerbrief* (EdF 294), Darmstadt: Wissenschaftliche Buchgesellschaft.
—(2001), *Studien zum Römerbrief* (WUNT 136), Tübingen: Mohr Siebeck.

Essays and Encyclopedia Articles
Ch. D. Myers Jr (1992), 'Romans, Epistle to the', *ABD* 5, New York, 816–30.
M. Theobald (2004), 'Art. Römerbrief', *RGG*^{4} 7, 611–18.
S. Vollenweider (2003), 'Art. Paulus', *RGG*^{4} 6, 1035–65.
O. Wischmeyer (2004), 'Die Religion des Paulus. Eine Problemanzeige', in dies., *Von Ben Sira zu Paulus. Ges. Aufsätze zu Texten, Theologie und Hermeneutik des Frühjudentums und des Neuen Testaments* (WUNT 173), Tübingen: Mohr Siebeck, 311–28.

Chapter 16

THEMES OF PAULINE THEOLOGY
Oda Wischmeyer

1
The Theology of Paul

Paul's Theology and the Theology of the New Testament
The *'Theology of the New Testament'*, the core of which is the *'Theology of Paul'*,[1] was devised as an independent subject in the context of the Enlightenment, Rationalism and Historicism. It came into being in the programmatic detachment from Protestant *Dogmatics* which until then had represented 'Theology' and in which 'the fundamental reference to the Bible (was) sometimes handled in a very formalistic way'.[2] Biblical statements and contents were fed into Dogmatics with the help of the so-called *dicta probantia* (today: 'the Biblical witness'). The basis of this construction was the early church conviction that 'Scripture' and 'Confession' corresponded in content. In this way Dogmatics constituted the hermeneutic framework of biblical-theological statements. The structure of this Dogmatics was composed of the main dogmatic concepts which for their part were taken from the Creeds but also, of course, from the Bible itself. Dogmatics served the 'a coherent account of the content of Christian proclamation'.[3] The influence of Dogmatics was to a large extent retained, at least in respect

---

1. More recent accounts of the 'Theology of Paul' are listed in the references at the end of this chapter.
2. F. Hahn, *Theologie I*, 2. Cf. *in toto* Hahn, *Theologie I*, 1–29. In greater depth: G. Strecker (1975), 'Das Problem der Theologie des Neuen Testaments', in *id.* (ed.), *Das Problem der Theologie des Neuen Testaments* (WdF 367), Darmstadt, 1–31. Cf. J. P. Gabler, 'Von der richtigen Unterscheidung der biblischen und der dogmatischen Theologie und der rechten Bestimmung ihrer beiden Ziele', in Strecker (ed.), *Problem*, 32–44. This contribution counts as the beginning of an independent theology of the New Testament. Cf. also O. Merk (2003), 'Anmerkungen zu Gablers Altdorfer Antrittsrede', in K.-W. Niebuhr and C. Böttrich (eds), *Johann Philipp Gabler 1753–1826 zum 250. Geburtstag*, Leipzig, 42–51. The first theology of the New Testament was then produced by G. L. Bauer (1800–1802), *Biblische Theologie des Neuen Testaments*, Vols I–IV, Leipzig. F. Hahn himself develops his own 'Theologie des Neuen Testaments', likewise in two volumes. Vol. 1 deals with the variety of New Testament writings and treats them theologically-historically. Vol. 2 proceeds thematically: In accordance with the significance of Christology Hahn starts from 'God's revelation in Jesus Christ' (Part II) and goes on to Soteriology (Part III). Ecclesiology (Part IV) and Eschatology (Part V) follow. Parts III–V are also conceived in a revelatory-theological way.
3. E. Herms (1999), 'Article: Dogmatics', *RPP* 4, 141–51 (141).

of terminology and structure, in the 'Theology of the New Testament' which was becoming independent and which was constituted as a historical representation. This conception based on Dogmatics has the advantage that it is easily oriented on the whole of theology and consequently it still tends to be used for the 'Theology of Paul'[4] even though since the nineteenth century this is in principle represented in its historical context and drawing on Paul's own terminology.

Accordingly for a basic orientation I start with a classic division of Pauline theology based on the important dogmatic topoi. Paul's specific theological themes can be integrated meaningfully within this framework:

Table 16.1

Theology	One God	Rom. 1.18ff.; 1 Cor. 8.1ff.; Gal. 3.20; 4.8–10; 1 Thess. 1.9
	Israel (1) as the people of God	Rom. 9–11
	Law (1) as a gift of God/Moses	Rom. 2; 3; 5.12 – 8.11; 10.1ff.; 2 Cor. 3; Gal. 3
	Creation	Rom. 1.18ff.
	God's justice and mercy	Rom. 1–3
	Abraham	Rom. 4; Gal. 3 and 4
	Holy Spirit (1)	Rom. 8; 1 Cor. 12
	Trinity	1 Cor. 12.4–6; 2 Cor. 13.13
Christology	Sonship/the sending of Christ (1)	Rom. 8.3; Gal. 4.4–6
	Sonship/the adoption of Christ (2)	Rom. 1.3–7
	Pre-existence of Christ	Phil. 2.6–11
	Christ's death, burial and resurrection	1 Cor. 15.1–11
Anthropology	Anthropological terms	
	Body	Rom. 12; 1 Cor. 6.12–20; 12; 15
	Flesh	Rom. 7.14–25; 8.1–17; Gal. 5.16–26
	Law (2) as indicator of sin	Rom. 5; 7; 10.1–5; Gal. 3
	Sin	Rom. 1–3; 5; 6; 7; 1 Cor. 6.18–20

---

4. Thus e.g. U. Schnelle, *The Apostle Paul Part Two: The Basic Structures of Pauline Thought*, 387–598. Schnelle divides into theology – soteriology – pneumatology – anthropology – ethics – ecclesiology – eschatology.

	Death	Rom. 5; 6; 7.7–25
	Israel (2) as part of humanity	Rom. 1–3
	Gentiles (1) as part of humanity	Rom. 1–3
	The state	Rom. 13
Soteriology	The righteousness of God/ justification	Rom. 1.16f.; 3.21–31; 10.1–4; 2 Cor. 5.21; Gal. 2.11–21; 3.10 –14; Phil. 3.9
	Sin/atonement	Rom. 3.25; 5.8; 8.32; 1 Cor. 11.25; 15.3b–5; Gal. 2.20; 1 Thess. 5.9f.
	Reconciliation	Rom. 5.6–11; 2 Cor. 5.11–21
	Redemption	Rom. 3.24; 1 Cor. 1.30
	Grace	Rom. 3.24; 5.15ff.
	Faith (1)	Rom. 1.16–18; 3.21–31; 4; 5.1–5; Gal. 2.16 – 3.29; 5.1–6; Abraham as father of faith (*v. supra*)
Ecclesiology	Understanding of ministry and apostle	Rom. 1.1–17; 15.14–21; 1 Cor. 1– 4 and 9; 2 Cor. 2.14 – 6.13; 10–13; Gal. 1 and 2; Phil. 3.4ff.
	Community as Body of Christ	Rom. 12; 1 Cor. 12
	Proclamation of the gospel	Rom. 1.16f.; 10.8–15; 1 Cor. 1–3; 15.1–11
	Baptism and Lord's Supper	Rom. 6.1–11; 1 Cor. 1.13–17; 12.
	Worship	1 Cor. 12–14
	Old Testament/Scripture	Rom. 4; 9.6–13; 1 Cor. 10.1–13; 2 Cor. 3; Gal. 3.6–9; 4.21–31
Ethics	Spirit (2) and spiritual gifts	Rom. 8; 1 Cor. 12–14; Gal. 3; 4.1–7; 5.16–26
	Paraenesis/way of life	Rom. 12ff.; 1 Cor. throughout; Gal. 5.1ff.; Phil. 2.5–18
	Righteousness	1 Cor. 5 and 6
	Faith (2) – Love – Hope	Rom. 8.1–30; 13.8–10; 1 Cor. 13
Eschatology	Resurrection	Rom. 6.1–11; 8.18–30; 1 Cor. 15; 2 Cor. 5.1–10; Phil. 1.21–24; 3. 20f.; 1 Thess. 4.13 – 5.10

Judgement	Rom. 1–3; 1 Cor. 3.5–17; 4.1–5; 6.2; 2 Cor. 5.10
Israel (3) as eschatological People of Salvation	Rom. 11
Gentiles (2) as important part of eschatology	Rom. 11

Rudolf Bultmann's 'Theology of Paul'

Since Ferdinand Christian Baur the theology of Paul is chiefly interpreted historically and imbedded in the development of the Christian Church.[5] Thereby the historical interpretation of statements in the New Testament entered alongside or before the dogmatic interpretation. The individual New Testament writings were taken on their own and interpreted by means of their main concepts and put into a connection of development and relationship. In addition dogmatic terms continued to be used. One arrangement, which was taken from the Pauline writings themselves and whose structure had proved able to stand until Bultmann's description, helped the follower of Schleiermacher, Leonhard Usteri[6] to make a breakthrough. Usteri divides as follows:

Table 16.2

First part	Second part
The pre-Christian Period or: *Paganism and Judaism* 1. The people before Christ 2. Sin 3. Sin – death – the Law 4. The Law – Righteousness 5. Nomos, pistis and pneuma 6. Yearning for Redemption	*Christianity* *To plērōma tou chronou* 1. Redemption 2. The Community of God A. Origin and formation B. Perfection

Rudolf Bultmann's 'Theologie des Neuen Testaments'[7] represents a new stage in the development of the subject 'Theology of the New Testament'. Theologically and with regard to its historical effect it is one of the determinative contributions of German-language New Testament scholarship of the twentieth century to theology as a whole and in particular to the theology of Paul. Two central features characterize Bultmann's work: First, with regard to Christian faith,

---

    5.   F.C. Baur (1853), *Geschichte des Christentums in den ersten drei Jahrhunderten*, Tübingen, and *id.* (1864), *Vorlesungen über neutestamentliche Theologie*, Leipzig.
    6.   L. Usteri (⁴1832), *Entwicklung des paulinischen Lehrbegriffs in seinem Verhältnis zur biblischen Dogmatik des Neuen Testaments*, Zürich.
    7.   R. Bultmann (1949–1953), *Theologie*; first appeared: Tübingen. The latest impression appeared in 1984 (edited by O. Merk).

Bultmann has it begin not with Jesus, but only with the Christian proclamation (*Kerygma*).[8]

The second characteristic relates to the task of theology. Bultmann understands every theology – and this includes New Testament theology – as a 'development of the ideas in which the Christian faith is assured of its subject, its foundation and its consequences'.[9]

Two consequences for the theology of the New Testament arise from this. The first consequence affects on the one hand the differentiation between the Kerygma of the original community and the pre-Pauline, Hellenistic community and that contemporary with him,[10] and on the other hand the Theology of Paul and that of John.[11] Bultmann clearly restricts the concept of theology when he understands the Kerygma of the original church and of the Hellenistic community merely as prerequisites of New Testament theology. In the second consequence Bultmann depicts *Pauline Theology as Anthropology*. This is basic for Bultmann's understanding of Paul and should be understood as the new element in the interpretation of Paul mentioned above. Bultmann's picture retains its epochal *theological* significance.[12] His approach to Paul's theology is outlined here:

- Paul's 'thinking and speaking' 'grow' from his basic theological standpoint.
- This basic standpoint is 'not a structure of theoretical thought... Rather Paul's theological thinking only lifts the knowledge inherent in faith itself into the clarity of conscious knowing... The act of faith is simultaneously an act of knowing... Therefore Pauline theology is not a speculative system'.[13]
- That is why Pauline theology 'deals with God not as He is in Himself but only with God as He is significant for man, for man's responsibility and man's salvation. Correspondingly, it does not deal with the world and man as they are in themselves but constantly sees the world in their relation to God.

---

8. Bultmann, *Theology*, 3: 'But Christian faith did not exist until there was a Christian Kerygma, i.e. a Kerygma proclaiming Jesus Christ to be God's eschatological act of Salvation.'
9. *Ibid.*, 3f.
10. Represented by Bultmann in the 'First part'.
11. Represented by Bultmann in the 'Second part'. Bultmann's 'Third part' is devoted to the development of church order, teaching and the lifestyle in the later New Testament writings. Here, too, Bultmann finds 'theology'.
12. This judgement holds true regardless of the fact that the *historical* reconstruction of Paul's religion has developed greatly since Bultmann, on the one hand through the extensive research on the subject of 'Paul and Judaism' (cf. on this Chapter 4 in this volume by J. Frey) and on the other through outlines of the theory of religion such as that by G. Theissen (2000), *Die Religion der ersten Christen. Eine Theorie des Urchristentums*, Gütersloh (*A Theory of Primitive Christian Religion*, London: SCM 1999 = *The Religion of the Earliest Churches. Creating a Symbolic World*, Minneapolis: Fortress 1999) and finally through the new questioning about the person of Paul: E.-M. Becker and P. Pilhofer (eds) (2005), *Biographie und Persönlichkeit des Paulus* (WUNT 187), Tübingen. Cf also Chapter 7 by E.-M. Becker on the person of Paul in this volume.
13. Bultmann, *Theology*, 190.

Every assertion about God is simultaneously an assertion about man and vice versa. For this reason and in this sense Paul's Theology is, at the same time, anthropology'. Correspondingly 'every assertion about Christ' is also 'an assertion about man and vice versa; and Paul's christology is simultaneously soteriology'.[14]

- It follows from this in the depiction of Pauline theology: 'Therefore, Paul's theology can best be treated as his doctrine of man: first, of man prior to the revelation of faith, and second, of man under faith, for in this way the anthropological and soteriological orientation of Paul's theology is brought out'.[15]

Table 16.3

Mankind before the revelation of pistis	Mankind under pistis
The anthropological terms	dikaiosynē theou
Flesh	charis
Sin	pistis
The World	eleutheria

Bultmann stretches the theological statements in Paul's epistles in a very unusual way in that he systematizes them far more than Paul himself does in the letter to the Romans.[16] At the same time Bultmann builds upon Paul's weight-bearing anthropological and soteriological vocabulary and in so doing takes account of Paul's theological language.

Bultmann perceives his own account in the strict sense as theological. According to his understanding Paul is the first Christian theologian, consequently a theological representation oriented on the conceptuality and the intrinsic style of Pauline thinking is apposite for Bultmann. Bultmann insists that Paul is misunderstood if one interprets him as a 'hero of godliness'.[17] The crucial factor remains the starting point of faith. That is why Bultmann's introduction closes with the sentence: 'Such a presentation presupposes, since theological understanding has its origin in faith, that man prior to the revelation of faith is so depicted by Paul as he is retrospectively seen from the standpoint of faith'.[18]

Bultmann's blueprint contains *one structural* flaw: he does not depict the significance of euangelion Iēsou Christou adequately. In Galatians, 1 Corinthians and Romans Paul on each occasion makes it abundantly clear that he understands his whole existence and his task and how he perceives them on the basis of the euangelion. In Rom. 1.16 he gives a classical formulation of the soteriological significance of the gospel. Ferdinand Hahn in Vol. 1 of his theology of

---

14. *Ibid.*, 191.
15. *Ibid.*
16. On the letter to the Romans cf. *ibid.*, 191.
17. *Ibid.*, 191.
18. *Ibid.*, 191.

the New Testament follows this theological train of thought.[19] The inclusion of the Gospel in his portrayal of Pauline thought goes beyond Bultmann's interpretation and should consequently be repeated here:

Table 16.4

1. The Gospel as proclamation of the fulfilment of the Salvation promised in the Old Testament
2. The Gospel as news about the person and work of Jesus
3. The Gospel as knowledge of humankind ... and the problem of the Law
4. The Gospel as an effective power of the donation of salvation (here: the Pauline message of justification)
5. The Gospel as foundation of the life in faith and in the community of believers
6. The Gospel as a message of salvation for the world
7. The Gospel as evidence of hope

Further kinds of portrayal or sketches of Pauline theology will not be surveyed here.[20] For New Testament studies it is particularly significant that the recent representations of Pauline theology predominantly continue to follow a historical and author- or work-related approach, i.e. one based on the history of theology or religion instead of Christian Dogmatics.

2
Paul's Theological Thinking

In this contribution a distinction will be made between a depiction of the '*Theology of Paul*' and the representation of '*Models and Themes of Pauline theological thinking*'. The description of a 'Theology of Paul' cannot and must not be reached here since this would only be possible and meaningful within a framework of a fully discussed, theologically reflected frame of reference.

---

19. Hahn, *Theologie I*, 187f. Hahn refers particularly to the commentaries of E. Käsemann, G. Bornkamm, G. Eichholz and J. Becker as well as P. Stuhlmacher. In a similar way he stresses the commentary on Romans by E. Lohse (2005), *Der Brief an die Römer* (KEK 4), Göttingen. Schnelle, *The Apostle Paul* 389ff. bears this in mind to such an extent that he begins the second main part with an introductory section entitled 'The presence of salvation as centre of Pauline theology'.

20. The following presentations are particularly important: P. Stuhlmacher, *Biblische Theologie I*, 221–392. Stuhlmacher places the pre-theological concept of *proclamation* at the centre of his representation, but then describes the 'origin and starting point of Pauline theology' (234ff.) as a 'definition of the relationship between the Torah and the Gospel of Christ' (243). Stuhlmacher determines the genre of Pauline theology as 'mission theology' (*ibid*.). Strecker, *Theologie*, 11–230 *begins* his description of theology as a whole with the theology of Paul. This he centres around the concepts of *liberation* and *freedom*. J. D. G. Dunn, *Theology*, broadly follows the thematic construction of the letter to the Romans, into which he then inserts the important themes of 1 Corinthians (Church, Communion). In a closing chapter he stresses the *central position of Christ* in Paul's theology. Cf. the introductions in Stuhlmacher, *Biblische Theologie I*, 234ff., and Hahn, *Theologie I*, 181ff.

A 'Theology of Paul' is part of the comprehensive, total theological task of a 'Theology of the New Testament' as Bultmann has shown in an exemplary fashion and as the history of the discipline clearly shows.[21]

This contribution does not outline a 'Theology of Paul'[22] but describes the types and themes of Paul's theological thinking, opinions and argumentation as we find them in his epistles.[23]

Theological Thinking

I begin with the question of how Paul's theological thinking can be described. This is a question of heuristics. If the dogmatic outline and the dogmatic concepts do not construct heuristics of Paul's theological thinking, heuristics must be developed from within the letters. This leads to the following conclusion: *Theological thinking arises for Paul in the course of his epistolary communication with his churches.* In his letters we find not only written communication but also a so-called *meta-communicative surplus*,[24] i.e. sections of the text which do not directly affect the communication with the addressees. Theological statements by Paul can be found in these *meta-communicative* passages in the text but always remain related to the situation of the letter. Bultmann made emphatic reference to this fact but at the same time rightly stressed that Paul's theology had its origin precisely in this limitation.[25] Eve-Marie Becker has described this fundamental fact on the basis of 2 Corinthians: 'When Paul speaks using meta-communication and in so doing formulates relevant letter-hermeneutic statements there arises a new, independent connection of thought and speech which ... departs from the actual content of the communication.' This '*meta-communicative surplus* in connection with the letter-hermeneutic statements generally has a linguistic and propositional theological character'[26] since Paul always argues within the framework of God and the eschatological rule of the Kyrios. *Theological statements and argumentation arise where Paul is thinking of phenomena such as*

21. This fact is not taken into account in any of the representations of Paul's theology mentioned above – including that of Bultmann.

22. This cannot be the task of a textbook on Paul since it requires a theological position of its own.

23. To this extent the same is true for the 'Theology of the New Testament' or its part, the 'Theology of Paul', as for the whole of Dogmatics: It belongs in the area of the *reception of the Pauline letters*, not in the *representation of the Pauline letters themselves*. (Cf. on this O. Wischmeyer (2004), *Hermeneutik des Neuen Testaments. Ein Lehrbuch* [NET 8], Tübingen, 63–90). This is also to be noted critically of Vol. II of F. Hahn's *Theologie des Neuen Testaments*.

24. E.-M. Becker (2004), 'Letter Hermeneutics in 2 Corinthians' (*JSNT*, Suppl. Series 279) T&T Clark: London/New York, 142: 'This term is used to characterize statements and forms of speech which have an independent theological content and which arise in the context of meta-communicative reflections'.

25. Bultmann, *Theology*, 190: Paul writes 'fragmentarily' and 'under the compulsion of a concrete situation'. Cf. on this E.-M. Becker (2002), *Schreiben und Verstehen. Paulinische Briefhermeneutik im Zweiten Korintherbrief* (NET 4), Tübingen, 133ff. and 275ff.

26. Becker, *Schreiben* (n. 25), 277.

his own person, the Christian communities, their opponents, Jews and Gentiles, the lifestyle and hope of the Christians – together with God, the Christ-event and the Last Days. This can be restricted to a concept or a clause, built up into a pattern such as 'the old and the new Adam'[27] or – on rare occasions – lead to a short theological exposition[28] or to a theological treatise (cf. 1 Cor. 15). In 2 Corinthians Paul pursues '*epistolary theology* in the extent to which he formulates important theological statements e.g. on the office of apostle (4.1f. or 6.1ff.), on eschatology (e.g. 5.10), soteriology (e.g. 5.20) or anthropology (e.g. 4.7ff.)'.[29]

Situations of Paul's Theological Thinking
This understanding of Paul's theological thinking based on his epistolary communication with the churches can be put in concrete terms by looking at the *models* of this *situation of communication which creates theology*, for the models of Pauline thinking are generated by particular typical situations:

The Theology of Proclamation/the Gospel
Theology arises for Paul from *the proclamation of the gospel of Jesus Christ*, for proclamation needs consolidating reflection. 1 Cor. 1.18 – 2.16 is an example of this. Here Paul reflects on his proclamation and lays the basis of a theology of the Cross.[30]

Theology in the Church
Theology arises against the *background of Church practice*. 1 Corinthians as a whole is the most important exemplification of this type. Even in Rom. 14 Paul treats a problem in the community in theological depth although he does not know the Roman Christians personally.

Polemical theology[31]
Theology arises to a considerable extent from the *confrontation with opponents*. 2 Corinthians is largely characterized by the confrontation about Paul's person: more precisely, about his understanding of 'apostle'. In Galatians the objective confrontation about the euangelion tou Christou (Gal. 1.6f.) predominates. Here personal and material confrontations are always tied to one another in Paul, as is already apparent in 1 Cor. 1–4.

Theology in Friendship
On the other side *communication with friends* can also lead to theological intensification. Examples of this are the letters to the Philippians and to Philemon.

27. Or: Revelation in Creation – Revelation in Christ (Rom. 1–3), Flesh and Spirit (1 Cor. 15 and often).
28. Thus 1 Cor. 7; 13 and Rom. 13.
29. Becker, *Schreiben*, 277.
30. Cf. Hahn, *Theologie I*, 260f. H. Weder (1985), *Das Kreuz Jesu bei Paulus* (FRLANT 125), Göttingen; T. Söding (1997), *Das Wort vom Kreuz* (WUNT 93), Tübingen.
31. To this category belong the anti-Jewish Theology of Righteousness by Faith and the anti-enthusiastic Theology of the Cross and of Suffering (*v. infra*, n. 102).

Autobiographical Theology
In Paul theology never arises without *reflection on his own religious biography*. Along with Gal. and 2 Cor. the autobiographical passages in Phil. and 1 Cor. are examples of this.[32] In Rom. 7 Paul engrosses these personal experiences and conceptualizes an adamitic anthropology.

Theology of Apostolate
Finally, theology arises in Paul most forcefully through the *necessity of self-presentation*. The documentation of such a self-presentation is the letter to the Romans in which Paul reveals the theology of his apostolate, gospel, righteousness and Israel.

The situations mentioned do not exclude one another. *One* epistle is usually witness to various situations and contains the appropriate statements. Thus Philippians, for example, does not contain only statements about friendship but has passages which are polemic, autobiographical, paraenetic and kerygmatic.

3
Characteristics of Pauline Theological Thinking

The representation chosen here of theological themes which Paul develops is connected, together with the theory of meta-communication, to *further insights* into Paul's way of thinking and working. I single out the most important aspects: changes, presuppositions and the impact of rhetoric.

Changes in Pauline Theology
Udo Schnelle, in his extensive representation of Paul, now treats the *historical and situative characteristics* of Paul's theological statements under the heading 'Changes'.[33] Although we can only follow approximately the last ten years of Paul's life through his letters,[34] the oft-repeated opinion that this period of time was too short for developments or changes cannot be upheld. For during the time of his mission Paul is involved in stormy confrontations which increase in problematic nature towards the end of his missionary activity in the east: 'The opposing front became ever larger and stronger near the end of Paul's ministry and this must have had a basis in the theological thinking of the Apostle himself. Jews regarded him as an apostate and radical Jewish-Christians as falsifier, i.e.

---

32. On this cf. O. Wischmeyer (2004), 'Die Religion des Paulus', in *id.*, *Von Ben Sira zu Paulus. Gesammelte Aufsätze zu Texten, Theologie und Hermeneutik des Frühjudentums und des Neuen Testaments* (WUNT 173), Tübingen, 311–28 and the contributions in Becker and Pilhofer, Biographie (n. 12).

33. Schnelle, *Paul*, 34f. Cf. especially n. 79 (pg. 42) with the literature and the critical discussion using the term 'development'. Cf. also the important article: H. D. Betz (1992), 'Paul', *ABD* 5, 186–201. Betz emphasizes: 'His theology is primarily the result of *processes of thought*' (192).

34. Here v. Chapter 5 in this volume by E. Ebel on the life of Paul.

they perceived Pauline's theology as hostile'.[35] Besides, new tasks brought with them new characteristic challenges. The letter to the Romans is an expression of this fact. Before his journeys to Jerusalem and Rome Paul thinks through his 'Gospel for the Gentiles' (Rom. 1.6) but also rethinks and augments the place of the Jews in the history of Salvation.

Presuppositions of Pauline Theology
A further dimension of Pauline theology lies in its *rootedness in facts handed down*: first in the *graphē* i.e. the 'Scriptures' of Israel, second in the *traditions of Jewish thinking*, third in the budding *traditions of the Christian communities* and fourth in a *stratum of contemporary ethics common to all in the Imperium Romanum*. For Paul is deliberating, certainly in a new and very creative way, but not in a 'vacuum'.[36] On the contrary he incorporates in very diverse depths and intensity the traditions mentioned into his own theological deliberations:

- 'Scripture'[37]
- principles of Pharisaic theology[38] and early Jewish Apocalyptic theology and literature[39]
- the tradition of the so-called Hellenistic congregations.[40]

Bultmann gave a detailed description of the 'Kerygma of the Hellenistic congregations before and at the time of Paul' as the basis of Pauline theology. In his 'Outline of the Theology of the New Testament' H. Conzelmann followed Bultmann,[41] but in so doing he gives up the differentiation between the Kerygma of the original Church and that of the Hellenistic congregations. F. Hahn now puts the early Christian tradition to which Paul refers within the framework of the individual theological topics.[42]

- In addition there is contemporary ethics.

35. Schnelle, *Paul*, 144.
36. The religio-historically directed examinations of Paul's theology present this phenomenon of Paul's rootedness in the world of thought around him. Currently in this area everything is concentrated on the so-called *New Perspective*, i.e. on the reconstruction of Paul's understanding of the Law. On this cf. Chapter 4 in this volume on Judaism by J. Frey.
37. Cf. on this fundamentally: D.-A. Koch (1986), *Die Schrift als Zeuge des Evangeliums. Untersuchungen zur Verwendung und zum Verständnis der Schrift bei Paulus* (BHTh 69), Tübingen; R. Hays (1989), Echoes of Scripture in the Letters of Paul, New Haven: Yale University Press.
38. In this cf. Chapter 4 on Judaism by J. Frey in this volume.
39. Cf. B. McGinn, J. J. Collins and S. Stein (eds) (2003), *The Continuum History of Apocalypticism*, New York/London. In this volume v. Chapter 4 by J. Frey on Judaism.
40. R. Bultmann determined what the tradition of the so-called Hellenistic congregations meant for Paul's theology: 'Not having been a personal disciple of Jesus, he has been won over to the Christian faith by the Kerygma of the Hellenistic church', Bultmann, *Theology*, 187f.
41. H. Conzelmann, *Grundriss*, 31–140.
42. Hahn, *Theologie I*, 164, 203ff. (sovereignty titles), 213 (Soteriology), 250 (Justification) etc.

To what extent Paul was aware of contemporary ethics in the form of popular philosophical teaching is difficult to reconstruct. It is clear, however, that there was a reservoir of ethical norms and advice or experiences common in content and in writing in which the philosophy of the early imperial period had a place as did the early Jewish and early Christian ethics.[43] The phenomenon of paraenesis can be found on numerous occasions in Paul.[44] A text such as Phil. 4.8 shows clearly that Pauline ethics is well aware of links with the ethics of the environment:

> Whatever is true, whatever is honourable, whatever is just, whatever is pure, whatever is lovely, whatever is gracious, if there is any excellence, if there is anything worthy of praise, think about these things.

The Theological Significance of Rhetoric and Epistolography in Paul

Hans Dieter Betz has drawn attention persistently to the significance of *rhetoric* for Paul's theology. Betz makes a very pointed statement in relation to the Corinthian opponents who compelled Paul to take part in a discussion on the relationship between rhetoric and theology: 'Without these challenges Paul's theology would never have been put on paper, and we would never have known about it'.[45] In general terms this means: Paul develops his theology in a critical inclusion of the contemporary practice of rhetoric as public argumentative speech based on conviction. On a Christian basis he develops a theological rhetoric of his own which is not simply a play on words but is 'a rhetoric designed to argue in rational arguments so that the truth may appear'.[46] Here we observe something like a second Socratic situation: Just as Socrates developed his questioning philosophical method in the clash with the Sophists, so Paul is brought by his opponents to his Christian, rhetorically argumentative theology – which is open and rational, is convincing and at the same time leaves space for divine action.[47]

Now, however, we possess this theology in an *epistolographic transformation*, in the genre of letters. The genre 'letter' 'is subjective, relevant to a situation, communicative, related to the addressees and – in the communicative and not the political sense – democratic'.[48] These aspects are a fundamental part of Pauline

---

43. Cf. Chapters 3 and 4 by B. Heininger and J. Frey in this volume.

44. Cf. J. Starr and T. Engberg-Pedersen (eds) (2004), *Early Christian Paraenesis in Context* (BZNW 125), Berlin/New York. Fundamental: A. Dihle (1966), 'Article: Ethik', *RAC* 6, 646–796.

45. H. D. Betz (1986), 'The Problem of Rhetoric and Theology According to the Apostle', in A. Vanhoye (ed.), *L'Apôtre Paul. Personalité, Style et Conception du Ministère* (BEThL 73), Leuven, 16–48, 47f.

46. *Ibid.*, 24 in relation to the letter to the Galatians.

47. H. D. Betz (1972), *Der Apostel Paulus und die sokratische Tradition. Eine exegetische Untersuchung zu seiner 'Apologie'* (BHTh 45), Tübingen.

48. Wischmeyer, *Hermeneutik* (n. 23), 33. More detailed in: H.-J. Klauck (2006), *Ancient Letter Writing and the New Testament: A Guide to Context and Exegesis*. With the

theology since Paul only wrote letters and did not make use of any other literary genre.

4
Topics of Theological Deliberation in the Pauline Letters

Within this section the individual theological topics will now be described. I proceed with an eye on the chronological sequence of the letters[49] and look for the theological motifs (1 Thess.) and themes (1, 2 Cor., Gal., Phil., Rom.) of the individual epistles.

1 Thessalonians

The first letter to the Thessalonians mentions a great variety of theological motifs without explaining them. All these motifs can be reinforced theologically and are starting points for theological deliberation as is shown in the later Pauline epistles:[50]

- Faith, Love, Hope, the so-called Triad 1.3 (cf. 1 Cor. 13.13)
- euangelion 1.5/ Word of the Lord 1.8; 2.13
- pistis 1.8; 3.5, 6, 10
- Conversion to God 1.9
- Jesus, Son of God, whom he raised from the dead 1.10; 4.14
- Apostolic self-introduction 2.1–12
- Jews 2.14–16
- Comfort in affliction 3.7
- agapē 3.12; 4.9ff.
- Christian peripatein, work 4.1–11; 5.12ff.
- Holiness of the congregation 4.3–8
- Soteriological dimension of the death of Jesus: 'hyper hymōn' 5.10.

The only theological theme where an attempt is made to elaborate is that of the so-called *Eschatology* in chapter 4.[51] Here there arises the need to teach (4.13 introductory formula for teaching), probably caused by an uncertainty in the church about the eschatological fate of members who had died (4.13ff.). In a

---

collaboration of Daniel W. Bailey, Waco, Tx.: Baylor University Press. Cf. the introduction to Part II and the contributions on the letters, particularly on Romans, in this volume.

49. On the chronology cf. Chapter 5 on the life of Paul by E. Ebel in this volume. On details cf. the chapters on the particular letters in this volume.

50. This contribution can neither look into the reappearance of these motifs nor investigate other motifs that are briefly mentioned in the later letters. Here it should simply be clear that in 1 Thess. on the one hand very many theological motifs are mentioned briefly but on the other only eschatology is given a more extensive clarification.

51. Fundamental for the historical background to New Testament eschatology is: P. Volz, *Die Eschatologie der jüdischen Gemeinde im neutestamentlichen Zeitalter*, [Tübingen 1934] reprinted Hildesheim 1996.

simple analogical conclusion (houtōs) Paul derives from the Kerygma of Christ in 4.14a that Jesus is also the Kyrios of those who have died (in Christ) and will lead them to God.[52] In 4.15–18 Paul sketches a short apocalyptic scenario in which the sequence of the eschatological events, in so far as they affect the Christians, is depicted: Resurrection of the Christians who have died, a common translation of all Christians to the Lord. The vision of the end is: 'pantote syn kyriō esometha' (4.17).

A further question relates to the *time* of the final event. Paul answers this question in 5.1–11 in the sense of 'unexpectedly soon'.[53] Here he is using as support a general early Christian knowledge that the 'Day of the Lord' – Paul uses the idea of the Day of Yahweh from the Old Testament which had already been revised in early Christianity – will come suddenly.[54] From this he derives, corresponding to the eschatology of the Synoptics, the ethos of watchfulness and of the Christian lifestyle (the Triad again in 5.8).

1 Corinthians

In the first letter to the Corinthians, as well as mentioning many theological motifs, Paul elaborates with the aid of particular motifs *individual theological topics* which require a detailed description – partly because the congregation has questions but also partly because he himself desires to clarify certain themes.

Chapters 1–4 apply to the function of the leader or founder of the church. Paul begins matter-of-factly with his commission to *proclaim the gospel* (1.17). From this he derives first the theological motif of the fellow worker (3.9) and steward (4.1) in the apostolate, second the motif of the apostolic suffering in lowliness, weakness and nearness to death (4.6–13) and third the theological conception of the Christian community, which is determined through unity (4.10ff.), modesty and holiness (3.16f.) and lifestyle after the example of the apostle (4.16). These basic elements of the *Theology of Apostolate* will be developed further by Paul particularly in 2 Corinthians. He reinforces the topic of the relationship between congregational leader and congregation in one decisive point: In 1.18 – 2.26 and 3.18–23 he outlines from his own commission to preach (1.17) a *Theology of Wisdom* marked by the circumstance of Christ's death on the Cross.[55] He isolates (2.2) and puts into concrete terms the first part of the tradition about Christ in 1 Cor. 15.3–5 (v. 3 hoti Christos apethanen) and fills the death on the Cross – which initially appears to be senseless (1.18) – with a soteriological significance against all the facts as proof of the specific power

---

52. Cf. on 1 Thess. 4.13 – 5.11 E. v. Dobschütz (1909), *Die Thessalonicher-Briefe* (KEK 10), Göttingen, 183–215.

53. Dobschütz, *Thessalonicher-Briefe* (n. 52), 204.

54. On the question as to whether a 'Word' of the Lord is the ground for this knowledge cf. v. Dobschütz, *Thessalonicher-Briefe* (n. 52), 204f.; Hahn, *Theologie I*, 311: Excursus 323–9. In general on the theology of 1 Thess. cf. T. Söding, 'Der Erste Thessalonicherbrief und die frühe paulinische Evangeliumsverkündigung', in *id.*, Wort (n. 30), 31–58.

55. Cf. Hahn, *Theologie I*, 260f. Söding, Wort (n. 30), there: 'Das Geheimnis Gottes im Kreuz Jesu (1 Kor. 2.1f., 7ff.)', 71–92; 'Kreuzestheologie und Rechtfertigungslehre', 153–84; 'God chose what is low and despised in the world' (1 Cor. 1.27), 260–71.

(dynamis) and wisdom (sophia) of God (1.24) which appear to be completely missing in this death. Paul develops this interpretation contrary to the facts in two directions: on the one hand pneumatologically with regard to the Christian dynamis of his own *person* (2.1–5) and the *church* (1.26–31), on the other in respect of a *personal Christological sophia* which is no longer the wisdom of Creation (1.18–21) but the eschatological wisdom of Redemption (2.6–9) and as such is a spiritual apocalypsis (2.10ff.). In 3.18–23 Paul formulates a critical closing thought: Christians possess the true wisdom and freedom.

In chapters 5 and 6 Paul expands the theological motif of the holiness of the congregation in 3.16f. He relates it to the holiness of the body, which prohibits immorality (ch. 5) and going to law in pagan courts (ch. 6). Alongside ethical regulations directed for use there arises here the outline of a theology of the *holiness of the body* of the members of the congregation in an ethical respect (6.19 taking up 3.16f.). Paul combines this idea here already with the theologumenon of the sōma Christou understood in a spiritual sense (3.17) which he develops in chapter 12 (6.15ff.).

In chapter 7 Paul inserts into the ethical instructions a significant eschatological motif: the *Eschaton* makes the things of the kosmos irrelevant, and so Christians should 'deal with the world (kosmos)' in such a way 'as though they had no dealings with it' (7.29ff.), in 'freedom from the world and its powers' and 'in the *distance of the hōs mē*'.[56]

In 8.1–6 Paul depicts his theology and parallel to it his Christology in its essential features in the confrontation with the Greco-Roman pantheon. In the course of chapters 8 to 10 Paul gives on this theological basis a complex instruction on how to deal with so-called *meat sacrificed to idols*. Theologically significant is the differentiation between mere food, which is soteriologically irrelevant (8.8), and the *conscience* (8.7) – here mentioned for the first time in the Pauline writings – of the apprehensive ('weak') Christians for whom the pagan gods still possess potential power and who consequently do not have the – theologically proper – freedom *not* to worry about the origin of the meat they eat. Here Paul does not really argue theologically but primarily pastorally: the 'weak' conscience must be spared (8.12f.). Paul is very well aware that in so saying he is falling behind his own theological possibilities and insights. In chapter 9 he names himself as an example for this self-denial.

In chapter 10.1–13 and 14–22 Paul delivers a warning, theologically based on 8.1–6, about too great certainty about the 'end of the ages' (10.11). Paul develops a '*Sacramental Theology*' *neither in 1 Cor. 10.14–22 nor in 11.17–34*. He simply gives a warning not to omit to distinguish to sōma (kyriou). Ethically unworthy participation in the Lord's Supper leads to punishment by the kyrios but not to eschatological damnation (v. 32). Paul considers illnesses and premature death as such punishments.

Chapters 12 to 14 develop within the framework of Pneumatology/doctrine of the Charismata practised in the church services (12.4–11) the theological

---

56. Bultmann, *Theology*, 351f.

metaphor of the church community as the *Body of Christ*, whereby the primacy is granted both ethically and eschatologically to agapē in chapter 13.

Chapter 15 contains the second longest theological exposition after chapter 2. Paul tackles the question of *resurrection* in a short theological treatise.[57] This is one of the rare, in the narrower sense theological, texts in Paul – induced on practical grounds (vv. 12,29), answered for personally, (vv. 8–11), accompanied by ethical advice (vv. 29–34) and concluding with apocalyptic (vv. 50–55). Paul uses the dominating analogy between the first and second Adam (vv. 20–28) and the analogous differentiation between the physical and the spiritual body. The aim of the theological discourse is to prove that the raising of Jesus from the dead was not a unique, ineffective act of the miraculous divine intervention in the *conditio humana* of dying but represents the eschatological beginning of the salvation of humankind. Paul understands Jesus Christ not as a divine hero but as the eschatological saviour, the one man, by whom 'has also come the resurrection of the dead' 15.21. To this extent chapter 15 is a true interpretation of that euangelion with which Paul introduces his treatise.

All in all, in this letter Paul constructs a coordinate theological system in which for the first time after 1.17f. he formulates the euangelion in his own characteristic way and inserts it into the eschatological framework provided by Jesus Christ as a new Adam and the forthcoming end of time. Ethical and eschatological questions of physicality (sōma), of participation in the eschatological sōma Christou and of the understanding of the Christian person, the Christian community and of the apostle are added here. The theology is based on the recognition of the *one* God and the confession of the *one kyrios Iēsous* (8.1–6; 12.1–3).

2 Corinthians

The second letter to the Corinthians is characterized throughout by a *Theology of Apostolate* which arose out of a situation which was highly polemical and which Paul treats autobiographically.[58]

In 2.14 – 6.10[59] Paul develops his Theology of Apostolate for apologetic reasons in the context of the Theology of the Spirit, Eschatology and Atonement-Christology. Consequently we have here a longer, very dense theological interrelation in which further theological motifs act in combination along with those named.

Paul understands himself – and his fellow workers (2.13ff.) – as bearers of the proclamation of Jesus Christ who in their work of preaching fulfil a soteriological function (2.14–16). The Christian community for its part is awarded

---

57. Cf. Lindemann, *Korintherbrief* (n. 51), 338f. and O. Wischmeyer, 'I Korinther 15. Der Traktat des Paulus über die Auferstehung der Toten in der Wahrnehmung unterschiedlicher Textzugänge', in *Id.*, *Ben Sira* (n. 32), 243–76.
58. On all details cf. Chapter 11 in this volume by E.-M. Becker. I do not refer here to the hypotheses of division but simply describe the elements of the Theology of Apostolate.
59. Here I am not dealing with a subsection of Letter A (v. Chapter 11 in this volume by E.-M. Becker).

the same function for those around it (3.1–3). The office of apostle (diakonia) is spiritual, life-giving and leads people to eschatological glory (3.4ff.). This gives it its honour and significance.

The text 3.4–18 deserves particular mention. Here Paul reasons using the outbiding (mallon 3.8) typology of Moses and the apostle as diakonos of the Old and the New Covenant which is only developed by Paul in relationship to the apostolate. Here Paul develops, as frequently, antithetical-corresponding series of concepts: Old and New Covenant, letter and spirit, tablets of stone and tablets of human hearts, death and life, Moses and the spirit, etc. The aim is to depict the glory and soteriological significance of the diakonia *of the apostle*. The metaphor of the covenant is connected to the Tablets of Moses, i.e. to the Decalogue, which in 3.14–16 represents the whole Torah. In 3.16 Paul formulates the hope that all Israel will be converted, which is set out in Rom. 11. In 3.17f. Paul sketches a Christology which is closely intertwined to the pneuma.

In 4.1–6 Paul makes it clear that the office of apostle (diakonia 4.1) is a public office and serves only the proclamation of Jesus Christ, not self-publicity. Consequently the office is service, not control. Its function is to enlighten people and make them aware of the majesty of God. In 4.7–18 Paul continues his theology of apostolate by developing the *theologumenon of the apostle's community with Christ in suffering and dying*. This leads him in 5.1–10 to depict an *eschatology of the individual* which is intensified autobiographically. Other than in 1 Cor. 15 Paul formulates here personally. He does not use the metaphor of the body but initially contrasts the human 'dwelling' and that which comes from God. Only in 5.5–10 does he return to the metaphor of the body, but here it is restricted to the earthly body. As a result there arises the idea of 'departing' from the body (5.8). Verse 5.10 connects the individual eschatology with the universal eschatology which is perceived apocalyptically. In 5.11–21 Paul succeeds in making a Christological amplification of the theme of the apostolate. The office of apostle is interpreted as an office of *reconciliation* (diakonia tēs katallagēs 5.18) derived from God's reconciling himself with humankind through Christ (5.17–21). The preaching of the gospel is in this context the logos tēs katallagēs (5.19).[60] Once again Paul makes the eschatological frame clear when he describes the Christian existence as a new creation: hōste ei tis en Christō kainē ktisis (5.17). The office of reconciliation becomes the office of ambassador (5.20 hyper Christou presbeuomen). Paul combines the Christology of Reconciliation with other Christological interpretations: the connection of the idea of Representation and the Christology of Incorporation (5.14f.), the non-inclusion of sins (5.13), the idea that Christ was free of sin (5.21) and the establishment of human righteousness in Christ (5.21, cf. 1 Cor. 1.30).

In 6.1–10 Paul visualizes in a list of afflictions formulated in an antithetical-paradoxical way the *suffering* of apostles as theou diakonoi (6.4) combined with the eschatological statement of time: 'Behold, now is the day of Salvation' (6.2).

60. On the Christology of Reconciliation cf. Hahn, *Theologie I*, 262f.

In chapters 10–12 Paul enlarges upon the *Theology of Apostolacy*, corroborated from his own experiences.[61] He defends himself against the accusation of personal weakness and illness by referring indirectly on the one hand to his Jewish-Pharisaic background (11.21f.), his mission (11.23,28f.), his charismata (12.12) and his religious experiences (12.1–5), but on the other hand he interprets his chronic illness itself as his actual strength (12.6–10 and the list of afflictions 11.23ff.). He supports this interpretation Christologically in quoting a personal message of the Kyrios to him: 'But he said to me, "My grace is sufficient for you, for my power is made perfect in weakness"' (12.9).[62]

The *metaphor of the fool* (aphrōn, aphrosynē) and the speaker in the '*Fool's Speech*' (12.17ff.) display bold theological means of style and thought which make it possible for Paul to develop verbally complex theological facts which break the rules of religious experience or even reverse them. Apostolic weakness is shown to be the strength based on Christ: 'For when I am weak, then I am strong' 'hotan gar asthenō, tote dynatos eimi' (12.10) reads the theological paradox.

In 2 Corinthians *criticism and polemic* also become theological media of style and thought with the aid of which the theology of fame and strength represented by the opponents is exposed as being directed against Christ.

Galatians

The first theological theme of the letter to the Galatians is the *unadulterated euangelion* in 1.6 – 2.21. The gospel is preached by the apostle, but he himself received it 'through a revelation of Jesus Christ'. At the same time the gospel refers to Jesus Christ. Here the question of the relationship between gospel and the Law – put in concrete terms in circumcision (2.3) and in the observance of the Jewish regulations relating to food (2.11ff. the 'Antiochian Incident') – is fundamental. To deal with this problem Paul develops the idea of a twofold form of gospel-proclamation: his own, devoted to the Gentiles which does *not* include living their lives according to Ioudaismos, and the one connected to Peter which is aimed at the Jews and does not insist on renunciation of the Law – although Peter himself appears to have been vacillating in his position on the law.[63] For Paul it is a necessary and obligatory part of the gospel *that Gentiles do not have to live like Jews*, i.e. do not have to conform to the Law in order to achieve righteousness before God (2.14–16). The polemical question in 2.14b: 'If you, though a Jew, live like a Gentile and not like a Jew, how can you compel the Gentiles to live like Jews?' contains a theological bombshell. Here Paul puts the Gentile (ethnikōs) way of life, i.e. non-observance of the laws in the Torah, on

---

61. Cf. Betz, *Apostel* (n. 47).
62. O. Wischmeyer, '2 Kor. 12.1–10. Ein autobiographisch-theologischer Text des Paulus', in *id.*, *Ben Sira* (n. 32), 277–87; *id.* (2004), '2 Korinther 12.7–8. Ein Gebet des Paulus', in R. Egger-Wenzel and J. Corley (eds), *Deuterocanonical and Cognate Literature Yearbook 2004. Prayer from Tobit to Qumran*, Berlin/New York, 467–80.
63. Peter, Barnabas and other Jewish-Christian missionaries do not always keep the Jewish laws relating to food, unlike James and his envoys (2.11ff.).

the same level as the Jewish (ioudaikōs) lifestyle, i.e. living in accordance with the Torah. The ioudaizein becomes in the process an ethnic characteristic and loses its soteriological quality. The physei-Ioudaioi-existence (v. 15) no longer has any power to save.

In so saying Paul comes to develop his second theological theme which continues the first and for which the stage has already been prepared in 2.16–21: *faith as opposed to works of the Law*. In 3.1–4.7 Paul begins a series of antithetical theological concepts:

Table 16.5

[hostile agitation]	[apostolic] proclamation of faith
Works of the Law	Faith/Righteousness
Flesh	Spirit

In this connection Paul interprets Abraham as a paradigm of faith, not of the Law. He follows this with further antithetical concepts:

Curse	Blessing
Carrying out the Law	Faith

The very intense argumentation in 3.10–14 using Deut. 27.26, Hab. 2.4 and Lev. 18.5 gives scriptural evidence for the fact that the Law is totally incapable of leading to life but has death (the curse) as its consequence. Paul inserts a chronological element in this argumentation: the vicarious (hyper hēmōn) cursing of Christ which quashed the curse of the Law for (Jewish-) Christians.

In 3.19 – 4.7 Paul asks the question which from a Jewish point of view is central: ti oun ho nomos? 'What then is the Law?' He answers in a special theological manner with a scheme relating to the history of salvation which again is connected to Christological thinking. God's actions from the very beginning led to Jesus Christ. He was born in the plērōma tou chronou (4.4). From this perspective the Law is a quantity bound to the epochs in the time before Christ. For this Paul uses the metaphor of the paidagōgos, the custodian of children (3.24f.). At the same time he consigns the Law to sin:

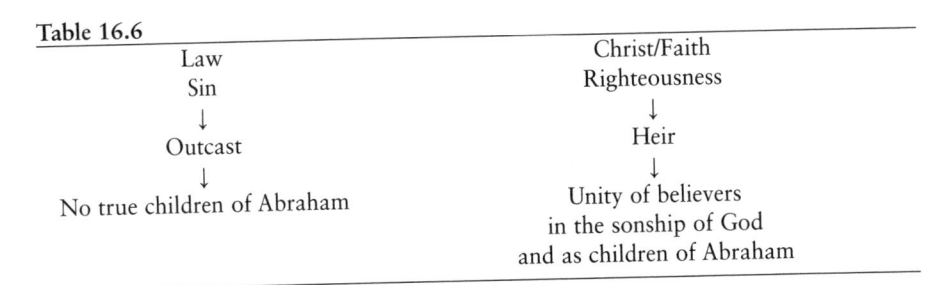

Table 16.6

Law	Christ/Faith
Sin	Righteousness
↓	↓
Outcast	Heir
↓	↓
No true children of Abraham	Unity of believers in the sonship of God and as children of Abraham

In 4.21–31 Paul intensifies the theological concept of sonship (of God) by interpreting (4.24) Gen. 16.15; 21.2,9. A further series of antithetical pairs of concepts begins:

Table 16.7

Son of the servant	Son of the free woman
according to the flesh	according to the promise
mother Hagar	(mother Sara)
Covenant of Mt Sinai	(New Covenant)
the present Jerusalem	the heavenly Jerusalem
slavery	freedom
(Jews)	Christians

In chapter 5 Paul locates the Christians within a topical theological framework:

Table 16.8

The yoke of slavery	Freedom
Circumcision of Christians	Uncircumcision
Law	Spirit
Falling from Grace	Righteousness
	Hope
Loss of Jesus Christ	Jesus Christ
	Faith

Finally in 5.13 – 6.10 Paul designs an outline of the Christian life in a *paraenesis* which interprets freedom ethically on the basis of the Commandment of love (5.13f.).

In the letter to the Galatians we find an almost totally polemical antithetical structure of basic theological concepts which starts from and is determined by the attempt of anti-Pauline Jewish-Christian missionaries to bring Gentile-Christians in Galatia to observe the Law, but at the same time thinks beyond this theological situation.[64]

Philippians

In the letter to the Philippians Paul interprets his *imprisonment* theologically as based on his mission to proclaim the gospel (1.16). Within this biographical framework, the 'letter of friendship', which is kept very personal, intensifies two theological motifs: Paul's relationship to Christ and the church's relationship to Christ.

In the letter to the Philippians Paul sees *his relationship to Christ* – taking up the theology of the first letter to the Corinthians – as physical: 'as it is my eager expectation and hope that I shall not be at all ashamed but that with full courage now as always Christ will be honoured in my body, whether by life or by death' (1.20).[65] The fulfilment of the union with Christ for which Paul longs is reserved

---

64. I. J. Elmer (2011), 'Pillars, Hypocrites and False Brothers. Paul's Polemic against Jerusalem in Galatians', in O. Wischmeyer and L. Scornaienchi, *Polemik in der frühchristlichen Literatur. Texte und Kontexte*, BZNW 170, Berlin/New York: de Gruyter, 123–54.

65. Here he is no doubt thinking of the idea formulated in 1 Cor. 15 of the sōma psychikon and the sōma pneumatikon (15.44ff.).

for the life after death (1.23). How this individual religious idea relates to 2 Cor. 5.1–10 and how it connects to the apocalyptic scenarios in 1 Thess. 4 and 1 Cor. 15 Paul does not make clear. It is, however, clear that Paul does not abandon the eschatology of the last judgement and Christ as judge which is depicted apocalyptically: 1.6,10 and 2.16 ('Day of Jesus Christ').[66]

Paul would like to see the *relationship of the church to Christ* marked by humility (tapeinophrosynē) and mutual service (2.3f.). He reinforces this way of living in agapē (2.1f.) Christologically by the reference to Jesus Christ. The church should live in Christ-like phronēsis (2.5). From the *Hymn of Christ* in 2.6–11[67] Paul takes the motif of self-abasement (v. 8) which finds its culmination in the death on the Cross.[68]

In Chapter 3 Paul speaks, with a more pointed polemic against competing hostile missionaries, about the dikaiosynē dia pisteōs Christou (v. 9). The text of 3.2–21 shows – in keeping with the genre of the personal 'letter of friendship' – an autobiographical approach to the theme of the dikaiosynē theou which, comparably to Gal. 1.10ff., develops the basic elements of Paul's so-called doctrine of justification from his own biography. In a bold theological metaphor Paul claims the covenantal sign of circumcision (peritomē) for Christians (3.3) by interpreting their circumcision as spiritual and the Jewish sign of the Covenant polemically as 'fleshly' (sarx), i.e. he allocates it to the sinful self-interest of humanity – concretized in his conception of the Jewish religion (3.4–6). Paul combines 'Righteousness through Faith' with a Christology of Participation or Communion (koinōnia pathēmatōn Christou 3.10) from which he infers for himself, analogous to the Hymn of Christ, from the sharing in Christ's suffering and death participation in his Resurrection (3.9–14). In so saying he is once again an example for the congregation (3.15ff.). He does not provide a more detailed discussion of the relationship between justification by faith and participation in Jesus' resurrection through a Christ-like personal way of living. Chapter 3, however, suggests that the apostolic life of suffering (3.10) is an interpretation and concretization of the dikaiosynē dia pisteōs Christou (3.9). In Phil. 3.12–14 and 20f. Paul makes it clear that the existence of the one justified by faith takes place in suspense and anticipation. The *conditio christiana* is a Christological-apocalyptic one: ho kyrios engys (4.5).

In 4.8 Paul formulates in passing principles of Christian *ethics* on the basis of aretē (cf. already in 1 Thess. 5.21).

Romans

Exegetes for the most part are unanimous that in the letter to the Romans we not only have the most detailed and the most developed form of Paul's theology but also that only here does Paul draw up something like a consistent theology in the narrower sense and expound this in longer developments of argumentation. But

---

66. On this cf. F. Hahn, *Theologie I*, 313f. Hahn suspects that Paul himself reckons with an individual intermediate state for those who have died (cf. also 1 Cor. 15).
67. On all details cf. Chapter 14 in this volume by L. Bormann.
68. Cf. 1 Cor. 1.18ff. (*v. supra*).

this theological account also remains related to the situation: In the letter to the Romans the epistolary self-representation generates a homogenous picture of the self-understanding of the Pauline euangelion.

Theological Themes (in tabular form)

Table 16.9

1.16 – 4.25	*The gospel of the righteousness of God* which saves humanity through faith Example: Abraham (Gal. 3)
5	*Freedom from death* and Christ as a second Adam (cf. 1 Cor. 15)
6	*Freedom from sin*, substantiated Christologically and theologically through baptism
7	*Freedom from the Law* in spite of the entanglement of the ego in sin
8	*Freedom of the Christians* and life in the Spirit *Waiting for the eschatological liberation of the whole of Creation*
9–11	*The current position of Israel before God and Israel's eschatological perspective*
12 – 15.13	*The Christian ethos* *Special topics:* State 13.1–7 Love 13.8–10 Church 14.1 – 15.13
15.14–21	*The Theology of the Apostolate* (cf. 1.1–7).

The *propositio generalis* in 1.16f. makes a fundamental theological statement on the theme: For which class of humanity is the soteriological power of the euangelion theou affective? The statement reads: Affected are all people who believe the Gospel. In saying this Paul determines that faith is the power which saves people.

The statement is at first only understandable in the Jewish religious paradigm: Because of their sins people need to be saved. This salvation comes from God. In the Jewish paradigm, however, Jews are saved by living according to the Thora, but Gentiles can only be saved if they observe the Torah and – if they are male – receive the sign of the covenant, namely circumcision, i.e. if they become Jews. Paul on the other hand determines that faith in the euangelion is the saving power and stresses that this soteriological possibility is open not only for the Jews but likewise for the non-Jews, i.e. from Israel's perspective, the Gentiles.

Chapters 1.18 to 3.19 outline a *Fundamental Anthropology*. The basis of this anthropology is the righteousness through faith in the *propositio generalis*, for this deprives Judaism of its soteriological precedence or its singular right to salvation. It is not the Jew who observes the Torah but the person who believes the Gospel who will 'live' (1.17). The new anthropology which applies to the whole of humanity interprets the Gospel of Jesus Christ, the Son of God (1.1–4). To this extent it is already Christian anthropology since it, too, is formulated from a Christian perspective. Paul understands its spatial scope to be universal, i.e. in the dimension of the Imperium Romanum, the world known to him. In a similar way he depicts it as chronologically universal: from the Creation or from Adam (1.20; 5.12ff.; 8.18ff.) up to the end of the present world-time of Creation (8.18ff.; 13.11–14). In chapters 1–3 he places the fundamental anthropology under the revelation of the wrath of God (not only over the Gentiles but also over the Jews) and indicates the deadly guilt before God of all humanity (1.32; 3.9,19).

In 3.21 – 8.39 Paul brings into focus *a Christian anthropology* by picturing the effects the revelation of the righteousness of God in Jesus Christ has upon people who believe in Jesus Christ. He begins with a Christological-soteriological foundation in 3.21–26. In chapter 4 he interprets the Jewish patriarch, Abraham, as a prototype of faith and thereby makes him a universal person who belongs in the line that leads from Adam to Christ. In chapters 5–7 Paul depicts the new, already eschatological life of those people who believe in Jesus Christ and are justified so that they 'have peace with God' (5.1). These people[69] live in freedom from death (ch. 5), sin (ch. 6) and the Law (ch. 7). Paul understands this threefold eschatological freedom as a change of rule, not already as a new form of existence. Death no longer has any power over people who believe in Christ. But the eschatological life has first to gain control (5.21).[70] Paul makes this idea clear with the aid of the Adam-Christ typology in chapter 5. The liberation from sin is depicted in chapter 6 with the help of the Theology of Baptism. Again it is clearly a question of a change of rule from sin to righteousness (6.12,13), not of the state of existence of present freedom from sin (6.16).

In chapter 7 Paul comes to the most difficult topic: Freedom from the rule of the Law (7.1). To begin with he explains this freedom in using the analogy of the widow who after the death of her husband is freed from the 'law concerning her husband', i.e. from the marital state (7.1–6). In a similar manner the Christian is freed from the state of life under the Law. In 7.7–13 Paul discusses the further suspicion that the Law might itself be sin (7.7). He rejects this, from a Jewish point of view, outrageous and blasphemous insinuation and defines the function of the Law as positive: It functions as an indicator of human sin. Only the Law allows the wicked deed to appear as such in that it exposes this as a violation of the Law. Paul differentiates here between the desire to overstep the law and the rules behind it and the Law itself. In 7.14–25 he combines this desire with the human person so that the person is understood as the one who desires, i.e. is basically living against the Law and its rules. This fundamental anthropological idea intensifies the reign of sin to which Paul returns once again in 7.14–25.[71] A person cannot, however, be completely evil, for then he could not be saved.

---

69. Paul does not call them 'Christians' but 'we' in an inclusive sense.
70. Notice the future tense in 5.21.
71. 7.20: 'the sin which dwells within me'.

He remains God's creature. Paul expresses this with the philosophical term of the esō anthrōpos[72] who 'delights in the law of God' (7.22). Consequently there takes place a battle for the person between the 'inner man' and the likewise inner striving for power on the part of sin (7.23). Paul calls off this battle with the emphatic double cry in 7.24 and 25.

In Chapter 8 he then shows the glorious freedom of the children of God. Those who are 'in Christ Jesus' are no longer under the condemnation of chapter 3. They are freed from the rule (here nomos, v. 3) of sin, death and the Law (8.1 and 2). In the second part of chapter 8 Paul in closing sketches a spiritual ethic and an eschatological perspective, and that initially for the Christians and then from 8.18 for the whole of Creation. In this way he combines the fundamental-anthropological view with the Christian anthropology and inserts both into the eschatological destiny of 'Creation'.

Chapters 9–11 apply the *propositio generalis* specifically to the Jews, who, as Israelites, remain the chosen people. In Chapter 11 Paul comes to the fundamental theological statement relating to Israel: 'God has not rejected his people whom he has chosen' (11.2). In so saying Paul makes somewhat superfluous his reflections in 9.6–12 where he differentiates between the Israelites and Esau. His reflections based on the prophets about God's merciful choice and on the 'remnant' of Israel who would be saved (9.14–29) also recede behind the statements in Chapter 11. And 9.30–33 and 10.1–21 describe the 'current position' of Israel from the view of the *propositio generalis* but not its eschatological perspective. Not even the further Old Testament motif of the 'hardening' (11.1–10) is Paul's final theological word to Israel. Paul only comes in 11.11–34 to his true *Theology of Israel* in the light of the *propositio generalis*. It is the universal fundamental anthropology in chapters 1–3 which opens the way to salvation for the Israelites; for in the light of the *propositio generalis* Paul recognizes God's will for universal salvation which now holds good not only for the Gentiles but finally again – and that conclusively – for Israel (11.25–27). To the judgement to plērōma tōn ethnōn eiselthē (11.25) corresponds the other judgement: pas Israēl sōthesetai. To the *Universal Anthropology* of the *propositio generalis* (cf. also 11.32a) there corresponds the *Universal Soteriology* (11.32b) which is set forth in the remarks in 11.25–33.

5
Retrospective

When one looks at the themes of Pauline deliberation as they are developed in his epistles according to the situation at the time, a clear *thought structure* emerges. This deliberation relates first to Paul's revelation of Christ, subjectively experienced but at the same time objectively understood as affecting the whole

---

72. Cf. on this R. v. Bendemann (2004), *Die kritische Diastase von Wissen, Wollen und Handeln. Traditionsgeschichtliche Spurensuche eines hellenistischen Topos in Römer 7*, ZNW 95, 35–63.

world; and secondly to the situative and possibly fundamental problems that arise from this for the Christian communities and Paul's preaching.

1. The *basis* of Paul's theological thinking – the phenomenon that Bultmann describes as 'faith' – is his personal appointment by the risen Lord, the Son of God, to preach the gospel to the Gentiles.[73] He fulfils this commission in his apostolic preaching and effectiveness in an ecumenical breadth from Jerusalem to Rome.[74] Other than the wide *spatial* scope of his activity is the *temporal* determination of his apostolate. He is convinced that his activity is set in a narrow temporal frame: ho kairos synestalmenos estin.[75] The burden, only conceivable with difficulty, which his commission brings with it he can endure only through his closeness to the kyrios, which he can express with the emotiveness of yearning[76] or refer to obliquely as 'being with Christ'.[77] The reality of his existence as an apostle, however, he experiences as a life of afflictions,[78] weakness[79] and illness[80] and in the face of death.[81] Here, however, he is not alone but knows that he is supported by numerous co-workers.[82] But at the same time he is attacked by numerous opponents[83] and threatened in his work for the church.

2. The *foci* of Paul's theological deliberation develop out of his personal commission: the proclamation of the euangelion to the Gentiles.[84]

- The first problem which Paul must deal with theologically in this connection is so-called *eschatology*. We can see in the first letter to the Thessalonians the origin of the problem: Christians have died[85] before the Kyrios has returned. In view of this fact Paul develops theological statements on the future of Christians and the cosmos, initially relating to the Parousia of Christ and the fate of the Christians who have died and those who are still alive.[86] Going far beyond this theologically he drafts the idea of the first and second Adam,[87] of the physical and spiritual person[88] and of the eschatological revelation of the New Creation.[89]

73. Gal. 1.16; Rom. 1.1–6; 15.14–21.
74. Rom. 15.19.
75. 1 Cor. 7.29; cf. Rom. 13.11f. and 1 Cor. 15.50ff.
76. Rom. 8.18–30; 2 Cor. 5.1–10; Phil. 1.20–26.
77. 1 Thess. 4.17; Phil. 1.23.
78. 1 Cor. 4.9–13; 2 Cor. 11.23–33.
79. 1 Cor. 2.1–5.
80. 2 Cor. 12.1–10.
81. Phil. 1.19f.
82. Phil. 1.14ff.; 1 Cor. 3.5ff.; esp. Rom. 16 throughout.
83. 2 Cor. 11.22; Gal. 4.17; 5.12; 6.12.f.; Phil. 1.15ff.; 3.2.
84. Gal. 1.16.
85. 1 Thess. 4.13.
86. 1 Thess. 4 and 5; 1 Cor. 15; 2 Cor. 5; Phil. 3.10ff.
87. 1 Cor. 15; Rom. 5.
88. 1 Cor. 15; Rom. 6.1–11.
89. Rom. 8.18ff.

- A second problem arises from the fact that Paul wins Gentiles for the gospel and admits them into the ekklēsia which he founds without their endorsing Ioudaismos, i.e. observing the Torah and – if they are male – being circumcised.[90] To observance of the Torah there belong according to the perception of Jews and Jewish-Christians above all purity,[91] questions relating to calendar and feast days[92] and circumcision. Paul has these questions clarified at the apostolic council in Jerusalem (49 CE) in favour of the *Law-free mission to the Gentiles*.[93] But the problems and uncertainties remain and result in the theological question as to what theological function the Law and circumcision have for the Gentile-Christians. In the end the question here is whether or to what extent the way of life of the Jewish-Christians is meaningful and soteriologically relevant. Paul battles persistently with these questions, develops his 'doctrine of justification through faith' in the letter to the Galatians[94] and the letter to the Philippians[95] in a polemical form, in the letter to the Romans in a more didactic version and develops this doctrine in the context of a soteriology supported by faith.[96] In the letter to the Romans he finally sketches a perspective of salvation for Israel as the People of God which rests on the preceding conversion of the Gentiles.[97] The questions relating to Paul's Law-free mission lead in the letter to the Romans[98] to a universal anthropological perspective *coram deo*. Before God's court Judaism loses its precedence for salvation and moves alongside heathenism. From this perspective which is opened up in Rom. 1–3 neither can Israel be saved by its own efforts nor is there a possibility of salvation for the Gentiles. Paul however, even in these fundamental anthropological texts, is clearly not considering specifically the theological position of the Jewish-Christians. Even his own position as a Jewish-Christian – which he in fact was – remains strangely vague.[99]
- Third, theology develops from the problem of the new ekklēsia theou or Iēsou Christou. The *churches* need a theological self-understanding in the crosshairs of eschatology and soteriology; for they are not simply Hellenistic-Roman societies or a further Jewish sect (hairesis), but Paul describes them as an

---

90. Gal. 2.3–10 and 5.1–12.
91. Particularly in respect of the laws relating to food, 1 Cor. 8–10; Gal. 2.11f.; Rom. 14.
92. Rom. 14.5; Gal. 4.10.
93. Gal. 2.1–10.
94. Gal. 2.11ff.; 2.16ff.; 3.1 – 5.12.
95. Phil. 3.1ff.
96. Gal. 2.16ff.; Rom. 1.16f. and 1.18 – 8.39 along with 1 Cor. 15.
97. Rom. 9–11.
98. But also in the letter to the Galatians as was explained above (in 4.4).
99. Cf. 1 Cor. 9.19–23. Such texts were certainly incomprehensible for devout Jewish-Christians such as James. Whether and to what extent Paul himself observed the Torah in spite of polemical texts such as Phil. 3.2–11 does not emerge from his epistles. He mainly developed *theologically* the argumentation of a Law-free mission to the Gentiles.

eschatological community[100] and as a participatory, spiritual community,[101] namely as the 'body of Christ' and as people who live in the Spirit.[102] Both these aspects of the ekklēsia hold true also for her individual members and for the apostle himself,[103] who for his part is an example for the churches.[104] The Christ-like existence of the congregation is shown in concrete form in lowliness, suffering and persecution.[105] Here, too, Paul understands himself as a model for the Christian communities.

- Fourth, there emerges for the churches a further requirement that gives rise to theology: They need an ethos of their own to take the place of the Torah. Paul sketches approaches to a Christian *ethic*[106] in the sense of a thematically open paraenesis to the churches which he can theologically substantiate as 'life in the Spirit',[107] in the Last Days[108] or in the state of the holiness of the body[109] or understands as a 'rational worship of God'[110] or as every conceivable 'good'.[111]

The four problems mentioned which lead to the formulation of theology are closely connected and represent aspects of the development of the *one* euangelion Iēsou Christou.[112] This means: the unity of the aspects portrayed does not lie in a theological meta-structure or in a basic theological principle – be it 'Christological', one based on a 'theology of revelation', a 'soteriological' or a pneumatological/anthropological approach.[113] Consequently the four aspects cannot be subordinated to *one* central theological concept and brought into a hierarchical dependency one upon another. Rather they are individual reflected and argumentative forms of the theological thinking which mediates between the *message of the Risen Kyrios Jesus Christ*, the Son of God [114] and the temporal-spatial-individual and social *conditions of life of the Christians*, and takes into consideration and formulates the consequences of the gospel for how one lives. For Paul understands the Christians[115] as people who believe the euangelion Iēsou

---

100. 1 Cor. 5–7.
101. Cf. G. Theissen (2002), *Das Neue Testament* (Beck Wissen 2192), Munich, 40–61. Theissen orders the letters according to theological features into situative (1 Thess.), anti-Judaistic (Gal.; Phil.), anti-Enthusiastic (1/2 Cor.) and theological-synthetic epistles (Rom.). E. P. Sanders, *Paulus*, stresses the participatory side of Pauline theology.
102. 1 Cor. 12–14 and Rom. 12; Gal. 5.16,25.
103. Eschatologically: Phil. 3.12–16; participatory: Phil. 1.20–24.
104. 1 Cor. 4.16; 11.1; Phil. 3.17.
105. 1 Cor. 1–4; 2 Cor. *passim*.
106. Rom. 12ff.; 1 Cor. *passim*; Gal. 5ff.
107. Gal. 5.16.
108. 1 Cor. 7.29f.
109. 1 Cor. 6.12ff.
110. Rom. 12.2.
111. Phil. 4.8f.
112. Cf .what was said above on F. Hahn's approach.
113. Christological: e.g. G. Strecker; theology of revelation: e.g. F. Hahn; soteriological: e.g. Melanchthon; pneumatological: e.g. E. P. Sanders; anthropological: e.g. R. Bultmann.
114. Rom. 1.3f.
115. He does not use this expression (cf. Acts 11.26).

Christou and base the way they live, understand their life and the world and their hope on the euangelion.

As far as we can see Paul is not only the one early Christian apostle who took part in a high-quality, detailed epistolary correspondence with his churches[116] but the one who developed from this literary communication theology in the sense of *individual aspects and elements of apostolic teaching and instruction. In so doing Paul stands at the beginning of Christian theology.*

References

General Literature

R. Bultmann (⁹1984), *Theologie des Neuen Testaments*, durchges. u. erg. von O. Merk (UTB 630), Tübingen: Mohr. English translation: (2007), *Theology of the New Testament* (trans. K. Grobel), 2 vols., Waco, TX: Baylor University Press.

G. B. Caird (1994), *New Testament Theology*, completed and edited by L. D. Hurst, Oxford: Clarendon Press.

H. Conzelmann (⁵1992), *Grundriß der Theologie des Neuen Testaments*, bearb. von A. Lindemann (UTB 1446), Tübingen: Mohr.

Ph. F. Esler (2005), *New Testament Theology. Communion and Community*, Minneapolis, MN: Fortress Press.

F. Hahn (2003), *Theologie des Neuen Testaments, Bd. 1: Die Vielfalt des Neuen Testaments. Theologiegeschichte des Urchristentums; Bd. 2: Die Einheit des Neuen Testaments. Thematische Darstellung*, Tübingen.

H. Marshall (2004), *New Testament Theology: Many Witnesses, One Gospel*, Downers Grove/Leicester: Inter-Varsity Press.

U. Schnelle (2007), *Theologie des Neuen Testaments*, Göttingen: Vandenhoeck & Ruprecht.

Thomas R. Schreiner (2008), *New Testament Theology: Magnifying God in Christ*, Grand Rapids, MI: Baker Academic.

G. Strecker (1995), *Theologie des Neuen Testaments*, bearb., erg. u. hg. von F. W. Horn, Berlin/New York: De Gruyter.

P. Stuhlmacher (1992/1999), *Biblische Theologie des Neuen Testaments, Bd. 1: Grundlegung. Von Jesus zu Paulus; Bd. 2: Von der Paulusschule zur Johannesoffenbarung. Der Kanon und seine Auslegung*, Göttingen: Vandenhoeck & Ruprecht.

Monographs

J. D. G. Dunn (1998), *The Theology of Paul the Apostle*, Grand Rapids, MI: Eerdmans.

E. P. Sanders (1977), *Paul and Palestinian Judaism,* London: SCM (Paulus und das palästinische Judentum [StUNT 17], Göttingen: Vandenhoeck & Ruprecht, 1985).

—(1991), *Paul*, Oxford: Oxford University Press.

U. Schnelle (2005), *Apostle Paul. His Life and Theology*, Grand Rapids, MI: Baker Academic (U. Schnelle, *Paulus. Leben und Denken*, Berlin/New York: De Gruyter, 2003).

---

116. Cf. the contribution on the second letter to the Corinthians in this volume.

Part III

Reception of Paul

Chapter 17

Introduction to Part III
Oda Wischmeyer

Paul is the person who, in the earliest days of emerging Christianity, generated the greatest impact. This is true not only for his own life and activity, which are discussed in Part I of this volume, and for his epistles and theological deliberation, which are represented in Part II, but also for the influence of his person after his death.

As an apostle who put his thoughts into writing Paul was effective in shaping 'education' and theology.

His pupils come on the scene as authors in their own right, without, however, mentioning their names. They write pseudonymously, i.e. under the name of their teacher, Paul. This is true of the letter to the Colossians, the letter to the Ephesians and the second letter to the Thessalonians. These *so-called Deutero-Pauline letters* were written using the stylistic device of literary fiction to the churches Paul had founded in Thessalonica, Colossae and Ephesus. They continue the cast of the letter to the Romans, coming from matters relating to the situation to general theological statements and making personal communication a literary fiction. The *Pastoral letters* – likewise literary fabrications – are addressed to Paul's fellow workers, Timothy and Titus. Here post-Pauline church leaders encourage one another by confirming the authority of the apostle and his best-known co-workers. All in all the Deutero-Pauline letters and the Pastoral epistles[1] introduce into new situations radical concerns of Pauline thought and apostolic leading of the church. What is crucial is that the Pauline impulses of the literary genre of the congregational letter and of the development of theological deliberation were developed by his pupils in his name, but commensurately adapted to fit new situations. At the same time in the author of Acts we find a writer who describes the activity of Paul as a decisive part of the apostolic period of the rise of Christianity and creates a second source for Paul's life and activity alongside the genuine Pauline letters (Acts 9–28).[2] This literary genre, too, developed its own further effect in the apocrypha which are dedicated to Paul and his followers.

---

1.   Cf. on this B. Heininger's contribution on 'The Reception of Paul in the First Century', Chapter 18 in this volume.
2.   Cf. the contribution by B. Heininger mentioned in n. 1.

In the Early Church, however, Paul's influence soon no longer continues in the literary sense of pseudepigraphical Pauline letters and new 'Acts' of the apostle[3] but it enters into the process of the canonization of the writings of the so-called Age of the New Testament. The core of the 'New Testament' that was arising were the first collections of Pauline letters. In the course of the second century we have the first of the commentaries on the Pauline letters.[4]

Since Origen's commentaries on the Pauline letters Christian theology has to a considerable extent taken the form of interpretation of Paul's letters.

High points of this continuing reception and effect of Paul's letters and their theological themes are to be found in Augustine, Luther and Calvin, and in the twentieth century in Barth and Bultmann.

The chapters in Part III are devoted to the Deutero- and Trito-Pauline writings (Chapter 18), the reception of Paul in the second century (Chapter 19) and the history of the influence and reception of Paul in the course of the history of Christianity (Chapter 20).

---

3. Here cf. Chapter 19 in this volume by A. Lindemann.
4. On this and further developments cf. Chapter 20 in this volume by W. Wischmeyer.

Chapter 18

The Reception of Paul in the First Century. The Deutero- and Trito-Pauline Letters and the Image of Paul in Acts

Bernhard Heininger

Table 18.1

Deutero-Paulines	
The letter to the Colossians	*c.*70–75 CE
The letter to the Ephesians	*c.*85–95 CE
Second Thessalonians	end of the first century
Trito-Paulines	
First letter to Timothy	*c.*100 CE
Second letter to Timothy	*c.*100 CE
Letter to Titus	*c.*100 CE

Note: The so-called *Letters from Prison* are written in italics.

Paul's death certainly meant a sharp break for the early Christians but in no way did it signify the end of Pauline theology. Even during the apostle's lifetime his *co-workers* carried and characterized the Pauline mission to a considerable extent; the Proto-Paulines alone mention around 40 people who are to be seen as fellow-workers of the apostle. One may suspect that Paul's work within this large circle of co-workers was scarcely limited merely to questions of organization, but that particularly in the closer circle of fellow workers intensive theological work took place, the literary expression of which is to be found in the pseudepigraphical Pauline letters. The very letters that scholarship names the Deutero- and Trito-Paulines provide evidence that Paul's legacy was not only tended but was reflected upon theologically and adapted to fit a situation which had changed. In the writings mentioned, Paul's doctrine of justification moves into the background while problems of church law and ethics become central, e.g. because of the appearance of heretical teachers. In this situation the suffering Paul – Col., Eph. and 2 Tim. purport to be letters from prison – becomes *the* authority of the early period, even being given a soteriological quality on occasion (cf. Col. 1.24; Eph. 3.1). The group of six pseudonymous

Pauline letters[1] make use of the stylistic device of pseudepigraphy, i.e. feigned authorship. They borrow Paul's literary and church-leading authority to enable them to lead and further develop the churches after his death. Simultaneously they develop on their part their picture of Paul parallel to that given in Acts: Paul the sufferer, the prisoner, the strict teacher (2 Thess. 3.14) and the generous teacher (1 Tim. 5.23). To this picture there also belong biographical details such as in 1 Tim. 18–20; 5.23; 2 Tim. 4.9–21; Tit. 3.12f.

A problem of a different kind is whether one should assign the writings mentioned to a 'school'. Presumably there are as many advocates for this view as there are opponents, and the answer to this question depends above all on what one understands by a 'school': Does it mean an organized educational concern which can be localized, such as the ancient schools of the philosophers (e.g. in Ephesus) or merely a phenomenon of the transmission and actualization in emulation of Paul which took on varying forms in different regions and situations?[2] Final answers, in spite of considerable scholarly efforts, have yet to be found.[3]

1
The Letter to the Colossians

The reason for the composition of the letter to the Colossians is the emergence of a certain 'philosophy' (2.8), the outlines of which become more evident in Col. 2.16–19,21. Evidently taboos relating to food and perhaps also sexual matters play a central part,[4] and the representatives of this 'philosophy' also demand the keeping of certain festal periods and of the Sabbath, from which we can conclude a Jewish background. In general the piety of this group is marked by self-abasement (2.18: tapeinophrosynē); no less important for them is the worship of angels. In all probability they pride themselves also on visionary experiences or transportations into heaven, if one may interpret thus the difficult ha heoraken embateuōn (who boasts of what he has seen) in 2.18. This 'philosophy' clearly represents a serious threat for the addressees because of which the author sees himself obliged to intervene. He does this using Paul's authority and as means also chooses Paul's characteristic form of communication, the letter.

The Development of the Text
The letter to the Colossians is based on the form of the Pauline letter. After a

---

1. Cf. U. Schnelle (⁵2005), *Einleitung in das Neue Testament* (UTB 1830), Göttingen; A. Merz, *Selbstauslegung*.
2. Thus P. Müller, *Anfänge*, 325.
3. On this cf. particularly the recent work of T. Schmeller (2001), *Schulen im Neuen Testament? Zur Stellung des Urchristentums in der Bildungswelt seiner Zeit*. Mit einem Beitrag von C. Cebulj zur johanneischen Schule (HBS 30), Freiburg im Breisgau.
4. Thus M. Wolter, *Brief*, 151; J. Gnilka, *Kolosserbrief*, 158 on Col. 2.21 ('Do not handle!')

brief prescript which names Timothy as a co-sender (1.1,2)[5] there follows a longer proemium (1.3–23) in which the typical epistolary elements of thanksgiving (1.3–8) and intercession (1.9–14) are amplified with a 'eulogy of Christ' (praise or hymn 1.15–20) together with an application to the church (1.21–23). As regards its contents, in verses 3ff. the well-known Pauline triad from 1 Cor. 13.13, 'Faith – Hope – Love', catches one's eye – which, however, is 'quoted' in the sequence as in 1 Thess. 1.3. The apostle's 'self-testimonial' which follows (1.24 – 2.5), by means of which 'Paul' describes his function in the event of the revelation given to him – namely as servant of the Church and of the gospel – is often assigned to the body of the letter but, analogous to 1 Tim. 1.12–17, it should be seen as an independent part between the introduction and the body of the letter which functions as a hinge.[6] A classic epistolary topos appears in the talk of absence 'in the body' and presence 'in spirit' (2.5); the inclusion of agonistic vocabulary in 1.29 (kopiō agōnizomenos) and 2.1 (agōna echo hyper hymōn)[7] awaken memories of the 'real' Paul.

The body of the letter extends from 2.6 – 4.6[8] and is divided, perhaps more clearly than is the case in the Proto-Paulines, into a didactic (2.6 – 3.4) and a paraenetic part (3.5 – 4.6). Verses 2.6–8 present the theme: The addressees stand before the alternatives, either 'to walk in Christ' (v. 6: en autō peripateite) or to lead a life according to the 'elemental spirits of the universe' such as a virulent 'philosophy' (v. 8) in the community clearly desires! The author meets this danger in two ways: First, he inserts a kind of reminder of their baptism (2.9–15) which refreshes the addressees' memory again of their 'state of salvation in Christ': They are circumcised, not by a circumcision by hand, have put off the 'fleshly body' and have been buried and raised (!) with Christ, with the result that they have rid themselves of any other lord or powers. Why, then, should they again accept rules in the form of taboos relating to foods or observation of a particular calendar of Feasts as the author sets out in the following refutation of the opposing position (2.16–23)? Far more, reads the final section of the didactic part (3.1–4), because of the fact that they have 'been raised with Christ' they should endeavour to seek 'things that are above' (ta anō) and not 'things that are on earth' (ta epi tēs gēs). On the one hand this is a delicate riposte with a touch of irony to the opponents who worship angels and presumably refer to experiencing visions (2.18: on this more later); on the other the author of Col. takes up again the opposition between a way of life kata Christon and life kata ta stoicheia tou kosmou introduced in 2.6–8 in a slightly changed linguistic form so that the sections 2.6–8 and 3.1–4 build a splendid *inclusio* (frame) around 2.9–23.

5. Timothy is also co-sender in Phil. 1.1; 1 Thess. 1.1; 2 Thess. 1.1 (on each occasion along with Silvanus); Phlm. 1.
6. Wolter, *Brief*, 98; I. Maisch, *Brief*, 25.
7. Cf. 1 Thess. 2.1f., 19; 1 Cor. 9.24–27; Gal. 2.2; 5.7; Rom. 9.16; 15.30; Phil. 1.27, 30; 3.12–16; 4.1, 3; here see U. Poplutz (2004), *Athlet des Evangeliums. Eine motivgeschichtliche Studie zur Wettkampfmetaphorik bei Paulus* (HBS 43), Freiburg im Breisgau.
8. J. Becker and U. Luz, *Briefe*, 184 and Maisch, *Brief*, 25 consider that the main part closes with 4.1 and assign the closing exhortations in 4.2–6 to the ending of the letter.

The paraenetic part subdivides, according to whether one includes 4.2–6 or not, into two/three sections. First, Col. 3.5–17 converts the indicative of the reminder of baptism in 2.9–15 into the imperative: The 'change of garments' which took place in baptism, i.e. the putting off of the old and the putting on of the new person,[9] must find a response in corresponding deeds, which the author puts in concrete terms with the aid of traditional lists of sins (3.5,8) and virtues (3.12). The following *Haustafel* ('Rules for the Household') (3.18 – 4.1) is addressed in turn to wives and husbands, children and parents/fathers as well as slaves and masters. From the wives subordination is requested, from children and slaves, obedience; in return the men should love their wives, not make their children discouraged and treat their slaves fairly and justly. General closing exhortations, such as to continue steadfastly in prayer or to conduct themselves wisely, close the body of the letter (4.2–6).

The conclusion of the letter (4.7–18) initially promises the arrival of the envoys, Tychicus and Onesimus (4.7–9); then follow the sending of greetings, commissions to give greetings and recommendations (4.10–17) before a greeting in his own hand (a literary stylistic touch quoting 1 Cor. 16.21) and a wish for grace close the epistle (4.18).

Table 18.2

The beginning of the letter	1.1,2		Epistolary prescript
	1.3–23		Introduction
	1.3–8		Thanksgiving
	1.9–14		Intercession
	1.15–20		The Christ-Hymn
	1.21–23		Application to the church
	1.24–25		The apostle's self-testimonial
The body of the letter	2.6 – 4.6	2.6–8	*Theme*: Appeal to remain 'in Christ' against the philosophy
		2.9–15	*Reminder*: In Christ the church already has the fullness of Salvation
		2.16–23	*Refutation*: The church needs no other doctrine of salvation
		3.1–4	*Invitation*: To orient themselves on the Risen Christ
		3.5 – 4.1	*Ethical admonition*: 3.5–17 on the old and the new person 3.18–41 Wives – Husbands Children – Parents Slaves – Free people

---

9. At this point the author also falls back on 2.9–15 linguistically: apekdysamenoi v. 15 takes up again the apekdysei tou sōmatos tēs sarkos in 2.11!

		4.2–6	Closing exhortations
Ending of the letter	4.7–18	4.7–9	The 'apostolic' parousia
		4.10–17	Greetings, requests to greet and recommendations
		4.18	Note on personal writing

Genesis of the Text
The Question of the Author
Literary and theological arguments speak against the attribution of the letter to the Colossians to the historical Paul. Typical Pauline expressions, i.e. concepts and phrases which are familiar to us from the letters which are universally accepted as genuine, such as dikaiosynē and dikaioun, eleutheria, koinōnia, nomos or sōtēria, are missing in Col.[10] On the other hand Col. uses 28 words which are certainly found in other New Testament writings but not in the Proto-Paulines. To these are added 37 hapax legomena. And while Paul thinks and formulates in an adversative way, the letter to the Colossians favours the loose, associative combination of thoughts through using the genitive, participial constructions, relative clauses and the like.[11]

The theological differences, however, are more significant than the linguistic and stylistic divergences. The cosmic dimension of Christology which can be seen at most in an initial stage in Paul (cf. 1 Cor. 8.6; 2 Cor. 4.4; Phil. 2.6–11) becomes a general topic in Col.: As Lord of Creation Christ rules over all that has been created, he is the Head of all authorities (2.10) and triumphs over the cosmic powers (2.15). The cosmos owes its continued existence to him. The central metaphor of Col., the sōma, receives similar treatment. While Paul calls the concrete local church the Body of Christ,[12] in Col. the global Church appears as a body to which Christ is now assigned as head (Col. 1.18; cf. 1.24; 2.19; 3.15). In the background stands the mythical idea of the world as a gigantic body of an all-embracing deity. There are also differences in eschatology, which in Col. is oriented in the present and precisely in the interpretation of baptism marks a significant difference from Paul: According to Col. 2.12 the faithful are already 'raised with' Christ (cf. the opposite of this in Rom. 6.3–5!) or, as it says in an earlier verse, 'transferred us to the kingdom of his beloved Son' (1 Cor. 1.13).[13] Finally the author works in the paraenesis with a new literary genre, the *Haustafeln* which also does not do justice to the original Paul in the matter of the subordination of the woman to the man.[14]

---

10. A complete list in E. Lohse, *Briefe*, 135.
11. Researched in depth by W. Bujard (1973), *Stilanalytische Untersuchungen zum Kolosserbrief als Beitrag zur Methodik von Sprachvergleichen* (StUNT 11), Göttingen.
12. Cf. 1 Cor. 12.27; slightly varied in Rom. 12.5: 'one body in Christ'.
13. Cf. however the remarkable observations in T. D. Still, *Eschatology*, 128–35, on the futuristic elements in the eschatological conception of Col.
14. Unless, however, we count 1 Cor. 14.34f. as part of the original stock of 1 Cor. and do *not* consider it a post-Pauline gloss. The difficulties of balancing this with 11.4f., where the praying of women during the service of worship is taken for granted, is obvious. Cf. recently

If, then, Paul is not the author of Col., who is? The close contacts which the list of greetings at the end of the letter (4.10–17) has with Phlm. 23 is sometimes evaluated to the effect that Col. was composed by a co-worker of Paul during his lifetime, since Paul himself was in prison. In such cases one often thinks of Timothy, who is named as co-sender, or the founder of the congregation, Epaphras (Col. 1.7).[15] Paul 'gave his blessing' as it were to the letter with an autographical note (4.18). But: Bujard's meticulous examinations of language and style, the letter's own theological cast and not least the 'deutero-Pauline' portrayal of the apostle in the self-recommendation in 1.24 – 2.5 – where the apostle becomes himself a part of the proclamation (1.24!) – speak for an author unknown to us from the Pauline school. Since Eph. uses Col. (*v. infra*) and since Col. must have been written after the death of Paul, a date around 70–75 CE is possible for its composition.

Addressees
Even if a considerable number of exegetes date Col. substantially earlier (in the case of the secretary-hypothesis) or occasionally still believe that Paul was the author of the letter, this also affects the naming of the addressees; for the town of Colossae, *c.*170 kilometres east of Ephesus in the Lycos valley, probably no longer existed in the period between 70–75 CE. The Roman author Tacitus reports at the beginning of the second century CE that an earthquake in 60/61 destroyed Laodicea and that Colossae, which was only 14 kilometres distant, may likewise have been affected detrimentally. Later authors (Eusebius, Orosius) also note that three towns in Asia fell: Laodicea, Hierapolis and Colossae. Consequently no Christian community existed in Colossae around 70 CE. On the other hand a reconstruction of the town is not entirely ruled out, and two inscriptions from the time of Trajan and Hadrian, together with the discoveries of coins from the second/third centuries, appear to point to the continuing existence of Colossae.

These archaeological data, however, must not be interpreted to the effect that Col. must inevitably have been written before 60/61 CE. The very non-existence of the Colossian church makes the possibility of the epistolary fiction easier: if an author who is no longer alive writes to a church which no longer exists, questions about the authenticity of the writer no longer arise! On the other hand the question of the real addressees of the letter becomes even more important: Are they perhaps the Laodiceans mentioned in 4.16 (but this town was also destroyed by the earthquake), or is the letter directed to a third church in Asia Minor not too close to Colossae and Laodicea? An indisputable answer to these questions has yet to be offered.

M. Crüsemann (2001), 'Unrettbar frauenfeindlich: Der Kampf um das Wort von Frauen in 1 Kor. 14, 34–35 im Spiegel antijudaistischer Elemente der Auslegung', in C. Janssen et al. (eds), *Paulus. Umstrittene Traditionen – lebendige Theologie. Eine feministische Lektüre*, Gütersloh, 23–41. Cf. Chapter 10 by O. Wischmeyer on the first letter to the Corinthians in this volume.

15. Timothy: E. Schweizer, *Brief*, 26; Luz, *Briefe*, 185f.; Epaphras: J. Lähnemann (1971), *Der Kolosserbrief. Komposition, Situation und Argumentation*, Gütersloh.

Theological Profile

The already-mentioned 'high' Christology of Col., which sees in Jesus Christ the head of all cosmic authorities and powers and in consequence the whole fullness of deity dwells in him (2.9f.), must be considered against the background of the confrontation with the Colossian philosophy. Their worship of angels – i.e. numinous beings in the air and the heavenly regions (as Eph. will formulate later) – and the accompanying 'observance of the law', i.e. the carrying out of taboos relating to foods and festal periods, would have called into question a fundamental datum of Pauline theology, namely the freedom from the Law. So that this does not happen the author basically employs two theological arguments: With the aid of the Christ-encomium (1.15–20) taken from tradition he makes it clear, first, who is 'master of the house' i.e. of the cosmos: none other than Jesus Christ! The 'thrones, dominions, principalities and authorities' named in the encomium, behind which we may with good reason suspect angelic powers, owe their existence *to him* (mediation of Creation), and it is also he who reconciles the universe to himself (1.20). The fragility and instability of the world, which was experienced by ancient mankind according to the then (Middle-Platonic) conception, was the result of a permanent conflict-situation between the elements and powers in the world. The resulting worldly fears consequently can no longer be overcome by asceticism (propagated by 'philosophy') and cultic worship which guide the world but by 'holding fast' to the 'Head' of the world, Christ. And, so the second argument: This should already have been bequeathed to them in flesh and blood because they were buried with Christ in baptism and raised form the dead/made alive (2.11–13). But as people who have been baptized they are no longer subject to the constraints of their earthly existence but have become members of the heavenly world (3.1–4). The strong present characteristic of the eschatology in the letter to the Colossians, which certainly diverges considerably from the Pauline eschatology, which is oriented on the eschaton, therefore has its 'Sitz im Leben' in the clash with heresy.

Ecclesiologically, Colossians likewise leads away from Paul. On the one hand the author no longer understands ekklēsia to mean a single church but considers it as the global Body of Christ through which Christ as the 'Head of the Body' brings into being his cosmic rule. And on the other hand the actual house-churches, which clearly exist in the area around Colossae (cf. 4.15!), receive through the *Haustafeln*, taken over from the ancient economic literature,[16] a significantly patriarchal structure (or at least they should) which demands from wives subordination to their husbands and insists on absolute obedience from children and slaves. These demands are, to be sure, christologically cushioned (en kyriō); but this in no way changes the fact that women in particular are clearly worse off in comparison to the Pauline statements (Gal. 3.28!).

---

16. More details on this recently in J. Woyke (2000), *Die neutestamentlichen Haustafeln. Ein kritischer und konstruktiver Forschungsüberblick* (SBS 184), Stuttgart, 34–6; in detail M. Gielen (1990), *Tradition und Theologie der neutestamentlichen Haustafelethik* (BBB 75), Bonn.

2
The Letter to the Ephesians

The Development of the Text

As with Col., the letter to the Ephesians poses as a writing of Paul composed during his imprisonment (Eph. 3.1; 4.1; 6.21). But in this case, too, important considerations speak against a Pauline authorship. Alongside a series of linguistic peculiarities[17] are, above all, the structure of the church which is much changed from that in Paul (cf. 4.11f.) and the manner in which reference is made to the person and work of Paul – there is no longer any trace of arguments about his apostolate. In Eph. 3.1–13 Paul appears alongside the apostles and prophets as *the* recipient of the revelation of God which led to the universal Church of Jews and Gentiles.

But the strongest argument for a Deutero-Pauline authorship is the fact that the writer of the letter to the Ephesians knew Col. Not only the affected style of the document speaks for this – the ornate sentences with their many participial and relative constructions and numerous chains of genitives find their closest analogy in Col. – but above all the common factors in construction and content. Between the prescript (Eph. 1.1f.) – which unlike Col. abstains from mentioning Timothy as co-sender – and the conclusion of the letter (6.21–24; note in vv. 21f. the note about Tychicus is almost identical with that in Col. 4.7f.) the author places an 'epistolary speech' (Sellin) which is at one time address and treatise, letter and tract, and particularly in the first, didactic part (1.3 – 3.21), but perhaps also in the second, paraenetic section (4.1 – 6.9), shows a cyclic structure. To the eulogy to God the Father and his plan of Salvation in 1.3–14 corresponds the doxology in 3.20–21, to the thanksgiving and intercession for the addressees in 1.15–23, the intercessions in 3.14–19. Between these come three didactic sections. Verses 2.1–10 pursue the pattern of 'then' and 'now' and clearly depict the new existence of the Christians: With Christ we are raised (cf. Col. 3.1!), yes, made to 'sit with him in the heavenly places' (2.6)! To Eph. 2.1–10 corresponds 3.1–13, a section on the apostle's function as a mediator of Salvation. The ecclesiological section in 2.11–22, the unity of the Church made up of Jews and Gentiles, constitutes the core.

In the second, paraenetic section the proximity to Col. is particularly striking. Eph. 4.1–17 'takes up' Col. 3.12–15 (motif of love) and reminds the addressees of various basic positions (lowliness, meekness, patience, love); it is a question, in the words of Eph. 4.3 of 'maintaining the unity of the Spirit in the bond of peace'. Eph. 4.17–24 appeals for the prevailing over the pagan way of life and, relating to this, also takes up the metaphor of clothing

---

17. As such would be: 35 hapax legomena as e.g. enotēs (Eph. 4.3,13), kosmokratōr (Eph. 6.12), mesotoichon (Eph. 2.14) or politeia (2.12), numerous phrases which do not appear in the proto-Paulines but which characterize the theology of Eph.; finally the writer shares with Col. the predilection for extra-long sentences (Eph. 1.3–14!) and the stringing together of synonymous words. Further, the exclusive use of adnominal genitive constructions is conspicuous, cf. G. Sellin (1992), *Über einige ungewöhnliche Genitive im Epheserbrief*, ZNW 83, 85–107.

known from Col. 3.5–10 (putting off of the old person/putting on the new). Then Eph. 4.25 – 5.20 offers numerous individual exhortations with the call to the *imitatio dei* in the centre (5.1f.), whereby the framework again clearly borrows from the lists of virtues and vices in Col. 3.5–9,12–14 and develops these further. One should perhaps consider whether one should not excerpt vv. 15–20 as a textual segment of its own ('Spirit-filled life') since the metaphor of light and darkness which begins in Eph 5.8 with the quotation from an early Christian baptismal hymn to Christ, the light, finds an ending in 5.14. The *Haustafeln* (5.21 – 6.9) which follow individual exhortations can be read as a continuation of Col. 3.18 – 4.1, whereby the author among other things intensifies the Old Testament references of the individual exhortations. We cannot make a clear decision as to whether we should assign Eph. 6.10–20 with its military metaphor as a final paraenesis to the ending of the letter or whether it should be left as part of the body of the letter. Unlike Col., Eph. closes almost entirely without greetings, plans for journeys or personal news (6.21–24).

Table 18.3

Beginning of the letter	1.1,2	Epistolary prescript	
Body of the letter	1.3 – 3.21	I. *The indicative of Salvation*	
		1.3–14	Introductory epistolary eulogy
		1.15–23	Thanksgiving
		2.1–10	The new life of the addressees
		2.11–22	The unity of Jews and Gentiles in Christ
		3.1–13	The role of the apostle in the process of Salvation
		3.14–19	Intercession
		3.20,21	Doxology
	4.1 – 6.9	II. *The paraenetic imperative*	
		4.1–16	Unity (metaphor of the ties)
		4.17–24	The lifestyle of the old and the new person
		4.25–32	Individual exhortations (I)
		5.1,2	*Imitatio dei*
		5.3–14	Individual exhortations (II)
		5.15–20	Life in the Spirit
		5.21 – 6.9	*Haustafeln*
Close of the letter	6.10–20 6.21–24	Concluding exhortations Ending of the letter	

The Genesis of the Text

If little more can be said about the author of the letter than that he knows the letter to the Colossians (and also probably Rom., 1 and 2 Cor. and Gal.), belonged to the 'school of Paul' and was perhaps a Hellenistic Jewish-Christian,[18] it appears that we can determine the addressees more precisely. As identification in Eph. 1.1 the author uses the phrase 'to the saints who are also faithful to Christ Jesus at Ephesus'. Admittedly the en Ephesō is dubious in the view of textual criticism because the oldest and most valuable manuscripts (𝔭46, ℵ, B) do not include this detail of addressees. From this we may conclude that from the very beginning Eph. was considered as a 'catholic' epistle for the whole of the province of Asia, for which 'Ephesus' was inserted metonymically in later manuscripts. Although a specific situation is lacking, perhaps the idea of unity, which is mentioned several times and particularly intensified with regard to the surmounting of the separation of Jews and Gentiles in the one church, allows us to conclude that the congregations addressed are in danger of fragmentation or that the increasing dominance of the Gentile Christians is threatening the existence of the Jewish-Christians. The most likely place of writing was Ephesus (if we locate the school of Paul there). Because of the dependence on Col. and the fact that Eph. 5.25,29 is quoted by Ignatius and 5.1 by Polycarp (110 CE) the date of its composition can be put no earlier than 80 CE but at the latest in the 90s of the first century. This fits with the impression that the apostles and prophets described in Eph. 2.20 as foundation of the church appear to be important figures in the past and contribute new services in the present for the development of the church (Eph. 4.11).

Theological Profile
The dependence on Col. conditions a certain closeness theologically; nevertheless Eph. sets its own accents. Even more clearly than Col., the author of Eph. thinks cosmologically: The universe (ta panta) is composed of five regions which lie one above/below the other: 'above all the heavens' God sits enthroned with Jesus at his right hand; the heavenly region and the air are the realm of the 'principalities and powers' (archai kai exousiai) i.e. the demonic forces; earth is reserved for humankind and the lowest of the regions of the earth for the dead. Even more emphatically than in Col. the risen Christ rules over the universe: God has put all things under his feet and given him, literally, to the Ecclesia as Head hyper panta (1.22). Christ fills the universe with his plērōma (1.23; 4.10). A certain corrective to this Christology of enhancement and power – which could perhaps be misinterpreted as slightly triumphalistic – is found in the scattered references to Jesus' death on the Cross which brings redemption and establishes peace (1.7; 2.13–16; 5.25).

But the central theme of Eph. is the Church which – consistent with Paul (1 Cor. 12.12–16; Rom. 12.4f.) and Col. 1.18 – is depicted as the sōma Christou with Christ as her Head (Eph. 1.22f.; 2.16; and frequently). Moreover, she is the 'bride of Christ' (5.31f.), whereby the author emphasizes the inseparable connection of Church and Christ: one does not exist without the other. The section pivotal for the Ecclesiology, 2.11–22, appears to be strongly marked

---

18. Cf. R. Schnackenburg, *Brief*, 32f.; differently A. Lindemann, *Bemerkungen*, 247, who considers the author as not Jewish by birth.

by the theology of the temple. The author of Eph. imagines the picture of the church, well known from 1 Cor. 3.9–11,16f., as the house or Temple of God, as it were against the background of the Jerusalem Temple: The antithesis of 'near' and 'far off' (Eph. 2.13) taken from Isa. 57.19 relates already there to the Temple; likewise the separating wall (of the Law) could refer to the Temple barriers which deny the Gentiles entry to the inner Forecourt of the Jews. The statement that, since Christ's death on the Cross, all have access to the Father could be a contrast to the entry reserved to the High Priest into the Holy of Holies on Yom Kippur. By and large this section is on the whole borne by the idea of a Church made up of Jews and Gentiles, whereby in contrast to Paul it is not the local church but the Church as a whole which is envisaged. On this matter the series of offices or functions within the Church in 4.11 is interesting: 'And he made some apostles, others prophets, others evangelists, others pastors and teachers'. This is presumably to be understood in this way: The apostles and prophets function as standardizing important figures in the past (cf. 2.20!), the missionary proclamation is entrusted to the evangelists, the leading of the congregations to the pastors, and the teachers are responsible for the didaskalia, i.e. for the preaching, teaching and instruction in the local churches.

In its eschatology, Eph. again takes paths similar to Col. Statements relating to the present come strongly to the forefront, those relating to the future are scarce but not completely absent, spatial categories take priority over temporal categories. In the author's opinion the Church already possesses Salvation (2.5f.: 'God has ... raised us up with him, and made us sit with him in the heavenly places in Jesus Christ') which, however, does not mean that all has already been won. We still need to put on the whole armour of God in order to be able to withstand 'in the evil day' (6.13).

3
The Second Letter to the Thessalonians

The cause for the writing of this pseudepigraphical letter, which can be dated towards the end of the first century CE or a little earlier, was the expectation of the 'imminent return' which had become a problem: According to 2 Thess. 2.2 the addressees have lost their composure 'through a spirit, or by a word or letter purporting to be from us' – i.e. through a prophetic speech by an oracle, through preaching or oral teaching or through a document, whereby in all probability 1 Thess. is meant (or more precisely, 1 Thess. 4.13 – 5.11)[19] – to such an extent 'as if the Day of the Lord has come'. The author responds to this with a kind of eschatological timetable (2 Thess. 2.3–12), which not only moves the Parousia of Christ into an indeterminate future but also makes it conditional upon certain happenings taking place prior to it: a general 'rebellion' (apostasia) and the appearance of a 'man of lawlessness' (ho anthropos tēs anomias). This

---

19. This is the majority opinion. A. Wanamaker, however, is dubious, *Epistles*, 239; he sees in 2 Thess. the older, genuine letter! On the discussion cf. H. Roose, *Polyvalenz*, 253–65.

man is also called the 'son of perdition' who opposes everything or exalts himself above everything which is called god or object of worship, and who in the end takes his seat in the temple of God and claims himself to be God (2 Thess. 2.3f.). However, the appearance of this 'Antichrist' – the term itself is not mentioned but the matter meant is described accurately by it – is yet to come; responsible for this is the *one* or *thing* 'restraining' him, who cannot be identified more precisely (2 Thess. 2.6f.). This qualifies the present as a time of postponement and pulls the ground from under an imminent expectation for the return of Christ.

Table 18.4

Beginning of the letter	1.1–2	Epistolary prescript	
	1.3–12	proemium (Thanksgiving)	
Body of the letter	2.1 – 3.13	2.1–12	Eschatological instruction
		2.13–17	Thanks and request to stand fast in the traditions
		3.1–5	Paul asks for their prayers and prays for them
		3.6–13	Exhortations on how to deal with the disorderly
Ending of the letter	3.14–16	Instructions about the reception of the letter	
	3.17,18	Postscript	

The material used by the author for the eschatological timetable stems from Jewish Apocalypticism as is also the case for the so-called 'Little Apocalypse' in 2 Thess. 1.5–10 where a future court of repayment is envisaged (where each one is repaid according to his deeds). That a general decline in faith precedes the end is also a conviction as widespread as that of the appearance of an ungodly figure.[20] Dan. 11.21–39 says, for example, that a 'contemptible person' will arise for whom the royal majesty was not intended but who will still do whatever he wishes: '... he shall exalt himself and consider himself greater than any god and shall speak horrendous things against the God of gods' (Dan. 11.36). This relates to Antiochus IV Epiphanes, and similarly concrete were also the *Sibylline Oracles* when, with regard to Nero, they established: 'But he shall vanish without a trace, the devil, and will come again, making himself equal to God (isazōn theō auton) who, however, will show him that he is not.'[21]

Concretizations of this kind – e.g. with regard to the Cult of the Emperor – are not apparent in 2 Thess. and consequently provide few clues for a precise dating of the letter. The sitting in the Temple of God thematized in 2 Thess. 2.4 should be understood symbolically and not evaluated as a reference to the Jerusalem Temple which still existed.[22]

With this we have mentioned the significant points which give 2 Thess. a character of its own. Everything else, beginning with the almost identical prescript (2 Thess. 1.1f.; cf. 1 Thess. 1.1) through the conspicuous doubling

20. Cf. Dan. 11.32; Jub. 23.14–21; 4 Ezra 5.1–12; in the New Testament e.g. Mk 13.5–23; Mt. 24.10–12; 1 Tim. 4.1; 2 Tim. 3.1ff.; Jude 17–19.
21. Or Sib 5.33f.
22. E. Reinmuth, *Brief*, 179.

of the proemium-like thanksgiving to be found already in 1 Thess. (2 Thess. 2.13; cf. 1 Thess. 2.13) to the prayerful wishes like the conclusion of a letter (2 Thess. 2.17; cf. 1 Thess. 3.12f.), leans so closely on 1 Thess.[23] that one can really come to no other conclusion than that here a theologian unknown to us at the end of the first century CE created, on the basis of Paul's authentic letter to the Thessalonians, a new document to correct a false expectation of the Parousia with the authority of the 'real Paul' (cf. in this respect the stamp of authenticity in 2 Thess. 3.17: 'I, Paul, write this greeting with my own hand. This is the mark in every letter of mine; it is the way I write'). Syntactic and semantic observations also point in the same direction: The verbatim correspondences and expressions parallel to 1 Thess. mount up to such an extent as is not even faintly the case between other Pauline epistles. Consequently anyone who holds or desires to hold to the authenticity of the letter (as once again Malherbe) must also explain how Paul, in a relatively brief space of time (the letter is usually calculated to have been written shortly after 1 Thess.) could have made such an eschatological volte-face (from an imminent expectation of Christ's return to a prolongation of the time). The post-Pauline author of 2 Thess. can be located temporally and spatially only with difficulty: he could be indigenous either in Greece or in Asia Minor. Because he reveals hardly any common ground with the Pauline disciples responsible for Col. and Eph. (apart, perhaps, from the syntax) it is questionable whether he belonged to the Pauline school.[24]

4
The Pastoral Letters

The Genesis of the Texts
Like the author of Col. the writer of the *Pastoral letters* – since the eighteenth century the comprehensive term for 1 and 2 Tim. and Tit. – has to contend with teachers of false doctrine who have clearly already begun their destructive work within the Christian community: 'They are upsetting whole families by teaching for base gain what they have no right to teach' (Tit. 1.10). According to 2 Tim. 3.6 they have a disastrous influence on women in particular. A very Jewish, perhaps even Jewish-Christian, colouring of this group is unmistakable: They come above all 'from the circumcision party' (Tit. 1.10) and pass on Jewish myths and genealogies (Tit. 1.14; 1 Tim. 1.3f.). In a similar manner to the Colossian 'philosophy' they subscribe to a strict asceticism, i.e. they forbid marriage and enjoin abstinence from foods (1 Tim. 4.3). This all comes to a head, so to speak, in a present eschatology: 'They say that the resurrection is past already' (2 Tim. 2.18). While the author describes this heresy in 1 Tim. 6.20 as 'Gnosis' one would not be wrong in assuming that the heretical teachers

---

23. Cf. the detailed treatment of the question in H.-J. Klauck (2006), *Ancient Letters and the New Testament: A Guide to Context and Exegesis*. With the collaboration of Daniel W. Bailey, Waco, Tx.: Baylor.
24. W. Trilling, *Brief*, 27f.; Schmeller, *Schulen* (n. 3), 248.

combatted are to be classified as part of a Jewish-Christian Gnosis which is in the process of developing.[25]

The insertion of this heresy in the history of religion then also forbids a too early dating of the Pastorals. Since a developed Gnosis can only be reckoned with from the middle of the second century CE one cannot set the Pastoral letters earlier than the turn from the first to the second centuries CE. There are also further relevant grounds for this late dating and the assessment of the Pastorals caused by this as a *double pseudepigraphy* – not only the sender, Paul, but also the addressees, Timothy and Titus, are a literary fiction. Language and style are not Pauline; alongside the 158 hapax legomena[26] it is highly significant that the author does not employ a series of Pauline key concepts (dikaiosynē theou, eleutheria etc.) or gives them a different meaning: pistis, for example, describes simply the content of faith (1 Tim. 3.9 and often) or the loyalty to this, but no longer the human correlate to God's act of salvation as in Paul. Moreover, there are important differences in the ecclesiology. The biographical details about Paul and his co-workers also do not correspond easily with the epistles and the details in Acts. Added together this leads to the following conclusion: The Pastoral letters were composed around 100 CE, their authors unknown to us. As place of origin the missionary area in Asia Minor can be considered, more precisely perhaps Ephesus (cf. 1 Tim. 1.3) but Rome is also mentioned.[27]

In recent years, however, objections to the 'consensus' have again been raised. In particular Johnson has subjected the arguments for a pseudepigraphical composition of the Pastorals and the situative location tied to this (school of Paul; against Gnosticizing Jewish-Christian teachers of false doctrine) to a detailed analysis and criticism. Johnson rightly finds fault with the insufficient differentiation between the individual letters and questions their being grouped into a uniform closed textual body. For example, in view of the church order which deviates from Paul one should remember that in 2 Tim. this is not important and in Tit. it is at most mentioned in passing. But the authenticity of *all three* letters represented by Johnson is not convincing precisely against this background (that the three epistles should be assessed differently).

The Pastoral letters were from the start conceived by their author as a unified corpus and perhaps were intended to be read in the sequence 1 Tim., Tit. and 2 Tim.[28]

---

25. Cf. the detailed discussion in G. Häfner, *Belehrung*, 18–41.

26. The details are according to Schnelle, *Einleitung* (n. 1), 377; it is also conspicuous that the Pastorals, in comparison with the genuine Pauline epistles, have at their disposal a relatively high special vocabulary (R. Morgenthaler [1958], *Statistik des neutestamentlichen Wortschatzes*, Zürich, 38).

27. A. Weiser, *Brief*, 59 is one who votes for Ephesus; for Rome J. D. Quinn, *Letter*, 21.

28. Thus J. Roloff, 'Article: Pastoralbriefe', 57; *id.*, *Brief*, 45. But at the same time Roloff emphasizes that on this point no conclusive clarity can be established. Klauck, *Ancient Letters* (n. 23), then also thinks differently. He (with many others) votes for the order Tit. – 1 Tim. – 2 Tim. The Pauline self-presentation in 1 Tim. 1.12–17 perhaps speaks for 1 Tim. as the beginning of the triad of letters, the testamentary character of 2 Tim. for its place at the end.

The Composition of the Texts
1 Tim. diverges from the form of the Pauline letters to the extent that 'Paul' does without the customary proemium after the prescript (1.1,2) and instead, in a certain respect comparable to Gal., immediately 'blurts things out': in 1.3–11 he warns most strongly against the teachers of false doctrine and underlines this in 1.9f. with a relatively detailed list of vices which presents for the first time what in the end is the central concept of the Pastorals, the 'saving doctrine'. There follows a self-presentation similar to that in Col. 1.24 – 2.5 (1.12–17) and the committing of his mission to Timothy (1.18–20). In the body of the letter (2.1 – 6.2) the imperative is dominant; the indicative of Salvation characteristic of the Proto-Paulines is clearly repressed:[29] 2.1–7 urges to prayers for everyone, but particularly for those who rule (cf. Rom. 13.1–7), 2.8–15 lays down the conduct of men and women in the service of worship, 3.1–13 imposes guidelines for the execution of the office of bishop and deacon. After a *volte* against the teachers of heresy (4.1–5) the author again turns directly to Timothy from 4.6: Timothy is instructed to the effect that he should reject the 'profane myths and old wives' tales' (4.7) and himself be an 'example for the believers in speech' (4.12). The instructions for his dealings with men and women, older and younger (5.1f.) then lead into directions for the care of widows (5.3–16), whereby the traditional verses 9 and 10 demand a clearly defined state of widowhood (cf. also v. 5). Exhortations relating to dealings with the elders (5.17–25) and instructions for slaves (6.1f.) close the body of the letter. The closing paraenesis (6.3–19) attacks the teachers of heresy again and rails critically against those who desire to become rich (6.9f.) or are already so (6.17–19), again taking up a new theme. Although the postscript (6.20f.) turns directly to Timothy, the concluding wish for grace ('Grace be with you') is formulated in the plural!

As regards contents, *Titus* represents an abbreviated duplicate of 1 Tim. As in the latter it also lacks a proemium. The body of the letter (1.5 – 3.11) follows immediately after the prescript (1.1–4). It contains a detailed description of the office of apostle entrusted to Paul and the attribution characteristic of the Pastoral letters of God *and* Christ as *sōtēr*, before – again typically Pauline – final instructions and greetings close the writing (3.12–15). From the body of the epistle we learn first that Titus has remained in Crete to appoint elders to act as episkopoi over the respective churches and these consequently must be correspondingly morally qualified (1.5–9) for teachers of false doctrine 'from the circumcision party' have appeared (1.10–16). In 2.1 – 3.11 the proper behaviour and true faith are the order of the day – in 2.1–10 in the form of instructions to men, women and slaves (cf. 1 Tim. 5.1f.; 6.1f.) which bring to mind the *Haustafeln* in Col. and Eph.,[30] in 2.11 – 3.11 in the sketching of Christian life as a life between the two *Epiphanies* of Christ, i.e. his Incarnation

---

29. An exception is the Christ-hymn taken over in 1 Tim. 3.16; further, one can consider whether the 'Pauline' self-presentation in 1.12–17 should not be read as indicative: Paul was chosen 'to be an example to those who were to believe in him for eternal life' (1.16)!

30. On the discussion as to whether the code for bishops and deacons in the pastorals can be classified as *Haustafeln* or not cf. Gielen, *Tradition* (n. 16)

and hoped-for Parousia (cf. 2.11–13). To this belongs submission to the governing authorities (3.1–3) and avoidance of controversies about the (Jewish) Law (3.9–11).

In genre, both writings are occasionally likened to Jewish and Early Christian rules for the Church (1QS; the Didache; Didaskalia Apostolorum), yet in this way the epistolary character of both these letters falls by the wayside. Consequently there is more to be said for the reference to Hellenistic royal letters and Roman imperial letters as being most closely analogous in genre. In this connection the reference to the *mandata principis*, standardized official instructions for newly appointed office-bearers in the Roman Provinces set by the imperial chancellery,[31] deserves particular mention.

2 Tim. differs from both epistles above both in genre and in content. The document, which contains four chapters, comes very close to the genre of the friendly letter, its central theme being the koinōnia between the apostle, who is near to death, and Timothy. Everything is concentrated on the preparing of the pupil to succeed the apostle. In consequence the letter bears in long stretches the characteristic of a literary legacy; analogies to Jewish and early Christian testamentary literature cannot be missed (Test XII; Lk. 22.25–38; Jn 13–16). Above all the proximity to Paul's farewell speech in Miletus in Acts 20.17–38 has – in common with a series of contacts in content – on several occasions supported the thesis that Luke was the author of 2 Tim. or, if one proceeds from a unified writing, the author of all three letters. Yet such hypotheses are just as tenuous as the assumption of a literary dependence of 2 Tim. on Acts.[32]

The writer, who consequently remains anonymous, places behind the prescript (1.1f.) a preface which aims to encourage courageous witness (1.3–18); the main section of the letter (2.1 – 4.8) indicates the sufferings of persecution (2.1–13), calls for confrontation with the heretics (2.14–26), warns of the separation from God which is imminent for mankind (3.1–9) and shows them the paradigmatic lifestyle of the office-bearers (3.10–17). Finally, in view of the imminent death of Paul, the difficulties of congregational life are dramatized (4.1–8). Personal messages (4.9–18) and greetings by name (4.19–22) close the epistle.

---

31. To these correspond in form in 1 Tim. 1.3 and Tit. 1.5 that in place of the customary thanksgiving there is a reminder to one of the addressees left behind in Ephesus/on Crete of the relative mission. More detail in M. Wolter, *Pastoralbriefe*, 161–77.

32. Cf. A. Weiser, *Brief*, 66–70, with the account of the findings and a very respectable discussion of the hypotheses mentioned.

Table 18.5
1 Timothy

Beginning of the letter	1.1,2	Prescript
	1.3–11	Topic and situation (autobiographical)
	1.12–20	Thanksgiving (autobiographical)
Body of the letter	2.1 – 3.16	1 Main section
		General paraclesis (parakalo ⁻ 2.1) for all Christians, especially for men, women, bishops and deacons
	4.1 – 6.19	2 Main section
		Teaching directed to Timothy (didaskalia 4.1) about godliness (eusebeia 4.7; 6.6) particularly for older people, widows, elders and slaves
Ending of the letter	6.20f.	Closing exhortation and greeting

Table 18.6
2 Timothy

Beginning of the letter	1.1,2	Prescript	
	1.3–5	Thanksgiving (biographical)	
Body of the letter	1.6 – 2.13	1 Main section	
		1.6–18	Epistolary self-presentation (autobiographical)
		2.1–13	Paul as witness of Jesus Christ
	2.14 – 4.8	2 Main section	
		2.14–26	Exhortation to personal probation
		3.1–9	Eschatological instruction
		3.10–17	Timothy's succession in teaching
		4.1–8	'Paul's Testament'
Ending of the letter	4.9–18	Autobiographical news and epistolary instructions	
	4.19–21	Greetings	
	4.22	Benediction	

Table 18.7
Titus

Beginning of the letter	1.1–4	Prescript
Body of the letter	1.5–16	Church order for elders and bishops against teachers of heresy
	2.1 – 3.11	Teaching (didaskalia) for the church: old people, the young and slaves, against a teacher of heresy (hairetikos anthrōpos 3.10)
Ending of the letter	3.12–14	Epistolary instructions
	3.14	Greetings Benediction

Theological Profile

The Pastorals receive a particular theological profile from their ecclesiology based on the metaphor of the household (oikos/oikia). Formal principles of the ancient extended family should also – in spite of the universal orientation – apply to the Church understood as the local congregation: God is the master of the house (2 Tim. 2.21: despotēs) who has appointed the leader of the local church as oikonomos (Tit. 1.7). This steward performs the function of the *pater familias*; it is a mark of his qualification for this that he is a good manager of his own household (1 Tim. 3.5). Matching this, instructions for men and women (1 Tim. 2.8–15; 5.1f.; Tit. 2.1–6), old and young (1 Tim. 5.1f.; 2.1–6) as well as for masters and slaves (1 Tim. 6.1f.; Tit 2.9f.) – similar to the *Haustafeln* in Col. and Eph. – are issued. A new factor is that widows are now also included in these regulations (1 Tim. 5.3–16). Presumably the 'widows in the congregation' have an established place in the church.

What is more, the concept of a patriarchially ordered congregation coming to light in such a way emphasizes relatively clearly the institutional features of the church. Alongside diverse measures for church discipline (cf. 1 Tim. 1.20; 2 Tim. 2.25) the instructions for the structuring of the offices of the church leadership in relation to these catch one's eye. The development which was already taking place in its early stages in the Pauline churches (Phil. 1.1) is driven forward in two established offices tied to persons: In each church there should be an episkopos, who is responsible as manager of the house as it were for the routine; to each of these there are assigned several diakonoi whose duties should lie mainly in the area of administration and in the care of the poor (1 Tim. 3.8–13). The Constitution of the Elders which still existed in some of the churches is brought closer or opened to the Constitution of Bishops (1 Tim. 5.17; Tit. 1.5f.). Thereby the way is prepared for the principle of Monepiscopacy, even if it in fact has not already come into existence in the churches in the catchment area of the Pastorals.

The central task of the church leadership is teaching; the bishop must 'hold firm to the sure word as taught, so that he may be able to give sound doctrine and also to confute those who contradict it' (Tit. 1.9). The authoritative norm for 'sound doctrine' is the Pauline tradition which is summed up in the key-concept of paratheke (1 Tim. 6.20; 2 Tim. 1.12,14). The concept relates to the stock of writings at hand, i.e. the Corpus Paulinum and the Pastorals and declares these to be an untouchable legacy which must be preserved at all costs. Typically pneuma occurs almost exclusively in the context of statements about the office-bearers (2 Tim. 1.7,14; 4.22), and ordination is named alone of the charismata (1 Tim. 4.14; 2 Tim. 1.6).

Women also drop out of the running. The – if one desires to express it positively – openness for the non-Christian society and its ways of life, which repressed all that which could contradict the ethical ideas of worth and the social role-expectation passed down led to the exclusion of Christian women from any active participation in the structuring of the service of worship (1 Tim. 2.8–13). The social ideal of the woman who is silent in public, restricted solely to the domestic front, is transposed to the Church (1 Tim. 5.14; Tit. 2.5). The woman is tainted by the sin of Eve and her salvation (sōzō) is connected to the bearing of children and bringing them up as Christians (1 Tim. 2.13–15). In a similar manner Christian slaves are warned almost apprehensively of any emancipatory tendency; they should do all that is required in that subordination which society expects of them.

The Picture of Paul
But the main feature of the Pastorals is their exclusive Paulinism. When 'Paul' describes himself in the *superscriptio* (1 Tim. 1.1; 2 Tim. 1.1; Tit. 1.1) as 'an apostle of Jesus Christ' this is initially in line with what Paul himself also does in his letters to the Corinthians, Galatians or Romans. By contrast there is no reference in the Pastorals to 'the apostles before me'. Paul is *the* apostle! His apostolate, in comparison with the following description in Acts which will be discussed below, is interpreted relatively one-sidedly as a vocation to teaching or the responsible administration of such. Paul is not only *the* apostle; he is also *the* teacher, whose doctrine and its proclamation possess the quality of revelation (cf. Tit. 1.3!). Consequently it must be passed on as an inalterable paratheke. Again 'Paul' gives the guidelines for this transmission: 2 Tim. 2.2 raises the personal succession stemming from Paul into the scheme which is intended to show the unbroken continuity between teacher and pupil. Here the personal example of the suffering apostle (2 Tim. 2.12; 2.8–13) is in no small way decisive. Anyone who stands up for the gospel must be prepared, like Paul, to bear resistance and suffering. This is important particularly in view of the current confrontation with the teachers of false doctrine (2 Tim. 2.14–21).

Paul, however, in the Pastorals is not only *the* model for potential office-bearers but is also the 'archetype' of everyone who believes, and as such can be compared with Abraham, the prototype of the receiver of salvation in early Judaism as the prototype of the faithful in early Christianity. His Damascus Road experience has a paradigmatic significance. Paul received mercy, according to 1 Tim. 1.16, so 'that in me, as the foremost, Jesus Christ might display the utmost patience, making me an example to those who would come to believe in him for eternal life'.

5
The Picture of Paul in Acts

Synopsis

We encounter a completely different world, however, in Acts, which was conceived as a continuation of the Gospel of Luke and was probably written at the beginning of the 90s of the first century CE.[33] Certainly there are points of contact with the Deutero- and Trito-Paulines (Eph., Pastorals), particularly in respect of the unmistakable interest which Acts also shows in the questions of church order and office (cf. Acts 20.17–38); but the great theological themes known from the authentic Pauline epistles such as the doctrine of justification, the ecclesiological model of the Church as the body of Christ developed in the Corinthian letters and Romans and the eschatological ideas Paul developed in several places (cf. 1 Thess. 4.13–17; 1 Cor. 15.1–58; 2 Cor. 5.1–10 etc.) are missing or only appear in a very rudimentary form. In place of these there is in Acts a decided interest in the Pauline biography (even if not in the modern sense): From Acts 7.58 where Paul as an uninvolved bystander was present at the stoning of Stephen to the end in Acts 28.31 we accompany Paul on practically all of the most important stages of his activity.

We are witness to his raging against the 'Way' as Luke describes the Christians (8.3; 9.1f.), of his 'conversion' outside Damascus (9.1–19a) and his first attempts to preach there and in Jerusalem (9.19b–30); we experience how Paul, together with Barnabas, develops from a simple envoy of the church at Antioch into a church missionary who first proselytized in Cyprus and large parts of Asia Minor (the so-called First Missionary Journey; cf. Acts 13–14) and later, after the council of apostles in Jerusalem – where according to Luke Paul had literally nothing to say (15.1–34) – and after the parting from Barnabas, he ventured the leap to Europe together with Silas and Timothy and there continued his missionary activity in almost all the large Greek centres (Philippi, Thessalonica, Athens, Corinth: 15.35 – 18.22). The account of the Third Missionary Journey (18.23 – 21.17) includes a longer sojourn teaching in Ephesus and takes Paul, after a further detour to Greece and the farewell speech before the elders in Miletus (20.17–38) finally to Jerusalem where he was taken prisoner, and after his scourging was prevented by the reference to his rights as a Roman citizen

---

33. If one presumes that Luke's Gospel was written between 80 and 85 CE this chronological estimate seems reasonable. Later datings (after 100 CE) are ruled out because then Acts must in one form or another have adopted the collections of Pauline epistles which were available towards the end of the first century CE. We can only speculate on where Acts was written; the place most often named is Rome, but Greece, Asia Minor and even Syrian Antioch also come into consideration. Cf. recently Schnelle, *Einleitung* (n. 1), 306f.; J. Zmijewski, *Apostelgeschichte*, 14–16.

(22.23–29) and a planned attack upon his life which was thwarted with the help of his nephew (23.12–22) he was handed over to the governor, Felix, in Caesarea. The parallels to the arrest and process against Jesus in Luke's Gospel which are already well known are strengthened in what follows. During the stay in Caesarea, which lasted two years (24.1 – 26.32), Paul is charged by the High Priest before the Roman governor, Felix, and as formerly Pilate in the case of Jesus, Felix brings Paul before a Jewish ruler (here Agrippa with his wife, Bernice, Acts 25.13–17; cf. Luke 23.6–12). The crossing to Rome reported in 27.1 – 28.15 gives the impression of an eyewitness account ('we') but includes motifs typical of ancient Roman literature with the motif of the shipwreck and the miraculous deliverance of the passengers on the island of Malta.[34] Acts closes with information on the stay and activity of the apostle in Rome; the author gives no information about his death although he certainly knows about it.[35]

Stations of Paul according to Acts 8–28:[36]

Table 18.8

	[Tarsus]
7.58 – 8.1, 3; 9.1f.	*Jerusalem*
9.3–8	Near *Damascus*, vocation
9.9–25	In *Damascus* by Ananias; first preaching and flight
9.26–29	In *Jerusalem*, first contact with the Christians
9.30	In *Caesarea* and *Tarsus*
11.25f.	From *Tarsus* to *Antioch*, there a year together with Barnabas, teaching
11.30	The collection brought about by Agabus is taken to *Jerusalem*
13.1 – 14.28	*First Missionary Journey: Barnabas and Paul* Cyprus with *Salamis* and *Paphos* *Perge*/Pamphylia *Antioch*/Pisidia *Iconium* *Lystra* *Derbe* Return to *Antioch* by way of *Attalia*
15.1–29	The Apostolic Council in *Jerusalem*

---

34. This is in itself accepted by all, cf. R. I. Pervo (1987), *Profit with Delight. The Literary Genre of the Acts of the Apostles*, Philadelphia, 53. Critical, however, once again M. Reiser, 'Von Cäsarea nach Malta. Literarischer Charakter und historische Glaubwürdigkeit von Act 27', in F. W. Horn, *Ende*, 49–74.

35. A detailed account in H. Omerzu, 'Das Schweigen des Lukas. Überlegungen zum offenen Ende der Apostelgeschichte', in Horn, *Ende*, 127–56.

36. Cf. in this volume the table of the chronology of Paul in Chapter 5 by E. Ebel, 'The Life of Paul', and in Chapter 6 'Paul's Missionary Activity' the section on Paul's journeys.

15.30–35	Paul and Barnabas as teachers and preachers in *Antioch*
15.36 – 18.22	*Second Missionary Journey: Paul and Silas (and Timothy)* Derbe Lystra Phrygia Galatia Mysia Troas Greece (Macedonia and Achaia) Samothrace *Neapolis* *Philippi* *Amphipolis* *Apollonia* *Thessalonica* Beroea Athens Corinth Cenchreae Ephesus Caesarea Jerusalem Antioch
18.23 – 21.17	*Third Missionary Journey: Paul* Galatia Phrygia *Ephesus* (two years teaching in the school of Tyrannus) Macedonia Hellas Macedonia *Philippi* Troas Assos *Mitylene* – Chios – Samos *Miletus* Kos – Rhodes – *Patara* – *Tyre* – *Ptolemais* – *Caesarea* – *Jerusalem*
21.18 – 23.30	In *Jerusalem*
23.31 – 26.32	Imprisoned in *Caesarea*
27.1 – 28.15	On the way to Rome as a prisoner Sidon – Myra – Salmone – *Lasea* (Crete) – Malta – *Syracuse* – *Rhegium* – *Puteoli* – *Rome*
28.16–30	Paul as an imprisoned preacher and teacher in *Rome* (two years)

Traditions

The portrait of Paul which appears in this way as a man who developed from a furious persecutor to the most successful missionary up until then of the Early Church and carried the new faith against all opposition and challenges to Rome itself is not only due to Luke's creative hand. The author of Acts can fall back on a series of separate traditions which, however, differ greatly in form and character. They may already have come into being during the lifetime of the apostle (cf. Gal. 1.23!) and turned increasingly into a 'Legend of Paul'. To these belong individual miraculous tales and legends which were circulating (such as e.g. 13.8–12; 14.8–18; 16.16–18) which were due to 'the theological desire in the circles rooted in unlettered Christianity for uplifting news of the former proof of power shown by the Apostle who had become an honoured miracle-worker'.[37] There were also secular anecdotes which were transferred to Paul (such as 19.13–16; 20.7–12; 28.3–6), the underlying tradition of his conversion (9.1–19) which perhaps represents a local Damascene tradition[38] and naturally notes on journeys which, however, would be second or even third-hand. The reminder of the apostle's sufferings was also not completely forgotten in the legend of Paul (cf. Acts 14.19f.; 16.19–24; 19.23–40) even though the contribution of tradition is hard to determine in each case and the picture of the miracle-worker clearly predominates.

The Lucan Picture of Paul

The stylization of Paul to a miracle-worker also reveals a characteristic which clearly differentiates the Paul of Acts from the Paul of the letters. Certainly Paul himself in Rom. 15.18f. and 2 Cor. 12.12 acknowledges that he has worked the 'signs of a true Apostle ... in all patience, with signs and wonders and mighty works', but it is only Acts which paints the picture of Paul as a miracle-worker with 'a magical touch'.[39] The first miracle is a punishing miracle, the blinding of the Jewish rival, Bar-Jesus Elymas (Acts 13.4–12), and then follow the healing of a lame man in Lystra (14.8–20), the exorcism of a spirit of divination in Philippi (16.16–18) and the healing of many ill people in Ephesus (19.8–10), which has a special element in that Paul no longer heals them directly but by means of his handkerchiefs and aprons to which the power of the miracle-worker apparently adheres magically.[40] To these are also added the raising of a dead man in Troas (20.7–12) and a healing from a fever and the curing of the rest of the invalids on Malta (28.8–10) after Paul, immediately prior to this, had survived a snake-bite without any ill effects (28.3–6). Other than in Lystra, where Paul had still refused the godlike worship granted to himself and Barnabas (15.12–17), he no

---

37. E. Plümacher, 'Article: Apostelgeschichte', 499.
38. In detail on this, B. Heininger (1996), *Paulus als Visionär. Eine religionsgeschichtliche Studie* (HBS 9), Freiburg im Breisgau, 211–34.
39. Cf. B. Kollmann (2000), 'Paulus als Wundertäter', in *id., Paulinische Christologie. Exegetische Beiträge, Festschrift H. Hübner*, Göttingen, 76–96.
40. Here cf. B. Heininger, *Dunstkreis*; further, H.-J. Klauck (1996), *Magie und Heidentum in der Apostelgeschichte* (SBS 167), Stuttgart.

longer contradicts the view of the bystanders – 'he is a god' (28.6) at the end of Acts – an indication that the apostle (although Luke refuses him this title) under the hand of the author of Acts develops *peu à peu* into the theios anēr, the 'divine human'. Thereby he not only far outstrips Peter, the dominant figure in the first part of Acts but also comes significantly close to Jesus of Nazareth, the hero of the first Lucan work.

But in Acts Paul is not only a miracle-worker but also a (philosophical) teacher.[41] If he still functions on the First Missionary Journey as a kind of junior partner to Barnabas, he emancipates himself rapidly in the Second Missionary Journey and rises to become himself the leader of a missionary team. His bearing in Athens (17.16–34) is then unmistakably modelled on the example of Greek philosophers. This is not only due to the fact that he gets into conversation with Epicurean and Stoic philosophers but also because of Luke's very cleverly carried out mimesis of Socrates[42] and the rhetorical speech constructed according to all the rules of this art (with *captatio benevolentiae* etc.) which combines the Hellenistic Kerygma of mission (renunciation of vain idols; turning to the one God) with Stoic theologumena. It also lies on this line that the time of teaching in Ephesus which lasted for two years takes place in the 'hall of Tyrannus' in the style of philosophical teaching (19.8–10!).

But the historical and theological significance of Paul is in no way exhausted in his characterization as a miracle-worker and a philosophically educated nomadic teacher who missionizes. His historical significance can be seen far more in how the way of the Church from Judaism to the Gentile world is paradigmatically illustrated in his person, precisely against the background of a – to a large extent – unsuccessful mission to the Jews, the failure of which is already noticed on the First Missionary Journey (13.46) and which is interpreted in 28.25-27 as due to stubbornness to which on the other side corresponds the willingness to listen and believe on the part of the Gentiles. Luke depicts Paul very deliberately as a Jew faithful to the Torah and Temple, who embodies Israel's own best hopes. In so doing he guarantees at the same time the continuity of the history of salvation within the turning of the history of the Early Christian mission from the Jews to the Gentiles. As a result Paul is for Luke *the* representative of the second generation of Christians. Or, once again, put in another way: 'Paul has become the identification-figure for the Church of Luke through whom she understands and overcomes the turnaround which has taken place in her own history'.[43]

But the person of Paul would still not be sufficiently understood if the reference to his qualification as witness and the associated willingness to suffer were lacking. Both in his apologia before the Jewish people and in his apologia before King Agrippa Paul emphasizes that his vocation on the road to Damascus served no other purpose than to choose him as a witness to what he had seen

---

41. On this in detail, B. Heininger, *Tarsus*, 125–43.
42. To this belong: (1) the circumstance that Paul speaks to passers-by who chance to be in the marketplace, (2) that he is called a preacher of foreign divinities and (3) the address andres Athēnaioi in v. 22.
43. J. Roloff, *Paulus-Darstellung*, 520.

and heard (cf. 22.14; 26.16). The Lucan Paul knows that he can only possess this life as a witness at the cost of suffering. Consequently he is ready 'not only to be imprisoned but even to die at Jerusalem for the name of the Lord Jesus' (21.13). Luke translates this in such a narrative way that he on several occasions models Paul's sufferings on the example of Jesus' Passion in the Gospel. In Paul we can see that the way of the individual believer, like the way of the whole church, is one of suffering obedience (Acts 14.22) which corresponds to the norm set by Jesus in the evidence of his suffering.

References

Letter to the Colossians
Commentaries
J.-N. Aletti (1993), *Saint Paul. L'Épître aux Colossiens. Introduction, traduction et commentaire* (ÉtB n.s. 20), Paris: J. Gabalda.
J. Becker and U. Luz (1998), *Die Briefe an die Galater, Epheser und Kolosser* (NTD 8/1), Göttingen: Vandenhoeck & Ruprecht.
J. Gnilka (1980), *Der Kolosserbrief* (HThK 10/1), Freiburg: Herder.
H. Hübner (1997), *An Philemon. An die Kolosser. An die Epheser* (HNT 12), Tübingen: Mohr Siebeck.
E. Lohse (^{15}1997), *Die Briefe an die Kolosser und Philemon* (KEK 9/2), Göttingen.
I. Maisch (2003), *Der Brief an die Gemeinde in Kolossä* (Theol. Komm. zum NT 12), Stuttgart: Kohlhammer.
M. MacDonald (2000), *Colossians and Ephesians* (Sacra pagina 17), Collegeville, MN: Liturgical Press.
P. Pokorný (^{2}1990), *Der Brief des Paulus an die Kolosser* (ThHK 10/1), Berlin: Evangelische Verlagsanstalt.
E. Schweizer (^{3}1989), *Der Brief an die Kolosser* (EKK 12), Zürich: Benziger; Neukirchen-Vluyn: Neukirchener Verlag.
M. Wolter (1993), *Der Brief an die Kolosser. Der Brief an Philemon* (ÖTK 12), Gütersloh: Gütersloher Verlagshaus Gerde Mohn.

Monographs
C. E. Arnold (1995), *The Colossian Syncretism. The Interface between Christianity and Folk Belief at Colossae* (WUNT II/77), Tübingen, J. C. B. Mohr.
A. R. Bevere (2003), *Sharing in the Inheritance. Identity and the Moral Life in Colossians* (JSNT.S 226), Sheffield: Sheffield Academic Press.
M. Dübbers (2005), *Christologie und Existenz im Kolosserbrief. Exegetische und semantische Untersuchungen zur Intention des Kolosserbriefs* (WUNT II/191), Tübingen: Mohr Siebeck.
R. Hoppe (1994), *Der Triumph des Kreuzes. Studien zum Verhältnis des Kolosserbriefes zur paulinischen Kreuzestheologie* (SBB 28), Stuttgart: Verlag Katholisches Bibelwerk.
J. Lähnemann (1971), *Der Kolosserbrief. Komposition, Situation und Argumentation* (StNT 3), Gütersloh: Gütersloher Verlagshaus Gerd Mohn.
P. Müller (1988), *Anfänge der Paulusschule. Dargestellt am Zweiten Thessalonicherbrief und am Kolosserbrief* (AThANT 74), Zürich: Theologischer Verlag.
A. Standhartinger (1999), *Studien zur Entstehungsgeschichte und Intention des Kolosserbriefs* (NT.S 94), Leiden: Brill.

Chr. Stettler (2000), *Der Kolosserhymnus. Untersuchungen zu Form, traditionsgeschichlichem Hintergrund und Aussage von Kol 1,15–20* (WUNT II/131), Tübingen: Mohr Siebeck.

Essays and Encyclopedia Articles

J.-N. Aletti (2001), 'Art. Kolosserbrief', in *RGG*[4] 4, 1502f.

A. Dettwiler (2002), 'Das Verständnis des Kreuzes Jesu im Kolosserbrief', in A. Dettwiler and J. Zumstein (Hgg.), *Kreuzestheologie im Neuen Testament* (WUNT 151), Tübingen: Mohr Siebeck, 81–105.

J. Ernst (1990), 'Art. Kolosserbrief', in *TRE* 19, 370–6.

H. Hübner (2003), 'Die Diskussion um die deuteropaulinischen Briefe seit 1970. I. Der Kolosserbrief (I.II)', *ThR* 68, 263–85, 395–440.

J. Luttenberger (2005), 'Der gekreuzigte Schuldschein: Ein Aspekt der Deutung des Todes Jesu im Kolosserbrief', *NTS* 51, 80–95.

H. O. Maier (2005), 'A Sly Civility: Colossians and Empire', *JSNT* 27, 323–49.

—(2005), 'Barbarians, Scythians and Imperial Iconography in the Epistle to the Colossians', in A. Weissenrieder u.a. (ed.), *Picturing the New Testament. Studies in Ancient Visual Images* (WUNT II/193), Tübingen: Mohr Siebeck, 385–406.

H. Merklein (1987), 'Paulinische Theologie in der Rezeption des Kolosser- und Epheserbriefes', in ders., *Studien zu Jesus und Paulus* (WUNT 43), Tübingen, 409–53.

A. Standhartinger (2004), 'Colossians and the Pauline School', *NTS* 50, 572–93.

T. D. Still (2004), 'Eschatology in Colossians: How Realized is It?' *NTS* 50, 125–38.

Letter to the Ephesians
Commentaries

J.-N. Aletti (2001), *Saint Paul épitre aux Éphésiens* (EtB 42), Paris: J. Gabalda.

F. Mußner (1982), *Der Brief an die Epheser* (ÖTK 10), Gütersloh: Gütersloher Verlagshaus Gerd Mohn.

P. Pokorný (1992), *Der Brief des Paulus an die Epheser* (ThHK 10/2), Leipzig: Evangelische Verlagsanstalt.

R. Schnackenburg (1982), *Der Brief an die Epheser* (EKK 10), Zürich: Benziger; Neukirchen-Vluyn: Neukirchener Verlag.

G. Sellin (2008), *Der Brief an die Epheser* (KER8), Göttingen: Vandenhoeck & Ruprecht.

Monographs

N. A. Dahl (2000), *Studies in Ephesians. Introductory Questions, Text- & Edition-Critical Issues, Interpretation of Texts and Themes* (WUNT 131), ed. by D. Hellholm, V. Blomkvist and T. Fornberg, Tübingen: Mohr Siebeck.

G. H. van Kooten (2003), *Cosmic Christology in Paul and the Pauline School. Colossians and Ephesians in the Context of Graeco-Roman Cosmology. With a New Synopsis of the Greek Texts* (WUNT II/171), Tübingen: Mohr Siebeck.

A. C. Mayer (2002), *Sprache der Einheit im Epheserbrief und in der Ökumene* (WUNT II/150), Tübingen: Mohr Siebeck.

R. Schwindt (2002), *Das Weltbild des Epheserbriefes. Eine religionsgeschichtlich-exegetische Studie* (WUNT II/148), Tübingen: Mohr Siebeck.

Essays and Encyclopedia Articles

B. Fiore (2003), 'Household Rules at Ephesus. Good News, Bad News, No News', in J. T. Fitzgerald (ed.), *Early Christianity and Classical Culture. Comparative Studies in Honor of Abraham J. Malherbe* (NT.S 110), Leiden: Brill, 589–607.

T. K. Heckel (2000), 'Juden und Heiden im Epheserbrief', in M. Karrer (Hg.), *Kirche und Volk Gottes, FS J. Roloff*, Neukirchen-Vluyn, 176–94.
G. Hotze (2003), 'Paradebeispiele der Paulusschule: Der Kolosser und der Epheserbrief', *BiLi* 76, 207–11, 285–9.
A. Lindemann (1976), 'Bemerkungen zu den Adressaten und zum Anlaß des Eph', *ZNW* 67, 235–71.
M. Y. MacDonald (2004), 'The Politics of Identity in Ephesians', *JSNT* 26, 419–44.
F. Mußner (1982), 'Art. Epheserbrief', *TRE* 9, 743–53.
H. Roose (2005), 'Die Hierarchisierung der Leib-Metapher im Kolosser- und Epheserbrief als "Paulinisierung": Ein Beitrag zur Rezeption paulinischer Tradition in pseudo-paulinischen Briefen', *NT* 47, 117–41.
R. Schnackenburg (1991), 'Art. Epheserbrief', *NBL* I, 549–51.
G. Sellin (1999), 'Art. Epheserbrief', *RGG*[4] 2, 1344–7.
—(2004), 'Monotheismus im Epheserbrief – jenseits von Theokratie und Ekklesiokratie', in W. Popkes and R. Brucker (Hg.), *Ein Gott und ein Herr. Zum Kontext des Monotheismus im Neuen Testament* (BThSt 68), Neukirchen-Vluyn, 41–64.
O. Wischmeyer (2004), 'Machtverständnis und Geschlechterdifferenz im Urchristentum am Beispiel des Epheserbriefs', in B. Heininger, S. Böhm and U. Sals (Hg.), *Machtbeziehungen, Geschlechterdifferenz und Religion* (Geschlecht – Symbol – Religion 2), Münster, 87–95.
T. Witulski (2005), 'Gegenwart und Zukunft in den eschatologischen Konzeptionen des Kolosser- und des Epheserbriefes', *ZNW* 96, 211–42.

Second Letter to the Thessalonians
Commentaries
A. J. Malherbe (2000), *The Letters to the Thessalonians. A New Translation with Introduction and Commentary* (AncB 32B), New York: Doubleday.
L. Morris (1995), *The First and Second Epistles to the Thessalonians* (NICNT), Grand Rapids, MI.
P.-G. Müller (2001), *Der erste und zweite Brief an die Thessalonicher* (RNT), Regensburg: Friedrich Pustet.
E. Reinmuth (1998), *Der zweite Brief an die Thessalonicher* (NTD 8/2), Göttingen: Vandenhoeck & Ruprecht, 157–202.
E. J. Richard (1995), *First and Second Thessalonians* (Sacra Pagina 11), Collegeville, MN: Liturgical Press.
W. Trilling (1980), *Der zweite Brief an die Thessalonicher* (EKK 14), Zurich: Benziger; Neukirchen-Vluyn: Neukirchener Verlag.
C. A. Wanamaker (1990), *The Epistles to the Thessalonians. A Commentary on the Greek Text* (NIGTC), Grand Rapids, MI: Eerdmans.

Monographs
Ch. vom Brocke (2001), *Thessaloniki – Stadt des Kassander und Gemeinde des Paulus* (WUNT II/125), Tübingen: Mohr Siebeck.
G. S. Holland (1988), *The Tradition That You Have Received from Us: 2 Thessalonians in the Pauline Tradition* (HUTh 24), Tübingen: J. C. B. Mohr.
P. Metzger (2005), *Katechon. II Thess 2,1–12 im Horizont apokalyptischen Denkens* (BZNW 135), Berlin.

Essays and Encyclopedia Articles

R. F. Collins (1988), 'Letters That Paul Did not Write: The Letters to the Hebrews and the Pauline Pseudepigrapha' (GNS 28), Wilmington, DE: Michael Glazier 209–41.

G. Hotze (1999), 'Die Christologie des 2. Thessalonicherbriefes', in K. Scholtissek (Hg.), *Christologie in der Paulus-Schule. Zur Rezeptionsgeschichte des paulinischen Evangeliums* (SBS 181), Stuttgart, 124–48.

M. Karrer (2003), '2 Thess 2,1–4 und der Widersacher Gottes', in R. Gebauer (Hg.), *Die bleibende Gegenwart des Evangeliums* (MThSt 76), FS O. Merk, Marburg, 171–88.

F. Laub (2001), 'Art. Thessalonicherbriefe', *NBL* 3, 832–5.

E. E. Popkes (2004), 'Die Bedeutung des zweiten Thessalonicherbriefs für das Verständnis paulinischer und deuteropaulinischer Eschatologie', *BZ NF* 48, 39–64.

H. Roose (2005), 'Polyvalenz durch Intertextualität im Spiegel der aktuellen Forschung zu den Thessalonicherbriefen', *NTS* 51, 250–69.

A. Schmidt (1992), 'Erwägungen zur Eschatologie des 2 Thessalonicher und 2 Johannes', *NTS* 38, 477–80.

Pastoral Letters
Commentaries

N. Brox ([5]1989), *Die Pastoralbriefe. 1 Timotheus, 2 Timotheus, Titus* (RNT), Regensburg: Verlag F. Pustet.

L. T. Johnson (2001), *The First and Second Letters to Timothy* (The Anchor Yale Bible Commentaries), New Haven, CT: Yale University Press.

L. Oberlinner (1994/1995/1996), *Die Pastoralbriefe. Erste Folge: Kommentar zum Ersten Timotheusbrief* (HThK 11/2/1); *Zweite Folge: Kommentar zum zweiten Timotheusbrief* (HThK 11/2/2); *Dritte Folge: Kommentar zum Titusbrief* (HThK 11/2/3), Freiburg: Herder.

J. D. Quinn (1990), *The Letter to Titus. A New Translation with Notes and Commentary and an Introduction to Titus, I and II Timothy, the Pastoral Epistles* (AncB 35), New York: Doubleday.

J. D. Quinn and W. C. Wacker (2000), *The First and Second Letters to Timothy. A New Translation with Notes and Commentary* (Eerdmans Critical Commentary), Grand Rapids, MI: Eerdmans.

J. Roloff (1988), *Der erste Brief an Timotheus* (EKK 15), Zürich: Benziger Verlag; Neukirchen-Vluyn: Neukirchener Verlag.

A. Weiser (2003), *Der zweite Brief an Timotheus* (EKK 16/1), Düsseldorf: Benziger Verlag; Neukirchen-Vluyn: Neukirchener Verlag.

Monographs

G. Häfner (2000), *'Nützlich zur Belehrung' (2 Tim 3,16). Die Rolle der Schrift in den Pastoralbriefen im Rahmen der Paulusrezeption* (HBS 25), Freiburg: Herder.

A. Merz (2004), *Die fiktive Selbstauslegung des Paulus. Intertextuelle Studien zur Intention und Rezeption der Pastoralbriefe* (NTOA 52), Göttingen: Vandenhoeck & Ruprecht; Freiburg: Academic Press.

L. K. Pietersen (2004), *The Polemic of the Pastorals. A Sociological Examination of the Development of Pauline Christianity* (JStNT.S 264), London: T&T Clark.

W. A. Richards (2002), *Difference and Distance in Post-Pauline Christianity. An Epistolary Analysis of the Pastorals* (SBL 44), New York: P. Lang.

R. van Neste (2004), *Cohesion and Structure in the Pastoral Epistles* (JSNT.S 280), Edinburgh: T&T Clark.

U. Wagner (1994), *Die Ordnung des 'Hauses Gottes'. Der Ort von Frauen in der Ekklesiologie und Ethik der Pastoralbriefe* (WUNT II/65), Tübingen.

M. Wolter (1988), *Die Pastoralbriefe als Paulustradition* (FRLANT 146), Göttingen: Vandenhoeck & Ruprecht.

Essays and Encyclopedia Articles

J. W. Aageson (2004), 'The Pastoral Epistles, Apostolic Authority, and the Development of Pauline Scriptures', in S. E. Porter (ed.), *The Pauline Canon (Pauline Studies 1)*, Leiden: Brill, 5–26.

—(2003), 'EUSEBEIA: Roman Imperial Family Values and the Sexual Politics of 4 Maccabees and the Pastorals', *Biblical Interpretation* 11, 139–65.

M. R. D'Angelo (2003), '"Knowing how to preside over his own Household". Imperial Masculinity and Christian Asceticism in the Pastorals, Hermas, and Luke-Acts', in S. D. Moore and J. C. Anderson (eds), *New Testament Masculinities* (SBL Semeia Studies 45), Atlanta, 265–95.

R. F. Collins (2003), 'Art. Pastoralbriefe', *RGG*[4] 6, 988–91.

M. Frenschkowski (2001), 'Pseudepigraphie und Paulusschule. Gedanken zur Verfasserschaft der Deuteropaulinen, insbesondere der Pastoralbriefe', in F. W. Horn (Hg.), *Das Ende des Paulus. Historische, theologische und literaturgeschichtliche Aspekte* (BZNW 106), Berlin: De Gruyter, 239–72.

G. Häfner (2001), 'Die Gegner in den Pastoralbriefen und die Paulusakten', *ZNW* 92, 64–77.

J. Herzer (2004), 'Abschied vom Konsens? Die Pseudepigraphie der Pastoralbriefe als Herausforderung an die neutestamentliche Wissenschaft', *ThLZ* 129, 1267–82.

H. Ritt (2001), 'Art. Pastoralbriefe', *NBL* 3, 81–7.

J. Roloff (1996), 'Art. Pastoralbriefe', *TRE* 26, 50–68.

H. Roose (2003), 'Dienen und Herrschen: Zur Charakterisierung des Lehrens in den Pastoralbriefen', *NTS* 49, 440–6.

Acts and Luke
Commentaries

J. Jervell (1998), *Die Apostelgeschichte* (KEK 3), Göttingen: Vandenhoeck & Ruprecht.

L. T. Johnson (1992), *The Acts of the Apostles* (Sacra Pagina 5), Collegeville, MN: Liturgical Press.

J. Roloff ([2]1988), *Die Apostelgeschichte* (NTD 5), Göttingen: Vandenhoeck & Ruprecht.

R. I. Pervo (2009), *Acts, a commentary*, Hermeneia Minneapolis, MN: Fortress Press.

G. Schneider (1980/1982), *Die Apostelgeschichte. 1. Teil: Einleitung, Kommentar zu Kap. 1,1–8,40; 2. Teil: Kommentar zu Kap. 9,1–28,28,31* (HThK 5/1.2), Freiburg: Herder.

A. Weiser (1981/1985), *Die Apostelgeschichte. 1: Kapitel 1–12; 2: Kapitel 13–28* (ÖTK 5/1.2), Gütersloh/Würzburg: Mohn.

J. Zmijewski (1994), *Die Apostelgeschichte* (RNT), Regensburg: F. Pustet.

Monographs

F. W. Horn (Hg.) (2001), *Das Ende des Paulus. Historische, theologische und literaturgeschichtliche Aspekte* (BZNW 106), Berlin: De Gruyter.

J. C. Lentz (1993), *Luke's Portrait of Paul* (MSSNTS 77), Cambridge: Cambridge University Press.

S. E. Porter (1999), *The Paul of Acts. Essays in Literary Criticism, Rhetoric, and Theology* (WUNT 115), Tübingen: Mohr Siebeck.

Essays and Encyclopedia Articles

D. L. Balch (1998), 'Art. Apostelgeschichte', *RGG*[4] 1, 642–8.

R. von Bendemann (1998), 'Paulus und Israel in der Apostelgeschichte des Lukas', in K. Wengst and G. Saß (Hg.), *Ja und Nein. Christliche Theologie im Angesicht Israels*, FS W. Schrage, Neukirchen-Vluyn: Neukirchener, 291–303.

R. Bondi (1997), 'Become such as I am: St. Paul in the Acts of the Apostles', *BTB* 27, 164–77.

B. Heininger (1998), 'Einmal Tarsus und zurück (Apg 9,30; 11,25–26). Paulus als Lehrer nach der Apostelgeschichte', *MThZ* 49, 125–43.

—(2005), 'Im Dunstkreis der Magie: Paulus als Wundertäter nach der Apostelgeschichte', in E.-M. Becker and P. Pilhofer (Hg.), *Biographie und Persönlichkeit des Paulus* (WUNT 178), Tübingen: Mohr Siebeck, 271–91.

E. Plümacher (1978), 'Art. Apostelgeschichte', *TRE* 3, 483–528.

J. Roloff (1979), 'Die Paulus-Darstellung des Lukas. Ihre geschichtlichen Voraussetzungen und ihr theologisches Ziel', *EvTh* 39, 510–31.

G. Schneider (1991), 'Art. Apostelgeschichte', *NBL* 1, 138–41.

A. Weiser (2000), 'Das Paulusbild der Apostelgeschichte', *BiKi* 55, 83–6.

Chapter 19

THE RECEPTION OF PAUL IN THE SECOND CENTURY
Andreas Lindemann

The extraordinary effect of the apostle Paul can be seen not only in the fact that very soon after his death letters were written in his name but also that already in the first century in theological argumentation reference was made expressly to Paul and to his special authority; the oldest witness to this is the Lucan Acts. On the legacy of Paul and his theology in the second century, however, an exegetical perception exists, which can almost be called 'popular', saying that Paul was immediately considered as 'the apostle of the heretics', above all through a Gnostic reception of Paul, and the 'orthodox' Church therefore had great problems in referring to Paul and preserving the legacy of the Pauline letters. This picture, which depends above all on the corresponding formulation of the Church Father, Tertullian,[1] can be refuted by the literary sources of the second century; the statement of Tertullian mentioned itself appears in a totally different light if one reads it in context: Tertullian is arguing with the theology of Marcion which he regards as heretical, and in so doing he shows that the statements which appear to corroborate Marcion's thinking in fact speak for the position of the 'orthodox' Church. Concerning the key words 'apostle of the heretics' the actual question is about the legitimacy of interpreting the Old Testament allegorically, which Marcion denies;[2] here Tertullian shows, using 1 Cor. 9.9, that Paul – the *haereticorum apostolus* – himself practised precisely this method of interpretation. Incidentally, the fifth book of Tertullian's work 'Adversus Marcionem' is above all a broadly structured refutation of Marcion's interpretation of Paul from the perspective of the 'orthodox' Church.

That Paul and his epistles were an absolutely recognized authority for the church at the end of the second century is proved by Irenaeus of Lyon in his work 'Adversus Haereses'; for him it is an indication of the 'heresy' of the Jewish-Christian sect of the Ebionites that they reject Paul (I 26.2) while he himself without any discussion refers to Paul as a matter of course to clarify theological facts.

What did the history of the reception and interpretation of Paul look like in the second century? To be able to answer this question we must direct our attention to the few extant Christian writings from this period. In the last decades of the first century, letters were composed and circulated in Paul's name which the Church then accepted as genuine Pauline letters. At roughly the same time,

---

1. Tertullian, Adversus Marcionem III 5.4: *haereticorum apostolus*.
2. Marcion did not, as is often said, 'reject the Old Testament' but read it in the tradition of the Creator God who is not identical with the Redeemer God revealed in Christ (*v. infra*).

various churches began to make copies of the letters written to them available to other churches and to bring the letters together into a collection.[3] Consequently Christian authors at the turn from the first to the second centuries[4] could refer specifically to Paul and use his epistles for their argumentation. The difference is clear: while the authors of the pseudo-Pauline letters slip into the mask of the apostle and compose their texts in such a way as if they in fact stemmed from Paul himself, the later authors who are represented below refer back to Paul expressly as an authority, whereby they clearly can assume that the addressees of their letters also recognize this authority.[5]

The following texts play a part in the reception of Paul in the second century:

Table 19.1

The first letter of Clement	End of the first century CE (?)
The letters of Ignatius to Ephesus to Magnesia to Tralles to Rome to Philadelphia to Smyrna to Polycarp	c.130/140 CE (?)
Polycarp to the Philippians	around 135 CE
The writing of Diognetus	end of the 2nd century (?)
The Prayer of the Apostle Paul	second half of the 2nd or 3rd
The Apocalypse of Paul	second half of the 2nd
[The Writings of Marcion]	mid-2nd century
The Acts of the Martyrs of Scili	end of the 2nd century
The Acts of Paul Third letter to the Corinthians 'Acta Pauli et Theclae'	end of the 2nd century
[Kerygmata Petrou]	2nd century

3. Cf. on this A. Lindemann (2003), 'Die Sammlung der Paulusbriefe im 1. und 2. Jahrhundert', in J.-M. Auwers and H. J. de Jonge (eds), *The Biblical Canons* (BEThL 163), Leuven, 321–51.

4. Details such as 'first' or 'second' century are naturally misleading in that the year 100 in the Christian calendar was, of course, not seen by anyone as a 'turn of the century'. Nevertheless, for the sake of simplicity, this terminology is retained.

5. The production of pseudo-Pauline epistles admittedly did not cease: There is, for example, a 'letter to the Laodiceans' which takes up Col. 4.16, a 'third letter to the Corinthians' and even an exchange of letters between Paul and the philosopher, Seneca. But these writings were always immediately recognized as literary forgeries because of their character.

1
1 Clement

The oldest of these documents is the first letter of Clement which was written in the last decade of the first century in Rome. In this extremely extensive letter the church (ekklēsia) in Rome advises the church (ekklēsia) in Corinth.[6] The cause for writing was the fact that some elders in the Corinthian congregation had been removed from office; the church in Rome or at least the author of 1 Clement[7] saw in this unbearable signs of 'argument and turmoil' (3.2) which – as is expressly said in 2.6 – up until that time had been unheard of in Corinth. One is aware in Rome that the church in Corinth was founded by Paul; one is also aware that once before, in the time of Paul, there had been schisms there (cf. 1 Cor. 1–3) but in comparison to the recent events these must be considered as comparatively harmless (*v. infra*).

From 1 Clement 47 it follows that the people in Rome are aware of the letter to the Corinthians and know that it makes a great deal of sense to remind the Corinthian Christians of the statements in this epistle. The formulation in 47.1: 'Take up the letter (tēn epistolēn) of the blessed Apostle Paul' allows us inquire whether the second letter to the Corinthians was not known or whether it possibly did not yet exist as such;[8] but the allusions in 1 Clement 47.1–4 refer so clearly to Paul's first letter to the Corinthians that negative conclusions in respect of the 'second letter to the Corinthians' should not be drawn.

It does not emerge from 1 Clem. what exactly had happened in Corinth and why the presbyters had lost their position; according to the author the elders had discharged their office 'blamelessly' (44.4), but whether this judgement was in accordance with the facts we are not in a position to tell. At any rate the fact that 1 Clem. was preserved and was later regularly read out in Corinth[9] would indicate that the letter from Rome appears to have understood correctly the main features of the situation in Corinth.

At the beginning of 1 Clem.[10] examples are mentioned of how already in biblical times 'emulation and envy, strife and sedition' (ch. 3) ruled among

---

6. The name of Clement, who is said to have been the third Roman bishop, was only connected at a later date with this letter: the name 'Clement' does not appear in 1 Clement itself. For information on 1 Clement see A. Lindemann (2010), 'The First Epistle of Clement', in W. Pratscher (ed.), *The Apostolic Fathers. An Introduction*, Waco, TX, 47–69.

7. 1 Clement was certainly drawn up by a single individual and not by a group although probably on the instruction or with the express approval of the Roman church.

8. In exegesis it is frequently – in my view correctly – assumed that 2 Cor. is the result of a secondary editing of what were originally several shorter letters; cf. H. Conzelmann and A. Lindemann (1988), *Interpreting the New Testament. An Introduction to the Principles and Methods of N.T. Exegesis*, Peabody Mass., 190–2. In this volume cf. Chapter 11 by E.-M. Becker on 2 Cor.

9. Eusebius, h.e. IV 23.11 quotes from a letter of Dionysios who reports around 170 that 1 Clem. was read aloud in the service in Corinth; cf. A. Lindemann (1992), *Die Clemensbriefe* (HNT 17: Die Apostolischen Väter I) Tübingen, 11f.

10. The quotations from 1 Clem. are taken from A. Roberts and J. Donaldson (eds) (1989), *The Ante-Nicene Fathers (Vol I)*, Edinburgh/Grand Rapids.

humanity – the author quotes in detail the story of Cain and Abel (4.1–6) and finally refers to David's persecution by Saul (4.13). But even in the recent past there have been 'noble examples' that envy and jealousy have led to the persecution and death 'of the greatest and most righteous pillars [of the Church]' (5.2); named are 'the illustrious apostles' (5.3), first Peter in a few words and then Paul fairly fully.

Peter, through unrighteous envy, endured not one or two but numerous labours; and when he had at length suffered martyrdom (houtō martyrēsas), departed to the place of glory due (to him). Owing to envy Paul also obtained the reward of patient endurance, after being seven times thrown into captivity, compelled to flee and stoned. After preaching both in the east and west he gained the illustrious reputation due to his faith, having taught righteousness to the whole world, and come to the extreme limit of the west and suffered martyrdom (martyrēsas) under the prefects. Thus was he removed from the world and went into the holy place, having proved himself a striking example of patience.

The statements about Paul, although very much more detailed than those about Peter, hardly allow us to recognize historical details of the life of Paul; the picture portrayed is very stylized, perhaps it takes its form from the list of peristases in 2 Cor. 11.23–27. At least the statement in 5.7 that Paul 'taught righteousness' to the whole world (dikaiosynēn didaxas holon ton kosmon) might be a vague allusion to the Pauline speech about the righteousness of God.[11] The comment that Paul came to the extreme limit of the west and suffered martyrdom under the prefects (epi tōn hēgoumenōn) could be an early indication of the tradition that Paul suffered martyrdom during Nero's persecution of the Christians in Rome. In this connection the statement about the 'extreme limit of the west' to which Paul came (epi to terma tēs dyseōs elthōn) is completely unclear: Is the author thinking of Spain and possibly explicitly of the 'Pillars of Hercules' which were considered to be the 'extreme west', and would 1 Clem. then be a witness for the actual implementation of Paul's mission to Spain planned in Rom. 15.24? Or is he thinking of the most westerly point in Paul's life, i.e. Rome? This may certainly appear disconcerting in a letter written in Rome but might also have been written from the perspective of the Corinthian addressees.[12] Decisive is: It is said of Paul, of whose work the Corinthians are naturally aware, that he became 'a striking example of patience' (hypomonēs genomenos megistos hypogrammos). Peter and particularly Paul count as people who, in contrast to the latest events in Corinth, did not practise envy, strife and sedition but on the contrary had to suffer envy and jealousy and thus after death reached 'the place of glory' (topon tēs doxēs, 5.4) or 'the holy place' (eis ton hagion topon, 5.7).

As far as we know 1 Clem. is the first document in which we encounter expressly that idea which later is described by the term 'apostolic succession': the apostles were 'appointed for the gospel' by Christ (euangelisthēsan, 42.1),

---

11. In 1 Clem. 31.33 there is then, even without an express mention of Paul, a very detailed reference to the thoughts on righteousness through faith for which Abraham is cited as proof (31.2; cf. 32.4).

12. On the discussion cf. Lindemann, *Clemensbriefe* (n. 9), 39.

and they, for their part, appointed in the countries and towns their 'first fruits' (tas aparcha autōn) as 'bishops and deacons' of those who should afterwards believe, according to the Scriptural saying, 'in a certain place' (pou): 'I will appoint their bishops in righteousness and their deacons in faith.'[13] For the author of 1 Clem. the presbyters, whose position he identifies as an 'office of supervision' (episkopē), were appointed by the apostles because they were aware, through Christ, that there would be strife on account of this office (1 Clem. 44). Possibly the Corinthian presbyters were removed from office on the grounds that Paul himself had not appointed any presbyters. In 1 Clem. also then it is not said that the dismissed presbyters (or their predecessors) owed their office to the apostle; but the author does refer to the fact that Paul himself once made a critical judgement on the building of parties in Corinth (47.1). But if the events then were still tolerable because the parties had allied themselves to two apostles (Peter and Paul) and a 'man whom they had approved' (Apollos), the 'one or two persons' who have now led the Corinthian church to sedition against its presbyters cannot in any way be compared with them:

> But now reflect who these are that have perverted you, and lessened the renown of your far-famed brotherly love. It is disgraceful, beloved, yea, highly disgraceful, and unworthy of your Christian profession (anaxia tēs en Christō agōgēs) that such a thing should be heard of as that the most steadfast and ancient church of the Corinthians should, on account of one or two persons, engage in sedition against its presbyters. And this rumour has reached not only us, but those also who are unconnected with us; so that, through your infatuation, the name of the Lord is blasphemed, while danger is also brought upon yourselves. (47.5–7)

A little later (49.1) the author establishes that one who has love en Christō should keep Christ's commandments, which reminds us of the Pauline determining of the relationship between 'indicative' and 'imperative'. In the closer description of what 'love' means he then (49.5) refers to 1 Cor. 13 in clear and very full allusions.

The first letter of Clement shows that, towards the end of the first century, i.e. about 30 or 40 years after the death of Paul, Paul's letter to the Romans was obviously known but so also was known in Rome his first (extant) letter to the church at Corinth, whereby one can at the same time presume that this letter was obviously 'on hand' in Corinth (47.1). The Pauline epistles have of course as yet no 'canonical' quality,[14] i.e. they do not yet have equal rights with

---

13. The author quotes, even if inexactly, Isa. 60.17b LXX: ... kai dōsō tous archontas sou en eirēnē kai tous episkopous sou en dikaiosynē. With the concept episkopoi which is only encountered here and in 42.5 (and also as a predicate of God in 59.3) 'bishops' are not meant but simply people who occupy an office of 'oversight' (cf. in the NT Phil. 1.1).

14. The use of the term 'canon' at this point in time is in any case incorrect; cf. D. Lührmann (2004), *Die apokryph gewordenen Evangelien. Studien zu neuen Texten und zu neuen Fragen* (NT.S 112), Leiden, 1–54. Cf. also B. M. Metzger (1987), *The Canon of the New Testament*, Oxford.

the biblical writings[15] which are frequently quoted in detail in 1 Clem. On the other hand, however, we should not overlook the fact that other early Christian writings which later become part of the 'New Testament' which was gradually coming into being in the second century are not mentioned or quoted in 1 Clem. To be sure there are in 13.1f. and 46.7f. quotations from the words of Jesus but in both cases no reference is made to a particular text, such as one of our New Testament Gospels.[16] Obviously there was a strong interest in Paul, although less in the reception of the contents or even the further development of Pauline theology than in regarding Paul as a guarantor of the developing church order. That it was necessary in so doing to defend Paul against attack or that it counted as a 'risk' to refer to him is not discernible. Conversely we can regard even the fact that 1 Clem. was written – and also the form chosen for it – as an indication that the Pauline letters had served the author or the Roman church at least as a formal model.

2
The Letters of Ignatius

The second early Christian author in whom we can detect an explicit reference to Paul is *Ignatius of Antioch*. The question as to when the letters of Ignatius were written, which were directed to Christian communities in towns in Asia Minor and Rome and to Polycarp of Smyrna, has again been for some time the subject of academic controversy; in this connection the question is once more under discussion whether the letters can be described as 'real' in the historical sense.[17] The question of authenticity may be answered as before positively; there is no explanation why, in the last third of the second century the pseudonym of an otherwise unknown episkopos at Antioch named Ignatius should have been chosen, especially when the letters contain no pointed reference to an (alleged) early dating. Hence it is very likely that the letters are 'real', i.e. that they were in

---

15. Perhaps it is different in 2 Pet. 3.15f. where Paul's letters are mentioned alongside 'the rest of the writings' without it being clear, however, which 'writings' are meant by the term hai loipai graphai.

16. 13.1b,2: 'Let us be mindful of the words of the Lord Jesus, which he spoke, teaching us meekness and long-suffering. For thus he spoke: Be ye merciful, that ye may obtain mercy; forgive, that it may be forgiven to you; as ye do, so shall it be done unto you ...' The series of sayings reminds us of the Sermon on the Mount without any textual passage being recognizable. 46.7b,8: 'Remember the words of our Lord Jesus Christ, how he said: Woe to that man! It would be better for him that he had never been born, than that he should cast a stumbling-block before one of my elect ...' This statement seems like a free combination of Mt. 26.24b and Mt. 18.6 (cf. Lindemann, *Clemensbriefe* [n. 9], 137).

17. Cf. R. M. Hübner (1997), 'Thesen zur Echtheit und Datierung der sieben Briefe des Ignatius von Antiochien', ZAC 1, 44–72; T. Lechner (1999), *Ignatius adversus Valentinianos? Chronologische und theologiegeschichtliche Studien zu den Briefen des Ignatius von Antiochien* (SVig Chr 47), Leiden; also A. Lindemann (1997), 'Antwort auf die „Thesen zur Echtheit und Datierung der sieben Briefe des Ignatius von Antiochien', ZAC 1, 185–94 and my review of Lechner's book in ZAC 6 (2002) 157–61.

fact written in the situation assumed in them: Ignatius is on the way as a prisoner from Syrian Antioch along the coast of Asia Minor to Rome, where he is to meet his death fighting animals in the arena.[18]

But the question whether the letters should be dated in the period 'around 110' – as has been assumed in research for a long time – is justifiable. This date for their composition arose from the frequently observed similarity to the correspondence between Pliny the Younger and the Emperor Trajan on the question of the legally justified action against Christians;[19] however, there are no specific parallels here. In addition, the picture of the episkopos, which becomes increasingly visible in the letters of Ignatius as the central figure not only in the guiding of the congregation but especially also in the conducting of the service of worship,[20] does not necessarily refer to a date of composition at the beginning of the second century.[21] Therefore, it is quite conceivable that the letters were written somewhat later, perhaps around 130.[22]

In Antioch Ignatius learned both the tradition of Jesus and also the tradition of Paul; but he wrote his letters under very difficult conditions, i.e. during his stays in prison – first in Smyrna then in Troas – and would have had no written sources at hand. The allusions to biblical – i.e. Old Testament texts – and to Christian literature are clearly formulated from memory. Ignatius mentions Paul by name twice in his letters, first in Eph. 12.2 and then in Rom. 4.3.[23]

> IgnEph. 12: 1.'I know both who I am, and to whom I write. I am a condemned man, you have been the objects of mercy; I am subject to danger, ye are established in safety. 2. Ye are the persons through whom those pass that are cut off for the sake of God. Ye are initiated into the mysteries of the Gospel (symmystai) with Paul, the holy, the martyred, the deservedly most happy, at whose feet may I be found when I shall attain to God; who in all his epistles makes mention of you in Christ Jesus.'
>
> IgnRom. 4: 1.'I write to all the churches and impress on them all that I shall willingly die for God when ye hinder me ... 2b. Entreat Christ for me that by these instruments (sc. wild bests in the arena) I may be found a sacrifice to God. I do not, as Peter and Paul, issue commandments (diatassomai) unto you. They were apostles; I am but a condemned man; they were free, while I am, even until now, a servant. But when I suffer, I shall be the freedman of Jesus and shall rise again emancipated in him (anastēsomai en autō eleutheros). And now, being a prisoner, I learn not to desire anything worldly or vain.'

18. Cf. W. R. Schoedel (1985), *Ignatius of Antioch. A Commentary on the Letters of Ignatius of Antioch, Hermeneia*, Philadelphia. H. Löhr, 'The Epistles of Ignatius of Antioch', in W. Pratscher (s. n. 6), 91–115.

19. Pliny, ep X. 96f. Cf. here K. Thraede (2004), 'Noch einmal: Plinius d.J. und die Christen', *ZNW* 95, 102–28.

20. In Ignatius the title episkopos can already be understood in the sense of 'bishop'.

21. In this case the letters of Ignatius would have been written at almost the same time as the New Testament Pastoral letters which, however – quite differently from Ignatius' letters – make hardly any differentiation between the presbyteroi and the episkopoi.

22. *Terminus post quem non* for the dating of the letters of Ignatius would be the letter of Polycarp (*v. infra*).

23. The quotations from the letters of Ignatius are taken from the edition mentioned in n. 10.

The first reference to the person of Paul is formulated very effusively and does not allow us to see any closer knowledge of him. What is surprising is above all Ignatius' assertion that Paul mentions the Ephesians 'in all his epistles' (en pasē epistolē).[24] At least Paul speaks of Ephesus expressly in 1 Cor. 15.32 and 16.8; and 'Asia', the capital of which was Ephesus, is mentioned in Rom. 16.5 and 2 Cor. 1.8 (cf. 1 Cor. 16.19). If one also takes into account that Ignatius knew and naturally considered authentic the New Testament letter to the Ephesians, and this might also be true of the Pastoral epistles,[25] and if, finally, it is taken into consideration that the New Testament 'Acts' describes a close and long-lasting relationship of Paul to Ephesus (Acts 19f.), then one would take the statement in IgnEph. 12.2 not necessarily as an indication of his ignorance of the actual facts. It appears that Ignatius wanted to show the church at Ephesus honour in a special way through the reference to Paul emphasized in this way.

The mention of Paul (after Peter[26]) in IgnRom. 4.3 on the other hand appears somewhat casual. Perhaps Ignatius understands the Pauline letter to the Romans, which he clearly knows, as a 'directive' such as he himself is not entitled to make (ouch ... diatassomai). But since the expression also relates to Peter it is unclear exactly what the Bishop of Antioch was thinking of in this statement.

In the theological expositions of Ignatius we can recognize in some themes *influences* of Pauline thinking or Pauline formulations without Ignatius expressly referring to Paul, or even quoting from one of his epistles. To the Pauline influence must belong the use of the set phrase en Christō (IgnEph. 20.2 'life in Jesus Christ'); and when in Eph. 18.1 we read that the Cross is for unbelievers a skandalon, 'but to us salvation and life eternal' and then the rhetorical questions: 'Where is the wise man? Where the disputer? Where is the boasting of those who are styled prudent?' this has not been written without knowledge of 1 Cor. 1.18–24.[27] In the letter to the church in Magnesia in Chapter 8f. Ignatius takes a critical look at the 'Judaist' tendencies, in a similar way to Paul in the letter to the Galatians; in so doing he speaks in 8.1 of life 'kata Ioudaismon', i.e. he uses the same phrase with which Paul characterized his past in Gal. 1.13f. On the other hand he combines charis with pisteuein in exactly the same way as Paul (8.2; 9.1)

In chapter 9 of the letter to the Christians in Tralles Ignatius warns of the dangers of a docetic Christology. Here we read:

---

24. The translation sometimes considered as 'in a whole letter', whereby the New Testament Eph. would be meant, is not possible linguistically.

25. Cf. my essay (1990): 'Paul in the Writings of the Apostolic Fathers', in W. S. Babcock (ed.), *Paul and the Legacies of Paul*, Dallas, 25–45. In the German translation (A. Lindemann [1999], *Paulus in den Schriften der Apostolischen Väter, in Paulus – Apostel und Lehrer der Kirche*, Tübingen, 252–79), I had written that it is 'wohl auszuschließen' ('probably ruled out') that Ignatius knew the Pastoral letters (269, n. 63); this judgement would have to be amended if the 'early dating' (around 110) of the letter of Ignatius should no longer apply (*v. supra*).

26. Cf. 1 Clem. 5.4–7 (*v. supra*).

27. Cf. IgnEph. 18.1: pou sophos? pou syzētētēs? pou kauchēsis tōn legomenōn synetōn? with Paul, 1 Cor. 1.19f.: gegraptai gar: apolō tēn sophian tōn sophōn kai synesin tōn synetōn athetēsō. pou sophos? pou grammateus? pou syzētētēs? pou syzētētēs tou aiōnos toutou? ouchi emōranen ho theos tēn sophian tou kosmou?

1. Stop your ears, therefore, when anyone speaks to you at variance with Jesus Christ, who was descended from David, and was also of Mary; who was truly (alēthōs) born, and did eat and drink. He was truly persecuted under Pontius Pilate; he was truly crucified, and (truly) died, in the sight of beings in heaven, and on earth, and under the earth. 2. He was also raised from the dead, his Father quickening him, even as after the same manner his Father will so raise up us who believe in him by Christ Jesus, apart from whom we do not possess the true life.

The scheme of the argumentation of deriving one's own resurrection through faith in the Resurrection of Jesus corresponds with the Pauline train of thought both in 1 Thess. 4.14 and in 1 Cor. 15.

A special analogy between Ignatius and Paul lies in the fact that – as far as we know – Ignatius was the first Christian author after Paul who wrote letters to churches in his own name. Certainly Ignatius did not make any claim of authority over the addressees of his letters,[28] but time after time he points in principle to his office as episkopos and he pleads emphatically that the churches to whom he writes should always follow their respective episkopos. To this extent there is some reason to suppose that Ignatius – even when he does not explicitly write this – considers himself as standing in the immediate succession of the apostles. One could, admittedly, object that with his formulation in IgnRom. 4.3 he rejects this idea (*v. supra*) but we cannot fail to notice that the statement there, taken as it stands, only leads to the thought that Ignatius might hold a position comparable to the apostolic authority.

3
Polycarp of Smyrna

Polycarp, Bishop of Smyrna,[29] who suffered martyrdom in the middle of the second century,[30] writes a letter[31] to the church at Philippi which allows us to see

---

28. This is basically true of Paul also; but the *Paulos apostolos* which usually opens the letters implies implicitly though unspoken that the writer of the letter presumes that he will receive special respect from the addressees.

29. On the epistle of Polycarp s. B. Dehandschutter in W. Pratscher (cf. n. 6), 117–33.

30. G. Buschmann (2003), 'Article: Polykarp', *RGG*[4] 6, 479f. names as the probable year of death 156 or 167. Cf. C. R. Moss (2010), 'On the Dating of Polycarp: Rethinking the Place of Martyrdom of Polycarp in the History of Christianity', *EC* 1, 539–74. She argues that the writing 'Martrydom of Polycarp' was written not earlier than in the third century.

31. This was a covering letter for the transmission of the letters of Ignatius to Philippi. In scholarship, however, it is disputed whether Polycarp's letter to the Philippians originally consisted of two letters; in PolPhil. 9 the death of Ignatius is taken for granted, whereas in chapter 13 (only extant in Latin) there is talk of Ignatius and those *qui cum eo sunt* (present) – i.e. Ignatius appears still to be alive. This literary-critical problem is admittedly of little importance for the question of dating the letter if – as hinted above – the letters of Ignatius were only written around 130/140. H. Paulsen dates Phil. 1–2 in the time 'around 135'.

that Polycarp is well informed about Paul's relationship to this community. In chapter 3[32] he writes:

> 1. These things, brethren, I write to you concerning righteousness, not because I take anything upon myself, but because ye have invited me to do so. 2. Fore neither I, nor any other such one, can come up to the wisdom of the blessed and glorified Paul. He, when among you, accurately and steadfastly taught the word of truth in the presence of those who were then alive. And when absent from you, he wrote you letters, which, if you carefully study, you will find to be the means of building you up in that faith which has been given you. 3. It (sc. faith) 'is the mother of us all', being followed by hope, and preceded by love towards God, and Christ and our neighbour. Fore if anyone be inwardly possessed of these graces, he hath fulfilled the command of righteousness, since he that hath love is far from all sin.

Not completely clear here is particularly the statement that Paul wrote letters (epistolas, plural) to Philippi. It is sometimes suspected that this is an indication that the hypothesis is correct which maintains that the Pauline letter to the Philippians was put together from what were originally several letters,[33] but even if the hypothesis were correct, it is still very unlikely that the editing of the letter to the Philippians which we now possess could not have been completed at the time when Polycarp wrote *his* letter to the Philippians. The assumption more likely is that a collection of Paul's letters was already available and that Polycarp with his remark wanted to express the idea that these letters were written 'for you' (apōn hymin egrapsen) over and above for the original various addressees. In PolPhil. 9.1, similarly to 1 Clem. 5, 'models of patience' are presented; these are, first, the contemporaries Ignatius, Zosimus and Rufus, but then 'Paul and the rest of the apostles', whereby the special emphasis on Paul may arise from the epistolary situation of PolPhil., but is nevertheless conspicuous.

In Chapter 11 Polycarp sharply criticizes a one-time presbyter of the church in Philippi named Valens who 'so underestimated' his office (*sic ignoret is locum*[34]), whereby the context makes it reasonable to suppose that it was a matter of a misdemeanour in the financial field. Polycarp writes:

> 2. If a man cannot govern himself in such matters, how shall he enjoin them in others? If a man does not keep himself from covetousness, he shall be defiled by idolatry and shall be judged as one of the heathen. But who of us are ignorant of the judgement of the Lord? Do we not know that the saints will judge the world, as Paul teaches? But I have neither seen nor heard of any such thing among you, in the midst of whom the blessed Paul laboured, and also are commended in the beginning of his Epistle. For he boasts of you in all those churches which also then knew the Lord; but we (of Smyrna) had not yet known him.

---

32.   The quotations from the letter of Polycarp are taken from the edition mentioned in n. 10.
33.   In my opinion the Pauline letter to the Philippians is a literary unity; v. Conzelmann and Lindemann, *Interpreting* (n. 8), 249f. Cf. chapter 13 by L. Bormann in this volume.
34.   PolPhil. 10–12 and 13.2b–14 are only preserved in the Latin translation.

The expression in 11.2, 'Do we not know that the saints will judge the world' (*aut nescimus, quia sancti mundum iudicabunt?*), is clearly a quotation of 1 Cor. 6.2 (there admittedly not *nescimus*, first person plural, but ouk oidate second person plural), whereby it is quite possible that the rhetorical question implies that the addressees in Philippi were already familiar with Paul's statement. The phrase 'as Paul teaches' (*sicut Paulus docet*) appears like a formula of quotation which almost corresponds to 'as is written' (Vulgate: *sicut scriptum est*) applied to biblical texts. In 11.3 Polycarp calls to mind Paul's activity in Philippi. The sense of the expression that the Philippians are mentioned 'in the beginning of the epistle' (*in principio epistulae eius*) is unclear and in a similar way it is not obvious what Polycarp is thinking about when he writes that Paul boasts of the Philippians *in omnibus ecclesiis* since the Pauline epistles, with the exception of Phil., contain no reference to Philippi. The statements certainly show that here, too, Polycarp, in a similar way as in 3.2, wishes to emphasize the close relationship between Philippi and Paul and that in so doing – consciously or unconsciously – expresses the praise of the church very effusively. *En passant*, Polycarp's letter to the Philippians allows us to detect in several passages that the episkopos of Smyrna is certainly familiar with Pauline theology or at least with individual theological statements of the apostle.[35] Conspicuous is a certain similarity with the Pastoral letters, which has led in research to the thesis – among others – that Polycarp himself was the author of the Pastoral letters;[36] but this is highly unlikely.

4
Further Writings

In closing, further writings from the second century, which contain references to Paul or – sometimes in a highly imaginative way – give reports about him, should be mentioned briefly.

1 The letter to Diognetus which belongs to the sphere of apologetic literature shows a clear propinquity to the ideas and statements of Pauline theology.[37] The dating of the writing is, however, highly controversial. If it were in fact composed in the second century it would be the great exception compared to the other apologetic writings, in which Paul is not only not mentioned by

---

35. The findings are somewhat complicated and consequently are not introduced in detail here; but cf. A. Lindemann (1979), *Paulus im ältesten Christentum. Das Bild des Apostels und die Rezeption des paulinischen Theologie in der frühchristlichen Literatur bis Marcion* (BHTh 58), Tübingen, 221–32.

36. Cf. H. von Campenhausen (1963), 'Polykarp von Smyrna und die Pastoralbriefe', in id., *Aus der Frühzeit des Christentums. Studien zur Kirchengeschichte des ersten und zweiten Jahrhunderts*, Tübingen, 197–252.

37. Text in English translation in the volume mentioned in n. 10, 25–30. On the Pauline reception cf. my essay: 'Paulinische Theologie im Brief an Diognet', in Lindemann, *Paulus* (n. 25), 280–93. Cf. H. E. Lona, 'Diognetus', in W. Pratscher (ed.) (n. 6), 197–213.

name but in which only a very modest influence of Pauline theology can be detected.[38]

2 The theologians who were critical of or rejected the 'orthodox church' which was coming into being also had a good look at Paul, whereby diverse tendencies are apparent. Two documents from the Coptic-Gnostic *Library of Nag Hammadi* refer to Paul according to their titles, but their dating is uncertain. The *'Prayer of the Apostle Paul'* (PrecPl, NHC I.1) was possibly written in the second century; it contains in lines A 11–14 an allusion to 1 Cor. 2.9: 'Grant what no angel eye has [seen] and no archon ear has heard and what has not entered into any human heart which came to be angelic and (modelled) after the image of the psychic God when it was formed in the beginning, since I have faith and hope!'[39] The *'Apocalypse of Paul'* (ApcPl) is transmitted in NHC V/2. It relates to Paul's translation 'up to the third heaven' mentioned in 2 Cor. 12.2–4 and describes how from there Paul reaches the tenth heaven; in the course of this he meets in the seventh heaven the Creator who desires to prevent his further ascension but then after a brief discussion must allow him to pass. Here, too, a date for composition in the second century is not inconceivable without our being able to mention any truly certain criteria.[40] The two 'Pauline' documents from Nag Hammadi admittedly provide no specific evidence for the closeness of Christian Gnosis to Paul because there are also Gnostic documents in this Corpus which are traced back, for example, to James, John and Peter, even to Peter and the twelve apostles.[41]

3 In the mid-second century Marcion,[42] who came from Pontus in Asia Minor, was active in Rome. After he was expelled from the congregation in 144 he founded his own church. Marcion had developed a theology of his own which was based on the idea of the existence of two Gods: The Old Testament testifies to the Creator God who is just and merciless and shows his imperfect Creation that he himself is imperfect. 'In the fifteenth year of

---

38. Cf. Lindemann, *Paulus im ältesten Christentum* (n. 35), 350–67.

39. Translation by Dieter Mueller (1988), in J. M. Robinson (ed.), *The Nag Hammadi Library in English*, Revised Edition, Leiden, 28. Mueller thinks that 'details such as the reference to the "psychic God" may indicate Valentinian connections. That association in turn suggests a date of origin between the second half of the second century and the end of the third century' (*ibid.*, 27).

40. On this cf. U.-K. Plisch (2003), in *Nag Hammadi Deutsch, 2 Band: NHC V.2 – XIII.1, BG 1 und 4* (GCS NF 12), Berlin/New York, 400: One 'can say no more than that the second century can be considered as the earliest possible period for its composition'. The Coptic-Gnostic ApcPl is, however, at any rate older than the complete apocryphal 'Apocalypse of Paul' extant only in a Latin translation (Visio Pauli); on the latter v. W. Schneemelcher (ed.) ([5]1989), *Neutestamentliche Apokryphen in deutscher Übersetzung, II. Band, Apostolisches, Apokalypsen und Verwandtes*, Tübingen, 644–75.

41. On the reception of Pauline theology in the Christian Gnosis of the second century including the Nag Hammadi texts v. Lindemann, *Paulus im ältesten Christentum* (n. 33), 297–343, further A. Lindemann, 'Der Apostel Paulus im 2. Jahrhundert', in *id.*, *Paulus, Apostel*, 294–322, here 306–15.

42. On Marcion see S. Moll (2010), *The Arch-Heretic Marcion* (WUNT 250), Tübingen.

the reign of Tiberius Caesar' (Lk. 3.1) the perfect, benevolent Redeemer God revealed himself in contrast to him and brought humanity liberation from the power of the Creator. In his opus, 'Antitheses', which has been lost, Marcion contrasted biblical ('Old Testament') statements with Christian tradition, in the course of which he presupposed that the Old Testament texts should be interpreted literally and not allegorically.[43] Marcion created for himself a collection of authoritative Christian writings made up of Luke's Gospel and the Pauline letters (without the Pastorals). In so doing Marcion was convinced that these documents were without exception adulterated and consequently had to be 'cleansed' of 'Jewish' alterations. He therefore removed a number of passages from the Pauline epistles as 'interpolations', for example the greater part of Rom. 9–11. Moreover, by the abbreviation of several texts he made objective corrections in favour of the doctrine he stood for.[44] Marcion's work and also his 'canon' have admittedly not been preserved but can only be reconstructed indirectly from the anti-Marcion writings of some Church Fathers, especially from the five-volume work 'Adversus Marcionem' by Tertullian.[45] Whether Marcion was the first to compile a 'New Testament' or whether in so doing he forced the main Church to react or conversely his action presupposed a collection of writings which already counted as authoritative in the Church cannot be said with certainty.[46] At any rate the polemic of the Church Fathers presents the picture that Marcion made an arbitrary choice from the wealth of Christian tradition of those which corresponded to his own interests. Certainly Paul and his epistles appear in Marcion as 'the apostle'; but in fact it was the 'bowdlerized' Paul whom Marcion believed he could bring on to the field as a main authority for his theology. In the end this is proof that Paul was already an established authority in the Church while Marcion saw himself forced to modify Paul's texts to the extent necessary to fit his own interests.[47]

---

43. When, for example, God calls to Adam in Paradise, 'Where are you?' (Gen. 3.9), this shows that he really did not know where Adam was.

44. V. further G. May (2002), 'Article: Markion/Markioniten', *RGG*[4] 5, 834–6.

45. On the reconstruction of Marcion's text of Paul v. U. Schmid (1995), *Marcion und sein Apostolos. Rekonstruktion und historische Einordnung der marcionistischen Paulusbriefausgabe* (ANTF 25) Berlin/New York. A. v. Harnack ([2]1924) undertook an attempt to reconstruct the 'Antithesen': *Marcion. Das Evangelium vom fremden Gott. Eine Monographie zur Geschichte der Grundlegung der katholischen Kirche. Neue Studien zu Marcion*. Leipzig, 89–92, 256–313.

46. Cf. on the reaction of the Church to Marcion, Lindemann, *Paulus im ältesten Christentum* (n. 33), 390–5; A. M. Ritter (1993), 'Zur Kanonbildung in der Alten Kirche', in *id.*, *Charisma und Caritas. Aufsätze zur Geschichte der Alten Kirche*, Göttingen, 265–80, here 267: It 'appears in all likelihood that it would have come to the development of a two-part canon of the New Testament ... even without Marcion from purely inner-Church attempts and stimuli. But Marcion's emergence would have hastened this development to a considerable extent'.

47. On Marcion's reception of Paul v. Lindemann, *Paulus im ältesten Christentum* (n. 33) 378–90.

4 In the report of the trial of the *Martyrs of Scili* on 17 July 180[48] it is said that the accused had with them a receptacle, and when the examining Proconsul Saturninus asked them what was in this receptacle they replied: 'Books and letters by Paul, a just man'.[49] That Paul is described as a *vir iustus* (and not e.g. as 'blessed' or as 'apostle') would be connected with the situation in court. What is meant exactly by the formulation *libri et epistulae Pauli* cannot be said: The statement shows at any rate that collections of Pauline letters existed in North Africa which were clearly also available to individual Christians.

5 Towards the end of the second century the *Acta Pauli* was written. According to Tertullian it was a presbyter in Asia Minor who, 'from love of Paul', wrote this document 'recently'.[50] Parts of the Acta Pauli are the *'third letter to the Corinthians'*[51] and above all the *'Acts of Paul and Thecla'*. To its exceptional details belongs a description of the person of Paul on his arrival at Iconium (ActPauli et Theclae 2f.):

> 2. And a man named Onesiphorus, who had heard that Paul was coming to Iconium, went to meet Paul taking his children Simmias and Zeno and his wife, Lectra, to offer him hospitality. Titus had told him what Paul looked like, for he had not seen him (previously) in the flesh but only in the spirit. 3. And he went on the royal road which leads to Lystra, took up position there to wait for him and looked at (all) who went past with Titus' description in mind. But he saw Paul coming: a man small in stature with a bald head and bow legs, a noble posture, with eyebrows which met and a nose which protruded just a little, completely friendly; for one moment he appeared like a human being, the next with the face of an angel.

In Iconium Thecla then sees the apostle, and because of his preaching immediately decides to terminate her engagement and henceforth to live abstinently. Thecla is condemned to fight wild animals, but while the animals fall upon her she jumps into a water-ditch and baptizes herself in anticipation of her death. In fact, however, she remains unscathed and is pardoned. Then she meets Paul again in Iconium and dies only after a long period of missionary activity in Seleucia. This tradition in a remarkable way results

---

48. V. on this H. R. Drobner (1994), *Lehrbuch der Patrologie*, Freiburg, 76f. The precise date emerges from the introductory clause: 'Praesente bis et Claudiano consulibus, XVI Kalendas Augustas ... (When Praesens for the second time and Claudianus were consuls, on the sixteenth day before the Kalends of August ...)'.

49. Text in G. Krüger (ed.) (⁴1965), *Ausgewählte Märtyrerakten*, with a postscript by G. Ruhbach (SQS NF 3), Tübingen.

50. Tertullian, De baptismo 17. The text of the Acta Pauli can be found in W. Schneemelcher, 'Paulusakten' in *id*., *Apokryphen* (n. 38), 193–242. Tertullian composed his work around 200, which means that the Acta Pauli would probably have been written around 180/190.

51. V. on this the study by V. Hovhanessian (2000), *Third Corinthians. Reclaiming Paul for Christian Orthodoxy* (Studies in Biblical Literature 18), New York etc.

in the fact that the oldest pictorial representations of Paul show the apostle accompanied by Thecla.[52]

6 A fundamental rejection of Paul and his theology is seen in Jewish-Christian communities, which hold fast to the Law: The Church Fathers in their corresponding papers on 'Heretics' emphasize this.[53] Direct textual sources have not survived; but one of the source-documents of the 'Pseudoclementines', the so-called '*Kerygmata Petrou*' at one place shows massive polemic by Peter against 'Simon Magus' (cf. Acts 8.9–24), in the course of which the statements allow us to perceive that in fact *Paul* is meant by this Simon Magus. Peter accuses him of not being a true apostle because he was not called by the earthly Jesus but through a vision; what is more, he has opposed him, who is the 'rock': 'If you were not an enemy then you would not have slandered me and reviled my preaching so that I find no belief when I preach what I in my own person heard from the Lord, as if I am indubitably condemned while you are praised'.[54] The allusions to Gal. 2.11–14 are clear; what is remarkable is that Paul is clearly not attacked directly but that the author of the Kerygmata Petrou had to choose a pseudonym.

5
Summary

Two lines are significant for the question of Paul's legacy in the second century: On the one hand we can detect references to Paul in almost every sector of the Church; and even where in Jewish-Christian communities observant of the Law there is polemic against Paul, this also shows that Paul has in no way been forgotten. Second, these references to Paul allow us to see that the collection of the Pauline letters and their circulation within the Church had already begun. This process led logically and without discussion to the 'canonization' of these letters within the New Testament.

References

A. Lindemann (2005), 'Paul's Influence on "Clement" and Ignatius', in A. F. Gregory and Chr. M. Tuckett (eds), *Trajectories through the New Testament and the Apostolic Fathers*, Oxford: Oxford University Press, 9–24.
H. O. Maier, 'The Politics and Rhetoric of Discord and Concord in Paul and Ignatius', ibid. 307–24.

---

52. E. Dassmann (1982), *Paulus in frühchristlicher Frömmigkeit und Kunst*, 25–32 (Picture 40ff.). Cf. J. N. Brenner (1996), *The Apocryphal Acts of Paul and Thecla*, Kampen.
53. Lindemann, *Paulus im ältesten Christentum* (n. 33), 101–9; 367–71.
54. Homilien VXII 19.4: v. G. Strecker, 'Kerygmata Petrou', in Schneemelcher, *Apokryphen* (n. 38), 479–88.

P. Oakes, 'Leadership and Suffering in the Letters of Polycarp and Paul to the Philippians', *ibid.*, 353–73.

W. Pratcher (ed.), (2010) *The Apostolic Fathers. An Introduction*, Waco, TX: Baylor University Press.

Chapter 20

THE RECEPTION OF PAUL IN THE HISTORY OF THE CHURCH
Wolfgang Wischmeyer

1
Main Lines of Development in Early Church History

After the genuine Pauline letters, the Deutero-Paulines and Acts reveal the first sign of the continued existence of the Pauline tradition which we can outline in seven points:

1 *The name*: The name 'Paul' remains alive and with the name the person lives on.
2 *The letters*: Paul as the author of letters remains in memory and stimulates the further writing of letters under his name.[1]
3 *The journeys*: That Paul visited many places and was in contact with numerous towns in the Roman Empire was fused with the addressees of his letters and the reports of his journeys in Acts to establish a picture of the character of the 'ecumenical apostle'. This perception also found its expression in the conviction that the apostle's journey to Spain *did* take place: hence he had travelled from east to west through the whole ancient world.
4 *The themes*: One can observe a partial identity of many of the themes which are connected with the name of Paul even if the way they are treated and the theological questions related to them clearly differ from those in the genuine Pauline epistles.
5 *The hermeneutics*: Here, however, we can detect a first clear sign of the reception of Paul. The Pauline hermeneutics of the Deutero- and Trito-Paulines lay the foundation for the Christian stream of continuity of Christian theological hermeneutics.
6 *The imitatio Paulina*: An *imitatio Paulina*[2] corresponding to the *imitatio Jesu* which was perhaps suggested by Acts is known to us only in the literary form of the apocryphal Acts of the Apostles, e.g. the Acta Pauli, partly with

---

1.   Cf. J. Divjak (1989), 'Pseudo-Seneca, Briefwechsel mit Paulus', HLL 5, § 571.1
2.   See M. M. Mitchell (2010), *Paul, the Corinthians and the Birth of Christian Hermeneutics*, Cambridge: Cambridge University Press. Comparable is the phenomenon that the depictions of the life of Jesus, at least those of the first three Gospels, lead time and again to an imitation of Jesus (*imitatio Jesuana*).

apocalyptic features such as the *Revelatio (Visio) Pauli*. Here the connection to Thecla is particularly important (Acta Pauli et Theclae).[3]

7 *The Martyrdom*: Certainly there were many martyrs before, at the same time and above all after Paul, but it is remarkable how much value is placed in the church and in the history of theology on the tradition of Paul's Roman martyrdom on the road to Ostia (*S. Paolo fuori le mura*) under Nero. To this is added the old connection of Peter and Paul as the joint teachers and martyrs in the capital of the Roman Empire.[4]

Decisive here is the tradition of the Pauline letters[5] as an independent collection even before the beginning of the process of canonization and the arising of the conception of a new 'Holy Book' for Christians. This collection played a decisive part in the 'self-definition' of the Gentile church: In the clash over the Old Testament and its interpretation and in the development of a Christian ethic along with a mystically tinged Christian philosophy which took their origin from the so-called participatory tendencies in Paul and in part led to Gnostic doctrine.

> Ernst Dassmann consequently can record a twofold outcome from the first two centuries:
> A large number of writings in all genres and areas of Early Christian literature betray knowledge of the person and work of Paul. The extent of this knowledge varies greatly, the attitude to the apostle and the assessment of his theology is diversely graded in the individual documents ... In spite of this variety in proof and tradition Paul was never considered the only or even only the most important source or mediator of the Church's proclamation.[6]

This is also true for such a particular reception of Paul as that of Marcion.[7] A further important aspect of the reception of Paul begins with the commentaries on Paul and comments on him (Clement of Alexandria, Irenaeus of Lyon). The oldest commentary on Paul (around 200) is thought to go back to an otherwise unknown author named Heraclitus.[8]

---

3. See Chapter 19 by A. Lindemann in this volume.
4. D. L. Eastman (2010), 'Paul the Martyr: The Cult of the Apostle in the Latin West', *Writings from the Greco-Roman World Supplements* 4, Leiden: Brill.
5. On letters in general see Chapter 11 by E.-M. Becker on 2 Corinthians in this volume. The topic of canonization is treated in: H. v. Lips (2004), *Der neutestamentliche Kanon. Seine Geschichte und Bedeutung*, Zürich; S. E. Porter (2004), 'When and How was the Pauline Corpus Compiled? An Assessment of Theories', in *id*., (ed.) *The Pauline Canon* (PAST 1), Leiden, 95–127.
6. E. Dassmann, *Stachel*, 316f. Cf. *id*. (1982), *Paulus in frühchristlicher Frömmigkeit und Kunst* (RhWAW.VG 256), Opladen, on the later archaeological traces, reports of pilgrims, Pauline churches and scenic representations.
7. Cf. G. May (ed.) (2002), *Marcion und seine kirchengeschichtliche Wirkung* (TU 150), Berlin.
8. Euseb, h.e. 5,27: ta Hērakleitou eis ton apostolon, cf. Jerome vir il.46: Heraclitus sub Commodi Severique imperio in apostolum commentarios composuit; v. R. Hanig (2002), 'Heraclitus', *LACL*[3], 319.

2
The Third and Fourth Centuries and the Development in the East

Since Irenaeus and the beginning of the School of Alexandria (see Gal. 3.24 'the Law is our paidagogos' as a model for the writing and the concept of the 'paidagogos' of Clement of Alexandria) it is clear 'how Paul together with John the Christian theologian from that time on delivers the decisive constituents from which the load-bearing pillars of christology, soteriology, anthropology and eschatology are constructed'.[9]

Of Origen's commentary on the apostle, which contained Rom. (15 books), 1 Cor., Gal., Eph., Col., 1 Thess., 2 Thess., Tit., Phil., Phlm. and Heb. only fragments have been preserved apart from the ten books of Rufinus' Latin translation of the commentary on Romans.[10] But this record, mostly in the Catenae, shows the significant effect of Origen's exegesis e.g. on the problem area of election and – a prominently emphasized – freedom of will. The exegetical work of Greek theology is then driven forward particularly by Theodore of Mopsuestia and Theodoret of Cyrus[11] and reaches its high point in John Chrysostom, from whom in addition to smaller works altogether 259 homilies[12] on all 14 letters have been preserved.[13] This exegesis became known in the west through Jerome. Chrysostom's picture of Paul can be found particularly in the seven homilies, *De laudibus S. Pauli*, which celebrate Paul, the theologian of the Cross, the 'archetype of virtue', as an orator who is superior to the angels in his paradoxical self-praise but does not lose sight of the question of social ethics.

3
Augustine

The African professor of Rhetoric, Augustine, learned this Antiochene interpretation of Paul from Bishop Ambrosius in Milan. Alongside this came the Neo-Platonic philosophical interpretation of Paul as it was represented in the work of the first Latin commentator of Paul, C. Marius Victorinus, which remained vivid in the Latin Pauline renaissance in Milan in the fourth century. These encounters with Paul finally led to the conversion and baptism of

---

9. S. Vollenweider, 'Article: Paulus', 1066. Vollenweider does not mention Heraclitus. On commentary in general cf. L. Fladerer and D. Börner-Klein (2004), 'Article: Kommentar', *RAC* 21, 274–329.

10. Cf. T. Heither (ed. and trans.) (1990–1999), *Origenes. Commentarii in epistolam ad Romanas* [Latin–German] 1–4 (FC 2), Freiburg; *id.* (1990), *Translatio religionis. Die Paulusdeutung des Origenes in seinem Kommentar zum Römerbrief*, Cologne.

11. K. Staab (ed.) (²1984), *Pauluskommentare aus der griechischen Kirche aus Katenen*, Münster.

12. CPG 4427–40.

13. F. Field (1845–1862), *Iohannis Chrysostomi interpretatio omnium epistularum Paulinarum 1–7*, Oxford; M. M. Mitchell (2000), *The Heavenly Trumpet. John Chrysostom and the art of Pauline interpretation* (HUT 40), Tübingen.

Augustine and to his decision to fulfil with a circle of friends a philosophical ideal of a life of asceticism and seclusion from the world.

Further encounters with Paul ensue in the course of Augustine's episcopacy. Through the primary task of preaching on a text Augustine saw himself increasingly referred to textual exegesis. This was particularly important for his constantly increasing confrontation on the question of theodicy, first with the Manichaeans and then with the Pelagians. Particularly in the face of the followers of Pelagius, who used very varied arguments, and especially against Julian of Aeclanum, a splendidly educated intellectual and outstanding representative of the School of Antioch, he became absorbed in his last two decades once again in his interpretation of Paul. This received in the final form of Augustinian theology such a status that one can say: From the late works of Augustine the reception of Paul in the history of the western Church and theology is for the most part also the reception of Augustine. Of the purely exegetical works of Augustine on Paul we have the *Expositio quarumdam propositionum ex epistula ad Romanos*, the *Epistulae ad Romanos inchoata expositio*, and the *Epistulae ad Galatas expositio*.[14]

Augustine extols Paul as follows: *unus apostolus Paulus cogit nos diligentius cogitare et perscrutari*[15] ('the apostle Paul alone compels us to think and scrutinize more diligently'). What fascinated the orator and then the bishop as long as he lived about Paul can be summarized in three points:

- the *relation to the text*, for all Christian theology must be biblical theology
- Paul's exemplary hermeneutical treatment of the texts from the *Old Testament*
- the *language* of the apostle, particularly the use of antithetical speech, which within the normative hermeneutical horizon of the Bible can even allow the paradox of the double command of love grounded in God and his sole working to stand.[16]

4

The Middle Ages in the West until Humanism

In addition to the Augustinian tradition, above all the *Expositio XIII epistularum Pauli* by Pelagius[17] with its influential prologues and similar works[18] was likewise important for further exegesis and interpretation of Paul in the medieval

14. J. Divjak (ed.), *Sancti Aurelii Augustini Opera IV/1* (CSEL 84), 1–181.
15. D. E. Dekkers and J. Fraipont (eds), *Enarratio in psalmos 49,9,12* (CCSL 38).
16. The formulation following K. Pollmann (2002), *Aurelius Augustinus. Die christliche Bildung (De doctrina christiana)*, Stuttgart, 278; cf. id. (1996), *Doctrina Christiana. Untersuchungen zu den Anfängen der christlichen Hermeneutik unter besonderer Berücksichtigung von Augustins De doctrina christiana* (Par. 41), Fribourg.
17. A. Souter (1922–1926), *Pelagius's Expositions of 13 Epistles of St. Paul* (TSt), Cambridge.
18. E.g. the Budapest Commentary on Paul: H. J. Frede (1973/1974), *Ein neuer Paulustext und Kommentar 1–2* (AGLB 7–8), Freiburg.

west. We find these first in the form of Catenae and glosses, then from the eleventh century in commentaries with *quaestiones*.

Abelard's commentary on the letter to the Romans was influential in its emphasis on the Apostle's rhetoric and dialectic.[19] He was the dialectician of the *sic et non*, a representative of the Parisian study-rules which made the fostering of Biblical Studies obligatory alongside Dogmatics and Philosophy. We must also mention the commentary on the *Corpus Paulinum* by Thomas Aquinas,[20] who interpreted the letters to the churches as the grace which had become real in the church, whereby in the letter to the Romans it was a matter of the *gratia secundum se*, in 1 and 2 Corinthians of the shape of grace in the sacraments and in the other letters of the *effectus unitatis* of grace.

An important factor for the history of exegesis in the Middle Ages is a development which also affects various important aspects of theology as a whole:

First, the unity of biblical and systematic theology is lost and biblical quotations increasingly become *dicta probantia*.

On the other hand the formalism of exegesis which from the thirteenth century is covered by the mnemonic *Littera gesta docet, quid credas allegoria, moralis quid agas, quid speres (quo tendas) anagogia* has a twofold result. It leads first to more careful interpretation of the text; second it rapidly flows, in connection with an anthropological concentration of the movements for reform in which one is concerned about one's own spiritual salvation, into emphasizing the literal sense and the biblical principle. This tendency increases in early Humanism and in manifold ways refers again to Paul and Augustine, as can be seen in Petrarch, Lorenzo Valla, Marsilio Ficino and Faber Stapulensis.

Finally, for Erasmus Paul is the outstanding witness of Christian Philosophy. When he calls for the Bible for the ploughman and the *muliercula* at her spinning-wheel, Paul is beside him, leading him as interpreter of the Bible as we can see in the *Paraphrasis in omnes epistolas apostolicas*.[21]

5
Reformation and Protestant Orthodoxy

Luther (1483–1546), coming from the contemporary Theology of Humility, from the winter of 1515–16 devoted himself as an exegete to Paul for his lectures on Romans. On the question of Justification he saw the reception of Paul as a mixture of the tradition of the Augustinian order and contemporary conceptions of Paul. For Luther, especially through the influence of Melanchthon's humanistic interest in Paul,[22] Paul was the well-established standard theologian.

---

19. R. Peppermüller, (trans.) (2000), *Petrus Abaelardus. Expositio in epistolam ad Romanos 1–3* (FC 26), Freiburg.
20. Cf. T. Domanyi (1979), *Der Römerbriefkommentar des Thomas von Aquin. Ein Beitrag zur Untersuchung seiner Auslegungsmethoden* (BSHST 39), Bern.
21. Desiderius Erasmus, Opera 7.6, Amsterdam 1997.
22. Cf. E. Bizer (1966), *Texte aus der Anfangszeit Melanchthons* (TGET 2,

In ApolCA 4.87 we then find the statement that in the letter to the Romans 'the whole substance of all the Epistles, indeed of the whole Bible, is contained'.[23]

In this way Paul became for the Wittenberg Reformation and its understanding of the gospel as *promissio* the hermeneutical key to the dialectics of the theological figures of *sola scriptura* and *solus Christus*. In the course of this the concepts of freedom borrowed from Paul which gave a boost to the Reformation in very different aspects and on various levels frequently led, combined with Erasmian motifs, beyond the Lutheran initial stages. This extended up to a continuing Reformation process among Baptists, Socinians and Evangelisti.

For the Southern German ('Oberdeutsch') and Swiss tradition, however, Paul and, once again, especially the letter to the Romans has just as great a significance as is shown by the commentaries of Oecolampadius, Bullinger and Bucer after 1523. Only glosses and annotations on Paul have survived from Zwingli – particularly on the matter of prophecy. Calvin (1509–64) began his exegetical activity in 1540. This embraces all Paul's epistles, starting with a commentary on Romans[24] which for him represented 'the open door to the immeasurable treasures of Scripture' and which for Karl Barth in 1918 would still be the '*non plus ultra*'.[25]

An exegetical work comparable to Melanchthon's researches on the Pauline letters is first to be found in the *Annotationes in Novum Testamentum* by Hugo Grotius (1583–1645), which appeared in 1641 to 1646. Some works against Orthodoxy by antideist authors of the Enlightenment such as John Locke's *A Paraphrase and Notes on the Epistles of St. Paul to the Galatians, 1 and 2 Corinthians, Romans, Ephesians*[26] followed. Translated in 1768/9 by Johann Georg Hofmann and with a preface by Johann David Michaelis it appeared in German and was intended to drive forward the discussion of Paul in the German Enlightenment[27] as Johann Friedrich Wilhelm Jerusalem also shows.

In his 'Geschichte der paulinischen Forschung' Albert Schweitzer (1875–1965) comes to the following assessment:

> The Reformation fought and conquered in the name of Paul. Consequently the teaching of the Apostle of the Gentiles took a prominent place in Protestant study. Nevertheless the labour expended on it did not, to begin with, advance the historical understanding of his system of thought. What men looked for in Paul's writings was proof-texts for Lutheran or Reformed theology; and that was what they found. Reformation exegesis

Neukirchen-Vluyn) and Melanchthon's large commentary on Paul from 1529/30.

23. BSLK (⁶1967), Göttingen, 178.
24. Calvin Studienausgabe 5.1. *Der Brief an die Römer. Ein Kommentar*, C. Link et al. (eds) (2005), Neukirchen-Vluyn.
25. K. Barth and E. Thurneysen (1973), *Briefwechsel 1: 1913–1921* (KBGA 5.1), Zurich, 260.
26. London 1706. Cf. the critical edition, J. Locke (1987), *A Paraphrase and Notes on the Epistles of St. Paul to the Galatians, 1 and 2 Corinthians, Romans, Ephesians*, edited by A. W. Wainwright, 2 vols, Oxford.
27. Cf. O. Merk, *Erwägungen*.

reads its own ideas into Paul, in order to receive them back again clothed with Apostolic authority.[28]

For theology this must be so: 'Paulinism belongs in the history of dogmatic Theology, since the formation of dogma begins immediately with the death of Jesus.'[29]

6
From the Enlightenment to Current Historical-Critical Research

Of considerable importance for the rise of a specialized exegetical research on Paul is Gotthold Ephraim Lessing (1729–81). Although he was no biblical theologian and certainly not a researcher of Paul in spite of his significance for the theology of his day in his battle against bibliolatry,[30] the New Testament documents were for him a significant *regula fidei* arising from books fundamental for the Christian religion – indeed, over and above this, those of a new third religion promised in the New Testament under the rule of the Spirit.[31] Indubitably Lessing's formula which was to be significant in the history of ideas: 'The letter is not the spirit; and the Bible is not religion', was stamped by Paul.

Johann Salomo Semler (1725–91) in his *Institutio ad doctrinam Christianam* (1774) treats Paul closer under the sign of his theory of Accommodation. Paul had to 'go to work with care and prudence, in the same way as Jesus himself earlier, when suppressing the false opinions of religion'; but: 'Of course such truths cannot be divine and Christian because they do not appear new and original'.[32] Consequently in his *Discourse on the free examination of the Canon* he describes the Pauline letters, following the Englishman, Thomas Chubb, as 'private opinions' or as 'a conversation with people at that time' with whom the apostle could speak 'in no other way than this' because of their preconceived opinions: 'When Paul wrote letters they were not directed to those Christians who certainly did not desire to belong to Paul's pupils and supporters'.[33]

28. A. Schweitzer, *Geschichte*, 1.
29. Schweitzer, *Geschichte*, VI.
30. Merk, *Erwägungen*, 71; cf. L. Zscharnak (1905), *Lessing und Semler. Ein Beitrag zur Entstehungsgeschichte des Rationalismus und der kritischen Theologie*, Giessen; K. Aner (1929), *Die Theologie der Lessingzeit*, Halle, here 27 n. 2, the reference to Lessing's review on 27.11.1751: 'Bekehrung und Apostelamt Pauli'; H. Schultze (1969), *Lessings Toleranzbegriff*, Göttingen; L. P. Wessel (1977), *G. E. Lessing's Theology. A Reinterpretation*, Den Haag; J. v. Lüpke (1989), *Weg der Weisheit. Studien zu Lessings Theologiekritik* (GTA 41), Goettingen; E. Quapp (1992), *Lessings Theologie statt Jacobis Spinozismus. Eine Interpretation der 'Erziehung des Menschengeschlechts' auf der Grundlage der Formel 'hen ego kai pan'*, Vol I §§ 1–25, Bern.
31. In the concept of 'spirit' here Pauline and Johannine connotations are perceptible.
32. Zscharnack, *Lessing* (n. 30), 135.
33. Quotations from Zscharnack, *Lessing* (n. 28), 135. Cf. the works of the Deist, T. Chubb (1738),

Only in connection with the sciences of history and their discussion of methods which develop in the eighteenth and nineteenth centuries and their reciprocal exchange with theology does it gradually come, within the historical-intellectual frame of sensibility, Romanticism, nationalism and Historicism, to critical philological research on the Pauline letters. At the beginning stood biographies of Paul as for example that by August Hermann Niemeyer (1754–1828), a great-grandson of August Hermann Francke, who was also an eminent educationalist. In his *'Charakteristik der Bibel'*[34] he gives Paul as a figure in the New Testament the most space and depicts him as a model of tolerance who had unfortunately been unjustly forgotten in the contemporary debate: 'I cannot understand how one can write whole books on tolerance and can quarrel about it without even touching upon such a unique example'.[35] In the series of biographies of Paul there are biographically oriented monographs and others which emphasize the history of religion such as that of Adolf Hausrath,[36] Ernest Renan[37] and Louis Auguste Sabatier,[38] who remains better known for his research on St Francis.

Ferdinand Christian Baur's (1792–1860) construction of a Petrine Jewish-Christianity and a Pauline Gentile-Christianity, which was determined by the dialectics of Idealism, influenced the discussion and the rapidly deepening development of scholarship in the nineteenth century after his two-part essay appeared in 1831 and 1836: *'Das Christentum in der korinthischen Gemeinde; der Gegensatz des petrinischen und paulinischen Christentums in der ältesten Kirche'*.[39]

Albert Schweitzer gives his opinion on the significance of Baur's research for the understanding of Paul:

- ... 'that the old dogma arose from the teaching of Jesus in an organic, logical process. The ... individual researches have shown that this assumption is false. We cannot speak of a "development" in the usual sense because the deeper examination does not confirm the natural connections which one would naturally like to take *a priori* as obvious but in their place allows inconceivable non-connections to come to light'.[40]
- 'No connections between Paulinism and ancient Greek dogma can be

---

The True Gospel of Jesus Christ asserted to which is added a Dissertation on Providence, London, and *id.* (1739),*The True Gospel of Jesus Christ vindicated*, London.

34. A. H. Niemeyer (1775–1782), *Charakteristik der Bibel*, 5 Vols, Halle.
35. Quoted after Aner, *Theologie* (n. 28), 150 n. 1.
36. A. Hausrath (1865), *Der Apostel Paulus*, Heidelberg.
37. E. Renan (1865), *St Paul*, Paris.
38. L. A. Sabatier (1870), *L'apôtre Paul*, Paris.
39. F. C. Baur (1831), 'Die Christuspartei in der korinthischen Gemeinde, der Gegensatz des petrinischen und paulinischen Christentums in der alten Kirche', *TZTh* H.4, 61–136; and *id.* (1836), 'Einige Bemerkungen über die Christuspartei in Korinth', *TZTh* H.4, 1–32; cf. also *id.* (1836), 'Über Zweck und Veranlassung des Römerbriefs', *TZTh* H.3, 59–178.
40. Schweitzer, *Geschichte*, vi.

detected. Ignatius and Justin do not take over his ideas but create again for their part something new'.[41]

In his survey of research on Paul, which as a whole concentrates exclusively on German protestant theology, Paul Feine outlines the four main routes taken from the time of the more recent Tübingen School up to the end of the first third of the twentieth century:[42]

1   the intellectual didactic reflection[43]
2   the religious studies reflection[44]
3   the eschatological reflection[45]
4   the change from the theological to the religious interpretation.[46]

With Karl Barth (1886–1968) who in his exegesis takes up almost anachronistically the theological interpretation of Paul at the time of the Reformation, begins the Pauline exegesis of dialectic theology which develops in detail in very different ways. Alongside Karl Barth[47] himself a discipline evolves which stretches from the so-called Luther Renaissance of Karl Holl (1866–1926) to the works on Paul by Rudolf Bultmann (1884–1976) and his followers, which were stamped by the philosophy of Martin Heidegger (1889–1976) and were at the same time a product of literary and religious studies.

This school of Pauline interpretation was definitive for the mid-twentieth century and will conclude this present survey. It began with Bultmann's interest in the style of the Pauline epistles in 1910[48] and became visibly more intense after

---

41.   Schweitzer, *Geschichte*, vii.

42.   P. Feine (1927), *Der Apostel Paulus. Das Ringen um das geschichtliche Verständnis des Paulus* (BFChTh 2,12), Gütersloh, vii; cf. the preparatory work, *id*. (1906), *Paulus als Theologe* (BZSF 2, 3–4), Berlin, and its stimulating first chapter: 'Paulus ist nicht Systematiker, wohl aber Theologe' (Paul is no systematic theologian, but theologian).

43.   R. A. Lipsius (who according to Feine, *Apostel* [n. 40], 22, still holds 'the view which has been abandoned by today's research that Paul's cardinal doctrine is that of justification, while we consider this as a doctrine of combat and simply as one of the ideas and doctrines in which he understands Christian salvation'), A. Ritschl, H. Lüdemann, O. Pfleiderer, H. J. Holtzmann, C. Weizsäcker, B. Weiss, W. Beyschlag and A. Harnack.

44.   A. Dieterich, R. Reitzenstein, W. Heitmüller, G. Heinrici, P. Wendland, E. Schwartz, E. Meyer, H. Gunkel, W. Wrede and W. Bousset.

45.   R. Kabisch, E. Teichmann, A. Schweitzer.

46.   W. Bornemann, A. Titius, P. Wernle, A. Schlatter, P. Feine (who refers here to his *Theologie des Neuen Testaments*, Leipzig [¹1910] ⁴1922, where he takes as his starting point the representation of Christ in Paul), H. Weinel, J. Weiss, A. Deissmann, R. Seeberg and K. Barth.

47.   K. Barth (⁶1926), *Der Römerbrief*, Munich; *id*. (²1925), *Die Auferstehung der Toten*, Munich; *id*. (1928), *Erklärung des Philipperbriefes*, Munich.

48.   R. Bultmann (1910), *Der Stil der paulinischen Predigt und die kynisch-stoische Diatribe* (FRANT 13), Göttingen.

his works on the Synoptics and John in the years 1929[49] to 1932.[50] Bultmann asks e.g. Wrede[51] and Bousset,[52] 'whether the picture of Paulinism which is full of contradictions is the picture which is properly observed; or whether a uniform purpose of Paul cannot be made clear which would explain the ambiguity of his language; whether he did not comprehend human existence in all its depth, from the Old Testament Jewish and Hellenistic-Gnostic ideas which in each case are given their proper rights and at the same time appear in a new sense.'[53] 'I believe that the more one realizes the existential character of Pauline thought the more one will see that Paul's significance for world history lies in nothing other than that he was a theologian.'[54]

After two millennia of reading and interpreting Paul, in an increasingly secularized context determined by lack of religion or pseudo-religiousness, we can formulate for European/North American Theology the task which is still open: an analysis of the theologian Paul as we encounter him in his letters, using the dialectical interplay of demythologization and hermeneutics in interpretation and exegesis. In so doing we should include and continue all the methods of theology appropriate to the texts, the ancient sciences and those of the civilized world, text and literature.[55]

References

J. W. Aageson (2008), *Paul, the Pastoral Epistles and the Early Church*, Peabody, MA: Hendrickson.

R. Bultmann (1929), 'Zur Geschichte der Paulusforschung', *ThR NF* 1, 26–59.

W. S. Campbell, P. S. Hawekins and B. D. Schilgen (2007), *Medieval Readings of Romans*, Harrisburg.

E. Dassmann (1979), *Der Stachel im Fleisch. Paulus in der frühchristlichen Literatur bis Irenäus*, Münster: Aschendorff.

D. L. Eastman (2010), 'Paul the Martyr: The Cult of the Apostle in the Latin West', *Writings from the Greco-Roman World Supplements 4*, Leiden: Brill.

B. D. Ehrman (2006), *Peter, Paul and Mary Magdalena: The Followers of Jesus in History and Legend*, New York: Oxford University Press.

L. J. Kreitzer (1999), *Pauline Images in Fiction and Film*, Sheffield: Sheffield Academic Press.

49. R. Bultmann, *Geschichte der Paulusforschung*; id. (1929), *Die Bedeutung der geschichtlichen Jesus für den Theologen Paulus*, ThBl 8, 137–51.
50. R. Bultmann (1932), 'Römer 7 und die Anthropologie des Paulus', in H. Bornkamm (ed.), *Imago Dei*, FS G. Krüger, Giessen, 53–62; id. (1932), 'Urchristentum und Religionsgeschichte' (on K. Holl's writing with the same title), *ThR NF* 4, 1–21 (originally in *SvTK* 6 [1930], 299–324).
51. W. Wrede (1904), *Paulus*, Halle.
52. W. Bousset (1913), *Kyrios Christos*, Göttingen.
53. Bultmann, *Geschichte der Paulusforschung*, 51–2.
54. Ibid., 59. See Feine, n. 42.
55. Cf. e.g. G. Agamben (2006), *Il tempo che resta. Un commentario alla lettera ai Romani*, Turin 2000: *Die Zeit die bleibt. Ein Kommentar zum Römerbrief*, Frankfurt.

A.-J. Levine and M. Blickenstaff (2004), *A Feminist Companion to Paul*, Cleveland, OH: Pilgrim Press.

O. Merk (1998), 'Erwägungen zum Paulusbild in der deutschen Aufklärung', in ders., *Wissenschaftsgeschichte und Exegese* (BZNW 95), Berlin, 71–97.

E. H. Pagels (1975), *The Gnostic Paul: Gnostic Exegesis of Paul's Letters*, Philadelphia, PA: Trinity Press.

R. I. Pervo (2010), *The Making of Paul. Constructions of the Apostle in Early Christianity*, Minneapolis, MN: Fortress Press.

A. Schweitzer (1911), *Geschichte der paulinischen Forschung von der Reformation bis in die Gegenwart*, Tübingen: J. C. B. Mohr.

R. P. Seesengood (2010), *Paul: A Brief History*, Oxford: Wiley-Blackwell.

S. Vollenweider (2003), 'Art. Paul', *RPP* 9, 625–43.

R. Walsh (2005), *Finding St. Paul in Film*, New York: T&T Clark.

Authors

Prof Dr. Eve-Marie Becker
Department of Biblical Studies
Faculty of Theology/Faculty of Arts
Aarhus University
Taasingegade 3
DK-8000 Aarhus

Prof. Dr. Lukas Bormann
Institut für Neues Testament
Evangelisch-theologische Fakultät
Universität Erlangen-Nürnberg
Kochstraße 6
91054 Erlangen

Dr. Eva Ebel
Institut Unterstrass an der Pädagogischen
Hochschule Zürich
Seminarstrasse 29
CH-8057 Zürich

Prof. Dr. Jörg Frey
Lehrstuhl für Neutestamentliche
Wissenschaft mit Schwerpunkt Antikes
Judentum
und Hermeneutik
Theologisches Seminar
Universität Zürich
Kirchgasse 9
CH-8001 Zürich

Prof. Dr. Bernhard Heininger
Institut für Biblische Theologie
Katholisch-Theologische Fakultät
Universität Würzburg
Sanderring 2
97070 Würzburg

Prof. em. Dr. Andreas Lindemann
Lehrstuhl für Neues Testament
Kirchliche Hochschule Bethel
Remterweg 45
33617 Bielefeld

Prof. em. Dr. Andreas Mehl
Institut für Altertumswissenschaften
Lehrstuhl für Alte Geschichte
Martin-Luther-Universität Halle-Wittenberg
Universitätsplatz 12
06108 Halle/Saale

Prof. em. Dr. Oda Wischmeyer
Institut für Neues Testament
Evangelisch-Theologische Fakultät
Universität Erlangen-Nürnberg
Kochstraße 6
91054 Erlangen

Prof. Dr. Wolfgang Wischmeyer
Lehrstuhl für Kirchengeschichte, Christliche
    Archäologie und Kirchliche Kunst
Evangelisch-Theologische Fakultät
Universität Wien
Rooseveltplatz 10

INDEX OF PERSONS

Aelius Aristides 36, 37
Agrippa I 10, 108
Agrippa II 10, 108
Alexander the Great 35, 63
Alexander Jannaeus 73, 75
Ananias 329
Antiochus III (the Great) 64
Antiochus IV Epiphanes 64, 70, 78, 320
Apollonius of Tyana 37, 39, 40
Apollos 127, 151, 168, 343
Apuleius of Madaura 33, 44
Aquila and Prisca/Priscilla 99, 117, 118, 255, 259, 261
Areius Didymus 48
Augustine 87, 125, 128, 308, 357–9
Augustus 5–11, 14–21, 29, 41–3, 108, 126, 187

Bar-Jesus Elymas 331
Barnabas 23, 113–18, 208, 211, 222, 294, 328–32

Caesar 9, 11, 33, 41, 126, 186, 230
Caligula 8, 10, 14, 16, 20, 42, 65, 108
Chrysippus 49
Cicero 41, 48, 191, 257
Claudius 7–10, 12–14, 16–18, 20, 42, 97–9, 103, 107, 145, 260
Clement of Alexandria 31, 34, 52, 356
Cleopatra VII 8
Cornutus 49

Dio Cassius 20, 40–2, 97, 99, 260

Epaphroditus 111, 224, 227, 229, 231–4
Epictetus 45, 48–51, 121
Epicurus 46–8, 69, 257
Eusebius of Caesarea 230, 314, 341, 356

Felix 99, 104, 106, 108, 329

Galba 15

Gallio 97–9, 104, 108, 186, 187
Gamaliel I. 58, 68, 103
Germanicus 9

Hadrianus 43, 314
Heiracleides Ponticus 39
Heraclitus 49, 356
Herod I (the Great) 8, 10, 68, 108
Herodes Antipas 116
Hierocles of Alexandria 49
Hippolytus of Rome 31, 49, 54

Ignatius of Antiochia 62, 221, 318, 340, 344–8, 353, 363
Irenaeus 52, 55, 339, 356
Izates II 75

Jerome 59, 101, 104, 356
John Chrysostomus 357
John Hyrcanus 72
John Mark 114
Jonathan 72
Josephus 20, 65, 68, 71–3, 101, 126, 128, 211
Julian of Aeclanum 358
Junia(s) 28, 118, 255

Livy 7, 8, 156
Lucretius 48
Luke 3, 23, 46, 57–9, 61, 63, 97, 99–102, 104–6, 112, 116, 128, 143, 208, 215, 236, 241, 324, 328, 331–3, 336, 351
Lydia 229

Manilius 49
Marcion 174, 200, 221, 247, 339, 349–51, 356
Marcus Aurelius 48
Marcus Iulius Agrippa II *see* Agrippa II
Marius Victorinus 357
Mark Anthony 8
Mattathias 70

Musonius 46, 49

Nero 5, 9, 13, 15–17, 20, 21, 42–5, 48, 50, 107, 109, 260, 320, 342, 356

Octavian *see* Augustus
Onesimus 127, 135, 237–43, 312
Orosius 99, 260, 314

Pausanias 25, 37
Pelagius 358
Persius 49
Peter 52, 106, 117, 129, 136, 165, 201, 215–17, 294, 332, 342, 345, 350, 353, 356, 364
Petronius 13
Philemon 100, 104, 135, 224, 230–2, 237, 239–43, 285, 333
Philo of Alexandria 27, 55, 64, 67, 70, 76, 78, 80, 82, 100, 187, 208
Philodemus of Gadara 48
Philostratus 37, 39
Phoebe 28, 118, 255, 259
Pliny the Older 37
Pliny the Younger 43, 345
Plotina 48
Plutarch 31, 33, 36, 46, 47
Polycarp of Smyrna 224, 318, 340, 344, 347–9, 354
Pontius Pilate 8, 347
Porcius Festus 109

Quintus Sergius Paul[l]us 108, 113

Rufinus 357

Salome Alexandra 73
Seneca the Younger 20, 48–51, 97, 123, 257, 340, 355
Silas/Silvanus 114, 117, 143, 328, 330
Simon Magus 54, 353
Stephanas 160
Stephen 104, 128, 328
Strabo 48
Suetonius 21, 41, 99, 107, 260

Tacitus 15, 21, 36, 107, 145, 260, 314
Tertullian 44, 174, 200, 339, 351
Thecla 40, 340, 352, 356
Theodor of Mopsuestia 357
Theodoret of Cyrus 357
Tiberius 9, 13, 16, 19–21, 42, 97, 108, 187, 260, 351
Timothy 51, 79, 111, 114, 117, 127, 135, 139, 142–4, 162, 173, 185, 223, 227, 229, 231–7, 240, 307, 309, 311, 314, 316, 322–5, 328, 330, 336, 357
Titus 122, 183, 190, 217, 307, 309, 322, 326, 336, 352
Trajan 6, 43, 48, 314, 345

Vegetius 112
Vespasian 7
Virgil 7, 14, 48

Zeno 48

INDEX OF CITIES

Alexandria 12, 14, 49, 52, 55, 65, 78, 116, 169
Alexandria Troas 112, 114, 190, 330, 345
Amphipolis 114, 330
Ancyra 207
Antioch/Orontes 12, 60, 64, 79, 83, 85, 93, 95, 103, 107, 113–17, 119, 201, 209, 211, 216, 222, 294, 328–30, 344–6, 357
Antioch/Pisidia 103, 114, 119, 208, 211, 329
Apollonia 114, 330
Assos 114, 330
Athens 7, 24, 31, 46, 48, 111, 114, 143, 186, 242, 328, 330, 332
Attalia 114, 329

Beroea 114, 119, 143, 330

Caesarea 9, 43, 88, 106, 109, 113–15, 230, 329
Cenchreae 28, 114, 330
Chios 114, 330
Colossae 239, 307, 314, 333
Corinth 27, 37, 51, 98–100, 103, 106, 108, 111, 114, 117–19, 127, 130, 139, 144, 149, 151–3, 156, 159–63, 165, 167–74, 177, 179, 182–96, 213, 245, 255, 259, 261, 274, 328, 330, 341–3
Corope 37
Ctesiphon 15

Damascus 4, 60, 83, 95, 105, 107, 112, 126, 209, 327–9, 331,
Delphi 24, 35, 98, 107, 186
Derbe 114, 117, 208, 210, 329
Didyma 26, 35
Dodona 36

Elephantine 64
Eleusis 29–33
Ephesus 23, 25, 39, 41, 43, 108, 113–15, 118, 149, 160, 183–5, 187, 190, 199, 212, 223, 230, 237, 240, 261, 307, 309, 314, 316, 318, 322, 324, 328, 330–5, 346, 360
Epidaurus 37
Eresos 42

Gischala 59, 101, 104

Herculaneum 48
Hierapolis 314

Iconium 114, 122, 208, 211, 329, 352

Jerusalem 8, 9, 10, 11, 58, 60, 63–7, 70, 75, 78, 100, 103–9 112–16, 128, 136, 145, 161, 168, 177, 192, 194, 201, 205, 208, 210–12, 214–17, 252, 259, 261, 274, 287, 296, 301, 319, 328–30, 333, 360

KaloiLimenes 116
Kos 37, 330

Laodicea 314, 340
Lasaea 330
Lystra 23, 114, 122, 208, 329–31, 352

Magnesia 44, 340, 346
Miletus 35, 41, 106, 114, 324, 328, 330
Mitylene 114, 330
Myra 42, 116, 330

Nag Hammadi 52, 350
Neapolis 112, 114, 330
Nicopolis 48

Oasis Siva 35

Paphos 114, 329
Patara 115, 330
Pergamum 8, 37, 41–3
Perge 115, 208, 329
Pessinus 207
Philippi 23, 40, 103, 111, 114, 117, 119,

135, 140, 143, 186, 223–6, 238, 328, 330, 347–9, 354
Phratrai 37
Pompei 21, 33
Priene 42
Ptolemais 115, 330
Puteoli 116, 330

Rhegium 116, 330
Rome 5–22, 106, 245–76

Salamis 114, 329
Salmone 330
Scili 340, 352

Seleucia 15, 114, 352
Sidon 116, 330
Smyrna 42, 340, 344, 347–9
Syracuse 116, 330

Tarsus 58–60, 63, 70, 101, 216, 329, 332, 337
Tavium 207
Thessalonica 114, 117, 119, 135, 139–48, 186, 227, 307, 328, 330
Troas *see* Alexandria Troas
Tyre 115, 330

Zeugma 14